HEROES OF THE RANGE

Yesteryear's Saturday Matinee Movie Cowboys

by

BUCK RAINEY

The Scarecrow Press, Inc.

Metuchen, N.J., and London, 1987

Library of Congress Cataloging in Publication Data

Rainey, Buck.
   Heroes of the range.

   Includes index.
   1. Western films--History and criticism. 2. Moving-
picture actors and actresses--United States--Biography.
I. Title.
PN1995.9.W4R32 1987   791.43'09'093278   85-2071
ISBN 0-8108-1804-3

All photographs used in this book are from
the collection of the author, Buck Rainey.

Manufactured in the United States of America

For

CHARLES STARRETT

As Fine a Gentleman As Ever Rode The Hollywood Range

Any boy was lucky who chose Charles for an idol and tried to walk in his footsteps, for nowhere along life's trails has he let his followers slip into troubled waters or the dark abyss of degradation out of neglect for where he himself was walking. He has extended a helping hand to one and all and held out his hand in friendship to anyone who would take it. For him there have been no "mighty" friends nor any "lowly" friends—just friends.

To have known this remarkable man has been one of life's great experiences for this author, and so it is a pleasure to here acknowledge Charles Starrett as a favorite among the Heroes of the Range.

CONTENTS

[v]

Acknowledgments

My special thanks are extended to these *compadres* and fellow film historians who provided much assistance and encouragement in the prepartion of this book. Their unselfish sharing of information has aided materially in making this book possible.

Les Adams

Janus Barfoed

Bill McDowell

Muchas gracias, good friends!

And in addition I am indebted to these friends who shared with me information they had and which is incorporated into the various chapters herein. Your contributions are appreciated.

Elizabeth Burbridge
Rod Cameron
Wayne J. Campbell
Buster Crabbe
Jose Simoes Filho
Russell Hayden
Berdee Holt
Jennifer Holt
Tim Holt
Al Hoxie
Gary Lease
Mike Marx
Mrs. Kermit Maynard
Don Miller
Cyril Nichols
George O'Brien

Duncan Renaldo
William Russell
Douglas Sanderson
Noreen Sather
Charles Starrett
Bob Steele
Ray Whitley
Nick Williams
W. C. Wilson

Preface

That the cowboy is one of the most romantic figures in American history is uncontested. Few other characters have received more attention in the pages of books and magazines, or have had more film footage devoted to them than has this almost legendary vestige of the West. Yet the true cowboy has seldom been discovered by either authors or directors. But it was the cinema cowboy of yesteryear, along with the cowboy of literary fiction, that has provided the basis for the popular misconception of the Wild West of the 1800s and 1900s.

There's an old saying that a cowboy is "a man with guts and a hoss." Perhaps it is, after all, as definitive and brief a definition of the cowboy as we can attain. But where do we go from there? Fiction has created a myth, and the myth has fashioned the cowboy into the most romantic occupant of the West, consistently gunning down badmen and saving virgins from "a fate worse than death." Yet, if the truth be known, there were neither enough badmen nor virgins available in the Old West for the involvement of any sizable number of cowboys in either of the activities. And besides, that was the job of the sheriff.

No, the real cowboy's life was anything but romantic or exciting. As historian Ramon F. Adams once said, "There was little romance in gettin' up at four o'clock in the mornin', eatin' dust behind a trail herd, swimmin' muddy and turbulent rivers, nor in doctorin' screw worms, pullin' stupid cows from bog holes, sweatin' in the heat of summer and freezin' in the cold of winter."

The cowboy captured the imagination of the world, and few groups have been commercialized as intensively as the poor cow tender. Yet the public, with an insatiable appetite, has continued to devour every morsel of "cowboydom" put on the market. As one of America's truly unique contributions to culture, the cowboy seems destined to live on forever in that favored corner of our hearts reserved for vicarious thoughts about experiences which—because of a combination of circumstances, era, and cowardice—we shall never have.

The movies have perpetuated, perfected, and extended the myth of the cowboy to such an extent that the average person cannot easily differentiate reality from myth when thinking about him. More likely than not, "cowboy" conjures up memories of those fabulous Saturdays of years past when a horde of saddle busters romped across the screen like a school of undernourished piranhas, and with a hint of improvisation and even uncertainty, became all-time heroes to the young at heart.

Mountains of epithets and hyperbole have been heaped upon these *Heroes of the Range,* expressing the inexpressible heights, and depths, and lengths, and breadth of the world's affection for them. The movie cowboy was not a hero to be circumscribed by ordinary rules and conventions, nor was he a nominal hero to be replaced easily in the heart and mind after a brief fling in the limelight. No American heroes have approached the sustained popularity of such cactus thriller favorites as Buck Jones, Tom Mix, John Wayne, and Roy Rogers.

From the days of Broncho Billy Anderson and William S. Hart to the era of Rex Allen and Monte Hale, cowboy heroes of the oats thrillers did their rip-snortin', boisterously harmless, broncho-busting stunts, stirring up the western dust literally and figuratively while Fairbanksing all over the footage in true (movie) Western style. Sagebrush eating audiences throughout the world found these rollicking horse flolics against scenic backgrounds delightfully palatable, and for half a century hay-burners constituted the main movie fare of a sizable clientele who devoured them ravishingly, as might a starving buffalo herd a valley of lush, green grass.

Red-blooded he-men, red-handed henchmen, rough-ridin' redmen, pretty prairie damsels, quick-witted horses, and dull-witted sidekicks set pulses throbbing and hearts beating madly in stories told and retold to the accompaniment of crackling gunfire and thudding hoofs in countless numbers of shoot-em-ups from 1903 through 1954, supported by a multitude of picture fans swearing faithfully by these heroes of the range as the greatest exponents of open-air adventure stories known to the screen.

This book is concerned with fifteen movie cowboys, seven of whom first earned their spurs in the silent era and eight of whom started their western careers in the sound era. The selection is not meant to imply that I believe these fifteen to constitute the hierarchy of movie cowboydom. In another book, *Saddle Aces of the Cinema* (A.S. Barnes & Company, 1980), I covered the careers of fifteen other famous cowboy aces. And there are many other great cowboy stars that I have not covered in either book—John Wayne, Tex Ritter, Bill Elliott, William S. Hart, Art Acord, Joel McCrea, Bob Custer, Neal Hart, and others. A single book, or two books, can be only so long. Some of the stars I chose not to include have been adequately treated in other books. Some yet remain to be given their just recognition.

I believe this book fills a gap in the history of the careers and achievements of specific cowboy personalities, presenting, as it does, as complete a record as has ever been assembled of each cowboy's film credits from his earliest walk-ons to his last fade-out, both western and non-western, silent and sound films. It is these painstakingly assembled data that make this book unique and, I believe, a valuable contribution to cinema history.

I hope that you will find merit in this book, enjoy it, and through it come to appreciate even more the cinematic achievements of these cowboy stalwarts who, for the most part, worked on the periphery of Hollywood fame and fortune. They found a permanent niche in the hearts and memories of those who, amid whoops, whistles, shrills, hand-clapping, and foot-stomping, lived a thousand vicarious adventures through the films of their idols. To some degree, through their low-budget morality plays that always emphasized good over evil, the "B" cowboys helped to instill in thousands of impressionable youth the virtues that would sustain them in adulthood. What other group of Hollywood stars have done as much? Society would seem to be the loser with the disappearance of...the **HEROES OF THE RANGE.**

Buddy Roosevelt

1 ● BUDDY ROOSEVELT

A Winsome Spirit Along the Trail

Buddy Roosevelt, one of the few surviving silent Western stars from Hollywood's Age of Innocence, was 75 years old when he died of cancer on October 6, 1973 at the Veterans Hospital in Meeker, Colorado. He had been born in the same city on June 25, 1898, the son of an Englishman who had come to America as the representative of a group of businessmen who wanted to establish a cattle empire in the West. Roosevelt, whose real name was Kenneth Standhope Sanderson, grew up in Meeker and in 1914 joined the C. B. Irwin Wild West Show, eventually landing in Inceville, California (now Culver City) where he went to work for Thomas Ince at the old Triangle Studios, working primarily in the William S. Hart pictures as a stuntman. He was in **Hell's Hinges,** Hart's classic Western of 1916. While at Triangle his salary rose to $22 a week plus board and room on the lot—pretty good wages for cowboys in those days.

Buddy was able to work consistently as a stuntman and trick rider and was easily supporting himself when World War I broke out. For awhile he worked on the ranch back home, as his father was having financial troubles in paying for and keeping the ranch going, but on September 26, 1917 Buddy quietly joined the navy in Grand Junction. After eight weeks of bootcamp at Goat Island in San Francisco he was shipped to Hampton Roads Naval Base at Norfolk, Virginia. His father died while he was there and Buddy took on the responsibility of partially supporting his mother and his younger sisters and brothers, who were left with a $5,000 mortgage on their mostly undeveloped land.

Although his pay was only $32.50 a month, Buddy took out a $20-a-month allotment for his mother and lived on $12.50, out of which he paid for an insurance policy listing his mother as beneficiary. He served throughout the war and was aboard the U.S.S. Norfolk when she was sunk in the Atlantic, forcing him to spend several days floating in a life ring before being picked up. During a flu epidemic when a number of men died, Buddy at one point was assumed dead and almost buried before someone noticed that there was still life in him. Toward the end of the war he served on the battleship Wyoming, which brought soldiers back from France. After his hitch at sea he was shipped to the U.S. Telegraphy Base at Cambridge, Massachusetts, and was discharged in March 1919. Returning home, he promised his mother and his family that he would stay for a year and help out with finances and running the ranch. He worked hard to put the ranch on its feet and, during the winter months, supplemented the family finances by working at Sims Moulton's store nearby. When the year was up Buddy got a job at a saw mill owned by the White River Lumber Company to earn enough ready cash to get back to Hollywood. It is clear that Roosevelt loved his mother, brothers, and sisters very much. They were a close-knit family. He continued to provide financial assistance for as long as they needed it. The more money he made, the more he sent home to his mother.

There was a boom on in Hollywood, especially in the production of westerns. Buddy easily found work. After years of stunting and bits (he set a precedent of $100 a week for stuntmen when he doubled for Rudolph Valentino in **The Sheik**) Roosevelt finally got a break at Universal, where he was on the payroll as double for

1

William Desmond. He began to work pretty steadily at the studio and developed an ambition to star in some of the two-reel westerns that the studio specialized in. He approached various directors on the lot about the possibilities. Director Nat Ross liked Buddy's looks and build and arranged to have him starred in **Down in Texas** (Universal, 1923). The film was typical of Universal's short Westerns—a little romance (with Lola Todd) and a terrific amount of fast-paced action. Roosevelt, athletic and a daring rider, came off well in his first starring oater and was billed under his real name of Kent Sanderson. Although the studio wanted him for more two-reelers (both Hoot Gibson and Pete Morrison were moving up to five-reel features), Buddy chose instead to make a six-reel feature entitled **Lure of the Yukon** (Dawn, 1924), filmed in Alaska for an independent producer. The lovely Eva Novak was the female lead and the film was heralded as a big production at the time. Universal had goofed in not signing Buddy to a six-picture contract; Buddy goofed in listening for a film cutter who steered him into discussions with the indie producer so that he might get the job of editing the film if the producer hired Buddy. It was a mistake not to have accepted the Universal contract; there, his career might have zoomed much higher than it ultimately did.

Buddy probably also made a mistake when he passed up the opportunity to work at Famous Players-Lasky and instead accepted a contract from Lester F. Scott, Jr., an independent producer who had just formed Action Pictures and was looking for a star for the cheapie Westerns he planned to produce. Because Scott wanted to capitalize on the popularity of ex-President Theodore Roosevelt's name, Kent Sanderson became "Buddy Roosevelt," a name calculated to have a magical quality that would draw attention. And so time

Violet La Plante, Terry Myles and Buddy Roosevelt in a scene from **Walloping Wallace** (Approved, 1924).

Buddy Roosevelt, Bud Osborne (in door), Norma Canterno, and others grace this scene from **Cyclone Buddy** (Approved, 1924).

proved, but Sanderson never appreciated the name. Scott would subsequently hire two other stars and change their names: Jay Wilsey to "Buffalo Bill, Jr." (the name Scott first tried to give to Sanderson, who refused to be saddled with it) and Floyd Alderson to "Wally Wales."

Roosevelt was signed to a five-year contract. It was supposed to be a one producer-one star arrangement, but when Scott got greedy and added the two other stars, the budgets for the Roosevelt westerns went down to partially compensate for the outlay on the other westerns. After his first series as a lead player, Buddy was wanted by other producers for better things. However, Scott asked too high a price for Buddy's contract. Buddy was trapped. He resigned himself to his fate and contented himself with sending his mother sizable sums of money each month for her and the children's support.

The story lines of the 25 westerns Roosevelt made for Action Pictures might be of interest, since the average western aficionado knows little about the Roosevelt features of the 1920s. Six features were released in each of 1924, 1925, 1926, and 1927, followed by one in 1928. As in evident from such titles as **Battling Buddy, Biff-Bang Buddy,** and **Cyclone Buddy,** our hero was generally "Buddy" in his films—"Buddy Benson," "Buddy West," "Buddy Walters," "Buddy Wallace," "Buddy Labrie," and so forth.

In **Rough Ridin'** ('24) Buddy abducts his sweetheart to get her out of the way while he clears up a crime which has involved his girl's brother. His objective in **Battling Buddy** ('24) is to prove his competency and win clear title to a ranch willed him by his uncle. **Biff Bang Buddy** ('24) finds him rescuing a girl, exposing an outlaw for what he is, and proving the girl's father innocent of any implication in the outlaw's skullduggery. In **Walloping Wallace** ('24) an incompetent cowhand is fired by ranch foreman Buddy, who has to whip the man in a fight. To get even the cowhand abducts the heroine, owner of the ranch, and forges her name to a bill of sale for cattle. Buddy is blamed but is able to rescue the girl, save the cattle, and capture the malefactor. **Rip-Roarin' Roberts** ('24) has Buddy as a deputy sheriff on the trail of "The Hawk," a notorious outlaw with a $1,000 price on his head, whereas in **Cyclone Buddy** ('24) he clears himself of murder charges after a daring escape from a courtroom, saves his boss's ranch, and wins approval to marry the boss's daughter.

Buddy is falsely accused of murder in **Gold and Grit** ('25) but uncovers the real criminal, prevents a fraudulent mine owner from making off with the gold, and wins the girl after proving she was tricked into accepting a proposal from a scoundrel. In **Fast Fightin'** ('25) he is employed as a cowboy on the ranch owned by the heroine, who accuses him of attempting to steal money from her. In reality it is her brother, in the clutches of the smooth crook, who is guilty. Naturally Buddy whips into action and prevents the theft, captures the crook, straightens out her brother, and wins the heroine's love. **Reckless Courage** ('25) has an interesting twist. A diamond necklace falls from the sky at Buddy's feet, followed by a girl parachutist with a gun pointed right at him. She proceeds to tie Buddy up and leaves. Later he rescues her from an accident and from jewel thieves who are after her valuable necklace. A head wound is suffered by Buddy, a secret service agent, in **Galloping Jinx** ('25), and he wanders on to a ranch where he is mistaken for the man the heroine is supposed to marry before noon on her 18th birthday in order to meet the terms of a will. Recovering, he brings to justice those who were trying to get the ranch

Buddy Roosevelt rescues Helen Foster in this scene from Reckless Courage (Action, 1925)

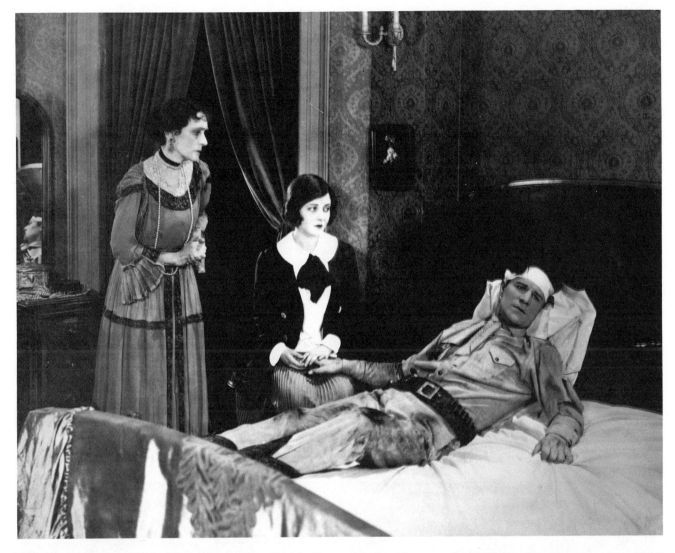

Billie Bennett and Gloria Heller look after Buddy Roosevelt in this scene from **Galloping Jinx** (Action, 1925).

from the girl (who should have had more sense than to marry a stranger in the first place), who by now is perfectly content to keep Buddy as her husband. In **Action Galore** ('25) Buddy is a ranger on the trail of an outlaw, who is not above a little claim jumping at the expense of the heroine. And **Thundering Through** ('25) finds him opposing a gang, secretly headed by the town banker, that is trying to gain control of certain ranches across which they know a railroad is to be built.

Hidden gold, a haunted ranch house, and a pretty girl combine to give Buddy an exciting time in **Hoodoo Ranch** ('26), the first release in his third series for Scott. In **Tangled Herds** ('26) he seeks to capture the man who has stolen pay dust from his gold mine, while also proving his own innocence of cattle rustling. A nice dual role as twin brothers—one a smuggler, the other a federal agent—is provided Buddy in **Twin Triggers** ('26). **Easy Going** ('26) has him intervening to protect

a rich young lady from being swindled by a smooth-talking villain. In **The Dangerous Dub** ('26) Buddy takes a job as a cowpuncher on the heroine's ranch because the two are attracted to each other. He thwarts the attempts of villains to wrest the ranch from the heroine's mother and marries the girl. Counterfeiters are brought to justice by Buddy, a bankers' association agent, in **The Ramblin' Galoot** ('26), whereas in **The Bandit Buster** ('26) he consorts with the heroine to abduct her banker father in order to force him to rest and get his mind off his business ventures. The plan backfires and when the father is really abducted for ransom by outlaws, the girl believes Buddy to be responsible and to have doublecrossed her.

In **Between Dangers** ('27), the first 1927 release, Buddy becomes innocently involved in a bank robbery after his identification papers, which show him to be heir to a ranch, are stolen. Two crooks attempt to do

5

Buddy Roosevelt and Robert Homans have the drop on Lafe McKee in **The Bandit Buster** (Action, 1926)

Togo Frye points Lafe McKee out to Buddy Roosevelt in this scene from **Twin Triggers** (Action, 1926)

away with him in order to use the ranch for their own purposes, but Buddy, with the aid and comfort of the heroine, brings justice about. **The Fightin' Comeback** ('27) revolves about Buddy's stealing money after being cheated in a card game and escaping to Mexico where he becomes a gang leader. Later he returns to make amends and meets a girl. Together they prove the stolen money is counterfeit and that the crooked gambler is responsible for Buddy's problems. The weak brother theme is used again in **Code of the Cow Country** ('27) as Buddy goes into action to help the boss's daughter, whom he loves, and her brother who is in hock to a notorious gambler. Another dual role comes Buddy's way in **The Phantom Buster** ('27) as he plays "look alikes"—one an outlaw and the other a Texas Ranger. He captures border smugglers and, in the process, the heart of the heroine, who was about to be forced into an unwanted marriage. In his last 1927 release, **Ride 'em High** ('27), Buddy aids the heroine and her father in a dispute with his own scoundrel cousin and, in the process, avenges his father's death.

Buddy's last film for Scott was the 1928 release, **The Cowboy Cavalier** ('28). A girl loses her memory when she witnesses her uncle being murdered. Later, the murderer and the girl's cousin, who is behind it all, kidnap and attempt to force her to sign a confession to the murder. Buddy, a deputy sheriff, steps in to solve the crime and marry the girl.

The Roosevelt films met with audience reception and made money. Although not works of art, the films, each produced in four to six days on budgets of around $20,000, were entertaining. Buddy was an interesting personality, sort of a poor man's Tom Mix, Buck Jones, and Hoot Gibson rolled into one. His films were released on a "states-right" basis and played mainly the second- and third-rate theatres, but he was one of the foremost "non-major" cowboy stars. Fast-moving and heavy on action, his films had a judicious sprinkling of deadpan comedy. Buddy was not unlike the more successful George O'Brien in his screen image. Although not the comedian, actor, or total extrovert that O'Brien was, there was a faint wisp of O'Brien in Buddy's screen characterizations. The potential for greatness as a performer seemed locked in Buddy, but was only partially released throughout his long career. Richard Thorpe as director, Betty Burbridge as scenarist, and Irving Reis as cameraman were highly competent at their trade and did their best to bring out what talent there might be in Buddy and magnify it.

Although there was a year to go on his five-year contract, Buddy obtained his release from Scott in January 1928 and signed for a series with Rayart (forerunner of Monogram). Trem Carr produced and J. P. McGowan directed the best Buddy Roosevelt oaters made up to

that time, although there was no appreciable improvement in story lines. **Painted Trails** ('28) has Buddy assigned to track down border smugglers. He pretends to be an outlaw in order to infiltrate the gang. In **Trailin' Back** ('28) Buddy is a sheriff in pursuit of a gang that he suspects is finding refuge on the ranch of the heroine and her father. **Trail Riders** ('28) revolves about a water rights dispute between adjacent ranch owners. Buddy exposes a cattle rustler who has misled the opposition, headed by a girl. With the water rights matter cleared up, the girl and Buddy find romance. **Lightnin' Shot** ('28) also has to do with a feud, this time between two ranchers. Their respective offspring would rather romance than fight, while a third rancher plots to keep the feud going so that he can ultimately obtain the land he wants. Buddy takes time out from wooing the maiden to put things in order. In **Devil's Tower** ('28) Roosevelt prevents destruction of a dam, extricates his father from trouble, captures a gang of crooks bent on destroying the construction project, and finds romance with the contractor's daughter. (I wonder why it is that heroines always had fathers but very seldom had a living mother?) The final film in the Rayart series was **Mystery Valley** ('28), released in July. In the story Buddy's father is killed before he can write informing his son of the location of the ranch title. His murderer, a gambler, takes over the ranch, on which gold is found. Buddy ultimately, with the help of his girlfriend, wages a battle against the gambler and his gang and proves his own claim to the ranch to be valid, as well as exposing the gambler's guilt.

A new Rayart contract was not forthcoming, as most studios were cutting back on the production of silent films and re-tooling for sound. But taking sound equipment into the outdoors created real technical problems, and it just wasn't being tried by the hoss opry producers at that time.

Buddy picked up what work he could for the next several years. Like a lot of people, he was hit hard by the depression and the collapse of financial institutions. As he put it, "All hell broke loose in the bankruptcy of the Guarantee Building and Loan Corporation of Hollywood, to the tune of $4 million. It cost me $36,000, peanuts compared to others—but it was about all I had."

Although Buddy didn't care much for hunting or fishing, he was a crack shot with both the rifle and hand guns and amazed his friends who knew that he seldom practiced. He got a real bang out of using the long bull whip and could pop the head off a chicken or a bird within range. He could make the whip pop like a gun and at the same time wrap it around a person's neck without hurting the victim. Another crazy pastime he had was throwing knives and bayonets, and he was particularly good at it. He had a mountain cabin at

Crestline Village not far from Arrowhead Lake in the San Bernadino Mountains where there were plenty of large trees to practice on during weekends. This was back in the bathtub gin days when Buddy and friends would sometimes get high on the homemade brew. As evening wore on, there would be one or two of his friends who would be feeling so good that they wanted to stand against a tree and have Buddy throw bayonets around them, "pinning them to the tree." Although he never hurt anyone, his brother, Douglas, was afraid that there would be an accident and took precautions to hide the knives and bayonets when Buddy himself seemed to have had a little too much spirits.

In the early 1930s Buddy starred in a few sound Westerns for Syndicate and Superior and thereafter reverted to stunting and supporting roles. The parts got smaller and smaller as the years went by. In the early Thirties he lost a chance to star in the Lonestar-Monogram series that ultimately went to John Wayne because Buddy's wife, Frances (a cousin of Clark Gable), "blew up" at the producer, Paul Malvern, just as Buddy was taking pen in hand to sign the contract. Her tantrum nixed the deal, caused a divorce, started the downhill slide of Buddy in movies, and aided Wayne in his climb to stardom. Buddy and Frances had been married at the "Little Church Around the Corner" in Hollywood in December 1929. An earlier marriage to Kathryn DeForest had lasted only a couple or three years. Buddy never got over his love for Frances and always regretted the divorce, although he would marry again. Another stroke of bad luck had befallen him a few years earlier when he possibly lost the chance to star as The Cisco Kid in **In Old Arizona** (Fox, '29), the role for which Warner Baxter won an academy award. Due to be tested for the role by his friend Raoul Walsh, the director, Buddy broke his leg and had to bow out. His career was plagued by such "lost chances."

During World War II Buddy served in the Coast Guard and, the war over, returned to Hollywood as a freelance actor and stuntman. For some time he was Ronald Colman's "stand-in" and the two were good friends. He was never able to stage a comeback as a featured player but he was able to support his wife and son during his downhill slide in pictures. Up until his retirement in 1962 Buddy appeared in scores of movies, accepting "bit" and "extra" roles wherever he could get them.

After becoming quite neurotic and sickly, Buddy was divorced a year or two before his death from his third wife, Wanda, and moved to his old hometown. His son was a disappointment to him and Buddy spent his last years neglected and alone except for his loyal and loving brothers and sister. A few friends, too, would occasionally drop by the Veterans hospital to see him, an event which never ceased to cheer him.

Buddy Roosevelt lived long enough to see the revival of interest in his screen work and to realize that he was not entirely forgotten. For this Western film fans can be grateful. And Buddy never completely lost his sense of humor. In the last years of declining health he liked to tell about receiving a fan letter from South America: it started with "Dear Pal," followed by a string of flowery words of praise, and ended with a postscript, "I always see your pictures because I never have to stand in line." That always struck Buddy as very funny. One of his favorite expressions was "May the sun always shine in your garden of happiness," and his own garden of happiness was brightened a little in the knowledge that there were those who remembered and appreciated him. To know that grown men still looked upon him as a cowboy hero who helped to shape their lives and their moral character was gratifying to him.

It is a shame that most readers missed the glorious Roosevelt years, 1924-'34, when he vied with the greatest for Western honors in wild and woolly action pictures. Buddy Roosevelt is gone, along with most of his cowboy contemporaries and the old Hollywood he helped to create, but he has left moviedom a legacy that deserves perpetuation. It is hoped that his films can be made available for a new generation to see, for they are part of a unique heritage.

Buddy Roosevelt in an unidentified western.

BUDDY ROOSEVELT Filmography

(Note: Roosevelt appeared in many films, both early and late in his career, that we have no record of at this point.)

HELL'S HINGES
(Ince/Triangle, February, 1916) 5 Reels
William S. Hart, Clara Williams, Alfred Hollingsworth, Jack Standing, Robert McKim, Louise Glaum, J. Frank Burke, Robert Kortman, Jean Hersholt, John Gilbert, Kent Sanderson *(Buddy Roosevelt)*
Director: William S. Hart
Story/Scenario: C. Gardner Sullivan
Producer: Thomas Ince

THE SHEIK
(Famous Players-Lasky/Paramount, November 20, 1921) 8 Reels
Agnes Ayres, Rudolph Valentino, Adolphe Menjou, Walter Long, Lucien Littlefield, George Waggner, Patsy Ruth Miller, F. R. Butler, *Buddy Roosevelt* (as double for Valentino)
Director: George Melford
Scenario: Monte M. Katterjohn
Story: Edith Maude Hull

BEASTS OF PARADISE
(Universal, October 1, 1923) 15 Chapters
William Desmond, Eileen Sedgwick, William H. Gould, Ruth Royce, Joe Bonomo, Margaret Morris, Alfred Fischer, Gordon McGregor, Clark Comstock, Slim Cole, William J. Welsh, *Buddy Roosevelt* (as double for Desmond)
Director: William Craft
Scenario: Val Cleveland
Story: Val Cleveland

DOWN IN TEXAS
(Universal, December 21, 1923) 2 Reels
Kent Sanderson *(Buddy Roosevelt)*, Lola Todd
Director: Nat Ross
Story: Arthur H. Gooden

LURE OF THE YUKON
(Norman Dawn Alaskan Company/Lee Bradford Corporation, August 1, 1924) 6 Reels
Eva Novak, Kent Sanderson *(Buddy Roosevelt)*, Spottiswoode Aitken, Arthur Jasmine, Howard Webster, Katherine Dawn, Eagle Eye
Director: Norman Dawn
Story/Scenario: Norman Dawn

ROUGH RIDIN'
(Approved Pictures/Weiss Brothers Artclass, July 15, 1924) 5 Reels
Buddy Roosevelt, Elsa Benham, Richard Thorpe, Joe Rickson, Frances Beaumont, Arthur Detlorf, Mike Ready
Director: Richard Thorpe
Scenario: Margaret M. Harris
Story: Elizabeth Burbridge
Producer: Lester F. Scott, Jr.

BATTLING BUDDY
(Approved Pictures/Weiss Brothers Artclass, August 15, 1924) 5 Reels
Buddy Roosevelt, Violet La Plante, William Lowery, Kewpie King, "Shorty" Hendrix, Charles E. Butler, "Pardner" (a horse)
Director: Richard Thorpe
Story: Elizabeth Burbridge
Producer: Lester F. Scott, Jr.

BIFF BANG BUDDY
(Approved Pictures/Weiss Brothers Artclass, September 15, 1924) 5 Reels
Buddy Roosevelt, Jean Arthur, Buck Connors, Robert Fleming, Al Richmond
Director: Frank L. Inghram
Story: Reginald C. Barker
Producer: Lester F. Scott, Jr.

WALLOPING WALLACE
(Approved Pictures/Weiss Brothers Artclass, October 15, 1924) 5 Reels
Buddy Roosevelt, Violet La Plante, Lew Meehan, N. E. Hendrix, Lillian Gale, Terry Myles, Olin Francis, Dick Bodkins
Director: Richard Thorpe
Scenario: Norbert Myles
Story: Robert J. Horton - "A Man of Action"
Producer: Lester F. Scott, Jr.

RIP ROARIN' ROBERTS
(Approved Pictures/Weiss Brothers Artclass, November 15, 1924) 5 Reels
Buddy Roosevelt, Brenda Lane, Joe Rickson, Al Richmond, John Webb Dillon, Bert Lindley, Lew Bennett
Director: Richard Thorpe
Story: Robert J. Horton
Producer: Lester F. Scott, Jr.

Billie Bennett tells Buddy Roosevelt to leave as Gloria Heller seems to be ready for a wedding in this scene from **Galloping Jinx** (Action, 1925).

CYCLONE BUDDY

(Approved Pictures/Weiss Brothers Artclass, December 15, 1924) 5 Reels

Buddy Roosevelt, Norma Conterno, Alfred Hewston, Bud Osborne, J. P. Lockney, Chet Ryan, Shorty Hendrix

Director/Story: Alvin J. Neitz
Producer: Lester F. Scott, Jr.

GOLD AND GRIT

(Approved Pictures/Weiss Brothers Artclass, January 15, 1925) 5 Reels

Buddy Roosevelt, Ann McKay, William H. Turner, L. J. O'Connor, Wilbur Mack, Nelson McDowell, Hank Bell

Director: Richard Thorpe
Story: Ned Nye
Producer: Lester F. Scott, Jr.

FAST FIGHTIN'

(Approved Pictures/Weiss Brothers Artclass, February 15, 1925) 5 Reels

Buddy Roosevelt, Neil Brantley, Joe Rickson, Emily Barrye, Sherry Tansey, Emma Tansey, Leonard Trainor, Hank Bell

Director: Richard Thorpe
Story: A. E. Serrao
Producer: Lester F. Scott, Jr.

RECKLESS COURAGE

(Action Pictures/Weiss Brothers Artclass, May, 1925) 5 Reels

Buddy Roosevelt, J. C. Fowler, Helen Foster, William McIllwain, Jay Morley, Jack O'Brien, N. E. Hendrix, Merrill McCormick, Eddie Barry, Princess Neola, Robert Burns

Director: Tom Gibson
Scenario: Betty Burbridge
Story: Victor Roberts
Producer: Lester F. Scott, Jr.

GALLOPING JINX

(Action Pictures/Weiss Brothers Artclass, September 24, 1925) 5 Reels

Buddy Roosevelt, Gloria Heller, J. Gordon Russell, Ralph Whiting, Billie Bennett, Louis Fitzroy, Jack O'Brien, Martha Dudley, Charles Colby, Clyde McClary, Sam Blum, Leonard Trainer

Director: Robert Eddy
Scenario: Betty Burbridge
Producer: Lester F. Scott, Jr.

ACTION GALORE

(Action Pictures/Weiss Brothers Artclass, November 3, 1925) 5 Reels

Buddy Roosevelt, Toy Gallagher, Charles Williams, Joe Rickson, Jack O'Brien, Raye Hampton, Ruth Royce
Director: Robert Eddy
Producer: Lester F. Scott, Jr.

THUNDERING THROUGH

(Action Pictures/Weiss Brothers Artclass, December 13, 1925) 5 Reels

Buddy Roosevelt, Jean Arthur, Charles Colby, Lew Meehan, Frederick Lee, L. J. O'Connor, Lawrence Underwood, George Marion, Raye Hampton
Director: Fred Bain
Story: Barr Cross
Producer: Lester F. Scott, Jr.
Scenario: Betty Burbridge

HOODOO RANCH

(Action Pictures/Weiss Brothers Artclass, January 22, 1926) 5 Reels

Buddy Roosevelt, Dixie Lamont, Frank Ellis, Nelson McDowell
Director: William Bertram
Producer: Lester F. Scott, Jr.

TANGLED HERDS

(Action Pictures/Weiss Brothers Artclass, March 8, 1926) 5 Reels

Buddy Roosevelt
Director: William Bertram
Producer: Lester F. Scott, Jr.

TWIN TRIGGERS

(Action Pictures/Weiss Brothers Artclass, April 13, 1926) 5 Reels

Buddy Roosevelt, Nita Cavalier, Frederick Lee, Laura Lockhart, Lafe McKee, Charles (Slim) Whitaker, Clyde McClary, Toyo Tuye, Hank Bell
Director: Richard Thorpe
Scenario: Betty Burbridge
Story: Jack Townley
Producer: Lester F. Scott, Jr.

EASY GOING

(Action Pictures/Weiss Brothers Artclass, May 22, 1926) 5 Reels

Buddy Roosevelt, Lew Meehan, Helen Foster
Director: Richard Thorpe
Producer: Lester F. Scott, Jr.

Nita Cavalier tells Buddy Roosevelt to go in this scene from **Twin Triggers** (Action, 1926).

THE DANGEROUS DUB
(Action Pictures/Associated Exhibitors, July 4, 1926) 5 Reels
Buddy Roosevelt, Peggy Montgomery, Joseph Girard, Fanny Midgley, Al Taylor, Curley Riviere
Director: Richard Thorpe
Scenario: Frank L. Inghram
Story: James Madison
Producer: Lester F. Scott, Jr.

THE RAMBLIN' GALOOT
(Action Pictures/Associated Exhibitors, November 21, 1926) 5 Reels
Buddy Roosevelt, Violet La Plante, Frederick Lee, Nelson McDowell
Director: Fred Bain
Story: Barr Cross
Producer: Lester F. Scott, Jr.

THE BANDIT BUSTER
(Action Pictures/Associated Exhibitors, December 19, 1926) 5 Reels
Buddy Roosevelt, Molly Malone, Lafe McKee, Winifred Landis, Robert Homans, Charles Whitaker, Al Taylor
Director: Richard Thorpe
Story: Frank L. Inghram
Producer: Lester F. Scott, Jr.

BETWEEN DANGERS
(Action Pictures/Pathe Exchange, February 13, 1927) 5 Reels
Buddy Roosevelt, Alma Rayford, Rennie Young, Al Taylor, Charles Thurston, Allen Sewall, Edward W. Borman, Hank Bell
Director: Richard Thorpe
Continuity: Richard Thorpe
Story: Walter J. Coburn - "Ride 'im Cowboy"
Producer: Lester F. Scott, Jr.

THE FIGHTIN' COMEBACK

(Action Pictures/Pathe, April 3, 1927) 5 Reels
Buddy Roosevelt, Clara Horton, Sidney M. Goldin,
Richard Neill, Robert Homans, Charles Thurston,
Richard Alexander
Director: Tenny Wright
Story: Walter J. Coburn - "The Sun Dance Kid"
Producer: Lester F. Scott, Jr.

CODE OF THE COW COUNTRY

(Action Pictures/Pathe, June 19, 1927) 5 Reels
Buddy Roosevelt, Elsa Benham, Hank Bell, Melbourne
MacDowell, Sherry Tansey, Richard Neill, Walter Maly,
Frank Ellis, Ruth Royce
Director: Oscar Apfel
Scenario: Betty Burbridge
Story: Wilton West
Producer: Lester F. Scott, Jr.

THE PHANTOM BUSTER

(Action Pictures/Pathe, August 14, 1927) 5 Reels
Buddy Roosevelt, Alma Rayford, Charles (Slim)
Whitaker, Boris Karloff, John Junior, Walter Maly,
Lawrence Underwood
Director: William Bertram
Scenario: Betty Burbridge
Story: Walter J. Coburn
Producer: Lester F. Scott, Jr.

RIDE 'EM HIGH

(Action Pictures/Pathe, October 9, 1927) 5 Reels
Buddy Roosevelt, Olive Hasbrouck, Charles K.
French, Robert Homans, George Magrill
Director: Richard Thorpe
Scenario: Frank L. Inghram
Story: Christopher B. Booth
Producer: Lester F. Scott, Jr.

THE COWBOY CAVALIER

(Action Pictures/Pathe, January 29, 1928) 5 Reels
Buddy Roosevelt, Olive Hasbrouck, Charles K.
French, Fannie Midgley, Robert Walker, Bob Clark,
William Ryno
Director: Richard Thorpe
Adaptation: Frank L. Inghram
Story: Lester F. Scott, Jr.

PAINTED TRAIL

(Trem Carr Productions/Rayart, February, 1928) 5 Reels
Buddy Roosevelt, Betty Baker, Leon De La Mothe,
Lafe McKee, Tommy Bay
Director: J. P. McGowan
Story/Scenario: Tom Roam

TRAILIN' BACK

(Trem Carr Productions/Rayart, March, 1928) 5 Reels
Buddy Roosevelt, Betty Baker, Lafe McKee, Leon De
La Mothe, Tommy Bay, Bert Sanderson, Al Bertram
Director/Scenario: J. P. McGowan
Story: Victor Rousseau

TRAIL RIDERS

(Trem Carr Productions/Rayart, April, 1928) 5 Reels
Buddy Roosevelt, Betty Baker, Lafe McKee, Pee Wee
Holmes, Paul Malvern, Leon De La Mothe, Tommy
Bay
Director/Scenario: J. P. McGowan
Story: Milton Angle

LIGHTNIN' SHOT

(Trem Carr Productions/Rayart, May, 1928) 5 Reels
Buddy Roosevelt, Carol Lane, J. P. McGowan, Frank
Earle, Jimmy Kane, Tommy Bay, Art Rowlands,
"Blanco"
Director/Scenario: J. P. McGowan
Story: Victor Rousseau

DEVIL'S TOWER

(Trem Carr Productions/Rayart, June, 1928) 5 Reels
Buddy Roosevelt, Thelma Pharr, Frank Earle, J. P.
McGowan, Art Rowlands, Tommy Bay
Director: J. P. McGowan
Scenario: Victor Rousseau

MYSTERY VALLEY

(Trem Carr Productions/Rayart, July, 1928) 5 Reels
Buddy Roosevelt, Carol Lane, Tommy Bay, Jimmy
Kane, Art Rowlands
Director/Scenario: J. P. McGowan
Story: Howard E. Morgan - "Snow Dust"

NAPOLEON'S BARBER

(Fox, November 24, 1928) 3 Reels
Otto Matiesen, Frank Reicher, Michael Mark, Natalie
Golitzen, Helen Darem, Philippe De Lacy, D'Arcy
Corrigan, Henry Herbert, Russ Powell, Kent Sanderson
(Buddy Roosevelt)
(Sound feature)
Director: John Ford
Story/Scenario: Arthur Caesar

STRONG BOY

(Fox, March 3, 1929) 6 Reels
(sound effects and music score)
Victor McLaglen, Leatrice Joy, J. Farrell MacDonald, Clyde Cook, Kent Sanderson *(Buddy Roosevelt)*, Douglas Scott, Slim Summerville, Tom Wilson, Eulalie Jensen, David Torrence, Dolores Johnson, Robert Ryan, Jack Pennick
Director: John Ford
Scenario: James Kevin McGuinness, Andrew Bennison, John McLain
Story: Frederick Hazlitt Brennan

BLACK WATCH

(Fox, May 26, 1929)
Victor McLaglen, Myrna Loy, Roy D'Arcy, Pat Somerset, David Rollins, Mitchell Lewis, Walter Long, David Percy, Lumsden Hare, Cyril Chadwick, David Torrence, Francis Ford, Claude King, Frederick Sullivan, Joseph Diskay, Richard Travers, Joyzelle, Kent Sanderson *(Buddy Roosevelt)*
Director: John Ford
Scenario: James K. McGuinness and John Stone
Story: Talbot Mundy - "King of the Khyber Rifles" (an all-talking feature)

WAY OUT WEST

(Metro-Goldwyn-Mayer, August 2, 1930) 8 Reels
(Sound)
William Haines, Leila Hyams, Polly Moran, Cliff Edwards, Francis X. Bushman, Jr., Vera Marsh, Charles Middleton, Jack Pennick, *Buddy Roosevelt,* Jay Wilsey (Buffalo Bill, Jr.)
Director: Fred Niblo
Story/Scenario: Bryan Morgan, Alfred Brock

WESTWARD BOUND

(Webb-Douglas Productions/Syndicate, January 25, 1931) 60 Minutes
Buffalo Bill, Jr., *Buddy Roosevelt,* Allene Ray, Yakima Canutt, Ben Corbett, Fern Emmett, Tom London, Robert Walker, Pete Morrison, Henry Roquemore, Wally Wales
Director: Harry Webb
Story: Carl Krusada
Producers: Harry Webb and F. E. Douglas

DISHONORED

(Paramount, April 4, 1931) 91 Minutes
Marlene Dietrich, Vitor McLaglen, Lew Cody, Gustav von Seyffertitz, Warner Oland, Barry Norton, Davison Clark, Wilfred Lucas, Ruth Mayhew, Alexis Davidoff, William B. Davidson, Ethan Laidlaw, Joseph Girald, George Irving, *Buddy Roosevelt*
Director/Story: Josef von Sternberg
Scenario: Daniel N. Rubin

LIGHTNIN' SMITH RETURNS

(Syndicate, August 31, 1931) 59 Minutes
Buddy Roosevelt, Barbara Worth, Tom London, Pee Wee Holmes, Jack Richardson, Fred Parker, William Bertram, Nick Dunray, Slim Whitaker, Sam Tittley
Director/Story/Producer: Jack Irwin
(Film also known as **Valley of the Badmen**)

WEST OF BROADWAY

(Metro-Goldwyn-Mayer, November 30, 1931) 71 Minutes
John Gilbert, El Brendel, Lola Moran, Madge Evans, Ralph Conroy, Gwen Lee, Hedda Hopper, Ruth Renick, Willie Fung, Kermit Maynard, *Buddy Roosevelt*
Director: Harry Beaumont
Story: Ralph Graves and Bess Meredyth
Adaptation: Gene Warkey

THE FOURTH HORSEMAN

(Universal, September 25, 1932) 63 Minutes
Tom Mix, Margaret Lindsay, Fred Kohler, Raymond Hatton, Rosita Matstini, *Buddy Roosevelt,* Edmund Cobb, Richard Cramer, Herman Nolan, Paul Shawhan, Donald Kirke, Harry Allen, Duke Lee, C. E. Anderson, Helene Millard, Martha Mattox, Frederick Howard, Grace Cunard, Walter Brennan, Pat Harmon, Hank Mann, Jim Corey, Delmar Watson, Fred Burns, Bud Osborne, Harry Tenbrook, Charles Sullivan, Sandy Sallee, Nip Reynolds, Henry Morris, Clyde Kinney, Jim Kinney, Ed Hendershot, Joe Balch, Augie Gomez, Frank Guskie, "Tony, Jr."
Director: Hamilton McGadden
Story: Nina Wilcox Putham
Screenplay: Jack Cunningham

WILD HORSE MESA

(Paramount, November 25, 1932) 65 Minutes
Randolph Scott, Sally Blaine, Fred Kohler, James Bush, George Hayes, Charley Grapewin, *Buddy Roosevelt,* Lucille LaVerne, Jim Thorpe, E. H. Calvert
Director: Henry Hathaway
Story: Zane Grey
Screenplay: Frank Clark, Harold Shumate

TEXAS TORNADO

(Kent, 1932)
Lane Chandler, *Buddy Roosevelt,* Doris Hill, Robert Gale, Yakima Canutt, Ben Corbett, Edward Hearn, Bart Carre, Mike Brand, Fred Burns, J. Frank Glendon, Pat Herly, Wes Warner, "Raven"
Director/Producer/Screenplay: Oliver Drake

WHAT NOT TO DO IN BRIDGE

(RKO-Radio, October 13, 1933) 2 Reels
Ely Culbertson, Josephine Culbertson, Chick Chandler, Lillian Rich, Ernie Shields, Phil Dunham, Eddie Boland, Harry Bowen, John Rand, Bill Franey, Al Kline, Nora Earl, *Buddy Roosevelt*, Robert Ripley, Harry Seymour, Eve Dennison, Bill Boggs, Jack Raymond, William Eddritt, Randolph Connolly, Harry Bradley
Director: Murray Roth
Supervisor: Lou Brock

OPERATOR 13

(Cosmopolitan/MGM, June 11, 1934) 9 Reels
Marion Davies, Gary Cooper, Jean Parker, Katherine Alexander, Ted Healy, Russell Hardie, Henry Wadsworth, Douglass Dumbrille, Willard Robertson, Fuzzy Knight, Sidney Toler, Robert McWade, Marjorie Gateson, Wade Boteler, Walter Long, Hattie McDaniel, Francis McDonald, William H. Griffith, James Marcus, The Mills Brothers (Vocal Group), Frank McGlynn, Jr., *Buddy Roosevelt*, Wheeler Oakman, Reginald Barlowe, Richard Powell, Ernie Alexander, Belle Daube, Wilfred Lucas, Bob Stevenson, Martin Turner, Frank Burt, Wallie Howe, William Henry, Richard Tucker, Arthur Grant, Sherry Tansey, Lia Lance, Charles Lloyd, DeWitt Jennings, Sam Ash, Ernie Adams, Clarence Wilson, Franklin Parker, Claudia Coleman, Sterling Holloway, Sherry Hall, Douglas Fowley, Frank Marlowe, Fred Warren, John Elliott, Frank Leighton, James C. Morton, Hattie Hill, John Kirkley, John Larkin, Poppy White
Director: Richard Boleslavsky
Producer: Lucien Hubbard
Screenplay: Harry Thew, Zelda Sears, Eve Greene
Story: Robert W. Chambers

BOSS COWBOY

(Superior Talking Pictures, 1934)
Buddy Roosevelt, Frances Morris, Sam Pierce, Fay McKenzie, Bud Osborne, George Chesebro, Lafe McKee, Merrill McCormack, Clyde McClary, Allen Holbrook
Director/Producer: Victor Adamson (Denver Dixon)
Story/Screenplay: Betty Burbridge

CIRCLE CANYON

(Superior Talking Pictures, 1934)
Buddy Roosevelt, June Mathews, Clarise Woods, Bob Williamson, Allen Holbrook, Harry Leland, George Hazle, Clyde McClary, Mark Harrison, Ernest Scott, Johnny Tyke
Director/Producer: Victor Adamson (Denver Dixon)
Story: "Gun Glory" - Burl Tuttle
Screenplay: B. R. (Burl) Tuttle

LIGHTNING RANGE

(Superior Talking Pictures, 1934)
Buddy Roosevelt, Patsy Bellamy, Betty Butler, Denver Dixon, Jack Evans, Si Jenks, Boris Bullock, Ken Broeker, Clyde McClary, Bart Carre, Olin Francis, Jack Bronston, Lafe McKee, Genee Boutell, Anne Howard, Merrill McCormack
Director/Producer: Victor Adamson (Denver Dixon)
Story: L. V. Jefferson

RANGE RIDERS

(Superior Talking Pictures, 1934)
Buddy Roosevelt, Barbara Starr, Merrill McCormack, Denver Dixon, Fred Parker, Clyde McClary, Horace B. Carpenter, Lew Meehan, Herman Hack
Director/Producer: Victor Adamson (Denver Dixon)
Screenplay: L. V. Jefferson

CALL OF THE SAVAGE

(Universal, June, 1935) 12 Chapters
Noah Beery, Jr., Dorothy Short, Harry L. Woods, Walter Miller, Bryant, Washburn, Frederic MacKaye, John Davidson, Eddie Kane, Stanley Andrews, Russ Powell, William Desmond, Frank Glendon, Viva Tattersall, Grace Cunard, Gwendolyn Logan, Don Brodie, H. Burroughs, Dick Jones, Wally Wales, Al Ferguson, *Buddy Roosevelt*, J. P. McGowan
Director: Louis Friedlander
Story: Otis Adelbert Kline - "Jan of the Jungle"
Screenplay: Nate Gazert, George Plympton, Basil Dickey
Chapter Titles: (1) Shipwrecked (2) Captured by Cannibals (3) Stampeding Death (4) Terrors of the Jungle (5) The Plunge of Peril (6) Thundering Waters (7) The Hidden Monster (8) Jungle Treachery (9) The Avenging Fire God (10) Descending Doom (11) The Dragon Strikes (12) The Pit of Flame

POWDERSMOKE RANGE

(RKO, September 27, 1935) 6 Reels
(First of the "3 Mesquiteers" films)
Harry Carey, Hoot Gibson, Bob Steele, Tom Tyler, Guinn "Big Boy" Williams, Boots Mallory, Wally Wales, Sam Hardy, Adrian Morris, Buzz Barton, Art Mix, Frank Rice, *Buddy Roosevelt*, Buffalo Bill, Jr., Franklyn Farnum, William Desmond, William Farnum, Ethan Laidlaw, Eddie Dunn, Ray Meyer, Barney Furey, Bob McKenzie, James Mason, Irving Bacon, Henry Rocquemore, Phil Dunham, Silver Tip Baker, Nelson McDowell, Frank Ellis
Director: Wallace Fox
Story: William Colt MacDonald
Screenplay: Adele Buffington
Producer: Cliff Reid

CAPTAIN BLOOD

(Cosmopolitan-Warner Brothers, December, 1935) 119 Minutes

Errol Flynn, Olivia DeHavilland, Lionel Atwill, Basil Rathbone, Ross Alexander, Guy Kibbee, Henry Stephenson, George Hassell, Forrester Harvey, Robert Barrat, Donald Meek, Hobart Cavanaugh, Frank McGlynn, Sr., David Torrence, J. Carrol Naish, Pedro de Cordoba, Leonard Mundie, Jessie Ralph, Stuart Casey, Halliwell Hobbes, Colin Kenny, E. E. Clive, Holmes Herbert, Mary Forbes, Reginald Barlowe, Ivan Simpson, Denis d'Auburn, Vernon Steele, Georges Renavent, Murray Kinnell, Harry Cording, Maude Leslie, Stymie Beard, Gardner James, Sam Appel, Chris-Pin Martin, Yola D'Arvil, Tina Menard, Frank Puglia, Art Ortego, Gene Alsace (also known as Buck Coburn and Rocky Camron), Kansas Moehring, Tom Steele, *Buddy Roosevelt,* William Yetter, Jim Thorpe, Blackie Whiteford, James Mason
Director: Michael Curtiz
Story: Rafael Sabatini
Screenplay: Casey Robinson
Producer: Hal B. Wallis
Associate Producers: Harry Joe Brown, Gordon Hollingshead

RAINBOW'S END

(First Division, 1935)
Hoot Gibson, June Gale, *Buddy Roosevelt,* Oscar Apfel, Warner Richmond, Ada Ince, Stanley Blystone, John Elliott, Henry Rocquemore, Fred Gilman
Director: Norman Spencer
Screenplay: Rollo Ward

GENERAL SPANKY

(Hal Roach Productions/Metro-Goldwyn-Mayer, December 11, 1936) 71 Minutes
George "Spanky" McFarland, Billie "Buckwheat" Thomas, Carl "Alfalfa" Switzer, Harold Switzer, Jerry Tucker, Flaette Roberts, Eugene "Porky" Lee, Rex Downing, Dickie De Nuet, Phillips Holmes, Ralph Morgan, Irving Pichel, Rosina Lawrence, James Burtis, Louise Beavers, Hobart Bosworth, Carl Voss, *Buddy Roosevelt,* Walter Gregory, Willie "Sleep 'n' Eat" Best, Jack Daugherty, Robert Middlemass, Henry Hall, Hooper Atchley, Karl Hackett, Frank H. LaRue, Ernie Alexander, Jack Hill, Ham Kinsey, Jack Cooper, Slim Whittaker, Harry Bernard, Alex Finlayson, Harry Strang, Richard Neill, Portia Lanning
Directors: Fred Newmeyer and Gordon Douglas
Screenplay/Story: John Guedel, Richard Flournoy, Carl Harbaugh, Hal Yates
Producer: Hal Roach

ROBINSON CRUSOE OF CLIPPER ISLAND

(Republic, 1936) 14 Chapters
Ray Mala, Mamo Clark, Herbert Rawlinson, William Newell, John Ward, John Dilson, Selmer Jackson, John Picorri, George Chesebro, Robert Kortman, George Cleveland, Lloyd Whitlock, Tiny Rowbuck, Tracy Layne, Herbert Weber, Anthony Pawley, Allen Connor, Evan Thomas, Larry Thompson, Allan Cavan, Ralph McCullough, Edmund Cobb, Ed Cassidy, Bud Osborne, Henry Sylvester, Jack Mack, Harry Strang, Oscar Hendrian, Val Duran, Al Taylor, Henry Hale, Lester Dorr, Jack Stewart, *Buddy Roosevelt,* Jerry Jerome, David Horsley, F. Herrick, Frazer Acosta, Francis Walker, Don Brodie, Frank Ellis
Directors: Mack V. Wright, Ray Taylor
Screenplay/Story: Morgan Cox, Barry Shipman, Maurice Geraghty
Associate Producer: Sol C. Siegel
Supervisor: J. Laurence Wickland

THE PLOUGH AND THE STARS

(RKO, January 15, 1937) 72 Minutes
Barbara Stanwyck, Preston Foster, Barry Fitzgerald, Dennis O'Dea, Eileen Crowe, Arthur Shields, Erin O'Brien-Moore, Brandon Hurst, F. J. McCormick, Una O'Connor, Moroni Olsen, J. M. Kerrigan, Neil Fitzgerald, Bonita Granville, Cyril McLaglen, Doris Lloyd, Mary Gordon, D'Arcy Corrigan, Wesley Barry, Robert Homans, *Buddy Roosevelt,,* Gaylord Pendleton, Michael Fitzmaurice, Mary Quinn
Director: John Ford
Scenario: Dudley Nichols
Story: Sean O'Casey
Associate Producers: Cliff Reid and Robert Sisk

DICK TRACY

(Republic, March, 1937) 15 Chapters
Ralph Byrd, Kay Hughes, Smiley Burnette, Lee Van Atta, John Picorri, Carleton Young, Fred Hamilton, Francis X. Bushman, John Dilson, Dick Beach, Wedgewood Nowell, Theodore Lorch, Edwin Stanley, Harrison Greene, Herbert Weber, *Buddy Roosevelt,* George DeNormand, Byron K. Foulger, Ed Platt, Lou Fulton, Nicholas Nelson, Bruce Mitchell, Sam Flint, John Holland, Monte Montague, Mary Kelley, Al Taylor, Forbes Murray, Hal Price, Ann Ainslee, Henry Sylvester, Milburn Morante, Kit Guard, William Stahl, Jack Ingram, Roy Barcroft, Leander de Cordova, Alice Fleming, I. Stanford Jolley, Jane Keckley, Wally West, Edward LeSaint, John Bradford, Jack Gardner, Bob Reeves, Lester Dorr, Kernan Cripps
Director: Ray Taylor, Alan James
Based on the comic strip by Chester Gould
Screenplay: Barry Shipman, Winston Miller

16

Story: Morgan Cox, George Morgan
Associate Producer: J. Laurence Wickland
Producer: Nat Levine
Chapter Titles: (1) The Spider Strikes (2) The Bridge of Terror (3) The Fur Pirates (4) Death Rides the Sky (5) Brother Against Brother (6) Dangerous Waters (7) The Ghost Town Mystery (8) Battle in the Clouds (9) The Stratosphere Adventure (10) The Gold Ship (11) Harbor Pursuit (12) The Trail of the Spider (13) The Fire Trap (14) The Devil in White (15) Brothers United

SOS COAST GUARD

(Republic, September, 1937) 12 Chapters
Ralph Byrd, Bela Lugosi, Maxine Doyle, Richard Alexander, Lee Ford, John Picorri, Lawrence Grant, Thomas Carr, Carleton Young, Allen Connor, George Chesebro, Ranny Weeks, Joe Mack, Herbert Weber, Dick Sheldon, Robert Walker, Gene Marvey, Eddie Phillips, Reed Sheffield, Frank Wayne, Warren Jackson, Dick Scott, Herbert Rawlinson, Jack Clifford, Jack Daley, Tom Ung, Lee Frederick, King Mojave, Curley Dresden, Henry Morris, Vinegar Roan, James Millican, Alexander Leftwich, Roy Barcroft, Joseph Girard, Lester Dorr, Edward Cassidy, Kit Guard, Frank Ellis, Rex Lease, Floyd Criswell, Jerry Frank, Frank Morgan, Audrey Gaye, Jack Ingram, Pat Mitchell, *Buddy Roosevelt*
Director: William Witney, Alan James
Story: Morgan Cox, Ronald Davidson
Screenplay: Barry Shipman, Franklyn Adreon
Associate Producer: Sol C. Siegel
Supervisor: Robert Beche
Chapter Titles: (1) Disaster at Sea (2) Barrage of Death (3) The Gas Chamber (4) The Fatal Shaft (5) The Mystery Ship (6) Deadly Cargo (7) Undersea Terror (8) The Crash (9) Wolves at Bay (10) The Acid Trail (11) The Sea Battle (12) The Deadly Circle

THE BUCCANEER

(Paramount, February 4, 1938) 13 Reels
Fredric March, Franciska Gaal, Akim Tamiroff, Margot Grahame, Walter Brennan, Anthony Quinn, Ian Keith, Douglass Dumbrille, Fred Kohler, Sr., Robert Barrat, Hugh Southern, John Rogers, Hans Steinke, Stanley Andrews, Beulah Bondi, Spring Byington, Montagu Love, Louise Campbell, Eric Stanley, Gilbert Emery, Holmes Herbert, Evelyn Keyes, Francis J. McDonald, Frank Melton, Jack Hubbard, Richard Denning, Lina Basquette, John Patterson, John Sutton, Mae Busch, Philo McCullough, James Craig, Rex Lease, *Buddy Roosevelt*, E. J. LeSaint, Ed Brady, Ralph Lewis, Charlotte Wynters, Maude Fealy, Jane Keckley, Barry Norton
Director/Producer: Cecil B. DeMille

Screenplay: Edwin Justus Mayer, Harold Lamb, and C. Gardner Sullivan
Adaptation: Jennie Macpherson
Story: Lyle Saxon - "Lafitte the Pirate"
Associate Producer: William H. Pine

THE FIGHTING DEVIL DOGS

(Republic, June, 1938) 12 Chapters
Lee Powell, Herman Brix, Eleanor Stewart, Montagu Love, Hugh Sothern, Lester Dorr, Stanley Price, Edwin Stanley, Sam Flint, Perry Ivins, Forrest Taylor, John Picorri, Carleton Young, John Davidson, Henry Otho, Reed Howes, Tom London, Edmund Cobb, Alan Gregg, Allan Mathews, Fred Schaefer, Harry Strang, Sherry Hall, Thomas Carr, Howard Chase, Lloyd Whitlock, Lee Baker, Jack Ingram, Robert Kortman, Bud Osborne, F. Herrick Herick, Ken Cooper, Jerry Frank, Jack O'Shea, Millard McGowan, Theodore Lorch, Al Taylor, Robert Wilbur, Harry Anderson, Monte Montague, Larry Steers, Bruce Lane, Lee Frederick, William Stahl, George Magrill, *Buddy Roosevelt*, Wesley Hopper, Edward Foster, Eddie Dew, Duke York, George DeNormand, Francis Sayles, John Hiestand, Joe Delacruz, Victor Wong
Director: William Witney, John English
Screenplay: Barry Shipman, Franklyn Adreon, Ronald Davidson, Sol Shor
Associate Producer: Robert Beche
Chapter Titles: (1) The Lightning Strikes (2) The Mill of Disaster (3) The Silenced Witness (4) Cargo of Mystery (5) Undersea Bandits (6) The Torpedo of Doom (7) The Phantom Killer (8) Tides of Trickery (9) Attack from the Skies (10) In the Camp of the Enemy (11) The Baited Trap (12) Killer at Bay

KING OF ALCATRAZ

(Paramount, October 12, 1938) 56 Minutes
Gail Patrick, Lloyd Nolan, Harry Carey, J. Carrol Naish, Robert Preston, Anthony Quinn, Richard Stanley (Dennis Morgan), Virginia Dabney, Emory Parnell, Dorothy Howe, John Hart, Philip Warren, Porter Hall, Richard Denning, Tom Tyler, Gustav von Seyfferitz, Monte Blue, Hooper Atchley, *Buddy Roosevelt*, Stanley Blystone
Director: Robert Florey
Story/Screenplay: Irving Reis

THE LONE RANGER RIDES AGAIN

(Republic, January 25, 1939) 15 Chapters
Robert Livingston, Chief Thundercloud, "Silver Chief" (a horse), Duncan Renaldo, Billy Bletcher, Jinx Falken, Ralph Dunn, J. Farrell MacDonald, Rex Lease, William Gould, Henry Otho, John Beach, Glenn Strange, Stanley Blystone, Eddie Parker, Al Taylor, Carleton

Young, Charles Whitaker, Bob Robinson, Ralph LeFever, Charles Regan, Fred Schaefer, David Sharpe, Art Felix, Chick Hannon, Eddie Dean, Bob McClung, Betty Roadman, Duke Lee, Howard Chase, Ernie Adams, Nelson McDowell, Walter Wills, Jack Kirk, Fred Burns, Buddy Mason, Lew Meehan, Wheeler Oakman, Forrest Taylor, Frank Ellis, Herman Hack, Bill Yrigoyen, Wesley Hopper, Bud Wolfe, Joe Yrigoyen, Duke Taylor, Forest Burns, George DeNormand, George Burton, Tommy Coats, Howard Hickey, Barry Hays, Ted Wells, Burt Dillard, Cecil Kellogg, Carl Sepulveda, Buddy Messenger, Jerome Ward, Roger Williams, *Buddy Roosevelt,* Jack Montgomery, Post Parks, Art Dillard, Horace Carpenter, Cactus Mack, Lafe McKee, Augie Gomez, Charles Hutchison, Monte Montague, Griff Barnette, Joe Perez
Directors: William Witney, John English
Screenplay: Franklyn Adreon, Ronald Davidson, Sol Shor, Barry Shipman
Associate Producer: Robert Beche
Chapter Titles: (1) The Lone Ranger Returns (2) Masked Victory (3) The Black Raiders Strike (4) The Cavern of Doom (5) Gents of Deceit (6) The Trap (7) The Lone Ranger at Bay (8) Ambush (9) Wheels of Doom (10) The Dangerous Captive (11) Death Blow (12) Blazing Peril (13) Exposed (14) Besieged (15) Frontier Justice

STAGECOACH
(United Artists, March 3, 1939) 96 Minutes
Claire Trevor, John Wayne, Thomas Mitchell, George Bancroft, Andy Devine, John Carradine, Louise Platt, Donald Meek, Berton Churchill, Tom Tyler, Tim Holt, Chris-Pin Martin, Elvira Rios, Billy Cody, *Buddy Roosevelt,* Yakima Canutt, Paul McVay, Joe Rickson, Harry Tenbrook, Jack Pennick, Kent Odell, William Hopper, Vester Pegg, Ted Lorch, Artie Ortego, Merril McCormack, Franklyn Farnum, James Mason, Si Jenks, Robert Homans, Chief White Horse, Bryant Washburn, Walter McGrail, Francis Ford, Chief Big Tree, Marga Daighton, Florence Lake, Duke Lee, Cornelius Keefe, Nora Cecil, Lou Mason, Mary Walker, Ed Brady
Director: John Ford
Story: Ernest Haycox - "Stage to Lordsburg"
Screenplay: Dudley Nichols
Producer: Walter Wanger

THE HUNCHBACK OF NOTRE DAME
(RKO, December 29, 1939) 115 Minutes
Charles Laughton, Maureen O'Hara, Edmond O'Brien, Sir Cedric Hardwicke, Thomas Mitchell, Walter Hampden, Harry Davenport, Alan Marshall, Katherine Alexander, George Zucco, Helene Whitney, Minna Gombell, Fritz Leiber, Etienne Giradot, Rod LaRocque,

Arthur Hohl, George Tobias, Spencer Charters, Fred Kohler, Jr., *Buddy Roosevelt*
Director: William Dieterle
Producer: Pandro S. Berman
Screenplay: Sonya Levien, Bruno Frank
Story: Victor Hugo

THE LONE RIDER RIDES ON
(PRC, January 10, 1941) 61 Minutes
(Lone Rider Series)
George Houston, Al St. John, Hillary Brooke, Lee Powell, *Buddy Roosevelt,* Al Bridge, Frank Hagney, Tom London, Karl Hackett, Forrest Taylor, Frank Ellis, Curley Dresden, Isabel LaMal, Harry Harvey, Jr., Don Forrest, Bob Kortman, Wally West, Steve Clark
Director: Sam Newfield
Screenplay: Joe O'Donnell
Producer: Sigmund Neufeld

BILLY THE KID'S RANGE WAR
(PRC, January 24, 1941) 57 Minutes
(Billy the Kid Series)
Bob Steele, Al St. John, Joan Barclay, Carleton Young, Rex Lease, *Buddy Roosevelt,* Milt Kibbee, Karl Hackett, Ted Adams, Julian Rivero, John Ince, Alden Chase, Howard Master, Ralph Peters, Charles King, George Chesebro, Steve Clark, Tex Palmer
Director: Peter Stewart (Sam Newfield)
Screenplay: William Lively
Producer: Sigmund Neufeld

THUNDER OVER THE PRAIRIE
(Columbia, July 30, 1941) 60 Minutes
Charles Starrett, Eileen O'Hearn, Cliff Edwards, Carl (Cal) Shrum and His Rhythm Rangers, Stanley Brown, Danny Mummert, David Sharpe, Joe McGuinn, Donald Curtis, Ted Adams, Jack Rockwell, Budd Buster, Horace B. Carpenter, *Buddy Roosevelt*
Director: Lambert Hillyer
Story: James L. Rubel
Screenplay: Betty Burbridge
Producer: William Berke

KING OF THE TEXAS RANGERS
(Republic, October 4, 1941) 12 Chapters
Sammy Baugh, Neil Hamilton, Pauline Moore, Duncan Renaldo, Charles Trowbridge, Herbert Rawlinson, Frank Darien, Robert O. Davis, Monte Blue, Stanley Blystone, Kermit Maynard, Roy Barcroft, Kenne Duncan, Jack Ingram, Robert Barron, Frank Bruno, Monte Montague, Joseph Forte, Lucien Prival, Paul Gustine, Henry Hall, William Kellogg, Richard Simmons, Alan Gregg, Iron Eyes Cody, Forrest Taylor, Lee Shumway, Ernest Sarracino, Bud Jamison, John James, Dick Scott,

Bud Wolfe, Barry Hays, Earl Bunn, George Burrows, Pat O'Shea, Bert LeBaron, Jerry Jerome, Bobby Barber, Forest Burns, Max Waizman, Charles Whitaker, Jack Chapin, Howard Hughes, Michael Owen, Ken Terrell, Hooper Atchley, Otto Reichow, Chick Hannon, Herman Hack, Tommy Coats, Charles Thomas, Bob Robinson, Edward Cassidy, *Buddy Roosevelt*, John Bagni, Eddie Dew, George Allen, Jimmy Fawcett, Al Taylor, Duke Green, Merlyn Nelson, Loren Riebe, David Sharpe, Cy Clocum, Tom Steele, Duke Taylor, Bill Wilkus, Joe Yrigoyen
Director: William Witney, John English
Screenplay: Ronald Davidson, Norman S. Hall, Joseph Poland, Joseph O'Donnell, William Lively
Associate Producer: Hiram S. Brown, Jr.
Chapter Titles: (1) The Fifth Column Strikes (2) Dead End (3) Man Hunt (4) Trapped (5) Test Flight (6) Double Danger (7) Death Takes the Witness (8) Counterfeit Trail (9) Ambush (10) Sky Raiders (11) Trail of Death (12) Code of the Rangers

DICK TRACY VS. CRIME, INC.
(Republic, 1941) 15 Chapters
Ralph Byrd, Michael Owen, Jan Wiley, John Davidson, Ralph Morgan, Kenneth Harlan, John Dilson, Howard Hickman, Robert Faazer, Robert Fiske, Jack Mulhall, Hooper Atchley, Anthony Warde, Chuck Morrison, Archie Twitchell, Frank Meredith, Jack Kenney, John Merton, Forrest Taylor, Terry Frost, Edward Hearn, Raphael Bennett, Jacques Lory, Joseph Kirk, Dick Lamarr, Barry Hays, Marjorie Kane, Bert LeBaron, Charles McAvoy, John James, Fred Schaefer, Duke Taylor, Frank Alten, George Peabody, Nora Lane, Sam Bernard, Robert Wilke, Fred Kohler Jr., Stanley Price, Walter Miller, Edmund Cobb, *Buddy Roosevelt*, Jimmy Fawcett, Al Seymour, C. Montague Shaw, Warren Jackson, William Hammer
Director: William Witney and John English
Screenplay: Ronald Davidson, Norman S. Hall, William Lively, Joseph O'Donnell, Joseph Poland
Based on the comic strip by Chester Gould
Associate Producer: W. J. O'Sullivan
Chapter Titles: (1) The Fatal Hour (2) The Prisoner Vanishes (3) Doom Patrol (4) Dead Man's Trap (5) Murder at Sea (6) Besieged (7) Sea Racketeers (8) Train of Doom (9) Beheaded (10) Flaming Peril (11) Seconds to Live (12) Trial by Fire (13) The Challenge (14) Invisible Terror (15) Retribution

SPY SMASHER
(Republic, 1942) 12 Chapters
Kane Richmond, Marguerite Chapman, Sam Flint, Hans Schumn, Tristram Coffin, Franco Corsaro, Hans Von Morhart, Georges Renavent, Robert O. Davis, Henry Zynda, Paul Bryar, Tom London, Richard Bond, Crane Whitley, John James, Yakima Canutt, Max Waizman, Howard Hughes, Charley Phillips, Martin Faust, Tom Steele, Eddie Jauregui, John Deheim, Bob Jamison, Walter Low, Jerry Jerome, Jack Arnold, Martin Garralaga, Robert Wilke, *Buddy Roosevelt*, Bud Wolfe, William Forrest, Nick Vehr, Duke Taylor, Sid Troy, Lee Phelps, Ken Terrell, Jimmy Fawcett, David Sharpe, Carleton Young, Roy Brent, Dudley Dickerson, George Sherwood, Lowden Adams, Jack O'Shea, Pat Moran, Robert Stevenson
Director: William Witney
Screenplay: Ronald Davidson, Norman S. Hall, William Lively, Joseph O'Donnell, Joseph Poland
Associate Producer: W. J. O'Sullivan
Chapter Titles: (1) American Beware (2) Human Target (3) Iron Coffin (4) Stratosphere Invaders (5) Descending Doom (6) The Invisible Witness (7) Secret Weapon (8) Sea Raiders (9) Highway Packetters (10) 2700° Fahrenheit (11) Hero's Death (12) V . . . —

SECRET SERVICE IN DARKEST AFRICA
(Republic, June, 1943) 15 Chapters
Rod Cameron, Joan Marsh, Duncan Renaldo, Lionel Royce, Kurt Kreuger, Frederic Brunn, Sigurd Tor, Georges Renavent, Kurt Katch, Ralf Harolde, William Vaughn, William Yetter, Hans Von Morhart, Erwin Goldi, Frederic Worlock, Paul Marion, Ken Terrell, Duke Green, Joe Yrigoyen, Eddie Phillips, Bud Geary, Reed Howes, Carey Loftin, Harry Semels, Tom Steele, Eddie Parker, Leonard Hampton, George Sorel, George J. Lewis, Jack LaRue, George DeNormand, Walter Fenner, Jacques Lory, Jack O'Shea, *Buddy Roosevelt*, John Davidson Frank Alten, Nino Bellini, Emily LaRue, Norman Nesbitt, John Royce, Ed Agresti
Director: Spencer Bennet
Screenplay: Royal Cole, Basil Dickey, Jesse Duffy, Ronald Davidson, Joseph O'Donnell, Joseph Poland
Associate Producer: W. J. O'Sullivan
Chapter Titles: (1) North African Intrigue (2) The Charred Witness (3) Double Death (4) The Open Grave (5) Cloaked in Flame (6) Dial of Doom (7) Murder Dungeon (8) Funeral Arrangements Completed (9) Invisible Menace (10) Racing Peril (11) Lightning Terror (12) Ceremonial (13) Unknown (14) Unknown (15) New Treachery Unmasked

ABILENE TOWN

(United Artists, January 11, 1946) 89 Minutes
Randolph Scott, Ann Dvorak, Edgar Buchanan, Rhonda Fleming, Lloyd Bridges, Helen Boyce, Howard Freeman, Richard Hale, Jack Lambert, Hank Patterson, Dick Curtis, Eddy Waller, *Buddy Roosevelt*
Director: Edwin L. Martin
Story: "Trail Town" - Ernest Haycox
Screenplay: Harold Shumate
Producer: Jules Levey

DAUGHTER OF DON Q

(Republic, February, 1946) 12 Chapters
Adrian Booth, Kirk Alyn, LeRoy Mason, Roy Barcroft, Claire Meade, Kernan Cripps, Jimmy Ames, Eddie Parker, Tom Steele, Dale Van Sickel, Fred Graham, Tom Quinn, John Daheim, Ted Mapes, I. Stanford Jolley, *Buddy Roosevelt*, Frederick Howard, George Chesebro, Michael Gaddis, Charles Sullivan, Arvon Dale, Maxine Doyle, Virginia Carroll, Jack O'Shea, George Magrill, Eddie Rocco, Matty Roubert, Joe Yrigoyen, Ken Terrell, Robert Wilke, Bud Wolfe, D'Arcy Miller, Betty Danko
Director: Spencer Bennet and Fred Brannon
Screenplay: Albert DeMond, Basil Dickey, Jesse Duffy, Lynn Perkins
Associate Producer: Ronald Davidson
Chapter Titles: (1) Multiple Murders (2) Vendetta (3) Under the Knives (4) Race to Destruction (5) Blackout (6) Forged Evidence (7) Execution by Error (8) Window to Death (9) The Juggernaut (10) Cremation (11) Glass Guillotine (12) Dead Man's Vengeance

BADMAN'S TERRITORY

(RKO, April 22, 1946) 98 Minutes
Randolph Scott, Ann Richards, George Hayes, Lawrence Tierney, Tom Tyler, John Halloran, Phil Warren, Steve Brodie, William Moss, James Warren, Isabel Jewell, Morgan Conway, Nestor Pavia, Chief Thunder Cloud, Ray Collins, Virginia Sale, Andrew Tombes, Harry Holman, Richard Hale, Emory Parnell, Ethan Laidlaw, Kermit Maynard, Bud Osborne, Chuck Hamilton, *Buddy Roosevelt*
Director: Tim Whelan
Screenplay: Jack Natteford, Luci Ward
Producer: Nat Holt

KING OF THE FOREST RANGERS

(Republic, April 27, 1946) 12 Chapters
Larry Thompson, Helen Talbot, Stuart Hamblen, Anthony Warde, LeRoy Mason, Scott Elliott, Tom London, Walter Soderling, Bud Geary, Harry Strang, Ernie Adams, Eddie Parker, Jack Kirk, Tom Steele, Dale Van Sickel, Stanley Blystone, Marin Sais, *Buddy Roosevelt*, Scott Elliott, Robert Wilke, Sam Ash, Carey Loftin,

Sailor Vincent, Jay Kirby, Joe Yrigoyen, Nick Warrick, Ken Terrell, Bud Wolfe, Wheaton Chambers, James Martin, Rex Lease, Charles Sullivan, David Sharpe
Director: Spencer Bennet and Fred Brannon
Screenplay: Albert DeMond, Basil Dickey, Jesse Duffy, Lynn Perkins
Associate Producer: Ronald Davidson
Chapter Titles: (1) The Mystery of the Towers (2) Shattered Evidence (3) Terror by Night (4) Deluge of Destruction (5) Pursuit into Perio (6) Brink of Doom (7) Design for Murder (8) The Flying Coffin (9) S.O.S. (10) The Death Detector (11) The Flaming Pit (12) Tower of Vengeance

BUCK PRIVATES COME HOME

(Universal, April, 1947) 77 Minutes
Bud Abbott, Lou Costello, Tom Brown, Joan Fulton, Nat Pendleton, Beverly Simmons, Don Beddoe, Don Porter, Donald MacBride, Lane Watson, William Ching, Peter Thompson, George Beban, Jr., Jimmie Dodd, Lennie Breman, Al Murphy, Bob Wilke, William Haade, Janna DeLoose, *Buddy Roosevelt*, Chuck Hamilton, Patricia Alphin, Joe Kirk, Ralph Dunn, Charles Trowbridge, Russell Hicks, John Sheehan, Cliff Clark, Jean Del Val, Frank Marlowe, Otola Nesmith, Eddie Dunn, Harlan Warde, Lyle Lattel, Myron Healy, James Farley, Rex Lease, Ernie Adams, Milburn Stone, Knox Manning
Director: Charles Barton
Screenplay: John Grant, Frederic I. Rinaldo, Robert Lees
Producer: Robert Arthur
Story: Richard MacCauley and Bradford Ropes

A DOUBLE LIFE

(Universal-International, February, 1948) 103 Minutes
Ronald Colman, Signe Hasso, Edmond O'Brien, Shelley Winters, Ray Collins, Phillip Loeb, Millard Mitchell, Joe Sawyer, Charles LaTorre, Whit Bissell, John Drew Colt, Marjorie Woodworth, Peter Thompson, Art Smith, Claire Carleton, Guy Bates Post, Elliott Reid, Nina Gilbert, John Derek, *Buddy Roosevelt*
Director: George Cukor
Screenplay: Ruth Gordon and Garson Kanin
Producer: Michael Kanin

FLAXY MARTIN

(Warner Brothers, January, 1949) 86 Minutes
Virginia Mayo, Zachary Scott, Dorothy Malone, Tom D'Andrea, Helen Westcott, Douglas Kennedy, Elisha Cook, Jr., Douglas Fowley, Monte Blue, Jack Overman, *Buddy Roosevelt*
Director: Richard Bare
Screenplay: David Lang
Producer: Saul Elkins

KING OF THE ROCKET MEN

(Republic, May, 1949) 12 Chapters
Tristram Coffin, Mae Clarke, Don Haggerty, House Peters, Jr., James Craven, I. Stanford Jolley, Douglas Evans, Ted Adams, Stanley Price, Dale Van Sickel, Tom Steele, David Sharpe, Eddie Parker, Michael Ferro, Frank O'Conner, *Buddy Roosevelt*, Arvon Dale, Bert LeBaron, Carey Loftin, Jack O'Shea, Art Gilmore
Director: Fred Brannon
Screenplay: Royal Cole, William Lively, Sol Shor
Associate Producer: Franklin Adreon

BEYOND THE FOREST

(Warner Brothers, October 22, 1949) 97 Minutes
Bette Davis, Joseph Cotten, David Brian, Ruth Roman, Minor Watson, Dona Drake, Regis Toomey, Sarah Selby, Mary Servoss, Frances Charles, Harry Tyler, Ralph Littlefield, Creighton Hale, Joel Allen, Ann Doran, *Buddy Roosevelt*, Bobby Henshaw, James Craven, Eve Miller, Gail Bonney, Hallene Hill, June Evans, Judith Wood, Eileen Stevens, Hal Gerard, Jim Haward, Charles Jordan, Frank Pharr
Director: King Vidor
Screenplay: Lenore Coffee
Story: Stuart Engstrand
Producer: Henry Blanke

COLT 45

(Warners, May 27, 1950) 70 Minutes
(Technicolor)
Randolph Scott, Zachary Scott, Ruth Roman, Lloyd Bridges, Alan Hale, Ian MacDonald, Chief Thundercloud, Walter Coy, Luther Crockett, Charles Evans, *Buddy Roosevelt*, Hal Taliaferro, Art Miles, Barry Reagan, Howard Negley, Aurora Navarro, Paul Newland, Franklin Farnum, Ed Peil, Sr., Jack Watt, Carl Andre, Royden Clark, Clyde Hudkins, Jr., Leroy Johnson, Ben Corbett, Kansas Moehring, Warren Fisk, Forrest R. Colee, Artie Orgego, Richard Brehm, Dick Hudkins, Leo McMahon, Bob Burrows, William Steele
Director: Edward L. Marin
Story/Screenplay: Thomas Blackburn
Producer: Saul Elkins

THE DESERT HAWK

(Universal-International, August, 1950) 77 Minutes
(Technicolor)
Yvonne De Carlo, Richard Green, Jackie Gleason, George Macready, Rock Hudson, Carl Esmond, Joe Besser, Ann Pearce, Marc Lawrence, Lois Andrews, Frank Puglia, Lucille Barkley, Donald Randolph, Ian MacDonald, Nestor Paiva, Richard Hale, Eileen Howe, Hazel Shaw, Mirian Dennish, Norma De Landa, Barbara Kelly, Vonne Lester, Mahmud Shaikhaly, *Buddy Roosevelt*, Virginia Hunter, Lester Sharpe, Ben Welden, Michael Ross, Lane Bradford, Shirley Ballard, Jack Raymond, Terry Frost, George Bruggerman, Michael Ansara, Fred Liddy, Bob Anderson, Jan Arvan, Milton Kibbee, Robert Filmer, Bob Wilke, Bruce Riley, Frank Lackteen, Dale Van Sickel, Shirley Ballard
Director: Frederick de Cordova
Screenplay: Aubrey Weisberg, Jack Pollexfen, Gerald Drayson Adams
Producer: Leonard Goldstein

KANSAS RAIDERS

(Universal-International, November, 1950) 80 Minutes
(Technicolor)
Audie Murphy, Brian Donlevy, Marguerite Chapman, Scott Brady, Anthony Curtis (Tony Curtis), Richard Arlen, Richard Long, James Best, John Kellogg, Dewey Martin, George Chandler, Charles Delaney, Richard Egan, David Wolfe, Mira McKinney, Sam Flint, *Buddy Roosevelt*, Larry McGrath, Ed Peril, Sr., Jack Perrin
Director: Ray Enright
Story/Screenplay: Robert L. Richards
Producer: Ted Richmond

DALLAS

(Warners, December 30, 1950) 94 Minutes
(Technicolor)
Gary Cooper, Ruth Roman, Steve Cochran, Raymond Massey, Barbara Payton, Leif Erickson, Antonio Moreno, Jerome Cowan, Reed Hadley, Gil Donaldson, Zon Murray, Will Wright, Monte Blue, Byron Keith, Jose Dominguez, Steve Dunhill, *Buddy Roosevelt*
Director: Stuart Heisler
Screenplay: John Twist
Producer: Anthony Veiller

ABBOTT AND COSTELLO IN THE FOREIGN LEGION

(Universal, 1950) 79 Minutes
Bud Abbott, Lou Costello, Patricia Medina, Walter Slezak, Douglas Dumbrille, Leon Balasco, Marc Lawrence, Tor Johnson, Wee Willie Davis, Sam Menacher, Fred Nurney, Paul Fierro, Henry Corden, Jack Raymond, Jack Shutta, Ernesto Morelli, Chuck Hamilton, Dan Seymour, Alberto Morin, Guy Beach, Ted Techt, Mahmud Shaikhaly, *Buddy Roosevelt*, Charmienne Harker, David Gorcey, Bobby Barber
Director: Charles Lamont
Producer: Robert Arthur
Screenplay: John Grant, Martin Pagaway, Leonard Stern
Story: D. D. Beauchamp

21

APACHE DRUMS

(Universal-Int., June 1, 1951) 75 Minutes
(Technicolor)

Stephen McNally, Doreen Gray, Willard Parker, Arthur Shields, James Griffith, Armando Silvestre, Georgia Backus, Clarence Muse, James Best, Ruthelma Stevens, Chinto Gusman, Ray Bennett, *Buddy Roosevelt*
Director: Hugo Fregonese
Story: David Chandler
Producer: Val Lewton

THE PRINCE WHO WAS A THIEF

(Universal, June, 1951) 88 Minutes

Tony Curtis, Piper Laurie, Everett Sloane, Jeff Corey, Betty Garde, Marvin Miller, Peggie Castle, Donald Randolph, Nita Bieber, Susan Cabot, King Donovan, Robert Rockwell, Frank Lackteen, Milada Maldova, Hayden Rorke, Carol Varga, *Buddy Roosevelt,* George Magrill
Director: Rudolph Mate
Screenplay: Gerald Drayson Adams and Aeneas MacKenzie
Story: Theodore Dreiser
Producer: Leonard Goldstein

THE OLD WEST

(Columbia, January 15, 1952) 61 Minutes
(Sepiatone)

Gene Autry, Gail Davis, Pat Buttram, Lyle Talbot, Louis Jean Heydt, House Peters, Sr., Dick Jones, Kathy Johnson, Don Harvey, Dee Pollack, Raymond L. Morgan, James Craven, Tom London, Frank Marvin, Syd Saylor, Bob Woodward, *Buddy Roosevelt,* Tex Terry, Pat O'Malley, Bobby Clark, Robert Hilton, John Merton, Frank Ellis
Director: George Archainbaud
Screenplay: Gerald Geraghty
Producer: Armand Schaefer

THE BELLE OF NEW YORK

(MGM, February, 1952) 82 Minutes
(Technicolor)

Fred Astaire, Vera-Ellen, Marjorie Main, Keenan Wynn, Alice Pearce, Clinton Sundberg, Gale Robbins, Lisa Ferraday, Henry Slate, Carol Brewster, Meredith Leeds, Lyn Wilde, Roger Davis, Dick Wessel, Percy Helton, Tom Dugan, *Buddy Roosevelt*
Director: Charles Walters
Producer: Arthur Freed
Screenplay: Robert O'Brien, Irving Elinson
Associate Producer: Chester Erskine
From a play by: Hugh Morton

HORIZONS WEST

(Universal-Int., October 1, 1952) 87 Minutes
(Technicolor)

Robert Ryan, Julia Adams, Rock Hudson, John McIntire, Judith, Braun, Raymond Burr, Frances Bavier, Dennis Weaver, Rodolfo Acosta, James Arness, Tom Powers, John Hubbard, Walter Reed, Tom Monroe, Douglas Fowley, Raymond Greenleaf, *Buddy Roosevelt,* Forbes Murray, Dan White, Robert Bice, Mae Clark, Alberto Morin, Eddie Parker, Monte Montague, John Harmon, Peter Mamakos, Paulette Turner
Director: Budd Boetticher
Story/Screenplay: Louis Stevens
Producer: Albert J. Cohen

THE REDHEAD FROM WYOMING

(Universal, December, 1952) 80 Minutes
(Technicolor)

Maureen O'Hara, Alex Nicol, Alexander Scourby, Jenne Cooper, Claudette Thornton, Palmer Lee (Gregg Palmer), Jack Kelly, William Bishop, Ray Bennett, Joe Bailey, Russ Williams, Dennis Weaver, David Alpert, Joe Bassett, Stacy Harris, Betty Allen, Robert Strauss, Larry Hudson, Edmund Cobb, Philo McCullough, Keith Kerrigan, Bob Merrick, Syd Saylor, George Taylor, Harold Goodwin, *Buddy Roosevelt,* Jack Hyde, Jack Perrin
Director: Lee Shoelm
Screenplay: Polly James and Herb Meadow
Producer: Leonard Goldstein

THE MISSISSIPPI GAMBLER

(Universal-Int., January, 1953) 98 Minutes
(Technicolor)

Tyrone Power, Piper Laurie, Julia Adams, John McIntire, William Reynolds, Paul Cavanaugh, Robert Warwick, John Baer, Ron Randell, Guy Williams, Ralph Dumke, King Donovan, Hugh Beaumont, Dennis Weaver, Gwen Vernon, Alan Dexter, Al Wyatt, Dale Van Sickel, Michael Dale, Bert LeBaron, Marcel De La Brosse, Frank Wilcox, Edward Earle, Dorothy Bruce, Angela Stevens, Rolfe Sedan, Saul Martell, Maya Van Horn, Tony Hughes, Fred Cavens, George Hamilton, David Newell, Eduardo Cansino, Jr., Jon Shepodd, *Buddy Roosevelt,* Anita Ekberg, Renate Hoy, Jackie Lougherty, Jeanne Thompson, Paul Bradley, Le Roi Antienne
Director: Rudolph Mate
Story/Screenplay: Seton I. Miller
Producer: Ted Richmond

LAW AND ORDER

(Universal-Int., May 1, 1953) 80 Minutes
(Technicolor)
Ronald Reagan, Dorothy Malone, Preston Foster, Alex Nicol, Ruth Hampton, Dennis Weaver, Chubby Johnson, Barry Kelly, *Buddy Roosevelt*
Director: Nathan Juran
Story: "Saint Johnson" - W. R. Burnett
Screenplay: John and Gwen Bagni, D. D. Beauchamp
Producer: John W. Rogers

RIDING SHOTGUN

(Warners, April 10, 1954) 75 Minutes
(WarnerColor)
Randolph Scott, Wayne Morris, Joan Weldon, Joe Sawyer, James Millican, Charles Buchinsky (Bronson), James Bell, Fritz Field, Richard Garrick, Victor Perrin, John Baer, William Johnstone, Kem Dibbs, Alvin Freeman, Edward Coch, Jr., Eva Lewis, Lonnie Price, Mary Lou Holloway, Boyd Morgan, Richard Benjamin, Jay Lawrence, George Ross, Ray Bennett, Jack Kenney, Jack Woody, Allegra Varron, Frosty Royse, Jimmy Mohley, Ruth Whitney, Bud Osborne, Budd Buster, *Buddy Roosevelt,* Dub Taylor, Joe Brockman, Harry Hines, Clem Fuller, Opan Evar, Morgan Brown, Bob Stephenson
Director: Andre de Toth
Story: Kenneth Perkins
Screenplay: Tom Blackburn
Producer: Ted Sherdeman

TALL MAN RIDING

(Warners, June 18, 1955) 83 Minutes
(Technicolor)
Randolph Scott, Dorothy Malone, Peggie Castle, William Ching, John Baragrey, Robert Barrat, John Dehner, Paul Richards, Lane Chandler, Mickey Simpson, Joe Bassett, Charles Watts, Russ Conway, Mike Reagan, Carl Andre, John Logan, Guy Hearn, Bill Faucett, Nolan Leary, Phil Rich, Eva Novak, *Buddy Roosevelt,* Jack Henderson, Bob Peoples, William Bailey, Patrick Henry, Joe Brooks, Vernon Rich, Bob Stephenson, Dub Taylor, Roger Creed
Director: Lesley Selander
Story: Norman A. Fox
Screenplay: Joseph Hoffman
Producer: David Wesibart

TRIBUTE TO A BADMAN

(MGM, April 13, 1956) 95 Minutes
(Eastman Color) (CinemaScope)
James Cagney, Don Dubbins, Stephen McNally, Irene Papas, Vic Morrow, James Griffith, Onslow Stevens, James Bell, Jeanette Nolan, Chubby Johnson, Royal Dano, Lee Van Cleef, Peter Chong, *Buddy Roosevelt,* Bud Osborne, Dennis Moore, Tom London, Tony Hughes, Roy Engel, John Halloran, Billy Dix, Clint Sharp
Director: Robert Wise
Story: Jack Schaefer
Screenplay: Michael Blankford
Producer: Sam Zimbalist

AROUND THE WORLD IN 80 DAYS

(Todd-AO, September, 1956) 175 Minutes
David Niven, Cantinflas, Robert Newton, Shirley MacLaine, Cameo performances by Charles Boyer, Joe E. Brown, Martine Carol, John Carradine, Charles Coburn, Ronald Colman, Melville Cooper, Noel Coward, Finlay Currie, Reginald Denny, Andy Devine, Marlene Dietrich, Luis Dominguin, Fernandel, Sir John Gielgud, Hermione Gingold, Jose Greco, Sir Cedric Hardwicke, Trevor Howard, Glynis Johns, Buster Keaton, Evelyn Lowe, A. E. Matthews, Col. Tim McCoy, Victor McLaglen, Mike Mazurki, John Mills, Alan Mowbray, Robert Morley, Jack Oakie, George Raft, Gilbert Roland, Cesar Romero, Frank Sinatra, Red Skelton, Ronald Squire, Basil Sydney, Harcourt Williams, *Buddy Roosevelt*
Director: Michael Anderson
Screenplay: S. J. Perelman
Story: Jules Verne
Producer: Michael Todd

SHOOT-OUT AT MEDICINE BEND

(Warners, May 4, 1957) 87 Minutes
Randolph Scott, James Craig, Angie Dickinson, Dani Crayne, James Garner, Gordon Jones, Trevor Bardette, Don Beddoe, Myron Healey, John Alderson, Harry Harvey, Sr., Robert Warwick, Howard Negley, Marshall Bradford, Ann Doran, Daryn Hinton, Dickie Bellis, Edward Hinton, Lane Bradford, Francis Morris, Robert Lynn, Sam Flint, Philip Van Zandt, Guy Wilkerson, Syd Saylor, Harry Rowland, Majorie Bennett, Jesslyn Fay, Marjorie Stapp, Nancy Kulp, George Meader, Rory Mallinson, Dee Carroll, Gerald Charlebois, Dale Van Sickel, Gil Perkins, Harry Lauter, George Russ, Carol Henry, George Pembroke, Tom Monroe, John Roy, *Buddy Roosevelt,* George Bell
Director: Richard L. Bare
Screenplay: John Tucker Battle and D. D. Beauchamp
Producer: Richard Wolfe

WESTBOUND

(Warners, April 25, 1925) 96 Minutes
(Warner Color)

Randolph Scott, Virginia Mayo, Karen Steele, Michael Dante, Andrew Duggan, Michael Pate, Wally Brown, John Day, Walter Barnes, Fred Sherman, Mack Williams, Ed Prentiss, Rory Mallinson, Rudi Dana, Tom Monroe, Jack Perrin, *Buddy Roosevelt,* Kermit Maynard, May Boss, William A. Green, Jack E. Henderson, Felice Richmond, Creighton Hale, Gertrude Keeler, Walter Reed, Jack C. Williams, Gerald Roberts, John Hudkins, Don Happy, Bobby Herron, Fred Stromscoe

Director: Budd Boetticher
Story: Berne Giler and Albert Shelby LeVino
Screenplay: Berne Giler
Producer: Henry Blanke

LI'L ABNER

(Paramount, October, 1959) 113 Minutes

Peter Palmer, Leslie Parrish, Stubby Kaye, Howard St. John, Julia Newmar, Stella Stevens, Billie Hayes, Joe E. Marks, Bern Hoffman, Al Nelson, Robert Strauss, William Lanteau, Ted Thurston, Carmen Alvarez, Alan Carney, Stanley Simmonds, *Buddy Roosevelt*

Director: Melvin Frank
Screenplay: Melvin Frank and Norman Panama
Producer: Norman Panama

THE MAN WHO SHOT LIBERTY VALANCE

(Paramount, April 11, 1962) 123 Minutes

John Wayne, James Stewart, Vera Miles, Lee Marvin, Edmond O'Brien, Andy Devine, Woody Strode, John Qualen, Jeanette Nolan, Lee Van Cleef, Strother Martin, Ken Murray, John Carradine, Willis Nouchey, Carleton Young, Denver Pyle, Robert F. Simon, O. Z. Whitehead, Paul Birch, Jack Pennick, Anna Lee, Charles Seel, Shug Fisher, Earle Hodgins, *Buddy Roosevelt,* Stuart Holmes, Dorothy Phillips, Gertrude Astor, Eva Novak, Slim Talbot, Monte Montana, Bill Henry, John B. Whiteford, Helen Gibson, Major Sam Harris

Director: John Ford
Screenplay: James Warner Bellah, Willis Goldbeck
Producer: Willis Goldbeck

2 ● GEORGE O'BRIEN

All Man and a Barrel of Fun

In the history of the genre only a handful of Western film stars ever achieved any real stature as dramatic actors, most being content to shoot, ride, fight, and sometimes romance their way through minor Western films called "programmers," "oaters," "B's," "giddy-ups," "sagebrushers," or "shoot-em-ups." Exceptions included Jack Holt, William Boyd, William Desmond, Harry Carey, Randolph Scott, William Farnum, and the subject of this chapter—George O'Brien.

O'Brien was for a decade one of the top luminaries in the Western film world, bringing to the genre a quality of acting and action seldom seen. A few men, such as Mix, Maynard, Jones, Hoxie, and Gibson, could match his daredevil antics on the screen; and a few, such as those mentioned in the opening paragraph above, could act as well as George—but Buck Jones was the only Western ace to challenge George seriously as **both** a top-flight actor and actioneer. Jones' acting talents, however, were pretty much limited to Westerns, whereas O'Brien spent several years as a major dramatic actor, starring in several classic films, before turning his attention to the Western. His career was very similar to William Boyd's in that they were both major stars before turning to Westerns exclusively; but, whereas Boyd was non-athletic, O'Brien was the personification of rugged manhood.

As any Western film buff knows, O'Brien was an extrovert without equal. At one time he was known as "The Chest," and his extrovertism, athletic prowess, dramatic ability, and comedy talents combined to make his films unique.

One of the last survivors of the old-time cowboy stars who were really big back in the '20s and '30s, O'Brien has crammed a lot of living into his 86 years. In World War I George was a seaman in the Navy, attained the rating of Pharmacist's Mate 3rd Class, and won the light-heavyweight boxing championship of the Pacific Fleet. George loved Navy life but, realizing his need for a formal education if he was going to accomplish much with his life, he left the Navy in '19 and entered college in California. However, he kept up his membership in the naval reserve for the next twenty years—right up to Pearl Harbor, and was called back into active service within a few days after the disaster. In '46 he was discharged as a commander but, the Navy was in his blood, he was soon back on active duty. George rose to the rank of captain and three times was recommended for admiral before going on inactive duty. He has a host of war medals.

George O'Brien was not born on a ranch as many cowboy stars were, nor did he enter movies via wild west shows, football, or as the result of having been seen and heard plucking a guitar in some "cotton field down south." He was born in San Francisco on April 19, 1900, the son of a man destined to be the city's chief of police and California's director of penology. As the result of an introduction to Tom Mix, who took a liking to him, George became second assistant cameraman with the Mix production unit at Fox. Eventually he got into stunting and "extra" jobs, and finally got small parts in several films. In one of his first screen appearances he doubled for a shark, swimming underwater with a tin fin fastened to his back. Another time, in a scene with the great Valentino, he was knocked from the rigging of a ship into the sea.

In '24, at the encourgement of John Ford, he tested

George O'Brien

26

for the lead in **The Iron Horse,** which Ford was to direct at Fox. He got the job over eighty aspirants after months of testing.

The Iron Horse was a grand-scale Western running 12 reels, but exciting stuff all the way. In it there are no useless images, no gratuitous events. Everything converges in the logical development of the action and the presentation of the characters. With it Ford attained a simple and naked beauty, still schematic in its development, but powerful, open, and vigorous. And Fox gave George the big play, using such statements in their ads as: "He's not a sheik or a cave man or a lounge lizard— He's a man's man and an idol of women!" George became a major star with the release of the film.

Naturally the studio tended to capitalize whenever possible on O'Brien's athletic prowess and his physique was often displayed for no other reason than to show off the body magnificent. But basically his early films were dramatic rather than action films, and George pleased even perfectionist John Ford with his acting ability. The two teamed frequently.

Three Bad Men (1926) was Ford's second masterpiece of the silent era and a triumph for O'Brien, who plays an expelled West Point cadet who joins the first settlers in the Dakota territory.

O'Brien continued to score heavily with each feature he made, reaching the heights as a dramatic actor in **Sunrise** (1927). Few films have displayed the honest emotion of love that is conveyed so beautifully in the film, directed by the famed German director, F. W. Murnau. O'Brien's performance as the happily married farmer who becomes infatuated with a temptress from the city was hailed by critics around the world.

On loan-out to Warners in '28 O'Brien starred in the part-talking **Noah's Ark.** The picture was a smash hit, one of the biggest of the year, and George's voice proved good for sound films.

By 1930 both Tom Mix and Buck Jones had departed from Fox, leaving the studio without a Western star. Having licked most of the technical problems associated with outdoor filming, and remembering the profits made on the Mix and Jones films, Fox decided to make a series of high-class Westerns, most of them based on the popular novels of Zane Grey. Not to be confused with the low-budget, quickie programmers of the '40s and '50s, the O'Brien Westerns were budgeted at up to $300,000 and four to six weeks were allocated for production of each, employing such locations as Monument Valley, various locales in California, and distant spots in Utah, Arizona, Colorado, Montana, and Nevada. In 1931 he was given the lead in **The Seas Beneath,** an especially gripping film directed by John Ford and set in World War I, with O'Brien as a

commander of a sailing ship which lured enemy submarines to destruction. Following completion of this film O'Brien and Ford took off on a "17-day" pleasure cruise to the South Pacific which stretched out to six months of frolicking in the sun and surf.

Back in harness at Fox, George completed twenty films from 1931 to 1936, seventeen of them Westerns. The O'Briens were on a par with the best of Buck Jones, Gene Autry, William Boyd, or Ken Maynard. And when Fox decided to end the long-running series, George signed with RKO for a similar series of quality Westerns. his first, **Daniel Boone** (1936), was a special and rates as both his favorite and that of film historians in so far as his RKO features are concerned. Two non-westerns followed and then came eighteen straight Westerns, costing from $200,000 to $260,000 each and with filming generally taking three to four weeks, mostly on location. O'Brien reports that as much as 47 per cent of the studio's overhead was charged against his films before he started the first day of production. Tim Holt, who succeeded O'Brien, also reported to the writer that his (Holt's) series had to pay most of the rent at the studio—and still the O'Brien and Holt films made money while carrying the expense of free-loading "arty" films!

The O'Brien Westerns were good, and all far superior to the mundane, downright bad sagebrushers produced in 3-4 days by PRC, Monogram, and Columbia during the late '40s, with as much as one-fourth of the running time taken up by stock footage from as far back as the late silents. George had no regular comic relief. Like Buck Jones and Hoot Gibson, he could make the audience laugh better than any two-bit comic sidekick if comedy was the order of the day.

George continually had offers from producers and agents representing other studio interests. Banks and independent money interests realized they would receive an immediate return of their investment because his films were sold to theatres before he made them. It was a great compliment to George to have his product in demand, and the theatres admitted to top profits on his films.

George never made a serial, nor did he ever travel as a paid member of a wild west show, circus, rodeo, etc., but he has appeared as a guest star and performer for charity benefits all over the world.

Returning from World War II O'Brien took featured roles in **My Wild Irish Rose** (1947), **Fort Apache** (1948), and **She Wore a Yellow Ribbon** (1949), and co-starred with The Three Stooges in **Gold Raiders** (1951). His last movie was **Cheyenne Autumn** (1964), his pal John Ford's epic account of the ill treatment of American Indians at the hands of whites. O'Brien has

Heather Angel quiets Aggie Herring as George O'Brien keeps an eye on Harry Cording in this scene from **DANIEL BOONE** (RKO, 1936)

produced and written scripts for movies and television and was in the stage production of "What Price Glory?" Travel for both pleasure and business has been a way of life for him, and he is independently wealthy. For years he lived in Tahiti while also maintaining a home in Los Angeles. George was divorced from his wife Marguerite in 1948. His son Darcy is a college professor of English and Irish literature and daughter Orin is with the New York Philharmonic Symphony Orchestra.

George likes to recall his past glories, but he is not one to live in the past. "My father taught me to live in the present, and I've been doing just that," said George in response to a comment that I made to the effect that it would be nice to turn back the clock and be a kid again, watching him perform in Westerns at my hometown theatre. "After four years in Vietnam," continued George, "plus the other wars I have come back from, I feel my life is at present 'all down hill and shady,' which is an old cowboy saying when everything is smooth, cool and happy."

George O'Brien is a fine fellow, one that Western buffs can be mighty proud of. He is truly humble, sincerely friendly, and genuinely respectable, with one of the most spotless reputations of any Hollywood personality. His boots would be hard to fill.

On a sadder note, George died at Broken Arrow, Oklahoma Wednesday, September 4, 1985. He had been living in a nursing home since a stroke left him partially paralyzed in 1979.

28

GEORGE O'BRIEN Filmography

WHITE HANDS
(Graf Productions/Wid Gunnings, January 9, 1932) 6 Reels
Hobart Bosworth, Robert McKim, Freeman Wood, Al Kaufman, Muriel Frances Dana, Elinor Fair, *George O'Brien*
Director/Scenario: Lambert Hillyer
Story: C. Gardner Sullivan
Producer: Max Graf

MORAN OF THE LADY LETTY
(Famous Players-Lasky, February 12, 1922) 7 Reels
Dorothy Dalton, Rudolph Valentino, Charles Brinley, Walter Long, Emil Jorgenson, Maude Wayne, Cecil Holland, George Kuwa, Charles K. French, *George O'Brien*
Director: George Melford
Adaptation: Monte M. Katterjohn
Story: Frank Norris

THE GHOST BREAKER
(Famous Players-Lasky/Paramount, September 10, 1922) 52 Minutes
Wallace Reid, Lila Lee, Walter Hiers, Arthur Carewe, J. Farrell MacDonald, Frances Raymond, Snitz Edwards, *George O'Brien*
Director: Alfred E. Green
Screenplay: Walter DeLeon
Adaptation: Jack Cunningham
Story: Paul Dickey and Charles W. Goddard — "The Ghost Breaker, A Melodramatic Farce in Four Acts"

THE NE'ER-DO-WELL
(Famous Players-Lasky/Paramount, April 29, 1923) 8 Reels
Thomas Meighan, Lita Lee, Gertrude Astor, John Miltern, Gus Weinberg, Sid Smith, *George O'Brien*
Director: Alfred E. Green
Scenario: Louis Stevens
Story: Rex Beach

WOMAN PROOF
(Famous Players-Lasky/Paramount, October 28, 1923) 8 Reels
Thomas Meighan, Lita Lee, John Sainpolis, Louise Dresser, Robert Agnew, Mary Astor, Edgar Norton, Charles A. Sellon, *George O'Brien,* Vera Reynolds, Hardee Kirkland, Martha Mattox, William Gonder, Mike Donlin
Director: Alfred E. Green
Scenario: Tom Geraghty
Story: George Ade

SHADOWS OF PARIS
(Famous Players-Lasky/Paramount, February, 1924) 66 Minutes
Pola Negri, Charles De Roche, Huntley Gordon, Adolphe Menjou, Gareth Hughes, Vera Reynolds, Rose Dione, Rosita Marstini, Edward Kipling, Maurice Cannon, Frank Nelson, *George O'Brien*
Director: Herbert Brenon
Scenario: Eve Unsell
Adaptation: Fred Jackson
Story: Andre Picard and Francis Carco — "Mon Homme; piece en 3 acts"

THE SEA HAWK
(Frank Lloyd Productions/Associated First National, June 2, 1924) 12 Reels
Milton Sills, Enid Bennett, Lloyd Hughes, Wallace MacDonald, Marc MacDermott, Wallace Beery, Frank Currier, Medea Radzina, William Collier, Jr., Lionel Belmore, Fred De Silva, Hector V. Sarno, George E. Romain, Robert Bolder, Christina Montt, Kathleen Key, Nancy Zann, Louis Morrison, Kate Price, Al Jennings, Bert Woodruff, Walter Wilkinson, Andrew Johnston, Henry Barrows, Edwards Davis, Claire Du Brey, Robert Spencer, Theodore Lorch, *George O'Brien*
Director: Frank Lloyd
Scenario: J. G. Hawks
Story: Rafael Sabatini

THE IRON HORSE
(Fox, August 28, 1924) 12 Reels
George O'Brien, Madge Bellamy, Cyril Chadwick, Fred Kohler, Gladys Hulette, James Marcus, J. Farrell MacDonald, James Welch, Walter Rogers, George Waggner, Jack Padjan, Charles O'Malley, Charles Newton, Charles Edward Bull, Colin Chase, Delbert Mann, Chief Big Tree, Chief White Spear, James Gordon, Winston Miller, Peggy Cartwright, Thomas Durant, Stanhope Wheatcroft, Frances Teague, Will Walling
Director: John Ford
Scenario: Charles Kenyon
Story: Charles Kenyon, John Russell

THE MAN WHO CAME BACK
(Fox, August 17, 1924) 9 Reels
George O'Brien, Dorothy Mackaill, Cyril Chadwick, Ralph Lewis, Emily Fitzroy, Harvey Clark, Edward Piel, David Kirby, James Gordon, Walter Wilkinson, Brother Miller
Director: Emmett Flynn
Scenario: Edmund Goulding
Story: John Fleming Wilson

THE PAINTED LADY

(Fox, September 28, 1924) 7 Reels
George O'Brien, Dorothy Mackaill, Harry T. Morey, Lucille Hutton, Lucille Ricksen, Margaret McWade, John Miljan, Frank Elliott, Lucien Littlefield
Director: Chester Bennett
Scenario: Thomas Dixon, Jr.
Story: Larry Evans

THE ROUGHNECK

(Fox, November, 1924) 8 Reels
George O'Brien, Billie Dove, Harry T. Morey, Cleo Madison, Charles A. Sellon, Anne Cornwall, Harvey Clark, Maryon Aye, Edna Eichor, Buddy Smith
Director: John Conway
Scenario: Charles Kenyon
Story: Robert William Service

THE DANCERS

(Fox, January 4, 1925) 7 Reels
George O'Brien, Alma Rubens, Madge Bellamy, Templar Saxe, Joan Standing, Alice Hollister, Freeman Wood, Walter McGrail, Noble Johnson, Tippy Grey
Director: Emmett J. Flynn
Scenario: Edmund Goulding
Story: Hubert Parsons

HAVOC

(Fox, September 27, 1925) 9 Reels
George O'Brien, Madge Bellamy, Walter McGrail, Eulalie Jensen, Margaret Livingston, Leslie Fenton, David Butler, Harvey Clark, Wade Boteler, Edythe Chapman, Capt. E. H. Calvert, Bertram Grassby
Director: Rowland V. Lee
Scenario: Edmund Goulding
Story: Henry Wall

THE FIGHTING HEART

(Fox, October 18, 1925) 7 Reels
George O'Brien, Billie Dove, J. Farrell MacDonald, Victor McLaglen, Diana Miller, Bert Woodruff, Francis Ford, Hazel Howell, Edward Piel, James Marcus
Director: John Ford
Scenario: Lillie Hayward
Story: Larry Evans - "Once to Every Man"

THANK YOU

(Fox, November 1, 1925) 7 Reels
George O'Brien, J. Farrell MacDonald, Alec B. Francis, Jacqueline Logan, George Fawcett, Cyril Chadwick, Edith Bostwick, Marion Harlan, Vivian Ogden, James Neill, Billy Rinaldi, Aileen Manning, Maurice Murphy, Robert Milasch, Ida Moore, Frankie Bailey
Director: John Ford
Scenario: Frances Marion
Story: Winchell Smith and Tom Cushing - "Thank You, A Play in Three Acts"

THE JOHNSTOWN FLOOD

(Fox, February 28, 1926) 6 Reels
George O'Brien, Florence Gilbert, Janet Gaynor, Anders Randolf, Paul Nicholson, Paul Panzer, George Harris, Max Davidson, Walter Perry, Sid Jordan
Director: Irving Cummings
Story/Scenario: Edfrid Bingham, Robert Lord

RUSTLING FOR CUPID

(Fox, April 11, 1926) 5 Reels
George O'Brien, Anita Stewart, Russell Simpson, Edith Yorke, Herbert Prior, Frank McGlynn, Jr., Sid Jordan
Director: Irving Cummings
Scenario: L. G. Rigby
Story: Peter B. Kyne

FIG LEAVES

(Fox, August 22, 1926) 7 Reels
George O'Brien, Olive Borden, Phyllis Haver, Andre de Beranger, William Austin, Heinie Conklin, Eulalie Jensen
Director/Story: Howard Hawks
Scenario: Hope Loring

THE SILVER TREASURE

(Fox, June 20, 1926) 6 Reels
George O'Brien, Jack Rollins, Helena D'Algy, Joan Renee, Evelyn Selbie, Lou Tellegen, Otto Matieson, Stewart Rome, Hedda Hopper, Daniel Makarenko, Fred Becker, Harvey Clark, Gilbert Clayton, Sidney De Grey, George Kuwa
Director: Rowland V. Lee
Scenario: Robert N. Lee
Story: Joseph Conrad - "Nostromo"

THREE BAD MEN

(Fox, August 13, 1926) 9 Reels
George O'Brien, Olive Borden, Lou Tellegen, J. Farrell MacDonald, Tom Santschi, Frank Campeau, George Harris, Jay Hunt, Priscilla Bonner, Otis Harlan, Walter Perry, Grace Gordon, Alec B. Francis, George Irving, Phyllis Haver, Vester Pegg, Bud Osborne
Director: John Ford
Adaptation/Scenario: John Stone
Story: Herman Whitaker - "Over the Border; a Novel"

THE BLUE EAGLE

(Fox, September 12, 1926) 7 Reels
George O'Brien, Janet Gaynor, William Russell, Robert Edeson, David Butler, Phil Ford, Ralph Sipperly, Margaret Livingston, Jerry Madden, Harry Tenbrook, Lew Short
Director: John Ford
Scenario: L. G. Rigby
Story: Gerald Beaumont - "The Lord's Referee"

IS ZAT SO?

(Fox, May 15, 1927) 7 Reels
George O'Brien, Edmund Lowe, Kathryn Perry, Cyril Chadwick, Doris Lloyd, Dione Ellis, Richard Maitland, Douglas Fairbanks, Jr., Philippe De Lacy, Jack Herrick
Director: Alfred E. Green
Scenario: Philip Klein
Story: James Gleason and Richard Taber - "Is Zat So? A Comedy in Three Acts"

PAID TO LOVE

(Fox, July 23, 1927) 7 Reels
George O'Brien, Virginia Valli, J. Farrell MacDonald, Thomas Jefferson, William Powell, Merta Sterling, Hank Mann
Director: Howard Hawks
Scenario: William M. Conselman, Seton I. Miller
Story: Harry Carr

SUNRISE

(Fox, September 23, 1927) 9 Reels
(Sound effects and music score)
George O'Brien, Janet Gaynor, Bodil Rosing, Margaret Livingston, J. Farrell MacDonald, Ralph Sipperly, Jane Winton, Arthur Housman, Eddie Arnold, Sally Eilers, Gino Corrado, Barry Norton, Robert Kortman
Director: F. W. Murnau
Scenario: Carl Mayer
Story: Hermann Sudermann - "A Trip to Tilsit"
Camera: Charles Rosher and Karl Struss (Rosher won an academy award for his camera work on this film)

EAST SIDE, WEST SIDE

(Fox, October 9, 1927) 9 Reels
George O'Brien, Virginia Valli, J. Farrell MacDonald, Dore Davidson, Sonia Nodaisky, June Collyer, John Miltern, Holmes Herbert, Frank Allsworth, William Fredericks, Jean Armour, Gordon McRae, Harold Levett
Director/Adaptation: Allan Dwan
Story: Felix Riesenberg

SHARP SHOOTERS

(Fox, January 15, 1928) 6 Reels
George O'Brien, Lois Moran, Noah Young, Tom Dugan, William Demarest, Gwen Lee, Josef Swickard
Director: J. G. Blystone
Scenario: Marion Orth
Story: Randall H. Faye

HONOR BOUND

(Fox, April, 1928) 7 Reels
George O'Brien, Estelle Taylor, Leila Hyams, Tom Santschi, Frank Cooley, Sam De Grasse, Al Hart, Harry Gripp, George Irving
Director: Alfred E. Green
Scenario: C. Graham Baker
Story: Jack Bethea

NOAH'S ARK

(Warner Brothers, June 15, 1929) 11 Reels
(Talking sequences and music score)
Dolores Costello, *George O'Brien*, Noah Beery, Louise Fazenda, Guinn 'Big Boy' Williams, Paul McAllister, Nigel De Brulier, Anders Randolf, Armand Kaliz, Myrna Loy, William V. Mong, Malcolm Waite, Noble Johnson, Otto Hoffman, Joe Bonomo
Director: Michael Curtiz
Screenplay: Anthony Coldeway

BLINDFOLD

(Fox, December 9, 1928) 6 Reels
(Music score)
Lois Moran, *George O'Brien*, Maria Alba, Earle Foxe, Don Terry, Fritz Feld, Andy Clyde, Crauford Kent, Robert E. Homans, John Kelly, Phillips Smalley
Director: Charles Klein
Scenario: Ewart Adamson
Adaptation: Robert Horwood
Story: Charles Francis Coe

TRUE HEAVEN

(Fox, January, 1929) 6 Reels
(sound effects)
George O'Brien, Lois Moran, Phillips Smalley, Oscar Apfel, Duke Martin, Andre Cheron, Donald MacKenzie, Hedwig Reicher, Will Stanton
Director: James Tinling
Adaptation: Dwight Cummins
Story: Charles Edward Montague - "Judith"

Sue Carol and George O'Brien cuddle in this scene from **The Lone Star Ranger** (Fox, 1930).

MASKED EMOTIONS
(Fox, June 23, 1929) 7 Reels
George O'Brien, Nora Lane, J. Farrell MacDonald, David Sharpe, James Gordon, Edward Peil, Sr., Frank Hagney
Director: David Butler, Kenneth Hawks
Scenario: Harry Brand, Benjamin Markson
Story: Ben Ames Williams - "A Son of Anak"

SALUTE
(Fox, September 1, 1929) 9 Reels
George O'Brien, Helen Chandler, Frank Albertson, William Janney, Clifford Dempsey, Lumsden Hare, Joyce Compton, David Butler, Stepin Fetchit, Rex Bell, John Breeden, John Wayne, Ward Bond
Director: John Ford
Screenplay: James K. McGuinness
Story: Tristram Tupper, John Stone

THE LONE STAR RANGER
(Fox, January 5, 1930) 5736 feet
George O'Brien, Sue Carol, Russell Simpson, Elizabeth Patterson, Dick Alexander, William Steele, Bob Fleming, Caroline Rankin, Lee Shumway, Joel Franz, Colin Chase, Oliver Eckhardt, Billy Butts, Ralph LeFevre, Roy Stewart, Warren Hymer, Joe Rickson, Delmar Watson
Director: A. F. Erickson
Story: Zane Grey
Screenplay: Seton Miller

ROUGH ROMANCE
(Fox, June 22, 1930) 4800 feet
George O'Brien, Helen Chandler, Antonio Moreno, Roy Stewart, Eddie Borden, Frank Lanning, Harry Cording, David Hartford, Noel Francis
Director: A. F. Erickson
Story: Kenneth Clark - "The Girl Who Wasn't Wanted"
Scenario: Elliott Lester

LAST OF THE DUANES

(Fox, August 31, 1930) 5580 feet

George O'Brien, Lucile Browne, Myrna Loy, Nat Pendleton, Walter McGrail, James Mason, Lloyd Ingraham, James Bradbury, Jr., Willard Robertson, Blanche Frederici, Frank Campeau

Director: Alfred L. Werker
Story: Zane Grey
Screenplay: Ernest Pascal

FAIR WARNING

(Fox, February 1, 1931) 74 Minutes

George O'Brien, Louise Huntington, Mitchell Harris, George Brent, Nat Pendleton, John Sheehan, Willard Robertson, Ernie Adams, Erwin Connelly, Alphonz Ethier

Director: Alfred Werker
Story: "The Untamed" - Max Brand
Screenplay: Ernest Pascal

SEAS BENEATH

(Fox, February, 1931) 99 Minutes

George O'Brien, Marion Lessing, Warren Hymer, William Collier, Sr., John Loder, Walter C. Kelly, Nat Pendleton

Director: John Ford
Screenplay: Dudley Nichols
Story: James Parker, Jr.

A HOLY TERROR

(Fox, July 19, 1931) 63 Minutes

George O'Brien, Sally Eilers, Rita LaFoy, Humphrey Bogart, James Kirkwood, Stanley Fields, Robert Warwick, Richard Tucker, Earl Pinegree

Director: Irving Cummings
Story: "Trailin" - Max Brand
Screenplay: Ralph Brock

RIDERS OF THE PURPLE SAGE

(Fox, October 28, 1931) 59 Minutes

George O'Brien, Marguerite Churchill, Noah Beery, Frank McGlynn, Yvonne Pelletier, James Todd, Stanley Fields, Lester Dorr, Shirley Nail

Director: Hamilton McFadden
Story: Zane Grey

RAINBOW TRAIL

(Fox, January 3, 1932) 60 Minutes

George O'Brien, Cecilia Parker, Roscoe Ates, James Kirkwood, Minna Gombell, Landers Stevens, Ruth Donnelly, Robert Frazer, Niles Welch, William L. Thorne

Director: David Howard
Story: Zane Grey
Screenplay: Barry Connors, Philip Klein

THE GAY CABALLERO

(Fox, February 14, 1932) 60 Minutes

George O'Brien, Victor McLaglen, Cecilia Parker, Weldon Heyburn, Linda Watkins, Conchita Montenegro, C. Henry Gordon, Willard Robertson, Wesley Giraud

Director: Alfred Werker
Story: Tom Gill
Screenplay: Barry Connors, Philip Klein

MYSTERY RANCH

(Fox, July 1, 1932) 65 Minutes

George O'Brien, Cecilia Parker, Charles Middleton, Roy Stewart, Charles Stevens, Forrest Harvey, Virginia Herdman, Noble Johnson, Russell Powell

Director: David Howard
Story: "The Killer" - Edward White
Screenplay: Al Cohn

THE GOLDEN WEST

(Fox, December 3, 1932) 74 Minutes

George O'Brien, Janet Chandler, Marion Burns, Onslow Stevens, Julia Swayne Gordon, Everett Corrigan, Edmund Breese, Sam West, Arthur Pierson, Bert Hanlon, Hattie McDaniel, Charles Stevens, Stanley Blystone, George Regas, Dorothy Ward, Sam Adams, Ed Dillon, Chief Big Tree, John War Eagle

Director: David Howard
Story: Zane Grey
Screenplay: Gordon Rigby

ROBBERS ROOST

(Fox, Januray 1, 1933) 64 Minutes

George O'Brien, Maureen O'Sullivan, Maude Eburne, William Pawley, Ted Oliver, Walter McGrail, Doris Lloyd, Reginald Owens, Frank Rice, Bill Nestell, Clifford Santley, Gilbert Holmes, Vinegar Roan

Director: David Howard
Story: Zane Grey
Screenplay: Dudley Nichols

SMOKE LIGHTNING

(Fox, February 17, 1933) 63 Minutes

George O'Brien, Virginia Sale, Douglass Dumbrille, Betsy King Ross, Nell O'Day, Frank Atkinson, Morgan Wallace, Clarence Wilson, George Burton, Fred Wilson

Director: David Howard
Story: "Canyon Walls" - Zane Grey
Screenplay: Gordon Rigby, Sidney Mitchell

LIFE IN THE RAW

(Fox, July 7, 1933) 62 Minutes
George O'Brien, Claire Trevor, Warner Richmond, Francis Ford, Greta Nilsen, Gaylord Pendleton, Alan Edwards, Nigel De Brulier
Director: Louis King
Story: Zane Grey
Screenplay: Stuart Anthony

THE LAST TRAIL

(Fox, August 25, 1933) 59 Minutes
George O'Brien, Claire Trevor, El Brendel, Lucille LaVerne, Matt McHugh, Edward J. LeSaint, J. Carrol Naish, Ruth Warren, George Reed, Luis Albertson
Director: James Tinling
Story: Zane Grey
Screenplay: Stuart Anthony

FRONTIER MARSHAL

(Fox, January 19, 1934) 66 Minutes
George O'Brien, Irene Bentley, George E. Stone, Alan Edwards, Ruth Gillette, Berton Churchill, Frank Conroy, Ward Bond, Edward J. LeSaint, Russell Simpson, Jerry Foster
Director: Lewis Seiler
Story: Stuart M. Lake
Screenplay: Stuart Anthony, William Counselman

THE DUDE RANGER

(Principal/Fox, September 29, 1934) 65 Minutes
George O'Brien, Irene Hervey, Syd Saylor, LeRoy Mason, Henry Hall, James Mason, Sid Jordan, Alma Chester, Lloyd Ingraham, Earl Dwire, Si Jenks, Lafe McKee, Jack Kirk, Hank Bell
Director: Edward F. Cline
Story: Zane Grey
Screenplay: Barry Barringer
Producer: Sol Lesser, John Zanft

Edgar Kennedy seems to like what George O'Brien is telling him in **The Cowboy Millionaire** (1935, Fox).

Barbara Fritchie and George O'Brien in a scene for **Thunder Mountain** (Fox, 1935)

WHEN A MAN'S A MAN
(Atherton/Fox, February 15, 1935) 7 Reels
George O'Brien, Dorothy Wilson, Paul Kelly, Harry Woods, Jimmy Butler, Richard Carlisle, Edgar Norton, Clarence Wilson
Director: Edward Cline
Story: Harold Bell Wright
Screenplay: Dan Jarrett
Producers: Sol Lesser, John Zanft

THE COWBOY MILLIONAIRE
(Atherton/Fox, April 25, 1935) 74 Minutes
George O'Brien, Evelyn Bostock, Edgar Kennedy, Alden Chase, Maude Allen, Dan Jarrett, Lloyd Ingraham, Thomas Curran
Director: Edward F. Cline
Screenplay: George Waggner, Dan Jarrett
Producer: Sol Lesser

HARD ROCK HARRIGAN
(Lesser-Zanft Productions/Atherton, July 19, 1935) 7 Reels
George O'Brien, Irene Hervey, Fred Kohler, Sr., Dean Benton, Frank Rice, Victor Potel, Olin Francis, William Gould, George Humbert, Edward Keane, Lee Shumway, Glenn Strange, Jack Kirk, Lee Phelps, Curley Dresden
Director: David Howard
Story: Charles Furthman
Screenplay: Raymond L. Schrock, Dan Jarrett

THUNDER MOUNTAIN
(Atherton/Fox, September 27, 1935) 7 Reels
George O'Brien, Barbara Fritchie, Frances Grant, Morgan Wallace, George Hayes, Edward J. LeSaint, Dean Benton, William N. Bailey
Director: David Howard
Story: Zane Grey
Screenplay: Dan Jarrett, Don Swift
Producer: Sol Lesser

35

WHISPERING SMITH SPEAKS

(Atherton Prod./20th C.-Fox, January, 1936) 7 Reels

George O'Brien, Irene Ware, Kenneth Thompson, Maude Allen, Spencer Charters

Director: David Howard
Screenplay: Don Swift, Dan Jarrett
Story: Frank H. Spearman
Adaptation: Gilbert Wright, Rex Taylor

O'MALLEY OF THE MOUNTED

(Principal/20th C.-Fox, March 27, 1936) 59 Minutes

George O'Brien, Irene Ware, Crauford Kent, James Bush, Victor Potel, Charles King, Stanley Fields, Tom London, Reginald Barlow, Richard Cramer, Olin Francis, Blackjack Ward

Director: David Howard
Story: William S. Hart
Screenplay: Dan Jarrett, Frank Howard Clark
Producer: Sol Lesser

THE BORDER PATROLMAN

(Principal/Fox, June 20, 1936) 60 Minutes

George O'Brien, Polly Ann Young, Roy (LeRoy) Mason, Mary Doran, Smiley Burnette, Tom London, William P. Carlton, Al Hill, Murdock McQuarrie, John St. Polis, Cyril Ring, Martin Garralaga, Chris-Pin Martin

Director: David Howard
Story/Screenplay: Dan Jarrett, Bennett Cohen
Producer: Sol Lesser

DANIEL BOONE

(RKO, October 16, 1936) 77 Minutes

George O'Brien, Heather Angel, John Carradine, Ralph Forbes, Clarence Muse, George Regas, Dickie Jones, Huntley Gordon, Harry Cording, Aggie Herring, Crauford Kent, Keith Kenneth

Director: David Howard
Story: Edgecumb Pinchon
Screenplay: Dan Jarrett
Producer: George A. Hirliman

George O'Brien gets friendly with Polly Ann Young in this scene from **The Border Patrolman** (Fox, 1936).

George O'Brien shows one of the comic touches he gave his films in **Park Avenue Logger** (RKO, 1937)

PARK AVENUE LOGGER
(RKO, March 16, 1937) 67 Minutes
George O'Brien, Beatrice Roberts, Willard Robertson, Ward Bond, Bert Hanlon, Gertrude Short, Lloyd Ingraham, George Rosenor, Robert E. O'Connor, Al Baffert, Dave Wengren
Director: David Howard
Story: From a *Saturday Evening Post* story by Bruce Hutchinson
Screenplay: Dan Jarrett, Ewing Scott
Producer: George A. Hirliman

HOLLYWOOD COWBOY
(RKO, May 28, 1937) 64 Minutes
(Reissued as "Wings Over Wyoming")
George O'Brien, Cecilia Parker, Maude Eburne, Joe Caits, Frank Milan, Charles Middleton, Lee Shumway, Walter DePalma, William Royle, Al Hill, Frank Hagney, Al Herman, Dan Wolheim, Slim Balch, Sid Jordan, Lester Dorr, Harold Daniels, Robert Walker, Donald Kerr, Hal Price, Horace B. Carpenter, Jack Evans
Director: Ewing Scott
Screenplay: Dan Jarrett, Ewing Scott
Producer: George A. Hirliman

WINDJAMMER
(RKO-Radio, August, 1937) 7 Reels
George O'Brien, Constance Worth, William Hall, Brandon Evans, Gavin Gordon, Stan Blystone
Director: Ewing Scott
Associate Producer: David Howard
Story: Raoul Haig
Screenplay: Dan Jarrett, James Gruen

GUN LAW
(RKO, May 13, 1938) 60 Minutes
George O'Brien, Rita Oehman, Ray Whitley, Paul Everton, Ward Bond, Francis McDonald, Edward Pawley, Robert Glecker, Frank O'Connor, Hank Bell, Paul Fix, Ethan Laidlaw, Lloyd Ingraham, Robert Burns, James Mason, Ken Card, Neal Burns, Ray Jones, Herman Hack
Director: David Howard
Story/Screenplay: Oliver Drake
Producer: Bert Gilroy

BORDER G-MAN

(RKO, June 24, 1938) 60 Minutes

George O'Brien, Laraine Johnson (Day), Ray Whitley, John Miljan, Rita LaRoy, Edgar Dearing, William Stalling, Edward Keane, Ethan Laidlaw, Robert Burns, Hugh Sothern, Ken Card
Director: David Howard
Screenplay: Oliver Drake, Bernard McConville
Producer: Bert Gilroy

THE PAINTED DESERT

(RKO, August 12, 1938) 59 Minutes

George O'Brien, Laraine Johnson (Day), Ray Whitley, Fred Kohler, Stanley Fields, Max Wagner, Harry Cording, Lee Shumway, Lloyd Ingraham, Maude Allen, William V. Mong, Lew Kelly, James Mason, Jack O'Shea, Ray Jones, Ken Card, The Phelps Brothers
Director: David Howard
Screenplay: John Rathmell, Oliver Drake
Producer: Bert Gilroy

THE RENEGADE RANGER

(RKO, September 16, 1938) 60 Minutes

George O'Brien, Rita Hayworth, Tim Holt, Ray Whitley, Lucio Villegas, William Royle, Cecelia Callejo, Neal Hart, Monte Montague, Bob Kortman, Charles Stevens, James Mason, Tom London, Guy Usher, Chris-Pin Martin, Tom Steele, Ken Card
Director: David Howard
Story/Screenplay: Bennett Cohen
Producer: Bert Gilroy

LAWLESS VALLEY

(RKO, November 4, 1938) 59 Minutes

George O'Brien, Kay Sutton, Chill Wills, Walter Miller, Fred Kohler, Sr., Fred Kohler, Jr., George McQuarrie, Lew Kelly, Earle Hodgins, Dot Farley, George Chesebro, Kirby Grant, Carl Stockdale, Ben Corbett, Robert McKenzie
Director: David Howard
Story: W. C. Tuttle
Screenplay: Oliver Drake
Producer: Bert Gilroy

ARIZONA LEGION

(RKO-Radio, January 20, 1939) 58 Minutes

George O'Brien, Laraine Johnson (Day), Chill Wills, Carlyle Moore, Jr., Edward J. LeSaint, Harry Cording, Tom Chatterton, William Royle, Glenn Strange, Monte Montague, Joe Rickson, Robert Burns, John Dilson, Lafe McKee, Guy Usher, Bob Kortman, Wilfred Lucas, James Mason, Art Mix
Director: David Howard
Story: "The Stagecoach Stops at Pinyon Gulch" - Bernard McConville
Screenplay: Oliver Drake
Producer: Bert Gilroy

TROUBLE IN SUNDOWN

(RKO, March 24, 1939) 60 Minutes

George O'Brien, Rosalind Keith, Ray Whitley, Chill Wills, Ward Bond, Cy Kendall, Howard Hickman, Monte Montague, John Dilson, Otto Yamaoka, Ken Card, Phelps Brothers, Earl Dwire, Robert Burns
Director: David Howard
Story: George F. Royal (Charles Francis Royal?)
Screenplay: Oliver Drake, Dorrell and Stuart McGowan
Producer: Bert Gilroy

RACKETEERS OF THE RANGE

(RKO, June 14, 1939) 62 Minutes

George O'Brien, Chill Wills, Marjorie Reynolds, Gay Seabrook, Robert Riske, Ray Whitley, John Dilson, Monte Montague, Ben Corbett, Bud Osborne, Cactus Mack, Frankie Marvin, Joe Balch, Dick Hunter, Ed Piel, Sr., Frank O'Connor, Mary Gordon, Stanley Andrews, Wilfred Lucas, Harry Cording, Clint Sharp, Del Maggert
Director: D. Ross Lederman
Story/Screenplay: Oliver Drake
Producer: Bert Gilroy

TIMBER STAMPEDE

(RKO, June 30, 1939) 59 Minutes

George O'Brien, Chill Wills, Marjorie Reynolds, Morgan Wallace, Guy Usher, Earl Dwire, Frank Hagney, Monte Montague, Robert Fiske, Robert Burns, William Benedict, Tom London, Elmo Lincoln, Bud Osborne, Bob Kortman, Ben Corbett, Cactus Mack, Hank Worden, Frank O'Connor, Sid Jordan, Herman Hack
Director: David Howard
Story: Bernard McConville, Paul Franklin
Screenplay: Morton Grant
Producer: Bert Gilroy

MARSHALL OF MESA CITY

(RKO, November 3, 1939) 63 Minutes

George O'Brien, Virginia Vale, Leon Ames, Henry Brandon, Harry Cording, Lloyd Ingraham, Slim Whitaker, Joe McGuinn, Mary Gordon, Frank Ellis, Wilfred Lucas, Carl Stockdale, Cactus Mack, Richard Hunter, Sid Jordan, Gaylord Pendleton, Spade Cooley, Bob Burns, Rube Schaefer, Edward Peil, Sr., Jack Cheatham, Bill Patton, Ed Brady, Speed Hanson, Harry Tenbrook, Monte Montague, Ben Corbett
Director: David Howard
Screenplay: Jack Lair, Jr.
Producer: Bert Gilroy

THE FIGHTING GRINGO
(RKO, November 28, 1939) 59 Minutes
George O'Brien, Lupita Tovar, Lucio Villegas, William Royle, Glenn Strange, Slim Whitaker, LeRoy Mason, Mary Field, Martin Garralaga, Dick Botiller, Bill Cody, Cactus Mack, Chris-Pin Martin, Ben Corbett, Forrest Taylor, Sid Jordan, Al Haskell, Hank Bell
Director: David Howard
Story/Screenplay: Oliver Drake
Producer: Bert Gilroy

LEGION OF THE LAWLESS
(RKO, January 5, 1940) 59 Minutes
George O'Brien, Virginia Vale, Herbert Heywood, Norman Willis, Hugh Sothern, William Benedict, Eddy Waller, Delmar Watson, Bud Osborne, Monte Montague, Slim Whitaker, Mary Field, Richard Cramer, John Dilson, Martin Garralaga, Ed Piel, Lloyd Ingraham, Henry Wills, Wilfred Lucas
Director: David Howard
Story: Berne Giler
Screenplay: Doris Schroeder
Producer: Bert Gilroy

BULLET CODE
(RKO Radio, April 12, 1940) 58 Minutes
George O'Brien, Virginia Vale, Slim Whitaker, Harry Woods, Robert Stanton (Kirby Grant), Walter Miller, William Haade, Bob Burns, Howard Hickman
Director: David Howard
Story: Bennett Cohen
Screenplay: Doris Schroeder
Producer: Bert Gilroy

PRAIRIE LAW
(RKO, June 14, 1940) 59 Minutes
George O'Brien, Virginia Vale, Dick Hogan, Slim Whitaker, J. Farrell MacDonald, Cy Kendall, Paul Everton, Henry Hall, Monte Montague, Quen Ramsey, Bud Osborne, Frank Ellis, John Henderson
Director: David Howard
Story: Bernard McConville
Screenplay: Doris Schroeder, Arthur V. Jones
Producer: Bert Gilroy

Virginia Vale stops George O'Brien in this moment from **Stage to Chino** (RKO, 1940)

STAGE TO CHINO

(RKO, July 26, 1940) 58 Minutes
George O'Brien, Virginia Vale, Hobart Cavanaugh, Roy Barcroft, Martin Garralaga, Carl Stockdale, Harry Cording, Ethan Laidlaw, William Haade, Glenn Strange, Tom London, Pals of the Golden West
Director: Edward Kelly
Screenplay: Morton Grant, Arthur V. Jones
Producer: Bert Gilroy

TRIPLE JUSTICE

(RKO, September 20, 1940) 66 Minutes
George O'Brien, Virginia Vale, Peggy Shannon, Harry Woods, Paul Fix, LeRoy Mason, Glenn Strange, Malcolm (Bud) McTaggart, Bob McKenzie, Wilfred Lucas, Herman Nolan, John Judd, Henry Rocquemore, Fern Emmett, Walter Patterson, Paul Everton, Lindeman Sisters
Director: David Howard
Story: Arnold Belgard, Jack Roberts
Screenplay: Arthur V. Jones, Morton Grant

MY WILD IRISH ROSE

(Warner Brothers, December 12, 1947) 101 Minutes
Dennis Morgan, Andrea King, Arlene Dahl, Alan Hale, George Tobias, *George O'Brien,* Sara Allgood, Ben Blue, William Frawley, Don McGuire, Charles Irwin, Clifton Young, Paul Stanton, George Cleveland, Oscar O'Shea, Ruby Dandridge, Grady Sutton, William B. Davidson, Douglas Wood, Charles Marsh, Andrew Toombes, Robert Lowell, Philo McCullough, Gino Corrado, Eddie Parker, Ross Ford, Eddie Kane, Tom Stevenson, Peggy Knudsen, Monte Blue, Wally Ruth, Emmett Vogan, Edward Clark, William Gould, Brandon Hurst, Forbes Murray, Winifred Harris, Billy Greene, Penny Edwards, Rodney Bell, Igor Dena, Pierre Andre, Lou Wills, Jr., The Three Dunhills
Director: David Butler
Story: Rita Olcott
Screenplay: Peter Milne
Producer: William Jacobs

FORT APACHE

(Argosy/RKO, March 9, 1948) 128 Minutes
John Wayne, Henry Fonda, Shirley Temple, John Agar, Ward Bond, *George O'Brien,* Victor McLaglen, Pedro Armendariz, Anna Lee, Irene Rich, Guy Kibbee, Grant Withers, Miguel Inclan, Jack Pennick, Mae Marsh, Dick Foran, Frank Ferguson, Francis Ford, Ray Hyke, Movita Castenada, Mary Gordon
Director: John Ford
Story: James Warner Bellah
Screenplay: Frank Nugent, Laurence Stallings
Producers: John Ford and Merian C. Cooper

SHE WORE A YELLOW RIBBON

(Argosy/RKO, October 22, 1949) 104 Minutes
(Technicolor)
John Wayne, Joanne Dru, John Agar, Ben Johnson, Harry Carey, Jr., Victor McLaglen, Mildred Natwick, *George O'Brien,* Arthur Shields, Harry Woods, Chief John Big Tree, Noble Johnson, Cliff Lyons, Tom Tyler, Mike Dugan, Mickey Simpson, Frank McGrath, Don Summer, Fred Libby, Jack Pennick, Billy Jones, Bill Goettinger (William Steele), Fred Graham, Fred Kennedy, Rudy Bowman, Post Parks, Ray Hyke, Lee Bradley, Francis Ford, Paul Fix, Dan White
Director: John Ford
Story: James Warner Bellah
Screenplay: Frank Nugent, Laurence Stallings
Producers: John Ford and Merian C. Cooper

GOLD RAIDERS

(Schwarz/United Artists, September 14, 1951) 56 Minutes
George O'Brien, The Three Stooges (Moe Howard, Shemp Howard, and Larry Fine), Sheila Ryan, Clem Bevins, Monte Blue, Lyle Talbot, John Merton, Al Baffert, Hugh Hooker, Bill Ward, Fuzzy Knight, Dick Crockett, Roy Canada
Director: Edward Bernds
Screenplay: Elwood Ullman (Daniel E. Ullman) and William Lively
Producer: Jack Schwarz

CHEYENNE AUTUMN

(Warner Brothers, December 19, 1964) 160 Minutes
(Technicolor) (Super PanaVision 70)
James Stewart, Richard Widmark, Carroll Baker, Ricardo Montalban, Karl Malden, Sal Mineo, Dolores Del Rio, Gilbert Roland, Arthur Kennedy, Patrick Wayne, Elizabeth Allen, John Carradine, Mike Mazurki, *George O'Brien,* Sean McClory, Judson Pratt, Carmen D'Antonio, Ken Curtis, Victor Jory, Edward G. Robinson, Walter Baldwin, Shug Fisher, Nancy Hsueh, Chuck Roberson, Harry Carey, Jr., Ben Johnson, Jimmy O'Hara, Chuck Hayward, Lee Bradley, Frank Bradley, Walter Reed, Willis Bouchey, Carleton Young, Denver Pyle, John Qualen, Dan Borzage, Nanomba "Moonbeam" Morton, Dean Smith, David H. Miller, Bing Russell
Director: John Ford
Story: Mari Sandoz
Screenplay: Joseph R. Webb
Producer: Bernard Smith

3 ● BOB STEELE

The Whirlwind Kid

During 1920-'21 movie audiences often got a bonus in the form of a one-reel short called a Pathegram sandwiched in between the feature and the serial episode. These Pathegrams were edited from extensive footage made by director Robert N. Bradbury of his twin sons Bill and Bob, during a vacation in the High Sierras. Pathe had liked the outdoor adventures of two young boys and proceeded to distribute the edited shorts under the general title "The Adventures of Bill and Bob." They proved popular and a second series was made in which there was more "plot" and "acting" *a la* Hollywood. One of the boys, Bill, grew up to become a doctor. The other, Robert N. Bradbury, Jr., became one of the most revered of all movie cowboys under the name Bob Steele, a name practically synonymous with Western adventure films. Few, if any, saddle aces have had screen careers as illustrious and long as the little giant of Westerns, the whirlwind kid whose heroics have encompassed silents, sound, and television over a span of sixty years.

Bob was born in Pendleton, Oregon on January 23, 1907. When he was still just a kid the family moved to Glendale and Robert Bradbury, Sr. became a movie director. It was in Glendale that Bob attended high school, excelling in a number of sports. And it was here, also, that he became good friends with a classmate named Marion Michael Morrison, better known in later years as John Wayne. The two would appear in five big-budget features together.

Upon graduation from high school Bob and brother Bill put together a comedy act and toured the vaudeville circuit billed as The Murdock Brothers. But Bill was soon off to college, while Bob decided to give movies a whirl. His dad was directing a series of historical Westerns for Sunset Productions and he was able to get Bob featured roles in **With Daniel Boone Thru the Wilderness** ('26), **With Davy Crockett at the Fall of the Alamo** ('26), **With Sitting Bull at the Spirit Lake Massacre** ('27), and possibly one or two others. Bob was a handsome youth, an all-around athlete, and an especially good horseman as a result of a natural fondness for horses and the opportunity to have spent much of his youth around them.

Because of his earlier adventure shorts and the skills and knowledge acquired in simply growing up within the film colony as the son of an action director, Bob demonstrated a degree of camera poise and acting finesse unusual for a 19-year-old. During the same period of time that he was doing work at Sunset he was sometimes employed at FBO. The most notable FBO film, from the standpoint of his career, was **The College Boob** ('26), in which he gave a good account of himself in support of Western star Lefty Flynn.

In spite of his youth—he was only 20—Bob was tested by FBO along with fifteen other aspirants for the lead in a planned series of feature Westerns. He won the contract. Although Buzz Barton and Newton House would star as juvenile Western leads, Bob was the youngest Western ace ever to assume full-fledged stardom playing an adult hero. His closest rival in this respect was Tim Holt, who was 21 when he started his RKO series.

Previously billed under his real name of Robert Bradbury, Jr., Bob assumed the screen name Bob Steele with his first starring cactus caper, **The Mojave Kid**, directed by his father and released in September 1927. The name and the man behind it would become legend

Bob Steele

in the history of Western filmmaking. Cowboys would come and go, some skyrocketing to incredible heights in popularity before their magnetism burned out and plunged them over the brink of fame onto the lonely range of cinema retirement ridden by many over-the-hill saddle busters. But Bob Steele would always be there, to the very end of the programmer era and beyond, working at his trade and consistently turning in a good performance regardless of the size and importance of his role or the budget of the film. It was a matter of pride. Bob always enjoyed being a part of the film world, although he never took his own popularity seriously, and worked hard at perfecting his talent.

Steele starred in thirteen whirlwind Westerns for FBO, most of them with running times of less than 50 minutes but making up in action content what they lacked in length. Bob was one of the smallest Western stars in stature, being only 5'10" tall and weighing around 160 pounds. However, he proved quickly that he could handle all of the action the script called for and became noted for his fight scenes in which he would slug away with both fists to an opponent's body until he got a chance to deliver the *coup-de-grace*. Bob had been a pretty good boxer before entering movies and that training carried over effectively to the screen, with the result that his films played up his fighting ability and gained him recognition as a first-rate screen scrapper.

Syndicate became home to Bob in '29, and he made a series of seven films directed by J. P. McGowan and scripted by Sally Winters. Two or three had music scores and sound effects; otherwise, they were very similar to the FBO dusties and none stood out perceptibly over the others.

By 1930 Bob had gone over to Tiffany and it was

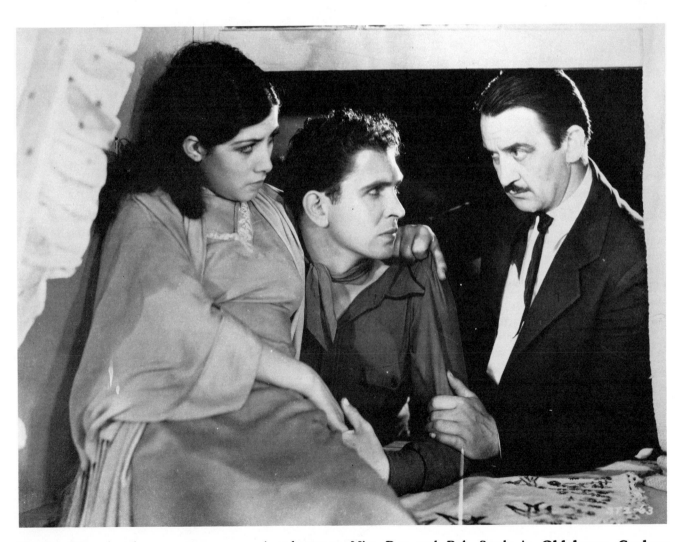

Charles King breaks up some romancing between Nita Ray and Bob Steele in **Oklahoma Cyclone** (Tiffany, 1930)

43

George Hayes, before his "Gabby" days, and Bob Steele in a publicity photo for **The Ranger's Code** (Monogram, 1931)

here that he made his first "all-talkie," **Near the Rainbow's End**. His voice registered well and he seemed at ease on a range suddenly filled with sound. Louise Lorraine was the femme interest, not a drawback for any cowboy flick. Lafe McKee, the grand old man of Westerns, also lent his charm to the plains meller. All in all, it came off well and critics were complimentary in their reviews. Seven more wild-and-woollies followed in the Trem Carr series for Tiffany, and then Carr and Steele teamed up for a series of six released through Sono Art/World Wide. Finally Carr took the Steele series with him when he became associated with Monogram, and it was under the Monogram logo that Steele appeared in 1932-'33.

The Steele films had their own distinctive style and were quite pleasant as simple little sagebrushers designed for the dueller-and-grinds market. There was no pretense of grandeur. Some of the plots were a little zany and incongruous but the films were generally well photographed, full of thrills, and replete with a mild range romance. Sometimes the locations used were different and interesting and the stories were a notch above the ordinary formula oaters. Robert N. Bradbury directed many of the films, and it was apparent that the father and son worked well together. No amount of elaboration could communicate effectively the charisma of the Monogram Steele Westerns. One really had to "live them" to appreciate them to the fullest. Later viewing on television did not provide the same satisfying feeling that original viewing in the Thirties did. They had a charm about them that was indubitably palatable.

The thing about Steele was that he kept working, consistently grinding out range mellers each year. Critics might write off his films as run-of-the-mill fare designed exclusively for the hick market and historians

44

might say he was not in a league with the super cowboys, but he worked—something the "Big Guns" couldn't always do. Perhaps Steele worried about critics' opinions as he made his deposits in the bank and accumulated the earnings which allowed him to enjoy early retirement. At an rate, he became one to the most likable and recognized heroes of the cinema range, without benefit of guitar, voice, or gimmick.

Steele's only serial, **Mystery Squadron**, was made for Mascot in 1933 and, as usual with Mascot cliffhangers, it contained a plethora of action and suspense and had a plot that was far-fetched and imaginative. A top cast headed by Lucile Browne, Guinn (Big Boy) Williams, Jack Mulhall, and Robert Kortman backed him up. The airplane motif was a popular one at the time and the serial was well received.

In 1934 Bob began his long-running series for A. W. Hackel, who released his product first through William Steiner, then through Supreme and Republic. Thirty-two of these minor sagebrushers were made before the series ended in 1938. Bob's father was still at the directorial helm in most of the films, and Sam Newfield, equally famed as an ace action director, put Steele through the paces in others. Even if he had made no other Westerns in his entire life, this long series alone would have been enough to establish Bob's credentials as one of the great Western performers. He was a scrappy son-of-a-gun and the stories, usually a little different, were as refreshing as a downpour of rain on a sunbaked desert in mid-August. In both '37 and '38 Bob ranked seventh in the Motion Picture Herald Poll of the most popular Western stars.

In 1939-'40 Steele completed eight films for Harry Webb, who released his indies through Metropolitan. He also was featured in Hal Roach's **Of Mice and Men** ('39), his role as "Curley" receiving wide acclaim from

Guinn "Big Boy" Williams, Lucile Brown, Lafe McKee, and Bob Steele examine one of the airplane symbols of the **Mystery Squadron** (Mascot, 1933).

Bob Steele is mad at whoever wounded Si Jenks in **The Great Train Robbery** (Republic, 1941)

the non-cowboy movie fraternity. He would later add to his acting credentials with meaty roles in such big-budget melodramas as **The Big Sleep** (WB, '46), **Killer McCoy** (MGM, '47), and **The Enforcer** (WB, '51).

PRC signed Bob in 1940 to star in a Billy the Kid series that featured Al St. John as his sidekick. Sigmund Neufeld produced and his brother Sam Newfield directed. Although cheaply made, the six films were fun to watch and carried on the traditional basic no-frills, no gimmicks, shoot-em-ups that were rapidly disappearing as a result of the Autry phenomenon.

Republic signed Bob for the "Tucson Smith" role in The Three Mesquiteers series in late 1940 and he made twenty of the popular trio oaters. Bob Livingston co-starred in seven of the films and Tom Tyler in thirteen others, while Rufe Davis had the comedy lead in fourteen and Jimmie Dodd in six. The series ranked in the top ten most popular Western series through 1943, the

last year of production. Bob made one non-Western during this time, **The Great Train Robbery** (Rep., '40). a railroad drama.

Without letting any grass grow under his horse, Steele stepped into the Trail Blazers series at Monogram in late '43, making five in that series and staying on for three more films as a co-star with Hoot Gibson. He then starred in a couple of cinecolor Westerns for Action Pictures before signing with PRC once more for his last series as a lead. Although **Thunder Town** ('46) brought his starring career to a close, it by no means closed the door on his movie activity.

From 1946 to 1973 Steele continued on screen as a character actor and assumed roles in big-budget features. Semi-retired for years, he chose only the roles that appealed to him. Work has not been a necessity but, as he put it, "How much golf can you play?" He has appeared often on television and was a regular on the

46

"F Troop" series for two seasons in the mid-sixties. His publicized appearance at a Western Film Festival in Memphis in 1974 drew huge crowds and long autograph lines. Good health has allowed him to do the things he has wanted to do, which includes a lot of golf, fishing, and relaxation at his cabin in the Sierras. His last known screen appearance was in 1973, but fans keep hoping that he will yet appear in "just one more Western"—a fine tribute for The Whirlwind Kid of half a century ago.

BOB STEELE Filmography

TRAPPING THE BOBCAT
(Pathe, April 6, 1921) 1 Reel
(Adventures of Bill and Bob Series)
William Bradbury and Robert N. Bradbury, Jr. *(Bob Steele)*
Producer/Director: Robert N. Bradbury, Sr.

OUTWITTING THE TIMBER WOLF
(Pathe, June 2, 1921) 1 Reel
(Adventures of Bill and Bob Series)
William Bradbury and Robert N. Bradbury, Jr. *(Bob Steele)*
Producer/Director: Robert N. Bradbury, Sr.

THE FOX
(Pathe, July 2, 1921) 1 Reel
(Adventures of Bill and Bob Series)
William Bradbury and Robert N. Bradbury, Jr. *(Bob Steele)*
Producer/Director: Robert N. Bradbury, Sr.

THE MOUNTAIN LION
(Pathe, July 19, 1921) 1 Reel
(Adventures of Bill and Bob Series)
William Bradbury and Robert N. Bradbury, Jr. *(Bob Steele)*
Producer/Director: Robert N. Bradbury, Sr.

TRAILING THE COYOTE
(Pathe, July 19, 1921) 1 Reel
(Adventures of Bill and Bob Series)
William Bradbury and Robert N. Bradbury, Jr. *(Bob Steele)*
Producer/Director: Robert N. Bradbury, Sr.

THE AMERICAN BADGER
(Pathe, July 19, 1921) 1 Reel
(Adventures of Bill and Bob Series)
William Bradbury and Robert N. Bradbury, Jr. *(Bob Steele)*
Producer/Director: Robert N. Bradbury, Sr.

CIVET CAT
(Pathe, September 7, 1921) 1 Reel
(Adventures of Bill and Bob Series)
William Bradbury and Robert N. Bradbury, Jr. *(Bob Steele)*
Producer/Director: Robert N. Bradbury, Sr.

THE SKUNK
(Pathe, October 19, 1921) 1 Reel
(Adventures of Bill and Bob Series)
William Bradbury and Robert N. Bradbury, Jr. *(Bob Steele)*
Producer/Director: Robert N. Bradbury, Sr.

A DAY IN THE WILDS
(Pathe, November 2, 1921) 1 Reel
(Adventures of Bill and Bob Series)
William Bradbury and Robert N. Bradbury, Jr. *(Bob Steele)*
Producer/Director: Robert N. Bradbury, Sr.

TRAPPING THE WEASEL
(Pathe, December 6, 1921) 1 Reel
(Adventures of Bill and Bob Series)
William Bradbury and Robert N. Bradbury, Jr. *(Bob Steele)*
Producer/Director: Robert N. Bradbury, Sr.

CAPTURING THE CANADIAN LYNX
(Pathe, March 4, 1922) 1 Reel
(Adventures of Bill and Bob Series)
William Bradbury and Robert N. Bradbury, Jr. *(Bob Steele)*
Producer/Director: Robert N. Bradbury, Sr.

MYSTERIOUS TRACKS
(Pathe, March 4, 1922) 1 Reel
(Adventures of Bill and Bob Series)
William Bradbury and Robert N. Bradbury, Jr. *(Bob Steele)*
Producer/Director: Robert N. Bradbury, Sr.

THE OPOSSUM
(Pathe, June 26, 1922) 1 Reel
(Adventures of Bill and Bob Series)
William Bradbury and Robert N. Bradbury, Jr. *(Bob Steele)*
Producer/Director: Robert N. Bradbury, Sr.

TRAPPING A RACCOON
(Pathe, release or copyright date unknown) 1 Reel
(Adventures of Bill and Bob series)
William Bradbury and Robert N. Bradbury, Jr. *(Bob Steele)*
Producer/Director: Robert N. Bradbury, Sr.

CAPTURING A KOALA BEAR

(Pathe, release or copyright date unknown) 1 Reel
(Adventures of Bill and Bob Series)
William Bradbury and Robert N. Bradbury, Jr. *(Bob Steele)*
Producer/Director: Robert N. Bradbury, Sr.

SECRET TRAILS

(Pathe, release or copyright date unknown) 1 Reel
(Adventures of Bill and Bob Series)
William Bradbury and Robert N. Bradbury, Jr. *(Bob Steele)*
Producer/Director: Robert N. Bradbury, Sr.

WITH DANIEL BOONE THRU THE WILDERNESS

(Sunset Productions, May 1, 1926) 56 Minutes
Roy Stewart, Kathleen Collins, Edward Hearne, Frank Rice, Emilie Gertes, Jay Morley, Tom Lingham, Bob Bradbury, Jr. *(Bob Steele)*
Director: Robert N. Bradbury
Producer: Anthony J. Xydias

WITH DAVY CROCKETT AT THE FALL OF THE ALAMO

(Sunset Productions, August 1, 1926) 55 Minutes
Cullen Landis, Kathryn MacQuire, Joe Rickson, Bob Fleming, Ralph McCullough, Fletcher Norton, Anne Berryman, Jay Morley, Tom Lingham, Frank Rice, Betty Brown, Bob Bradbury, Jr. *(Bob Steele)*, Steve Clemento
Director: Robert N. Bradbury
Adaptation: Ben Newman
Producer: Anthony J. Xydias

THE COLLEGE BOOB

(FBO, August 15, 1926) 53 Minutes
Lefty Flynn, Jean Arthur, Jimmy Anderson, Bob Bradbury, Jr. *(Bob Steele)*, Cecil Ogden, Dorthea Wolbert, William Nolan, Raymond Turner
Director: Harry Garson
Screenplay: Gerald C. Duffy
Story: Jack Casey

WITH SITTING BULL AT THE SPIRIT LAKE MASSACRE

(Sunset Productions, June 16, 1927) 52 Minutes
Bryant Washburn, Ann Schaeffer, Jay Morley, Shirley Palmer, Thomas Lingham, Chief Yowlachie, James O'Neil, Bob Bradbury, Jr. *(Bob Steele)*, Fred Warren, Leon Kent, Lucille Ballart
Director: Robert N. Bradbury
Adaptation: Ben Allah
Producer: Anthony J. Xydias

THE MOJAVE KID

(R-C Pictures/FBO, September 25, 1927) 49 Minutes
Bob Steele, Lilian Gilmore, Buck Connors, Bob Fleming, Jay Morley, Theodore Henderson, Nat Mills
Director: Robert N. Bradbury
Story: Oliver Drake
Assistant Director: Wallace Fox

THE BANDIT'S SON

(FBO, November 20, 1927) 48 Minutes
Bob Steele, Tom Lingham, Hal Davis, Stanley Taylor, Ann Sheridan, Bobby Mack, Finch Smiles, Barry Gilmore
Director: Wallace Fox
Story: Frank Howard Clark

DRIFTIN' SANDS

(FBO, January 1, 1928) 48 Minutes
Bob Steele, Gladys Quartaro, William H. Turner, Jay Morley, Carl Axzelle, Gladden James
Director: Wallace Fox
Adaptation: Oliver Drake
Story: W. C. Tuttle - "Fate of the Wolf"

THE RIDING RENEGADE

(FBO, February 19, 1928) 47 Minutes
Bob Steele, Dorothy Kitchen, Lafe McKee, Bob Fleming, Ethan Laidlaw, Nick Thompson, Pedro Riga
Director: Wallace Fox
Story/Screenplay: Frank Howard Clark

BREED OF THE SUNSETS

(FBO, March 5, 1928) 49 Minutes
Bob Steele, Nancy Drexel, George Bunny, Dorothy Kitchen, Leo White, Larry Fisher
Director: Wallace Fox
Adaptation: Oliver Drake
Story: S. E. V. Taylor

MAN IN THE ROUGH

(FBO, May 20, 1928) 48 Minutes
Bob Steele, Marjorie King, Tom Lingham, William Narton Bailey, Jay Morley
Director: Wallace Fox
Screenplay: Frank Howard Clark
Story: W. C. Tuttle

TRAIL OF COURAGE

(FBO, July 8, 1928) 47 Minutes
Bob Steele, Marjorie Bonner, Tom Lingham, Jay Morley
Director: Wallace Fox
Screenplay: Frank Howard Clark
Story: Kenneth Perkins - "Better Than a Rodeo"

CAPTAIN CARELESS

(FBO, August 26, 1928) 49 Minutes
Bob Steele, Mary Mabery, Perry Murdock, Jack Donovan, Barney Furey, Wilfred North
Director: Jerome Storm
Screenplay: Perry Murdock, Frank Howard Clark
Story: Bob Steele, Perry Murdock

LIGHTNING SPEED

(FBO, August 26, 1928) 46 Minutes
Bob Steele, Mary Mabery, Perry Murdock, Barney Furey, William Welsh
Director/Story/Screenplay: Robert North Bradbury

HEADIN' FOR DANGER

(FBO/RKO Radio, December 16, 1928) 52 Minutes
Bob Steele, Jola Mendez, Al Ferguson, Tom Forman, Frank Rice, Harry DeRoy, Leonard Trainer
Director: Robert N. Bradbury
Scenario: Frank Howard Clark

COME AND GET IT

(FBO/RKO Radio, February 3, 1929) 51 Minutes
Bob Steele, Jimmy Quinn, Betty Walsh, Jay Morley, James B. Leong, Harry O'Connor, Marin Sais, William Welsh
Director: Wallace Fox
Scenario: Frank Howard Clark

THE AMAZING VAGABOND

(FBO/RKO Radio, April 7, 1929) 51 Minutes
Bob Steele, Tom Lingham, Jay Morley, Perry Murdock, Lafe McKee, Thelma Daniels, Emily Gerdes
Director: Wallace Fox
Story/Screenplay: Frank Howard Clark

LAUGHING AT DEATH

(FBO/RKO Radio, June 2, 1929) 50 Minutes
Bob Steele, Natalie Joyce, Captain Vic, Kai Schmidt, Ethan Laidlaw, Armand Trillor, Hector V. Sarno, Golden Wadhams
Director: Wallace Fox
Scenario: Frank Howard Clark

THE INVADERS

(Big Production Film Corp./Syndicate, October, 1929) 62 Minutes (Music score and sound effects)
Bob Steele, Edna Aslin, Tom Lingham, J. P. McGowan, Celeste Rush, Tom Smith, Bud Osborne, Chief Yowlachie
Director: J. P. McGowan
Scenario: Walter Sterret
Story: Sally Winters

THE COWBOY AND THE OUTLAW

(Big Production Film Corp./Syndicate, October, 1929) 48 Minutes (Music score and sound effects)
Bob Steele, Edna Aslin, Bud Osborne, Tom Lingham, Cliff Lyons, J. P. McGowan, Alfred Hewston
Director: J. P. McGowan
Story: Sally Winters

A TEXAS COWBOY

(Big Production Film Corp./Syndicate, December 26, 1929) 50 Minutes
Bob Steele, Edna Aslin, Perry Murdock, J. P. McGowan, Bud Osborne, Alfred Hewston, Grace Stevens, Cliff Lyons
Director: J. P. McGowan
Story/Screenplay: Sally Winters

BREEZY BILL

(Big Production Film Corp./Syndicate, January 24, 1930) 46 Minutes
Bob Steele, Alfred Hewston, George Hewston, Edna Aslin, Perry Murdock, Bud Osborne, Cliff Lyons, J. P. McGowan
Director: J. P. McGowan
Story/Screenplay: Sally Winters

HUNTED MEN

(Big Production Film Corp./Syndicate, April, 1930) 48 Minutes
Bob Steele, Jean Reno, Lew Meehan, Mac V. Wright, Tom Lingham, Clark Comstock
Director: J. P. McGowan
Story/Scenario: Sally Winters

MAN FROM NOWHERE

(Big Production Film Corp./Syndicate, April, 1930) 49 Minutes
Bob Steele, Tone Reed, Clark Comstock, Bill Nestel, Perry Murdock, Tom Forman, Clark Coffey
Director: J. P. McGowan
Story/Scenario: Sally Winters
(Film also known as "Western Honor")

NEAR THE RAINBOW'S END

(Tiffany, June 10, 1930) 51 Minutes
(an "all-talkie" film)
Bob Steele, Louise Lorraine, Al Ferguson, Lafe McKee, Al Hewston, Hank Bell, Merrill McCormack
Director: J. P. McGowan
Screenplay: Sally Winters
Producer: Trem Carr

THE OKLAHOMA SHERIFF
(Big Production Film Corp./Syndicate, July 10, 1930) 49 Minutes (Steele's last silent film—made before "Near the Rainbow's End")
Bob Steele, Jean Reno, Perry Murdock, Cliff Lyons, Mac V. Wright, Tom Lingham, Clark Comstock
Director: J. P. McGowan
Story/Screenplay: Sally Winters

OKLAHOMA CYCLONE
(Tiffany, August 8, 1930) 59 Minutes
Bob Steele, Al St. John, Nita Ray, Charles King, Slim Whitaker, Shorty Hendricks, Emilio Fernandez, Hector Sarno, Fred Burns, Cliff Lyons, John Ince
Director: John P. McCarthy
Screenplay: Ford Beebe
Producer: Trem Carr

THE LAND OF MISSING MEN
(Tiffany, October 15, 1930) 52 Minutes
Bob Steele, Caryl Lincoln, Al St. John, Fern Emmett, S. S. Simmons, Emilio Fernandez, Noah Hendricks, Al Jennings, Eddie Dunn, C. R. DaFau, Fred Burns
Director: John P. McCarthy
Story/Screenplay: John P. McCarthy, Robert Quigley
Producer: Trem Carr

HEADIN' NORTH
(Tiffany, November 1, 1930) 53 Minutes
Bob Steele, Barbara Luddy, Perry Murdock, Walter Shumway, Eddie Dunn, Fred Burns, Gordon DeMain, Harry Allen, Gunner Davis, S. S. Simon, James Welsh, Jack Henderson
Director: J. P. McCarthy
Story/Screenplay: J. P. McCarthy
Producer: Trem Carr

SUNRISE TRAIL
(Tiffany, February 7, 1931) 65 Minutes
Bob Steele, Blanche Mehaffey, Jack Clifford, Eddie Dunn, Germaine De Neel, Fred Burns, Dick Alexander
Director: J. P. McCarthy
Story/Screenplay: Wellyn Totman
Producer: Trem Carr

THE RIDIN' FOOL
(Tiffany, May 31, 1931) 58 Minutes
Bob Steele, Frances Morris, Josephine Velez, Florence Turner, Eddie Fetherston, Ted Adams, Al Bridge, Fern Emmett, Gordon DeMain, Jack Henderson, Artie Ortego
Director: J. P. McCarthy
Story/Screenplay: Wellyn Totman
Producer: Trem Carr

THE NEVADA BUCKAROO
(Tiffany, September 27, 1931) 59 Minutes
Bob Steele, Dorothy Dix, George Hayes, Ed Brady, Glen Cavander, Billy Engle, Artie Ortego, Merrill McCormack
Director: John P. McCarthy
Story: Wellyn Totman
Producer: Trem Carr

NEAR THE TRAIL'S END
(Tiffany, September 30, 1931) 55 Minutes
Bob Steele, Marion Shockley, Jay Morley, Hooper Atchley, Si Jenks, Murdock McQuarrie, Henry Rocquemore, Fred Burns, Artie Ortego
Director: Wallace Fox
Story: Robert Quigley
Screenplay: G. A. Durlam
Producer: Trem Carr

SOUTH OF SANTA FE
(Sono Art-World Wide, January 8, 1932) 60 Minutes
Bob Steele, Janis Elliott, Chris-Pin Martin, Jack Clifford, Eddie Dunn, Robert Burns, Hank Bell, Allan Garcia
Director: Bert Glennon
Story/Screenplay: G. A. Durlam
Producer: Trem Carr

LAW OF THE WEST
(Sono Art-World Wide, March 20, 1932) 58 Minutes
Bob Steele, Nancy Drexel, Ed Brady, Hank Bell, Charles West, Earl Dwire, Dick Dickinson, Rose Plummer, Frank Ellis
Director: Robert N. Bradbury
Story/Screenplay: Robert N. Bradbury
Producer: Trem Carr

RIDERS OF THE DESERT
(Sono Art-World Wide, April 24, 1932) 59 Minutes
Bob Steele, Gertrude Messinger, George Hayes, Al St. John, Greg Whitespear, Horace B. Carpenter, Louise Carber, Joe Dominguez, John Elliott
Director: Robert N. Bradbury
Story/Screenplay: Wellyn Totman
Producer: Trem Carr

MAN FROM HELL'S EDGES
(Sono Art-World Wide, June 15, 1932) 61 Minutes
Bob Steele, Nancy Drexel, George Hayes, Earl Dwire, Robert Homans, Gilbert Holmes, Dick Dickinson, Perry Murdock, Julian Rivero, Blackie Whiteford
Director: Robert N. Bradbury
Story/Screenplay: Robert N. Bradbury
Producer: Trem Carr

SON OF OKLAHOMA

(Sono Art-World Wide, July 17, 1932) 55 Minutes
Bob Steele, Carmen LaRoux, Earl Dwire, Julian Rivero, Josie Sedgwick, Robert Homans, Henry Rocquemore, Jack Perrin
Director: Robert N. Bradbury
Story: Wellyn Totman
Screenplay: Burl Tuttle, George Hull
Producer: Trem Carr

HIDDEN VALLEY

(Monogram, October 10, 1932) 60 Minutes
Bob Steele, Gertrude Messinger, Francis McDonald, Ray Haller, John Elliott, Arthur Millet, V. L. Barnes, Joe De LaCruz, Dick Dickinson, George Hayes, Capt. Verner L. Smith, Tom London
Director: Robert N. Bradbury
Story/Screenplay: Wellyn Totman
Producer: Trem Carr

TEXAS BUDDIES

(Tiffany/World Wide, October 19, 1932) 59 Minutes
Bob Steele, Nancy Drexel, George Hayes, Francis McDonald, Harry Semels, Dick Dickinson, Slade Harulbert, William Dyer
Director: Robert N. Bradbury
Story/Screenplay: Robert N. Bradbury
Producer: Trem Carr

YOUNG BLOOD

(Monogram, November 5, 1932) 59 Minutes
Bob Steele, Helen Foster, Naomi Judge, Charles King, Henry Rocquemore, Art Mix, Hank Bell, Harry Semels, Lafe McKee, Perry Murdock, Roy Bucko
Director: Phil Rosen
Story/Screenplay: Wellyn Totman
Producer: Trem Carr

THE FIGHTING CHAMP

(Monogram, December 15, 1932) 59 Minutes
Bob Steele, Arletta Duncan, George Hayes, Charles King, Lafe McKee, Kit Guard, George Chesebro, Frank Ball, Henry Rocquemore, Hank Bell
Director: J. P. McCarthy
Story/Screenplay: Wellyn Totman
Producer: Trem Carr

BREED OF THE BORDER

(Monogram, May 10, 1933) 60 Minutes
Bob Steele, Marion Byron, George Hayes, Ernie Adams, Wilfred Lucas, Henry Rocquemore, Fred Cavens, Robert Cord, Perry Murdock
Director: Robert N. Bradbury
Story/Screenplay: Harry O. Jones
Producer: Trem Carr

THE GALLANT FOOL

(Monogram, May 24, 1933) 60 Minutes
Bob Steele, Arletta Duncan, George Hayes, John Elliott, Theodore Lorch, Perry Murdock, George Nash, Pascall Perry
Director: Robert N. Bradbury
Screenplay: Robert N. Bradbury, Harry O. Jones (Harry Fraser)
Producer: Trem Carr

GALLOPING ROMEO

(Monogram, August 5, 1933) 60 Minutes
Bob Steele, Doris Hill, George Hayes, Frank Ball, Ernie Adams, Lafe McKee, Ed Brady, George Nash, Earl Dwire
Director: Robert N. Bradbury
Story: Robert N. Bradbury
Screenplay: Harry O. Jones (Harry Fraser)
Producer: Trem Carr

THE RANGER'S CODE

(Monogram, August 15, 1933) 59 Minutes
Bob Steele, Doris Hill, George Hayes, George Nash, Ernie Adams, Ed Brady, Hal Price, Dick Dickinson, Frank Ball
Director: Robert N. Bradbury
Story: John T. Neville
Screenplay: Harry O. Jones (Harry Fraser)
Producer: Trem Carr

MYSTERY SQUADRON

(Mascot, December 22, 1933) 12 Chapters
Bob Steele, Guinn "Big Boy" Williams, Lucile Browne, Jack Mulhall, Purnell Pratt, Lafe McKee, Robert Kortman, Robert Frazer, Edward Hearn, Edward Piel, Kernan Cripps, Jack Mower, Jack Perrin, Lew Meehan, Frank Ellis, Wally Wales
Directors: Colbert Clark and David Howard
Story: Sherman Lowe, Al Martin
Screenplay: Barney Sarecky, Colbert Clark, David Howard, Wyndham Gittens
Chapter Titles: (1) The Black Ace (2) The Fatal Warning (3) The Black Ace Strikes (4) Men of Steel (5) The Death Swoop (6) Doomed (7) Enemy Signals (8) The Canyon of Calamity (9) The Secret of the Mine (10) Clipped Wings (11) The Beast at Bay (12) The Ace of Aces

TRAILING NORTH

(Monogram, 1933) 60 Minutes
Bob Steele, Doris Hill, George Hayes, Arthur Rankin, Fred Burns, Dick Dickinson, Norma Fensler
Director: J. P. McCarthy
Story: Harry O. Jones (Harry Fraser)
Screenplay: John Morgan
Supervisor: Trem Carr
Producer: Paul Malvern

51

A DEMON FOR TROUBLE

(Supreme/William Steiner, August 10, 1934) 58 Minutes
Bob Steele, Gloria Shea, Lafe McKee, Walter McGrail, Don Alvarado, Nick Stuart, Carmen LaRoux, Perry Murdock, Blackie Whiteford, Jimmy Aubrey, Buck Morgan
Director: Robert Hill
Story/Screenplay: Jack Natteford
Producer: A. W. Hackel

BRAND OF HATE

(Supreme/William Steiner, November 2, 1934) 63 Minutes
Bob Steele, Lucile Browne, William Farnum, Charles K. French, George Hayes, Jack Rockwell, Mickey Rentschiller, Archie Ricks, James Flavin
Director: Lew Collins
Story/Screenplay: Jack Natteford
Producer: A. W. Hackel

POWDERSMOKE RANGE

(RKO, September 27, 1935) 6 Reels
(First of the "3 Mesquiteers" films)
Harry Carey, Hoot Gibson, *Bob Steele,* Tom Tyler, Guinn "Big Boy" Williams, Boots Mallory, Wally Wales, Sam Hardy, Adrian Morris, Buzz Barton, Art Mix, Frank Rice, Buddy Roosevelt, Buffalo Bill, Jr., Franklyn Farnum, William Desmond, William Farnum, Ethan Laidlaw, Eddie Dunn, Ray Meyer, Barney Furney, Bob McKenzie, James Mason, Irving Bacon, Henry Rocquemore, Phil Dunham, Silver Tip Baker, Nelson McDowell, Frank Ellis
Director: Wallace Fox
Story: William Colt MacDonald
Screenplay: Adele Buffington
Producer: Cliff Reid

BIG CALIBRE

(Supreme/William Steiner, March 8, 1935)
Bob Steele, Peggy Campbell, Georgia O'Dell, Bill Quinn, Earl Dwire, John Elliott, Forrest Taylor, Perry Murdock, Si Jenks, Frank Ball, Frank McCarroll, Blackie Whiteford
Director: Robert N. Bradbury
Story: Perry Murdock
Producer: A. W. Hackel

TOMBSTONE TERROR

(Supreme/William Steiner, April 25, 1935) 58 Minutes
Bob Steele, George Hayes, Kay McCoy, Earl Dwire, John Elliott, Hortense Petro, Ann Howard, Nancy DeShon, Frank McCarroll, Artie Ortego, George Morrell, Herman Hack
Director/Screenplay: Robert N. Bradbury
Producer: A. W. Hackel

WESTERN JUSTICE

(Supreme/William Steiner, June 14, 1935)
Bob Steele, Renee Borden, Julian Rivero, Jack Cowell, Perry Murdock, Vane Calvert, Lafe McKee, Arthur Loft
Director/Screenplay: Robert N. Bradbury
Producer: A. W. Hackel

KID COURAGEOUS

(Supreme/William Steiner, July 26, 1935)
Bob Steele, Renee Borden, Kit Guard, Arthur Loft, Jack Powell, Lafe McKee, Vane Calvert, Barry Seury, Perry Murdock, John Elliott
Director/Screenplay: Robert N. Bradbury
Producer: A. W. Hackel

NO MAN'S RANGE

(Supreme/William Steiner, September 5, 1935)
Bob Steele, Roberta Gale, Buck Connors, Steve Clark, Charles K. French, Jack Rockwell, Roger Williams, Earl Dwire, Ed Cassidy, Jim Corey
Director: Robert N. Bradbury
Story/Screenplay: Forbes Parkhill
Producer: A. W. Hackel

SMOKEY SMITH

(Supreme/William Steiner, September 26, 1935) 57 Minutes
Bob Steele, Mary Kornman, George Hayes, Warner Richmond, Earl Dwire, Horace B. Carpenter, Tex Phelps, Archie Hicks
Director: Robert N. Bradbury
Story/Screenplay: Robert N. Bradbury
Producer: A. W. Hackel

THE RIDER OF THE LAW

(Supreme/William Steiner, October, 1935)
Bob Steele, Gertrude Messinger, Si Jenks, Earl Dwire, Forrest Taylor, Lloyd Ingraham, John Elliott, Sherry Tansey, Tex Palmer, Chuck Baldra
Director: Robert N. Bradbury
Story/Screenplay: Jack Natteford
Producer: A. W. Hackel

ALIAS JOHN LAW

(Supreme/William Steiner, November 5, 1935)
Bob Steele, Roberta Gale, Buck Connors, Earl Dwire, Bob McKenzie, Steve Clark, Jack Rockwell, Roger Williams, Jack Cowell, Horace Murphy
Director: Robert N. Bradbury
Screenplay: Forbes Parkhill
Producer: A. W. Hackel

TRAIL OF TERROR

(Supreme/William Steiner, December 20, 1935)
Bob Steele, Beth Marion, Forrest Taylor, Charles King, Lloyd Ingraham, Frank Lyman, Jr., Charles K. French, Richard Cramer, Nancy DeShon
Director/Screenplay: Robert N. Bradbury
Producer: A. W. Hackel

THE KID RANGER

(Supreme/William Steiner, February 5, 1936) 57 Minutes
Bob Steele, William Farnum, Joan Barclay, Earl Dwire, Charles King, Lafe McKee, Frank Ball, Reetsy Adams, Paul and Paulina, Buck Moulton
Director: Robert N. Bradbury
Story/Screenplay: Robert N. Bradbury
Producer: A. W. Hackel

SUNDOWN SAUNDERS

(Supreme/William Steiner, March 25, 1936) 59 Minutes
Bob Steele, Catherine Cotter, Earl Dwire, Milburn Morante, Ed Cassidy, Jack Rockwell, Frank Ball, Hal Price, Charles King, Horace Murphy, Edmund Cobb, Bob McKenzie, Jack Kirk, Herman Hack
Director/Story/Screenplay: Robert N. Bradbury
Producer: A. W. Hackel

LAST OF THE WARRENS

(Supreme/William Steiner, May 10, 1936) 60 Minutes
Bob Steele, Margaret Marquis, Charles King, Horace Murphy, Lafe McKee, Charles K. French, Blackie Whiteford, Steve Clark
Director/Story/Screenplay: Robert N. Bradbury
Producer: A. W. Hackel

THE LAW RIDES

(Supreme/William Steiner, June 25, 1936) 57 Minutes
Bob Steele, Harley Wood, Charles King, Buck Connors, Margaret Mann, Jack Rockwell, Norman Neilsen, Barney Furey, Ted Mapes
Director: Robert N. Bradbury
Story: Forbes Parkhill
Screenplay: Al Martin
Producer: A. W. Hackel

BRAND OF THE OUTLAW

(Supreme/William Steiner, August 15, 1936) 60 Minutes
Bob Steele, Margaret Marquis, Virginia True Boardman, Jack Rockwell, Edward Cassidy, Charles King, Frank Ball, Bud Osborne, Bob Kortman
Director: Robert N. Bradbury
Story/Screenplay: Forbes Parkhill
Producer: A. W. Hackel

CAVALRY

(Republic, October 5, 1936) 63 Minutes
Bob Steele, Frances Grant, Karl Hackett, William Welch, Earl Ross, Hal Price, Ed Cassidy, Perry Murdock, Martin Turner, Pinky Barnes, Budd Buster, William Desmond, Earl Dwire, Horace B. Carpenter
Director/Story: Robert N. Bradbury
Screenplay: George Plympton
Producer: A. W. Hackel

THE GUN RANGER

(Republic, February 9, 1937) 56 Minutes
Bob Steele, Eleanore Stewart, John Merton, Ernie Adams, Earl Dwire, Budd Buster, Frank Ball, Horace Murphy, Lew Meehan, Hal Taliaferro (Wally Wales), Horace B. Carpenter, Jack Kirk, George Morrell, Tex Palmer
Director: Robert N. Bradbury
Story: Homer Gordon
Screenplay: George Plympton
Producer: A. W. Hackel

Bob Steele has the drop on the saloon in **The Gun Ranger** (Republic, 1936).

LIGHTNIN' CRANDALL

(Republic, March 24, 1937) 60 Minutes

Bob Steele, Lois January, Dave O'Brien, Horace Murphy, Charles King, Ernie Adams, Earl Dwire, Frank LaRue, Lloyd Ingraham, Lew Meehan, Dick Cramer, Jack C. Smith, Sherry Tansey, Tex Palmer, Ed Carey, Art Felix

Director: Sam Newfield
Story: E. B. Mann
Screenplay: Charles Francis Royal
Producer: A. W. Hackel

THE TRUSTED OUTLAW

(Republic, May 4, 1937) 52 Minutes

Bob Steele, Lois January, Joan Barclay, Earl Dwire, Charles King, Dick Cramer, Hal Price, Budd Buster, Frank Ball, Oscar Gahan, George Morrell, Chick Hannon, Sherry Tansey, Clyde McClary, Wally West, Jack Rockwell, Joe Weaver, Ray Henderson

Director: R. N. Bradbury
Story: Johnston McCaulley
Screenplay: George Plympton, Fred Myton
Producer: A. W. Hackel

GUN LORDS OF STIRRUP BASIN

(Republic, May 18, 1937) 53 Minutes

Bob Steele, Louise Stanley, Karl Hackett, Ernie Adams, Frank LaRue, Frank Ball, Steve Clark, Lew Meehan, Frank Ellis, Jim Corey, Budd Buster, Lloyd Ingraham, Jack Kirk, Horace Murphy, Milburn Morante, Bobby Nelson, Tex Palmer, Emma Tansey, Horace B. Carpenter, Herman Hack

Director: Sam Newfield
Story: Harry Olmstead
Screenplay: George Plympton, Fred Myton
Producer: A. W. Hackel

BORDER PHANTOM

(Republic, June 7, 1937) 58 Minutes

Bob Steele, Harley Wood, Don Barclay, Karl Hackett, Perry Murdock, Frank Ball, Hans Joby, Miki Morita

Director: S. Roy Luby
Screenplay: Fred Myton
Producer: A. W. Hackel

DOOMED AT SUNDOWN

(Republic, July 7, 1937) 53 Minutes

Bob Steele, Lorraine Hays (Laraine Day), Dave Sharpe, Warner Richmond, Earl Dwire, Harold Daniels, Horace B. Carpenter, Sherry Tansey, Budd Buster, Jack C. Smith, Jack Kirk, Horace Murphy, Charles King, Lew Meehan, Jack Ingram

Director: Sam Newfield
Story: Fred Myton
Screenplay: George Plympton
Producer: A. W. Hackel

THE RED ROPE

(Republic, July 19, 1937) 56 Minutes

Bob Steele, Lois January, Horace Murphy, Charles King, Bobby Nelson, Ed Cassidy, Lew Meehan, Frank Ball, Forrest Taylor, Jack Rockwell, Karl Hackett

Director: S. Roy Luby
Screenplay: George Plympton
Producer: A. W. Hackel

ARIZONA GUNFIGHTER

(Republic, September 24, 1937) 58 Minutes

Bob Steele, Jean Carmen, Ted Adams, Ernie Adams, Lew Meehan, Steve Clark, John Merton, Karl Hackett, A. C. Anderson, Frank Ball, Sherry Tansey, Jack Kirk, Hal Price, Budd Buster, Horace B. Carpenter, Tex Palmer, Archie Ricks, Allen Greer, Roy Bucko, Oscar Gahan, Silver Tip Baker

Director: Sam Newfield
Story: Harry Olmstead
Screenplay: George Plympton
Producer: A. W. Hackel

RIDIN' THE LONE TRAIL

(Republic, November 1, 1937) 56 Minutes

Bob Steele, Claire Rochelle, Charles King, Ernie Adams, Lew Meehan, Julian Rivero, Steve Clark, Hal Price, Frank Ball, Jack Kirk

Director: Sam Newfield
Story: E. B. Mann
Screenplay: Charles Francis Royal
Producer: A. W. Hackel

COLORADO KID

(Republic, December 6, 1937) 56 Minutes

Bob Steele, Marion Weldon, Karl Hackett, Ernie Adams, Ted Adams, Frank LaRue, Horace Murphy, Kenne Duncan, Budd Buster, Frank Ball, John Merton, Horace B. Carpenter, Wally West

Director: Sam Newfield
Story: Harry Olmstead
Screenplay: Charles Francis Royal
Producer: A. W. Hackel

PAROLED TO DIE

(Republic, January 11, 1938) 55 Minutes

Bob Steele, Kathleen Eliot, Karl Hackett, Horace Murphy, Steve Clark, Budd Buster, Sherry Tansey, Frank Ball, Jack C. Smith, Horace B. Carpenter

Director: Sam Newfield
Story: Harry Olmstead
Screenplay: George Plympton
Producer: A. W. Hackel

Steve Clark and Rex Lease watch Marion Weldon and Bob Steele in **Desert Patrol** (Republic, 1938).

THUNDER IN THE DESERT

(Republic, March 7, 1938) 56 Minutes
Bob Steele, Louise Stanley, Don Barclay, Charles King, Ed Brady, Horace Murphy, Steve Clark, Lew Meehan, Ernie Adams, Dick Cramer, Budd Buster, Sherry Tansey
Director: Sam Newfield
Screenplay: George Plympton
Producer: A. W. Hackel

THE FEUD MAKER

(Republic, April 18, 1938) 55 Minutes
Bob Steele, Marion Weldon, Karl Hackett, Frank Ball, Budd Buster, Lew Meehan, Roger Williams, Forrest Taylor, Jack C. Smith, Steve Clark, Lloyd Ingraham, Sherry Tansey, Wally West, Tex Palmer
Director: Sam Newfield
Story: Harry Olmstead
Screenplay: George Plympton
Producer: A. W. Hackel

DESERT PATROL

(Republic, June 6, 1938) 56 Minutes
Bob Steele, Rex Lease, Marion Weldon, Ted Adams, Forrest Taylor, Budd Buster, Steve Clark, Jack Ingram, Julian Madison, Tex Palmer
Director: Sam Newfield
Story: Fred Myton
Producer: A. W. Hackel

DURANGO VALLEY RAIDERS

(Republic, August 22, 1938) 55 Minutes
Bob Steele, Louise Stanley, Karl Hackett, Forrest Taylor, Ted Adams, Steve Clark, Horace Murphy, Jack Ingram, Ernie Adams, Julian Madison, Budd Buster, Frank Ball
Director: Sam Newfield
Story: Harry Olmstead
Screenplay: George Plympton
Producer: A. W. Hackel

FEUD OF THE RANGE

(Metropolitan, January 15, 1939) 57 Minutes

Bob Steele, Richard Cramer, Gertrude Messinger, Frank LaRue, Jean Cranford, Robert Burns, Budd Buster, Jack Ingram, Charles King, Duke Lee, Denver Dixon, Carl Mathews

Director: Harry S. Webb
Screenplay: Carl Krusada
Producer: Harry S. Webb

SMOKEY TRAILS

(Metropolitan, March 3, 1939) 57 Minutes

Bob Steele, Jean Carmen, Murdock McQuarrie, Jimmy Aubrey, Frank LaRue, Bruce Dane, Ted Adams, Bob Terry, Frank Wayne, George Chesebro

Director: Bernard B. Ray
Screenplay: George Plympton
Producer: Harry S. Webb

MESQUITE BUCKAROO

(Metropolitan, May 1, 1939) 55 Minutes

Bob Steele, Carolyn (Clarene) Curtis, Frank LaRue, Juanita Fletcher, Charles King, Gordon Roberts, Ted Adams, Joe Whitehead, Ed Brady, Bruce Dane, Snub Pollard, John Elliott, Jimmy Aubrey, Carleton Young

Director/Producer: Harry S. Webb
Screenplay: George Plympton

RIDERS OF THE SAGE

(Metropolitan, August 1, 1939) 57 Minutes

Bob Steele, Claire Rochelle, Ralph Hoopers, James Whitehead, Earl Douglas, Ted Adams, Dave O'Brien, Frank LaRue, Bruce Dane, Jerry Sheldon, Reed Howes, Bud Osborne, Gordon Roberts (Carleton Young)

Director/Producer: Harry S. Webb
Story: Forrest Sheldon
Screenplay: Carl Krusada

THE PAL FROM TEXAS

(Metropolitan, November 1, 1939) 56 Minutes

Bob Steele, Claire Rochelle, Jack Perrin, Josef Swickard, Betty Mack, Ted Adams, Carleton Young, Jack Ingram, Robert Walker

Director/Producer: Harry S. Webb
Story: Forrest Sheldon
Screenplay: Carl Krusada

EL DIABLO RIDES

(Metropolitan, December 1, 1939) 57 Minutes

Bob Steele, Claire Rochelle, Kit Guard, Carleton Young, Ted Adams, Robert Walker, Bob Robinson, Hal Carey

Director: Ira Webb
Screenplay: Carl Krusada
Producer: Harry S. Webb

OF MICE AND MEN

(Hal Roach/United Artists, January 12, 1940) 107 Minutes

Burgess Meredith, Betty Field, Lon Chaney, Jr., Charles Bickford, Roman Bohnen, *Bob Steele,* Noah Beery, Jr., Oscar O'Shea, Granville Bates, Leigh Whipper, Leona Roberts, Helen Lynd, Barbara Pepper, Henriette Kaye, Eddie Dunn, Howard Mitchell, Whitney deRhan, Baldy Cooke, Charles Watt, Jack Lawrence, Carl Pitti, John Beach

Director: Lewis Milestone
Screenplay: Eugene Solow
Story: John Steinbeck

WILD HORSE VALLEY

(Metropolitan, March 1, 1940) 57 Minutes

Bob Steele, Phyllis Adair, Buzz Barton, Lafe McKee, Jimmy Aubrey, Ted Adams, Bud Osborne, George Chesebro

Director: Ira Webb
Screenplay: Carl Krusada
Producer: Harry S. Webb

PINTO CANYON

(Metropolitan, May 1, 1940) 55 Minutes

Bob Steele, Louise Stanley, Kenne Duncan, Ted Adams, Steve Clark, Budd Buster, Murdock McQuarrie, George Chesebro, Jimmy Aubrey, Carl Mathews

Director: Raymond Johnson
Story: Richard D. Pearsall
Screenplay: Carl Krusada
Producer: Harry S. Webb

THE CARSON CITY KID

(Republic, July 1, 1940) 57 Minutes

Roy Rogers, George Hayes, *Bob Steele,* Pauline Moore, Noah Beery, Jr., Francis McDonald, Hal Taliaferro, Arthur Loft, George Rosenor, Chester Gan, Hank Bell, Ted Mapes, Jack Ingram, Jack Kirk, Jack Rockwell, Tom Smith, Art Dillard, Hal Price, Yakima Canutt, Kit Guard, Curley Dresden, Oscar Gahan, Chick Hannon, Al Taylor

Director/Associate Producer: Joseph Kane
Story: Joseph Kane
Screenplay: Robert Yost, Gerald Geraghty

BILLY THE KID OUTLAWED

(PRC, July 20, 1940) 52 Minutes
(Billy the Kid Series)

Bob Steele, Al St. John, Louise Currie, Carleton Young, John Merton, Joe McGuinn, Ted Adams, Walter McGrail, Hal Price, Kenne Duncan, Reed Howes, George Chesebro, Steve Clark, Budd Buster, Sherry Tansey, Jack Ingram, Carl Sepulveda

Director: Peter Stewart (Sam Newfield)
Screenplay: Oliver Drake
Producer: Sigmund Neufeld

CITY FOR CONQUEST

(Warner Brothers/First National, September 21, 1940)
101 Minutes

James Cagney, Ann Sheridan, Frank McHugh, Frank Craven, Donald Crisp, Arthur Kennedy, George Tobias, Jerome Cowan, Anthony Quinn, Lee Patrick, Blanche Yurka, George Lloyd, Joyce Compton, Thurston Hall, Ben Welden, John Arledge, Edward Keane, Selmer Jackson, Joseph Crehan, *Bob Steele,* Billy Wayne, Pat Flaherty, Sidney Miller, Lee Phelps, Charles Wilson, Edward Gargan, Howard Hickman, Charles Lane, Dana Dale (later Margaret Hayes), Ed Pawley, William Newell, Lucia Carroll

Director/Producer: Anatole Litvak
Screenplay: John Wexley
Story: Aben Kandel

UNDER TEXAS SKIES

(Republic, September 20, 1940) 57 Minutes
(3 Mesquiteers Series)

Robert Livingston, *Bob Steele,* Rufe Davis, Lois Ranson, Henry Brandon, Wade Boteler, Rex Lease, Yakima Canutt, Jack Ingram, Walter Tetley, Earle Hodgins, Curley Dresden, Jack Kirk, Ted Mapes, Vester Pegg

Director: George Sherman
Story: Anthony Coldeway, Betty Burbridge
Screenplay: Anthony Coldeway, Betty Burbridge
Based on characters created by William Colt MacDonald
Associate Producer: Harry Grey

BILLY THE KID IN TEXAS

(PRC, September 30, 1940) 52 Minutes

Bob Steele, Al St. John, Terry Walker, Carleton Young, Charles King, John Merton, Frank LaRue, Slim Whitaker, Curley Dresden, Tex Palmer, Chick Hannon, Merrill McCormack, Denver Dixon, Bob Woodward, Sherry Tansey, Herman Hack, Pasquel Perry, George Morrell, Lew Meehan, Al Haskell, Oscar Gahan

Director: Peter Stewart (Sam Newfield)
Screenplay: Joseph O'Donnell
Producer: Sigmund Neufeld

THE TRAIL BLAZERS

(Republic, November 11, 1940) 58 Minutes
(3 Mesquiteers Series)

Robert Livingston, *Bob Steele,* Rufe Davis, Pauline Moore, Rex Lease, Weldon Heyburn, Carroll Nye, Tom Chatterton, Si Jenks, Mary Field, John Merton, Robert Blair, Barry Hayes, Pascale Perry, Harry Strang

Director: George Sherman
Story: Earle Snell
Screenplay: Barry Shipman
Based on characters created by William Colt MacDonald
Associate Producer: Harry Grey

LONE STAR RAIDERS

(Republic, December 23, 1940) 57 Minutes
(3 Mesquiteers Series)

Robert Livingston, *Bob Steele,* Rufe Davis, June Johnson, George Douglas, Sarah Padden, John Elliott, John Merton, Rex Lease, Bud Osborne, Jack Kirk, Tom London, Hal Price

Director: Hal Price
Screenplay: Joseph March, Barry Shipman
Based on characters created by William Colt MacDonald
Associate Producer: Louis Grey

BILLY THE KID'S GUN JUSTICE

(PRC, December 27, 1940) 59 Minutes
(Billy the Kid Series)

Bob Steele, Al St. John, Louise Currie, Carleton Young, Charles King, Rex Lease, Ted Adams, Kenne Duncan, Forrest Taylor, Al Ferguson, Karl Hackett, Edward Piel, Sr., Julian Rivero, Blanca Vischer, Joe McGuinn, George Morrell

Director: Peter Stewart (Sam Newfield)
Screenplay: Joseph O'Donnell
Producer: Sigmund Neufeld

BILLY THE KID'S RANGE WAR

(PRC, January 24, 1941) 57 Minutes
(Billy the Kid Series)

Bob Steele, Al St. John, Joan Barclay, Carleton Young, Rex Lease, Buddy Roosevelt, Milt Kibbee, Karl Hackett, Ted Adams, Julian Rivero, John Ince, Alden Chase Howard Masters, Ralph Peters, Charles King, George Chesebro, Steve Clark, Tex Palmer

Director: Peter Stewart (Sam Newfield)
Screenplay: William Lively
Producer: Sigmund Neufeld

PRAIRIE PIONEERS

(Republic, February 16, 1941) 58 Minutes

Robert Livingston, *Bob Steele,* Rufe Davis, Esther Estrella, Robert Kellard, Guy D'Ennery, Davidson Clark, Jack Ingram, Kenneth MacDonald, Lee Shumway, Mary MacLaren, Yakima Canutt, Jack Kirk, Carleton Young, Wheaton Chambers, Frank Ellis, Cactus Mack, Curley Dresden, Frank McCarroll

Director: Les Orlebeck
Story: Karl Brown
Screenplay: Barry Shipman
Based on character created by William Colt MacDonald
Associate Producer: Louis Gray

THE GREAT TRAIN ROBBERY

(Republic, February 28, 1941) 61 Minutes

Bob Steele, Claire Carleton, Milburn Stone, Helen MacKeller, Si Jenks, Monte Blue, Hal Taliaferro, George Guhl, Jay Novello, Dick Wessel, Yakima Canutt, Lew Kelly, Guy Usher

Director: Joseph Kane

Screenplay: Olive Cooper, Garnett Weston, Robert T. Shannon

Associate Producer: Joseph Kane

PALS OF THE PECOS

(Republic, April 8, 1941) 56 Minutes

(Three Mesquiteers Series)

Robert Livingston, *Bob Steele,* Rufe Davis, June Johnson, Dennis Moore, Roy Barcroft, Pat O'Malley, Robert Frazer, John Holland, Tom London, Robert Winkler, George Chesebro, Chuck Morrison, Bud Osborne, Jack Kirk, Forrest Taylor, Frank Ellis, Eddie Dean

Director: Les Orlebeck

Story: Oliver Drake

Screenplay: Oliver Drake, Herbert Delmas

Based on characters created by William Colt MacDonald

Associate Producer: Louis Grey

BILLY THE KID'S FIGHTING PALS

(PRC, April 18, 1941) 62 Minutes

(Billy the Kid Series)

Bob Steele, Al St. John, Phyllis Adair, Carleton Young, Charles King, Curley Dresden, Edward Piel, Sr., Hal Price, George Chesebro, Forrest Taylor, Budd Buster, Julian Rivero, Ray Henderson, Wally West, Art Dillard

Director: Sherman Scott (Sam Newfeld)

Screenplay: George Plympton

Producer: Sigmund Neufeld

SADDLEMATES

(Republic, May 16, 1941) 56 Minutes

(Three Mesquiteers Series)

Robert Livingston, *Bob Steele,* Rufe Davis, Gale Storm, Forbes Murray, Cornelius Keefe, Peter George Lynn, Marin Sais, Matty Faust, Glenn Strange, Ellen Lowe, Iron Eyes Cody, Chief Yowlachie, Bill Hazlett, Henry Wills, Major Bill Keefer

Director: Les Orlebeck

Story: Bernard McConville, Karen DeWolf

Screenplay: Albert Demond, Herbert Dalmas

Based on characters created by William Colt MacDonald

Associate Producer: Louis Gray

GANGS OF SONORA

(Republic, July 10, 1941) 56 Minutes

(Three Mesquiteers Series)

Robert Livingston, *Bob Steele,* Rufe Davis, June Johnson, Bud McTaggart, Helen MacKellar, Robert Frazer, William Farnum, Budd Buster, Hal Price, Wally West, Bud Osborne, Bud Geary, Jack Kirk, Al Taylor, Griff Barnette, Curley Dresden, Jack Lawrence

Director: John English

Screenplay: Albert DeMond, Doris Schroeder

Associate Producer: Louis Gray

BILLY THE KID IN SANTA FE

(PRC, July 11, 1941) 56 Minutes

(Billy the Kid Series)

Bob Steele, Al St. John, Rex Lease, Marin Sais, Dennis Moore, Karl Hackett, Steve Clark, Hal Price, Charles King, Frank Ellis, Dave O'Brien, Kenne Duncan, Curley Dresden, Tex Palmer

Director: Sherman Scott (Sam Newfeld)

Screenplay: Joseph O'Donnell

Producer: Sigmund Neufeld

OUTLAWS OF THE CHEROKEE TRAIL

(Republic, September 10, 1941) 56 Minutes

(Three Mesquiteers Series)

Bob Steele, Tom Tyler, Rufe Davis, Lois Collier, Tom Chatterton, Rex Lease, Joel Friedkin, Roy Barcroft, Philip Trent, Peggy Lynn, Bud Osborne, Chief Yowlachie, John James, Lee Shumway, Karl Hackett, Chuck Morrison, Billy Burtis, Griff Barnette, Bud Geary, Al Taylor, Henry Wills, Sarah Padden, Iron Eyes Cody, Cactus Mack

Director: Les Orlebeck

Screenplay: Albert DeMond

Based on characters created by William Colt MacDonald

GAUCHOS OF ELDORADO

(Republic, October 24, 1941) 56 Minutes

(Three Mesquiteers Series)

Bob Steele, Tom Tyler, Rufe Davis, Lois Collier, Duncan Renaldo, Rosani Galli, Norman Willis, Yakima Canutt, William Ruhl, Tony Roux, Ray Bennett, Bud Geary, Edmund Cobb, Eddie Dean, John Merrill Holmes, Terry Frost, John Merton, Virginia Farmer, Si Jenks, Ted Mapes, Bob Woodward, Ray Jones, Horace B. Carpenter

Director: Les Orlebeck

Story: Earle Snell

Based on characters created by William Colt MacDonald

Associate Producer: Louis Gray

WEST OF CIMARRON

(Republic, December 15, 1941) 56 Minutes

(Three Mesquiteers Series)

Bob Steele, Tom Tyler, Rufe Davis, Lois Collier, James Bush, Guy Usher, Hugh Prosser, Cordell Hickman, Roy Barcroft, Budd Buster, Mickey Rentschiller, John James, Bud Geary, Stanley Blystone

Director: Les Orlebeck

Screenplay: Albert DeMond, Don Ryan

Based on characters created by William Colt MacDonald

Associate Producer: Louis Gray

CODE OF THE OUTLAW

(Republic, January 30, 1942) 57 Minutes

(Three Mesquiteers Series)

Bob Steele, Tom Tyler, Rufe Davis, Weldon Heyburn, Melinda Leighton, Don Curtis, John Ince, Kenne Duncan, Phil Dunham, Max Walzman, Chuck Morrison, Carleton Young, Al Taylor, Robert Frazer, Dick Alexander, Forrest Taylor, Jack Ingram, Wally West, Edward Piel, Sr., Bud Osborne, Hank Worden, Cactus Mack

Director: John English

Screenplay: Barry Shipman

Associate Producer: Louis Gray

Based on characters created by William Colt MacDonald

RAIDERS OF THE RANGE

(Republic, March 18, 1942) 55 Minutes

(Three Mesquiteers Series)

Bob Steele, Tom Tyler, Rufe Davis, Lois Collier, Frank Jacquet, Fred Kohler, Jr., Dennis Moore, Tom Chatterton, Charles Miller, Max Walzman, Hal Price, Charles Phillips, Bud Geary, Jack Ingram, Al Taylor, Chuck Morrison, Joel Friedkin, Bob Woodward, Tom Steele, Monte Montague, Ken Terrell, Dick Alexander, Cactus Mack, John Cason

Director: John English

Story: Albert DeMond

Screenplay: Barry Shipman

Based on character created by William Colt MacDonald

Associate Producer: Louis Gray

WESTWARD HO

(Republic, April 24, 1942) 56 Minutes

(Three Mesquiteers Series)

Bob Steele, Tom Tyler, Rufe Davis, Evelyn Brent, Donald Curtis, Lois Collier, Emmett Lynn, John James, Tom Seidel, Jack Kirk, Kenne Duncan, Milton Kibbee, Edmund Cobb, Monte Montague, Al Taylor, Bud Osborne, Jack Montgomery, Horace B. Carpenter, John L. Cason, Jack O'Shea, Ray Jones, Tex Palmer, Curley Dresden, Budd Buster

Director: John English

Story: Morton Grant

Screenplay: Morton Grant, Doris Schroeder

Based on characters created by William Colt MacDonald

Producer: Louis Gray

THE PHANTOM PLAINSMEN

(Republic, June 16, 1942) 65 Minutes

(Three Mesquiteers Series)

Bob Steele, Tom Tyler, Rufe Davis, Lois Collier, Robert O. Davis, Charles Miller, Alex Callam, Monte Montague, Henry Roland, Richard Crane, Jack Kirk, Edward Cassidy, Vince Barnett, Lloyd Ingraham, Al Taylor, Bud Geary, Herman Hack

Director: John English

Story: Robert Yost

Screenplay: Robert Yost, Barry Shipman

Based on characters created by William Colt MacDonald

Associate Producer: Louis Gray

SHADOWS ON THE SAGE

(Republic, September 24, 1942) 58 Minutes

(Three Mesquiteers Series)

Bob Steele, Tom Tyler, Jimmie Dodd, Cheryl Walker, Harry Holman, Yakima Canutt, Tom London, Bryant Washburn, Griff Barnette, Freddie Mercer, Rex Lease, Curley Dresden, Eddie Dew, Horace B. Carpenter, Frank Brownlee, John Cason, Pascale Perry

Director: Les Orlebeck

Screenplay: J. Benton Cheney

Based on characters created by William Colt MacDonald

Associate Producer: Louis Gray

VALLEY OF HUNTED MEN

(Republic, November 13, 1942) 60 Minutes
(Three Mesquiteers Series)

Bob Steele, Tom Tyler, Jimmie Dodd, Anna Marie Stewart, Edward Van Sloan, Roland Varno, Edythe Elliott, Arno Frey, Richard French, Robert Stevenson, George Neiss, Duke Aldon, Budd Buster, Hal Price, Billy Benedict, Charles Flynn, Rand Brooks, Kenne Duncan, Jack Kirk, Kermit Maynard

Director: John English
Story: Charles Tetford
Screenplay: Albert DeMond, Morton Grant
Based on characters created by William Colt MacDonald
Associate Producer: Louis Gray

THUNDERING TRAILS

(Republic, January 25, 1943) 56 Minutes
(Three Mesquiteers Series)

Bob Steele, Tom Tyler, Jimmie Dodd, Nell O'Day, Sam Flint, Karl Hackett, Charles Miller, John James, Forrest Taylor, Ed Cassidy, Forbes Murray, Reed Howes, Bud Geary, Budd Buster, Vince Barnett, Lane Bradford, Cactus Mack, Edwin Parker, Al Taylor, Art Mix, Jack O'Shea

Director: John English
Screenplay: Norman S. Hall, Robert Yost
Based on characters created by William Colt MacDonald
Associate Producer: Louis Gray

THE BLOCKED TRAIL

(Republic, March 12, 1943) 58 Minutes
(Three Mesquiteers Series)

Bob Steele, Tom Tyler, Jimmie Dodd, Helen Deverall, George J. Lewis, Walter Sodering, Charles Miller, Kermit Maynard, Pierce Lyden, Cart Mathews, Hal Price, Budd Buster, Earle Hodgins, Bud Osborne, Al Taylor, Art Dillard, Bud Geary

Director: Elmer Clifton
Screenplay: John K. Butler, Jacquin Frank
Based on characters created by William Colt MacDonald
Associate Producer: Louis Gray

SANTA FE SCOUTS

(Republic, April 16, 1943) 57 Minutes
(Three Mesquiteers Series)

Bob Steele, Tom Tyler, Jimmie Dodd, Lois Collier, John James, Tom Chatterton, Elizabeth Valentine, Tom London, Budd Buster, Jack Ingram, Kermit Maynard, Rex Lease, Ed Cassidy, Yakima Canutt, Jack Kirk, Curley Dresden, Reed Howes, Bud Geary, Carl Sepulveda, Al Taylor, Kenne Duncan

Director: Howard Bretherton
Screenplay: Morton Grant, Betty Burbridge
Based on characters created by William Colt MacDonald
Producer: Louis Gray

RIDERS OF THE RIO GRANDE

(Republic, May 21, 1943) 55 Minutes
(Three Mesquiteers Series)

Bob Steele, Tom Tyler, Jimmie Dodd, Lorraine Miller, Edward Van Sloan, Rick Vallin, Harry Worth, Roy Barcroft, Charles King, Jack Ingram, John James, Jack O'Shea, Henry Hall, Bud Osborne

Director: Howard Bretherton
Screenplay: Albert DeMond
Based on characters created by William Colt MacDonald
Associate Producer: Louis Gray

REVENGE OF THE ZOMBIES

(Monogram, September 17, 1943) 61 Minutes

John Carradine, Gale Storm, Robert Lowery, Mantan Moreland, *Bob Steele,* Veda Ann Borg, Barry McCollu, Mauritz Hugo, James Baskett, Sybil Lewis

Director: Steve Sekely
Screenplay: Edmund Kelso, Van Norcross

DEATH VALLEY RANGERS

(Monogram, December 3, 1943) 59 Minutes
(Trail Blazers Series)

Ken Maynard, Hoot Gibson, *Bob Steele,* Linda Brent, Kenneth Harlan, Bob Allen, Charles King, George Chesebro, John Bridges, Al Ferguson, Steve Clark, Wally West, Glenn Strange, Forrest Taylor, Lee Roberts, Weldon Heyburn, Karl Hackett

Director: Robert Tansey
Screenplay: Robert Emmett, Frances Kavanaugh, Elizabeth Beecher
Producer: Robert Tansey

WESTWARD BOUND
(Monogram, January 17, 1944) 54 Minutes
(Trail Blazers Series)
Ken Maynard, Hoot Gibson, *Bob Steele,* Betty Miles,
John Bridges, Harry Woods, Karl Hackett, Weldon
Heyburn, Hal Price, Roy Brent, Frank Ellis, Curley
Dresden, Dan White, Al Ferguson
Director/Producer: Robert Tansey
Screenplay: Frances Kavanaugh

ARIZONA WHIRLWIND
(Monogram, February 21, 1944) 49 Minutes
(Trail Blazers Series)
Ken Maynard, Hoot Gibson, *Bob Steele,* Ian Keith,
Myrna Dell, Donald Stewart, Charles King, Karl
Hackett, George Chesebro, Dan White, Charles
Murray, Jr., Frank Ellis, Chief Soldani, Willow Bird
Director/Producer: Robert Tansey
Screenplay: Frances Kavanaugh

OUTLAW TRAIL
(Monogram, April 18, 1944) 53 Minutes
(Trail Blazers Series)
Hoot Gibson, *Bob Steele,* Chief Thunder Cloud,
Jennifer Holt, Cy Kendall, Rocky Cameron, George
Eldridge, Charles King, Hal Price, John Bridges, Bud
Osborne, Jim Thorpe, Frank Ellis, Al Ferguson, Warner
Richmond, Tex Palmer, Charles Murray, Jr., Lee
Roberts
Director/Producer: Robert Tansey
Story: Alvin J. Neitz (Alan James)
Screenplay: Frances Kavanaugh

SONORA STAGECOACH
(Monogram, June 10, 1944) 61 Minutes
(Trail Blazers Series)
Hoot Gibson, *Bob Steele,* Chief Thunder Cloud,
Rocky Cameron, Betty Miles, Glenn Strange, George
Eldridge, Karl Hackett, Henry Hall, Charles King, Bud
Osborne, Charles Murray, Jr., John Bridges, Al
Ferguson, Frank Ellis, Hal Price, Rodd Redwing, John
Cason, Horace B. Carpenter
Director/Producer: Robert Tansey
Screenplay: Frances Kavanaugh

Bob Steele disarms Charles King as Hoot Gibson supports Cy Kendall in **The Outlaw Trail** (Monogram, 1944)

Bob Steele smiles at pretty Veda Ann Borg in **Marked Trails** (Monogram, 1945)

THE UTAH KID
(Monogram, July 26, 1944) 55 Minutes
Hoot Gibson, *Bob Steele,* Beatrice Gray, Evelyn Eaton, Ralph Lewis, Mike Letz, Mauritz Hugo, Jammison Shade, Dan White, George Morrell, Bud Osborne
Director: Vernon Keyes
Screenplay: Victor Hammond
Producer: William Strobach

MARKED TRAILS
(Monogram, July 29, 1944) 58 Minutes
Hoot Gibson, *Bob Steele,* Veda Ann Borg, Ralph Lewis, Mauritz Hugo, Steve Clark, Charles Stevens, Lynton Brent, Bud Osborne, George Morrell, Allen B. Sewell, Ben Corbett
Director: J. P. McCarthy
Screenplay: J. P. McCarthy, Victor Hammond
Producer: William Strobach

TRIGGER LAW
(Monogram, September 30, 1944) 56 Minutes
Hoot Gibson, *Bob Steele,* Beatrice Gray, Ralph Lewis, Edward Cassidy, Jack Ingram, George Eldridge, Pierce Lyden, Lane Chandler, Bud Osborne, George Morrell
Director: Vernon Keyes
Screenplay: Victor Hammond
Producer: Charles J. Bigelow

WILDFIRE
(Action Pictures, July 18, 1945) 57 Minutes
(Cinecolor)
Bob Steele, Sterling Holloway, John Miljan, William Farnum, Virginia Maples, Eddie Dean, Sarah Padden, Wee Willie David, Rocky Camron, Al Ferguson, Francis Ford, Frank Ellis, Hal Price
Director: Robert Tansey
Story: W. C. Tuttle
Screenplay: Frances Kavanaugh
Producer: William B. David

THE NAVAJO KID

(PRC, November 21, 1945) 59 Minutes

Bob Steele, Syd Saylor, Edward Cassidy, Caren Marsh, Stanley Blystone, Edward Howard, Charles King, Bud Osborne, Budd Buster, Henry Hall, Gertrude Glorie, Bert Dillard, Rex Rossi

Story/Screenplay: Harry Fraser
Producer: Arthur Alexander

NORTHWEST TRAIL

(Action Pictures/Lippert, November 30, 1945) (Cinecolor)

Bob Steele, John Litel, Joan Woodbury, Madge Bellamy, George Meeker, Ian Keith, Raymond Hatton, Poodles Hanaford, John Hamilton, Charles Middleton, Grace Hanaford, Bill Hammond, Bud Osborne, Al Ferguson, Bob Duncan, Josh (John) Carpenter

Director: Derwin Abrahams
Screenplay: Harvey Gates, L. J. Swabacher
Producers: William B. David and Max M. King

SIX GUN MAN

(PRC, February 1, 1946) 57 Minutes

Bob Steele, Syd Saylor, Jean Carlin, I. Stanford Jolley, Brooke Temple, Bud Osborne, Budd Buster, Jimmie Martin, Stanley Blystone, Roy Brent, Steve Clark, Dorothy Whitmore, Ray Jones

Director/Screenplay: Harry Fraser
Producer: Arthur Alexander

AMBUSH TRAIL

(PRC, February 17, 1946) 60 Minutes

Bob Steele, Syd Saylor, Lorraine Miller, I. Stanford Jolley, Charles King, Bob Cason, Budd Buster, Kermit Maynard, Frank Ellis, Edward Cassidy, Roy Brent

Director: Harry Fraser
Screenplay: Elmer Clifton
Producer: Arthur Alexander

SHERIFF OF REDWOOD VALLEY

(Republic, March 29, 1946) 54 Minutes
(Red Ryder Series)

Bill Elliott, Bobby Blake, Alice Fleming, *Bob Steele,* Peggy Stewart, Arthur Loft, James Craven, Tom London, Kenne Duncan, Bud Geary, John Wayne Wright, Tom Chatterton, Budd Buster, Frank McCarroll, Frank Linn

Director: R. G. Springsteen
Screenplay: Earle Snell
Associate Producer: Sidney Picker

THUNDER TOWN

(PRC, April 12, 1946) 57 Minutes

Bob Steele, Syd Saylor, Ellen Hall, Bud Geary, Charles King, Edward Howard, Steve Clark, Bud Osborne, Jimmy Aubrey, Pascale Perry

Director: Harry Fraser
Screenplay: James Oliver
Producer: Arthur Alexander

THE BIG SLEEP

(Warner Brothers-First National, August 31, 1946) 114 Minutes

Humphrey Bogart, Lauren Bacall, John Ridgley, Martha Vickers, Dorothy Malone, Peggy Knudsen, Regis Toomey, Charles Waldron, Charles D. Brown, *Bob Steele,* Elisha Cook, Jr., Louis Jean Heydt, Sonia Darrin, James Flavin, Thomas Jackson, Tom Rafferty, Theodore von Eltz, Dan Wallace, Joy Barlowe, Tom Fadden, Ben Welden, Trevor Bardette

Director/Producer: Howard Hawks
Screenplay: William Faulkner, Leigh Brackett, Jules Furthman
Story: Raymond Chandler

RIO GRANDE RAIDERS

(Republic, September 9, 1946) 56 Minutes

Sunset Carson, Linda Stirling, *Bob Steele,* Tom London, Tris Coffin, Edmund Cobb, Jack O'Shea, Tex Terry, Kenne Duncan, Al Taylor, Blackie Whiteford, Roy Bucko, Fred Burns

Director: Thomas Carr
Screenplay: Norton S. Parker
Associate Producer: Bennett Cohen

TWILIGHT ON THE RIO GRANDE

(Republic, April 1, 1947) 71 Minutes

Gene Autry, Sterling Holloway, Adele Mara, *Bob Steele,* Charles Evans, Martin Garralaga, Howard J. Negley, George J. Lewis, Nacho Falindo, Tex Terry, George Magril, Bob Burns, Enrique Acosta, Frankie Marvin, Barry Norton, Gil Perkins, Nina Campana, Kenne Duncan, Tom London, Alberto Morin, Keith Richards, Anna Camargo, Donna Martell, Jack O'Shea, Steve Soldi, Bud Osborne, Frank McCarroll, Bob Wilke, Alex Montoya, Connie Menard, Joaquin Elizondo, The Cass County Boys, "Champion, Jr."

Director: Frank McDonald
Screenplay: Dorrell and Stuart McGowan
Associate Producer: Armand Schaefer

CHEYENNE

(Warner Brothers, June 14, 1947) 100 Minutes
Dennis Morgan, Jane Wyman, Arthur Kennedy, Janis Paige, Bruce Bennett, Barton MacLane, *Bob Steele,* Tom Tyler, Monte Blue, Britt Wood, Alan Hale
Director: Raoul Walsh
Screenplay: Alan Lemay, Thomas Williamson
Story: Paul I. Wellman

EXPOSED

(Republic, September 8, 1947) 59 Minutes
Robert Armstrong, Adele Mara, Adrian Booth, Robert Scott, *Bob Steele,* William Haade, Harry Shannon, Charles Evans, Joyce Compton, Russell Hicks, Colin Campbell, Paul E. Burn, Edward Gargan, Mary Gordon, Partricia Knox
Director: George Blair
Story: Charles Moran
Screenplay: Royal K. Cole, Charles Moran
Associate Producer: William O'Sullivan

KILLER MCCOY

(MGM, December 5, 1947) 104 Minutes
Mickey Rooney, Brian Donlevy, Ann Blythe, James Dunn, Tom Tully, Sam Levene, Walter Sande, Mickey Knox, James Bell, Gloria Holden, June Storey, Douglas Croft, *Bob Steele,* David Clarke
Director: Roy Rowland
Story/Screenplay: Thomas Lennon, George Bruce, George Oppenheimer
Producer: Sam Zimbalist

BANDITS OF DARK CANYON

(Republic, December 15, 1947) 59 Minutes
Allan Lane, *Bob Steele,* Eddy Waller, Roy Barcroft, John Hamilton, Linda Johnson, Gregory Marshall, Francis Ford, Eddie Acuff, LeRoy Mason, Jack Norman, "Black Jack"
Director: Phillip Ford
Screenplay: Bob Williams
Associate Producer: Gordon Kay

SOUTH OF ST. LOUIS

(Warner Brothers, 1949) 88 Minutes
(Technicolor)
Joel McCrea, Dorothy Malone, Zachary Scott, Alan Hale, Victor Jory, *Bob Steele,* Douglas Kennedy, Art Smith, Monte Blue, Nacho Galindo
Director: Ray Enright
Story/Scenario: James R. Webb, Zachary Gold

THE SAVAGE HORDE

(Republic, May 22, 1950) 90 Minutes
William (Bill) Elliott, Adrian Booth, Grant Withers, Barbara Fuller, Noah Beery, Jr., Jim Davis, Douglass Dumbrille, *Bob Steele,* Will Wright, Roy Barcroft, Earle Hodgins, Stuart Hamblen, Hal Taliaferro, Lloyd Ingraham, Marshall Reed, Crane Whitley, Charles Stevens, James Flavin, Edward Cassidy, Kermit Maynard, George Chesebro, Jack O'Shea, Monte Montague, Bud Osborne, Reed Howes
Director: Joseph Kane
Story: Thams Williamson and Gerald Geraghty
Screenplay: Kenneth Gamet
Associate Producer: Joseph Kane

THE ENFORCER

(United States Pictures/Warner Brothers, February 24, 1951) 87 Minutes
Zero Mostel, Ted Decorsia, Everett Sloan, Roy Roberts, Michael Tolan, *Bob Steele,* King Donovan, Pat Joiner, Don Beddoe, Tito Vuolo, John Kellogg, Jack Lambert, Adelaide Klein, Susan Cabot, Mario Siletti
Director: Bretaigne Windust
Producer: Milton Sperling
Screenplay/Story: Martin Rackin

SILVER CANYON

(Columbia, June 20, 1951) 70 Minutes
(Sepiatone)
Gene Autry, Pat Buttram, Gail Davis, Jim Davis, *Bob Steele,* Edgar Dearing, Dick Alexander, Terry Frost, Peter Mamakos, Steve Clark, Stanley Andrews, Duke York, Eugene Borden, Bobby Clark, Frankie Marvin, Boyd Stockman, Sandy Sanders, Kenne Duncan, Bill Hale, Jack O'Shea, Frank Matts, Stanley Blystone, John Merton, Jack Pepper, Pat O'Malley, Martin Wilkins, Jim Magill, John R. McKee, "Champion, Jr."
Director: John English
Story: Alan James
Screenplay: Gerald Geraghty
Producer: Armand Schaefer

FORT WORTH

(Warners, July 14, 1951) 80 Minutes
(Technicolor)
Randolph Scott, David Brian, Phyllis Thaxter, Helena Carter, Dick Jones, Ray Teal, Lawrence Tolan, Paul Picerni, Emerson Treacy, *Bob Steele,* Walter Sande, Chubby Johnson, Kermit Maynard
Director: Edwin L. Marin
Story/Screenplay: John Twist
Producer: Anthony Vellier

CATTLE DRIVE

(Universal-International, August 1, 1951) 77 Minutes
(Technicolor)

Joel McCrea, Dean Stockwell, Chill Wills, Leon Ames, Henry Brandon, Howard Pietre, *Bob Steele,* Griff Barnett

Director: Kurt Neumann
Screenplay: Jack Natteford and Lillie Hayward
Producer: Aaron Rosenberg

ROSE OF CIMARRON

(Alco/20th C.-Fox, April 1, 1952) 72 Minutes
(Natural Color)

Jack Buetel, Mala Powers, Bill Williams, Jim Davis, Dick Curtis, Lane Bradford, William Phipps, *Bob Steele,* Alex Gerry, Lillian Bronson, Art Smith, Monte Blue, Argentina Brunetti, John Doucette

Director: Harry Keller
Screenplay: Maurice Geraghty
Producer: Edward L. Alperson

THE LION AND THE HORSE

(Warners, April 19, 1952) 83 Minutes
(WarnerColor)

Steve Cochran, Ray Teal, *Bob Steele,* Harry Antrim, George O'Hanlon, Sherry Jackson, William Fawcett, House Peters, Jr., Lane Chandler, Lee Roberts, Charles Stevens, Jack Williams, Tom Tyler, Billy Dix, Steve Peck

Director: Louis King
Story/Screenplay: Crane Wilbur
Producer: Bryan Foy

SAN ANTONE

(Republic, 1953) 90 Minutes

Rod Cameron, Arleen Whelan, Forrest Tucker, Katy Jurado, Rodolfo Acosta, Roy Roberts, *Bob Steele,* Harry Carey, Jr., James Lilburn, Douglas Kennedy, George Cleveland

Director/Asssociate Producer: Joseph Kane
Story: Curt Carroll - "The Golden Herd"
Screenplay: Steve Fisher

SAVAGE FRONTIER

(Republic, May 15, 1953) 54 Minutes

Allan Lane, Eddy Waller, *Bob Steele,* Dorothy Patrick, Roy Barcroft, Richard Avonde, Bill Phipps, Jimmy Hawkins, Lane Bradford, John Cason, Kenneth MacDonald, Bill Henry, Gerry Flash, "Black Jack"

Director: Harry Keller
Screenplay: Dwight Babcock, Gerald Geraghty
Associate Producer: Ruby Ralston

COLUMN SOUTH

(Universal-International, June 1, 1953) 84 Minutes
(Technicolor)

Audie Murphy, Joan Evans, Robert Sterling, Ray Collins, Palmer Lee, Ralph Moody, Dennis Weaver, Johnny Downs, Russell Johnson, *Bob Steele,* Jack Kelly, Raymond Montgomery, Richard Garland, James Best, Ed Rand, Rico Alanix

Director: Frederick de Cordova
Story/Screenplay: William Sackheim
Producer: Ted Richmond

ISLAND IN THE SKY

(Warner Brothers, September 5, 1953) 109 Minutes

John Wayne, Lloyd Nolan, Walter Abel, James Arness, Andy Devine, Allyn Joslyn, James Lydon, Harry Carey, Jr., Hal Baylor, Sean McClory, Wally Cassell, Gordon Jones, Frank Fenton, Robert Keys, Sumner Getchell, Regis Toomey, Paul Fix, Jim Dugan, George Chandler, Louis Jean Heydt, *Bob Steele,* Darryl Hickman, Michael Connors, Carl Switzer, Cass Gidley, Guy Anderson, Ann Doran, Dawn Bender

Director: William A. Wellman
Story/Screenplay: Ernest K. Gann
Producer: Robert Fellows

DRUMS ACROSS THE RIVER

(Universal-International, June 1, 1954) 78 Minutes
(Technicolor)

Audie Murphy, Lisa Gaye, Lyle Bettiger, Walter Brennan, Mara Corday, Hugh O'Brien, Jay Silverheels, Regis Toomey, Morris Ankrum, James Anderson, George Wallace, *Bob Steele,* Lane Bradford, Emile Meyer, Gregg Barton, Howard McNear, Ken Terrell

Director: Nathan Juran
Screenplay: John D. Butler
Producer: Melville Tucker

THE OUTCAST

(Republic, August 15, 1954) 90 Minutes
(Trucolor)

John Derek, Joan Evans, Jim Davis, Catherine McLeod, Ben Cooper, Taylor Holmes, Nana Bryant, Slim Pickens, Frank Ferguson, James Millican, *Bob Steele,* Nacho Galindo, Harry Carey, Jr., Robert "Buzz" Henry, Nicolas Coster

Director: William Witney
Story: From *Esquire* magazine by Todhunter Ballard
Screenplay: John K. Butler and Richard Wormser
Associate Producer: William J. O'Sullivan

LAST OF THE DESPERADOS

(Associated, December 1, 1955) 70 Minutes
James Craig, Jim Davis, Barton MacLane, Margia Dean, Donna Martell, Myrna Dell, *Bob Steele,* Stanley Clements, Jack Perrin
Director: Sam Newfield
Screenplay: Orville Hampton
Producer: Sigmund Neufeld

THE FIGHTING CHANCE

(Republic, December 15, 1955) 70 Minutes
Rod Cameron, Julie London, Ben Cooper, Taylor Holmes, Howard Wendell, Mel Wells, *Bob Steele,* Paul Birch, Carl Milletaire, Rodolfo Hoyos, Jr.
Director: William Witney

THE SPOILERS

(Universal-International, January 2, 1956) 84 Minutes
(Technicolor)
Anne Baxter, Jeff Chandler, Rory Calhoun, Ray Danton, Barbara Britton, John McIntire, Carl Benton Reid, Wallace Ford, Raymond Walburn, Dayton Lummis, Willis Bouchey, Roy Barcroft, Ruth Donnelly, Forrest Lewis, Jack Perrin, *Bob Steele,* Arthur Spann, Lane Bradford, Terry Frost, Dave McGuire, Frank Sully, John Harmon
Director: Jesse Hibbs
Story: Rex Beach
Screenplay: Oscar Brodney and Charles Hoffman
Producer: Ross Hunter

THE STEEL JUNGLE

(Warner Brothers, March 31, 1956) 86 Minutes
Perry Lopez, Beverly Garland, Walter Abel, Ted DeCorsia, Kenneth Tobey, Allison Hayes, Gregory Walcott, Leo Gordon, Kay Kutar, *Bob Steele,* Ralph Moody, Stafford Repp, Billy Vincent
Director/Screenplay: Walter Doniger
Producer: David Weisbart

PARDNERS

(Paramount, August 1, 1956) 88 Minutes
(Technicolor) (VistaVision)
Dean Martin, Jerry Lewis, Lori Nelson, Jeff Morrow, Jackie Loughery, John Baragrey, Agnes Moorehead, Lon Chaney, Jr., Milton Frome, Richard Aherne, Lee Van Cleef, Stuart Randall, Scott Douglas, Jack Elam, *Bob Steele,* Mickey Finn, Douglas Spencer, Philip Tonge
Director: Norman Taurog
Story: Marvin J. Houser
Screenplay: Sidney Sheldon and Jerry Davis
Producer: Paul Jones

DUEL AT APACHE WELLS

(Republic, January 25, 1957) 70 Minutes
(Naturama)
Anna Marie Alberghetti, Ben Cooper, Jim Davis, Harry Shannon, Francis McDonald, *Bob Steele,* Frank Puglia, Argentina Brunetti, Ian MacDonald, John Dierkes, Ric Roman
Director: Joseph Kane
Screenplay: Bob Williams
Producer: Joseph Kane

GUN FOR A COWARD

(Universal-International, March 1, 1957) 88 Minutes
(Eastman Color) (CinemaScope)
Fred MacMurray, Jeffrey Hunter, Janice Rule, Chill Wills, Dean Stockwell, Josephine Hutchinson, Betty Lynn, Iron Eyes Cody, Robert Hoy, Jane Howard, Marjorie Stapp, John Leach, Paul Birch, *Bob Steele,* Frances Morris
Director: Abner Biberman
Screenplay: H. Wright Campbell
Producer: William Alland

BAND OF ANGELS

(Warner Brothers, August 3, 1957) 107 Minutes
Clark Gable, Yvonne de Carlo, Sidney Poitier, Efrem Zimbalist, Jr., Patric Knowles, Rex Reason, Torin Thatcher, Andrea King, Ray Teal, Russ Evans, Carol Drake, Raymond Bailey, Tommie Moore, William Forrest, Noreen Corcoran, *Bob Steele*
Director: Raoul Walsh
Screenplay: John Twist, Ivan Goff
Story: Robert Penn Warren

THE PARSON AND THE OUTLAW

(Columbia, September 1, 1957) 71 Minutes
(Technicolor)
Anthony Dexter, Sonny Tufts, Marie Windsor, Charles "Buddy" Rogers, Jean Parker, Robert Lowery, Madalyn Trahey, *Bob Steele*
Director: Oliver Drake
Screenplay: Oliver Drake, John Mantley
Producers: Robert Gilbert, Charles Rogers

DECISION AT SUNDOWN

(Columbia, November 10, 1957) 77 Minutes
(Technicolor)
Randolph Scott, John Carroll, Karen Steele, Valerie French, Noah Beery, Jr., John Archer, Andrew Duggan, James Westerfield, John Litel, Ray Teal, Vaughn Taylor, Richard Deacon, H. M. Wynant, Guy Wilkerson, *Bob Steele*
Director: Budd Boetticher
Screenplay: Charles Lang, Jr.
Producers: Harry Joe Brown, Randolph Scott

GIANT FROM THE UNKNOWN

(Screencraft-Astor, April 9, 1958) 77 Minutes
Edward Kemmer, Sally Fraser, Buddy Baer, Morris Ankrum, *Bob Steele,* Joline Brand
Director: Richard Cunha
Producer: Arthur A. Jacobs
Screenplay: Frank Hart Taussig, Ralph Brooke

THE BONNIE PARKER STORY

(American-International, May, 1958) 79 Minutes
Dorothy Provine, Jack Hogan, Richard Bakalyan, Joseph Turkel, William Stevens, Pat Huston, Douglas Kennedy, Joel Colin, Jim Beck, Karl Davis, *Bob Steele,* Edmund Cobb
Director: William Witney
Producer/Screenplay: Stanley Sheptner

ONCE UPON A HORSE

(Universal-International, September, 1958) 85 Minutes (CinemaScope)
Dan Rowan, Dick Martin, Martha Hyer, Leif Erickson, Nita Talbot, James Gleason, John McGiver, David Burns, Dick Ryan, Max Baer, Buddy Baer, Steve Pendleton, Sydney Chatton, Paul Anderson; Guest Stars: Tom Keene, Bob Livingston, Kermit Maynard, *Bob Steele*
Director/Screenplay/Producer: Hal Kanter
Story: Henry Gregor Felsen

RIO BRAVO

(Armada/Warners, April 4, 1959) 141 Minutes (Technicolor)
John Wayne, Dean Martin, Ricky Nelson, Angie Dickinson, Walter Brennan, Ward Bond, John Russell, Pedro Gonzales-Gonzales, Estelita Rodriguez, Claude Akins, Malcolm Atterbury, Harry Carey, Jr., *Bob Steele,* Bing Russell, Myron Healey, Eugene Iglesias, Fred Graham, Tom Monroe, Riley Hill
Director: Howard Hawks
Story: B. H. McCampbell
Screenplay: Leigh Brackett and Jules Furthman
Producer: Howard Hawks

PORK CHOP HILL

(Melville-United Artists, May, 1959) 97 Minutes
Gregory Peck, Harry Guardino, Rip Torn, George Peppard, James Edwards, *Bob Steele,* Woody Strode, Norman Fell, Robert Blake, Biff Elliott, Barry Atwater, Ken Lynch, Abel Fernandez, Martin Landau, Kevin Hagen, Gavin McLeod, Chuck Hayward, Robert Williams
Director: Lewis Milestone
Producer: Sy Bartlett
Screenplay: James R. Webb

THE ATOMIC SUBMARINE

(Gorham Productions/Allied Artists, November 29, 1959) 73 Minutes
Arthur Franz, Dick Foran, Brett Halsey, Tom Conway, Paul Dubov, *Bob Steele,* Joi Lansing, Victor Varconi, Selmer Jackson, Jack Mulhall, Jean Moorhead, Richard Tyler, Sid Melton, Ken Becker
Director: Spencer G. Bennett
Screenplay: Orville Hampton
Producer: Alex Gordon

HELL BENT FOR LEATHER

(Universal-International, February, 1960) 82 Minutes (Eastman Color) (CinemaScope)
Audie Murphy, Felicia Farr, Stephen McNally, Robert Middleton, Rad Fultom, Jan Merlin, Herbert Rudley, Malcolm Atterbury, Joseph Ruskin, Allan Lane, John Qualen, Eddie Little Sky, Steve Gravers, Beau Gentry, *Bob Steele,* Kermit Maynard
Director: George Sherman
Story: Ray Hogan
Screenplay: Christopher Knopf
Producer: Gordon Kay

THE COMANCHEROS

(20th C.-Fox, October 30, 1961) 107 Minutes (DeLuxe Color) (CinemaScope)
John Wayne, Stuart Whitman, Ina Balin, Nehemiah Persoff, Lee Marvin, Michael Ansara, Pat Wayne, Bruce Cabot, Joan O'Brien, Jack Elam, Edgar Buchanan, Henry Daniell, Richard Devon, Steve Baylor, John Dierkes, Roger Mobley, *Bob Steele,* Luisa Triana, Iphigenie Castiglioni, Aissa Wayne, George J. Lewis, Greg Palmer, Don Brodie, Jon Lormer, Phil Arnold, Alan Carney, Dennis Cole
Director: Michael Curtiz
Story: Paul I. Wellman
Screenplay: James Edward Grant, Clair Huffaker
Producer: George Sherman

THE WILD WESTERNERS

(Columbia, June, 1962) 70 Minutes (Eastman Color)
James Philbrook, Nancy Kovack, Duane Eddy, Guy Mitchell, Hugh Sanders, Elizabeth MacRae, Marshall Reed, Nestor Pavia, Harry Lauter, *Bob Steele,* Lisa Burkett, Terry Frost, Hans Wedemeyer, Don Harvey, Elizabeth Harrower, Francis Osborne, Tim Sullivan, Pierce Lyden, Joe McGuinn, Charles Horvath, Marjorie Stapp
Director: Oscar Rudolph
Screenplay: Gerald Drayson Adams
Producer: Sam Katzman

SIX BLACK HORSES

(Universal-International, June, 1962) 80 Minutes
(Eastman Color)
Audie Murphy, Dan Duryea, Joan O'Brien, George Wallace, Roy Barcroft, *Bob Steele,* Henry Wills, Phil Chambers, Charles Regis, Dale Van Sickel
Director: Harry Keller
Screenplay: Burt Kennedy
Producer: Gordon Kay

McLINTOCK

(Batjac/United Artists, November 13, 1963) 127 Minutes
(Technicolor) (PanaVision)
John Wayne, Maureen O'Hara, Yvonne De Carlo, Patrick Wayne, Stefanie Powers, Jack Kruschen, Chill Wills, Jerry Van Dyke, Edgar Buchanan, Bruce Cabot, Perry Lopez, Michael Pat, Strother Martin, Gordon Jones, Robert Lowery, Ed Faulkner, H. W. Gim, Aissa Wayne, Chuck Roberson, Hal Needham, Pedro Gonzales, Jr., Hank Worden, Ralph Volkie, Dan Borzage, John Stanley, Karl Noven, Mari Blanchard, Leo Gordon, *Bob Steele,* John Hamilton
Director: Andrew V. McLaglen
Screenplay: James Edward Grant
Producer: Michael Wayne

4 FOR TEXAS

(Warner Brothers, January 4, 1964) 124 Minutes
(Technicolor)
Frank Sinatra, Dean Martin, Anita Ekberg, Ursula Andress, Charles Bronson, Victor Buono, Edric Connor, Nick Dennis, Richard Jaeckel, Mike Mazurki, Wesley Addy, Marjorie Bennett, Jack Elam, Fritz Feld, Percy Helton, Jonathan Hale, Jack Lambert, Paul Langton, Teddy Buckner and His All Stars, The Three Stooges, *Bob Steele,* Virginia Christine, Ralph Volkie, Ellen Corby, Jesslyn Fax, Allyson Ames, Arthur Godfrey
Director: Richard Thorpe
Screenplay: Allan Weiss
Producer: Hal Wallis

BULLET FOR A BADMAN

(Universal, September 2, 1964) 80 Minutes
(Eastman Color)
Audie Murphy, Darren McGavin, Ruta Lee, Beverly Owen, Skip Homeier, George Tobias, Alan Hale, Jr., Berkeley Harris, Edward C. Platt, Kevin Tate, Cece Whitney, Mort Wills, Budd Brady, *Bob Steele,* Ray Teal
Director: R. G. Springsteen
Story: Marvin H. Albert - "Renegade Posse"
Screenplay: Mary and Willard Willingham
Producer: Gordon Kay

TAGGART

(Universal, December 24, 1964) 85 Minutes
(Color)
Tony Young, Dan Duryea, Dick Foran, Elsa Cardenas, John Hale, Emile Meyer, David Carradine, Peter Duryea, Tom Reese, Ray Teal, Claudia Barrett, Stuart Randall, Harry Carey, Jr., Bill Henry, Sarah Selby, George Murdock, Arthur Space, *Bob Steele*
Director: R. G. Springsteen
Story: Louis L'Amour - "Taggart"
Screenplay: Robert Creighton Williams
Producer: Gordon Kay

SHENANDOAH

(Universal, June 3, 1965) 105 Minutes
(Technicolor)
James Stewart, Doug McClure, Glenn Corbett, Patrick Wayne, Rosemary Forsyth, Philip Alford, Katherine Ross, Charles Robinson, James McMullan, Tim McIntyre, Eugene Jackson, Jr., Paul Fix, Denver Pyle, George Kennedy, James Best, Tom Simcox, Berkeley Harris, Harry Carey, Jr., Kevin Hagen, Dabbs Greer, Strother Martin, Kelly Thordsen, *Bob Steele*
Director: Andrew V. McLaglen
Screenplay: James Lee Barrett
Producer: Robert Arthur

THE BOUNTY KILLER

(Embassy, June, 1965) 92 Minutes
(Technicolor) (TechniScope)
Dan Duryea, Rod Cameron, Audrey Dalton, Richard Arlen, Buster Crabbe, Fuzzy Knight, Johnny Mack Brown, *Bob Steele,* Bronco Billy Anderson, Peter Duryea, Eddie Quillan, Norman Willis, Edmund Cobb, I. Stanford Jolley, Frank Lackteen, Dan White, Grady Sutton, Emory Parnell, Duana Ament, Red Morgan, John Reach, Dolores Domansin, Dudley Ross, Ronn Delanor, Tom Kennedy, Michael Hinn
Director: Spencer G. Bennet
Screenplay: R. Alexander, Leo Gordon
Producer: Alex Gordon

REQUIEM FOR A GUNFIGHTER

(Embassy, June 30, 1965) 91 Minutes
(Technicolor) (TechniScope)
Rod Cameron, Stephen McNally, Mike Mazurki, Olive Sturgess, Tim McCoy, Johnny Mack Brown, *Bob Steele,* Lane Chandler, Raymond Hatton, Chet Douglas, Dick Jones, Chris Hughes, Rand Brooks, Dale Van Sickel, Frank Lackteen, Ron Murray, Ronn Delanor, Edmund Cobb, Margo Williams, Doris Spiegel, Dick Alexander, Fred Carson, Red Morgan
Director: Spencer G. Bennet
Story: Evans W. Corness, Guy J. Tedesco
Screenplay: R. Alexander
Producer: Alex Gordon

TOWN TAMER

(Paramount, July 7, 1965) 89 Minutes
(Technicolor) (TechniScope)

Dana Andrews, Terry Moore, Pat O'Brien, Lon Chaney, Bruce Cabot, Lyle Bettger, Coleen Gray, Richard Arlen, Barton MacLane, Richard Jaeckel, Philip Carey, DeForest Kelley, Sonny Tufts, Roger Torrey, James Brown, Richard Webb, Jeanne Cagney, Donald Barry, *Bob Steele*, Robert Ivers, Dale Van Sickel, Dinny Powell, Frank Gruber
Director: Lesley Selander
Story/Screenplay: Frank Gruber
Producer: A. C. Lyles

HANG 'EM HIGH

(Malpaso/United Artists, July 31, 1968) 114 Minutes
(Deluxe Color)

Clint Eastwood, Inger Stevens, Ed Begley, Pat Hingle, Arlene Golonka, Charles McGraw, Ruth White, James MacArthur, Bruce Dern, Alan Hale, Jr., James Westerfield, Dennis Hopper, L. Q. Jones, Bert Freed, Michael O'Sullivan, Tod Andrews, Rick Gates, Bruce Scott, Roy Glenn, Ben Johnson, Jack Ging, *Bob Steele*, Joseph Sirola, Russell Thorson, Ned Romero, Jonathan Lipe, Richard Guizon, Mark Lenard, Paul Sorenson, Richard Angarola, Larry Blake, Ted Thorpe, Robert B. Williams, Tony D'Milo, Dennis Dengate, William Zuckert
Director: Ted Post (Sergio Leone)
Screenplay: Leonard Freeman, Mel Goldberg
Producer: Leonard Freeman

THE GREAT BANK ROBBERY

(Warner Brothers-7 Arts, June 24, 1969) 98 Minutes
(Technicolor) (PanaVision)

Zero Mostel, Kim Novak, Clint Walker, Claude Akins, Akim Tamiroff, Larry Storch, John Anderson, Sam Jaffe, Elisha Cook, Math Warrick, John Fieldler, John Larch, Peter Whitney, Norman Alden, *Bob Steele,* Grady Sutton, Ben Aliza, William Zuckert, Mickey Simpson, Byron Keith, Kenny Endoso, Roy Ogata, George Sasaki, Yoneo Iguchi, Hiroshi Hissamuri, Bob Mitchell Boys Choir
Director: Hy Averback
Story: Frank O'Rourke
Screenplay: William Peter Blatty
Producer: Malcolm Stuart

RIO LOBO

(National General, December 16, 1970) 114 Minutes
(Technicolor) (Partly filmed in Mexico)

John Wayne, Jorge Rivero, Jennifer O'Neill, Jack Elam, Christopher Mitchum, Victor French, Susana Dosamantes, David Huddleston, Mike Henry, Bill Williams, Jim Davis, Sherry Lansing, Dean Smith, Robert Donner, George Plimpton, Edward Faulkner, Peter Jason, *Bob Steele*, Robert Rothwell, Chuck Courtney, Boyd (Red) Morgan, Hank Worden, Chuck Roberson, John Ethan Wayne, William Byrne, Donald (Red) Barry, Jose Angel Espinosa, Anthony Sparrow Hawk, Charles Longfoot, Frank Kennedy, John McKee, Stanley Corson, Chuck Hayward, Sandra Currie, Jim Prejean, Danny Sands, Harold Cops
Director: Howard Hawks
Story: Burton Wohl
Screenplay: Burton Wohl, Leigh Brackett
Producer: Howard Hawks

SKIN GAME

(Warner Brothers, October, 1971) 102 Minutes
(Technicolor) (PanaVision)

James Garner, Lou Gossett, Susan Clark, Brenda Sykes, Edward Asner, Andrew Duggan, Henry Jones, Neva Patterson, Parley Baer, George Tyne, Royal Dano, Pat O'Malley, Joel Fruellen, Napoleon Whiting, Juanita Moore, Dort Clark, *Bob Steele*
Director: Paul Bogart
Story: Richard Alan Simmons
Screenplay: Pierre Marton
Producer: Harry Keller

SOMETHING BIG

(National General, December, 1971) 108 Minutes
(Technicolor) (Filmed in Mexico)

Dean Martin, Brian Keith, Honor Blackman, Carol White, Ben Johnson, Albert Salmi, Don Knight, Joyce Van Patten, Denver Pyle, Merlin Olsen, Robert Donner, Harry Carey, Jr., Judi Meredith, Ed Faulkner, Paul Fix, Armand Alzamora, David Huddleston, *Bob Steele,* Shirlenna Manchur, Jose Angel Espinosa, Juan Garcia, Robert Gravage, Chuck Hicks, John Kelly, Enrique Lucerno, Lupe Amador
Director/Producer: Andrew V. McLaglen
Story/Screenplay: James Lee Barrett

NIGHTMARE HONEYMOON

(M-G-M, March, 1972) 88 Minutes

Dick Rambo, Rebecca Dianna Smith, John Beck, Pat Hingle, Roy Jenson, David Huddleston, Jay Robinson, Dennis Patrick, Jim Boles, Dennis Burkley, Pat Cranshaw, Richard O'Brien, Angela Clark, Jack Perkins, *Bob Steele*

Director: Elliot Silverstein
Scenario: S. Lee Pogostin
Story: Lawrence Block - "Deadly Honeymoon"
Producer: Hugh Benson

CHARLEY VARRICK

(Universal, September, 1973) 111 Minutes

Walter Matthau, Joe Don Baker, Felicia Farr, Andy Robinson, John Vernon, Sheree North, Norman Fell, Benson Fong, Woodrow Parfrey, William Schallert, Jacqueline Scott, Marjorie Bennett, Rudy Diaz, Colby Chester, Charlie Briggs, Priscilla Garcia, Tom Tully, Hope Summers, Charles Matthau, Albert Popwell, Kathleen O'Malley, Christina Hart, Craig Baxley, Donald Siegel, *Bob Steele,* Virginia Wing, Monica Lewis

Director: Don Siegel
Screenplay: Howard Rodman, Dean Riesner
Story: John Reese - "The Looters"
Producer: Don Siegel

4 ● KERMIT MAYNARD

Everybody's Nice Guy

The early Kermit Maynard films for Ambassador Pictures are noteworthy in showing what an independent producer, having a limited budget, can accomplish when the filmmaking crew work harmoniously, intelligently, and efficiently. Built for the Old Western market, and built well, the initial series of Maynard films were among the finest oaters produced by Poverty Row outfits in the mid-'30s and compared favorably with the more expensive products of the majors, shaping up as good stuff for the grinds and splits market.

Probably no group of Western indies have drawn as much favorable comment from critics and fans as have the two series of Maynard, released in 1935-'36. Possessing more action than the average, these oats operas each got off to a flying start and held the pace consistently, spaced nicely with comedy bits, but in the main tending strictly to business with a few refreshingly new twists. True, the first series, in which Kermit played a mountie, was the better of the two in terms of production. Quality declined in the second series, which consisted strictly of cowboy opuses or logging stories. But both series carried sufficient overall action, gunplay, and the usual theatrics to satisfy the Western audiences in secondary houses and the juvenile trade at the weekend matinees. There are the usual quota of script incongruities and a few directorial fumbles, but the wealth of action covers them sufficiently. And it is in the handling of the action that the films rise above their story level.

Kermit's athletic agility is aptly highlighted through the numerous instances of trick riding, trick roping, and stunting—the latter on the order of Douglas Fairbanks. Most of the films give story credit to James Oliver Cur-

wood and, as such, have locales in the northwest. It was somewhat refreshing to see films in this genre wherein snow and winter existed, rather than the sameness of mid-summer connected with most programmer Westerns.

There's plenty of zest and pace in the films, the casts are competent, technical niceties exist (e.g., wipes, running inserts, fades), and the footage is well stocked with rough-and-tumble fights, hard ridin' and heavy shootin'.

Most critics give Kermit the edge over his brother Ken in acting ability, although Kermit was no word twister himself when it came to dialogue. In his own inimitable way he shined most when in action. But certainly he was not the stone-faced, silent cowboy he appeared to be in his many films as a supporting player. He had a certain charm, smiled readily, handled mild comedy satisfactorily, and even sang in one film. In short, it is hard to realize that the breezy, handsome, good natured Kermit Maynard of 1935-'36 is the same Kermit Maynard so familiar to fans of the '40s as the sterlingly competent but deadpan outlaw who menaced the white-stetsoned heroes. It was quite a metamorphosis.

Kermit Maynard was born on September 30, 1897 in Vevay, Indiana. Brother Ken was also born there two years earlier. Their father was a working man. Kermit had a normal boyhood and was a good son to his parents, never displaying the wanderlust and rebelliousness that caused Ken to run away with a circus at an early age. Kermit's interests were sports and horses. He was an outstanding high school athlete and easily learned the fundamentals of horsemanship in his

Kermit Maynard

spare hours away from the athletic field, his studies, and his home chores.

At Indiana University Kermit lettered in football, basketball, baseball, and track. As a half-back on the football team he won a berth on the All-Western Conference team and had the thrill of playing against George Gipp and Knute Rockne's great Notre Dame team. Upon graduation he took a job with the George A. Hormel Packing Company as a claims agent. His second day on the job in Austin, Minnesota he met Edith Jessen on a triple date with friends. Kermit and Edith dated for two years and on February 23, 1924 were married in Minneapolis, where Edith was attending a school of music and where, on that particular Saturday, Kermit was playing in a semi-pro basketball game with the Hormel Club. Kermit loved sports and in addition to playing semi-pro ball for two years helped with the coaching of the high school and basketball teams at Austin just for the fun of it.

Edith finished out her term of school, commuting to Austin on weekends. Kermit was not happy in a desk job and gave it up to attend the 1926 summer session at Indiana University, having about decided to become a teacher-coach. Certainly an outdoors-oriented person like Kermit was not meant to be a white-collar worker all his life. Whether or not he would have been happy as a coach is academic; he never became one. Before he could make the plunge he received a letter from Ken, who was just starting his series at First National, urging him to come to California. Kermit and Edith decided to give it a whirl.

Arriving in Hollywood they found that Ken was off on location somewhere. They had just enough money to get an apartment for a month and buy $20 worth of groceries. However, Kermit landed a job in the sporting goods department at the May Company and Edith got temporary secretarial jobs. Ultimately Ken returned to town and through him Kermit met Harry Joe Brown, who gave him work as an extra. Soon he was working steadily as a stuntman, particularly at Fox, once it was known that he was a good horseman. Edith got a job at Fox and worked there until 1932. Kermit doubled for Milton Sills, Warner Baxter, George O'Brien, Edmund Lowe, and numerous other stars, and all the time he was practicing day-on-end to become the best trick rider in the business, determined to outdo his more famous brother.

Rayart Pictures took notice of Kermit and signed him for a starring series in 1927, billing him as Tex Maynard. Six pictures were made, Kermit receiving a total of $250 in salary—that's *total*, not a per picture amount! And he had to buy his own wardrobe and perform all his own rough stuff. No doubles. What with replacing the clothes torn as a result of his stunting, he realized practically nothing from the series except experience, slight recognition as a cowboy star, and many offers to do stuntwork, which he resumed when the series was dropped after one season.

About 1932 Kermit acquired his horse "Rocky" for $90. The dappled grey was only three years old. Kermit worked with him until he had mastered 62 different tricks, and the two hit the rodeo circuit between Kermit's assignments as a movie stuntman and occasional actor. Kermit's specialty was trick riding and trick roping and he won World Championships for both events in contests at Salinas, California in 1931 and 1933 and acknowledgment by Ken as the best in the world, bar none. As a matter of record, "Rocky" lived until 1958, dying at the age of 33.

It was in late 1934 that Maurice Conn, president of Ambassador Pictures, signed Kermit for the outdoor series that aficionados still talk about. The casts of these oaters were terrific. Heroines included Ann Sheridan, Beryl Wallace, Andrea Leeds, Evelyn Brent, Polly Ann Young, and Joan Barclay, and the rough-and-tough element contained the likes of Charles King, Fred Kohler, Wheeler Oakman, Yak Canutt, John Merton, Dick Curtis, Stanley Blystone, and Leroy Mason.

Following the termination of the series Kermit went back to stunting and character roles, rating as one of the best in each capacity. Sometime during the Fifties he co-starred with Bill Henry in a television pilot about bush pilots filmed in Idaho, but it did not sell. However, he worked up until 1961, retiring from acting to take a job with the Screen Extras' Guild. He worked as a representative of the Guild for nearly eight years, finally retiring from all work in 1969. He had undergone two operations in 1967 which aged him consideraly and left him with phlebitis.

Kermit loved golf and spent much of his time in retirement on the golf course. As with everything else he did, he tried to become the best. For eleven years he coached a little league baseball team and through his many athletic connections was able to get scholarships and other assistance for promising high school athletes whom he observed in the many games he attended.

Kermit Maynard was one of the Western filmdom's most beloved cowboys, respected by the film colony for his gentlemanly ways. Quite unlike his brother, Kermit did not drink, throw tantrums, or otherwise behave in an obnoxious way. Kermit liked people, appreciated his fans, and was kind and considerate of all people. He was deeply respected and loved by those with whom he worked.

On the evening of January 16, 1971 Kermit Maynard died of a heart attack as he stepped through the backdoor of his home.

KERMIT MAYNARD Filmography

WILD BULL OF THE CAMPUS
(FBO, 1926)
Lefty Flynn, *Kermit Maynard*

PRINCE OF THE PLAINS
(Rayart, September, 1927) 5 Reels
Tex *(Kermit) Maynard*, Betty Caldwell, Walter Shumway
Director: Robert Williamson
Scenario: Arthur Hoerl
Story: Victor Rousseau
Producer: Trem Carr

GUN-HAND GARRISON
(Rayart, October, 1927) 5 Reels
Tex *(Kermit) Maynard*, Ruby Blaine, Jack Anthony, Charles O'Malley, Charles Schaeffer, Edmund Heim, Arthur Witting, Paul Malvern
Director: Edward R. Gordon
Scenario: Arthur Hoerl
Producer: Trem Carr

RIDIN' LUCK
(Rayart, October, 1927) 5 Reels
Tex *(Kermit) Maynard*, Ruby Blaine, Jack Anthony, Charles O'Malley, Charles Schaeffer, Art Witting, Marshall Ruth
Director: Edward R. Gordon
Scenario: Arthur Hoerl
Story: Francis James
Producer: Trem Carr

WILD BORN
(Rayart, December, 1927) 5 Reels
Tex *(Kermit) Maynard*, Ruby Blaine, Charles Schaeffer, Jack Anthony, Arthur Witting, Edward Heim, Marshall Ruth, Patsy Page
Director: Edward R. Gordon
Adaptation: Arthur Hoerl
Story: Tom Roan
Producer: Trem Carr

WANDERER OF THE WEST
(Rayart, December, 1927) 5 Reels
Tex *(Kermit) Maynard*, Betty Caldwell, Frank Clark, Walter Shumway, Tom Brooker, Roy Watson, Al Rogers, M. S. Dickinson
Director: Robert E. Williamson
Scenario: Arthur Hoerl
Adaptation: Victor Rousseau
Story: W. Ray Johnston

THE DRIFTING KID
(Rayart, April 27, 1928) 5 Reels
Tex *(Kermit) Maynard*, Betty Caldwell
Director: Robert Williamson or Edward R. Gordon
Producer: Trem Carr

THE PHANTOM OF THE WEST
(Mascot, January 1, 1931) 10 Chapters
Tom Tyler, William Desmond, Tom Santschi, Dorothy Gulliver, Joe Bonomo, Tom Dugan, Philo McCullough, *Kermit Maynard*, Frank Lanning, Frank Hagney, Dick Dickinson, Halee Sullivan, Al Taylor, Ernie Adams
Director: Ross Lederman
Producer: Nat Levine
Chapter Titles: (1) The Ghost Riders, (2) The Stairway of Doom, (3) The Horror in the Dark, (4) The Battle of the Strong, (5) The League of the Lawless, (6) The Canyon of Calamity, (7) The Price of Silence, (8) The House of Hate, (9) The Fatal Secret, (10) Rogue's Roundup

WEST OF BROADWAY
(MGM, November 30, 1931) 71 Minutes
John Gilbert, El Brendel, Lola Moran, Madge Evans, Ralph Conroy, Gwen Lee, Hedda Hopper, Ruth Renick, Willie Fung, *Kermit Maynard*, Buddy Roosevelt
Director: Harry Beaumont
Story: Ralph Graves and Bess Meredyth
Adaptation: Gene Markey

LIGHTNING WARRIOR
(Mascot, December 1, 1931) 12 Chapters
Rin-Tin-Tin, Frankie Darro, George Brent, Georgia Hale, Yakima Canutt, *Kermit Maynard*, Bob Kortman, Lafe McKee, Hayden Stevenson, Pat O'Malley, Dick Dickinson, Ted Lorch, Frank Brownlee, Helen Gibson, William Desmon, Steve Clemente, Frank Lanning, Bertee Beaumont
Directors: Armand Schaefer, Benjamin Kline
Screenplay: Wyndham Gittens, Ford Beebe, Colbert Clark
Producer: Nat Levine
Chapter Titles: (1) Drums of Doom, (2) The Wolf Man, (3) Empty Saddles, (4) Flaming Arrows, (5) The Invisible Enemy, (6) The Fatal Name, (7) The Ordeal of Fire, (8) The Man Who Knew, (9) Traitor's Hour, (10) The Secret of the Cave, (11) Red Shadows, (12) Painted Faces

DYNAMITE RANCH

(KBS/World Wide, July 31, 1932) 59 Minutes
Ken Maynard, Ruth Hall, Jack Perrin, Arthur Hoyt, Allan Roscoe, Al Smith, John Beck, George Pierce, Lafe McKee, Moatha Mattox, Edmund Cobb, Charles Le Moyne, Cliff Lyons, *Kermit Maynard* (stuntman and double), "Tarzan"
Director: Forrest Sheldon
Story/Screenplay: Barry Barrington, Forrest Sheldon
Producers: Burt Kelly, Sam Bischoff, William Saal

OUTLAW JUSTICE

(Majestic, October 1, 1932) 61 Minutes
Jack Hoxie, Dorothy Gulliver, Chris-Pin Martin, Donald Keith, *Kermit Maynard*, Charles King, Jack Trent, Walter Shumway, Jack Rockwell, Tom London
Director: Armand Schaefer
Story: W. Scott Darling
Screenplay: Oliver Drake
Producer: Larry Darmour

DRUM TAPS

(KBS/World Wide, January 24, 1933) 61 Minutes
Ken Maynard, Dorothy Dix, Hooper Atchley, Junior Coghlan, Charles Stevens, *Kermit Maynard*, Al Bridge, Harry Semels, Slim Whitaker, James Mason, Leo Willis, Los Angles Boy Scout Troup 107, "Tarzan"
Director: J. P. McGowan
Screenplay: Alan James

42ND STREET

(Warner Bros., April, 1933) 89 Minutes
Warner Baxter, Bebe Daniels, George Brent, Una Merkel, Ruby Keeler, Guy Kibbee, Dick Powell, Ginger Rogers, George E. Stone, Robert McWade, Ned Sparks, Allen Jenkins, Henry B. Walthall, Jack LaRue, Dave O'Brien, Charles Lane, Lyle Talbot, *Kermit Maynard*
Director: Lloyd Bacon
Story: Bradford Ropes
Screenplay: Rian James, James Seymour

THE FIGHTING TROOPER

(Ambassador, November 1, 1934) 61 Minutes
Kermit Maynard, Barbara Worth, Walter Miller, Robert Frazer, LeRoy Mason, George Regas, Charles Delaney, Joe Girard, George Chesebro, Charles King, Artie Ortego, Lafe McKee, Milburn Norante, Gordon DeMain, Nelson McDowell, George Morrell, Merrill McCormack
Director: Ray Taylor
Story: James Oliver Curwood - "Footprints"
Screenplay: Forest Sheldon
Producer: Maurice Conn

NORTHERN FRONTIER

(Ambassador, February 1, 1935) 60 Minutes
Kermit Maynard, Eleanor Hunt, J. Farrell MacDonald, LeRoy Mason, Charles King, Ben Hendricks, Jr., Russell Hopton, Nelson McDowell, Walter Brennan, Gertrude Astor, Dick Curtis, Kernan Cripps, Jack Crisholm, Lloyd Ingraham, Lafe McKee, Tyrone Power, Jr., Artie Ortego, "Rocky"
Director: Sam Newfield
Story: James Oliver Curwood - "Four Minutes Late"
Screenplay: Barry Barringer
Producer: Maurice Conn

WILDERNESS MAIL

(Ambassador, March 9, 1935) 65 Minutes
Kermit Maynard, Fred Kohler, Doris Brook, Dick Curtis, Syd Saylor, Paul Hurst, Nelson McDowell, Kernan Cripps, "Rocky"
Director: Forrest Sheldon
Story: James Oliver Curwood
Screenplay: Bennett Cohen, Robert Dillon
Producer: Maurice Conn

CODE OF THE MOUNTED

(Ambassador, June 1, 1935) 60 Minutes
Kermit Maynard, Robert Warwick, Lilliam Miles, Jim Thorpe, Syd Saylor, Wheeler Oakman, Dick Curtis, Stanley Blystone, Roger Williams, "Rocky"
Director: Sam Newfield
Story: James Oliver Curwood - "Wheels of Fate"
Screenplay: George Sayre
Producers: Maurice Conn and Sigmund Neufeld

THE RED BLOOD OF COURAGE

(Ambassador, June 1, 1935) 55 Minutes
Kermit Maynard, Ann Sheridan, Reginald Barlow, Ben Hendricks, Jr., George Regas, Nat Carr, Charles King, "Rocky"
Director: Jack English
Story: James Oliver Curwood
Screenplay: Barry Barringer
Producers: Maurice Conn, Sigmund Neufeld

TRAILS OF THE WILD

(Ambassador, August 1, 1935) 60 Minutes
Kermit Maynard, Billie Seward, Fuzzy Knight, Monte Blue, Mathew Betz, Theodore von Eltz, Frank Rice, Robert Frazer, Wheeler Oakman, Roger Williams, Charles Delaney, John Elliott, Dick Curtis, "Rocky"
Director: Sam Newfield
Story: "Caryl of the Mountains" - James Oliver Curwood
Screenplay: Joseph O'Donnell
Producers: Sigmund Neufeld, Maurice Conn

Kermit Maynard keeps an Indian from knifing Wheeler Oakman in **Code of the Mounted** (Ambassador, 1935)

HIS FIGHTING BLOOD
(Ambassador, October 15, 1935) 60 Minutes
Kermit Maynard, Polly Ann Young, Ted Adams, Paul Fix, Joseph Girard, Ben Hendricks, Jr., Frank O'Connor, Charles King, Frank LaRue, Ed Cecil, Theodore Lorch, Jack Cheatham, The Singing Constables (Jack Kirk, Chuck Baldra, and Glenn Strange), "Rocky"
Director: John English
Story: James Oliver Curwood
Screenplay: Joseph O'Donnell
Producers: Maurice Conn, Sigmund Neufeld

TIMBER WAR
(Ambassador, November 1, 1935) 60 Minutes
Kermit Maynard, Lucille Lund, Lawrence Gray, Robert Warwick, Lloyd Ingraham, Wheeler Oakman, Roger Williams, George Morrell, James Pierce, Patricia Royal, "Rocky"
Director: Sam Newfield
Story: James Oliver Curwood
Screenplay: Joseph O'Donnell
Producers: Maurice Conn, Sigmund Neufeld

SONG OF THE TRAIL
(Ambassador, March 15, 1936) 59 Minutes
Kermit Maynard, Evelyn Brent, Fuzzy Knight, George Hayes, Wheeler Oakman, Antoinette Lees (Andrea Leeds), Lee Shumway, Lynette London, Roger Williams, Ray Gallagher, Charles McMurphy, Horace Murphy, Bob McKenzie, Frank McCarroll, Artie Ortego, "Rocky"
Director: Russell Hopton
Story: "Playing with Fire" - James Oliver Curwood
Screenplay: George Sayre, Barry Barrington
Producer: Maurice Conn

WILDCAT TROOPER
(Ambassador, July 1, 1936) 60 Minutes
Kermit Maynard, Hobart Bosworth, Fuzzy Knight, Lois Wilde, Yakima Canutt, Eddie Phillips, Jim Thorpe, John Merton, Frank Hagney, Roger Williams, Dick Curtis, Ted Lorch, Hal Price, "Rocky"
Director: Elmer Clifton
Story: "The Midnight Call" - James Oliver Curwood
Screenplay: Joseph O'Donnell
Producer: Maurice Conn

PHANTOM PATROL

(Ambassador, September 30, 1936) 60 Minutes
Kermit Maynard, Joan Barclay, Dick Curtis, Harry Worth, George Cleveland, Paul Fix, Julian Rivero, Eddie Phillips, Roger Williams, Lester Dorr, "Rocky"
Director: Charles Hutchison
Story: "Fatal Note" - James Oliver Curwood
Screenplay: Credited to Stephen Norris (Name of character in the film)
Producer: Maurice Conn

WILD HORSE ROUND-UP

(Ambassador, December, 1936) 5 Reels
Kermit Maynard, Betty Lloyd (Beth Marion), Dickie Jones, Budd Buster, John Merton, Frank Hagney, Roger Williams, Dick Curtis, Jack Ingram
Director: Alan James
Story: James Oliver Curwood
Screenplay: Joseph O'Donnell
Producer: Maurice Conn

VALLEY OF TERROR

(Ambassador, January 20, 1937) 58 Minutes
Kermit Maynard, Harley Wood, John Merton, Jack Ingram, Dick Curtis, Roger Williams, Frank McCarroll, Hank Bell, Hal Price, Slim Whitaker, Jack Casey, George Morrell, Blackie Whiteford, Herman Hack, "Rocky"
Director: Al Herman
Story: James Oliver Curwood
Producer: Maurice Conn

WHISTLING BULLETS

(Ambassador, May 3, 1937) 57 Minutes
Kermit Maynard, Harlene (Harley) Wood, Jack Ingram, Maston Williams, Bruce Mitchell, Karl Hackett, Sherry Tansey, Cliff Parkinson, Cherokee Alcorn, Herman Hack, Bill McCall, Buck Moulton
Director: John English
Story: James Oliver Curwood
Screenplay: Joseph O'Donnell
Producer: Maurice Conn

Kermit Maynard has Paul Fix and friend covered as Joan Barclay looks on in **Phantom Patrol** (Ambassador, 1936)

Kermit Maynard has a grip on Budd Buster in **The Fighting Texan** (Ambassador, 1937)

THE FIGHTING TEXAN

(Ambassador, June 1937) 59 Minutes
Kermit Maynard, Elaine Shepard, Frank LaRue, Budd
Buster, Ed Cassidy, Bruce Mitchell, Murdock
McQuarrie, Art Miles, Merrill McCormack, Blackie
Whiteford, Wally West, John Merton, Bob Woodward
Director: Charles Abbott
Story: James Oliver Curwood
Screenplay: Joseph O'Donnell
Producer: Maurice Conn

GALLOPING DYNAMITE

(Ambassador, July, 1937)
Kermit Maynard, Ariane Allen, John Merton, John
Ward, Stanley Blystone, David Sharpe, Earl Dwire,
Francis Walker, Tracy Layne, Bob Burns, Allen Greer,
Budd Buster
Director: Harry Fraser
Story: "Dawn Rider" - James Oliver Curwood
Screenplay: Jesse Duffy, Sherman Lowe, Charles
Condon
Producer: Maurice Conn

ROUGH RIDING RHYTHM

(Ambassador, August 15, 1937) 57 Minutes
Kermit Maynard, Beryl Wallace, Ralph Peters, Olin
Francis, Curley Dresden, Betty Mack, Cliff Parkinson,
Dave O'Brien, Newt Kirby, J. P. McGowan
Director: J. P. McGowan
Story: James Oliver Curwood - "Getting a Start in Life"
Screenplay: Arthur Everett
Producer: Maurice Conn

ROARING SIX GUNS

(Ambassador, September 1, 1937) 57 Minutes
Kermit Maynard, Mary Hayes, Sam Flint, John Merton,
Budd Buster, Robert Fiske, Edward Cassidy, Curley
Dresden, Dick Morehead, Slim Whitaker, Earle
Hodgins, Rene Stone
Director: J. P. McGowan
Story: James Oliver Curwood
Screenplay: Arthur Everett
Producer: Maurice Conn

WILD HORSE RODEO

(Republic, December 6, 1937) 55 Minutes
Bob Livingston, Ray Corrigan, Max Terhune, June Martel, Walter Miller, Edmund Cobb, William Gould, Jack Ingram, Fred "Snowflake" Toones, Henry Isabell, Art Dillard, Ralph Robinson, Dick Weston (Roy Rogers), Jack Kirk, *Kermit Maynard*
Director: George Sherman
Story: Oliver Drake, Gilbert Wright
Screenplay: Betty Burbridge
Producer: Sol C. Siegel

THE GREAT ADVENTURES OF WILD BILL HICKOK

(Columbia, June, 30, 1938) 15 Chapters
Gordon Elliott (Bill Elliott), Monte Blue, Carole Wayne, Frankie Darro, Dickie Jones, Sammy McKim, *Kermit Maynard,* Roscoe Ates, Monte Collins, Reed Hadley, Chief Thunder Cloud, George Chesebro, Mala (Ray Mala), Walter Wills, J. P. McGowan, Eddy Waller, Alan Bridge, Slim Whitaker, Walter Miller, Lee Phelps, Robert Fiske, Earle Hodgins, Earl Dwire, Ed Brady, Ray Jones, Edmund Cobb, Art Mix, Hal Taliaferro, Blackie Whiteford, Jack Perrin
Directors: Mack V. Wright, Sam Nelson
Screenplay: George Rosenor, Charles Arthur Powell, George Arthur Durlam
Producer: Harry Webb
Chapter Titles: (1) The Law of the Gun, (2) Stampede, (3) Blazing Terror, (4) Mystery Canyon, (5)Flaming Brands, (6) The Apache Killer, (7) Prowling Wolves, (8) The Pit, (9) Ambush, (10) Savage Vengeance, (11) Burning Waters, (12) Desperation, (13) Phantom Bullets, (14) The Lure, (15) Trail's End

Mary Hayes and Kermit Maynard in **Roaring Six Guns** (Ambassador, 1937)

THE LAW WEST OF TOMBSTONE

(RKO, November 18, 1938) 73 Minutes
Harry Carey, Tim Holt, Evelyn Brent, Jean Rouverol, Clarence Kolb, Esther Muir, Bradley Page, Paul Guilfoyle, Robert Moya, Allan Lane, Ward Bond, George Irving, Monte Montague, Bob Kortman, *Kermit Maynard* (unbilled)
Director: Glenn Tyron
Story: Clarence Upson Young
Screenplay: John Twist, Clarence Upson Young
Producer: Cliff Reid

WESTERN JAMBOREE

(Republic, December 2, 1938) 56 Minutes
Gene Autry, Smiley Burnette, Jean Rouveral, Esther Muir, Frank Darien, Joe Frisco, *Kermit Maynard,* Jack Perrin, Jack Ingram, Margaret Armstrong, Harry Holman, Edward Raquello, Bentley Hewitt, Georgia Walcott, Ray Teal, Frank Ellis, Eddie Dean, Davidson Clark, "Champion"
Director: Ralph Staub
Story: Patricia Harper
Screenplay: Gerald Geraghty
Associate Producer: Harry Grey

CODE OF THE CACTUS

(Victory, February 25, 1939) 56 Minutes
Tim McCoy, Dorothy Short, Ben Corbett, Dave O'Brien, Alden Chase, Ted Adams, Forrest Taylor, Bob Terry, Slim Whitaker, Frank Wayne, *Kermit Maynard,* Art Davis, Carl Sepulveda, Carl Mathews, Lee Burns, Clyde McCreary, Jack King, Rube Calroy
Director: Sam Newfield
Story/Screenplay: Edward Halperin
Producer: Sam Katzman

THE NIGHT RIDERS

(Republic, April 12, 1939) 58 Minutes
(Three Mesquiteers Series)
John Wayne, Ray Corrigan, Max Terhune, Ruth Rogers, Doreen McKay, George Douglas, Tom Tyler, Sammy McKim, *Kermit Maynard,* Walter Wills, Ethan Laidlaw, Ed Piel, Sr., Tom London, Jack Ingram, Bill Nestell, Cactus Mack, Lee Shumway, Hal Price, Hank Worden, Roger Williams, Olin Francis, Francis Walker, Hugh Prosser, Jack Kirk, Yakima Canutt, Glenn Strange, David Sharpe, Bud Osborne, Georgia Summers
Director: George Sherman
Screenplay: Betty Burbridge, Stanley Roberts
Associate Producer: William Berke
Based on characters created by William Colt MacDonald

COLORADO SUNSET

(Republic, July 31, 1939) 61 Minutes

Gene Autry, Smiley Burnette, June Storey, Larry "Buster" Crabbe, Barbara Pepper, Robert Barrat, Patsy Montana, Parnell Pratt, William Farnum, *Kermit Maynard,* Jack Ingram, Elmo Lincoln, Frank Marvin, Ethan Laidlaw, Fred Burns, Jack Kirk, Budd Buster, Ed Cassidy, Slim Whitaker, Murdock McQuarrie, Ralph Peters, The CBS-KMBC Texas Rangers, "Champion"

Director: George Sherman
Story: Luci Ward, Jack Natteford
Screenplay: Betty Burbridge, Stanley Roberts
Associate Producer: William Berke

CHIP OF THE FLYING U

(Universal, November 29, 1939) 55 Minutes

Johnny Mack Brown, Bob Baker, Fuzzy Knight, Doris Weston, Karl Hackett, Forrest Taylor, Anthony Warde, Henry Hall, Claire Whitney, Ferris Taylor, Cecil Kellogg, Hank Bell, Harry Tenbrook, Chester Conklin, Vic Potel, Hank Worden, Charles K. French, Al Ward, Budd Buster, Frank Ellis, *Kermit Maynard,* Jack Shannon, Chuck Morrison

Director: Ralph Staub
Story: B. M. Bower
Screenplay: Larry Rhine, Andrew Bennison

HEROES OF THE SADDLE

(Republic, January 12, 1940) 59 Minutes
(Three Mesquiteers Series)

Robert Livingston, Raymond Hatton, Duncan Renaldo, Patsy Lee Parsons, Loretta Weaver, Byron Foulger, Vince Barnett, William Royle, Jack Roper, Reed Howes, Ethel May Halls, Al Taylor, Patsy Carmichael, *Kermit Maynard,* Tom Hanlon, Tex Terry, Douglas Deems, Darwood Kaye, Matt McHugh, Harrison Greene

Director: William Witney
Screenplay: Jack Natteford
Associate Producer: Harry Grey
Based on characters created by William Colt MacDonald

THE SHOWDOWN

(Paramount, March 8, 1940) 65 Minutes
(Hopalong Cassidy Series)

William Boyd, Russell Hayden, Britt Wood, Morris Ankrum, Jane (Jan) Clayton, Wright Kramer, Donald Kirke, Roy Barcroft, *Kermit Maynard,* Walter Shumway, Eddie Dean, The King's Men

Director: Howard Bretherton
Story: Jack Jungmeyer
Screenplay: Howard and Donald Kusel
Producer: Harry Sherman
Based on characters created by Clarence E. Mulford

RIDERS OF PASCO BASIN

(Universal, April 5, 1940) 56 Minutes

Johnny Mack Brown, Fuzzy Knight, Bob Baker, Frances Robinson, Frank LaRue, Arthur Loft, James Guilfoyle, Lafe McKee, Chuck Morrison, Edward Cassidy, Robert Winkler, William Gould, Ted Adams, *Kermit Maynard,* David Sharpe, Hank Bell, Edward Peil, John Judd, Gordon Hart, Rudy Sooter and his Californians

Director: Ray Taylor
Story/Screenplay: Ford Beebe

WEST OF CARSON CITY

(Universal, May 13, 1940) 57 Minutes

Johnny Mack Brown, Bob Baker, Fuzzy Knight, Peggy Moran, Harry Woods, Robert Homans, Al Hall, Roy Barcroft, Charles King, Frank Mitchell, Edmund Cobb, Jack Roper, Ted Wells, Jack Shannon, Vic Potel, *Kermit Maynard,* Ernie Adams, Donald Kerr, Dick Carter, Al Bridge, The Notables Quartet

Director: Ray Taylor
Story: Milt Raison
Screenplay: Milt Raison, Sherman Lowe, Jack Bernhard

THE RANGE BUSTERS

(Monogram, August 22, 1940) 56 Minutes
(Range Busters Series)

Ray Corrigan, John King, Max Terhune, LeRoy Mason, Luana Walters, Earle Hodgins, Frank LaRue, *Kermit Maynard,* Bruce King, Duke (Carl) Mathews, Horace Murphy, Karl Hackett

Director: S. Roy Luby
Screenplay: John Rathmell
Producer: George W. Weeks

RAGTIME COWBOY JOE

(Universal, September 20, 1940) 58 Minutes

Johnny Mack Brown, Fuzzy Knight, Nell O'Day, Marilyn (Lynn) Merrick, Dick Curtis, Walter Sodering, Roy Barcroft, Harry Tenbrook, George Plues, Ed Cassidy, Buck Moulton, Harold Goodwin, Wilfred Lucas, *Kermit Maynard,* Viola Vonn, Jack Clifford, William Gould, Bud Osborne, The Texas Rangers, Bob O'Connor, Eddie Parker, Frank McCarroll, Slim Whitaker

Director: Ray Taylor
Screenplay: Sherman Lowe
Associate Producer: Joseph Sanford

NORTHWEST MOUNTED POLICE

(Paramount, October 22, 1940) 125 Minutes

Gary Cooper, Madeleine Carroll, Paulette Goddard, Preston Foster, Robert Preston, George Bancroft, Lynne Overman, Akim Tamiroff, Walter Hampden, Lon Chaney, Jr., Montague Love, Francis J. McDonald, George E. Stone, Willard Robertson, Regis Toomey, Richard Denning, Douglas Kennedy, Robert Ryan, James Seay, Lane Chandler, Ralph Byrd, Eric Alden, Wallace Reid, Jr., Bud Geary, Evan Thomas, Jack Pennick, Rod Cameron, Davidson Clark, Ed Brady, Monte Blue, Mala, Jack Chapin, Chief Thunder Cloud, Harry Burns, Lou Merrill, Clara Blandick, Ynez Seabury, Eva Puig, Julia Faye, Weldon Heyburn, Phillip Terry, George Regas, Jack Luden, Soledad Jimenez, Emory Parnell, William Haade, Nestor Paiva, Donald Curtis, Jane Keckley, Noble Johnson, Norma Nelson, John Hart, Ethan Laidlaw, Jim Pierce, *Kermit Maynard*, Franklyn Farnum, James Flavin

Director: Cecil B. DeMille
Story: "Royal Canadian Mounted Police" - R. G. Fetherstonhaugh
Screenplay: Alan LeMay, Jesse Lasky, Jr., C. Gardner Sullivan
Producer: Cecil B. DeMille
Associate Producer: William H. Pine

LAW AND ORDER

(Universal, November 28, 1940) 57 Minutes

Johnny Mack Brown, Fuzzy Knight, Nell O'Day, James Craig, Harry Cording, Ethan Laidlaw, Ted Adams, Harry Humphrey, Jimmy Dodd, William Worthington, George Plues, Earle Hodgins, Robert Fiske, *Kermit Maynard*, Frank McCarroll, Bob Kortman, Frank Ellis, Jim Corey, Lew Meehan, Charles King, The Notables Quartet

Director: Ray Taylor
Story: "Saint Johnson" - W. R. Burnette
Screenplay: Sherman Lowe, Victor McLeod

PONY POST

(Universal, December 1, 1940) 59 Minutes

Johnny Mack Brown, Fuzzy Knight, Nell O'Day, Lane Chandler, Edmund Cobb, *Kermit Maynard*, Dorothy Short, Tom Chatterton, Stanley Blystone, Jack Rockwell, Ray Teal, Lloyd Ingraham, Charles King, Frank McCarroll, Iron Eyes Cody, Jimmy Wakely and his Rough Riders

Director: Ray Taylor
Story/Screenplay: Sherman Lowe

TRAIL OF THE SILVER SPURS

(Monogram, January 4, 1941) 58 Minutes
(Range Busters Series)

Ray Corrigan, John King, Max Terhune, Dorothy Short, I. Stanford Jolley, Eddie Dean, Milburn Morante, George Chesebro, *Kermit Maynard*, Frank Ellis, Carl Mathews, Steve Clark

Director: S. Roy Luby
Story: Elmer Clifton
Screenplay: Earle Snell
Producer: George W. Weeks

WYOMING WILDCAT

(Republic, January 6, 1941) 56 Minutes

Don Barry, Julie Duncan, Syd Saylor, Frank M. Thomas, Dick Botiller, Edmund Cobb, Ed Brady, Edward Cassidy, George Sherwood, Ethan Laidlaw, Al Haskell, Frank Ellis, Curley Dresden, Art Dillard, Cactus Mack, *Kermit Maynard*, Frank O'Connor, Fred Burns

Director/Associate Producer: George Sherman
Story: Bennett Cohen
Screenplay: Bennett Cohen, Anthony Coldeway

BOSS OF BULLION CITY

(Universal, January 10, 1941)

Johnny Mack Brown, Fuzzy Knight, Nell O'Day, Maria Montez, Earle Hodgins, Harry Woods, Melvin Lang, Dick Alexander, Karl Hackett, George Humbert, Frank Ellis, *Kermit Maynard*, Tex Terry, Bob Kortman, Michael Vallon, The Guadalajara Trio, Bill Nestell

Director: Ray Taylor
Story: Arthur St. Claire
Screenplay: Arthur St. Claire, Victor McLeod
Associate Producer: Will Cowan

BURY ME NOT ON THE LONE PRAIRIE

(Universal, March 21, 1941) 57 Minutes

Johnny Mack Brown, Fuzzy Knight, Nell O'Day, Kathryn Adams, Lee Shumway, Frank O'Connor, Ernie Adams, Don House, Pat O'Brien, Bud Osborne, Ed Cassidy, Slim Whitaker, *Kermit Maynard*, William Desmond, Jack Rockwell, Bob Kortman, Jim Corey, Charles King, Ethan Laidlaw, Harry Cording, Frank Ellis, Jimmy Wakely's Rough Riders

Director: Ray Taylor
Story: Sherman Lowe
Screenplay: Sherman Lowe, Victor McLeod
Associate Producer: Will Cowan

BILLY THE KID

(M-G-M, May 30, 1941) 95 Minutes

Robert Taylor, Brian Donlevy, Ian Hunter, Mary Howard, Gene Lockhart, Lon Chaney, Jr., Henry O'Neill, Guinn Williams, Cy Kendall, Ted Adams, Frank Conlan, Frank Puglia, Mitchell Lewis, Dick Curtis, Grant Withers, Joe Yule, Earl Gunn, Eddie Dunn, Carl Pitti, *Kermit Maynard*, Ethel Griffies, Chill Wills, Olive Blakeney

Director: David Miller
Story: Walter Noble Burns
Screenplay: Gene Fowler
Producer: Irving Asher

BADLANDS OF DAKOTA

(Universal, September 5, 1941) 74 Minutes

Robert Stack, Ann Rutherford, Richard Dix, Frances Farmer, Brad Crawford, Hugh Herbert, Fuzzy Knight, Lon Chaney, Jr., Andy Devine, Addison Richards, Samuel S. Hinds, Eddie Dew, *Kermit Maynard*, Charles King, Hank Bell, Bradley Page, Carleton Young, Glenn Strange, Don Barclay, Emmett Vogan, Willie Fung, Edward Fielding, The Jesters (Dwight Latham, Walter Carlson & Guy Bonham)

Director: Alfred E. Breene
Story: Harold Shumate
Screenplay: Gerald Geraghty
Associate Producer: George Waggner

MAN FROM MONTANA

(Universal, September 5, 1941) 56 Minutes

Johnny Mack Brown, Fuzzy Knight, Nell O'Day, Butch and Buddy (Billy Lenhart and Kenneth Brown), Jeanne Kelly (Jean Brooks), William Gould, James Blaine, Dick Alexander, Karl Hackett, Edmund Cobb, Frank Ellis, *Kermit Maynard*, Jack Shannon, Murdock McQuarrie, Charles McMurphy, Blackjack Ward, The King's Men

Director: Ray Taylor
Screenplay: Bennett Cogen
Associate Producer: Will Cowan

BELLE STARR

(20th Century-Fox, September 12, 1941) 87 Minutes

Randolph Scott, Gene Tierney, Dana Andrews, John Sheppard, Elizabeth Patterson, Chill Wills, Louise Beavers, Olin Howlin, Paul Burns, Joseph Sawyer, Joseph Downing, Howard Hickman, Charles Trowbridge, James Flavin, Charles Middleton, Clarence Muse, George Melford, Mae Marsh, Herbert Ashley, Norman Willis, Billy Wayne, George Reed, Davidson Clark, Hugh Chapman, Clinton Rosemond, *Kermit Maynard*, Franklyn Farnum

Director: Irvin Cummings
Story: Niven Busch, Cameron Rogers
Screenplay: Lamar Trotti
Associate Producer: Kenneth McGowan

STICK TO YOUR GUNS

(Paramount, September 27, 1941) 63 Minutes
(Hopalong Cassidy Series)

William Boyd, Andy Clyde, Brad King, Jacqueline (Jennifer) Holt, Dick Curtis, Weldon Heyburn, Henry Hall, Joe Whitehead, Bob Card, Jack C. Smith, Homer (Heb) Holcomb, Tom London, *Kermit Maynard*, Frank Ellis, Jack Rockwell, Mickey Eissa, The Jimmy Wakely Trio (Jimmy Wakely, Johnny Bond and Dick Rinehart)

Director: Lesley Selander
Screenplay: J. Benton Cheney
Producer: Harry Sherman
Based on characters created by Clarence E. Mulford

KING OF THE TEXAS RANGERS

(Republic, October 4, 1941) 12 Chapters

Sammy Baugh, Neil Hamilton, Pauline Moore, Duncan Renaldo, Charles Trowbridge, Herbert Rawlinson, Frank Darien, Robert O. Davis, Monte Blue, Stanley Blystone, *Kermit Maynard*, Roy Barcroft, Kenne Duncan, Jack Ingram, Robert Barron, Frank Bruno, Monte Montague, Joseph Forte, Lucien Prival, Paul Gustien, Henry Hall, William Kellogg, Richard Simmons, Alan Gregg, Iron Eyes Cody, Forrest Taylor, Lee Shumway, Ernest Sarracino, Bud Jamison, John James, Dick Scott, Bud Wolfe, Barry Hays, Earl Bunn, George Burrows, Pat O'Shea, Bert LeBaron, Jerry Jerome, Bobby Barber, Forest Burns, Max Waizman, Charles Whitaker, Jack Chapin, Howard Hughes, Michael Owen, Ken Terrell, Hooper Atchley, Otto Reichow, Chick Hannon, Herman Hack, Tommy Coats, Charles Thomas, Bob Robinson, Edward Cassidy, Buddy Roosevelt, John Bagni, Eddie Dew, George Allen, Jimmy Fawcett, Al Taylor, Duke Green, Merlyn Nelson, Loren Riebe, David Sharpe, Cy Clocum, Tom Steele, Duke Taylor, Bill Wilkus, Joe Yrigoyen

Directors: William Witney, John English
Screenplay: Ronald Davidson, Norman S. Hall, Joseph Poland, Joseph O'Donnell, William Lively
Associate Producer: Hiram S. Brown, Jr.
Chapter Titles: (1) The Fifth Column Strikes (2) Dead End (3) Man Hunt (4) Trapped (5) Test Flight (6) Double Danger (7) Death Takes the Witness (8) Counterfeit Trail (9) Ambush (10) Sky Raiders (11) Trail of Death (12) Code of the Rangers

SIERRA SUE

(Republic, November 12, 1941) 64 Minutes

Gene Autry, Smiley Burnette, Fay McKenzie, Frank M. Thomas, Robert Homans, Earle Hodgins, Dorothy Christy, Jack Kirk, Eddie Dean, *Kermit Maynard*, Budd Buster, Rex Lease, Hugh Prosser, Vince Barnett, Hal Price, Syd Saylor, Roy Butler, Sammy Stein, Eddie Cherkose, Bob McKenzie, Marin Sais, Bud Brown, Gene Eblen, Buel Bryant, Ray Davis, Art Dillard, Frankie Marvin, "Champion"

Director: William Morgan
Screenplay: Earl Felton, Julian Zimet
Associate Producer: Harry Grey

THE ROYAL MOUNTED PATROL

(Columbia, November 13, 1941) 59 Minutes
Charles Starrett, Russell Hayden, Wanda McKay, Donald Curtis, Lloyd Bridges, *Kermit Maynard*, Evan Thomas, Ted Adams, Harrison Greene, Ted Mapes, George Morrell
Director: Lambert Hillyer
Screenplay: Winston Miller
Producer: William Berke

ARIZONA CYCLONE

(Universal, November 14, 1941) 59 Minutes
Johnny Mack Brown, Fuzzy Knight, Nell O'Day, Kathryn Adams, Dick Curtis, Herbert Rawlinson, Buck Moulton, Jack Clifford, *Kermit Maynard*, Frank Ellis, The Notables, Robert Strange, Glenn Strange, Carl Sepulveda, Chuck Morrison
Director: Joseph H. Lewis
Screenplay: Sherman Lowe
Associate Producer: Will Cowan

BELOW THE BORDER

(Monogram, January 30, 1942) 57 Minutes
(Rough Riders Series)
Buck Jones, Tim McCoy, Raymond Hatton, Linda Brent, Eva Puig, Charles King, Dennis Moore, Roy Barcroft, Ted Mapes, Bud Osborne, Merrill McCormack, Jack Rockwell, *Kermit Maynard*, Frank Ellis, Reed Howes
Director: Howard Bretherton
Screenplay: Jess Bowers (Adele Buffington)
Producer: Scott R. Dunlap

STAGECOACH BUCKAROO

(Universal, February 13, 1942) 58 Minutes
Johnny Mack Brown, Fuzzy Knight, Nell O'Day, Anne Nagel, Herbert Rawlinson, Glenn Strange, Ernie Adams, Henry Hall, Lloyd Ingraham, *Kermit Maynard*, Frank Brownlee, Jack C. Smith, Harry Tenbrook, Frank Ellis, Blackie Whiteford, Hank Bell, Ray Jones, Jim Corey, William Nestell, Carl Sepulveda, The Guardsman Quartet
Director: Ray Taylor
Story: "Shotgun Messenger" - Arthur St. Clair
Screenplay: Al Martin
Associate Producer: Will Cowan

ROCK RIVER RENEGADES

(Monogram, February 27, 1942) 56 Minutes
(Range Busters Series)
Ray Corrigan, John King, Max Terhune, Christine McIntyre, John Elliott, Weldon Heyburn, *Kermit Maynard*, Frank Ellis, Carl Mathews, Dick Cramer, Tex Palmer, Hank Bell, Budd Buster, Steve Clark
Director: S. Roy Luby
Story: Faith Thomas
Screenplay: John Vlahos, Earl Snell
Producer: George W. Weeks

SABOTEUR

(Universal, April 24, 1942) 108 Minutes
Robert Cummings, Priscilla Lane, Otto Kruger, Alan Baxter, Vaughn Glazer, Ian Wolfe, Dorothy Peterson, Norman Lloyd, Pedro de Cordoba, Kathryn Adams, Murray Alper. Billy Curtis, Rex Lease, Alan Bridge, Francis Carson, Will Wright, George Offerman, Jr., Frank Marlowe. Selmer Jackson, Pat Flaherty, Matt Willis, Dick York, Oliver Blake, Charles Halton, Ralph Dunn, Emory Parnell, James Flavin, Hans Conried, William Gould, Willian Ruhl, Belle Mitchell, Jeffrey Sayre, Lee Phelps, Milt Kibbee, *Kermit Maynard*
Director: Alfred Hitchcock
Screenplay: Peter Viertel, Joan Harrison, Dorothy Parker
Story: Alfred Hitchcock
Producers: Frank Lloyd, Jack Skirball

HOME IN WYOMIN'

(Republic, April 29, 1942) 67 Minutes
Gene Autry, Smiley Burnette, Fay McKenzie, Olin Howlin, Chick Chandler, Joe Strauch, Jr., Forrest Taylor, James Seay, George Douglas, Charles Lane, Hap Price, Bud Geary, Ken Cooper, Jean Porter, James McNamara, *Kermit Maynard*, Roy Butler, Billy Benedict, Cyril Ring, Spade Cooley, Ted Mapes, Jack Kirk, William Kellogg, Betty Farrington, Rex Lease, Tom Hanlon, Lee Shumway, "Champion"
Director: William Morgan
Story: Stuart Palmer
Screenplay: Robert Tasker, M. Coates Webster
Associate Producer: Harry Grey

PERILS OF THE ROYAL MOUNTED

(Columbia, May 24, 1942) 15 Chapters
Robert Stevens (Robert Kellard), Nell O'Day, Herbert Rawlinson, *Kermit Maynard*, Kenneth MacDonald, John Elliott, Nick Thompson, Art Miles, Richard Fiske, Richard Vallin, Forrest Taylor, Goerge Chesebro, Jack Ingram, Iron Eyes Cody
Director: James W. Horne
Screenplay: Basil Dickey, Scott Littleton, Jesse A. Duffy, Louis Heifetz
Producer: Larry Darmour
Chapter Titles: (1) The Totem Talks (2) The Night Raiders (3) The Water God's Revenge (4) Beware, The Vigilantes (5) The Masked Mountie (6) Underwater Gold (7) Bridge to the Sky (8) Lost in the Mine (9) Into the Trap (10) Betrayed by Law (11) Blazing Beacon (12) The Mountie's Last Chance (13) Painted White Man (14) Burned at the Stake (15) The Mountie Gets His Man

TEXAS TROUBLE SHOOTERS

(Monogram, June 12, 1943) 55 Minutes
(Range Busters Series)
Ray Corrigan, John King, Max Terhune, Julie Duncan, Glenn Strange, Roy Harris (Riley Hill), *Kermit Maynard*, Eddie Phillips, Frank Ellis, Ted Mapes, Steve Clark, Gertrude Hoffman, Jack Holmes, Dick Cramer, Carl Mathews
Director: S. Roy Luby
Story: Elizabeth Beecher
Screenplay: Arthur Hoerl
Producer: S. Roy Luby

PRAIRIE PALS

(PRC, September 4, 1942) 5 Reels
Bill (Cowboy Rambler) Boyd, Art Davis, Lee Powell, Charles King, Esther Estrella, John Merton, J. Merrill Holmes, *Kermit Maynard*, I. Stanford Jolley, Karl Hackett, Bob Burns, Al St. John, Al Taylor, Art Dillard, Curley Dresden, Frank McCarroll, Bill Patton, Carl Mathews, Frank Ellis, Jack Kinney, Morgan Flowers
Director: Peter Stewart (Sam Newfield)
Screenplay: Patricia Harper
Producer: Sigmund Neufeld

SHERIFF OF SAGE VALLEY

(PRC, October 2, 1942) 60 Minutes
(Billy the Kid Series)
Buster Crabbe, Al St. John, Tex (Dave) O'Brien, Maxine Leslie, Charles King, John Merton, *Kermit Maynard*, Hal Price, Curley Dresden, Jack Kirk, Lynton Brent, Budd Buster, Frank Ellis, Jack Evans, Carl Mathews, Merrill McCormack, Al Taylor
Director: Sherman Scott (Sam Newfield)
Screenplay: Milton Raison, George W. Sayre
Producer: Sigmund Neufeld

THE MYSTERIOUS RIDER

(PRC, November 20, 1942) 56 Minutes
(Billy the Kid Series)
Buster Crabbe, Al St. John, Caroline Burke, John Merton, *Kermit Maynard*, Jack Ingram, Slim Whitaker, Ted Adams, Guy Wilkerson, Edwin Brien, Frank Ellis
Director: Sam Newfield
Screenplay: Steve Braxton
Producer: Sigmund Neufeld

TRAIL RIDERS

(Monogram, December 4, 1942) 55 Minutes
(Range Busters Series)
John King, David Sharpe, Max Terhune, Evelyn Finley, Forrest Taylor, Lynton Brent, Charles King, *Kermit Maynard*, John Curtis, Steve Clark, Kenne Duncan, Frank LaRue, Bud Osborne, Tex Palmer, Dick Cramer, Frank Ellis
Director: Robert Tansey
Screenplay: Frances Kavanaugh
Producer: George W. Weeks

ARABIAN NIGHTS

(Universal, December 24, 1942) 86 Minutes
(Technicolor)
John Hall, Maria Montez, Sabu, Leif Erickson, Billy Gilbert, Edgar Barrier, Richard Lane, Turhan Bey, John Qualen, Shemp Howard, William 'Wee Willie' Davis, Thomas Gomez, Jeri Le Gon, Charles Coleman, Adia Kuznetzoff, Robin Raymond, Carmen D'Antonio, *Kermit Maynard*, Frank Lackteen, Elyse Knox, Acquanetta, David Sharp
Director: John Rawlins
Story/Screenplay: Michael Hogan
Producer: Walter Wanger

THE BLOCKED TRAIL

(Republic, March 12, 1943) 58 Minutes
(Three Mesquiteers Series)
Bob Steele, Tom Tyler, Jimmie Dodd, Helen Deverall, George J. Lewis, Walter Sodering, Charles Miller, *Kermit Maynard*, Pierce Lyden, Carl Mathews, Hal Price, Budd Buster, Earl Hodgins, Bud Osborne, Al Taylor, Art Dillard, Bud Geary
Director: Elmer Clifton
Screenplay: John K. Butler, Jacquin Frank
Based on characters created by William Colt MacDonald
Associate Producer: Louis Gray

FUGITIVE OF THE PLAINS

(PRC, April 1, 1943) 57 Minutes
(Billy the Kid Series)
Buster Crabbe, Al St. John, Maxine Leslie, *Kermit Maynard*, Jack Ingram, Karl Hackett, Hal Price, Budd Buster, Artie Ortego, Carl Sepulveda
Director: Sam Newfield
Screenplay: George Sayre
Producer: Sigmund Neufeld

SANTA FE SCOUTS

(Republic, April 16, 1943) 57 Minutes
(Three Mesquiteers Series)
Bob Steele, Tom Tyler, Jimmie Dodd, Lois Collier, John James, Tom Chatterton, Elizabeth Valentine, Tom London, Budd Buster, Jack Ingram, *Kermit Maynard*, Rex Lease, Ed Cassidy, Yakima Canutt, Jack Kirk, Curley Dresden, Reed Howes, Bud ·Geary, Carl Sepulveda, Al Taylor, Kenne Duncan
Director: Howard Bretherton
Screenplay: Morton Grant, Betty Burbridge
Based on characters created by William Colt MacDonald
Associate Producer: Louis Gray

CHEYENNE ROUNDUP

(Universal, April 29, 1943) 59 Minutes
Johnny Mack Brown, Fuzzy Knight, Tex Ritter, Jennifer Holt, Jimmy Wakely Trio (Jimmy Wakely, Johnny Bond, Scotty Harrell), Harry Woods, Roy Barcroft, Robert Barron, Budd Buster, Gil Patric, Carl Mathews, *Kermit Maynard*, William Desmond, Kenne Duncan, Buck Moulton, Lynton Brent, Roy Brent, Michael Vallon, Jim Mitchle, George Plues
Director: Ray Taylor
Story: Elmer Clifton
Screenplay: Elmer Clifton, Bernard McConville

DEATH RIDES THE PLAINS

(PRC, May 7, 1943)
(Lone Rider Series)
Bob Livingston, Al St. John, Nica Doret, Ray Bennett, I. Stanford Jolley, *Kermit Maynard*, George Chesebro, John Elliott, Slim Whitaker, Karl Hackett, Frank Ellis, Ted Mapes, Dan White, Jimmy Aubrey
Director: Sam Newfield
Story: Patricia Harper
Screenplay: Joe O'Donnell
Producer: Sigmund Neufeld

WESTERN CYCLONE

(PRC, May 14, 1943) 56 Minutes
(Billy the Kid Series)
Buster Crabbe, Al St. John, Marjorie Manners, Karl Hackett, Milt Kibbee, *Kermit Maynard*, Glenn Strange, Charles King, Hal Price, Frank Ellis, Frank McCarroll, Artie Ortego, Herman Hack, Al Haskell
Director: Sam Newfield
Screenplay: Patricia Harper
Producer: Sigmund Neufeld

BORDER BUCKAROOS

(PRC, June 1943)
(Texas Rangers Series)
Dave O'Brien, Jim Newill, Guy Wilkerson, Christine McIntyre, Eleanor Counts, Jack Ingram, Ethan Laidlaw, Charles King, Michael Vallon, Kenne Duncan, Reed Howes, *Kermit Maynard*, Bud Osborne
Director: Oliver Drake
Screenplay: Oliver Drake
Producer: Alfred Stern and Arthur Alexander

THE STRANGER FROM PECOS

(Monogram, July 17, 1943) 55 Minutes
Johnny Mack Brown, Raymond Hatton, Kirby Grant, Christine McIntyre, Steve Clark, Sam Flint, Roy Barcroft, Robert Frazer, Edmund Cobb, Charles King, Bud Osborne, Artie Ortego, Tom London, *Kermit Maynard*, Milburn Morante, Lynton Brent, Carol Henry, George Morrell
Director: Lambert Hillyer
Screenplay: Jess Bowers (Adele Buffington)
Producer: Scott R. Dunlap

SILVER SPURS

(Republic, August 12, 1943) 65 Minutes
Roy Rogers, Smiley Burnette, John Carradine, Phyllis Brooks, Jerome Cowan, Joyce Compton, Bob Nolan and the Sons of the Pioneers, Hal Taliaferro, Jack Kirk, *Kermit Maynard*, Dick Wessell, Forrest Taylor, Byron Foulger, Charles Wilson, Pat Brady, Jack O'Shea, Slim Whitaker, Arthur Loft, Eddy Waller, Tom London, Bud Osborne, Fred Burns, Henry Wills, "Trigger"
Director: Joseph Kane
Screenplay: John K. Butler, J. Benton Cheney
Associate Producer: Harry Grey

BLAZING FRONTIER

(PRC, September 4, 1943) 59 Minutes
(Billy the Kid Series)
Buster Crabbe, Al St. John, Marjorie Manners, Milt Kibbee, I. Stanford Jolley, *Kermit Maynard*, Frank Hagney, George Chesebro, Frank Ellis, Hank Bell, Jimmy Aubrey
Director: Sam Newfield
Screenplay: Patricia Harper
Producer: Sigmund Neufeld

BEYOND THE LAST FRONTIER

(Republic, September 18, 1943) 57 Minutes
(John Paul Revere Series)
Eddie Dew, Smiley Burnette, Lorraine Miller, Bob Mitchum, Harry Woods, *Kermit Maynard,* Ernie Adams, Richard Cramer, Charles Miller, Jack Kirk, Wheaton Chambers, Jack Rockwell, Cactus Mack, Al Taylor, Art Dillard, Frank O'Connor, Tom Steele, Henry Wills, Curley Dresden
Director: Howard Bretherton
Screenplay: John K. Butler, Morton Grant
Associate Producer: Louis Gray

RAIDERS OF RED GAP

(PRC, September 30, 1943)
(Lone Rider Series)
Bob Livingston, Al St. John, Myrna Dell, Ed Cassidy, Charles King, Slim Whitaker, *Kermit Maynard,* Roy Brent, Frank Ellis, George Chesebro, Bud Osborne, Jimmy Aubrey, Merrill McCormack, George Morrell, Wally West, Reed Howes
Director: Sam Newfield
Screenplay: Joe O'Donnell
Producer: Sigmund Neufeld

DEVIL RIDERS

(PRC, November 5, 1943)
(Billy Carson Series)
Buster Crabbe, Al St. John, Patty McCarthy, *Kermit Maynard,* Charles Merton, Frank LaRue, Jack Ingram, George Chesebro, Ed Cassidy, Al Ferguson, Frank Ellis, Bert Dillard, Bud Osborne, Artie Ortego, Herman Hack, Roy Bucko, Buck Bucko
Director: Sam Newfield
Screenplay: Joe O'Donnell
Producer: Sigmund Neufeld

TEXAS KID (THE)

(Monogram, November 26, 1943) 59 Minutes
Johnny Mack Brown, Raymond Hatton, Shirley Patterson, Marshall Reed, *Kermit Maynard,* Edmund Cobb, Robert Fiske, Stanley Price, Lynton Brent, Bud Osborne, John Judd, Charles King, Cyrus Ring, George J. Lewis
Director: Lambert Hillyer
Story: Lynton Brent
Screenplay: Jess Bowers (Adele Buffington)
Producer: Scott R. Dunlap

Kermit Maynard and Guy Wilkerson fight for the gun in **Gunsmoke Mesa** (PRC, 1944).

GUNSMOKE MESA

(PRC, January 3, 1944) 59 Minutes
(Texas Rangers Series)
Dave O'Brien, Jim Newill, Patti McCarty, Guy Wilkerson, Jack Ingram, *Kermit Maynard,* Robert Barron, Dick Alexander, Michael Vallon, Roy Brent, Jack Rockwell
Director: Harry Fraser
Screenplay: Elmer Clifton
Producer: Arthur Alexander

RAIDERS OF THE BORDER

(Monogram, January 31, 1944) 58 Minutes
Johnny Mack Brown, Raymond Hatton, Ellen Hall, Craig Wood, Stanley Price, Ray Bennett, Edmund Cobb, Lynton Brent, Dick Alexander, *Kermit Maynard,* Ernie Adams
Director: John P. McCarthy
Story: Johnston McCulley
Screenplay: Jess Bowers (Adele Huffington)
Producer: Scott R. Dunlap

FRONTIER OUTLAWS

(PRC, March 4, 1944) 56 Minutes
(Billy Carson Series)
Buster Crabbe, Al St. John, Frances Gladwin, Marin Sais, Charles King, Jack Ingram, *Kermit Maynard,* Edward Cassidy, Emmett Lynn, Budd Buster, Frank Ellis
Director: Sam Newfield
Screenplay: Joe O'Donnell
Producer: Sigmund Neufeld

THUNDERING GUN SLINGERS

(PRC, March 25, 1944) 59 Minutes
(Billy Carson Series)
Buster Crabbe, Al St. John, Frances Gladwin, Karl Hackett, Charles King, *Kermit Maynard,* Jack Ingram, Budd Buster, George Cheseboro
Director: Sam Newfield
Screenplay: Fred Myton
Producer: Sigmund Neufeld

THE WHISTLER

(Columbia, March 30, 1944) 59 Minutes
Richard Dix, Gloria Stuart, J. Carrol Naish, Alan Dinehart, Don Costello, Joan Woodbury, Cy Kendall, Otto Forrest, Bryon Foulger, Trevor Bardette, *Kermit Maynard*
Director: William Castle
Screenplay: Eric Taylor
Story: J. Donald Wilson

BUFFALO BILL

(20th Century-Fox, April 1, 1944) 90 Minutes
Joel McCrea, Maureen O'Hara, Linda Darnell, Thomas Mitchell, Edgar Buchanan, Anthony Quinn, Moroni Olson, Frank Fenton, Matt Briggs, George Lessey, Frank Orth, George Chandler, Chief Thunder Cloud, Sidney Blackmer, Edwin Stanley, Nick Thompson, Chief Many Treaties, John Dilson, Evelyn Beresford, William Haade, Merrill Rodin, Talzumbia Dupea, *Kermit Maynard*
Director: William A. Wellman
Story: Frank Winch
Screenplay: Aeneas MacKenzie, Delmente Ripley, Cecile Kramer
Producer: Harry Sherman

THE PINTO BANDIT

(PRC, April 27, 1944) 56 Minutes
(Texas Rangers Series)
Dave O'Brien, Jim Newill, Guy Wilkerson, Mady Lawrence, James Martin, Jack Ingram, Edward Cassidy, Budd Buster, Karl Hackett, Robert Kortman, Charles King, Jimmy Aubrey, *Kermit Maynard*
Director: Elmer Clifton
Screenplay: Elmer Clifton
Producer: Alfred Stern

THE DRIFTER

(PRC, June 14, 1944) 62 Minutes
(Billy Carson Series)
Buster Crabbe, Al St. John, Carol Parker, *Kermit Maynard,* Jack Ingram, Roy Brent, George Chesebro, Ray Bennett, Jimmy Aubrey, Slim Whitaker, Wally West
Director: Sam Newfield
Screenplay: Patricia Harper
Producer: Sigmund Neufeld

BRAND OF THE DEVIL

(PRC, July 30, 1944) 57 Minutes
(Texas Rangers Series)
Dave O'Brien, Jim Newill, Guy Wilkerson, Ellen Hall, I. Stanford Jolley, Charles King, Reed Howes, *Kermit Maynard,* Budd Buster, Karl Hackett, Ed Cassidy
Director: Harry Fraser
Screenplay: Elmer Clifton
Producer: Arthur Alexander

WILD HORSE PHANTOM

(PRC, October 28, 1944) 56 Minutes
(Billy Carson Series)
Buster Crabbe, Al St. John, Elaine Morey, *Kermit Maynard,* Budd Buster, Hal Price, Robert Meredith, Frank Ellis, Frank McCarroll, Bob Carson, John Elliott
Director: Sam Newfield
Screenplay: George Milton
Producer: Sigmund Neufeld

OATH OF VENGEANCE

(PRC, December 9, 1944) 57 Minutes
(Billy Carson Series)
Buster Crabbe, Al St. John, Mady Lawrence, Jack Ingram, Charles King, Marin Sais, Karl Hackett, *Kermit Maynard*, Hal Price, Frank Ellis, Budd Buster, Jimmy Aubrey
Director: Sam Newfield
Screenplay: Fred Myton
Producer: Sigmund Neufeld

THE DESERT HAWK

(Columbia, 1944) 15 Chapters
Gilbert Roland, Mona Maris, Ben Welden, Kenneth MacDonald, Frank Lackteen, I. Stanford Jolley, Charles Middleton, Egan Brecher, *Kermit Maynard*
Director: B. Reeves Eason
Screenplay: Sherman Lowe, Leslie Swabacker, Jack Stanley, Leighton Brill
Chapter Titles: (1) The Twin Brothers (2) The Evil Eye (3) The Mask of the Scimitar (4) A Caliph's Treachery (5) The Secret of the Palace (6) The Feast of the Beggars (7) Double Jeopardy (8) The Slave Traders (9) The Underground River (10) The Fateful Wheel (11) The Mystery of the Mosque (12) The Hand of Vengeance (13) The Sword of Fate (14) The Wizard's Story (15) The Triumph of Kasim

MARKED FOR MURDER

(PRC, February 8, 1945) 58 Minutes
(Texas Rangers Series)
Tex Ritter, Dave O'Brien, Guy Wilkerson, Marilyn McConnell, Hanry Hall, Edward Cassidy, Charles King, Jack Ingram, Bob Kortman, Wen Wright, The Milo Twins, *Kermit Maynard*
Director/Screenplay: Elmer Clifton
Producer: Arthur Alexander

CHINA SKY

(RKO, April 21, 1945) 78 Minutes
Randolph Scott, Ruth Warrick, Ellen Drew, Anthony Quinn, Carol Thurston, Richard Loo, "Ducky" Looie, Philip Ahn, Benson Fong, H. T. Tsiang, Chin Kuang Chow, James Leong, Jimmy Luno, Gerald Lee, Chung Owen Song, Bob Chinn, Lane Tom, Jr., Harold Fong, Jung Lim, Moy Ming, Audrey Chow, *Kermit Maynard*, Weaver Levy, Charles Lung, Albert Low
Director: Ray Enright
Screenplay: Brenda Weisberg
Story: Pearl S. Buck

ENEMY OF THE LAW

(PRC, May 7, 1945) 59 Minutes
(Texas Rangers Series)
Tex Ritter, Dave O'Brien, Guy Wilkerson, Kay Hughes, Jack Ingram, Charles King, Frank Ellis, *Kermit Maynard*, Henry Hall, Karl Hackett, Ed Cassidy, Ben Corbett
Director/Screenplay: Harry Fraser
Producer: Arthur Alexander

GANGSTER'S DEN

(PRC, June 14, 1945) 55 Minutes
(Billy Carson Series)
Buster Crabbe, Al St. John, Sidney Logan, Charles King, Emmett Lynn, *Kermit Maynard*, Edward Cassidy, I. Stanford Jolley, George Chesebro, Karl Hackett, Michael Owen, Bob Cason, Wally West
Director: Sam Newfield
Screenplay: George Plympton
Producer: Sigmund Neufeld

STAGECOACH OUTLAWS

(PRC, August 17, 1945) 55 Minutes
(Billy Carson Series)
Buster Crabbe, Al St. John, Frances Gladwin, *Kermit Maynard*, Ed Cassidy, I. Stanford Jolley, Bob Cason, Bob Kortman, Steve Clark, George Chesebro, Hank Bell
Director: Sam Newfield
Screenplay: Fred Myton
Producer: Sigmund Neufeld

FLAMING BULLETS

(PRC, October 15, 1945) 55 Minutes
(Texas Rangers Series)
Tex Ritter, Dave O'Brien, Guy Wilkerson, Patricia Knox, Charles King, Bud Osborne, I. Stanford Jolley, Bob Duncan, *Kermit Maynard*, Dick Alexander, Dan White
Director/Screenplay: Harry Fraser
Producer: Arthur Alexander

FIGHTING BILL CARSON

(PRC, October 31, 1945) 51 Minutes
(Billy Carson Series)
Buster Crabbe, Al St. John, Kay Hughes, I. Stanford Jolley, *Kermit Maynard*, John L. "Bob" Carson, Budd Buster, Bud Osborne, Charles King
Director: Sam Newfield
Story: Louise Rousseau
Screenplay: Louise Rousseau
Producer: Sigmund Neufeld

PRAIRIE RUSTLERS

(PRC, November 7, 1945) 56 Minutes

(Billy Carson Series)

Buster Crabbe, Al St. John, Evelyn Finley, Karl Hackett, Bud Osborne, Marin Sais, I. Stanford Jolley, *Kermit Maynard*, Herman Hack, George Morrell, Tex Cooper, Dorothy Vernon

Director: Sam Newfield
Story/Screenplay: Fred Myton
Producer: Sigmund Neufeld

THEY WERE EXPENDABLE

(MGM, December 30, 1945) 135 Minutes

Robert Montgomery, John Wayne, Donna Reed, Jack Holt, Ward Bond, Marshall Thompson, Paul Langton, Leon Ames, Arthur Walsh, Donald Curtis, Cameron Mitchell, Jeff York, Murray Alper, Harry Tenbrook, Jack Pennick, Alex Havier, Charles Trowbridge, Robert Barrat, Bruce Kellogg, Tim Murdock, Louis Jean Heydt, Russell Simpson, Pedro de Cordoba, Tom Tyler, Vernon Steele, Stubby Kruger, Trina Law, Sammy Stein, Blake Edwards, Michael Kirby, Robert Emmett O'Connor, Philip Ahn, Pacita Tod-Tod, William B. Davidson, Mag Ong, Bill Wilkerson, John Carlyle, Betty Blythe, *Kermit Maynard*

Producer/Director: John Ford
Associate Producer: Cliff Reid
Story: William L. White
Screenplay: Lieutenant Commander Frank Weed

JUNGLE RAIDERS

(Columbia, 1945) 15 Chapters

Kane Richmond, Eddie Quillan, Veda Ann Borg, Carol Hughes, Janet Shaw, John Elliott, Jack Ingram, Charles King, Ernie Adams, I. Stanford Jolley, *Kermit Maynard*, Budd Buster, George Turner, Nick Thompson, Jim Aubrey

Director: Lesley Selander
Screenplay: Andy Lamb and George H. Plympton
Producer: Sam Katzman
Chapter Titles: (1) Mystery of the Lost Tribe (2) Primitive Sacrifice (3) Prisoners of Fate (4) Valley of Destruction (5) Perilous Mission (6) Into the Valley of Fire (7) Devil's Brew (8) The Dagger Pit (9) Jungle Jeopardy (10) Prisoners of Peril (11) Vengeance of Zora (12) The Key to Arzec (13) Witch Doctor's Treachery (14) The Judgement of Rana (15) The Jewels of Arzec

AMBUSH TRAIL

(PRC, February 17, 1946) 60 Minutes

Bob Steele, Syd Saylor, Lorraine Miller, I. Stanford Jolley, Charles King, Bob Cason, Budd Buster, *Kermit Maynard*, Frank Ellis, Edward Cassidy, Roy Brent

Director: Harry Fraser
Screenplay: Elmer Clifton
Producer: Arthur Alexander

BADMAN'S TERRITORY

(RKO, April 22, 1946) 98 Minutes

Randolph Scott, Ann Richards, George Hayes, Lawrence Tierney, Tom Tyler, John Halloran, Phil Warren, Steve Brodie, William Moss, James Warren, Isabel Jewell, Morgan Conway, Nestor Pavia, Chief Thunder Cloud, Ray Collins, Virginia Sale, Andrew Tombes, Harry Holman, Richard Hale, Emory Parnell, Ethan Laidlaw, *Kermit Maynard*, Bud Osborne, Chuck Hamilton, Buddy Roosevelt

Director: Tim Whelan
Screenplay: Jack Natteford, Luci Ward
Producer: Nat Holt

GALLOPING THUNDER

(Columbia, April 25, 1946) 54 Minutes

(Durango Kid Series)

Charles Starrett, Smiley Burnette, Adelle Roberts, Richard Bailey, *Kermit Maynard*, Edmund Cobb, Ray Bennett, Curt Barrett, John Merton, Nolan Leary, Budd Buster, Forrest Taylor, Merle Travis and his Bronco Busters

Director: Ray Nazarro
Screenplay: Ed Earl Repp
Producer: Colbert Clark

UNDER ARIZONA SKIES

(Monogram, April 27, 1946) 59 Minutes

Johnny Mack Brown, Raymond Hatton, Reno Blair (Browne), Riley Hill, Tris Coffin, Reed Howes, Ted Adams, Ray Bennett, Frank LaRue, Steve Clark, Jack Rockwell, Bud Geary, Ted Mapes, *Kermit Maynard*, Ray Jones, Smith Ballew and the Sons of the Sage

Director: Lambert Hillyer
Screenplay: J. Benton Cheney
Producer: Scott R. Dunlap

TERRORS ON HORSEBACK

(PRC, May 1, 1946) 55 Minutes

(Billy Carson Series)

Buster Crabbe, Al St. John, Patti McCarty, I. Stanford Jolley, *Kermit Maynard*, Henry Hall, Karl Hackett, Marin Sais, Budd Buster, Steve Darrell, Steve Clark, Bud Osborne, Al Ferguson, George Chesebro, Frank Ellis, Jack Kirk, Lane Bradford

Director: Sam Newfield
Screenplay: George Milton
Producer: Sigmund Neufeld

PRAIRIE BADMAN

(PRC, July 17, 1946) 55 Minutes

(Billy Carson Series)

Buster Crabbe, Al St. John, Patricia Knox, Charles King, Edward Cassidy, *Kermit Maynard,* John I. Cason, Steve Clark, Frank Ellis, Budd Buster

Director: Sam Newfield
Screenplay: Fred Myton
Producer: Sigmund Neufeld

RUSTLER'S ROUNDUP

(Universal, August 9, 1946) 57 Minutes
Kirby Grant, Fuzzy Knight, Jane Adams, Earle Hodgins, Charles Miller, Mauritz Hugo, Eddy Waller, Roy Brent, Frank Marlo, Edmund Cobb, Ethan Laidlaw, Steve Clark, Hank Bell, Bud Osborne, Rex Lease, Budd Buster, George Morrell, Artie Ortego, *Kermit Maynard*
Director: Wallace Fox
Story: Sherman Lowe, Victor McLeod
Screenplay: Jack Natteford
Producer: Wallace Fox

'NEATH CANADIAN SKIES

(Screen Guild/Golden Gate, October 15, 1946) 40 Minutes
Russell Hayden, Inez Cooper, Douglas Fowley, Cliff Nazarro, I. Stanford Jolley, *Kermit Maynard*, Jack Mulhall, Dick Alexander, Pat Hurst, Gil Patrick, Boyd Stockman, Jimmie Martin
Director: B. Reeves Eason
Story: James Oliver Curwood
Screenplay: Arthur V. Jones
Producer: William B. David

TUMBLEWEED TRAIL

(PRC, October 28, 1946) 57 Minutes
Eddie Dean, Roscoe Ates, Shirley Patterson, Johnny McGovern, Bob Duncan, Ted Adams, *Kermit Maynard*, William Fawcett, Carl Mathews, Matty Roubert, Lee Roberts, Frank Ellis, The Sunshine Boys (M. H. Richman, J. O. Smith, A. L. Smith, Edward F. Wallace), "Flash"
Director/Producer: Robert Emmett Tansey
Screenplay: Frances Kavanaugh

STARS OVER TEXAS

(PRC, November 18, 1946) 57 Minutes
Eddie Dean, Roscoe Ates, Shirley Patterson, Lee Bennett, Lee Roberts, *Kermit Maynard*, Jack O'Shea, Hal Smith, Matty Roubert, Carl Mathews, William Fawcett, The Sunshine Boys, "Flash"
Director: Robert Emmett Tansey
Screenplay: Frances Kavanaugh

RENEGADE GIRL

(Affiliated/Screen Guild, December 25, 1946) 65 Minutes
Alan Curtis, Ann Savage, Edward Brophy, Russell Wade, Jack Holt, Ray Corrigan, John King, Chief Thunder Cloud, Edmund Cobb, Claudia Drake, Dick Curtis, Nick Thompson, James Martin, Harry Cording, *Kermit Maynard*
Director/Producer: William Berke
Screenplay: Edwin K. Westrate

DUEL IN THE SUN

(Selznick, April 1947) 134 Minutes
(Technicolor)
Jennifer Jones, Joseph Cotten, Gregory Peck, Lionel Barrymore, Herbert Marshall, Lillian Gish, Walter Huston, Charles Bickford, Harry Carey, Tilly Losch, Joan Tetzel, Sidney Blackmer, Francis McDonald, Victor Kilian, Griff Barnett, Butterfly McQueen, Frank Cordell, Scott McKay, Dan White, Otto Kruger, Steve Dunhill, Lane Chandler, Lloyd Shaw, Thomas Dillon, Robert McKenzie, Charles Kingle, Si Jenks, *Kermit Maynard,* Hank Worden, Hal Taliaferro, Guy Wilkerson, Rose Plummer, Johnny Bond, Hank Bell
Director: King Vidor
Story: Niven Busch
Screenplay: Oliver H. P. Garrett
Producer: David O. Selznick

THE VIGILANTE

(Columbia, May 22, 1947) 15 Chapters
Ralph Byrd, Ramsay Ames, Lyle Talbot, George Offerman, Jr., Robert Barron, Frank Marlo, Hugh Prosser, Jack Ingram, Eddie Parker, George Chesebro, Bill Brauer, Frank Ellis, Edmund Cobb, Terry Frost, Ted Adams, *Kermit Maynard,* Al Ferguson
Director: Wallace Fox
Story: Based on "The Vigilante" feature in Action Comics
Screenplay: George Plympton, Lewis Clay, Arthur Hoerl
Producer: Sam Katzman
Chapter Titles: (1) The Vigilante Rides Again (2) Mystery of the White Horses (3) Double Peril (4) Desperate Flight (5) In the Gorilla's Cage (6) Battling the Unknown (7) Midnight Rendevous (8) Blasted to Eternity (9) The Fatal Flood (10) Danger Ahead (11) X-1 Closes In (12) Death Rides the Rails (13) The Trap that Failed (14) Closing In (15) The Secret of the Skyroom

THE LAW COMES TO GUNSIGHT

(Monogram, May 24, 1947) 56 Minutes
Johnny Mack Brown, Raymond Hatton, Reno Blair (Browne), Lanny Rees, Zon Murray, Frank LaRue, Ernie Adams, *Kermit Maynard,* Ted Adams, Gary Garrett
Director: Lambert Hillyer
Screenplay: J. Benton Cheney
Producer: Barney Sarecky

ALONG THE OREGON TRAIL

(Republic, August 30, 1947) 64 Minutes
(TruColor)
Monte Hale, Adrian Booth, Max Terhune, Clayton Moore, Roy Barcroft, Will Wright, Wade Crosby, LeRoy Mason, Tom London, Forrest Taylor, *Kermit Maynard,* Foy Willing and the Riders of the Purple Sage
Director: R. G. Springsteen
Screenplay: Earle Snell
Associate Producer: Melville Tucker

RIDIN' DOWN THE TRAIL

(Monogram, October 4, 1947) 53 Minutes
Jimmy Wakely, Dub Taylor, Beverly Jons, Douglas Fowley, John James, Doug Aylesworth, Charles King, Matthew B. Slaven (Brad Slaven), *Kermit Maynard,* Harry Carr, Milburn Morante, Ted French, Post Park, Dick Rinehart, Don Weston, Jesse Ashlock, Stanley Ellison, Wayne Burson
Director: Howard Bretherton
Screenplay/Producer: Bennett Cohen

RETURN OF THE LASH

(PRC, October 11, 1947) 55 Minutes
Lash LaRue, Al St. John, Mary Maynard, Brad Slaven, George Chesebro, George DeNormand, Lee Morgan, Lane Bradford, John Gibson, Dee Cooper, Carl Mathews, Bud Osborne, Slim Whitaker, *Kermit Maynard,* Frank Ellis, Bob Woodward
Director: Ray Taylor
Screenplay: Joseph O'Donnell
Producer: Jerry Thomas

BUCKAROO FROM POWDER RIVER

(Columbia, October 14, 1947) 55 Minutes
(Durango Kid Series)
Charles Starrett, Smiley Burnette, Eve Miller, Forrest Taylor, Paul Campbell, Doug Coppin, Phillip Morris, Casey MacGregor, Ted Adams, Ethan Laidlaw, Frank McCarroll, The Cass County Boys, *Kermit Maynard*
Director: Ray Nazarro
Screenplay: Norman S. Hall
Producer: Colbert Clark

THE GALLANT LEGION

(Republic, May 24, 1948) 88 Minutes
William (Bill) Elliott, Adrian Booth, Joseph Schildkraut, Bruce Cabot, Andy Devine, Jack Holt, Grant Withers, Adele Mara, James Brown, Hal Landon, Max Terry, Lester Sharpe, Hal Taliaferro, Russell Hicks, Herbert Rawlinson, Marshall Reed, Steve Drake, Harry Woods, Roy Barcroft, Bud Osborne, Hank Bell, Jack Ingram, George Chesebro, Rex Lease, Noble Johnson, Emmett Vogan, John Hamilton, Trevor Bardette, Gene Stutenroth, Ferris Taylor, Iron Eyes Cody, *Kermit Maynard,* Jack Kirk, Merrill McCormack, Augie Gomez, Cactus Mack, Fred Kohler, Glenn Strange, Tex Terry, Joseph Crehan, Peter Perkins, Jack Perrin
Director/Associate Producer: Joseph Kane
Story: John K. Butler, Gerald Geraghty
Screenplay: Gerald Adams

NORTHWEST STAMPEDE

(Eagle Lion, July 28, 1948) 79 Minutes
(CineColor)
James Craig, Joan Leslie, Jack Oakie, Chill Wills, Victor Killian, Stanley Andrews, Ray Bennett, Lane Chandler, Harry Shannon, *Kermit Maynard*
Director: Albert S. Rogell
Story: "Wild Horse Roundup" - *Saturday Evening Post* article by Jean Muir
Screenplay: Art Arthur, Lillian Hayward
Producer: Albert S. Rogell

A SOUTHERN YANKEE

(MGM, September 24, 1948) 90 Minutes
Red Skelton, Brian Donlevy, Arlene Dahl, George Coulouris, Lloyd Gough, John Ireland, Charles Kingle, Joyce Compton, Reed Hadley, Arthur Space, Richard Simmons, Cliff Clark, Ian McDonald, Dick Wessel, Stanley Andrews, William Tannen, Paul Harvey, Henry Hall, Harry Cording, Ralph Sanford, Paul Newlan, Brad King, James Harrison, Bob Wilke, Gene Roth, *Kermit Maynard,* Weldon Heyburn, Sam Flint, Tom Quinn, John Hart
Director: Edward Sedgwick
Screenplay: Norman Panama, Melvin Frank
Producer: Paul Jones

FRONTIER REVENGE

(Western Adventure/Screen Guild, December 17, 1948)
55 Minutes
Lash LaRue, Al St. John, Jim Bannon, Peggy Stewart, Ray Bennett, Sarah Padden, Jimmie Martin, Jack Hendricks, Lee Morgan, Sandy Sanders, Billy Dix, Cliff Taylor, Steve Raines, Bud Osborne, George Chesebro, Forrest Matthews, *Kermit Maynard*
Story/Screenplay: Ray Taylor
Producer: Ron Ormond

THE PALEFACE
(Paramount, December 24, 1948) 91 Minutes
(Technicolor)
Bob Hope, Jane Russell, Robert Armstrong, Iris Adrian, Robert Watson, Jack Searl, Joseph Vitale, Charles Trowbridge, Clem Bevins, Jeff York, Stanley Andrews, Wade Crosby, Chief Yowlachie, Iron Eyes Cody, Jon Maxwell, Tom Kennedy, Henry Brandon, Francis McDonald, Frank Hagney, Skelton Knaggs, Olin Howlin, George Chandler, Nestor Paiva, Carl Andre, Ted Mapes, *Kermit Maynard*
Director: Norman Z. McLeod
Screenplay: Edmund Hartmann, Frank Tashlin, Jack Rose
Producer: Robert L. Welch

MASSACRE RIVER
(Windsor Prod./Allied Artists, April 1, 1949)
Guy Madison, Rory Calhoun, Johnny Sands, Carole Mathews, Cathy Downs, Minor Watson, *Kermit Maynard,* Steve Brodie, Art Baker, Iron Eyes Cody, Gregg Barton, Emory Parnell, Queenie Smith, James Bush, John Holland, Douglas Fowley
Director: John Rawlins

MIGHTY JOE YOUNG
(Argosy-RKO, May 31, 1949) 94 Minutes
Terry Moore, Ben Johnson, Robert Armstrong, Frank McHugh, Douglas Fowley, Dennis Green, Paul Guilfoyle, Nestor Paiva, Regis Toomey, James Flavin, Flora Lee Michel, *Kermit Maynard,* Jack Pennick, Irene Ryan, Archie Twitchell, Primo Carnera
Director: Ernest B. Schoedsack
Producers: John Ford and Merian C. Cooper

LUST FOR GOLD
(Columbia, June, 1949) 90 Minutes
Ida Lupino, Glenn Ford, Gig Young, William Prince, Edgar Buchanan, Will Geer, Paul Ford, Jay Silverheels, Eddy Waller, Will Wright, Virginia Mullen, Antonio Moreno, Myrna Dell, Tom Tyler, Elspeth Dudgeon, Paul Burns, Hayden Rorke, *Kermit Maynard*
Director: S. Sylvan Simon
Story: "Thunder God's Gold" - Barry Storm
Screenplay: Ted Sherdeman, Richard English
Producer: S. Sylvan Simon

THE MYSTERIOUS DESPERADO
(RKO, September 10, 1949) 61 Minutes
Tim Holt, Richard Martin, Movita, Edward Norris, Frank Wilcox, William Tannen, Robert Livingston, Robert B. Williams, Kenneth MacDonald, Frank Lackteen, *Kermit Maynard*
Director: Lesley Selander
Screenplay: Norman Houston
Producer: Herman Schlom

RIDERS IN THE SKY
(Columbia, November 1, 1949) 70 Minutes
Gene Autry, Gloria Henry, Pat Buttram, Mary Beth Hughes, Robert Livingston, Steve Darnell, Alan Hale, Jr., Tom London, Hank Patterson, Ben Welden, Dennis Moore, Joe Forte, Kenne Duncan, Frank Jacquet, Roy Gordon, Loi Bridge, Boyd Stockman, Vernon Johns, Pat O'Malley, John Parrish, *Kermit Maynard,* Bud Osborne, Lynton Brent, Isobel Withers, Sandy Sanders, Denver Dixon, Robert Walker, "Champion, Jr."
Director: John English
Story: Herbert A. Woodbury
Screenplay: Gerald Geraghty
Producer: Armand Schaefer

RANGE LAND
(Monogram, December 25, 1949) 56 Minutes
Whip Wilson, Andy Clyde, Reno Browne (Blaire), Reed Howes, Kenne Duncan, *Kermit Maynard,* Steve Clark, Stanley Blystone, Leonard Penn, John Cason, William M. Griffith, Michael Dugan, Carol Henry
Director: Lambert Hillyer
Screenplay: Adele Buffington
Producer: Eddie Davis

FIGHTING MAN OF THE PLAINS
(20th C.-Fox, December, 1949) 94 Minutes
(CineColor)
Randolph Scott, Bill Williams, Victor Jory, Jane Nigh, Dale Robertson, Douglas Kennedy, Joan Taylor, Barry Kroeger, Rhys Williams, Barry Kelly, James Todd, James Millican, Burk Symond, Herbert Rawlinson, J. Farrell MacDonald, Harry Cheshire, James Griffith, Tony Hughes, *Kermit Maynard*
Director: Edwin L. Marin
Story/Screenplay: Frank Gruber
Producer: Nat Holt

THE SAVAGE HORDE
(Republic, May 22, 1950) 90 Minutes
William (Bill) Elliott, Adrian Booth, Grant Withers, Barbara Fuller, Noah Beery, Jr., Jim Davis, Douglass Dumbrille, Bob Steele, Will Wright, Roy Barcroft, Earle Hodgins, Stuart Hamblen, Hal Taliaferro, Lloyd Ingraham, Marshall Reed, Crane Whitley, Charles Stevens, James Flavin, Edward Cassidy, *Kermit Maynard,* George Chesebro, Jack O'Shea, Monte Montague, Bud Osborne, Reed Howes
Director: Joseph Kane
Story: Thams Williamson and Gerald Geraghty
Screenplay: Kenneth Gamet
Associate Producer: Joseph Kane

Kermit Maynard has Whip Wilson covered in **Silver Raiders** (Monogram, 1950).

THE CARIBOO TRAIL
(20th C.-Fox, August 1, 1950) 81 Minutes
(CineColor)
Randolph Scott, George Hayes, Bill Williams, Karin
Booth, Victory Jory, Douglas Kennedy, Jim Davis, Dale
Robertson, Mary Stuart, James Griffith, Lee Tung Foo,
Tony Hughes, Mary Kent, Ray Hyke, Kansas
Moehring, Dorothy Adams, Jerry Root, Cliff Clark,
Fred Libby, Tom Montore, Michael Barret, *Kermit
Maynard,* Smith Ballew
Director: Edwin L. Marin
Story: John Rhodes Sturdy
Screenplay: Frank Gruber
Producer: Nat Holt

SILVER RAIDERS
(Monogram, August 20, 1950) 55 Minutes
Whip Wilson, Andy Clyde, Virginia Herrick, Leonard
Penn, Patricia Rios, Dennis Moore, *Kermit Maynard,*
Reed Howes, Riley Hill, Marshall Reed, George
DeNormand
Director: Wallace Fox
Screenplay: Dan Ullman
Producer: Vincent M. Fennelly

DEVIL'S DOORWAY
(MGM, September 15, 1950) 84 Minutes
Robert Taylor, Louis Calhern, Paula Raymond, Mar-
shall Thompson, James Mitchell, Edgar Buchanan, Rhys
Williams, Spring Byington, James Millican, Bruce
Cowling, Fritz Lieber, Chief Big Tree, *Kermit Maynard*
Director: Anthony Mann
Story/Screenplay: Guy Trosper
Producer: Nicholas Nayfack

LAW OF THE PANHANDLE
(Monogram, September 17, 1950) 55 Minutes
Johnny Mack Brown, Jane Adams, Riley Hill, Marshall Reed, Myron Healey, Ted Adams, Lee Roberts, *Kermit Maynard,* Carol Henry, Milburn Morante, Bob Duncan, Boyd Stockman, George DeNormand, Ted Palmer, Ray Jones
Director: Lewis Collins
Screenplay: Joseph Poland
Producer: Jerry Thomas

TRAIL OF ROBIN HOOD
(Republic, December 15, 1950) 67 Minutes
(TruColor)
Roy Rogers, Penny Edwards, Gordon Jones, Jack Holt, Emory Parnel, Clifton Young, James Magill, Carol Nugent, George Chesebro, Edward Cassidy, Foy Willing and The Riders of the Purple Sage, "Trigger," and Guest Stars: Tom Tyler, *Kermit Maynard,* Ray Corrigan, Tom Keene, Monte Hale, Rex Allen, Allan Lane, and William Farnum
Director: William Witney
Screenplay: Gerald Geraghty
Associate Producer: Eddy White

SHORT GRASS
(Allied Artists, December 24, 1950) 82 Minutes
Rod Cameron, Cathy Downs, Johnny Mack Brown, Raymond Walburn, Alan Hale, Jr., Morris Ankrum, Jonathan Hale, Harry Woods, Marlo Dwyer, Riley Hill, Jeff York, Stanley Andrews, Jack Ingram, Myron Healey, Tris Coffin, Rory Mallison, Felipe Turich, George J. Lewis, Lee Tung Foo, *Kermit Maynard,* Lee Roberts, Frank Ellis
Director: Lesley Selander
Story/Screenplay: Tom W. Blackburn
Producer: Scott R. Dunlap

THREE DESPERATE MEN
(Lippert, January 12, 1951) 71 Minutes
Preston Foster, Jim Davis, Virginia Grey, Ross Latimer, Monte Blue, Sid Melton, Rory Mallison, John Brown, Margaret Seddon, House Peters, Jr., Joel Newfield, Lee Bennett, Steve Belmont, Carol Henry, *Kermit Maynard,* Bert Dillard, Gene Randall, Milton Kibbee, William N. Bailey
Director: Sam Newfield
Story/Screenplay: Orville Hampton
Producer: Sigmund Neufeld

IN OLD AMARILLO
(Republic, May 15, 1951) 67 Minutes
Roy Rogers, Estelita Rodriguez, Penny Edwards, Pinky Lee, Roy Barcroft, Pierre Watkin, Ken Howell, Elizabeth Risdon, William Holmes, *Kermit Maynard,* Alan Bridge, Roy Rogers Riders, "Trigger"
Director: William Witney
Screenplay: Sloan Nibley
Associate Producer: Eddy White

FORT WORTH
(Warners, July 14, 1951) 80 Minutes
(Technicolor)
Randolph Scott, David Brian, Phyllis Thaxter, Helena Carter, Dick Jones, Ray Teal, Lawrence Tolan, Paul Picerni, Emerson Treacy, Bob Steele, Dick Jones, Walter Sande, Chubby Johnson, *Kermit Maynard*
Director: Edwin L. Marin
Story/Screenplay: John Twist
Producer: Anthony Vellier

FORT DODGE STAMPEDE
(Republic, August 24, 1951) 60 Minutes
Allan Lane, Chubby Johnson, Mary Ellen Kay, Roy Barcroft, Trevor Bardette, Bruce Edwards, Wesley Hudman, William Forrest, Chuck Roberson, Rory Mallison, Jack Ingram, Frank O'Connor, *Kermit Maynard,* "Black Jack"
Director/Associate Producer: Harry Keller
Screenplay: Richard Wormser

GOLDEN GIRL
(20th C.-Fox, November, 1951) 108 Minutes
(Technicolor)
Mitzi Gaynor, Dale Robertson, Dennis Day, Una Merkel, Raymond Walburn, Gene Sheldon, Carmen D'Antonio, Michael Ross, Harry Carter, Lovyss Bradley, Emory Parnell, Luther Crockett, Harris Brown, *Kermit Maynard,* Robert Nash, Jessie Arnold
Director: Lloyd Bacon
Story: Albert Lewis, Arthur Lewis, Edward Thompson
Screenplay: Walter Bullock, Charles O'Neal, Gladys Lehman

THE BLACK LASH
(Western Adventure, January 2, 1952)
Lash LaRue, Al St. John, Peggy Stewart, *Kermit Maynard,* Ray Bennett, Byron Keith, Jimmie Martin, John (Bob) Cason, Clarke Stevens, Bud Osborne, Roy Butler, Larry Barton
Director/Producer: Ron Ormond
Screenplay: Kathy McKeel

RANCHO NOTORIOUS
(RKO-Fidelity, March 1, 1952) 70 Minutes
(Technicolor)
Marlene Dietrich, Arthur Kennedy, Mel Ferrer, Gloria Henry, William Frawley, Lisa Ferraday, John Raven, Jack Elam, George Reeves, Frank Ferguson, Francis McDonald, Dan Seymour, John Kellogg, Rodd Redwing, Stuart Randall, Roger Anderson, I. Stanford Jolley, Felipe Turich, John Doucette, Jose Dominguez, William Lee, *Kermit Maynard*
Director: Fritz Lang
Story: Sylvia Richards
Screenplay: Daniel Taradash
Producer: Howard Welsh

HELLGATE
(Lippert, September 5, 1952) 87 Minutes
Sterling Hayden, Joan Leslie, Ward Bond, James Arness, Peter Coe, John Pickard, Robert Wilke, Lyle James, Richard Emory, Richard Paxton, William R. Hamel, Marshall Bradford, Sheb Wooley, Rory Mallison, Pat Coleman, Timothy Carey, Kyle Anderson, Rodd Redwing, Stanley Price, *Kermit Maynard*
Director/Screenplay: Charles Marquis Warren
Producer: John C. Champion

THE EDDIE CANTOR STORY
(Warner Bros., January 30, 1953) 118 Minutes
(Technicolor)
Keefe Brasselle, Marilyn Erskine, Aline McMahon, Arthur Franz, Alex Gerry, Greta Granstedt, Gerald Mohr, William Forrest, Jackie Barnett, Richard Monda, Marie Windsor, Douglas Evans, Ann Doran, Hal March, Susan Odin, Owen Pritchard, Will Rogers, Jr., James Flavin, Chick Chandler, Tristram Coffin, Larry Blake, Arthur Space, Mickey Simpson, Bobby Jordan, *Kermit Maynard,* Ida Cantor, Eddie Cantor
Director: Alfred Green
Screenplay: Jerome Weidman, Tod Sherdeman, Sidney Skolsky
Producer: Sidney Skolsky

THE COMMAND
(Warners, February 13, 1953) 88 Minutes
(CinemaScope) (WarnerColor)
Guy Madison, Joan Weldon, James Whitmore, Carl Benton Reid, Harvey Lembeck, Ray Teal, Bob Nichols, Don Sheldon, Gregg Barton, Boyd (Red) Morgan, Zachary Yaconelli, Renata Vanni, Tom Monroe, *Kermit Maynard*
Director: David Butler
Story: "The White Invader" - James Warner Bellah
Screenplay: Russell Hughes, Samuel Fuller
Producer: David Weisbart
THE GREAT SIOUX UPRISING

(Univ-Int., July 17, 1953) 80 Minutes
(Technicolor)
Jeff Chandler, Faith Domergue, Lyle Bettger, Peter Whitney, John War Eagle, Stephen Chase, Stacey Harris, Walter Sande, Clem Fuller, Glenn Strange, Ray Bennett, Charles Arnt, Rosa Rey, Jack Ingram, *Kermit Maynard*
Director: Lloyd Bacon
Screenplay: Melvin Levy, J. Robert Bren, and Gladys Atwater
Producers: Albert J. Cohen, Leonard Goldstein

PACK TRAIN
(Columbia, July 30, 1953) 57 Minutes
(Sepiatone)
Gene Autry, Smiley Burnette, Gail Davis, Kenne Duncan, Sheila Ryan, Tom London, Harry Lauter, Melinda Plowman, B. G. Norman, Louise Lorimer, Frankie Marvin, Norman E. Westcoatt, Tex Terry, Wesley Hudman, *Kermit Maynard,* Frank Ellis, Frank O'Connor, Dick Alexander, Jill Zeller, Herman Hack
Director: George Archainbaud
Screenplay: Norman S. Hall
Producer: Armand Schaefer

THE YELLOW MOUNTAIN
(Univ-Int, December 1, 1954) 78 Minutes
(Technicolor)
Lex Barker, Mala Powers, Howard Duff, William Demarest, John McIntire, Leo Gordon, Hal K. Dawson, Dayton Lummis, *Kermit Maynard*
Director: Jesse Hibbs
Story: Harold Channing Wire
Screenplay: George Zuckerman, Russell Hughes, Robert Blees
Producer: Ross Hunter

WICHITA
(Allied Artists, July 3, 1955) 81 Minutes
(Technicolor) (CinemaScope)
Joel McCrea, Vera Miles, Lloyd Bridges, Wallace Ford, Edgar Buchanan, Peter Graves, Keith Larsen, Carl Benton Reid, John Smith, Walter Coy, Walter Sande, Robert J. Wilke, Rayford Barnes, Jack Elam, Mae Clark, Gene Wesson, *Kermit Maynard,* and the voice of Tex Ritter
Director: Jacques Tourneur
Story/Screenplay: Daniel B. Ullman
Producer: Walter Mirisch

THE LAST COMMAND

(Republic, August 3, 1955) 110 Minutes
(Trucolor)
Sterling Hayden, Anna Maria Alberghetti, Richard Carlson, Arthur Hunnicutt, Ernest Borgnine, J. Carrol Naish, Ben Cooper, John Russell, Virginia Grey, Jim Davis, Edward Franz, Otto Kruger, Russell Simpson, Roy Roberts, Slim Pickens, Hugh Sanders, *Kermit Maynard*
Director: Frank Lloyd
Story: Sy Bartlett
Screenplay: Warren Duff
Associate Producer: Frank Lloyd

APACHE AMBUSH

(Columbia, September 1, 1955) 68 Minutes
Bill Williams, Richard Jaeckel, Alex Montoya, Movita, Adele August, Tex Ritter, Ray "Crash" Corrigan, Ray Teal, Don Harvey, James Griffith, James Flavin, George Chandler, Forrest Lewis, George Keymas, Victor Milan, Harry Lauter, Bill Hale, Robert Foulk, *Kermit Maynard*
Director: Fred F. Sears
Story/Screenplay: David Lang
Producer: Wallace MacDonald

THE OX-BOW INCIDENT

(20th C.-Fox-TV, November, 1955)
Robert Wagner, Cameron Mitchell, Raymond Burr, E. G. Marshall, Wallace Ford, Hope Emerson, Eddie Firestone, James Westerfield, Taylor Holmes, Ray Teal, Walter Sande, Robert Adler, Nacho Galindo, Russell Simpson, Robert Foulk, Willis Bouchey, Elisha Cook, Jr., *Kermit Maynard*

A LAWLESS STREET

(Scott-Brown/Columbia, December 15, 1955)
78 Minutes (Technicolor)
Randolph Scott, Angela Lansbury, Warner Anderson, Jean Parker, Wallace Ford, John Emery, James Bell, Ruth Donnelly, Michael Pate, Don Megowan, Jeanette Nolan, Peter Ortiz, Don Carlos, Frank Hagney, Charles Williams, Frank Ferguson, Harry Tyler, Harry Antrim, Jay Lawrence, Reed Howes, Guy Teague, Hal K. Dawson, Pat Collins, Frank Scannell, Stanley Blystone, Barry Brooks, Edwin Chandler, Jack Perrin, *Kermit Maynard*
Director: Joseph H. Lewis
Story: "Marshal of Medicine Bend" - Brad Ward
Screenplay: Kenneth Gamet
Producers: Harry Joe Brown, Randolph Scott

PERILS OF THE WILDERNESS

(Columbia, January 6, 1956) 15 Chapters
Dennis Moore, Richard Emory, Eve Anderson, Kenneth MacDonald, Rich Vallin, John Elliott, Don Harvey, Terry Frost, Al Ferguson, Bud Osborne, Rex Lease, Pierce Lyden, John Mitchum, Lee Roberts, Stanley Price, Ed Coch, *Kermit Maynard*
Director: Spencer G. Bennet
Screenplay: George H. Plympton
Producer: Sam Katzman
Chapter Titles: (1) The Voice from the Sky (2) The Mystery Plane (3) The Mine of Menace (4) Ambush for a Mountie (5) Laramie's Desperate Chance (6) Trapped in the Flaming Forest (7) Out of the Trap (8) Laramie Rides Alone (9) Menace of the Medicine Man (10) Midnight Marauders (11) The Falls of Fate (12) Rescue from the Rapids (13) Little Bear Pays a Debt (14) The Mystery Plane Flies Again (15) Laramie Gets His Man

THE LONE RANGER

(Wrather/Warners, February 25, 1956) 86 Minutes
(WarnerColor)
Clayton Moore, Jay Silverheels, Lyle Bettger, Bonita Granville, Perry Lopez, Robert Wilke, John Pickard, Beverly Washburn, Michael Ansara, Frank de Kova, Charles Meredith, Mickey Simpson, Zon Murray, Lane Chandler, *Kermit Maynard*
Director: Stuart Heisler
Screenplay: Herb Meadow
Based on: "The Lone Ranger Legend"
Producer: Willis Goldbeck

RED SUNDOWN

(Univ-Int, March 1, 1956) 82 Minutes
(Technicolor)
Rory Calhoun, Martha Hyer, Dean Jagger, Robert Middleton, James Millican, Lita Baron, Grant Williams, Trevor Bardette, David Kasday, Stevie Wootton, Leo Gordon, Steve Darrell, *Kermit Maynard,* John Carpenter, Henry Wills, Alex Sharpe
Director: Jack Arnold
Story: Martin Berkeley
Producer: Albert Zugsmith

BLACKJACK KETCHUM, DESPERADO

(Clover/Columbia, April 1, 1956) 76 Minutes
Howard Duff, Victor Jory, Maggie Mahoney, Angela Stevens, David Orrick, William Tannen, Ken Christy, Martin Garralaga, Robert Roark, Don C. Harvey, Pat O'Malley, Jack Littlefield, Sidney Mason, Ralph Sanford, George Edward Mather, Charles Wagenheim, Wes Hudman, *Kermit Maynard*
Director: Earl Bellamy
Story: Louis L'Amour
Screenplay: Luci Ward, Jack Natteford
Producer: Sam Katzman

GREAT DAY IN THE MORNING

(RKO, May 16, 1956) 92 Minutes
(Technicolor) (SuperScope)
Virginia Mayo, Robert Stack, Ruth Roman, Alex Nicol, Raymond Burr, Leo Gordon, Donald McDonald, Regis Toomey, Peter Whitney, Dan White, *Kermit Maynard,* Carleton Young, George Wallace, Dennis Moore, Ben Corbett, Bill Phipps, Lane Chandler, Paul McGuire, Syd Saylor, Burt Mustin, Lee Ericson
Director: Jacques Tourneur
Story: Robert Hardy Andrews
Screenplay: Lesser Samuels
Producer: Edmund Grainger

STAR IN THE DUST

(Univ-Int, June 1, 1956) 80 Minutes
(Technicolor)
John Agar, Mamie Van Doren, Richard Boone, Leif Erickson, Coleen Gray, James Gleason, Randy Stuart, Terry Gilkyson, *Kermit Maynard*
Director: Charles Haas
Story: Lee Leighton
Screenplay: Oscar Brodney
Producer: Albert Zugsmith

GUNSLINGER

(American Releasing Corp., June 15, 1956) 83 Minutes
(Pathe Color)
John Ireland, Beverly Garland, Allison Hayes, Martin Kingsley, Jonathan Haze, Chris Alcaide, Richard Miller, Bruno De Sota, Margaret Campbell, William Schallert, Aaron Saxon, Chris Miller, *Kermit Maynard*
Director/Producer: Roger Corman
Screenplay: Mark Hanna, Charles B. Griffith

THE RAWHIDE YEARS

(Univ-Int, July 1, 1956) 85 Minutes
(Technicolor)
Tony Curtis, Colleen Miller, Arthur Kennedy, William Demarest, William Gargan, Peter Van Eyck, Minor Watson, Donald Randolph, Chubby Johnson, James Anderson, Bob Wilke, Trevor Bardette, Robert Foulk, Leigh Snowden, Don Beddoe, Jack Perrin, Rex Lease, *Kermit Maynard*
Director: Rudolph Mate
Story: Norman A. Fox
Screenplay: Earl Felton, Robert Presnell, Jr., and D. D. Beauchamp
Producer: Stanley Rubin

THE FASTEST GUN ALIVE

(MGM, July 6, 1956) 92 Minutes
Glenn Ford, Jeanne Crain, Broderick Crawford, Russ Tamblyn, Allyn Joslin, Leif Erickson, John Dehner, Noah Beery, Jr., J. M. Kerrigan, Rhys Williams, Virginia Gregg, Chubby Johnson, John Coucette, William Phillips, Chris Olson, Paul Birch, Florenz Ames, Joseph Sweeney, *Kermit Maynard*
Director: Russell Rouse
Story: "The Last Notch" - Frank D. Gilroy
Screenplay: Frank D. Gilroy and Russell Rouse
Producer: Clarence Greene

REBEL IN TOWN

(Bel-Air/United Artists, July 30, 1956) 78 Minutes
John Payne, Ruth Roman, J. Carrol Naish, Ben Cooper, John Smith, James Griffith, Mary Adams, Bobby Clark, Mimi Gibson, Ben Johnson, Sterling Frank, Joel Ashley, Jack Perrin, *Kermit Maynard*
Director: Alfred Werker
Story/Screenplay: Danny Arnold
Producer: Aubrey Schenck

BLAZING THE OVERLAND TRAIL

(Columbia, August 4, 1956) 15 Chapters
Lee Roberts, Dennis Moore, Norma Brooks, Gregg Barton, Don Harvey, Lee Morgan, Ed Coch, Pierce Lyden, Reed Howes, *Kermit Maynard,* Al Ferguson, Pete Kellett
Director: Spencer Gordon Bennet
Screenplay: George H. Plympton
Producer: Sam Katzman
Chapter Titles: (1) Gun Emperor of the West (2) Riding the Danger Trail (3) The Black Raiders (4) Into the Flames (5) Trapped in a Runaway Wagon (6) Rifles for Redskins (7) Midnight Attack (8) Blast at Gunstock Pass (9) War at the Wagon Camp (10) Buffalo Stampede (11) Into the Fiery Blast (12) Cave-In (13) Bugle Call (14) Blazing Peril (15) Raiders Unmasked

THE FIRST TRAVELING SALESLADY

(RKO, August 15, 1956) 92 Minutes
(Technicolor)
Ginger Rogers, Barry Nelson, Carol Channing, David Brian, James Arness, Clint Eastwood, Robert Simon, Frank Wilcox, Dan White, Harry Cheshire, John Eldredge, Robert Hinkle, Jack Rice, Kate Drain Lawson, Edward Cassidy, Fred Essler, *Kermit Maynard*
Director/Producer: Arthur Lubin
Screenplay: Stephen Longstreet and Devery Freeman

FLESH AND THE SPUR
(American-International, September 25, 1956)
80 Minutes (Pathe Color)
John Agar, Marla English, Touch (Mike) Connors, Raymond Hatton, Maria Monay, Joyce Meadows, Kenne Duncan, Frank Lackteen, Mel Gaines, Michael Harris, Eddie Kafafain, Dick Alexander, *Kermit Maynard,* Bud Osborne, Buddy Roosevelt
Director: Edward L. Cahn
Screenplay: Charles B. Griffith and Mark Hanna
Producer: Alex Gordon

RUNAWAY DAUGHTERS
(American International, October 21, 1956) 91 Minutes
Marla English, Anna Sten, John Litel, Lance Fuller, Adele Jergens, Mary Ellen Kay, Gloria Castillo, Jay Adler, Steven Terrell, Nicky Blair, Frank J. Gorshin, Maureen Cassidy, Reed Howes, Anne O'Neal, Edmund Cobb, Snub Pollard, Jack Perrin, *Kermit Maynard*
Director: Edward L. Cahn
Producer: Alex Gordon
Executive Producer: Samuel Z. Arkoff

FRIENDLY PERSUASION
(United Artists, November 25, 1956) 140 Minutes
(DeLuxe Color)
Gary Cooper, Dorothy McGuire, Marjorie Main, Anthony Perkins, Richard Eyer, Phyllis Love, Robert Middleton, Mark Richman, Walter Catlett, Richard Hale, Joel Fluellen, Theodore Newton, John Smith, Mary Carr, Edna Skinner, Marjorie Durant, Frances Farwell, Russell Simpson, Charles Halton, Everett Glass, *Kermit Maynard*
Director: William Wyler
Story: Jessamyn West
Producers: William Wyler, Robert Wyler

GIANT
(Warner Brothers, November 24, 1956) 201 Minutes
(WarnerColor)
Elizabeth Taylor, Rock Hudson, James Dean, Carroll Baker, Chill Wills, Jane Withers, Mercedes McCambridge, Sal Mineo, Dennis Hopper, Judith Evelyn, Paul Fix, Rod Taylor, Earl Holliman, Robert Nichols, Alexander Scourby, Fran Bennett, Charles Watts, Eliza Cardenas, Carolyn Craig, Monte Hale, Mary Ann Edwards, Sheb Wooley, Victor Millan, Mickey Simpson, Pilar de Rey, Maurice Java, Ray Whitley, Noreen Nash, Tina Menard, Max Terhune, Jack Perrin, *Kermit Maynard*
Director: George Stevens
Story: Edna Ferber
Screenplay: Fred Gudil, Ivan Moffat
Producer: George Stevens

DRANGO
(Earlmar Productions/United Artists, January 2, 1957)
96 Minutes
Jeff Chandler, Joanne Dru, Julie London, Ronald Howard, Donald Crisp, John Lupton, Morris Ankrum, Helen Wallace, Walter Sande, Parley Baer, Amzie Stirkland, Charles Horvath, Barney Phillips, David Stollery, Mimi Gibson, Paul Lukather, Damian O'Flynn, Edith Evanson, Phil Chambers, David Saber, Chuck Webster, Katherine Warren, Chubby Johnson, Milburn Stone, Anthony Jochim, Maura Murphy, *Kermit Maynard*
Directors: Hall Bartlett and Jules Bricken
Screenplay/Producer: Hall Bartlett

THE WINGS OF EAGLES
(MGM, February 22, 1957) 110 Minutes
John Wayne, Dan Dailey, Maureen O'Hara, Ward Bond, Ken Curtis, Edmund Lowe, Kenneth Tobey, James Todd, Barry Kelley, Sig Rumann, Henry O'Neill, Willis Bouchey, Dorothy Jordan, Peter Ortiz, Louis Jean Heydt, Tige Andrews, Dan Borzage, William Tracy, Harlan Warde, Jack Pennick, William Henry, Alberto Morin, Mimi Gibson, Evelyn Rudie, Charles Trowbridge, Mae Marsh, Olive Carey, Chuck Roberson, Fred Graham, William Forrest, Robert Armstrong, Ray Hyke, James Flavin, Dale Van Sickel, *Kermit Maynard,* Harry Strang, Cliff Lyons, Veda Ann Borg
Director: John Ford
Screenplay: Frank Fenton and William Wister Haines
Producer: Charles Schnee

FURY AT SHOWDOWN
(Goldstein Productions/United Artists, April 1, 1957)
75 Minutes
John Derek, John Smith, Carolyn Craig, Nick Adams, Gage Clarke, Robert E. Griffin, Malcolm Atterbury, Rusty Lane, Sidney Smith, Frances Morris, Tyler McDuff, Robert Adler, Norman Leavitt, Ken Christy, Tom McKee, *Kermit Maynard*
Director: Gerd Oswald
Story: Lucas Todd
Screenplay: Jason James
Producer: John Beck

THE OKLAHOMAN
(Allied Artists, May 19, 1957) 81 Minutes
(DeLuxe Color) (CinemaScope)
Joel McCrea, Barbara Hale, Brad Dexter, Gloria Talbott, Michael Pate, Verna Felton, Douglas Dick, Anthony Caruso, Esther Dale, Adam Williams, Ray Teal, Peter Votrian, John Pickard, Mimi Gibson, I. Stanford Jolley, Jody Williams, *Kermit Maynard*
Director: Francis D. Lyon
Story/Screenplay: Daniel B. Ullman
Producer: Walter Mirisch

RUN OF THE ARROW
(RKO, September 1, 1957) 85 Minutes
(Technicolor)
Rod Steiger, Sarita Montiel, Brian Keith, Ralph Meeker, Jay C. Flippen, Colonel Tim McCoy, Frank De Kova, Stuart Randall, Charles Bronson, Olive Carey, H. M. Wynant, Neyle Morrow, Frank Warner, Billy Miller, Chuck Hayward, Chuck Roberson, *Kermit Maynard*
Director/Screenplay/Producer: Samuel Fuller

GUN BATTLE AT MONTEREY
(Allied Artists, October 27, 1957) 67 Minutes
Sterling Hayden, Pamela Duncan, Ted de Corsica, Mary Beth Hughes, Lee Van Cleef, Charles Cane, Pat Comiskey, Byron Foulger, Maruita Hugo, I. Stanford Jolley, Fred Sherman, George Baxter, Michael Vallon, John Dalmer, *Kermit Maynard*
Directors: Carl K. Hittleman, Sidney A. Franklin, Jr.
Screenplay: Jack Leonard, Lawrence Resner
Producer: Carl K. Hittleman

THE DOMINO KID
(Columbia, October, 1957) 73 Minutes
Rory Calhoun, Kristine Miller, Andrew Duggan, Yvette Dugay, Peter Whitney, Eugene Iglesias, Robert Burton, Bart Bradley, James Griffith, Roy Barcroft, Denver Pyle, Ray "Crash" Corrigan, Wes Christenson, Don Orlando, Fred Graham, Regis Parton, Paul E. Burns, Thomas Browne, Tom London, Don Harvey, Dennis Moore, Harry Tyler, Frank Sully, *Kermit Maynard,* Ethan Laidlaw, Snub Pollard
Director: Ray Nazarro
Screenplay: Kenneth Gamet
Producers: Rory Calhoun, Victor Orsatti

LES GIRLS
(MGM, November, 1957) 116 Minutes
Gene Kelly, Mitzi Gaynor, Kay Kendall, Taina Elg, Jacques Bergerac, Leslie Phillips, Henry Daniell, Patrick Macnee, Stephen Vercoe, Philip Tonge, Nestor Paiva, Alberto Morin, Dick Alexander, *Kermit Maynard*
Director: George Cukor
Story: Vera Caspary
Screenplay: John Patrick
Producer: Sol C. Siegel

THE HARD MAN
(Romson/Columbia, December 1, 1957) 80 Minutes
(Technicolor)
Guy Madison, Valerie French, Lorne Greene, Barry Atwater, Robert Burton, Rudy Bond, Trevor Bardette, Renata Vanni, Rickie Sorenson, Frank Richards, Myron Healey, Robert B. Williams, *Kermit Maynard*
Director: George Sherman
Story/Screenplay: Leo Katcher
Producer: Helen Ainsworth

MAN FROM GOD'S COUNTRY
(Allied Artists, February 9, 1958) 70 Minutes
(DeLuxe Color) (CinemaScope)
George Montgomery, Randy Stuart, James Griffith, House Peters, Jr., Susan Cummings, Kim Charney, Frank Wilcox, Greg Barton, Philip Terry, Al Wyatt, *Kermit Maynard*
Director: Paul Landres
Screenplay: George Waggner
Producer: Scott R. Dunlap

COLE YOUNGER, GUNFIGHTER
(Allied Artists, March 30, 1958) 78 Minutes
(DeLuxe Color) (CinemaScope)
Frank Lovejoy, James Best, Abby Dalton, Jan Merlin, Douglas Spencer, Ainslie Pryor, Frank Ferguson, Myron Healey, George Keymas, Dan Sheridan, John Mitchum, *Kermit Maynard*
Director: R. G. Springsteen
Story: Clifton Adams
Screenplay: Daniel Mainwaring
Producer: Ben Schwald

THE SHEEPMAN
(Metro-Goldwyn-Mayer, May 16, 1958) 85 Minutes
(MetroColor) (CinemaScope)
Glenn Ford, Shirley MacLaine, Leslie Neilsen, Mickey Shaughnessy, Edgar Buchanan, Willis Bouchey, Pernell Roberts, Slim Pickens, Buzz Henry, Pedro Gonzales-Gonzales, *Kermit Maynard*
Director: George Marshall
Screenplay: William Bowers, James Edward Grant
Producer: Edmund Grainger

ONCE UPON A HORSE
(Univ-Int., September, 1958) 85 Minutes
(CinemaScope)
Dan Rowan, Dick Martin, Martha Hyer, Leif Erickson, Nita Talbot, James Gleason, John McGiver, David Burns, Dick Ryan, Max Baer, Buddy Baer, Steve Pendleton, Sydney Chatton, Paul Anderson, Guest Stars: Tom Keene, Bob Livingston, *Kermit Maynard,* Bob Steele
Director/Screenplay/Producer: Hal Kanter
Story: Henry Gregor Felsen

GUNMEN FROM LAREDO
(Columbia, March 1, 1959) 67 Minutes
(Columbia Color)
Robert Knapp, Jani Davi, Walter Coy, Paul Birch, Don C. Harvey, Clarence Straight, Jerry Barclay, Ron Hayes, Charles Horvath, Jean Moorehead, X. Brands, Harry Antrim, *Kermit Maynard*
Director: Wallace MacDonald
Screenplay: Clark E. Reynolds
Producer: Wallace MacDonald

WESTBOUND
(Warners, April 25, 1959) 96 Minutes
(Warner Color)
Randolph Scott, Virginia Mayo, Karen Steele, Michael Dante, Andrew Duggan, Michael Pate, Wally Brown, John Day, Walter Barnes, Fred Sherman, Mack Williams, Ed Prentiss, Rory Mallinson, Rudi Dana, Tom Monroe, Jack Perrin, Buddy Roosevelt, *Kermit Maynard,* May Boss, William A. Green, Jack E. Henderson, Felice Richmond, Creighton Hale, Gertrude Keeler, Walter Reed, Jack C. Williams, Gerald Roberts, John Hudkins, Don Happy, Bobby Herron, Fred Stromscoe
Director: Budd Boetticher
Story: Berne Giler and Albert Shelby LeVino
Screenplay: Berne Giler
Producer: Henry Blanke

CAST A LONG SHADOW
(Mirisch/United Artists, July 27, 1959) 82 Minutes
Audie Murphy, Terry Moore, John Dehner, James Best, Rita Flynn, Denver Pyle, Ann Doran, Stach B. Harris, Robert Foulk, Wright King, *Kermit Maynard*
Director: Thomas Carr
Story: Wayne D. Overholser
Screenplay: Martin G. Goldsmith, John McGreevey
Producer: Walter Mirisch

HELL BENT FOR LEATHER
(Univ-Int., February, 1960) 82 Minutes
(Eastman Color) (CinemaScope)
Audie Murphy, Felicia Farr, Stephen McNally, Robert Middleton, Rad Fulton, Jan Merlin, Herbert Rudley, Malcom Atterbury, Joseph Ruskin, Allan Lane, John Qualen, Eddie Little Sky, Steve Gravers, Beau Gentry, Bob Steele, *Kermit Maynard*
Director: George Sherman
Story: Ray Hogan
Screenplay: Christopher Knopf
Producer: Gordon Kay

TOBY TYLER
(Buena Vista, February, 1960) 96 Minutes
Kevin Corcoran, Henry Calvin, Gene Sheldon, Bob Sweeney, Richard Eastham, James Drury, Barbara Beaird, Dennis Joel, Edith Evanson, Tom Fadden, Ollie Wallace, Jesse Kirkpatrick, Guy Wilkerson, Howard Negley, *Kermit Maynard,* William Challee, Wilima Newell, Robert Shayne, Earl Hodgins, Dale Van Sickel
Director: Charles Barton
Screenplay: Bill Walsh, Lillie Hayward
Story: James Otis Kaler
Associate Producer: Bill Walsh

NOOSE FOR A GUNMAN
(United Artists, May, 1960) 69 Minutes
Jim Davis, Lyn Thomas, Ted de Corsica, Walter Sande, Barton MacLane, Harry Carey, Jr., Lane Chandler, John Hart, Leo Gordon, William Tannen, Jan Arvan, Bob Tetrick, William Remick, *Kermit Maynard,* William Challee, Cecil Weston
Director: Edward L. Cahn
Screenplay: Robert B. Gordon
Producer: Robert E. Kent

ONE FOOT IN HELL
(20th C.-Fox, August, 1960) 90 Minutes
(DeLuxe Color) (CinemaScope)
Alan Ladd, Don Murray, Dan O'Herlihy, Dolores Michaels, Barry Cox, Larry Gates, Karl Swenson, John Alexander, Rachel Stephens, Henry Norell, Harry Carter, Ann Morriss, *Kermit Maynard*
Director: James B. Clark
Story/Screenplay: Aaron Spelling
Producer: Sidney Boehm

HIGH TIME
(20th C.-Fox, October, 1960)
Bing Crosby, Fabian Forte, Tuesday Weld, Nicole Maurey, Richard Beymer, Patrick Adiarte, Yvonne Craig, J. Boyd, Gavin McLeod, Kenneth McKenna, Nina Shipman, Paul Schreiber, Angus Duncan, Dick Crockett, Frank Scannell, Douglass Dumbrille, James Lanphier, Ernestine Wade, Harry Carter, Jeffrey Sayre, *Kermit Maynard*
Director: Blake Edwards
Screenplay: Frank and Tom Waldman
Story: Garson Kanin
Producer: Charles Brackett

NORTH TO ALASKA
(20th C.-Fox, November 7, 1960) 122 Minutes
(DeLuxe Color) (CinemaScope)
John Wayne, Stewart Granger, Ernie Kovaks, Fabian, Capucine, Mickey Shaughnessy, Karl Swenson, Jr., Joe Sawyer, Kathleen Freeman, John Qualen, Stanley Adams, Stephen Courtleigh, Douglas Dick, Jerry O'Sullivan, Ollie O'Toole, Tudor Owen, Lilyan Chauvin, Marcel Hillaire, Richard Deacon, James Griffith, Max Hellinger, Richard Collier, Fortune Gordien, Roy Jensen, Charles Seel, Esther Dale, Rayford Barnes, Fred Graham, Alan Carney, Peter Bourne, Tom Dillon, Arlene Harris, Paul Maxey, Oscar Beregi, Johnny Lee, *Kermit Maynard,* Pamela Raymond, Maurice Delamore, Patty Wharton
Director/Producer: Henry Hathaway
Screenplay: John Lee Mahin, Martin Rackin, Claude Binyon
Story: Laszlo Fodor (from an idea by John Kafka)

CIMARRON

(Metro-Goldwyn-Mayer, December 8, 1960)
147 Minutes (MetroColor) (CinemaScope)
Glenn Ford, Maria Schell, Anne Baxter, Arthur O'Connell, Russ Tamblyn, Mercedes McCambridge, Vic Morrow, Robert Keith, Charles McGraw, Henry (Harry) Morgan, David Opatoshu, Aline MacMahon, Lili Darvas, Edgar Buchanan, Mary Wickes, Royal Dano, L. Q. Jones, George Brenlin, Vladimir Sokoloff, Ivan Tissault, John Cason, Dawn Little Sky, Eddie Little Sky, *Kermit Maynard*

Director: Anthony Mann
Story: Edna Ferber
Screenplay: Arnold Schulman
Producer: Edmund Grainger

POCKETFUL OF MIRACLES

(United Artists, December 18, 1961) 136 Minutes
Glenn Ford, Bette Davis, Hope Lange, Arthur O'Connell, Peter Falk, Thomas Mitchell, Edward Everett Horton, Mickey Shaughnessy, David Brian, Sheldon Leonard, Peter Mann, Ann Margret, Barton MacLane, John Litel, Jerome Cowan, Jay Novello, Frank Ferguson, Willis Bouchey, Fritz Feld, Gavin Gordon, Ellen Corby, Benny Rubin, Jack Elam, Mike Mazurki, Hayden Rorke, Doodles Weaver, Paul E. Burns, Angelo S. Rossitto, Edgar Stehli, George E. Stone, William F. Sauls, Tom Fadden, Snub Pollard, Peter Hanson, Harry Wilson, Dick Wessel, Mike Ross, James Griffith, Marc Cavell, Byron K. Foulger, Richard Karlan, Kem Dibbs, Kelly Thordsen, Paul Newlan, Billy Nelson, *Kermit Maynard,* Stuart Holmes, Betty Bronson, Andy Albin

Director/Producer: Frank Capra
Screenplay: Hal Danter and Harry Tugend
Story: Damon Runyon
Associate Producers: Glenn Ford and Joseph Sistrom

TARAS BULBA

(Hecht-Curteigh Prod./United Artists, December 19, 1962) 122 Minutes (Eastman Color) (PanaVision)
Tony Curtis, Yul Brynner, Christine Kaufman, Sam Wanamaker, Brad Dexter, Guy Rolfe, Perry Lopez, George Macready, Ilka Windish, Vladimir Sokoloff, Vladimir Irman, Daniel Ocko, Abraham Sofaer, Mickey Finn, Richard Rust, Ron Weyant, Vitina Marcus, Martine Milner, Chuck Hayward, Syl Lamont, Ellen Davalos, Marvin Goux, Jack Raine, *Kermit Maynard*

Director: J. Lee Thompson
2nd Unit Director: Cliff Lyons
Screenplay: Waldo Salt, Karl Tunberg
Producer: Harold Hecht
Story: Nikolay Vasilyevich Gogol — "Taras Bulba"

Tim McCoy

5 ● TIM McCOY

Dignity in the Saddle

Tim McCoy, whether you realized it or not as a popcorn-munching kid, was different. You really didn't expect, if you will but think back, to see him crawl up on a bucking bronc like Gibson or Mix, engage in fantastic riding stunts such as were performed by Maynard or Jones, or give-and-take in a face-to-face slugfest with a half-dozen villains in every picture. Somehow it wasn't expected of this straight-backed, coldly reserved, glove-wearing protagonist with the distinguishing black suit and wide-brimmed white stetson. Rather, it was expected that in an eyeball-to-eyeball confrontation his icy stare would melt even the most courageous soul, that he would draw his pearl-handled pistols with the speed of greased lightning when the occasion demanded, foil the attempts of all who would despoil and bring dishonor to the range, win the hand of the prima donna if he so pleased, and bring a quality of acting and charm to the screen not usually seen in Westerns of the "B" category. And this he did with gusto. In a starring career that lasted sixteen years McCoy became one of Western filmdom's all-time greats, sharing world acclaim for outstanding contributions to the genre with such other cowboy favorites as Buck Jones, Tom Mix, Gene Autry, and Ken Maynard

Tim was born April 10, 1891, long before the motion picture industry was even a dream. He attended public schools in Michigan and eventually entered St. Ignatius College in Chicago. But he was more enticed by the call of the West than by Shakespeare, law, or science, and so, after being emotionally charged at seeing the Miller Brothers 101 Ranch Wild West Show, he heeded the call of adventure and drifted westward in 1907, winding up in Wyoming. There he quickly endeared

himself to the Indians of the Wind River Country by mastering their sign language and becoming an astute student of all aspects of the Indian culture. Tim worked as a wrangler for various Wyoming cattle outfits and quickly became a proficient cowpoke. Saving his money and living frugally, he was able in a short while to purchase his own ranch, one which grew to exceed 5,000 acres.

McCoy was accepted into Officers Candidate School in World War I and was graduated as a cavalry officer. Later he served in the artillery under famed General Hugh Scott. Following the war Tim was made adjutant general of Wyoming and worked tirelessly to help his Indian friends.

In 1922 Tim left the army to accept a job as technical advisor on **The Covered Wagon,** the super Western being filmed by Jesse L. Lasky for Paramount. Tim was fascinated with the world of make-believe, and he and a troupe of Indians appeared for over a year on the stage in this country and Europe with a prologue act to the film itself. There was a lot of ham in McCoy, but audiences loved it.

Quite taken with show business, Tim, after returning from the European stint, decided to stick around Hollywood awhile. Paramount cast him in Jack Holt's **The Thundering Herd** in 1925. He also served as technical advisor on **The Vanishing American,** a Richard Dix starrer that same year.

Irving Thalberg, production head of MGM, was quite aware of the success of **The Covered Wagon** and of Tim's part in it. He had been impressed with Tim's stage delivery of the prologue to the film and his expertise in Indian customs. Then he saw McCoy in the Holt feature. Realizing that Tim was star material, he signed him to an MGM contract and put him into a series of historical films—some Westerns and some colonial pieces. Cost per film ranged from $125,000 down to $60,000, whereas many "B" Westerns were being produced for from $15,000 to $40,000.

By 1929 sound had shaken the industry, and Westerns, with peculiar outdoor technical problems, were in both a production and box office slump. MGM decided against continuing the McCoy series. Assuming his movie-making days were over, Tim went back to work as an honest-to-goodness rancher. But Universal beckoned before long and Tim was once again enticed away from the real range to ride the "reel" range in a serial called **The Indians Are Coming** ('29), produced in both a silent and a sound version. The serial was the first to gross $1 million and helped to rejuvenate interest in the Western genre. Tim did a second serial for Universal, a non-Western entitled **Heroes of the Flames,** but declined to star in a third. Instead, he signed for a Western series with Columbia.

Tim was fortunate in landing the Columbia contract, for few of the major companies were making Westerns in 1931, and most Western stars, if they were working at all, were plodding away at the independent studios in "cheapie" oaters. He made sixteen Western thrillers between '31 and '33, becoming one of the most popular of Saturday matinee saddle aces. Countering violence with craft and confounding gunmen by superior finesse and bull strength, Tim faithfully upheld the tradition of the Wild West, complete with fast shooters and inveterate gamblers, its chivalry and its villainy. The result was above-par mustang mellers that delighted all cow-loving customers and a sizable number of city slickers too. McCoy could be counted on for more than ample action and thrills during the unreeling of his prairie epics, and audiences could usually cheer the arrival of the hero at the psychological moment.

Columbia starred Tim in a series of non-Westerns in 1933-'34, modeled somewhat after the Jack Holt melodramas for the same studio. The studio would probably have continued using McCoy in such vehicles except that Buck Jones packed his saddlebags and moved over to the Universal pasture, leaving Columbia with a Western backlot and no cowboy star to gallop down its dusty streets. Consequently, Tim was heaved back into the saddle, Columbia's boss Harry Cohn believing that Tim might make a bigger contribution to profits as a Western star than as a meller star. **The Prescott Kid** was the first in a series of eight Westerns made in 1934-'35. David Selman directed most of the films, with Ford Beebe active on the screenplays. All in all, the series was one of the best produced in the mid-'30s.

In mid-1935 Tim signed with Puritan Pictures, an independent, and made ten pictures, receiving his usual $4,000 per picture, just about the same salary he had been paid for the far-superior MGM and Columbia Westerns. Competent actors, loved but nameless to most matinee audiences, added their professional touch to the enjoyment of the series. In general they were enjoyable flicks, and those who can remember those golden years of the movies will, no doubt, fondly recall Tim's chilling glare as he stepped through the swinging doors of a saloon, his fast draw, and the rip-snortin' gun-fight scenes. In his blue shirt, orange neckerchief, and white hat Tim was a sight guaranteed to bring forth shrills, shrieks, and whistles as he rode into action atop his steed "Pal."

Tim always liked the thrill of the circus and wild west show; in between picture assignments he managed to squeeze in three circus tours. He was featured in the concert of the Sells-Floto (1935) Circus and the Ring-ling Brothers and Barnum and Bailey Circus (1936, 1937), scoring a smashing success with the wild west aftershow. Sawdust and spangles were definitely in his blood and a great part of his life would be spent in one-night stands with traveling shows. Starting to work to form his own organization and frame a show in the fall of 1937, his dream reached fruition on April 14, 1938 when Colonel Tim McCoy's Real Wild West and Rough Riders of the World premiered in the International amphitheatre in Springfield, Missouri.

McCoy sank $100,000 into the show and owned 51 per cent of the stock. Although the show was first-class in every respect, it was in trouble from the beginning. Under-capitalization, heavy competition, the Depression, poor advance advertising, and other factors combined to bring down the last great wild west show ever assembled, the death blow coming on May 4, 1938, three weeks after its highly touted opening. Operating expenses alone had been $5,000 a day. Sadly, Tim had learned a lesson already learned by other cinema cowboys: great "giddy-up" stars are not necessarily astute businessmen.

Monogram came to Tim's rescue with an offer to do four pictures. Then Sam Katzman's Victory Pictures starred him in a series of old-fashioned shoot-'em-ups. Tim had a field day impersonating Mexicans, Chinese, Englishmen, and assorted brigands. He was an innate ham, and director Sam Newfield gave him free rein. Old-time comic Ben Corbett served as sidekick throughout the eight-picture series.

Tim did a PRC series in 1940-'41 and then signed with Monogram again to co-star with Buck Jones and Raymond Hatton in the highly successful "Rough Riders" series. Incredibly, this trio of old-time "has-beens" came off well in competition with the singing cowboys then

Roy Barcroft and Harry Woods watch as Buck Jones threatens Tim McCoy in **West of the Law** (Monogram, 1942).

in vogue. With production budgets of around $60,000 per picture the series rejuvenated interest in strictly action Westerns and in "trio oaters." It was refreshing, even to kids who had not known McCoy or Jones in their heydays, to see these non-crooning Western flickers built upon solid scripts, plentiful action, highly competent acting, a rousing musical score, and outstanding photography and stuntwork. They were undoubtedly among the best series Westerns ever produced by Monogram.

McCoy ran unsuccessfully for the U.S. Senate in Wyoming on the Republican ticket in 1942. Upon completion of **West of the Law,** eighth in the series and the last under his contract, Tim applied for and was granted active military status as a lieutenant-colonel, and subsequently rose to the rank of full colonel. He spent most of the war years in the European theatre and accumulated a galaxy of decorations, among them the

Bronze Star, Legion of Honor, and France's Air Medal. In 1945, at the age of 55, Tim retired from the service, a little old to resume active screen cowboyin'. He made personal appearances, sold his Wyoming ranch and moved east with a new wife, a Danish journalist. He made a film entitled **Injun Talk** for the Sinclair Oil Company in the early Fifties and also had a syndicated television show devoted to narratives of the Old West and especially to Indian culture.

During much of the last thirty years of his life Tim traveled with circuses and other shows, among them the Al G. Kelly & Miller Bros. Circus, the Carson-Barnes Circus, and Tommy Scott's Country Caravan and Wild West Show. He only retired at the age of 83. Tim had built a home in Nogales, Arizona, and it is here that he lived out his final years, passing away on January 29, 1978 in the army hospital at Ft. Huachuca, Arizona at the age of 86. Tim had been inducted into the

National Cowboy Hall of Fame two years before his death and his book, *Tim McCoy Remembers the West,* received recognition as the best book of the year in 1978 at the National Cowboy Hall of Fame Awards Banquet in Oklahoma City.

Colonel Tim McCoy was a legend in his own lifetime. He brought to the screen a sophisticated, suave personality and an approach to Westerns that was unique. He was a credit to the genre. Not only was he a great Western actor and a great showman, he was a gentleman—"the real McCoy."

TIM McCOY Filmography

THE COVERED WAGON
(Famous Players Lasky/Paramount, March 16, 1923) 10 Reels
Lois Wilson, J. Warren Kerrigan, Ernest Torrence, Charles Ogle, Ethel Wales, Alan Hale, Tully Marshall, Guy Oliver, John Fox, *Tim McCoy*
Director/Producer: James Cruze
Screenplay: Jack Cunningham
Story: Emerson Hough
Technical Advisor: Colonel Tim McCoy

THE THUNDERING HERD
(Famous Players Lasky/Paramount, March 7, 1925) 7 Reels
Jack Holt, Lois Wilson, Noah Beery, Sr., Raymond Hatton, Charles Ogle, *Tim McCoy,* Fred Kohler, Lillian Leighton, Eulalia Jensen, Stephen Carr, Pat Hardigan, Maxine Elliott, Edward Brady, Robert Perry
Director: William K. Howard
Scenario: Lucien Hubbard
Story: Zane Grey

WAR PAINT
(MGM, October 10, 1926) 6 Reels
Tim McCoy, Pauline Starke, Charles K. French, Karl Dane, Chief Yowlachie
Director: W. S. Van Dyke
Story: Peter B. Kyne
Continuity: Charles Maigne

Pauline Starke and Tim McCoy in **War Paint** (MGM, 1926).

WINNERS OF THE WILDERNESS

(MGM, January 15, 1927) 7 Reels
(Technicolor Sequences)
Tim McCoy, Joan Crawford, Roy D'Arcy, Louise Lorraine, Lionel Belmore, Edward Hearn, Frank Currier, Tom O'Brien, Edward Connelly, Will R. Walling, Chief Big Tree, Jean Arthur
Director: W. S. Van Dyke
Story: John Thomas Neville
Continuity: Josephine Chippo

CALIFORNIA

(MGM, May 23, 1927) 5 Reels
Tim McCoy, Dorothy Sebastian, Sam Appel, Frank Currier, Marc McDermott, Lillian Leighton, Fred Warren, Edwin Terry
Director: W. S. Van Dyke
Continuity: Frank Davis
Story: Peter B. Kyne - "Desert of Odyssey"

THE FRONTIERSMAN

(MGM, June 11, 1927) 5 Reels
Tim McCoy, Claire Windsor, Chief Big Tree, May Foster, Frank S. Hagney, Louise Lorraine, Tom O'Brien, Russell Simpson, Lillian Leighton, John Peters
Director: Reginald H. Barker
Story: Ross B. Wills
Scenario: L. G. Rigby

THE ADVENTURER

(MGM, July 14, 1928) 5 Reels
Tim McCoy, Dorothy Sebastian, Charles Delaney, George Cowl, Gayne Whitman, Michael Visaroff, Alex Melesh, Katherine Block
Director: Viatcheslav Tourjansky
Story: Leon Abrams
Scenario: Jack Cunningham

FOREIGN DEVILS

(MGM, September 3, 1927) 5 Reels
Tim McCoy, Claire Windsor, Cyril Chadwick, Frank Currier, Emily Fitzroy, Frank Chew, Lawson Butt, Sojin
Director: W. S. Van Dyke
Story: Peter B. Kyne
Scenario: Marian Ainslee

SPOILERS OF THE WEST

(MGM, December 10, 1927) 6 Reels
Tim McCoy, Marjorie Daw, William Fairbanks, Chief Big Tree, Charles Thurston
Director: W. S. Van Dyke
Story: John Thomas Neville
Scenario: Madeleine Ruthven

WYOMING

(MGM, March 24, 1928) 5 Reels
Tim McCoy, Dorothy Sebastian, Charles Bell, William Fairbanks, Bert Henderson, Blue Washington, Goes in the Lodge, Chief Big Tree
Director/Story: W. S. Van Dyke
Screenplay: Madeleine Ruthven, Ross R. Wills

THE LAW OF THE RANGE

(MGM, January 21, 1928) 6 Reels
Tim McCoy, Joan Crawford, Rex Lease, Bodil Rosing, Tenen Holtz
Director: William Nigh
Story: Norman Houston
Scenario: Richard Schayer

RIDERS OF THE DARK

(MGM, April 2, 1928) 6 Reels
Tim McCoy, Dorothy Dwan, Rex Lease, Roy D'Arcy, Frank Currier, Bert Roach, Dick Sutherland
Director: Nick Grinde
Story/Continuity: W. S. Van Dyke

BEYOND THE SIERRAS

(MGM, September 15, 1928) 6 Reels
Tim McCoy, Sylvia Beecher, Roy D'Arcy, Polly Moran, J. Gordon Russell, Richard R. Neill
Director: Nick Grinde
Story: John Thomas Neville
Screenplay: Robert Lord

THE BUSHRANGER

(MGM, November 17, 1928) 7 Reels
Tim McCoy, Marion Douglas, Russell Simpson, Arthur Lubin, Richard Neill, Dale Austen, Ed Brady, Frank Baker, Rosemary Cooper
Director: Chet Withey
Story: Madeleine Ruthven
Continuity: George C. Hull

MORGAN'S LAST RAID

(MGM, January 5, 1929) 6 Reels
Tim McCoy, Dorothy Sebastian, Wheeler Oakman, Allan Garcia, Hank Mann, Montague Shaw
Director: Nick Grinde
Story: Madeleine Ruthven, Ross B. Wills
Continuity: Bradley King

THE OVERLAND TELEGRAPH

(MGM, March 2, 1929) 6 Reels
Tim McCoy, Dorothy Janis, Frank Rice, Lawford Davidson, Clarence Geldert
Director: John Waters
Story: Ward Wing
Scenario: George C. Hull

SIOUX BLOOD

(MGM, April 20, 1929) 6 Reels
Tim McCoy, Robert Frazer, Marion Douglas, Clarence Geldert, Chief Big Tree, Sidney Bracy
Director: John Waters
Scenario: George C. Hull
Adaptation: Houston Branch
Story: Harry Sinclair Drago

A NIGHT ON THE RANGE

(MGM or Fox, April, 1929) 10 Minutes
(sources disagree as to releasing company and the film was not copyrighted)
Tim McCoy
Director: Nick Grinde

THE DESERT RIDER

(MGM, May 11, 1929) 6 Reels
Tim McCoy, Raquel Torres, Bert Roach, Harry Woods, Edward Connelly, Jess Cavin
Director: Nick Grinde
Story: Ted Shayne, Milton Bren
Screenplay: Oliver Drake

THE INDIANS ARE COMING

(Universal, October 20, 1930) 12 Chapters
Tim McCoy, Allene Ray, Edmund Cobb, Francis Ford, Wilbur McGough, Bud Osborne, Charles Royal, Don Francis, "Dynamite" (a dog), Lafe McKee, Tex Phelps
Director: Henry MacRae
Story: "The Great West That Was" - William F. Cody
Screenplay: Ford Beebe, George Plympton
Producer: Henry MacRae
Chapter Titles: (1) Pals in Buckskin (2) A Call to Arms (3) A Furnace of Fear (4) The Red Terror (5) The Circle of Death (6) Hate's Harvest (7) Hostages of Fear (8) The Dagger Duel (9) The Blast of Death (10) Redskin's Vengeance (11) Frontiers Aflame (12) The Trail's End

Raquel Torres and Tim McCoy in **The Desert Rider** (MGM, 1929)

Virginia Lee Corbin gets a hug from Tim McCoy in **Shotgun Pass** (Columbia, 1931)

HEROES OF THE FLAMES

(Universal, June, 1931) 12 Chapters
Tim McCoy, William Gould, Grace Cunard, Marion Shockley, Bobby Nelson, Gayne Whitman, Beulah Hutton, Monte Montague, Charles Lemoyne, Joe Bonomo, Bud Osborne, Andy Devine, Buck Moulton, Ed Cobb, Marshall Ruth, Bruce Cabot, Walter Brennan
Director: Robert F. Hill
Continuity: George Morgan, Basil Dickey, George H. Plympton
Chapter Titles: (1) The Red Peril (2) Flaming Hate (3) The Fire Trap (4) Death's Chariot (5) The Avalanche (6) The Jaws of Death (7) Forests of Fire (8) Blank Cartridges (9) The House of Terror (10) The Depths of Doom (11) A Flaming Death (12) The Last Alarm

THE ONE WAY TRAIL

(Columbia, October 15, 1931) 60 Minutes
Tim McCoy, Polly Ann Young, Doris Hill, Al Ferguson, Carrol Nye, Bud Osborne, Slim Whitaker, Jack Ward, Herman Hack
Director: Ray Taylor
Story: Claude Rister
Screenplay: George Plympton

SHOTGUN PASS

(Columbia, November 1, 1931) 58 Minutes
Tim McCoy, Virginia Lee Corbin, Frank Rice, Dick Stewart, Joe Marba, Monty Vandergrift, Ben Corbett, Albert J. Smith, Archie Hicks
Director: J. P. McGowan
Story/Screenplay: Robert Quigley

THE FIGHTING MARSHAL
(November 25, 1931) 58 Minutes
Tim McCoy, Dorothy Gulliver, Matthew Betz, Mary Carr, Pat O'Malley, Edward J. LeSaint, Lafe McKee, W. A. Howell, Dick Dickinson, Bob Perry, Harry Todd, Ethan Laidlaw, Lee Shumway, Blackjack Ward, Blackie Whiteford
Director: D. Ross Lederman
Story/Screenplay: Frank Clark

THE FIGHTING FOOL
(Columbia, January 20, 1932) 58 Minutes
Tim McCoy, Marceline Day, Robert Ellis, Ethel Wales, Dorothy Granger, Bob Kortman, Arthur Rankin, Harry Todd, William V. Mong, Mary Carr, Herman Hack, Ray Henderson, Al Taylor, Dick Dickinson
Director: Lambert Hillyer
Story/Screenplay: Frank Clark

TEXAS CYCLONE
(Columbia, February 4, 1932) 58 Minutes
Tim McCoy, Shirley Grey, Wheeler Oakman, John Wayne, Wallace MacDonald, Harry Cording, Vernon Dent, Walter Brennan, Mary Gordon, James Farley
Director: D. Ross Lederman
Story: William Colt MacDonald
Producer: Randall Faye

THE RIDING TORNADO
(Columbia, May 4, 1932) 64 Minutes
Tim McCoy, Shirley Grey, Wallace MacDonald, Russell Simpson, Art Mix, Montague Love, Wheeler Oakman, Vernon Dent, Lafe McKee, Bud Osborne, Hank Bell, Art Mix, Silver Tip Baker, Tex Palmer, Artie Ortego
Director: D. Ross Lederman
Story: William Colt MacDonald
Screenplay: Burt Kempler

Tim McCoy looks angry as Shirley Grey supports a wounded John Wayne in **Texas Cyclone** (Columbia, 1932)

J. Carrol Naish threatens Tim McCoy in **Silent Men** (Columbia, 1933)

TWO-FISTED LAW

(Columbia, June 8, 1932) 64 Minutes
Tim McCoy, Alice Day, Wheeler Oakman, Tully Marshall, Wallace MacDonald, John Wayne, Walter Brennan, Dick Alexander
Director: D. Ross Lederman
Screenplay: Burt Kempler
Story: William Colt MacDonald

DARING DANGER

(Columbia, July 27, 1932) 57 Minutes
Tim McCoy, Alberta Vaughn, Wallace MacDonald, Robert Ellis, Edward J. LeSaint, Bobby Nelson, Max Davidson, Dick Alexander, Vernon Dent, Murdock MacQuarrie, Edmund Cobb, Charles Brinley, Art Mix
Director: D. Ross Lederman
Story/Screenplay: William Colt MacDonald, Michael Trevelyan

CORNERED

(Columbia, August 5, 1932) 58 Minutes
Tim McCoy, Shirley Grey, Niles Welch, Raymond Hatton, Lloyd Ingraham, Claire McDowell, Charles King, John Eberts, John Elliott, Walter Long, Bob Kortman, Art Mix, Merrill McCormack, Noah Beery, Sr., Artie Ortego, Jim Corey, Edward Peil, Roy Jones, Jack Evans, Blackie Whiteford, Tom London, Edmund Cobb, Jack Kirk
Director: B. Reeves Eason
Story: Ruth Todd
Screenplay: Wallace MacDonald

SCREEN SNAPSHOTS

(Columbia, August, 1932) 1 Reel
Hoot Gibson, Mary Pickford, Clark Gable, *Tim McCoy,* Lina Basquette, William S. Hart, Mary Brian, Will Rogers, Sally Eilers, Lew Cody, Jackie Searl
Producers: Jack Cohn, Louis Lewyn

THE WESTERN CODE
(Columbia, September 16, 1932) 61 Minutes
Tim McCoy, Nora Lane, Mischa Auer, Wheeler Oakman, Gordon DeMain, Mathew Betz, Dwight Frye, Bud Osborne, Emilio Fernandez, Cactus Mack, Chuck Baldra
Director: J. P. McCarthy
Screenplay: Milton Krims
Story: William Colt MacDonald

FIGHTING FOR JUSTICE
(Columbia, October 29, 1932) 61 Minutes
Tim McCoy, Joyce Compton, Hooper Atchley, William Norton Bailey, Walter Brennan, Lafe McKee, Harry Todd, Harry Cording, Robert Frazer, Murdock Mac-Quarrie, William V. Mong, Charles King
Director: Otto Brower
Story: Gladwell Richardson
Screenplay: Robert Quigley

END OF THE TRAIL
(Columbia, December 9, 1932) 59 Minutes
Tim McCoy, Luana Walters, Wheeler Oakman, Wally Albright, Lafe McKee, Wade Boteler, Chief White Eagle
Director: D. Ross Lederman
Story/Screenplay: Stuart Anthony

MAN OF ACTION
(Columbia, January 20, 1933) 57 Minutes
Tim McCoy, Caryl Lincoln, Wheeler Oakman, Walter Brennan, Stanley Blystone, Charles K. French, Julian Rivero
Director: George Melford
Story: William Colt MacDonald
Screenplay: Robert Quigley

Tim McCoy enjoying a good story with friends between takes of **Rusty Rides Alone** (Columbia, 1933)

Ward Bond dislikes the attention Tim McCoy is giving Evalyn Knapp in **A Man's Game** (Columbia, 1934)

SILENT MEN

(Columbia, March 3, 1933) 68 Minutes

Tim McCoy, Florence Britton, Wheeler Oakman, J. Carrol Naish, Walter Brennan, Joe Girard, Mathew Betz, Lloyd Ingraham, Steve Clark, William V. Mong, Syd Saylor

Director: D. Ross Lederman
Story: Walt Coburn
Screenplay: Jack Cunningham, Stuart Anthony, Gerald Geraghty

THE WHIRLWIND

(Columbia, April 14, 1933) 62 Minutes

Tim McCoy, Alice Dahl, Pat O'Malley, J. Carrol Naish, Mathew Betz, Joe Girard, Lloyd Whitcomb, William McCall, Stella Adams, Theodore Lorch, Hank Bell, Mary Gordon, Joe Dominguez

Director: D. Ross Lederman
Screenplay: Stuart Anthony

RUSTY RIDES ALONE

(Columbia, May 26, 1933) 58 Minutes

Tim McCoy, Barbara Weeks, Dorothy Burgess, Wheeler Oakman, Ed Burns, Rockcliffe Fellows, Edmund Cobb, Clarence Geldert, "Silver King"

Director: D. Ross Lederman
Story: Walt Coburn
Screenplay: Robert Quigley

POLICE CAR 17

(Columbia, September 27, 1933) 6 Reels

Tim McCoy, Evalyn Knapp, Wallis Clark, Ward Bond, Harold Huber, Edwin Maxwell, DeWitt Jennings

Director/Story/Screenplay: Lambert Hillyer

HOLD THE PRESS

(Columbia, November 5, 1933) 6 Reels

Tim McCoy, Shirley Grey, Henry Wadsworth, Oscar Apfel, Wheeler Oakman, Samuel S. Hinds

Director: Phil Rosen
Screenplay: Horace McCoy

STRAIGHTAWAY

(Columbia, January 2, 2934) 6 Reels
Tim McCoy, Sue Carol, William Bakewell, Ward Bond, Francis McDonald, Samuel S. Hinds, Arthur Rankin
Director: Otto Brower
Story/Screenplay: Lambert Hillyer

SPEEDWINGS

(Columbia, February 12, 1934) 6 Reels
Tim McCoy, Evalyn Knapp, William Bakewell, Ward Bond, Vincent Sherman, Hooper Atchley, Jack Long
Director: Otto Brower
Story/Screenplay: Horace McCoy

VOICE IN THE NIGHT

(Columbia, March 24, 1934) 5 Reels
Tim McCoy, Billie Seward, Joseph Crehan, Ward Bond, Kane Richmond, Francis McDonald, Guy Usher
Director: Charles Clifford Coleman
Story/Screenplay: Harold Shumate

HELL BENT FOR LOVE

(Columbia, May 10, 1934) 6 Reels
Tim McCoy, Lillian Bond, Bradley Page, Vincent Sherman, Guy Usher, Lafe McKee
Director: David Ross Lederman
Story/Screenplay: Harold Shumate

A MAN'S GAME

(Columbia, June 18, 1934) 6 Reels
Tim McCoy, Evalyn Knapp, Ward Bond, DeWitt Jennings, Wade Boteler, Bob Kortman, Alden Chase
Director: David Ross Lederman
Story/Screenplay: Harold Shumate

BEYOND THE LAW

(Columbia, July 31, 1934) 60 Minutes
Tim McCoy, Shirley Grey, Lane Chandler, Addison Richards, Dick Rush, Harry Bradley, Morton Laverre (John Merton)
Director: D. Ross Lederman
Story/Screenplay: Harold Shumate

THE PRESCOTT KID

(Columbia, November 8, 1934) 60 Minutes
Tim McCoy, Sheila Mannors, Alden Chase, Hooper Atchley, Joseph Sauers (Joe Sawyer), Albert J. Smith, Carlos De Veldez, Ernie Adams, Steve Clark, Slim Whitaker, Charles King, Bud Osborne, Art Mix, Tom London, Edmund Cobb, Walter Brennan, Lew Meehan, Jack Rockwell
Director: David Selman
Story: Claude Rister
Screenplay: Ford Beebe

THE WESTERNER

(Columbia, December 1, 1934) 58 Minutes
Tim McCoy, Marion Schilling, Joseph Sauers (Joe Sawyer), Hooper Atchley, Edward J. LeSaint, Edmund Cobb, John Dilson, Bud Osborne, Albert Smith, Harry Todd, Slim Whitaker, Lafe McKee, Merrill McCormack
Director: David Sellman
Story: Walt Coburn
Screenplay: Harold Shumate

SQUARE SHOOTER

(Columbia, January 21, 1935) 57 Minutes
Tim McCoy, Jacqueline Wells (Julie Bishop), Erville Alderson, Charles Middleton, John Darrow, J. Farrell MacDonald, Wheeler Oakman, Steve Clark, William V. Mong, Jack Evans
Director: David Selman
Story/Screenplay: Harold Shumate

LAW BEYOND THE RANGE

(Columbia, February 15, 1935) 60 Minutes
Tim McCoy, Billie Seward, Robert Allen, Guy Usher, Harry Todd, Walter Brennan, Si Jenks, J. B. Kenton, Ben Hendricks, Jr., Jules Cowles, Tom London, Jack Rockwell, Alan Sears, Charles King, Jack Kirk
Director: Ford Beebe
Story: Lambert Hillyer
Screenplay: Ford Beebe

THE REVENGE RIDER

(Columbia, March 18, 1935) 60 Minutes
Tim McCoy, Robert Allen, Billie Seward, Edward Earle, Frank Sheridan, Jack Clifford, Jack Mower, George Pierce, Alan Sears, Harry Semels, Joseph Sauers (Joe Sawyer), Lafe McKee
Director: David Selman
Story/Screenplay: Ford Beebe

FIGHTING SHADOWS

(Columbia, April 18, 1935) 58 Minutes
Tim McCoy, Robert (Bob) Allen, Geneva Mitchell, Ward Bond, Si Jenks, Otto Hoffman, Edward J. LeSaint, Bud Osborne, Alan Sears, Ethan Laidlaw
Director: David Selman
Story/Screenplay: Ford Beebe

JUSTICE OF THE RANGE

(Columbia, May 25, 1935) 58 Minutes
Tim McCoy, Billie Seward, Ward Bond, Guy Usher, Edward J. LeSaint, Alan Sears, Jack Rockwell, Jack Rutherford, George Hayes, Bill Patton, Stanley Blystone, Earl Dwire, Dick Rush, J. Frank Glendon, Frank Ellis, Tom London, Bud Osborne, Dick Botiller
Director: David Selman
Story/Screenplay: Ford Beebe

THE OUTLAW DEPUTY
(Puritan, June 20, 1935) 56 Minutes
Tim McCoy, Nora Lane, Bud Osborne, George Offerman, Jr., Si Jenks, Jack Montgomery, George Holtz, Hank Bell, Tex Cooper, Jim Corey, Eddie Gribbon
Director: Otto Brower
Story: "King of Cactusville" - Johnston McCulley
Screenplay: Ford Beebe, Dell Andrews
Adaptation: Ford Beebe
Producer: Nat Ross

RIDING WILD
(Columbia, June 28, 1935) 57 Minutes
Tim McCoy, Billie Seward, Niles Welch, Edward J. LeSaint, Dick Alexander, Dick Botiller, Edmund Cobb, Jack Rockwell, Bud Osborne, Wally West, Al Haskell, Si Jenks
Director: David Selman
Story/Screenplay: Ford Beebe

THE MAN FROM GUNTOWN
(Puritan, August 15, 1935) 61 Minutes
Tim McCoy, Billie Seward, Rex Lease, Jack Clifford, Wheeler Oakman, Bob McKenzie, Jack Rockwell, George Chesebro, George Pierce, Ella McKenzie, Horace B. Carpenter, Hank Bell, Eddie Gribbon, Charles King, Oscar Gahan
Director/Story: Ford Beebe
Screenplay: Ford Beebe, Thomas H. Ince, Jr.
Producer: Nat Ross

BULLDOG COURAGE
(Puritan, December 30, 1935) 67 Minutes
Tim McCoy, Joan Woodbury, Karl Hackett, John Cowells, Eddie Buzzard, John Elliott, Edward Cassidy, Edmund Cobb, George Morrell, Paul Fix, Jack Rockwell, Bud Osborne, Blackjack Ward
Director: Sam Newfield
Screenplay: Joseph O'Donnell, Frances Guihan
Producers: Sigmund Neufeld, Leslie Simmonds

ROARIN' GUNS
(Puritan, January 27, 1936) 67 Minutes
Tim McCoy, Rosalinda Price, Wheeler Oakman, Rex Lease, Karl Hackett, John Elliott, Tommy Bupp, Jack Rockwell, Lew Meehan, Frank Ellis, Edward Cassidy, Dick Alexander, Artie Ortego, Tex Phelps, Al Taylor, Jack Evans, Roger Williams
Director: Sam Newfield
Screenplay: Joseph O'Donnell
Producers: Sigmund Neufeld, Leslie Simmonds

BORDER CABALLERO
(Puritan, March 1, 1936) 59 Minutes
Tim McCoy, Lois January, Ralph Byrd, Ted Adams, J. Frank Glendon, Earle Hodgins, John Merton, Oscar Gahan, Robert McKenzie, Frank McCarroll, George Morrell, Jack Evans, Ray Henderson, Tex Phelps, Bill Patton
Director: Sam Newfield
Story: Norman S. Hall
Screenplay: Joseph O'Donnell
Producers: Sigmund Neufeld, Leslie Simmonds

LIGHTNIN' BILL CARSON
(Puritan, April 15, 1936) 70 Minutes
Tim McCoy, Lois January, Rex Lease, Harry Worth, Karl Hackett, John Merton, Lafe McKee, Frank Ellis, Slim Whitaker, Edmund Cobb, Jack Rockwell, Jimmy Aubrey, Artie Ortego, Oscar Gahan, Herman Hack, Tom Smith, Franklyn Farnum, George Morrell
Director: Sam Newfield
Story: George Arthur Durlam
Screenplay: Joseph O'Donnell
Producers: Sigmund Neufeld, Leslie Simmonds

ACES AND EIGHTS
(Puritan, June 6, 1936) 62 Minutes
Tim McCoy, Luana Walters, Wheeler Oakman, Rex Lease, Joe Girard, John Merton, Charles Stevens, Jimmy Aubrey, Earle Hodgins, J. Frank Glendon, Tom Smith, Frank Ellis, Jack Evans
Director: Sam Newfield
Story/Screenplay: George A. Durlam
Producers: Sigmund Neufeld, Leslie Simmonds

THE LION'S DEN
(Puritan, July 8, 1936) 59 Minutes
Tim McCoy, Joan Woodbury, Don Barclay, J. Frank Glendon, John Merton, Dick Curtis, Arthur Millet, Art Felix, Jack Rockwell, Karl Hackett, Jack Evans, Bud McClure, Frank Ellis
Director: Sam Newfield
Story: L. V. Jefferson
Screenplay: John T. Neville
Producers: Sigmund Neufeld, Leslie Simmonds

GHOST PATROL
(Puritan, August 3, 1936) 58 Minutes
Tim McCoy, Claudia Dell, Walter Miller, Wheeler Oakman, Lloyd Ingraham, Dick Curtis, Slim Whitaker, Jim Burtis, Jack Casey, Artie Ortego, Art Dillard, Fargo Bussey
Director: Sam Newfield
Story: Joseph O'Donnell
Screenplay: Wyndham Gittens
Producers: Sigmund Neufeld, Leslie Simmonds

THE TRAITOR

(Puritan, August 29, 1936) 57 Minutes

Tim McCoy, Frances Grant, Wally Wales, Karl Hackett, Jack Rockwell, Pedro Regas, Frank Melton, Dick Curtis, Dick Botiller, Edmund Cobb, Wally West, Tina Menard, Soledad Jiminez, J. Frank Glendon, Frank McCarroll, Oscar Gahan, Julian Rivero, Jack Kirk, Al Taylor, Jack King, Ray Henderson, Charles Whitaker, Buck Morgan

Director: Sam Newfield
Story: John Thomas Neville
Screenplay: Joseph O'Donnell
Producers: Sigmund Neufeld, Leslie Simmonds

WEST OF RAINBOW'S END

(Concord/Monogram, January 12, 1928) 57 Minutes

Tim McCoy, Kathleen Eliot, Walter McGrail, Frank LaRue, George Chang, Mary Carr, Ed Coxen, George Cooper, Bob Kortman, Jimmy Aubrey, Reed Howes, Ray Jones, Sherry Tansey

Director: Alan James
Story: Robert Emmett (Tansey)
Screenplay: Stanley Roberts, Gennaro Rea
Producer: Maurice Conn

CODE OF THE RANGERS

(Monogram, April 8, 1938) 56 Minutes

Tim McCoy, Rex Lease, Judith Ford, Wheeler Oakman, Frank LaRue, Roger Williams, Kit Guard, Frank McCarroll, Jack Ingram, Loren Riebe, Budd Buster, Ed Peil, Hal Price, Zeke Clemens, Herman Hack

Director: Sam Newfield
Screenplay: Stanley Roberts
Producer: Maurice Conn

TWO GUN JUSTICE

(Concord/Monogram, April 30, 1928) 58 Minutes

Tim McCoy, Betty Compson, John Merton, Joan Barclay, Lane Chandler, Al Bridge, Tony Paton, Alan Cavan, Harry Strang, Earl Dwire, Enid Parrish, Olin Francis, Curley Dresden, Jack Ingram

Director: Alan James
Story/Screenplay: Fred Myton
Producer: Maurice Conn

PHANTOM RANGER

(Monogram, May 27, 1938) 54 Minutes

Tim McCoy, Suzanne Kaaren, John St. Polis, Karl Hackett, Charles King, Tom London, John Merton, Dick Cramer, Herb Holcombe, Harry Strang, Wally West, Horace B. Carpenter, Sherry Tansey, George Morrell, Herman Hack, Bob McKenzie, Jimmy Aubrey, Bruce Warren, Edward Earle, Frank Ellis, Roy Henderson

Director: Sam Newfield
Story: Stanley Roberts
Screenplay: Joe O'Donnell
Producer: Maurice Conn

LIGHTNING CARSON RIDES AGAIN

(Victory, October 10, 1938) 58 Minutes

Tim McCoy, Joan Barclay, Bob Terry, Frank Wayne, Ben Corbett, Ted Adams, Karl Hackett, Forrest Taylor, Frank LaRue, James Flavin, Reed Howes, Jane Keckley, Slim Whitaker, Wally West

Director: Sam Newfield
Story/Screenplay: Joseph O'Donnell
Producer: Sam Katzman

SIX-GUN TRAIL

(Victory, November 25, 1938) 59 Minutes

Tim McCoy, Nora Lane, Alden Chase, Ben Corbett, Karl Hackett, Donald Gallagher, Ted Adams, Kenne Duncan, Sherry Tansey, Bob Terry, Frank Wayne, Hal Carey, Jimmy Aubrey, George Morrell

Director: Sam Newfield
Screenplay: Joseph O'Donnell
Producer: Sam Katzman

CODE OF THE CACTUS

(Victory, February 25, 1939) 56 Minutes

Tim McCoy, Dorothy Short, Ben Corbett, Dave O'Brien, Alden Chase, Ted Adams, Forrest Taylor, Bob Terry, Slim Whitaker, Frank Wayne, Kermit Maynard, Art Davis, Carl Sepulveda, Carl Mathews, Lee Burns, Clyde McCreary, Jack King, Rube Dalroy

Director: Sam Newfield
Story/Screenplay: Edward Halperin
Producer: Sam Katzman

TEXAS WILDCATS

(Victory, April 10, 1939) 57 Minutes

Tim McCoy, Joan Barclay, Ben Corbett, Forrest Taylor, Ted Adams, Dave O'Brien, Frank Ellis, Carl Mathews, Bob Terry, Slim Whitaker, Reed Howes, George Morrell

Director: Sam Newfield
Story/Screenplay: George H. Plympton
Producer: Sam Katzman

OUTLAWS PARADISE

(Victory, April 10, 1939) 62 Minutes

Tim McCoy, Ben Corbett, Joan Barclay, Dave O'Brien, Ted Adams, Forrest Taylor, Bob Terry, Don Gallaher, Jack Mulhall, Carl Mathews, Jack C. Smith, George Morrell

Director: Sam Newfield
Story/Screenplay: Basil Dickey
Producer: Sam Katzman

THE FIGHTING RENEGADE

(Victory, September 1, 1939) 58 Minutes
Tim McCoy, Joyce Bryant, Dave O'Brien, Budd Buster, Ben Corbett, Forrest Taylor, Ted Adams, Reed Howes, John Elliott, Carl Mathews
Director: Sam Newfield
Story/Screenplay: William Lively
Producer: Sam Katzman

STRAIGHT SHOOTER

(Victory, 1939) 54 Minutes
Tim McCoy, Julie Sheldon, Ben Corbett, Ted Adams, Reed Howes, Forrest Taylor, Budd Buster, Wally West, Carl Mathews, Jack Ingram
Director: Sam Newfield
Screenplay: Joseph O'Donnell, Basil Dickey
Producer: Sam Katzman

TRIGGER FINGERS

(Victory, 1939) 60 Minutes
Tim McCoy, Ben Corbett, Jill Martin, Joyce Bryant, John Elliott, Ted Adams, Ralph Peters, Bud McTaggart, Forrest Taylor, Kenne Duncan, Carleton Young, Carl Mathews
Director: Sam Newfield
Story/Screenplay: Basil Dickey
Producer: Sam Katzman

TEXAS RENEGADES

(PRC, January 17, 1940) 59 Minutes
Tim McCoy, Nora Lane, Harry Harvey, Kenne Duncan, Lee Prather, Earl Gunn, Hal Price, Joe McGuinn, Edward Cassidy
Director: Peter Stewart (Sam Newfield)
Screenplay: Joe O'Donnell
Producer: Sigmund Neufeld

FRONTIER CRUSADER

(PRC, June 1, 1940) 62 Minutes
Tim McCoy, Dorothy Short, Lou Fulton, Karl Hackett, Ted Adams, John Merton, Forrest Taylor, Hal Price, Frank LaRue, Kenne Duncan, George Chesebro, Frank Ellis, Carl Mathews, Reed Howes, Herman Hack, Sherry Tansey, Lane Bradford, Ray Henderson
Director: Peter Stewart (Sam Newfield)
Story: Arthur Durlam
Screenplay: William Lively
Producer: Sigmund Neufeld

GUN CODE

(PRC, August 3, 1940) 54 Minutes
Tim McCoy, Inna Gest (Ina Guest), Lou Fulton, Alden Chase, Ted Adams, Dave O'Brien, Carleton Young, Robert Winkler, John Elliott, George Chesebro, Jack Richardson, Carl Mathews
Director: Peter Stewart (Sam Newfield)
Screenplay: Joseph O'Donnell
Producer: Sigmund Neufeld

ARIZONA GANGBUSTERS

(PRC, September 16, 1940) 57 Minutes
Tim McCoy, Pauline Haddon, Lou Fulton, Forrest Taylor, Julian Rivero, Arno Frey, Kenne Duncan, Jack Rutherford, Elizabeth LaMal, Otto Reichow, Lita Cortez, Carl Mathews, Ben Corbett, Frank Ellis, Curley Dresden
Director: Peter Stewart (Sam Newfield)
Screenplay: Joseph O'Donnell
Producer: Sigmund Neufeld

RIDERS OF BLACK MOUNTAIN

(PRC, November 11, 1940) 57 Minutes
Tim McCoy, Pauline Haddon, Rex Lease, Ralph Peters, Edward Peil, Sr., George Chesebro, Dirk Thane, Carl Mathews
Director: Peter Stewart (Sam Newfield)
Screenplay: Joe O'Donnell
Producer: Sigmund Neufeld

OUTLAWS OF THE RIO GRANDE

(PRC, March 7, 1941) 63 Minutes
Tim McCoy, Virginia Carpenter, Charles King, Ralph Peters, Rex Lease, Kenne Duncan, Karl Hackett, Philip Turich, Frank Ellis, Thornton Edwards, Joe Dominguez, George Chesebro, Sherry Tansey
Director: Peter Stewart (Sam Newfield)
Screenplay: George Plympton
Producer: Sigmund Neufeld

THE TEXAS MARSHAL

(PRC, July 13, 1941) 58 Minutes
Tim McCoy, Art Davis and His Rhythm Riders, Kay Leslie, Karl Hackett, Edward Peil, Sr., Charles King, Dave O'Brien, Budd Buster, John Elliott, Wilson Edwards, Byron Vance, Frank Ellis
Director: Peter Stewart (Sam Newfield)
Screenplay: William Lively
Producer: Sigmund Neufeld

ARIZONA BOUND

(Monogram, July 19, 1941) 57 Minutes
(Rough Riders Series)
Buck Jones, *Tim McCoy,* Raymond Hatton, Tris Coffin, Dennis Moore, Luana Walters, Kathryn Sheldon, Gene Alsace, Slim Whitaker, Artie Ortego, I. Stanford Jolley, Horace Murphy, Hal Price, Jack Daley, Augie Gomez, "Silver"
Director: Spencer G. Bennet
Story: Oliver Drake
Screenplay: Jess Bowers (Adele Buffington)
Producer: Scott R. Dunlap

THE GUNMAN FROM BODIE

(Monogram, September 26, 1941) 62 Minutes
(Rough Riders Series)

Buck Jones, *Tim McCoy*, Raymond Hatton, Christine McIntyre, David O'Brien, Robert Frazer, Frank LaRue, Charles King, Lynton Brent, Max Walzman, Gene Alsace, John Merton, Jerry Sheldon, Jack King, Earl Douglas, Warren Jackson, Billy Carro, Frederick Gee, "Silver"

Director: Spencer G. Bennet
Screenplay: Jess Bowers (Adele Buffington)
Producer: Scott R. Dunlap

FORBIDDEN TRAILS

(Monogram, December 26, 1941) 54 Minutes
(Rough Riders Series)

Buck Jones, *Tim McCoy*, Raymond Hatton, Tris Coffin, Charles King, Glenn Strange, Lynton Brent, Jerry Sheldon, Hal Price, Dave O'Brien, Christine McIntyre, Dick Alexander, "Silver"

Director: Robert North Bradbury
Screenplay: Jess Bowers (Adele Buffington)
Story: Oliver Drake
Producer: Scott R. Dunlap

BELOW THE BORDER

(Monogram, January 30, 1942) 57 Minutes
(Rough Riders Series)

Buck Jones, *Tim McCoy,* Raymond Hatton, Linda Brent, Eva Puig, Charles King, Dennis Moore, Roy Barcroft, Ted Mapes, Bud Osborne, Merrill McCormack, Jack Rockwell, "Silver"

Director: Howard Bretherton
Screenplay: Jess Bowers (Adele Buffington)
Producer: Scott R. Dunlap

GHOST TOWN LAW

(Monogram, March 27, 1942) 62 Minutes
(Rough Riders Series)

Buck Jones, *Tim McCoy,* Raymond Hatton, Virginia Carpenter, Murdock MacQuarrie, Charles King, Howard Masters, Ben Corbett, Tom London, "Silver"

Director: Howard Bretherton
Screenplay: Jess Bowers (Adele Buffington)
Producer: Scott R. Dunlap

RIDERS OF THE WEST

(Monogram, August 21, 1942) 58 Minutes
(Rough Riders Series)

Buck Jones, *Tim McCoy*, Raymond Hatton, Sarah Padden, Dennis Moore, Harry Woods, Christine McIntyre, Walter McGrail, Harry Frazer, Bud Osborne, Charles King, Lee Phelps, Kermit Maynard, Milburn Morante, Edward Peil, Sr., Lynton Brent, J. Merrill Holmes, George Morrell, Tom London, "Silver"

Director: Howard Bretherton
Screenplay: Jess Bowers (Adele Buffington)
Producer: Scott R. Dunlap

WEST OF THE LAW

(Monogram, October 2, 1942) 60 Minutes
(Rough Riders Series)

Buck Jones, *Tim McCoy*, Raymond Hatton, Evelyn Cook, Milburn Morante, Harry Woods, Roy Barcroft, Bud McTaggart, George DeNormand, Jack Daley, Bud Osborne, Lynton Brent, "Silver"

Director: Howard Bretherton
Screenplay: Jess Bowers (Adele Buffington)
Producer: Scott R. Dunlap

AROUND THE WORLD IN 80 DAYS

(Todd-AO, September, 1956) 175 Minutes

David Niven, Cantinflas, Robert Newton, Shirley MacLaine, Charles Boyer, Joe E. Brown, Martine Carol, John Carradine, Charles Coburn, Ronald Colman, Melville Cooper, Noel Coward, Finlay Currie, Reginald Denny, Andy Devine, Marlene Dietrich, Luis Dominguin, Fernandel, Sir John Gielgud, Hermione Gingold, Jose Greco, Sir Cedric Hardwicke, Trevor Howard, Glynis Johns, Buster Keaton, Evelyn Love, A. E. Matthews, *Col. Tim McCoy*, Victor McLaglen, Mike Mazurki, John Mills, Alan Mowbray, Robert Morley, Jack Oakie, George Raft, Gilbert Roland, Cesar Romero, Frank Sinatra, Red Skelton, Ronald Squire, Basil Sydney, Harcourt Williams, Buddy Roosevelt

Director: Michael Anderson
Screenplay: S. J. Perelman
Story: Jules Verne
Producer: Michael Todd

RUN OF THE ARROW

(RKO, September 1, 1957) 85 Minutes
(Technicolor)

Rod Steiger, Sarita Montiel, Brian Keith, Ralph Meeker, Jay C. Flippen, *Colonel Tim McCoy*, Frank De Kova, Stuart Randall, Charles Bronson, Olive Carey, H. M. Wynant, Neyle Morrow, Frank Warner, Billy Miller, Chuck Hayward, Chuck Roberson, Kermit Maynard

Director/Screenplay/Producer: Samuel Fuller

REQUIEM FOR A GUNFIGHTER

(Embassy, June 30, 1965) 91 Minutes
(Technicolor) (TechniScope)

Rod Cameron, Stephen McNally, Mike Mazurki, Olive Sturgess, *Tim McCoy*, Johnny Mack Brown, Bob Steele, Lane Chandler, Raymond Hatton, Chet Douglas, Dick Jones, Chris Hughes, Rand Brooks, Dale Van Sickel, Frank Lackteen, Zon Murray, Ronn Delanor, Edmund Cobb, Margo Williams, Doris Spiegel, Dick Alexander, Fred Carson, Red Morgan

Director: Spencer G. Bennet
Story: Evans W. Cornell, Guy J. Tedesco
Screenplay: R. Alexander
Producer: Alex Gordon

6 ● JACK HOXIE

A Giant in the Saddle

Few names are more revered in the chronicle of cactus capers than that of "Hoxie," made famous by the brothers Jack and Al back in the early days of flicker magic when making buckaroo film dramas was just as hard work as riding the line, rounding up stock, and trail herding ever were in the palmy days of the open range. Of course, it paid a lot better, but it was still a job for tough hombres who could take it. Jack and Al had done both kinds of work and knew.

Although most authors have stated that Jack was born on Kingfisher Creek in Indian Territory in 1888, such is apparently not the case, according to brother Al. A notation in the family Bible, placed there by his mother, indicates that Jack was born January 11, 1888 in Kansas. Probably the actual birthplace was just a short distance from the Indian Territory, where the family soon settled in a small cabin built by the elder Hoxie, a veterinarian, on a plot of land he got in the Oklahoma land rush.

Indian Territory was a rough, wild country at the turn of the century and Jack early experienced sunup-to-sundown labor as a farmhand and cowpoke. Rodeoing appealed to him, both as a respite from the drudgery of long days in the fields and as a source of much needed money. While barely a teenager he had won several pots and trophies. And when his parents decided to pull up roots and move to Idaho, Jack became a full-fledged working cowboy. His parents had a ranch and maybe 600 head of cattle in Northern Idaho in the Salmon River Country.

When his folks disposed of the ranch following a terrible winter, Jack moved into Boise, where he got a job as head packer for the fort there. His brief marriage to

a girl named Pearl Gage had just ended, so there was little reason to remain in the Salmon River country. His job often required him to take about 20 mules and as many soldiers on packing trips into the hills, where he would teach the soldiers how to pack, survive in the wilds, etc. His skill and riding ability made him popular in many rodeos as bronc buster and bulldogger. He was winner of a bulldogging championship at Bakersfield, California and won many other awards during his early years.

In 1909 Jack signed on as a bronc rider and bulldogger with the Dick Stanley Wild West Show, the first of many circus/wild west shows with which he would tour. He had met Hazel Panky at the show when it was in Boise and had married her during one of the performances. The same evening he rode "Dynamite" to win a championship and an invitation to join the circus. So, newlyweds Jack and Hazel were off with the show.

Jobless and stranded in California at the end of the season, bronc-busting Jack overnight became Hartford Hoxie, fledging motion picture actor. The year was 1911 or 1912. With his riding ability it was easy to pick up jobs at various studios as a stuntman, extra, and bit player. Gradually, he rose to more important roles, one of his most notable early ones being in **The Dumb Girl of Portici** at Universal in 1916. Other early-day appearances included **The Hazards of Helen** (a serial), **Blue Blazes Rawden, Man from Nowhere, Iron Test, Sparks of Flint, Told in the Hills, Valley of the Giants, Nan of Music Mountain,** and **Johnny Get Your Gun.** He had billing in all of these action films and in at least two films—**The Man from Tiajuana** (1917) and **The Wild Engine** (1919)—he was

Jack Hoxie

featured. Marin Sais had the female lead in **The Man from Tiajuana** and subsequently became Hoxie's wife after he and his second wife, Hazel Panky, were divorced. Jack and Hazel had two children, Ramona and Pearl, who were taken back to San Antonio by their mother after the marriage ended. The marriage with Marin Sais was a good one in many respects and Marin gave Jack what polish he might have had, a thin veneer at best.

In 1919 Jack supported William Duncan and Edith Johnson in the Vitagraph serial, **A Fight for Millions.** And then came his big chance. He was signed by National Film Corporation to co-star with Ann Little in **Lightning Bryce,** a 15-chapter cliffhanger well received by audiences of the day. Jack was kept on to star in **Thunderbolt Jack,** another serial. His wife played opposite him and brother Al, a 19-year old fresh from Oregon, played Marin's brother, using the screen name Alton J. Stone so as not to conflict with Jack's name.

Scoring big again with the action fans in this second serial outing, Jack was signed by Arrow Films for a Western series, most of the films being produced by Ben Wilson, an adventure star himself. Thirteen whirlwind sagebrushers were churned out by Jack in 1921 and 1922. And although later film historians would usually disparage Jack's thespian talents, the less critical audiences of the '20s couldn't have cared less about his emoting. Jack was a mighty man on a horse and in a screen brawl. Tom Mix himself was little better as an actor, so Hoxie was accepted readily and rose to a leading position among silent film cowboys. He looked like a million dollars astride his horse "Scout," and on a horse is where his fans kept him for a decade. The fact that his appraised value as a boudoir romeo was more like fifty cents was unimportant to those who faithfully followed Jack's range escapdes from week to week. His giddyups usually conformed 100% to the old-time idea of what a rousing mustanger should be.

In 1922 Jack signed with Universal, the greatest studio of them all when it came to making fine little Westerns. Carl Laemmle, founder of Universal, loved westerns and made more money from them than any other type of film. He provided each of the Universal cowboy stars his own barn and horses and a group of cowboys who worked almost exclusively with him. Horses were Jack's real love and he had 25 of them at one time during his plush days as a top gun.

Jack's first Universal film was **Don Quickshot of the Rio Grande,** directed by George Marshall. He went on to star in about 35 slick oaters for Universal, at a beginning salary of $500 a week. His second contract with Laemmle gave him $1,000 a week. The Hoxie programmers were good, according to those who can remember

them. Most of the films are not in existence today, which means that the writers who debunk Jack's films are probably basing their evaluation of his work almost strictly on the low-budget "quickie" talkies he made in 1932-'33, and perhaps one or two silents they might have seen. It is not a fair judgment of the man and his films. In the '20s he was second only to Hoot Gibson in the Universal corral of popular cowboys.

Hoxie's opuses were always full of fast riding and hard shooting, with a number of rough-and-tumble fights, all of which provided plenty of diversion for devotees who went for this type of screen antics. A combination of Universal's high technical skills backed the Hoxie pictures to give them a physical wallop, and so Jack's wide-awake wits and ready fists continued not only to non-plus the on-screen villains but also to fill the seats of the neighborhood theatres. While on screen men guffawed at the bar, the bartender polished his glasses, and smoke-rings curled in the air above card-players, goose bumps would rise among the audience as old reliable Jack would slide through the swinging doors of that basic commodity of all shoot-em-ups—the saloon—with a determined glint in his steel-blue eyes which suggested that he was about to sweep all hell of its varmints.

Jack and Al spent a lot of time together during the '20s. Jack had a ten-acre ranch in San Fernando Valley where he liked to take care of horses. He didn't fish, play golf, gamble, or do much of anything else. He had no hobbies, except horses. He would, however, spend hours bending Al's ear either about how he could make a million dollars in some wild scheme or about the movies and the circus.

Tall, stalwart, handsome, a fearless rider and a matchless roper and rifleman, Jack Hoxie, as he thundered across the screen in the Universal Westerns of 1923-1927, might have ridden straight out of the past. In a thousand theatres in a thousand towns Jack Hoxie and his horse "Scout" and his dog "Bunkie" provided goose-pimple thrills for audiences throughout rural America, making the old West come alive again for the price of a dime or a quarter. "Scout" was more than just another horse. He had a whole repertoire of tricks which he performed in movies. Jack acquired him at the beginning of his movie career and kept him until the horse's death around 1939. The dog "Bunkie," sometimes called "Bunkie Bean," was brought from Australia as a pup and appeared in many oaters with Jack and "Scout."

The film that Hoxie himself loved and the only one he looked back on with much affection was Metropolitan's **The Last Frontier** (1926). In it, he plays Buffalo Bill Cody. William Boyd (yet several years away from Western fame as "Hopalong Cassidy") and

George K. French and Ena Gregory look down the stairs at Jack Hoxie in **Red Hot Leather** (Universal, 1926)

Marguerite De La Motte were co-starred with him in this film conceived by Thomas H. Ince, then turned over to Hunt Stromberg who eventually sold the rights to Metropolitan to complete it.

Something happened between Jack and Universal in 1927, with the result that Jack tore up his contract. It was like signing his own death warrant. From that day he was washed up in the movies, though he would yet make a few. Nat Levine had formed Mascot Pictures to produce serials about this time and signed Jack to head up an all-star cast in one of the last of the silent cliffhangers, a semi-oater titled **Heroes of the Wild.** After that, there were no offers. Most of the studios were re-tooling for sound.

Jack cashed in on his name and talent by taking to the sawdust trail once again as a circus headliner for the Charles Sparks Circus. He also moved to Anderson, Arizona, along with his 22 horses, and tried to start

a dude ranch. All of his horses except Scout died from eating loco weed, and the dude ranch turned out to be pretty much of a fiasco. Jack later joined the Miller Brothers 101 Ranch Show with a good, fast-moving act in which he was assisted by the female trick rider Dixie Starr (whom he is reputed to have married), his famous steed "Scout," and his dog "Bunkie." With the possible exception of Reb Russell, Hoxie has the best act of the movie cowboys from the standpoint of raw action. He did not just "appear"—he performed the daredevil stunts so characteristic of his movies.

In 1932 and 1933 Jack made his first and last series of sound Westerns. It was a cheap group of "quickies" put out by Majestic Pictures that did nothing to bolster his sagging popularity with the movie patrons who were turning to the new breed of cowboys. Although Jack could still ride and fight with the best of them, the dialogue did him in. His voice wasn't very good for sound and he had trouble with the scripts. Although he was not illiterate, as some have claimed, it was true that he could read and write only poorly. He retired permanently from the screen.

Jack knew nothing but movies, the circus, and horses. So, with the movies behind him, he hit the sawdust trail with the Jack Hoxie Circus in 1937 and 1938. In 1939 he headed up Lewis Brothers Circus. In 1944, after marrying for the final time, to Bonnie Showwalter, Jack joined the Mills Brothers Circus and traveled with them for five seasons. Over the years he traveled with other shows, culminating his circus activity with the Bill Tatum Circus in 1959. After that he lived on his small ranch in Mulberry, Arkansas for several years until leukemia put a stop to his activities. In the early '60s, he moved to Keyes, Oklahoma on a little place his mother had owned, and it was here he spent his last days quietly, often reminiscing with fans who remembered him and sought him out.

Jack Hoxie died on March 27, 1965 at Elkhart, Kansas and was buried at Keyes. He was 77 years old. It had been 30 years since he retired from the screen, but his place as one of filmdom's greatest cowboys was assured. His reputation has survived him, although few of his great silent films remain today for viewing. He breathed life into the cinema Western and earned himself a niche in the hearts of Western film buffs throughout the world, long before the crooners with their guitars and fancy duds and automobiles appeared on the range to spoil it. The Hoxie range was filled with real cowboys, cows, and cow-dung. He probably would not have wanted it any other way.

JACK HOXIE Filmography

BROUGHT TO BAY
(Kalem, May 13, 1913) 2 Reels
Helen Holmes, Jack Conway, Hart *(Jack)* *Hoxie,* Steve Banner, May Madden, Pete Frawley, Joe Temple, William Brunton
Director: J. P. McGowan

TRAGEDY OF BIG EAGLE MINE
(Kalem, May 31, 1913) 2 Reels
Jane Wolfe, Carlyle Blackwell, Knute Rahmn, Hart *(Jack)* *Hoxie*

THE INVADERS
(Kalem, August, 1913) 2 Reels
Paul Hurst, Jane Wolfe, Marin Sais, Carlyle Blackwell, William West, Charles French, James Horne, Rhys Pryce, Hart *(Jack)* *Hoxie,* Knute Rahmn
Director: George Melford
Story: John Lloyd

BATTLE AT FORT LARAMIE
(Kalem, 1913) 2 Reels
Helen Holmes, Leo Maloney, G. A. Williams, Hart *(Jack)* *Hoxie,* Alice Dexter, Charles Gillette
Director: J. P. McGowan

BIG HORN MASSACRE
(Kalem, December 24, 1913) 2 Reels
Billie Rhodes, Hart *(Jack)* *Hoxie,* Paul Hurst
Director: unknown (possibly Paul Hurst)

THE CONDUCTOR'S COURTSHIP
(Kalem, June, 1914)
Hart *(Jack)* *Hoxie*

THE IDENTIFICATION
(Kalem, July, 1914) 2 Reels
Helen Holmes, J. P. McGowan, Hart *(Jack)* *Hoxie*
Director: J. P. McGowan

THE OPERATOR AT BLACK ROCK
(Kalem, August 1, 1914) 2 Reels
Helen Holmes, G. A. Pulliam, Bert C. Hadley, Hart *(Jack)* *Hoxie*
Director: J. P. McGowan
Story: E. W. Matlock

NEAR DEATH'S DOOR
THE CAR OF DEATH
(These are Kalem titles that Hoxie is rumored to have been in, but the author so far has uncovered no backup information on them)

THE HAZARDS OF HELEN
(Kalem, November 13, 1914) 119 Chapters
Helen Holmes, Helen Gibson, Robyn Adair, Ethel Clisbee, Tom Trent, G. A. Williams, Pearl Anibus, P. S. Pembroke, Roy Watson, Hoot Gibson, Hartford *(Jack)* *Hoxie,* Harry Schumm, O. Fillipi, George Routh
(Hoxie was featured prominently in Episode No. 26, "The Wild Engine" and probably appeared in other episodes of the long-running serial as well)
Directors: J. P. McGowan and James Davis
(Mr. McGowan directed the segments with Miss Holmes (Nos. 1-48) and Mr. Davis directed those with Miss Gibson (Nos. 49-119))

THE SCARLET SIN
(Broadway Universal Special, July 31, 1915) 4 Reels
Hobart Bosworth, Jane Novak, Hart *(Jack)* *Hoxie,* Grace Thompson, Frank Elliott, Ed Brown, Wadsworth Harris, Helen Wright
Director/Producers: Otis Turner, Hobart Bosworth
Scenario: James Dayton
Story: Olga Printzlau Clark

THE GOPHER

(Universal-Bison, August 13, 1915) 2 Reels
Herbert Rawlinson, Ann Little, Hart *(Jack) Hoxie,* Jack Pyles
Director/Producer: William Worthington
Screenplay: Harvey Gates

FATHERHOOD

(Broadway Universal, September 20, 1915) 4 Reels
Hobart Bosworth, Joseph Flores, Hart *(Jack) Hoxie,* Helen Wolcott, Lydia Yeamans, Titus C. Stevens
Story/Screenplay: Hobart Bosworth
Story: Julia Crawford Ivers

BLIND FURY

(Universal-Laemmle, December 31, 1915) 1 Reel
Jack Livingston, Leon D. Kent, Mina Jeffries, Bud Osborne, Hart *(Jack) Hoxie*
Producer: Leon D. Kent
Scenario: G. E. Jenks, Leon D. Kent

BUCK SIMMONS, PUNCHER

(Universal-Bison, January 22, 1916) 2 Reels
Leon Kent, Pat Rooney, Edna Maison, Malcolm Blevin, Hart *(Jack) Hoxie*
Producer/Story: Leon Kent

BLIND FURY

(Laemmle, January, 1916)
Jack Livingston, Leon D. Kent, Mina Jeffries, Bud Osborne, Malcolm Blevins, Hart *(Jack) Hoxie*
Director: Leon D. Kent
Scenario: J. E. Jenks

THE QUARTER BREED

(Universal-Bison, March 3, 1916) 3 Reels
Mina Cunard, Jack Livingston, Bud Osborne, Malcolm Blevins, Hart *(Jack) Hoxie*
Director/Story: Leon D. Kent

THE DUMB GIRL OF PORTICI

(Universal, April 13, 1916) 10 Reels
Anna Pavlova, Rupert Julian, Douglas Gerrard, Betty Schade, John Hunt, Jack Holt, Hart *(Jack) Hoxie,* Lois Wilson
Director/Adaptation: Lois Weber
Story: from the opera based on the life of Masaniello by Daniel Francois Esprit Auber
Producers: The Smalleys

A YOUTH OF FORTUNE

(Universal-Red Feather, April 26, 1916) 5 Reels
Mr. and Mrs. Carter DeHaven, Hart *(Jack) Hoxie*
Director: Otis Turner
Scenario: Ford Beebe

THE THREE GODFATHERS

(Universal-Bluebird, May 31, 1916) 6 Reels
Harry Carey, Stella Razetto, George Berrell, Frank Lanning, Hart *(Jack) Hoxie,* Joe Rickson
Director: Edward LeSaint
Screenplay: Edward LeSaint and Harvey Gates
Story: Peter B. Kyne

THE GIRL FROM FRISCO

(Kalem, 1916) 16 Chapters
Marin Sais, True Boardman, Frank Jonasson, Ronald Bradbury, Josephine West, Steve Murphy, Karl Formes, Jr., Edward Clisbee, Barney Furey, Jack Hutchinson, E. Forrest Taylor, Hart *(Jack) Hoxie,* Jack McDonald
Director: James W. Horne
Story: Robert Welles Ritchie
Chapter Titles: (1) The Fighting Heiress (2) The Turquoise Mine Conspiracy (3) The Oil Field Plot (4) Tiger Unchained (5) The Ore Plunderers (6) The Treasure of Cibola (7) The Gun Runners (8) A Battle in the Dark (9) The Web of Guilt (10) The Reformation of Dog Hole (11) Secret of a Box Car (12) Hurled Thru the Drawbridge (13) The Yellow Hand (14) The Resurrection of Gold Bar (15) False Prophet (16) Fight for Paradise Valley

JOAN THE WOMAN

(Cardinal Film Co./Paramount, January 4, 1917) 10 Reels
Geraldine Farrar, Raymond Hatton, Hobart Bosworth, Theodore Roberts, Wallace Reid, Charles Clary, James Neill, Tully Marshall, Lawrence Peyton, Horace B. Carpenter, Cleo Ridgely, Lillian Leighton, Marjorie Daw, Stephen Gray, Ernest Joy, John Oaker, Hugo B. Koch, William Conklin, Walter Long, Billy Elmer, Emilius Jorgenson, Ramon Samaniegos (Novarro), Hartford *(Jack) Hoxie*
Director/Producer: Cecil B. DeMille
Scenario: Jeanie MacPherson

THE SECRET OF THE LOST VALLEY

(Kalem, March, 1917) 2 Reels
(The American Girl Series)
Marin Sais, Frank Jonasson, Edward Hearn, Edward Clisbee, R. E. Bradbury, Knute Rahmn, Hart *(Jack) Hoxie,* Grace Johnson

THE VULTURES OF SKULL MOUNTAIN

(Kalem, April, 1917) 2 Reels
(The American Girl Series)
Marin Sais, Frank Jonasson, Edward Hearn, Ronald Bradbury, Edward Clisbee, Hart *(Jack) Hoxie*

THE WOLF AND HIS MATE
(Universal Butterfly, 1917) 5 Reels
Hart *(Jack) Hoxie,* Louise Lovely, Betty Schade, Hector Dion
Director: Edward J. LeSaint
Scenario: Doris Schroeder
Story: Julia Maier

JACK AND JILL
(Oliver Morosco Photoplay for Paramount, November 12, 1917) 5 Reels
Jack Pickford, Louise Huff, Hart *(Jack) Hoxie,* Leo Houck, Don Bailey, J. H. Holland, Colonel Lenone, Beatrice Burnham
Director: William D. Taylor
Story: Margaret Turnbull
Screenplay: Gardner Hunting

NAN OF MUSIC MOUNTAIN
(Famous Players Lasky/Paramount, December 12, 1917) 5 Reels
Wallace Reid, Ann Little, Theodore Roberts, James Cruze, Charles Ogle, Raymond Hatton, Hart *(Jack) Hoxie,* Ernest Joy, Guy Oliver, James Mason, Horace Carpenter, Henry Woodward, Alice Marc
Director: George H. Melford
Scenario: Beulah Marie Dix
Story: Frank H. Spearman

THE MAN FROM TIAJUANA
(Kalem, 1917) 1 Reel
(The American Girl Series)
Marin Sais, Edward Hearn, Hart *(Jack) Hoxie*

BLUE BLAZES RAWDEN
(Artcraft, February, 1918) 2 Reels
William S. Hart, Hart *(Jack) Hoxie,* Maud George, Gertrude Claire, Robert McKim, Robert Gordon
Director/Producer: William S. Hart
Supervisor: Thomas H. Ince
Screenplay: J. G. Hawks

HIS MAJESTY, BUNKER BEAN
(Famous Players-Lasky/Paramount, March, 1918) 5 Reels
Jack Pickford, Louise Huff, Hart *(Jack) Hoxie,* Jack McDonald
Director: William Desmond Taylor
Screenplay: Julia Crawford Ivers
Story: Harry Leon Wilson

A FIGHT FOR MILLIONS
(Vitagraph, July 15, 1918) 15 Chapters
William Duncan, Edith Johnson, Joe Ryan, Walter Rodgers, S. E. Jennings, Leo Maloney, Hart *(Jack) Hoxie,* Willie Calles, Vincente Howard
Director: William Duncan
Story: Albert E. Smith, Cyrus Townsend Brady
Adaptation: Graham Baker
Chapter Titles: (1) The Snare (2) Flames of Peril (3) The Secret Stockade (4) The Precipice of Horror (5) The Path of Thrills (6) The Spell of Evil (7) The Gorge of Destruction (8) In the Clutches (9) The Escape (10) The Secret Tunnel (11) The Noose of Death (12) The Tide of Disaster (13) The Engine of Terror (14) The Decoy (15) The Sealed Envelope

THE IRON TEST
(Vitagraph, October 21, 1918) 15 Chapters
Antonio Moreno, Carol Holloway, Hart *(Jack) Hoxie,* Barney Furey, Chet Ryan, Frank Jonasson, Charles G. Rich
Directors: R. N. Bradbury, Paul C. Hurst
Story: Albert E. Smith, Cyrus Townsend Brady
Scenario: Graham Baker
Chapter Titles: (1) Ring of Fire (2) Van of Disaster (3) Blade of Hate (4) The Noose (5) Tide of Death (6) Fiery Fate (7) The Whirling Trap (8) The Man Eater (9) The Pit of Lost Hope (10) In the Coils (11) The Red Mask's Prey (12) The Span of Terror (13) Hanging Peril (14) Desperate Odds (15) Riding with Death

NOBODY'S WIFE
(Universal, 1918) 5 Reels
Hart *(Jack) Hoxie,* Louise Lovely, Alfred Allen, Betty Schade, H. G. Kenyon, Grace McLean
Director: Edward J. LeSaint
Story: Robert N. Bradbury, F. Clark
Scenario: Charles Kenyon

JOHNNY GET YOUR GUN
(Artcraft/Paramount, January 24, 1919) 5 Reels
Fred Stone, Mary Anderson, Casson Ferguson, Dan Crimmings, James Cruze, Sylvia Ashton, Nina Byron, Fred Huntley, Raymond Hatton, Ernest Joy, Hart *(Jack) Hoxie,* Noah Beery, Clarence Geldart
Director: Donald Crisp
Story: Edmund L. Burke
Scenario: Gardner Hunting

VALLEY OF THE GIANTS

(Artcraft/Paramount, July 24, 1919) 5 Reels
Wallace Reid, Grace Darmond, William Brunton, Charles Ogle, Ralph Lewis, Alice Taaffe, Kay Laurel, Hart *(Jack) Hoxie,* Noah Beery, Guy Oliver, William H. Brown, Virginia Fultz
Director: James Cruze
Screenplay: Marion Fairfax
Story: Peter B. Kyne

TOLD IN THE HILLS

(Famous Players-Lasky/Paramount, August 15, 1919) 6 Reels
Robert Warwick, Ann Little, Tom Forman, Wanda Hawley, Charles Ogle, Monte Blue, Margaret Loomis, Eileen Percy, Hart *(Jack) Hoxie,* Jack Herbert, Guy Oliver
Director: George Melford
Scenario: Will M. Ritchey
Story: Marah Ellis Ryan

LIGHTNING BRYCE

(National Film Corp./Arrow, October 15, 1919) 15 Chapters
Jack Hoxie, Ann Little, Steve Clemento, Ben Corbett, Walter Patterson, George Champion, Slim Lucas, George Hunter, Paul C. Hurst
Director: Paul C. Hurst
Story: Joe Brandt
Scenario: Harvey Gates
Chapter Titles: (1) The Scarlet Moon (2) Wolf Nights (3) Perilous Trails (4) The Noose (5) The Dragon's Den (6) Robes of Destruction (7) Bared Fangs (8) The Yawning Abyss (9) The Voice of Conscience (10) Poison Waters (11) Walls of Flame (12) A Voice From the Dead (13) Battling Barriers (14) Smothering Tides (15) The End of the Trail

THUNDERBOLT JACK

(Arrow, November 1, 1920) 10 Chapters
Jack Hoxie, Marin Sais, Chris Frank, Steve Clemento, Alton (Al) Hoxie, Edith Stayart
Directors: Murdock MacQuarrie, Francis Ford
Chapter Titles: (1) The Thunderbolt Strikes (2) Eight to One (Copyright records do not indicate titles of the remaining 8 chapters) (10) Dungeon of Death

THE MAN FROM NOWHERE

(Ben Wilson Productions/Arrow, December, 1920) 5 Reels
Jack Hoxie, Vera Sisson, Pansy Porter, Fred Moore, Francis Ford, Sam Polo
Director: Francis Ford

A MAN'S COUNTRY

(Unity Photoplays/Arrow, 1920) 5 Reels
Jack Hoxie
Director: Francis Ford
Story: Arthur Chapman
Scenario: B. Reeves Eason
Producer: Ben Wilson

CYCLONE BLISS

(Unity Photoplays/Arrow, January, 1921) 5 Reels
Jack Hoxie, Evelyn Nelson, Frederick Moore, Fred Kohler, Steve Clemento, William Dyer, James Kelly, Phil Ford
Director: Francis Ford
Producer: Ben Wilson

THE SHERIFF OF HOPE ETERNAL

(Unity Photoplays/Arrow, March, 1921) 5 Reels
Jack Hoxie, Marin Sais, Joseph Girard, William Dyer, Bee Monson, Theodore Brown, Wilbur McGaugh
Director/Producer: Ben Wilson

DEAD OR ALIVE

(Unity Photoplays/Arrow, March, 1921) 5 Reels
Jack Hoxie, Marin Sais, Joseph Girard, C. Ray Florhe, Wilbur McGaugh, Evelyn Nelson
Director: Dell Henderson
Producer: Ben Wilson

CUPID'S BRAND

(Unity Photoplays/Arrow, April, 1921) 6 Reels
Jack Hoxie, Mignon Anderson, Wilbur McGaugh, Charles Force, William Dyer, A. T. Van Sickle
Director: Rowland V. Lee
Producer: Ben Wilson

DEVIL DOG DAWSON

(Unity Photoplays/Arrow, May, 1921) 5 Reels
Jack Hoxie, Helen Rosson, Evelyn Selbie, Wilbur McGaugh, Arthur Mackley, William Dyer
Directors: King Gray, William Dyer
Story: Karl Coolidge
Producer: Ben Wilson

THE BROKEN SPUR

(Ben Wilson Productions/Arrow, July, 1921) 5 Reels
Jack Hoxie, Marin Sais, Evelyn Nelson, Jim Welch, Wilbur McGaugh, Edward Berman, Harry Rattenberry
Director: Ben Wilson

HILLS OF HATE

(Ben Wilson Productions/Arrow, July, 1921) 5 Reels
Jack Hoxie

THE DOUBLE O
(Ben Wilson Productions/Arrow, November 29, 1921)
5 Reels
Jack Hoxie, Evelyn Nelson, Steve Clemento, William Lester, Ed La Niece
Director/Story/Scenario: Roy Clements

SPARKS OF FLINT
(Ben Wilson Productions/Arrow, December 10, 1921)
5 Reels
Jack Hoxie, Dorothy Holmes
Director/Scenario: Roy Clements

TWO-FISTED JEFFERSON
(Ben Wilson Productions/Arrow, January 14, 1922)
5 Reels
Jack Hoxie, Evelyn Nelson, Claude Payton, Bill White, Steve Clemento, James Welch, Ed La Niece, Buck Connors
Director/Scenario: Roy Clements

THE DESERT'S CRUCIBLE
(Ben Wilson Productions/Arrow, April 23, 1922) 5 Reels
Jack Hoxie, Andrea Tourneur, Claude Payton, Evelyn Nelson, Thomas Lingham, Walter Williamson
Director/Story: Roy Clements

A DESERT BRIDEGROOM
(Ben Wilson Productions/Arrow, May 28, 1922) 5 Reels
Jack Hoxie, Evelyn Nelson, Bill White, Olin Francis
Director/Story: Roy Clements

THE MARSHAL OF MONEYMINT
(Ben Wilson Productions/Arrow, June 14, 1922) 5 Reels
Jack Hoxie, Andrea Tourneur, Jim Welch, James Rock, William Lester, Claude Payton, Goldie Madden
Director/Story: Roy Clements

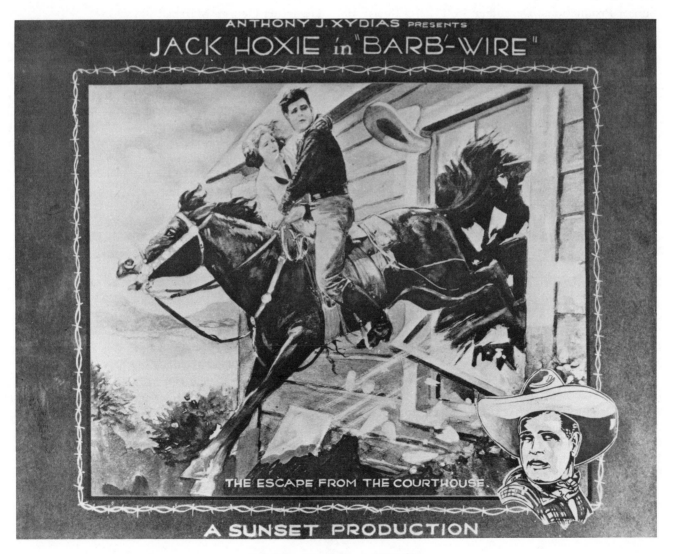

A Lobby Card for a 1922 film.

BARB'-WIRE
(Sunset Productions/Aywon, June, 1922) 5 Reels
Jack Hoxie, Jean Porter, Olah Norman, William Lester, Joe McDermott, Jim Welsh
Director: Frank Grandon
Story: William Lester, Marin Sais

THE CROW'S NEST
(Sunset Prod./Aywon, September 15, 1922) 5 Reels
Jack Hoxie, Evelyn Nelson, Ruddel Weatherwax, Tom Lingham, William Lester, William Dyer, Mary Bruce, Bert Lindley, Augustina Lopez
Director: Paul Hurst
Story: William Lester

BACK FIRE
(Sunset Prod./Aywon, November 1, 1922) 5 Reels
Jack Hoxie, Marin Sais, Thomas Lingham, Jack Pierce, Pat Harmon, Frank Rice
Director/Screenplay: Robert N. Bradbury

RIDERS OF THE LAW
(Sunset Productions, December 15, 1922) 5 Reels
Jack Hoxie, Marin Sais, Thomas Lingham, Jack Pierce, Pat Harmon, Frank Rice
Director/Screenplay: Robert N. Bradbury

THE FORBIDDEN TRAIL
(Sunset Productions, February 1, 1923) 5 Reels
Jack Hoxie, Evelyn Nelson, Frank Rice, William Lester, Joe McDermott, Tom Lingham, Steve Clemento
Director/Story/Screenplay: Robert N. Bradbury

GALLOPIN' THROUGH
(Sunset Productions, March 15, 1923) 5 Reels
Jack Hoxie, Priscilla Bonner, William Lester, Janet Ford, Doreen Turner
Director: Robert N. Bradbury

WOLF TRACKS
(Sunset Productions, April, 1923) 5 Reels
Jack Hoxie, Marin Sais, James Welch, Tom Lingham, Kate Price, Andrea Tourneur, William Lester
Director: Robert N. Bradbury
Story: William Lester

DESERT RIDER
(Sunset Productions, June, 1923) 5 Reels
Jack Hoxie, Evelyn Nelson, Frank Rice, Claude Payton, Tom Lingham, Walter Wilkinson, "Scout"
Director: Robert North Bradbury
Story: Frank Howard Clark

DON QUICKSHOT OF THE RIO GRANDE
(Universal, June 4, 1923) 5 Reels
Jack Hoxie, Elinor Field, Emmett King, Fred C. Jones, William Steele, Bob McKenzie, Harry Woods, Hank Bell, Ben Corbett, Skeeter Bill Robbins, "Scout"
Director: George Marshall
Scenario: George Hively
Story: Stephen Chambers

WHERE IS THIS WEST?
(Universal, September 17, 1923) 5 Reels
Jack Hoxie, Mary Philbin, Bob McKenzie, Sid Jordan, Slim Cole, Joseph Girard, Bernard Siegel, "Scout"
Director: George Marshall
Scenario: George C. Hively
Story: George C. Hull

MEN IN THE RAW
(Universal, October 16, 1923) 5 Reels
Jack Hoxie, Marguerite Clayton, Sid Jordan, J. Morris Foster, Tom Kerrick, William A. Lowry, Art Manning, "Scout"
Director: George Marshall
Scenario: George C. Hively
Story: Bert W. Foster

THE RED WARNING
(Universal, December 17, 1923) 5 Reels
Jack Hoxie, Elinor Field, Fred Kohler, Frank Rice, Jim Welsh, William Welsh, Ben Corbett, Ralph Fee McCullough, Al Hoxie, "Scout"
Director: R. N. Bradbury
Story/Scenario: Isadore Bernstein

THE MAN FROM WYOMING
(Universal, January 28, 1924) 5 Reels
Jack Hoxie, Lillian Rich, William Welsh, Claude Peyton, Ben Corbett, Lon Poff, George Kuwa, James Corrigan, "Scout"
Director: R. N. Bradbury
Adaptation/Continuity: Isadore Bernstein
Story: William McLeod Raine - "Wyoming, A Story of the Outdoor West"

THE PHANTOM HORSEMAN
(Universal, March 3, 1924) 5 Reels
Jack Hoxie, Lillian Rich, Neil McKinnon, Wade Boteler, William McCall, Ben Corbett, George A. Williams, Rudy Lafayette, "Scout"
Director: Robert N. Bradbury
Story/Scenario: Isadore Bernstein

THE GALLOPING ACE
(Universal, March 31, 1924) 5 Reels
Jack Hoxie, Margaret Morris, Robert McKim, Frank Rice, Fred Humes, Julia Brown, Dorthea Wolbert, "Scout"
Director: Robert N. Bradbury
Story: Jacques Jaccard - "Hard Rock"
Screenplay: Isadore Bernstein

RIDGEWAY OF MONTANA
(Universal, May 12, 1924) 5 Reels
Jack Hoxie, Olive Hasbrouck, Herbert Fortier, Lew Meehan, Charles Thurston, Pat Harmon, Lyndon Hobart, "Scout"
Director: Cliff Smith
Scenario: E. Richard Schayer
Story: William McLeod Raine - "A Sacrifice to Mammon"

THE BACK TRAIL
(Universal, June 16, 1924) 5 Reels
Jack Hoxie, Eugenia Gilbert, Alton Stone (Al Hoxie), Claude Payton, William Lester, Bill McCall, Buck Connors, Pat Harmon, "Scout"
Director: Cliff Smith
Scenario: Isadore Bernstein
Story: Walter J. Coburn

FIGHTING FURY
(Universal, August 24, 1924) 5 Reels
Jack Hoxie, Helen Holmes, Fred Kohler, Duke R. Lee, Bert DeMarc, Al Jennings, George "Buck" Connors, Art Manning, "Scout"
Director: Cliff Smith
Story: Walter J. Coburn - "Triple Cross for Danger"
Scenario: Isadore Bernstein

THE WESTERN WALLOP
(Universal, October 10, 1924) 5 Reels
Jack Hoxie, Margaret Landis, James Gordon Russell, Charles Brinley, Duke R. Lee, Fred Burns, Jack Pratt, Herbert Fortier, Joseph W. Girard, William Welsh, "Scout"
Director: Cliff Smith
Screenplay: Wyndham Gittens
Story: Adolph Bannauer - "On Parole"

DARING CHANCES
(Universal, October 19, 1924) 5 Reels
Jack Hoxie, Alta Allen, Claude Payton, Jack Pratt, Catherine Wallace, Doreen Turner, Genevieve Danninger, Newton Campbell, William McCall, "Scout"
Director: Cliff Smith
Continuity: Wyndham Gittens
Story: Isadore Bernstein

THE CITY OF STARS
(Universal, 1924) 28 Minutes
William Desmond, Norman Kerry, Jean Hersholt, Reginald Denny, *Jack Hoxie,* Laura LaPlante, Pat O'Malley, Alice Joyce, Clive Brook, Hoot Gibson, May McAvoy, Marian Nixon
Director: H. Bruce Humberstone
(This was some kind of promotional release filmed in and around Universal City, with many of the studio's stars being seen at work and play)

THE SIGN OF THE CACTUS
(Universal, January 4, 1925) 5 Reels
Jack Hoxie, Helen Holmes, J. Gordon Russell, Francis Ford, Josef Swickard, Frank Newbert, Jack Pratt, Bobby Gordon, Muriel Frances Dana, "Scout"
Director: Cliff Smith
Scenario: Isadore Bernstein
Story: Norman Wilde

A ROARING ADVENTURE
(Universal, February 8, 1925) 5 Reels
Jack Hoxie, Mary McAllister, Marin Sais, J. Gordon Russell, Jack Pratt, Francis Ford, Margaret Smith, "Scout"
Director: Cliff Smith
Continuity: Percy Heath
Adaptation: Isadore Bernstein
Story: Jack Rollens - "The Tenderfoot"

FLYING HOOFS
(Universal, February 8, 1925) 5 Reels
Jack Hoxie, Charlotte Stevens, Bartlett Carre, William Welsh, J. Gordon Russell, Alys Murrell, Duke R. Lee, "Scout"
Director: Cliff Smith
Story: Clee Woods - "Beyond the Law"

RIDIN' THUNDER
(Universal, June 14, 1925) 5 Reels
Jack Hoxie, Katherine Grant, Jack Pratt, Francis Ford, George (Buck) Connors, Bert De Mare, William McCall, Broderick O'Farrell, Al Hoxie, "Scout"
Director: Cliff Smith
Continuity: Carl Krusada
Adaptation: Isadore Bernstein
Story: B. M. Bower - "Jean of Lazy A"

DON DAREDEVIL
(Universal, July 18, 1925) 5 Reels
Jack Hoxie, Cathleen Calhoun, Duke Lee, William Welsh, Thomas G. Lingham, Evelyn Sherman, William A. Steele, Cesare Gravina, Tommy Grimes, Demetrius Alexis, "Scout"
Director: Cliff Smith
Story/Scenario: Wyndham Gittens

A Lobby Card from Universal (1926) showing Olive Hasbrouck and Jack Hoxie.

THE RED RIDER
(Universal, August 2, 1925) 5 Reels
Jack Hoxie, Mary McAllister, Jack Pratt, Natalie War-field, William McCall, Marin Sais, Francis Ford, George Connors, Frank Lanning, Clark Comstock, Duke R. Lee, Chief Big Tree, William Welsh, Virginia True Boardman, "Scout"
Director: Cliff Smith
Story: Isadore Bernstein, Wyndham Gittens

THE WHITE OUTLAW
(Universal, September 6, 1925) 5 Reels
Jack Hoxie, Marceline Day, William Welsh, Duke Lee, Floyd Shackleford, Charles Brinley, "Scout"
Director: Cliff Smith
Screenplay: Isadore Bernstein

BUSTIN' THRU
(Universal, October 18, 1925) 5 Reels
Jack Hoxie, Helen Lynch, William Norton Bailey, Alfred Allen, George Grandee, "Scout"
Director: Cliff Smith
Story/Continuity: Buckleigh F. Oxford

HIDDEN LOOT
(Universal, October 31, 1925) 5 Reels
Jack Hoxie, Olive Hasbrouck, Edward Cecil, Jack Kenny, Buck Connors, Bert De Marc, Charles Brinley, "Scout"
Director: Robert N. Bradbury
Story: William J. Neidig
Scenario: Harry Dittmar

TWO FISTED JONES
(Universal, December 6, 1925) 5 Reels
Jack Hoxie, Kathryn McGuire, William Steele, Harry Todd, Frank Rice, Paul Grimes, William Welsh, Frederick Cole, Byron Douglas, Ed Burns, Art Ortego, "Scout"
Director: Edward Sedgwick
Story: Sarah Saddoris
Screenplay: W. Scott Darling

THE DEMON
(Universal, January 31, 1926) 5 Reels
Jack Hoxie, Lola Todd, William Welsh, Jere Austin, Al Jennings, Georgie Grandee, Harry Semels, "Scout"
Director: Cliff Smith
Continuity: Buckleigh F. Oxford
Story: Buckleigh F. Oxford

A SIX SHOOTIN' ROMANCE
(Universal, March 7, 1926) 5 Reels
Jack Hoxie, Olive Hasbrouck, William A. Steele, Carmen Phillips, Robert McKenzie, Mattie Peters, Virginia Bradford, "Scout"
Director: Cliff Smith
Scenario: Alvin J. Neitz
Story: Ruth Comfort Mitchell - "Dashing"

THE BORDER SHERIFF
(Universal, April 25, 1926) 5 Reels
Jack Hoxie, Olive Hasbrouck, S. E. Jennings, Gilbert Holmes, Buck Moulton, Tom Lingham, Bert De Marc, Frank Rice, Floyd Criswell, Leonard Trainer, "Scout"
Director/Continuity: Robert N. Bradbury
Story: W. C. Tuttle - "Straight Shootin' "

LOOKING FOR TROUBLE
(Universal, May 30, 1926) 5 Reels
Jack Hoxie, Marceline Day, Gordon Russell, Clark Comstock, Edmund Cobb, Bud Osborne, Peggy Montgomery, William Dyer, "Scout"
Director: Robert N. Bradbury
Scenario: George C. Hively
Story: Stephen Chalmers

THE FIGHTING PEACEMAKER
(Universal, July 7, 1926) 5 Reels
Jack Hoxie, Lola Todd, Ted Oliver, William A. Steele, Bob McKenzie, Clark Comstock, Frank Rice, "Scout"
Director: Cliff Smith
Scenario: Alvin J. Neitz, Harrison Jacobs
Story: W. C. Tuttle - "Peace Medicine"

THE LAST FRONTIER
(Metropolitan/Producers Dist. Co., August 16, 1926) 8 Reels
William Boyd, Marguerite De La Motte, *Jack Hoxie,* Junior Coghlan, Mitchell Lewis, Gladys Brockwell, Frank Lackteen, J. Farrell MacDonald, Sally Rand
Director: George B. Seitz
Adaptation: Will M. Ritchey
Story: Courtney Ryley Cooper

THE WILD HORSE STAMPEDE
(Universal, September 5, 1926) 5 Reels
Jack Hoxie, Fay Wray, William Steele, Marin Sais, Clark Comstock, Jack Pratt, George Kesterson (Art Mix), Bert De Marc, Monte Montague, "Scout"
Director: Albert Rogell
Scenario: Doris Malloy
Story: W. C. Tuttle - "Blind Trails"

RED HOT LEATHER
(Universal, October 17, 1926) 5 Reels
Jack Hoxie, Ena Gregory, William Malan, Tom Shirley, William H. Turner, George French, Billy Engle, Jim Corey, Leo (Syd) Saylor, "Scout"
Director/Story: Albert Rogell
Adaptation/Scenario: Harrison Jacobs, Albert Rogell

ROUGH AND READY
(Universal, January 9, 1927) 5 Reels
Jack Hoxie, Ena Gregory, Jack Pratt, William A. Steele, Monte Montague, Clark Comstock, Marin Sais, Bert De Marc, "Scout"
Director: Albert Rogell
Continuity: William Lester
Story: Gardner Bradford

THE WESTERN WHIRLWIND
(Universal, February 20, 1927) 5 Reels
Jack Hoxie, Margaret Quimby, Claude Payton, "Scout"
Director/Story: Albert Rogell
Scenario: Harrison Jacobs

THE RAMBLING RANGER
(Universal, April 10, 1927) 5 Reels
Jack Hoxie, Dorothy Gulliver, C. E. Anderson, Monte Montague, Charles Avery, Monte Montague, Jr., "Scout," "Bunk" (a dog)
Director: Dell Henderson
Story/Scenario: George C. Hively

Fay Wray holds the hand of Jack Hoxie in **Wild Horse Stampede** (Universal, 1926)

GRINNING GUNS
(Universal, May 22, 1927) 5 Reels

Jack Hoxie, Ena Gregory, Robert Milasch, Arthur Morrison, George French, Dudley Hendricks, Alphonse Martell, "Scout"
Director: Albert Rogell
Story/Scenario: Grover Jones

MEN OF DARING
(Universal, June 5, 1927) 6 Reels

Jack Hoxie, Ena Gregory, Marin Sais, Francis Ford, James Kelly, Ernie Adams, Robert Milash, Bert Lindley, Bert Apling, William Malan, John Hall, Joseph Bennett, "Scout"
Director: Albert Rogell
Story/Scenario: Marion Jackson

THE FIGHTING THREE
(Universal, July 3, 1927) 5 Reels

Jack Hoxie, Olive Hasbrouck, Marin Sais, Fanny Warren, William Malan. Buck Connors, William Dyer, Henry Roquemore, William Norton Bailey, "Scout"
Director: Albert Rogell
Story/Scenario: William Lester

HEROES OF THE WILD
(Mascot, November 1, 1927) 10 Chapters

Jack Hoxie, Josephine Hill, T. Bryant, Helen Gibson, Linda Loredo, Joe Bonomo, "Tornado" (a dog), "White Fury" (a horse)
Director: Harry Webb
Chapter Titles: (1)Heroes of the Wild (2) Sword to Sword (3) The Plunge of Peril (4) The Slide of Life (5) The Trap of Death (6) The Flaming Fiend (7) The Clutching Hand (8) The Broken Cable (9) The Fatal Hour (10) The Crown of the Incas

A Lobby Card from 1932 showing Tom London and Jack Hoxie.

133

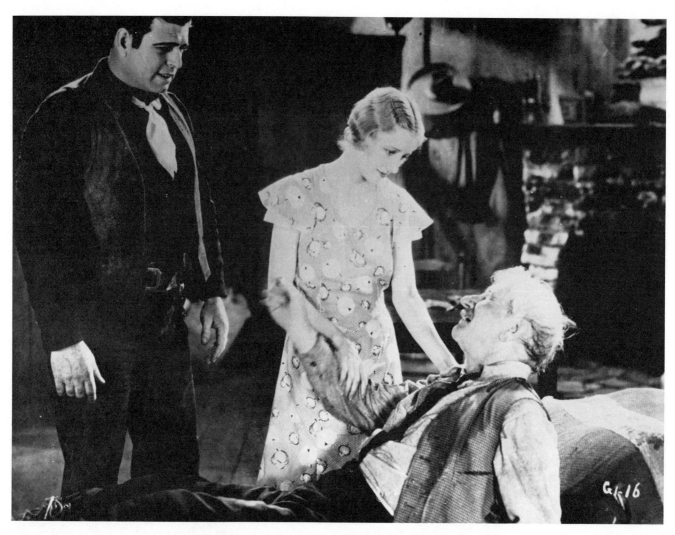

Jack Hoxie and Alice Day comfort Lafe McKee in **Gold** (Majestic, 1932).

OUTLAW JUSTICE

(Majestic, October 1, 1932) 61 Minutes
Jack Hoxie, Dorothy Gulliver, Chris-Pin Martin, Donald Keith, Kermit Maynard, Charles King, Jack Trent, Walter Shumway, Jack Rockwell, Tom London, "Scout"
Director: Armand Schaefer
Story: W. Scott Darling
Screenplay: Oliver Drake
Producer: Larry Darmour

GOLD

(Majestic, October 5, 1932) 48 Minutes
Jack Hoxie, Alice Day, Hooper Atchley, Jack Clifford, Bob Kortman, Tom London, Lafe McKee, Mathew Betz, Harry Todd, Archie Ricks, Jack Kirk, Jack Byron, "Scout"
Director: Otto Brower
Story: Jack Natteford
Screenplay: W. Scott Darling
Producer: Larry Darmour

LAW AND LAWLESS

(Majestic, November 30, 1932) 59 Minutes
Jack Hoxie, Hilda Moore, Wally Wales, Yakima Canutt, Julian Rivero, Jack Mower, J. Frank Glendon, Edith Fellows, Helen Gibson, Robert Burns, Alma Rayford, Joe De LaCruz, Fred Burns, Elvero Sonchez, William Quinn, Al Taylor, Dixie Starr, "Scout"
Director: Armand Schaefer
Story/Screenplay: Oliver Drake
Producer: Larry Darmour

VIA PONY EXPRESS

(Majestic, February 6, 1933) 60 Minutes
Jack Hoxie, Marceline Day, Lane Chandler, Julian Rivero, Doris Hill, Mathew Betz, Joe Girard, Charles K. French, Bill Quinlan, "Scout"
Director: Lew Collins
Screenplay: Lew Collins, Oliver Drake
Producer: Larry Darmour

GUN LAW
(Majestic, April 1, 1933) 59 Minutes
Jack Hoxie, Betty Boyd, J. Frank Glendon, Paul Fix,
Mary Carr, Harry Todd, Ben Corbett, Dick Botiller,
Edmund Cobb, Robert Burns, Jack Kirk, Horace B.
Carpenter, "Scout"
Director: Lew Collins
Screenplay: Lew Collins, Oliver Drake
Producer: Larry Darmour

TROUBLE BUSTERS
(Majestic, May 15, 1933) 55 Minutes
Jack Hoxie, Lane Chandler, Kaye Edwards, Ben Corbett, Harry Todd, Slim Whitaker, William Burt, Roger
Williams, "Scout"
Director: Lew Collins
Story: Oliver Drake
Screenplay: Oliver Drake, Lew Collins
Producer: Larry Darmour

Tom Tyler

7 ● TOM TYLER

Like a Whiff of Honeysuckle Across a Cow-dung Pasture

In 1950 a once great cowboy ace, then only a shadow of the superb physical speciman he once was, played heavies in a series of six cheap Westerns starring Jimmy Ellison and Russell Hayden, produced back-to-back in a matter of days, and released by Lippert, a small independent studio. Along about the same time he could also be seen menacing Tim Holt and Lash LaRue in programmers and Glenn Ford, Randy Scott, Robert Mitchum, and Robert Ryan in larger-scale Westerns. His last recognition as a Western titan came in late 1950 when he had a brief guest-star cameo in the Roy Rogers starrer, **Trail of Robin Hood.** His many fans were both elated and pained—elated at the brief recognition afforded an old favorite, pained as they remembered the muscular athlete of only seven or eight years before who had thrilled audiences as Captain Marvel.

Tom Tyler made only a handful of pictures after the Rogers film. His roles were hardly more than bits. Crippling arthritis had gripped him about 1945 and his health failed rapidly. After dropping out of films for nearly two years, Tom tried to make a comeback as a character actor. To a degree he succeeded, for his performances in such films as **Cheyenne** (WB, '47), **Return of the Badman** (RKO, '48), **Blood on the Moon** (RKO, '48), and **The Younger Brothers** (WB, '49), though only minor roles, were good. But his illness grew worse and by 1952 he was unable to work. Penniless, and only 48 years old, he returned to his sister's home in Detroit where he lived until a heart attack felled him at age 50 on May 1, 1954. Very little news coverage was given his death and only a few fans were ever aware of his long illness and death. It was hardly an ending befit-

ting one of Tom Tyler's stature in the Western and serial genres. In his day he had been a real powerhouse in the rough-and-tumble market, and his flicks were generally okay for solo one-day showings and espcially safe on double grind bills.

Tyler was agile and pleasant and put plenty of realism into his work, whether doing a rescue, a slam-bang saloon fight or a wild canter over the plains. His climactic fistic battles were sometimes teeth-rattling affairs. His were what might be called substantial Westerns, typical in plot, characters, surroundings, and undoubtedly produced in the best interests of that elusive patronage in uncharted parts of the country. Tom often had most of his personality wrapped up in a whimsical smile, but his knack for hard riding and putting on the semblance of a good fist fight was ever apparent.

Tom was born Vincent Markowski on August 9, 1903 in Port Henry, New York, hardly a name or a desirable birthplace for a hero of the Old West. His childhood was spent mostly in Port Henry. About the time of his high school graduation the family moved to Detroit and he spent some time there. Tom had excelled in athletics and during the next few years he perfected his skill as a weight lifter while working as a seaman on a merchant steamer, mining coal in Pennsylvania, lumbering in the Northwest, performing as a boxer and muscleman in a circus sideshow, and a few other assorted jobs. His ambition since high school had been the movies, and he finally worked his way to Hollywood in late 1923, armed with a portfolio of photographs of himself. He soon found an agent and work.

Tyler's first known role was a bit in **Three Weeks** ('24) for Goldwyn Pictures. In **Leatherstocking,** the Pathe serial of 1924, he played an Indian in the Edna Murphy-James Pierce starrer, giving little indication that he would one day be one of the more important thrillmakers of serialdom.

While a member of the Los Angeles Athletic Club, Tyler created a new world's amateur record in the right-hand clean and jerk lift of 213 pounds. He scaled at 197 pounds in his prime and was over 6 feet tall, a perfect specimen of the all-around athlete. In 1928 he set a new world's record in weight-lifting in the heavyweight class when he lifted 760 pounds. This record stood for fourteen years.

While working in the film **Ben Hur** at MGM, Tom was signed for a Western series by an agent of R-C Pictures, releasing through FBO. Although he had never ridden a horse, he jumped at the chance to be a cowboy star and quickly learned the rudiments of horsemanship, eventually becoming an expert rider. His first Western was **Let's Go Gallagher** ('25), and go he did—galloping through smoke and bullets with six-shooter blazing in a red-hot action story. His billing was as Tom Tyler. Never again would he be known as Vincent Markowski.

Twenty-eight more whirlwind thrillers followed for RC-FBO, with fast, furious action, gunplay galore, and Tom himself in some of the most daring stunts ever filmed. He was only 23 and in the pink of condition. What he didn't have in thespian talents he more than made up for in red-blooded stories built around his athletic prowess. Little Frankie Darro was in most of the Tyler Westerns, and the two worked well together. It was refreshing to see stories built around a talented youngster of Darro's caliber and not have to be subjected to ludicrousness of an all-thumbs, cornball-acting sidekick with the brains of a cow. Some interesting

Tom Tyler disarms a villain in an unusual way in **Terror of the Plains** (Reliable, 1934)

Ray Bennett, Rufe Davis, Norman Willis (a.k.a. Jack Norman), Tom Tyler and Bob Steele in **Gauchos of El Dorado**
(Republic, 1941)

stories resulted from the involvement of a boy in the cow-country goings-on. Doris Hill, Peggy Montgomery, Jean Arthur, and Nora Lane were among the bevy of heroines gracing the Tyler Westerns and although romance was never really played up much in these action opuses, their talent and beauty added considerably to the overall enjoyment of the films, for they had above-average acting ability and succeeded in making a name for themselves as Western heroines.

When FBO temporarily ceased making Westerns in 1929, Tyler moved over to Syndicate, as did Bob Steele, Bob Custer, and some others. He made a total of eight silent Westerns, most of them directed by J. P. McGowan and scripted by Sally Winters. While Syndicate was tooling up for the production of sound features Mascot hired Tyler for the lead in the sound serial, **The Phantom of the West** ('30). His deep, commanding voice registered satisfactorily and was in

keeping with his physical appearance; thus, it was an asset rather than, as with John Gilbert, Art Acord, and Tom Mix, a liability.

Fast-moving action was the basic ingredient of serials, with romance, heavy drama, and realistic stories usually cast aside in the pursuit of a film print capable of producing shrieks and shrills from an audience of juveniles. Tyler was ideally suited as a bigger-than-life hero and was enthusiastically accepted by Saturday matinee audiences. In fact, only Buster Crabbe exceeded him in popularity as a cliffhanger super hero in the sound era. In the next thirteen years Tom was to star in six more serials: **Battling with Buffalo Bill** (Univ., '31), **Jungle Mystery** (Univ., '31), **Clancy of the Mounted** (Univ., '31), **The Phantom of the Air** (Univ., '33), **Adventures of Captain Marvel** (Rep., '41), and **The Phantom** (Col., '43). All in all Tom starred in roughly 28 to 30 hours of escapist fare spread

139

out over 85 weeks in 20-25-minute segments. Thus, the serials gave him a lot of exposure and his later features benefited from his serial popularity.

Tom's first sound features were for Syndicate, beginning with **West of Cheyenne** ('31) and followed by **God's Country and the Man** ('31) and **A Rider of the Plains** ('31). During the 1931-'32 season he completed eight Westerns for the newly-formed Monogram Pictures, them moved over to Freuler-Monarch for four of the better independent Westerns of 1933.

Tyler signed with Bernard B. Ray's Reliable Pictures (releasing through William Steiner) in 1934 and kicked up a lot of trail dust as he charged through eighteen slam-bang shoot-em-ups as the virtuous hero determined to see justice triumph and the heroine's virtue remain spotless. In a change of character, though, he played Sundown Saunders, a gunman with a conscience, in RKO's all-star western **Powdersmoke Range** ('35), and an unsympathetic gang leader in the same studio's **The Last Outlaw** ('36). Both films starred Harry Carey and Hoot Gibson. Thereafter Tom took on offbeat character roles now and then in addition to playing the stalwart hero. Tom could change from white hat to black hat and back again with little difficulty.

In 1936-'37 Tyler made eight programmers for Sam Katzman's Victory Pictures and then toured for a season with the Wallace Brothers Circus as its stellar attraction. Besides being a Western movie star, Tom was good on the horizontal bars.

Back in Hollywood after the circus tour, Tom was unable to land another series and so began to play villainous and character roles. His portrayal as Luke Plummer in John Ford's classic **Stagecoach** (UA, '39) was convincing evidence that Tom was capable of more than simply "They went that-a-way" dramatics. **Frontier Marshal** (Fox, '39), **Gone with the Wind** (MGM, '39), **Brother Orchid** (WB, '40), **Cherokee Strip** (Par., '40), **Texas Rangers Ride Again** (Par., '40), **The Grapes of Wrath** (20th C.-Fox, '40), and **The Mummy's Hand** (Univ., '40) gave him further opportunities to expand his dramatic boundaries.

In 1941 Robert Livingston dropped out of the popular 3 Mesquiteers series at Republic and was replaced by Tyler in the "Stony Brooke" role. Co-starring in the trio with him was his old friend from the FBO and Syndicate days, Bob Steele. Rufe Davis was the comic in the first six features that Tom made as a Mesquiteer, and Jimmie Dodd took over for the next six. Republic turned out a glossy product that spelled quality in the low-budget field and the trio was a popular one, making the "Top 10" list in 1941, '42, and '43. Several non-western roles were taken by Tom during this period of time, most notable being the lead in **The Adventures of Captain Marvel**; it was based on the comic strip and

was one of the most popular serials ever produced by Republic. Tyler's last serial, also casting him as a comic-strip hero, was **The Phantom** (Col., '43), a run-of-the-mill cliffhanger from the technical standpoint but a popular film with the juvenile trade. Columbia also gave Tyler one of the leads in **Sing Me a Song of Texas** ('45), a musical western with Rosemary Lane, The Hoosier Hot Shots, and Guinn (Big Boy) Williams also featured.

After 1945 it was all downhill for Tom as the crippling arthritis and other physical complications sapped away at his once great physique. His last several years on the screen were spent mostly playing heavies, at which he was very good. Few could portray a bad gunman more convincingly than Tom.

And so the last sunset arrived for yet another great cowboy. Tom Tyler will be remembered for as long as there are those who can recall the days of the 'B' Western when heroic saddle aces engaged in thrilling conflicts of wits, fists, knives, horsemanship, and guns, the *beau ideal* of open-air adventure entertainment. The Tyler sagas usually contained a punch in every minute of action without a lingering pause until the amazing cyclonic finish when Tom produced more dazzling gunplay, hard riding, and desperate fighting than you could find in any other two stories of the wide open spaces.

TOM TYLER Filmography

THREE WEEKS
(Goldwyn Pictures/Goldwyn-Cosmopolitan, February 10, 1924) 8 Reels
Aileen Pringle, Conrad Nagel, John Sainpolis, H. Reeves Smith, Stuart Holmes, Mitchell Lewis, Robert Cain, Nigel De Brulier, Claire De Lorez, Dale Fuller, Helen Dunbar, Alan Crosland, Jr., Joan Standing, William Haines, George Tustain, Dane Rudhyar, Vincent Markowski *(Tom Tyler)*
Director: Alan Crosland
Scenario/Story: Elinor Glyn
Adaptation: Carey Wilson

LEATHERSTOCKING
(Pathe, March 23, 1924) 10 Chapters
Edna Murphy, James Pierce, Harold Miller, David Dunbar, Frank Lackteen, Whitehorse, Vincent Markowski *(Tom Tyler)*
Director: George B. Seitz
Story: Robert Dillon
Based on novels by James Fenimore Cooper
Chapter Titles: (1) The Warpath (2) The Secret Trail (3) The Hawk's Eyes (4) The Paleface Law (5) Ransom (6) The Betrayal (7) Rivenoak's Revenge (8) Out of the Storm (9) The Panther (10) Mingo Torture

LET'S GO GALLAGHER
(R-C Pictures/FBO, September 20, 1924) 52 Minutes
Tom Tyler, Barbara Starr, Olin Francis, Sam Peterson, Alfred Hewston, Frankie Darro
Director: Robert De Lacey, James Gruen
Story/Continuity: Percy Heath, James Gruen

THE WYOMING WILDCAT
(R-C Pictures/FBO, November 1, 1925) 52 Minutes
Tom Tyler, Virginia Southern, Billie Bennett, Gilbert Clayton, Ethan Laidlaw, Alfred Hewston, Thomas Delmar, Frankie Darro
Director: Robert De Lacey
Story/Scenario: Percy Heath

THE ONLY THING
(MGM/Metro-Goldwyn Dist. Corp., November 22, 1925) 58 Minutes
Eleanor Boardman, Conrad Nagel, Edward Connelly, Louis Payne, Arthur Edmund Carewe, Vera Lewis, Carrie Clark Ward, Constance Wylie, Dale Fuller, Ned Sparks, Mario Carillo, David Mir, Mary Hawes, Michael Pleschkoff, Buddy Smith, Joan Crawford, Frank Braidwood, Derek Glynne, Vincent Markowski *(Tom Tyler)*
Director: Jack Conway
Story/Adaptation: Elinor Glyn

THE COWBOY MUSKETEER
(R-C Pictures/FBO, December 13, 1925) 45 Minutes
Tom Tyler, Frances Dare, Frankie Darro, Jim London, David Dunbar, "Beans" (a dog)
Director: Robert De Lacey
Story/Scenario: Buckleigh Oxford - "Up and at 'Em"

BORN TO BATTLE
(R-C Pictures/FBO, January 24, 1926) 52 Minutes
Tom Tyler, Jean Arthur, Ray Childs, Fred Gambold, Frankie Darro, Buck Black, Leroy Mason, Ethan Laidlaw, Irvin Renard, "Beans" (a dog)
Director: Robert De Lacey
Story/Scenario: William E. Wing

THE ARIZONA STREAK
(R-C Pictures/FBO, March 7, 1926) 47 Minutes
Tom Tyler, Alfred Hewston, Ada Mae Vaughn, Frankie Darro, Dave Ward, Leroy Mason, Ed Smith, Mary Lane, Jack Anthony, "Beans" (a dog)
Director: Robert De Lacey
Story: George Worthington Yates, Jr.
Continuity: Lanier Bartlett

WILD TO GO
(R-C Pictures/FBO, April 18, 1926) 46 Minutes
Tom Tyler, Eugenie Gilbert, Frankie Darro, Fred Burns, Ethan Laidlaw, Earl Haley, "Sitting Bull" (a dog)
Director: Robert De Lacey
Story/Adaptation: F. A. E. Pine

THE MASQUERADE BANDIT
(R-C Pictures/FBO, May 30, 1926) 49 Minutes
Tom Tyler, Dorothy Dunbar, Ethan Laidlaw, Alfred Hewston, Ray Childs, Raye Hamilton, Earl Haley, Frankie Darro
Director: Robert De Lacey
Scenario: William E. Wing
Story: Enid Hibbard, Ethel Hill

THE COWBOY COP
(R-C Pictures/FBO, July 11, 1926) 44 Minutes
Tom Tyler, Jean Arthur, Irvin Renard, Frankie Darro, Pat Harmon, Earl Haley, "Beans" (a dog)
Director: Robert De Lacey
Story: Frank Richard Pierce
Continuity: F. A. E. Pine

TOM AND HIS PALS
(R-C Pictures/FBO, September 4, 1926) 44 Minutes
Tom Tyler, Doris Hill, Frankie Darro, Dickey Brandon, Helen Lynch, Leroy Mason, Frank Woods, "Beans" and "Sitting Bull" (both dogs)
Director: Robert De Lacey
Story: Frederick Arthur Mindlin - "Cowpunching for Cupid"
Continuity: F. A. E. Pine

OUT OF THE WEST
(R-C Pictures/FBO, September 26, 1926) 46 Minutes
Tom Tyler, Bernice Welch, Harry J. O'Connor, Ethan Laidlaw, Alfred Hewston, Frankie Darro, Gertrude Claire, Barney Furey, "Beans" (a dog)
Director: Robert De Lacey
Story: Frederick Arthur Mindlin
Continuity: Wyndham Gittens

RED HOT HOOFS
(R-C Pictures/FBO, December 19, 1926) 47 Minutes
Tom Tyler, Frankie Darro, Dorothy Dunbar, Stanley Taylor, Harry O'Connor, Al Kaufman, Barney Furey
Director: Robert De Lacey
Story: George Worthington Yates - "The Kid's Last Fight"
Adaptation/Continuity: F. A. E. Pine

LIGHTNING LARIATS

(R-C Pictures/FBO, January 30, 1927) 46 Minutes
Tom Tyler, Dorothy Dunbar, Frankie Darro, Ruby Blaine, Fred Holmes, Irvin Renard, Carl Silvera, LeRoy Scott
Director: Robert De Lacey
Scenario: F. A. E. Pine
Story: George Worthington Yates, Jr. - "The Cowboy and the King"

THE SONORA KID

(R-C Pictures/FBO, March 13, 1927) 46 Minutes
Tom Tyler, Peggy Montgomery, Billie Bennett, Mark Hamilton, Jack Richardson, Ethan Laidlaw, Bruce Gordon, Barney Furey, Vic Allen, "Beans" (a dog)
Director: Robert De Lacey
Scenario: J. G. Hawks
Continuity: Percy Heath
Story: William Wallace Cook - "A Knight of the Range"

CYCLONE OF THE RANGE

(R-C Pictures/FBO, April 24, 1927) 48 Minutes
Tom Tyler, Elsie Tarron, Harry O'Connor, Richard Howard, Frankie Darro, Bert Hadley, Harry Woods, "Beans" (a dog)
Director: Robert De Lacey
Story: Oliver Drake
Continuity: Arthur Statter

SPLITTING THE BREEZE

(R-C Pictures/FBO, May 29, 1927) 50 Minutes
Tom Tyler, Peggy Montgomery, Harry Woods, Barney Furey, Tom Lingham, Red Lennox, Alfred Hewston, Barbara Starr, "Beans" (a dog)
Director: Robert De Lacey
Story/Continuity: Frank Howard Clark

TOM'S GANG

(R-C Pictures/FBO, July 10, 1927) 50 Minutes
Tom Tyler, Sharon Lynn, Frankie Darro, Harry Woods, Frank Rice, Barney Furey, Tom Lingham, Jack Anthony, "Beans" (a dog)
Director: Robert De Lacey
Story/Continuity: Frank Howard Clark

THE FLYING U RANCH

(R-C Pictures/FBO, September 4, 1927) 49 Minutes
Tom Tyler, Nora Lane, Bert Hadley, Grace Woods, Frankie Darro, Olin Francis, Barney Furey, Dudley Hendricks, Bill Patton, "Beans" (a dog)
Director: Robert De Lacey
Scenario: Oliver Drake
Story: B. M. Bower - "The Flying U Ranch"

BEN-HUR

(MGM, October 8, 1927) 117 Minutes
(Technicolor sequences) (Film actually completed in 1925)
Ramon Novarro, Francis X. Bushman, May McAvoy, Betty Bronson, Claire McDowell, Kathleen Key, Carmel Myers, Nigel De Brulier, Mitchell Lewis, Leo White, Frank Currier, Charles Belcher, Dale Fuller, Winter Hall, Vincent Markowski *(Tom Tyler)*
Director: Fred Niblo
Scenario: Bess Meredyth, Carey Wilson
2nd Unit Director: Reaves Easton
Story: Lew Wallace - "Ben-Hur, A Tale of the Christ"
Producers: Louis B. Mayer, Samuel Goldwyn, Irving Thalberg

THE CHEROKEE KID

(FBO, October 30, 1927) 49 Minutes
Tom Tyler, Sharon Lynn, Jerry Pembroke, Robert Burns, Robert Reeves, Ray Childs, James Van Horn, Carol Holloway, Frankie Darro, Thomas Lingham, Barney Furey, "Beans" (a dog)
Director: Robert De Lacey
Story: Joseph Kane
Adaptation/Continuity: Oliver Drake

THE DESERT PIRATE

(FBO, December 25, 1927) 5 Reels
Tom Tyler, Frankie Darro, Duane Thompson, Edward Hearn, Tom Lingham, Vester Pegg, Alfred Hewston, "Beans" (a dog)
Director: James Dugan
Story: Frank Howard Clark
Adaptation/Continuity: Oliver Drake

WHEN THE LAW RIDES

(FBO, February 26, 1928) 49 Minutes
Tom Tyler, Ione Reed, Frankie Darro, Harry O'Connor, Harry Woods, Charles Thurston, Bill Nestel, Barney Furey
Director: Robert De Lacey
Story/Continuity: Oliver Drake

PHANTOM OF THE RANGE

(FBO, April 22, 1928) 48 Minutes
Tom Tyler, Duane Thompson, Frankie Darro, Charles McHugh, James Pierce, Marjorie Zier, "Beans" (a dog)
Director: James Dugan
Story: Oliver Drake
Continuity: Frank Howard Clark

THE TEXAS TORNADO
(FBO, June 24, 1928) 48 Minutes
Tom Tyler, Nora Lane, Frankie Darro, Jack Anthony, Frank Whitson, Bob Burns, "Beans" (a dog)
Director/Story/Scenario: Frank Howard Clark

TERROR MOUNTAIN
(FBO, August 19, 1928) 49 Minutes
Tom Tyler, Ione Reed, Al Ferguson, Jules Cowles, Frankie Darro
Director: Louis King
Story: Wyndham Gittens
Continuity: Frank Howard Clark

THE AVENGING RIDER
(FBO, October 7, 1928) 48 Minutes
Tom Tyler, Florence Allen, Frankie Darro, Al Ferguson, Bob Fleming, Arthur Thalasso, Mal Davis
Director: Wallace Fox
Scenario: Frank Howard Clark
Story: Adele Buffington - "Dancing Hoofs"

TYRANT OF RED GULCH
(FBO, November 25, 1928) 48 Minutes
Tom Tyler, Frankie Darro, Josephine Borio, Harry Woods, Serge Temoff, Barney Furey
Director: Robert De Lacey
Story/Continuity: Oliver Drake

TRAIL OF THE HORSE THIEVES
(FBO/RKO, January 13, 1929) 48 Minutes
Tom Tyler, Sharon Lynn, Frankie Darro, Harry O'Connor, Barney Furey, Bill Nestell, Vic Allen, Ray Childs, Lee Willett
Director: Robert De Lacey
Screenplay: Frank Howard Clark
Story: William E. Wing - "Desert Madness"

GUN LAW
(FBO/RKO, March 3, 1929) 48 Minutes
Tom Tyler, Ethlyne Clair, Barney Furey, Frankie Darro, Lew Meehan, Tom Brooker, Harry Woods
Director: Robert De Lacey
Story/Scenario: Oliver Drake

IDAHO RED
(FBO/RKO, April 21, 1929) 48 Minutes
(Music and Sound Effects)
Tom Tyler, Frankie Darro, Patricia Caron, Barney Furey, Lew Meehan, Albert J. Smith, Yakima Canutt
Director: Robert De Lacey
Story/Screenplay: Frank Howard Clark

THE PRIDE OF PAWNEE
(FBO/RKO, June 9, 1929) 47½ Minutes
Tom Tyler, Ethlyne Clair, Frankie Darro, Barney Furey, Jack Hilliard, Lew Meehan, Jimmy Casey
Director: Robert De Lacey
Story: Joseph Kane
Screenplay: Frank Howard Clark

LAW OF THE PLAINS
(J. P. McGowan Productions/Syndicate, August 19, 1929) 48 Minutes
Tom Tyler, Natalie Joyce, Al Ferguson, J. P. McGowan, William Nolte, Francis Walker
Director: J. P. McGowan

THE MAN FROM NEVADA
(J. P. McGowan Productions/Syndicate, August, 1929) 47½ Minutes
Tom Tyler, Natalie Joyce, Al Ferguson, Alfred Hewston, Kip Cooper, Godfrey Craig, Frank Crane, Bill Nolte, Andrew Heragi, Cliff Lyons
Director: J. P. McGowan
Story/Scenario: Sally Winters

THE PHANTOM RIDER
(J. P. McGowan Productions/Syndicate, September 24, 1929) 48 Minutes
Tom Tyler, Lotus Thompson, Harry Woods, J. P. McGowan
Director: J. P. McGowan

'NEATH WESTERN SKIES
(J. P. McGowan Productions/Syndicate, October 18, 1929) 49 Minutes
Tom Tyler, Lotus Thompson, Hank Bell, Harry Woods, J. P. McGowan, Bobby Dunn, Alfred Hewston, Barney Furey
Director: J. P. McGowan
Story/Scenario: Sally Winters

THE LONE HORSEMAN
(J. P. McGowan Productions/Syndicate, November, 1929) 5 Reels
Tom Tyler, Charlotte Winn, J. P. McGowan, Black Jack Ward, Mrs. B. Tansey, Tom Bay, Mack V. Wright
Director: J. P. McGowan
Story/Scenario: Sally Winters

PIONEERS OF THE WEST

(J. P. McGowan Prod./Syndicate, November, 1929)
5 Reels
Tom Tyler, Charlotte Winn, J. P. McGowan, George Brownhill, Mack V. Wright, Tommy Bay
Director/Scenario: J. P. McGowan
Story: Sally Winters

HALF-PINT MOLLY

(Pathe, 1930) 2 Reels
(Rodeo Comedy Series)
Tom Tyler, Mona Ray, Hank McFarlene, Tom McFarlene, Bud Osborne, Marcio Manning, Harry O'Connor, Al Smith, Robert Dunn, Charles Clary
Producer: E. B. Derr

THE CANYON OF MISSING MEN

(J. P. McGowan Prod./Syndicate, February, 1930)
47½ Minutes
Tom Tyler, Sheila LeGay, Tom Forman, Bud Osborne, J. P. McGowan, Cliff Lyons, Bobby Dunn, Arden Ellis
Director: J. P. McGowan
Story: George H. Williams
Screenplay: Sally Winters

CALL OF THE DESERT

(J. P. McGowan Prod./Syndicate, March 1, 1930)
48 Minutes (Music Score)
Tom Tyler, Sheila LeGay, Bud Osborne, Cliff Lyons, Bobby Dunn
Director: J. P. McGowan
Story/Screenplay: Sally Winters

THE PHANTOM OF THE WEST

(Mascot, November 1, 1930) 10 Chapters
Tom Tyler, William Desmond, Dorothy Gulliver, Tom Santschi, Joe Bonomo, Tom Dugan, Philo McCullough, Kermit Maynard, Frank Lanning, Frank Hagney, Dick Dickinson, Halee Sullivan, Al Taylor, Ernie Adams, James Carlyle, Pee Wee Holmes
Director: Ross Lederman
Story/Screenplay: Wyndham Gittens, Ford Beebe, Bennett Cohen
Photography: Benjamin Kline, Ernest Miller, Joe Novak
Producer: Nat Levine
Chapter Titles: (1) The Ghost Riders (2) The Stairway of Doom (3) The Horror in the Dark (4) The Battle of the Strong (5) The League of the Lawless (6) The Canyon of Calamity (7) The Price of Silence (8) The House of Hate (9) The Fatal Secret (10) Rogue's Roundup

WEST OF CHEYENNE

(Syndicate, January 15, 1931) 56 Minutes
Tom Tyler, Josephine Hill, Harry Woods, Robert Walker, Ben Corbett, Fern Emmett, Lafe McKee, Lew Meehan, Charles Whitaker
Director/Producer: Harry S. Webb
Story/Screenplay: Bennett Cohen, Oliver Drake

GOD'S COUNTRY AND THE MAN

(Syndicate, May 1, 1931) 59 Minutes
Tom Tyler, Betty Mack, George Hayes, Ted Adams, Julian Rivero, Al Bridge, John Elliott, Gordon DeMain, Artie Ortego, William Bertram, Merrill McCormack, Carmen LaRoux, Slim Whitaker, Blackie Whiteford, Henry Roquemore, Al Haskell
Director: J. P. McCarthy
Story: John P. McCarthy, Alan Bridge
Screenplay: Wellyn Totman
Producer: Trem Carr
(Film also known as "Rose of the Rio Grande")

A RIDER OF THE PLAINS

(Syndicate, April 1, 1931) 57 Minutes
Tom Tyler, Andy Shuford, Lillian Bond, Alan Bridge, Gordon DeMain, Ted Adams, Fern Emmett, Slim Whitaker, Jack Perrin
Director: J. P. McCarthy
Story/Screenplay: Wellyn Totman
Producer: Trem Carr

PARTNERS OF THE TRAIL

(Monogram, July 11, 1931) 63 Minutes
Tom Tyler, Betty Mack, Lafe McKee, Reginald Sheffield, Horace B. Carpenter, Pat Rooney, Hank Bell, Art Ortego
Director: Wallace Fox
Story/Screenplay: G. A. Durlam
Producer: Trem Carr

THE MAN FROM DEATH VALLEY

(Monogram, September 9, 1931) 64 Minutes
Tom Tyler, Betty Mack, John Oscar, Si Jenks, Gino Corrado, Stanley Blystone, Hank Bell
Director: Lloyd Nosler
Story/Screenplay: George Arthur Durlam
Producer: Trem Carr

TWO-FISTED JUSTICE

(Monogram, October 20, 1931) 63 Minutes
Tom Tyler, Barbara Weeks, Bobby Nelson, Yakima Canutt, John Elliott, G. D. Wood, Gordon DeMain, Kit Guard, William Walling, Pedro Regas, Carl DeLoue, Joe Mills, Si Jenks
Director/Story/Screenplay: G. Arthur Durlam
Producer: Trem Carr

BATTLING WITH BUFFALO BILL

(Universal, November 23, 1931) 12 Chapters

Tom Tyler, Rex Bell, Lucile Browne, William Desmond, Chief Thunderbird, Francis Ford, Yakima Canutt, Bud Osborne, John Beck, George Regas, Joe Bonomo, Jim Thorpe, Bobby Nelson, Edmund Cobb, Fred Haynes, Art Mix, Franklyn Farnum, Joe Miles, William Rambeau, William Patton, Edward Anton, Jim Corey

Director: Ray Taylor
Story: William Cody
Screenplay: George Plympton, Ella O'Neill
Producer: Henry MacRae
Chapter Titles: (1) Captured by Redskins (2) Circling Death (3) Between Hostile Tribes (4) The Savage Horde (5) The Fatal Plunge (6) Trapped (7) The Unseen Killer (8) Sentenced to Death (9) The Death Trap (10) A Shot from Ambush (11) The Flaming Death (12) Cheyenne Vengeance

GALLOPING THRU

(Monogram, December 5, 1931) 58 Minutes

Tom Tyler, Betty Mack, Al Bridge, Si Jenks, Stanley Blystone, G. D. Woods (Gordon DeMain), John Elliott, Artie Ortego, Lafe McKee, Frank Ellis, Hank Bell, Art Mix, Jack Evans

Director: Lloyd Nosler
Story/Screenplay: Wellyn Totman
Producer: Trem Carr

SINGLE-HANDED SANDERS

(Monogram, February 10, 1932) 61 Minutes

Tom Tyler, Margaret Morris, Robert Manning, G. D. Woods, John Elliott, Hank Bell, Lois Bridge, Fred Toones

Director: Lloyd Nosler
Screenplay: Charles A. Post
Producer: Trem Carr

THE MAN FROM NEW MEXICO

(Monogram, April 1, 1932) 60 Minutes

Tom Tyler, Caryl Lincoln, Robert Walker, Jack Richardson, Lafe McKee, Frank Ball, Lewis Sargent, Blackie Whiteford, Slim Whitaker, Frederick Ryter, Jack Long, William Nolte, C. H. (Fargo) Bussey, Lee Timm

Director: J. P. McCarthy
Story: "Fang Branded" - Frederick Ryter
Screenplay: Harry O. Hoyt
Producer: Trem Carr

VANISHING MEN

(Monogram, April 15, 1932) 62 Minutes

Tom Tyler, Adele Lacy, Raymond Keane, Willia L. Thorne, John Elliott, Robert Manning, Charles King, James Marcus, Dick Dickins

Director: Harry Fraser
Story/Screenplay: Wellyn Totman
Producer: Trem Carr

HONOR OF THE MOUNTED

(Monogram, June 20, 1932) 62 Minutes

Tom Tyler, Cecilia Ryland, Francis McDonald, Charles King, Tom London, Stanley Blystone, William Dyer, Arthur Millet, Gordon Wood (Gordon DeMain), Ted Lorch

Director/Story/Screenplay: Harry Fraser
Producer: Trem Carr

JUNGLE MYSTERY

(Universal, August, 1932) 12 Chapters

Tom Tyler, Cecelia Parker, William Desmond, Philo McCullough, Noah Beery, Jr., Carmelita Geraghty, Sam Baker

Director: Ray Taylor
Screenplay: Ella O'Neill, George Plympton, Basil Dickey, George Morgan
Story: Talbot Mundy - "The Ivory Trail"
Chapter Titles: (1) Into the Dark Continent (2) The Ivory Trail (3) The Death Scream (4) Poisoned Fangs (5) The Mystery Cavern (6) Daylight Doom (7) The Jaws of Death (8) Trapped by the Enemy (9) The Jungle Terror (10) Ambushed (11) The Lion's Fury (12) Buried Treasure

THE FORTY-NINERS

(Freuler/Monarch, October 28, 1932) 59 Minutes

Tom Tyler, Betty Mack, Al Bridge, Fern Emmett, Gordon Wood (Gordon DeMain), Mildred Rogers, Fred Ritter, Frank Ball, Florence Wells

Director: John P. McCarthy
Story/Screenplay: F. McGrew Willis
Producer: Trem Carr

WHEN A MAN RIDES ALONE

(Freuler/Monarch, January 15, 1933) 60 Minutes

Tom Tyler, Adele Lacy, Alan Bridge, Robert Burns, Frank Ball, Alma Chester, Duke Lee, Barney Furey, Lee Cordova, Lillian Chay, Jack Rockwell, Bud Osborne, Ed Burns, Jack Kirk, Herman Hack

Director: J. P. McGowan
Story: F. McGrew Willis
Screenplay: Oliver Drake
Producer: Burton King

CLANCY OF THE MOUNTED

(Universal, February 27, 1933) 12 Chapters
Tom Tyler, Jacqueline Wells (Julie Bishop), William Desmond, Rosalie Roy, Francis Ford, Earl McCarthy, Tom London, Edmund Cobb, William Thorne, Leon Duval, Al Ferguson, Frank Lanning, Fred Humes, Monte Montague, Frank Lackteen, Steve Clemente
Director: Ray Taylor
Story: Based on the poem by Robert W. Service
Screenplay: Basil Dickey, Harry O. Hoyt, Ella O'Neill
Producer: Henry MacRae
Chapter Titles: (1) The Black Ghost Rides (2) The Thundering Herd (3) The Black Ghost Strikes (4) A Single Shot (5) Clutching Hands (6) The Terror Trail (7) Doomed! (8) Facing Death (9) Thundering Doom (10) The Life Line (11) Driving Danger (12) The Black Ghost's Last Ride

DEADWOOD PASS

(Freuler/Monarch, May 5, 1933) 62 Minutes
Tom Tyler, Alice Dahl, Wally Wales, Buffalo Bill, Jr., Lafe McKee, Bud Osborne, Edmund Cobb, Slim Whitaker, Merrill McCormack, Charlote (Carlotta) Monti, Duke Lee, Blackie Whiteford, Bill Nestell
Director: J. P. McGowan
Story: John Wesley Patterson
Screenplay: Oliver Drake
Producer: Burton King

WAR ON THE RANGE

(Freuler/Monarch, September 22, 1933) 59 Minutes
Tom Tyler, Caryl Lincoln, Lane Chandler, Lafe McKee, Slim Whitaker, Ted Adams, Charles K. French, William Malan, Fred Burns, Billy Franey, Joseph Giraud
Director: J. P. McGowan
Screenplay: Oliver Drake
Producer: Burton King

Dick Alexander and Charles Whitaker are going to give Tom Tyler a surprise in **Coyote Trails** (Reliable, 1935)

THE PHANTOM OF THE AIR

(Universal, 1933) 12 Chapters
Tom Tyler, Gloria Shea, LeRoy Mason, Hugh Enfield, William Desmond, Sidney Bracey, Walter Brennan, Jennie Cramer, Cecil Kellogg
Director: Ray Taylor
Story: Ella O'Neill
Screenplay: Basil Dickey, George Plympton
Chapter Titles: (1) The Great Air Meet (2) The Secret of the Desert (3) The Avenging (4) The Battle in the Clouds (5) Terror of the Heights (6) A Wild Ride (7) The Jaws of Death (8) Aflame in the Sky (9) The Attack (10) The Runaway Plane (11) In the Enemy's Hands (12) Safe Landing

Tom Tyler has just escaped in **COYOTE TRAILS** (Reliable, 1935)

RIDIN' THRU

(Reliable/William Steiner, November 26, 1934) 55 Minutes
Tom Tyler, Ruth Hiatt, Lafe McKee, Philo McCullough, Ben Corbett, Lew Meehan, Bud Osborne, Colin Chase, Jane Regan, Buck Morgan
Director: Harry S. Webb
Story: Carol Shanoren
Screenplay: Rose Gordon, Carl Krusada
Associate Producer: Harry S. Webb

THE UNCONQUERED BANDIT

(Reliable/William Steiner, January 8, 1935) 57 Minutes
Tom Tyler, Lillian Gilmore, Slim Whitaker, William Gould, John Elliott, Earl Dwire, Joe De LaCruz, George Chesebro, Lew Meehan, Dick Alexander, George Hazle, Ben Corbett, Wally Wales, Culin Chase, Frank Ellis, Herman Hack, Ray Henderson
Director: Harry S. Webb
Story: Carl Krusada
Screenplay: Rose Gordon, Lou C. Borden
Producer: Bernard B. Ray
Associate Producer: Harry S. Webb

THE FIGHTING HERO

(Reliable/William Steiner, January, 1935) 55 Minutes
Tom Tyler, Renee Bordon, Edward Hearn, Dick Botiller, Ralph Lewis, Murdock McQuarrie, Nelson McDowell, Tom London, George Chesebro, Rosa Rosanova, J. P. McGowan, Lew Meehan, Jimmy Aubrey, Chick Baldra
Director: Harry S. Webb
Story: C. E. Roberts (Charles)
Screenplay: Rose Gordon, Carl Krusada
Producer: Bernard B. Ray
Associate Producer: Harry S. Webb

TRACY RIDES

(Reliable/William Steiner, February 26, 1935) 51 Minutes
Tom Tyler, Virginia Brown Faire, Edmund Cobb, Charles K. French, Carol Shandrew, Lafe McKee, George Chesebro, Robert Walker, Jimmy Aubrey, Dick Botiller
Director: Harry S. Webb
Story: Norman Hughes
Screenplay: Rose Gordon, Betty Burbridge
Producer: Bernard B. Ray

COYOTE TRAILS

(Reliable/William Steiner, February, 1935) 65 Minutes
Tom Tyler, Helen Dahl, Ben Corbett, Lafe McKee, Dick Alexander, Roger Williams, George Chesebro, Slim Whitaker, Jack Evans, Lew Meehan, Art Dillard, Jimmy Aubrey, Bud McClure, Tex Palmer, Si Jenks
Director: B. B. Ray
Screenplay: Carl Krusada
Producer: Bernard B. Ray

MYSTERY RANCH

(Reliable/William Steiner, April 12, 1935) 56 Minutes
Tom Tyler, Roberta Gale, Jack Gable (Jack Perrin),
Frank Hall Crane, Louise Gabo, Charles King, Tom
London, George Chesebro, Lafe McKee, Jimmy
Aubrey, Robert Walker
Director: Ray Bernard (Bernard B. Ray)
Story: J. K. Henry
Screenplay: Rose Gordon, Carl Krusada
Producer: Bernard B. Ray
Associate Producer: Harry S. Webb

BORN TO BATTLE

(Reliable/William Steiner, April, 1935) 63 Minutes
Tom Tyler, Jean Carmen, Earl Dwire, Julian Rivero,
Nelson McDowell, William Desmond, Dick Alexander,
Charles King, Ralph Lewis, Ben Corbett, George
Chesebro, Robert Walker, Blackie Whiteford, Jack
Evans, Jimmy Aubrey, Roger Williams, Hank Bell
Director: Harry S. Webb
Story: Oliver Drake
Screenplay: Carl Krusada, Rose Gordon
Producer: Bernard B. Ray

THE SILVER BULLET

(Reliable/William Steiner, May 11, 1935) 59 Minutes
Tom Tyler, Jayne Regan, Lafe McKee, Charles King,
Slim Whitaker, Franklyn Farnum, George Chesebro,
Lew Meehan, Walt Williams (Wally Wales), Nelson
McDowell, Robert Brower, Blackie Whiteford, Hank
Bell, Allen Greer, Tom Smith, Tex Palmer, Fern
Emmett, Jack Evans, Bruce Mitchell, Bill Patton, Robert
Walker, Herman Hack, Barney Beasley
Director: Bernard B. Ray
Story: William L. Nolte
Screenplay: Rose Gordon, Carl Krusada
Producer: B. B. Ray
Associate Producer: Harry S. Webb

SILENT VALLEY

(Reliable/William Steiner, May, 1935) 56 Minutes
Tom Tyler, Nancy DeShon, Wally Wales, Charles King,
Alan Bridge, Murdock McQuarrie, Art Miles, George
Chesebro, Charles Whitaker, Jimmy Aubrey, Frank
Ellis, Budd Buster
Director/Producer: Bernard B. Ray
Screenplay: Carl Krusada, Rose Gordon
Story: Carl Krusada
Associate Producer: Harry S. Webb

Nancy DeShon looks worried as Tom Tyler stops Charles King from choking Wally Wales in **Silent Valley**
(Reliable, 1935).

TERROR OF THE PLAINS
(Reliable/William Steiner, June 27, 1935) 58 Minutes
Tom Tyler, Roberta Gale, William Gould, Charles (Slim) Whitaker, Fern Emmett, Nelson McDowell, Frank Rice, Ralph Lewis, Robert Walker, Murdock McQuarrie, Budd Buster, Jack Kirk, Jimmy Aubrey, Jack Cross, Herman Hack
Director: Harry S. Webb
Story: Charles E. Roberts
Screenplay: Carl Krusada, Rose Gordon
Producer: Bernard B. Ray
Associate Producer: Harry S. Webb

THE LARAMIE KID
(Reliable/William Steiner, June, 1935) 57 Minutes
Tom Tyler, Alberta Vaughn, Al Ferguson, Murdock McQuarrie, George Chesebro, Snub Pollard, Steve Clark, Artie Ortego, Nelson McDowell, Wally Wales, Budd Buster, Jimmy Aubrey, Charles Whitaker, Herman Hack
Director: Harry S. Webb
Story: C. C. Church
Screenplay: Carl Krusada, Rose Gordon
Producer: Bernard B. Ray
Associate Producer: Harry S. Webb

RIO RATTLER
(Reliable/William Steiner, August, 1935) 58 Minutes
Tom Tyler, Marion Shilling, Eddie Gribbon, William Gould, Tom London, Slim Whitaker, Lafe McKee, Ace Cain, Frank Ellis, Jimmy Aubrey, Blackie Whiteford, Nelson McDowell, Lane Chandler, Tom Brower, Herman Hack
Director: Franklin Shamray (B. B. Ray)
Story: Bennett Cohen
Screenplay: Carl Krusada
Producer: Bernard B. Ray
Associate Producer: Harry S. Webb

POWDERSMOKE RANGE
(RKO, September 27, 1935) 6 Reels, 71 Minutes
(First of the "3 Mesquiteers" films)
Harry Carey, Hoot Gibson, Bob Steele, *Tom Tyler,* Guinn "Big Boy" Williams, Boots Mallory, Wally Wales, Sam Hardy, Adrian Morris, Buzz Barton, Art Mix, Frank Rice, Buddy Roosevelt, Buffalo Bill, Jr., Franklyn Farnum, William Desmond, William Farnum, Ethan Laidlaw, Eddie Dunn, Ray Meyer, Barney Furey, Bob McKenzie, James Mason, Irving Bacon, Henry Rocquemore, Phil Dunham, Silver Tip Baker, Nelson McDowell, Frank Ellis
Director: Wallace Fox
Story: William Colt MacDonald
Screenplay: Adele Buffington
Producer: Cliff Reid

FAST BULLETS
(Reliable/William Steiner, February 23, 1936) 57 Minutes
Tom Tyler, Rex Lease, Margaret Nearing, Al Bridge, William Gould, Robert Walker, James Aubrey, Slim Whitaker, Charles King, Lew Meehan, Nelson McDowell, Jack Evans, Frank Ellis, George Chesebro
Director: Henri Samuels (Harry S. Webb)
Story: Jay J. Bryan
Screenplay: Rose Gordon, Carl Krusada
Producer: Bernard B. Ray

RIDIN' ON
(Reliable/William Steiner, February 29, 1936) 56 Minutes
Tom Tyler, Geraine Geear (John Barclay), Rex Lease, John Elliott, Earl Dwire, Bob McKenzie, Roger Williams, Slim Whitaker, Wally West, Jimmy Aubrey, Francis Walker, Dick Cramer, Jack Evans, Shawn Tansey, Tex Palmer, Chick Morrison, Milburn Morante
Director: Bernard B. Ray
Story: "Feud of the Jay Bar Dee" - Arthur Carhart
Screenplay: John T. Neville
Producer: Bernard B. Ray
Associate Producer: Harry S. Webb

ROAMIN' WILD
(Reliable/William Steiner, April 29, 1936) 58 Minutes
Tom Tyler, Max Davidson, Carol Wyndham, Al Ferguson, George Chesebro, Fred Parker, Slim Whitaker, Bud Osborne, Wally West, Earl Dwire, Lafe McKee, John Elliott, Frank Ellis, Sherry Tansey, Buck Morgan, Jimmy Aubrey
Director/Producer: Bernard B. Ray
Screenplay/Story: Robert Tansey

PINTO RUSTLERS
(Reliable/William Steiner, May 14, 1936) 56 Minutes
Tom Tyler, George Walsh, Al St. John, Catherine Cotter, Earl Dwire, William Gould, George Chesebro, Roger Williams, Bud Osborne, Slim Whitaker, Murdock McQuarrie, Milburn Morante, Sherry Tansey, Charles King, Bob Burns, Wally West, Tex Palmer
Director: Henri Samuels (Harry S. Webb)
Story/Screenplay: Robert Tansey
Producer: Bernard B. Ray
Associate Producer: Harry S. Webb

THE LAST OUTLAW
(RKO, June 19, 1936) 62 Minutes
Harry Carey, Hoot Gibson, *Tom Tyler,* Henry B. Wathall, Margaret Callahan, Ray Meyer, Harry Jans, Frank M. Thomas, Russell Hopton, Frank Jenks, Maxine Jennings, Joe Sawyer, Fred Scott
Director: Christy Cabanne
Story: John Ford, E. Murray Campbell
Screenplay: John Twist, Jack Townley
Producer: Robert Sisk

SANTE FE BOUND

(Reliable/William Steiner, August 15, 1936) 56 Minutes
Tom Tyler, Jeanne Martel, Richard Cramer, Charles (Slim) Whitaker, Edward Cassidy, Dorothy Woods, Charles King, Lafe McKee, Earl Dwire, Wally West, Ray Henderson
Director: Henri Samuels (Harry S. Webb)
Story: Rose Gordon
Screenplay: Carl Krusada
Producer: Bernard B. Ray
Associate Producer: Harry S. Webb

RIP ROARIN' BUCKAROO

(Victory, October 15, 1936) 58 Minutes
Tom Tyler, Beth Marion, Sammy Cohen, Charles King, Forrest Taylor, Dick Cramer, John Elliott
Director: Robert Hill
Screenplay: William Buchanan
Producer: Sam Katzman

THE PHANTOM OF THE RANGE

(Victory, November 28, 1936) 57 Minutes
Tom Tyler, Beth Marion, Sammy Cohen, Soledad Jiminez, Forrest Taylor, Charles King, John Elliott, Dick Cramer
Director: Bob Hill
Story/Screenplay: Basil Dickey
Producer: Sam Katzman

TRIGGER TOM

(Reliable/William Steiner, 1936) 57 Minutes
Tom Tyler, Al St. John, Bernadene Hayes, William Gould, John Elliott, Bud Osborne, Lloyd Ingraham, Wally Wales, Jack Evans
Director: Henri Samuels (Harry S. Webb)
Story: "The Swimming Herd" - George Cory Franklin
Screenplay: Tom Gibson
Producer: Bernard B. Ray

CHEYENNE RIDES AGAIN

(Victory, January 7, 1937) 56 Minutes
Tom Tyler, Lucile Browne, Creighton Chaney (Lon Chaney, Jr.), Roger Williams, Carmen LaRoux, Ed Cassidy, Ted Lorch, Bud Pope, Francis Walker, Slim Whitaker, Merrill McCormack, Wilbur McCauley, Jimmy Fox, Tommy Rix
Director: Robert Hill
Screenplay: Basil Dickey
Producer: Sam Katzman

THE FEUD OF THE TRAIL

(Victory, March 1, 1937) 56 Minutes
Tom Tyler, Harlene Wood, Milburn Morante, Roger Williams, Lafe McKee, Jim Corey, Dick Alexander, Roger Williams, Vane Calvert, Slim Whitaker, Eddie Gribbon, Francis Walker
Director: Robert Hill
Story/Screenplay: Basil Dickey
Producer: Sam Katzman

MYSTERY RANGE

(Victory, May 1, 1937) 56 Minutes
Tom Tyler, Jerry Bergh, Milburn Morante, Lafe McKee, Roger Williams, Dick Alexander, Jim Corey, Slim Whitaker, George Morrell
Director: Bob Hill
Story/Screenplay: Basil Dickey
Producer: Sam Katzman

ORPHAN OF THE PECOS

(Victory, June 5, 1937) 55 Minutes
Tom Tyler, Jeanne Martel, Lafe McKee, Forrest Taylor, Ted Lorch, Slim Whitaker, John Elliott, Marjorie Beebe, Howard Bryant, Roger Williams, Lafe McKee, Eddie Gribbon, John Elliott
Director: Sam Katzman
Story/Screenplay: Basil Dickey
Producer: Sam Katzman

BROTHERS OF THE WEST

(Victory, September 30, 1937) 58 Minutes
Tom Tyler, Lois Wilde, Dorothy Short, Lafe McKee, Bob Terry, Roger Williams, Jim Corey, James C. Morton, Tiny Lipson
Director/Producer: Sam Katzman
Story/Screenplay: Basil Dickey

LOST RANCH

(Victory, November, 1937) 56 Minutes
Tom Tyler, Jeanne Martel, Marjorie Beebe, Howard Bryant, Ted Lorch, Slim Whitaker, Forrest Taylor, Lafe McKee, Roger Williams
Director/Producer: Sam Katzman
Story/Screenplay: Basil Dickey

KING OF ALCATRAZ

(Paramount, October 12, 1938) 55 Minutes
Gail Patrick, Lloyd Nolan, J. Carrol Naish, Harry Carey, Robert Preston, Anthony Quinn, Richard Stanley, Dennis Morgan, Virginia Dabney, Nora Cecil, Emory Parnell, Dorothy Howe, John Hart, Philip Warren, Porter Hall, Richard Denning, *Tom Tyler,* Konstantin Shayne, Harry Worth, Edward Marr, Clay Clement, Gusav von Seyfferitz, Monte Blue, Hooper Atchley, Buddy Roosevelt, Stanley Blystone, Dick Rich, Joseph Eggenton, Pierre Watkin, Paul Fix
Director: Robert Florey
Story/Screenplay: Irving Reis

STAGECOACH

(United Artists, March 3, 1939) 96 Minutes

Claire Trevor, John Wayne, Thomas Mitchell, George Bancroft, Andy Devine, John Carradine, Louise Platt, Donald Meek, Berton Churchill, *Tom Tyler,* Tim Holt, Chris-Pin Martin, Elvira Rios, Bill Cody, Buddy Roosevelt, Yakima Canutt, Paul McVay, Joe Rickson, Harry Tenbrook, Jack Pennick, Kent Odell, William Hopper, Vester Pegg, Ted Lorch, Artie Ortego, Merrill McCormack, Franklyn Farnum, James Mason, Si Jenks, Robert Homans, Chief White Horse, Bryant Washburn, Walter McGrail, Francis Ford, Chief Big Tree, Marga Daighton, Florence Lake, Duke Lee, Cornelius Keefe, Nora Cecil, Lou Mason, Mary Walker, Ed Brady

Director: John Ford
Story: "Stage to Lordsburg" - Ernest Haycox
Screenplay: Dudley Nichols
Producer: Walter Wanger

THE NIGHT RIDERS

(Republic, April 12, 1939) 58 Minutes
(Three Mesquiteers Series)

John Wayne, Ray Corrigan, Max Terhune, Ruth Rogers, Doreen McKay, George Douglas, *Tom Tyler,* Sammy McKim, Kermit Maynard, Walter Willis, Ethan Laidlaw, Ed Peil, Sr., Tom London, Jack Ingram, Bill Nestell, Cactus Mack, Lee Shumway, Hal Price, Hank Worden, Roger Williams, Olin Francis, Francis Walker, Hugh Prosser, Jack Kirk, Yakima Canutt, Glenn Strange, David Sharpe, Bud Osborne, Georgia Summers

Director: George Sherman
Screenplay: Betty Burbridge, Stanley Roberts
Based on characters created by William Colt MacDonald
Associate Producer: William Berke

FRONTIER MARSHAL

(20th C.-Fox, July 28, 1939) 71 Minutes

Randolph Scott, Nancy Kelly, Cesar Romero, Binnie Barnes, John Carradine, Edward Norris, Eddie Foy, Jr., Ward Bond, Lon Chaney, Jr., *Tom Tyler,* Joe Sawyer, Del Henderson, Harry Hayden, Harlan Briggs, Dick Alexander, Harry Woods, Dick Cramer, Dick Elliott, Hank Bell

Director: Allan Dwan
Story: "Wyatt Earp, Frontier Marshal" - Stuart Lake
Screenplay: Sam Hellman
Producer: Sol Wurtzel

DRUMS ALONG THE MOHAWK

(20th C.-Fox, November 10, 1939) 103 Minutes

Claudette Colbert, Henry Fonda, Edna May Oliver, Eddie Collins, John Carradine, Doris Bowdon, Jessie Ralph, Arthur Shields, Robert Lowery, Roger Imhof, Francis Ford, Ward Bond, Kay Linaker, Russell Simpson, Spencer Charters, Si Jenks, Jack Pennick, Arthur Aylesworth, Chief John Big Tree, Charles Tannen, Paul McVey, Elizabeth (Tiny) Jones, Beulah Hall Jones, Edwin Maxwell, Robert Greig, Clara Blandick, *Tom Tyler,* Lionel Pape, Noble Johnson, Clarence H. Wilson, Mae Marsh

Director: John Ford
Based on the novel by Walter D. Edmonds
Screenplay: Lamar Trotti and Sonya Levien
Associate Producer: Raymond Griffith

GONE WITH THE WIND

(David O. Selznick/MGM, December 13, 1939) 225 Minutes

Clark Gable, Vivien Leigh, Olivia de Havilland, Leslie Howard, Thomas Mitchell, Hattie McDaniel, Fred Crane, George Reeves, Everett Brown, Zack Williams, Oscar Polk, Barbara O'Neill, Victor Jory, Evelyn Keyes, Ann Rutherford, Butterfly McQueen, Howard Hickman, Rand Brooks, Carroll Nye, Marcella Sartin, James Bush, Laura Hope Crews, Harry Davenport, Leona Roberts, Albert Morin, Mary Anderson, Terry Shero, William McClain, Eddie Anderson, Jackie Moran, Cliff Edwards, Ona Munson, Ed Chandler, George Hackathorne, Roscoe Ates, John Arledge, Eric Linden, Guy Wilkerson, *Tom Tyler,* Frank Faylen, William Bakewell, Lee Phelps, Paul Hurst, Ernest Whitman, Robert Elliott

Directors: Victor Fleming, Sam Wood, George Cukor
Story: Margaret Mitchell
Screenplay: Sideny Howard, F. Scott Fitzgerald, John Van Druten, Ben Hecht
Producer: David O. Selznick

THE LIGHT OF WESTERN STARS

(Paramount, April 10, 1940) 67 Minutes

Russell Hayden, Victor Jory, Jo Ann Sayers, Noah Beery, Jr., J. Farrell MacDonald, Ruth Rogers, *Tom Tyler,* Rad Robinson, Eddie Dean, Esther Estrella, Alan Ladd

Director: Lesley Selander
Story: "The Light of Western Stars" - Zane Grey
Screenplay: Norman Houston
Producer: Harry Sherman

THE GRAPES OF WRATH

(20th C.-Fox, January 24, 1940) 129 Minutes
Henry Fonda, Jane Darwell, John Carradine, Charley Grapewin, Doris Bowdon, Russell Simpson, O. Z. Whitehead, John Qualen, Eddie Quillan, Zeffie Tilbury, Frank Sully, Frank Darien, Darryl Hickman, Shirley Mills, Roger Imhof, Grant Mitchell, Charles D. Brown, John Arledge, Ward Bond, Harry Tyler, William Pawley, Arthur Aylesworth, Charles Tannen, Selmer Jackson, Charles Middleton, Eddy Waller, Paul Guilfoyle, David Hughes, Cliff Clark, Joe Sawyer, Adrian Morris, Hollis Jewell, Robert Homans, Irving Bacon, Kitty McHugh, Frank Faylen, *Tom Tyler,* Mae Marsh, Norman Willis, Peggy Ryan, Wally Albright, Erville Anderson, Barry Strang, Rex Lease, Louis Mason, Harry Tenbrook, Ralph Dunn, Frank O'Connor, Herbert Heywood, Walter Miller, Gaylord Pendleton, Robert Shaw, Lee Shumway, Dick Rich, James Flavin, George O'Hara, Thornton Edwards, Trevor Bardette, Jack Pennick, Walter McGrail, George Breakston, William Haade, Ted Oliver, Ben Hall, Gloria Roy
Director: John Ford
Story: John Steinbeck
Screenplay: Nunnally Johnson
Producer: Darryl F. Zanuck

BROTHER ORCHID

(Warner Bros., June 8, 1940) 91 Minutes
Edward G. Robinson, Ann Sothern, Humphrey Bogart, Ralph Bellamy, Donald Crisp, Allen Jenkins, Charles D. Brown, Cecil Kellaway, Joseph Crehan, Wilfred Lucas, Morgan Conway, Richard Lane, John Ridgely, Dick Wessell, *Tom Tyler,* Paul Phillips, Don Rowan, Granville Bates, Nanatte Vallon, Paul Guilfoyle, Tim Ryan, Joe Caits, Pat Gleason, Tommy Baker, G. Pat Collins, John Qualen, Leonard Mudie, Charles Coleman, Edgar Norton, Jean Del Val, Charles de Ravenne, Paul Porcasi, James Flavin, Sam McDaniel, Lee Phelps, Mary Gordon, George Renavent, Frank Faylen, William Hoppper, Creighton Hale, George Haywood
Director: Lloyd Bacon
Story: Richard Connell
Screenplay: Earl Baldwin
Executive Producer: Hal B. Wallis
Associate Producer: Mark Hellinger

THE MUMMY'S HAND

(Universal, September 20, 1940) 67 Minutes
Dick Foran, Peggy Moran, Wallace Ford, Eduardo Cianelli, George Zucco, Cecil Kellaway, *Tom Tyler,* Charles Trowbridge, Sig Arno, Eddie Foster, Harry Stubbs, Michael Mark, Maria Tarta, Leon Belasco
Director: Christy Cabanne
Story: Griffin Jay
Screenplay: Maxwell Shane, Griffin Jay
Associate Producer: Ben Pivar

THE WESTERNER

(United Artists, September 20, 1940) 100 Minutes
Gary Cooper, Walter Brennan, Fred Stone, Doris Davenport, Dana Andrews, Forrest Tucker, Chill Wills, Lillian Bond, Paul Hurst, Arthur Aylesworth, Trevor Bardette, *Tom Tyler,* Stanley Andrews
Director: William Wyler
Story: Stuart Lake
Screenplay: Jo Swerling, Niven Busch
Producer: Samuel Goldwyn

CHEROKEE STRIP

(Paramount, October 11, 1940) 86 Minutes
Richard Dix, Florence Rice, William Henry, Victor Jory, Andy Clyde, *Tom Tyler,* George E. Stone, Morris Ankrum, Charles Trowbridge, Douglas Fowley, Addison Richards, William Haade, Ray Teal, Hal Taliaferro, Jack Rockwell, Tex Cooper
Director: Lesley Selander
Story: Bernard McConville
Screenplay: Norman Houston, Bernard McConville
Producer: Harry Sherman

TEXAS RANGERS RIDE AGAIN

(Paramount, December 13, 1940) 68 Minutes
John Howard, Ellen Drew, Akim Tamiroff, Broderick Crawford, May Robson, Charley Grapewin, John Miljan, Anthony Quinn, *Tom Tyler,* Donald Curtis, Eddie Acuff, Ruth Rogers, Robert Ryan, Eva Puig, Monte Blue, James Pierce, William Duncan, Harvey Stephens, Harold Goodwin, Edward Pawley, Eddie Foy, Jr., Joseph Crehan, Stanley Price, Charles Lane, Jack Perrin, Gordon Jones, John Miller, Henry Rocquemore
Director: James Hogan
Screenplay: William Lipman, Horace McCoy

BUCK PRIVATES

(Universal, January 31, 1941) 82 Minutes
Bud Abbott, Lou Costello, Andrews Sisters, Lee Bowman, Alan Curtis, Jane Frazee, Nat Pendleton, Don Raye, Dora Clement, J. Anthony Hughes, Hughie Prince, Leonard Elliott, Jeanne Kelly, Elaine Morey, Kay Leslie, Harry Strang, Frank Cook, Samuel S. Hinds, Shemp Howard, James Flavin, Mike Frankovich, Jack Mulhall, Nella Walker, Douglas Wood, Charles Coleman, Selmer Jackson, *Tom Tyler,* Harold Goodwin, Bud Harris, Al Billings, Frank Penny, Frank Grandetta, Bob Wayne
Director: Arthur Lubin
Screenplay: Arthur T. Horman
Producer: Alex Gottlieb

BORDER VIGILANTES

(Paramount, April 18, 1941) 62 Minutes
(Hopalong Cassidy Series)

William Boyd, Russell Hayden, Andy Clyde, Victor Jory, Morris Ankrum, Frances Gifford, Ethel Wales, *Tom Tyler,* Hal Taliaferro, Jack Rockwell, Britt Wood, Hank Worden, Hank Bell, Edward Earle, Al Haskell, Curley Dresden, Chuck Morrison, Ted Wells

Director: Derwin Abrahams
Screenplay: J. Benton Cheney
Based on characters created by Clarence E. Mulford
Producer: Harry Sherman

RIDERS OF THE TIMBERLINE

(Paramount, September 17, 1941) 59 Minutes
(Hopalong Cassidy Series)

William Boyd, Brad King, Andy Clyde, J. Farrell Mac-Donald, Eleanor Stewart, Anna Q. Nilsson, Edward Keane, Hal Taliaferro, Victor Jory, *Tom Tyler,* Mickey Essia, Hank Bell, The Guardsman Quartet

Director: Lesley Selander
Screenplay: J. Benton Cheney
Based on characters created by Clarence E. Mulford
Producer: Harry Sherman

GAUCHOS OF ELDORADO

(Republic, October 24, 1941) 56 Minutes
(Three Mesquiteers Series)

Bob Steele, *Tom Tyler,* Rufe Davis, Lois Collier, Duncan Renaldo, Rosani Galli, Norman Willis, Yakima Canutt, William Ruhl, Tony Roux, Ray Bennett, Bud Geary, Edmund Cobb, Eddie Dean, John Merrill Holmes, Terry Frost, John Merton, Virginia Farmer, Si Jenks, Ted Mapes, Bob Woodward, Ray Jones, Horace B. Caprenter

Director: Les Orlebeck
Story: Earle Snell
Based on characters created by William Colt MacDonald
Associate Producer: Louis Gray

WEST OF CIMARRON

(Republic, December 15, 1941) 56 Minutes
(Three Mesquiteers Series)

Bob Steele, *Tom Tyler,* Rufe Davis, Lois Collier, James Bush, Guy Usher, Hugh Prosser, Cordell Hickman, Roy Barcroft, Budd Buster, Mickey Rentschiller, John James, Bud Geary, Stanley Blystone

Director: Les Orlebeck
Screenplay: Albert Demond, Don Ryan
Based on characters created by William Colt MacDonald
Associate Producer: Louis Gray

ADVENTURES OF CAPTAIN MARVEL

(Republic, 1941) 12 Chapters

Tom Tyler, Frank Coghlan, Jr., William Benedict, Louise Currie, Robert Strange, Harry Worth, Gerald Mohr, Bryant Washburn, John Davidson, George Pembroke, Peter George Lynn, Reed Hadley, Jack Mulhall, Kenne Duncan, Nigel de Brulier, John Bagni, Carleton Young, Leyland Hodgson, Stanley Price, Ernest Sarracino, Tetsu Komai, Paul Lopez, Chuck Morrison, Francis Sayles, Eddie Dew, Loren Riebe, Edward Cassidy, Ted Mapes, Ken Terrell, Al Taylor, Curley Dresden, Henry Wills, Bud Geary, Armand Cortes, Major Sam Harris, Loren Riebe, Lynton Brent, Ray Hanson, David Sharpe, Al Kikume, Marten Lamont, Carl Zwolsman, Wilson Benge, Jerry Jerome, Dick Crockett

Directors: William Witney, John English
Screenplay: Ronald Davidson, Norman S. Hall, Aach B. Heath, Joseph Poland, Sol Shor
Associate Producer: Hiram S. Brown, Jr.
Chapter Titles: (1) Curse of the Scorpion (2) The Guillotine (3) Time Bomb (4) Death Takes the Wheel (5) The Scorpion Strikes (6) Lens of Death (7) Human Targets (8) Boomerang (9) Dead Man's Trap (10) Doom Ship (11) Valley of Death (12) Captain Marvel's Secret

CODE OF THE OUTLAW

(Republic, January 30, 1942) 57 Minutes
(Three Mesquiteers Series)

Bob Steele, *Tom Tyler,* Rufe Davis, Weldon Heyburn, Melinda Leighton, Don Curtis, John Ince, Kenne Duncan, Phil Dunham, Max Walzman, Chuck Morrison, Carleton Young, Al Taylor, Robert Frazer, Dick Alexander, Forrest Taylor, Jack Ingram, Wally West, Edward Peil, Sr., Bud Osborne, Hank Worden, Cactus Mack

Director: John English
Screenplay: Barry Shipman
Based on characters created by William Colt MacDonald
Associate Producer: Louis Gray

RAIDERS OF THE RANGE

(Republic, March 18, 1942) 55 Minutes
(Three Mesquiteers Series)

Bob Steele, *Tom Tyler,* Rufe Davis, Lois Collier, Frank Jacquet, Fred Kohler, Jr., Dennis Moore, Tom Chatterton, Charles Miller, Max Walzman, Hal Price, Charles Phillips, Bud Geary, Jack Ingram, Al Taylor, Chuck Morrison, Joel Friedkin, Bob Woodward, Tom Steele, Monte Montague, Ken Terrell, Dick Alexander, Cactus Mack, John Cason

Director: John English
Story: Albert DeMond
Screenplay: Barry Shipman
Based on characters created by William Colt MacDonald
Associate Producer: Louis Gray

WESTWARD HO
(Republic, April 24, 1942) 56 Minutes
Bob Steele, *Tom Tyler*, Rufe Davis, Evelyn Brent, Donald Curtis, Lois Collier, Emmett Lynn, John James, Tom Siedel, Jack Kirk, Kenne Duncan, Milton Kibbee, Edmund Cobb, Monte Montague, Al Taylor, Bud Osborne, Jack Montgomery, Horace B. Carpenter, John L. Cason, Jack O'Shea, Ray Jones, Tex Palmer, Curley Dresden, Budd Buster
Director: John English
Story: Morton Grant
Screenplay: Morton Grant, Doris Schroeder
Based on characters created by William Colt MacDonald
Producer: Louis Gray

THE PHANTOM PLAINSMEN
(Republic, June 16, 1942) 65 Minutes
(3 Mesquiteers Series)
Bob Steele, *Tom Tyler*, Rufe Davis, Lois Collier, Robert O. Davis, Charles Miller, Alex Callam, Monte Montague, Henry Roland, Richard Crane, Jack Kirk, Edward Cassidy, Vince Barnett, Lloyd Ingraham, Al Taylor, Bud Geary, Herman Hack
Director: John English
Story: Robert Yost
Screenplay: Robert Yost, Barry Shipman
Based on characters created by William Colt MacDonald
Associate Producer: Louis Gray

THE TALK OF THE TOWN
(Columbia, August 20, 1942) 118 Minutes
Cary Grant, Jean Arthur, Ronald Colman, Edgar Buchanan, Glenda Farrell, Charles Dingle, Emma Dunn, Rex Ingram, Leonid Kinskey, *Tom Tyler*, Don Beddoe, George Watts, Clyde Filmore, Frank M. Thomas
Director/Producer: George Stevens
Associate Producer: Fred Guiol
Story: Sidney Harmon
Screenplay: Irwin Shaw, Sidney Buckman

SHADOWS ON THE SAGE
(Republic, September 24, 1942) 58 Minutes
(3 Mesquiteers Series)
Bob Steele, *Tom Tyler*, Jimmie Dodd, Cheryl Walker, Harry Holman, Yakima Canutt, Tom London, Bryant Washburn, Griff Barnette, Freddie Mercer, Rex Lease, Curley Dresden, Eddie Dew, Horace B. Carpenter, Frank Brownlee, John Cason, Pascale Perry
Director: Les Orlebeck
Screenplay: J. Benton Cheney
Based on characters created by William Colt MacDonald
Associate Producer: Louis Gray

THE MUMMY'S TOMB
(Universal, October 23, 1942) 61 Minutes
Lou Chaney, Dick Foran, John Hubbard, Elyse Knox, George Zucco, Wallace Ford, Turhan Bey, Virginia Brissac, Cliff Clark, Mary Gordon, Paul E. Burns, Frank Reicher, Emmett Vogan, *Tom Tyler*
Director: Harold Young
Story: Neil Varnick
Screenplay: Griffin Jay, Henry Sucher
Associate Producer: Ben Pivar

VALLEY OF HUNTED MEN
(Republic, November 13, 1942) 60 Minutes
(3 Mesquiteers Series)
Bob Steele, *Tom Tyler*, Jimmie Dodd, Anna Marie Stewart, Edward Van Sloan, Roland Varno, Edythe Elliott, Arno Frey, Richard French, Robert Stevenson, George Neiss, Duke Aldon, Budd Buster, Hal Price, Billy Benedict, Charles Flynn, Rand Brooks, Kenne Duncan, Jack Kirk, Kermit Maynard
Director: John English
Story: Charles Tetford
Screenplay: Albert DeMond, Morton Grant
Based on characters created by William Colt MacDonald
Associate Producer: Louis Gray

THUNDERING TRAILS
(Republic, January 25, 1943) 56 Minutes
(3 Mesquiteers Series)
Bob Steele, *Tom Tyler*, Jimmie Dodd, Nell O'Day, Sam Flint, Karl Hackett, Charles Miller, John James, Forrest Taylor, Ed Cassidy, Forbes Murray, Reed Howes, Bud Geary, Budd Buster, Vince Barnett, Lane Bradford, Cactus Mack, Edwin Parker, Al Taylor, Art Mix, Jack O'Shea
Director: John English
Screenplay: Norman S. Hall, Robert Yost
Based on characters created by William Colt MacDonald
Associate Producer: Louis Gray

THE BLOCKED TRAIL
(Republic, March 12, 1943) 58 Minutes
(3 Mesquiteers Series)
Bob Steele, *Tom Tyler*, Jimmie Dodd, Helen Deverall, George J. Lewis, Walter Sodering, Charles Miller, Kermit Maynard, Pierce Lyden, Carl Mathews, Hal Price, Budd Buster, Earl Hodgins, Bud Osborne, Al Taylor, Art Dillard, Bud Geary
Director: Elmer Clifton
Screenplay: John K. Butler, Jacquin Frank
Based on characters created by William Colt MacDonald
Associate Producer: Louis Gray

SANTA FE SCOUTS
(Republic, April 16, 1943) 57 Minutes
(3 Mesquiteers Series)
Bob Steele, *Tom Tyler*, Jimmie Dodd, Lois Collier, John James, Tom Chatterton, Elizabeth Valentine, Tom London, Budd Buster, Jack Ingram, Kermit Maynard, Rex Lease, Ed Cassidy, Yakima Canutt, Jack Kirk, Curley Dresden, Reed Howes, Bud Geary, Carl Sepulveda, Al Taylor, Kenne Duncan
Director: Howard Bretherton
Screenplay: Morton Grant, Betty Burbridge
Based on characters created by William Colt MacDonald
Associate Producer: Louis Gray

RIDERS OF THE RIO GRANDE
(Republic, May 21, 1943) 55 Minutes
(3 Mesquiteers Series)
Bob Steele, *Tom Tyler*, Jimmie Dodd, Lorraine Miller, Edward Van Sloan, Rick Vallin, Harry Worth, Roy Barcroft, Charles King, Jack Ingram, John James, Jack O'Shea, Henry Hall, Bud Osborne
Director: Howard Bretherton
Screenplay: Albert DeMond
Based on characters created by William Colt MacDonald
Associate Producer: Louis Gray

WAGON TRACKS WEST
(Republic, October 28, 1943) 55 Minutes
Bill Elliott, George Hayes, *Tom Tyler*, Anne Jeffreys, Rick Vallin, Robert Frazer, Roy Barcroft, Charles Miller, Tom London, Cliff Lyons, Jack Rockwell, Kenne Duncan, Minerva Urecal, Hal Price, William Nestell, Frank Ellis, Hank Bell, Jack O'Shea, Ray Jones, Jack Ingram, Curley Dresden, Frank McCarroll, Marshall Reed, Ben Corbett, Jack Montgomery, Tom Steele, J. W. Cody, Roy Butler
Director: Howard Bretherton
Screenplay: William Lively
Associate Producer: Louis Gray

THE PHANTOM
(Columbia, 1943) 15 Chapters
Tom Tyler, Kenneth MacDonald, Frank Shannon, Jeanne Bates, Ace (The Wonder Dog), Guy Kingsford, Joe Devlin, Ernie Adams, John S. Bagni
Director: B. Reeves Eason
Screenplay: Morgan B. Cox, Victor McLeod, Sherman Lowe, Leslie J. Swabacker
Chapter Titles: (1) The Sign of the Skull (2) The Man Who Never Dies (3) A Traitor's Code (4) The Seat of Judgment (5) The Ghost Who Walks (6) Jungle Whispers (7) The Mystery Well (8) In Quest of the Keys (9) The Fire Princess (10) The Chamber of Death (11) The Emerald Key (12) The Fangs of the Beast (13) The Road To Zoloz (14) The Lost City (15) Peace in the Jungle

GUN TO GUN
(Warner Brothers, January 8, 1944) 20 Minutes
(Santa Fe Trail Series)
(Technicolor)
Robert Shayne, Lupita Tovar, Pedro de Cordova, Harry Woods, *Tom Tyler*, Anita Camargo, Roy Bucko, Julian Rivero
Director: D. Ross Lederman
Story: Lanier and Virginia Stivers Bartlett
Screenplay: Ed Earl Repp

THE NAVY WAY
(Paramount, February 25, 1944)
Robert Lowery, Jean Parker, William Henry, Roscoe Karns, Sharon Douglas, Robert Armstrong, Richard Powers, Larry Nunn, Mary Treen, Joseph Crehan, Edward Earle, Sarah Padden, Ralph Peters, George Humbert, Horace McMahon, Roy Gordon, Lyle Latell, *Tom Tyler*, Will Wright, Al Hill, Edward Keane
Director: William Berke
Producer: William Pine, William Thomas

BOSS OF BOOMTOWN
(Universal, May 22, 1944) 58 Minutes
Rod Cameron, Fuzzy Knight, *Tom Tyler*, Vivian Austin (Vivian Coe), Ray Whitley, Jack Ingram, Robert Barron, Marie Austin, Max Wagner, Sam Flint, Dick Alexander, Forrest Taylor, Tex Cooper, Hank Bell, Ray Jones, Ray Whitley's Bar-6 Cowboys
Director: Ray Taylor
Screenplay: William Lively
Associate Producer: Oliver Drake

LADIES OF WASHINGTON
(20th Century-Fox, May 25, 1944)
Trudy Marshall, Ronald Graham, Anthony Quinn, Sheila Ryan, Robert Bailey, Beverly Whitney, Jackie Paley, Carleton Young, John Philliber, Robin Raymond, Doris Merrick, Barbara Booth, Jo-Carroll Dennison, Lillian Porter, Harry Shannon, Ruby Dandridge, Charles D. Brown, Pierre Watkin, Nella Walker, Inna Gest, Rosalind Keith, Edna Mae Jones, *Tom Tyler*
Director: Louis King
Producer: William Girard

SING ME A SONG OF TEXAS
(Columbia, February 8, 1945) 66 Minutes
Tom Tyler, Rosemary Lane, Hal McIntyre and his Orchestra, The Hoosier Hotshots, Guinn "Big Boy" Williams, Slim Summerville, Carole Matthews, Noah Beery, Sr., Pinky Tomlin, Marie Austin, Foy Willing and his Riders of the Purple Sage
Director: Vernon Keays
Screenplay: J. Benton Cheney, Elizabeth Beecher
Producer: Colbert Clark

THE PRINCESS AND THE PIRATE

(Regent/RKO, 1944) 94 Minutes

Bob Hope, Virginia Mayo, Walter Slezak, Victor McLaglen, Marc Lawrence, Hugo Haas, Maude Eburne, Adia Kuznetzoff, Brandon Hurst, Tom Kennedy, Stanley Andrews, Robert Warwick, *Tom Tyler,* Rondo Hatton, Richard Alexander, Ernie Adams, Ralph Dunn, Bert Roach, Francis Ford, Edwin Stanley, Ray Teal, Weldon Heyburn, Edward Peil, Crane Whitley, James Flavin, Alan Bridge, Al Hill, Dick Rich, Mike Mazurki, Jack Carr, Colin Kenney, Bing Crosby (guest bit)

Director: David Butler

Screenplay: Don Hartman, Melville Shavelson, Everett Freeman

Story: Sy Bartlett

Producer: Samuel Goldwyn

SAN ANTONIO

(Warner Brothers, December 29, 1945) 111 Minutes

Errol Flynn, Alexis Smith, S. Z. "Cuddles" Sakall, Victor Francen, Florence Bates, John Litel, Paul Kelly, Robert Shayne, John Alvin, Monte Blue, Robert Barrat, Pedro de Cordoba, *Tom Tyler,* Chris-Pin Martin, Charles Stevens, Poodles Hanaford, Doodles Weaver, Dan White, Ray Spikes, Hap Winters, Harry Cording, Chalky Williams, Wallis Clark, Bill Steele, Allen Smith, Howard Hill, Arnold Kent

Director: David Butler

Screenplay: Alan LeMay, W. R. Burnett

Producer: Robert Buckner

THEY WERE EXPENDABLE

(MGM, December 30, 1945) 135 Minutes

Robert Montgomery, John Wayne, Donna Reed, Jack Holt, Ward Bond, Marshall Thompson, Paul Langton, Leon Ames, Arthur Walsh, Donald Curtis, Cameron Mitchell, Jeff York, Murray Alper, Harry Tenbrook, Jack Pennick, Alex Havier, Charles Trowbridge, Robert Barrat, Bruce Kellogg, Tim Murdock, Louis Jean Heydt, Russell Simpson, Pedro de Cordoba, *Tom Tyler,* Vernon Steele, Stubby Kruger, Trina Lowe, Sammy Stein, Blake Edwards, Michael Kirby, Robert Emmett O'Connor, Philip Ahn, Pacita Tod-Tod, William B. Davidson, Mag Ong, Bill Wilkerson, John Carlyle, Betty Blythe, Kermit Maynard

Director/Producer: John Ford

Story: William L. White

Screenplay: Lieut. Commander Frank Weed

Associate Producer: Cliff Reid

BADMAN'S TERRITORY

(RKO, April 22, 1946) 98 Minutes

Randolph Scott, Ann Richards, George Hayes, Lawrence Tierney, *Tom Tyler,* John Halloran, Phil Warren, Steve Brodie, William Moss, James Warren, Isabel Jewell, Morgan Conway, Nestor Paiva, Chief Thunder Cloud, Ray Collins, Virginia Sale, Andrew Tombes, Harry Holman, Richard Hale, Emory Parnell, Ethan Laidlaw, Kermit Maynard, Bud Osborne, Chuck Hamilton, Buddy Roosevelt

Director: Tim Whelan

Screenplay: Jack Natteford, Luci Ward

Producer: Nat Holt

NEVER SAY GOODBYE

(Warner Brothers, November 9, 1946) 97 Minutes

Errol Flynn, Eleanor Parker, S. Z. Sakall, Hattie McDaniel, Lucile Watson, Forrest Tucker, Donald Woods, Peggy Knudsen, Tom D'Andrea, Charles Coleman, Patti Brady, *Tom Tyler*

Director: James V. Kern

Story: Ben and Norma Barzman

Adaptation: Lewis R. Foster

Screenplay: I. A. L. Diamond, James V. Kern

Producer: William Jacobs

CHEYENNE

(Warner Brothers, June 14, 1947) 100 Minutes

Dennis Morgan, Jane Wyman, Arthur Kennedy, Janis Paige, Bruce Bennett, Barton MacLane, Bob Steele, *Tom Tyler,* Monte Blue, Britt Wood, Alan Hale

Director: Raoul Walsh

Story: Paul I. Wellman

Screenplay: Alan Lemay, Thomas Williamson

THE DUDE GOES WEST

(King Bros./Allied Artists, May 30, 1948) 86 Minutes

Eddie Albert, Gale Storm, James Gleason, Gilbert Roland, Binnie Barnes, Barton MacLane, Douglas Fowley, *Tom Tyler,* Harry Hayden, Chief Yowlachie, Sarah Padden, Catherine Doucet, Edward Gargan, Frank Yaconelli, Olin Howlin, Charles Williams, Francis Pierlot, Dick Elliott, Lee "Lasses" White, Si Jenks, George Meeker, Ben Welden

Director: Kurt Neumann

Screenplay: Richard Sale and Mary Loos

Producers: Frank and Maurice King

RETURN OF THE BAD MEN

(RKO, July 17, 1948) 96 Minutes

Randolph Scott, Robert Ryan, Anne Jeffreys, George Hayes, Jacqueline White, Richard Powers (Tom Keene), *Tom Tyler,* Steve Brodie, Robert Bray, Lex Barker, Walter Reed, Michael Harvey, Dan White, Robert Armstrong, Lew Harvey, Gary Gray, Walter Baldwin, Minna Gombell, Warren Jackson, Robert Clarke, Jason Robards, Sr., Ernie Adams, Bud Osborne, Forrest Taylor, Lane Chandler, Charles Stevens, Kenneth Mac-Donald, Earle Hodgins, Harry Shannon, Larry McGrath, Billy Vincent, Brandon Beach, Ida Moore, John Hamilton

Director: Ray Enright

Screenplay: Charles O'Neal, Jack Natteford, Luci Ward

Producer: Nat Holt

THE GOLDEN EYE

(Monogram, August 29, 1948) 69 Minutes

Roland Winters, Mantan Moreland, Victor Sen Yung, Tim Ryan, Bruce Kellogg, Wanda McKay, Ralph Dunn, Forrest Taylor, Lois Austin, Evelyn Brent, Edmund Cobb, Lee "Lasses" White, *Tom Tyler,* George L. Spaulding, Barbara Jean Wong, Lee Tung Foo, Richard Loo, Bill Walker, Herman Cantor, John Merton

Director: William Beaudine

Screenplay: W. Scott Darling

Based on characters created by Earl Derr Biggers

Producer: James S. Burkett

RED RIVER

(Monterey/United Artists, September 17, 1946) 125 Minutes

John Wayne, Montgomery Clift, Joanne Dru, Walter Brennan, Coleen Gray, John Ireland, Noah Beery, Jr., Chief Yowlachie, Harry Carey, Sr., Harry Carey, Jr., Mickey Kuhn, Paul Fix, Hank Worden, Ivan Parry, Hal Taliaferro, Paul Fiero, Billy Self, Ray Hyke, Glenn Strange, *Tom Tyler,* Dan White, Lane Chandler, Lee Phelps, George Lloyd, Shelley Winters

Director: Howard Hawks

Story: Borden Chase - "The Chisholm Trail" (also titled "Red River")

Screenplay: Borden Chase, Charles Schnee

Producer: Howard Hawks

BLOOD ON THE MOON

(RKO Radio, November 9, 1948) 88 Minutes

Robert Mitchum, Barbara Bel Geddes, Robert Preston, Walter Brennan, Phyllis Thaxter, Frank Faylen, Tom Tully, Charles McGraw, *Tom Tyler,* Richard Powers (Tom Keene), Clifton Young, George Cooper, Bud Osborne, Zon Murray, Robert Bray, Ben Corbett, Harry Carey, Jr., Chris-Pin Martin, Al Ferguson, Iron Eyes Cody, Ruth Brennan, Erville Alderson, Joe Devlin, Al Murphy, Robert Malcolm

Director: Robert Wise

Story: Luke Short

Screenplay: Harold Shumate, Luke Short

Producer: Sid Rogell

THE THREE MUSKETEERS

(MGM, November 26, 1948) 125 Minutes

Lana Turner, Gene Kelly, June Allison, Van Heflin, Angela Lansbury, Frank Morgan, Vincent Price, Keenan Wynn, John Sutton, Gig Young, Robert Coote, Reginald Owen, Ian Keith, Patricia Medina, Richard Stapley, Byron Foulger, Sol Gorss, Richard Simmons, Robert Warwick, William Phillips, Albert Morin, Norman Leavett, Marie Windsor, Ruth Robinson, *Tom Tyler,* Kirk Alyn, John Holland, Reginald Sheffield, William Edmunds, Irene Seldner, Francis McDonald, Paul Maxey, Arthur Hohl, Gil Perkins, Mickey Simpson

Director: George Sydney

Story: Alexandre Dumas

Screenplay: Robert Ardrey

Producer: Pandro S. Berman

I SHOT JESSE JAMES

(Lippert/Screen Guild, February 26, 1949) 81 Minutes

John Ireland, Preston Foster, Barbara Britton, J. Edward Bromberg, Victor Killian, Barbara Woodell, *Tom Tyler,* Reed Hadley, Tommy Noonan, Byron Foulger, Eddie Dunn, Jeni Le Gon, Robin Short

Director/Screenplay: Samuel Fuller

Story: Homer Croy

Producers: Robert L. Lippert, Carl Hittleman

THE YOUNGER BROTHERS

(Warner Brothers, May 25, 1949) 77 Minutes

Wayne Morris, Janis Paige, Bruce Bennett, Geraldine Brooks, Robert Hutton, Alan Hale, Sr., Fred Clark, *Tom Tyler,* Ian Wolfe, William Forrest, Monte Blue

Director: Edwin L. Marin

Story: Morton Grant - "Three Bad Men"

Screenplay: Edna Anhalt

Producer: Saul Elkins

LUST FOR GOLD

(Columbia, June, 1949) 90 Minutes
Ida Lupino, Glenn Ford, Gig Young, William Prince, Edgar Buchanan, Will Geer, Paul Ford, Jay Silverheels, Eddy Waller, Will Wright, Virginia Mullen, Antonio Moreno, Myrna Dell, *Tom Tyler,* Elspeth Dudgeon, Paul Burns, Hayden Rorke, Kermit Maynard
Director: S. Sylvan Simon
Story: Barry Storm - "Thunder God's Gold"
Screenplay: Ted Sherdeman, Richard English
Producer: S. Sylvan Simon

MASKED RAIDERS

(RKO, August 15, 1949) 60 Minutes
Tim Holt, Richard Martin, Marjorie Lord, Gary Gray, Frank Wilcox, Charles Arnt, *Tom Tyler,* Harry Woods, Housley Stevenson, Clayton Moore, Bill George
Director: Lesley Selander
Screenplay: Norman Houston
Producer: Herman Schlom

SAMSON AND DELILAH

(Paramount, October 21, 1949) 128 Minutes
Victor Mature, Hedy Lamarr, George Sanders, Angela Lansbury, Henry Wilcoxon, Olive Deering, Fay Holden, Julia Faye, Russell Tamblyn, William Farnum, Lane Chandler, Moroni Olsen, Francis J. McDonald, William Davis, John Miljan, Arthur Q. Bryan, Laura Elliot, Victor Varconi, John Parrish, Frank Wilcox, Russell Hicks, Boyd Davis, Fritz Leiber, Mike Mazurki, Davidson Clark, George Reeves, Pedro de Cordoba, Frank Reicher, Colin Tapley, Nils Asther, Crauford Kent, Pierre Watkin, *Tom Tyler,* Fred Kohler, Jr., Philo McCullough, Greta Granstedt, Karen Morley, Robert St. Angelo, Charles Judels, Charles Meredith, Frank Mayo
Director/Producer: Cecil B. DeMille
Screenplay: Jesse L. Lasky, Jr., Frederic M. Frank
Adaptation: Harold Lamb
Story: The story of Samson and Delilah in the Holy Bible and Vladimir Jabotinsky's novel, "Judge and Fool"

SHE WORE A YELLOW RIBBON

(Argosy/RKO, October 22, 1949) 104 Minutes (Technicolor)
John Wayne, Joanne Dru, John Agar, Ben Johnson, Harry Carey, Jr., Victor McLaglen, Mildred Natwick, George O'Brien, Arthur Shields, Harry Woods, Chief John Big Tree, Noble Johnson, Cliff Lyons, *Tom Tyler,* Mike Dugan, Mickey Simpson, Frank McGrath, Don Summer, Fred Libby, Jack Pennick, Billy Jones, Bill Goettinger (William Steele), Fred Graham, Fred Kennedy, Rudy Bowman, Post Parks, Ray Hyke, Lee Bradley, Francis Ford, Paul Fix, Fred Graham, Dan White
Director: John Ford
Story: James Warner Bellah
Screenplay: Frank Nugent, Laurence Stallings
Producers: John Ford and Merian C. Cooper

SQUARE DANCE JUBILEE

(Donald Barry Prods./Lippert, November 11, 1949) 69 Minutes
Donald Barry, Mary Beth Hughes, Wally Vernon, Max Terhune, Thurston Hall, John Eldredge, Tom Kennedy, Britt Wood, Marshall Reed, *Tom Tyler,* Chester Clute, Lee Roberts, Alex Montoya, Cliff Taylor, Ralph Moody, Hazel Nilson, Snub Pollard, Tex Cooper, Dorothy Vernon, Slim Gault, Hal King, Spade Cooley and his Band, Lloyd "Cowboy" Copas, Claude Casey, The Brown Brothers, Smiley & Kitty, Dana Gibson, Herman the Hermit, Ray Vaughn, Charles Grillo, Buddy McDowell, The Tumble Weeds, Dot Remy, The Elder Lovies and Les Gotcher (World's Champion Square Dance Caller)
Director: Paul Landers
Producer: Ron Ormond

RIDERS OF THE RANGE

(RKO, February 11, 1950) 57 Minutes
Tim Holt, Richard Martin, Jacqueline White, Reed Hadley, Robert Barrat, *Tom Tyler,* Robert Clarke, William Tannen
Director: Lesley Selander
Screenplay: Norman Houston
Producer: Herman Schlom

THE DALTONS' WOMEN

(Western Adventure/Howco, February 25, 1950) 80 Minutes
Lash LaRue, Al St. John, Jack Holt, Tom Neal, Pamela Blake, Jacqueline Fontaine, Raymond Hatton, Lyle Talbot, *Tom Tyler,* J. Farrell MacDonald, Terry Frost, Stanley Price, Bud Osborne, Cliff Taylor, Buff Brown, Clarke Stevens, Lee Bennett, Jimmie Martin, Archie Twitchell
Director: Thomas Carr
Screenplay: Ron Ormond and Maurice Tombragel
Producer: Ron Ormond

HOSTILE COUNTRY

(Lippert, March 24, 1950) 60 Minutes
Jimmy Ellison, Russell Hayden, Fuzzy Knight, Raymond Hatton, Betty (Julie) Adams, *Tom Tyler,* Dennis Moore, George J. Lewis, John Cason, Stanley Price, Stephen Carr, George Chesebro, Bud Osborne, Jimmie Martin, Judith Webster, Jimmy Van Horn, Cliff Taylor, Ray Jones, I. Stanford Jolley, George Sowards, J. Farrell MacDonald
Director: Thomas Carr
Screenplay: Maurice Tombragel, Robert Lippert
Producer: Ron Ormond

MARSHAL OF HELDORADO

(Lippert, April 21, 1950) 53 Minutes
Jimmy Ellison, Russell Hayden, Raymond Hatton, Fuzzy Knight, Betty (Julie) Adams, *Tom Tyler,* George J. Lewis, John Cason, Stanley Price, Stephen Carr, Dennis Moore, George Chesebro, Jimmie Martin, Cliff Taylor, Ned Roberts, Jack Hendricks, Wally West, James Van Horn, Jack Geddes, Bud Osborne, Carl Mathews
Director: Thomas Carr
Screenplay: Ron Ormond, Maurice Tombragel
Producers: Ron Ormond, Murray Lerner

COLORADO RANGER

(Lippert, May 12, 1950) 59 Minutes
Jimmy "Shamrock" Ellison, Russell "Lucky" Hayden, Fuzzy Knight, Raymond Hatton, Betty (Julie) Adams, George J. Lewis, *Tom Tyler,* John Cason, Stanley Price, Stephen Carr, Dennis Moore, George Chesebro, Bud Osborne, Jimmie Martin, Gene Roth, I. Stanford Jolley, Joseph Richards
Director: Thomas Carr
Screenplay: Ron Ormond and Maurice Tombragel
Producers: Ron Ormond, Murray Lerner

WEST OF THE BRAZOS

(Lippert, June 2, 1950) 58 Minutes
Jimmy Ellison, Russell Hayden, Raymond Hatton, Fuzzy Knight, Betty (Julie) Adams, *Tom Tyler,* Stanley Price, Dennis Moore, George J. Lewis, John Cason, Bud Osborne, George Chesebro, Judith Webster, Gene Roth, Jimmie Martin, Stephan Carr
Director: Thomas Carr
Screenplay: Ron Ormond, Maurice Tombragel
Producers: Ron Ormond, Murray Lerner

CROOKED RIVER

(Lippert, June 9, 1950) 55 Minutes
Jimmy Ellison, Russell Hayden, Fuzzy Knight, Raymond Hatton, Betty (Julie) Adams, *Tom Tyler,* George J. Lewis, John Cason, Stanley Price, Stephen Carr, Dennis Moore, George Chesebro, Bud Osborne, Jimmie Martin, Cliff Taylor, Helen Gibson, Carl Mathews, George Sowards, Scoop Martin, Joe Phillips
Director: Thomas Carr
Screenplay: Ron Ormond and Maurice Tombragel
Producers: Ron Ormond and Murray Lerner

FAST ON THE DRAW

(Lippert, June 30, 1950)
Jimmy Ellison, Russell Hayden, Raymond Hatton, Fuzzy Knight, Betty (Julie) Adams, *Tom Tyler,* George J. Lewis, John Cason, Dennis Moore, Judith Webster, Bud Osborne, Helen Gibson, Cliff Taylor, Stanley Price, Jimmy Van Horn, Bud Hooker, Ray Jones, I. Stanford Jolley
Director: Thomas Carr
Screenplay: Maurice Tombragel, Ron Ormond
Producer: Ron Ormond

RIO GRANDE PATROL

(RKO, October 21, 1950) 60 Minutes
Tim Holt, Richard Martin, Jane Nigh, Douglas Fowley, Cleo Moore, *Tom Tyler,* Rick Vallin, John Holland, Larry Johns, Harry Harvey, Forrest Burns
Director: Lesley Selander
Screenplay: Norman Houston
Producer: Herman Schlom

TRAIL OF ROBIN HOOD

(Republic, December 15, 1950) 67 Minutes
(TruColor)
Roy Rogers, Penny Edwards, Gordon Jones, Jack Holt, Emory Parnel, Clifton Young, James Magill, Carol Nugent, George Chesebron, Edward Cassidy, Foy Willing and The Riders of the Purple Sage, "Trigger," and Guest Stars: *Tom Tyler,* Kermit Maynard, Ray Corrigan, Tom Keene, Monte Hale, Rex Allen, Allan Lane, William Farnum
Director: William Witney
Screenplay: Gerald Geraghty
Associate Producer: Eddy White

THE GREAT MISSOURI RAID

(Paramount, February 22, 1951) 83 Minutes
(Technicolor)
Wendell Corey, MacDonald Carey, Ellen Drew, Ward Bond, Bruce Bennett, Bill Williams, Anne Revere, Edgar Buchanan, Lois Chastland, Louis Jean Heydt, Barry Kelly, James Millican, Guy Wilkerson, Ethan Laidlaw, *Tom Tyler,* Paul Fix, James Griffith, Whit Bissell, Steve Pendleton, Paul Lees, Bob Brey, Alan Wells
Director: Gordon Douglas
Story/Screenplay: Frank Gruber
Producer: Nat Holt

BEST OF THE BADMEN

(RKO, June 9, 1951) 84 Minutes
(Technicolor)
Robert Ryan, Claire Trevor, Jack Buetel, Robert Preston, Walter Brennan, Bruce Cabot, John Archer, Lawrence Tierney, Barton MacLane, *Tom Tyler,* Bob Wilke, John Cliff, Lee MacGregor, Emmett Lynn, Carleton Young, Byron Foulger, William Tannen, Harry Woods, Everett Glass
Director: William D. Russell
Story: Robert Hardy Andrews
Screenplay: Robert Hardy Andrews, John Twist
Producer: Herman Schlom

ROAD AGENT

(RKO, March 29, 1952) 60 Minutes

Tim Holt, Richard Martin, Noreen Nash, Mauritz Hugo, Dorothy Patrick, Bob Wilke, *Tom Tyler,* Guy Edward Hearn, William Tannen, Sam Flint, Forbes Murray, Stanley Blystone, Tom Kennedy

Director: Lesley Selander
Screenplay: Norman Houston
Producer: Herman Schlom

THE LION AND THE HORSE

(Warners, April 19, 1952) 83 Minutes
(WarnerColor)

Steve Cochran, Ray Teal, Bob Steele, Harry Antrim, George O'Hanlon, Sherry Jackson, William Fawcett, House Peters, Jr., Lane Chandler, Lee Roberts, Charles Stevens, Jack Williams, *Tom Tyler,* Billy Dix, Steve Peck

Director: Louis King
Story/Screenplay: Crane Wilbur
Producer: Bryan Foy

WHAT PRICE GLORY?

(20th C.-Fox, August, 1952)

James Cagney, Corinne Calvet, Dan Dailey, William Demarest, Craig Hill, Robert Wagner, Casey Adams, James Gleason, Wally Vernon, Henry Lefondal, Fred Libby, Ray Hyke, Paul Fix, James Lilburn, Henry Morgan, Dan Borzage, Bill Henry, Henry Kulley, Jack Pennick, Stanley Johnson, Luis Alberni, Barry Norton, Alfred Ziesler, George Braggeman, Scott Forbes, Mickey Simpson, *Tom Tyler*

Director: John Ford
Story: Maxwell Anderson, Laurence Stallings
Screenplay: Phoebe Ephren, Henry Ephren
Producer: Sol C. Siegel

COW COUNTRY

(Allied Artists, April 26, 1953) 82 Minutes

Edmond O'Brien, Helen Westcott, Robert Lowery, Barton MacLane, Peggie Castle, Robert Barrat, James Millican, Don Beddoe, Robert Wilke, Raymond Hatton, Chuck Courtney, Steve Clark, Rory Mallison, Marshall Reed, Brett Houston, *Tom Tyler,* Sam Flint, Jack Ingram, George J. Lewis

Director: Lesley Selander
Story: Adele Buffington
Associate Producer: Tom W. Blackburn
Producer: Scott R. Dunlap

8 ● BUSTER CRABBE

Thrill-Maker Nonpareil

Lucky is the individual who is old enough to have clung to his seat at the neighborhood theatre and swung, swum, ridden, flown, fought, and loved with Larry (Buster) Crabbe through 30 years of action films as Tarzan, Flash Gordon, Buck Rogers, Red Barry, Billy the Kid, Billy Carson, Captain Gallant, Thunda, and assorted other heroes. The undisputed King of Sound Serials, Buster provided the heroics in no less than nine serials and 122 episodes of pulse-pounding action, an eternity in the lives of the young who impatiently waited for each Saturday to arrive to see Buster thwart the villains, only to find himself once again in jeopardy at the conclusion of the second reel.

Larry Crabbe was born Clarence Linden Crabbe in Oakland, California on February 7, 1908 and grew up in Hawaii where he excelled in swimming, baseball, football, track and boxing. In '28 and '32 he participated in the Olympic Games, winning a gold medal for the 400-meter free-style event in the '32 meet. Before the end of '33, Buster had set a dozen world records in swimming; forty years later he would still be setting world records in the "senior citizen" competition. Thus his nickname "Buster" was an appropriate moniker, for he "busted" about all existing swimming records. But actually his father had given him the nickname when Larry was just a boy in Hawaii.

Continuing a collegiate education at the University of Southern California that was begun at the University of Hawaii, Buster was signed to a contract by Paramount following the '32 Olympics and after a few brief stints as an extra. He never got around to finishing his senior year as a law student.

Paramount gave Buster a small role in **Island of Lost Souls,** a film featuring Richard Arlen and Charles Laughton, and then gave him the lead in **King of the Jungle** ('33). Playing a Tarzan-type role as Kaspa, The Lion Man, Buster emoted with Frances Dee and Sidney Toler (of Charlie Chan fame) and received good reviews for his performance as the jungle man unwilling to cope with the civilized world and people's cruelty to animals.

Buster's first Western role followed, a good part in the Randolph Scott vehicle, **Man of the Forest** ('33), which, besides Buster, featured a dynamic group of supporting players headed by Harry Carey and Noah Beery, Sr.

On loan to Sol Lesser's Principal Pictures, Buster became Tarzan the Ape Man in his first serial, **Tarzan the Fearless** ('33), a 12-chapter cliffhanger also released in an edited feature version prior to the release of the serial version. Although Crabbe would never again play the role of Tarzan, he would always be identified with the character and was considered by many as the best of the many actors who have undertaken the role. The serial was weak in many production aspects, but it successfully launched Buster into the circle of top adventure actors. His exploits as the jungle lord are still entertaining television and cinema art audiences today, a generation of viewers not even born when he made the film.

Paramount eventually launched Crabbe on a series of Zane Grey Westerns that put him into the list of top ten Western stars in the Motion Picture Herald Poll of 1936. Things were picking up for Buster, but neither he nor anyone else at the time realized how fortunate

Buster Crabbe as **The Sea Hound** (Columbia, 1947)

A Lobby Card from 1933.

he was in '36 to be selected by Universal for the title role in **Flash Gordon,** a 13-episode serial based on Alex Raymond's popular comic strip. It was a smashingly successful film and resulted in two sequels in 1938 and 1940, as well as two serials based on the comic-strip heroes **Buck Rogers** and **Red Barry,** respectively. Buster continued to be used by Paramount in relatively unimportant roles until his contract expired in 1939. In spite of the success of the Crabbe serials, Universal never offered him leads in feature films and Paramount did not keep him in Westerns although he had quickly made the "Big 10." But PRC capitalized on his popularity, first with a jungle cheapie titled **Jungle Man** ('41), then with a long-running "Billy the Kid" series of Westerns. Teamed with Buster was veteran comic Al St. John, a holdover from the Keystone Kop days. They proved a popular duo.

Both "quickie" and "cheapie" describe the PRC

Westerns, not only those with Crabbe but with all the other cowboys who made pictures back-to-back and side-to-side at the little studio. But these low-grade horse operas found a steady market, and they were quite often entertaining in their own unique way. Some of the films were even good. Forty-six sagebrushers were made by Buster between '41 and '46, none of which won an academy award nor even honorable mention. But they were horse operas, and their appeal lay in the fact that Buster was tough and implacable, St. John was funny, the girls stayed pretty much out of the way, and the outlaws were familiar and predictable.

Although lacking in budget, the films did not lack for names long associated with Westerns. Reliables such as Slim Whitaker, I. Stanford Jolley, Glenn Strange, and George Chesebro were much in evidence throughout the series. But more than any others, it was Charles King and Kermit Maynard who slugged it out with

163

Crabbe, King appearing in 21 films and Maynard in 17 films of the long-running series. Crabbe did the best he could with poor scripts and St. John was quite often amusing as "Fuzzy Q. Jones," but production standards were far below those at Republic, Columbia, RKO, and even Monogram. Retakes were a luxury the studio hardly ever indulged in, and muffed lines and inept action sequences were all too apparent to adult audiences. Running inserts, camera finesse, rehearsals, and picturesque locations were among the little extras that PRC sacrificed in order to make a profit.

Crabbe's non-Westerns for PRC, besides **Jungle Man,** were **Jungle Siren** ('42), **Queen of Broadway** ('42), **Nabonga** ('44), and **The Contender** ('44). **Jungle Siren** was obviously designed to capitalize on the charms of Ann Corio, a famous burlesque stripper, as well as an ex-Tarzan Crabbe. **Queen of Broadway** had Buster playing opposite Rochelle Hudson in a standard B-melodrama. **Nabonga** (also known as **The Girl and the Gorilla**) provided good, well-paced escapist material that found a receptive audience, particularly among younger theatre-goers who took delight in animal antics, savages, and elemental battles to the death. **The Contender** contrives to rise above an oft-repeated story of a prizefighter who allows success to go to his head. It is well-paced and for an obviously low-budget picture packs a lot of entertainment, despite a too-frequent insertion of antiquated stock fight shots. Crabbe does well in his role as a heel.

Buster freelanced after 1946, appearing in several features before signing with Columbia for the lead in **The Sea Hound** ('47), his seventh serial. Two more serials followed for Columbia, **Pirates of the High Seas** ('50) and **King of the Congo** ('52). In each of these cliffhangers Buster had ample opportunity to flex his muscles, expand his chest, and display his swimming

Frank Shannon and Jean Rogers watch as Buster Crabbe makes a friendly overture to Emperor Ming's men in **Flash Gordon** (Universal, 1936).

164

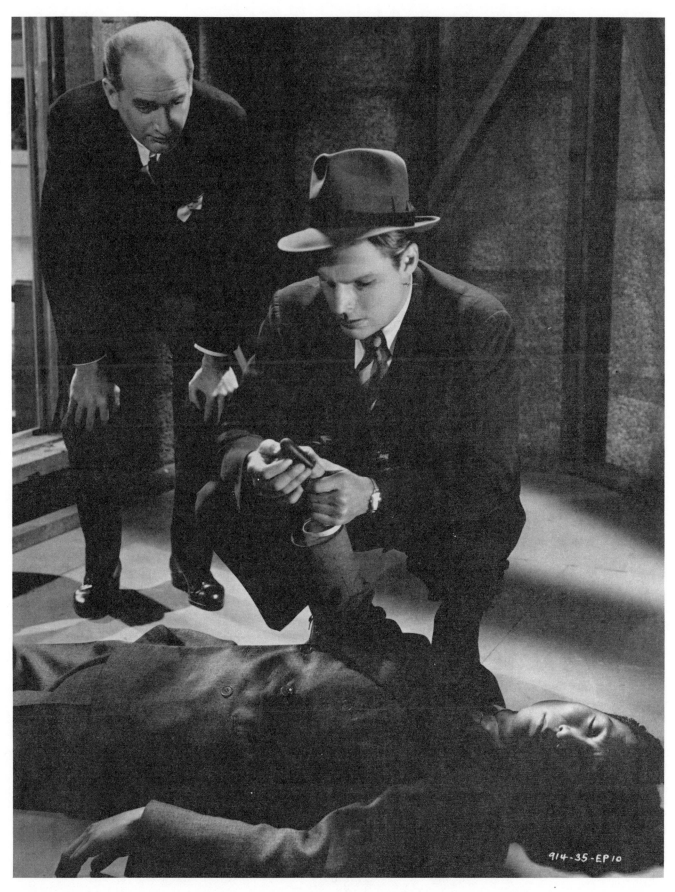

William Ruhl watches Buster Crabbe take something out of the death grip of Philip Ahn in **Red Barry** (Universal, 1938).

Buster Crabbe and Rusty Westcott fight for the knife in **Pirates of the High Seas** (Columbia, 1950).

ability, and in the latter film he is back in a Tarzan-type role.

After 1952, Buster turned his attention to television and other business interests, making only six pictures between '52 and '66. For awhile he hosted a television show in New York City, showing his old movies and commenting on their production. He also had a physical fitness show and traveled with his own water show. For several years he operated a boys' camp in New York's Catskills during the summer months and served as Director of Water Sports at the Concord Hotel on weekends. An investment in a swimming pool company paid off rather well, and he was seen in various TV commercials.

For two seasons, '55-'57, Buster starred in **Captain Gallant of the Foreign Legion**, a syndicated television series filmed in Morocco. His son Cullen and veteran comic Fuzzy Knight supported him. Just a few

of the approximately 70 titles in the series are "One Accident Too Many," "Rescue," "Masquerade," "Dr. Legionnaire," "The Evil Men Do," "Boy Who Found Christmas," "Constance Missile," "Captive Oasis," "The Long Night," "Water," "Man with Map," "Tola's Secret," "Carnival in Zogora," "Revenge," "Ring of Steel," "Prayer Rug," "The Informer's Map," "Out of Bounds," "Long Legionnaire," "Fuzzy's Furlough," "Ransom," "Too Many Suspects," "Man from Cairo," "Sword of El Kiri," "Magic Lamp," "Tina," "Legion—Our Home," "The Hat," "Shifting Sands," "Court Martial," and "Hana of Fatima."

Buster's last Western, **Comeback Trail**, shot in color in the early 1970s, is yet unreleased due to Buster's insistence that sex scenes shot without his knowledge be deleted from the release print. So far the producer has balked, and the film remains on the shelf. It is unlikely that it will ever be released. It is too bad that

166

producer Harry Hurwitz will not clean it up, for Buster's performance is one of his best.

To date 70,000 copies of Buster's physical fitness book *Energistics* have been sold in paperback by Playboy Press. In 1979 he appeared in the made-for-television movie, **Buck Rogers in the 25th Century**, as a space warrior coming out of retirement in an emergency, adding a touch of nostalgia to the proceedings.

For the last several years of his life Buster lived in Scottsdale, Arizona. To the very end he looked as if he could put on a loincloth and swing through the trees with Cheeta or cavort through the wilds of Mongo, battle sea pirates, or clean out a den of Western renegades. Apparently his exploits will be viewed at serial and Western film festivals, on TV, and by private collectors of 16mm prints and video cassettes for years to come—a tribute to the effulgence of a Western and Serial titan nonpareil.

Buster Crabbe passed away in his home on April 23, 1983 while sitting in his living room with his wife, preparing to catch a plane in order to make a live television appearance in another state. Cause of death was a heart attack. He was 75 years old.

BUSTER CRABBE Filmography

THE THUNDERING HERD

(Paramount, March 1, 1933) 59 Minutes
(Reissued as "Buffalo Stampede")
Randolph Scott, Judith Allen, Barton MacLane, Harry Carey, Larry *"Buster" Crabbe*, Dick Rush, Frank Rice, Buck Connors, Charles Murphy, Noah Beery, Sr., Raymond Hatton, Blanche Frederici, Monte Blue, Al Bridge
Director: Henry Hathaway
Story: Zane Grey
Screenplay: Jack Cunningham, Mary Flannery

KING OF THE JUNGLE

(Paramount, March 9, 1933) 75 Minutes
Buster Crabbe, Frances Dee, Disney Toler, Nydia Westman, Douglass Dumbrille, Robert Adair, Florence Britton, Ronnie Crosby, Robert Barrat, Sam Baker, Patricia Farley, Irving Pichel, Warner Richmond
Director: H. Bruce Humberstone
Screenplay: Philip Wylie and Fred Niblo, Jr.
Story: Charles Thurley Stoneham - "The Lion's Way"

MAN OF THE FOREST

(Paramount, August 25, 1933) 62 Minutes
Randolph Scott, Harry Carey, Verna Hillie, Noah Beery, Larry *Buster Crabbe*, Barton MacLane, Guinn Williams, Vince Barnett, Blanche Frederici, Tempe Piggot, Tom Kennedy, Frank McGlynn, Jr., Duke Lee, Lew Kelly, Merrill McCormack
Director: Henry Hathaway
Story: Zane Grey
Screenplay: Jack Cunningham, Harold Shumate

TO THE LAST MAN

(Paramount, September 15, 1933) 70 Minutes
Randolph Scott, Esther Ralston, Noah Beery, Jack LaRue, Larry *Buster Crabbe*, Fuzzy Knight, Barton MacLane, Gail Patrick, Muriel Kirkland, Egon Brecher, James Eagles, Eugenie Besserer, Harlan Knight, Shirley Temple
Director: Henry Hathaway
Story: Zane Grey
Screenplay: Jack Cunningham

HOLLYWOOD ON PARADE #17

(Paramount, November, 1933) 1 Reel
Buster Crabbe, Cecil B. DeMille, Mae West, George Raft, Jack Oakie, Mary Pickford, Polly Moran, Groucho Marx, Zeppo Marx, Chico Marx, Charlie Chaplin, Paulette Goddard, Gary Cooper, Loretta Young, Fredric March
Producer: Louis Lewyn

TARZAN THE FEARLESS

(Principal, 1933) 12 Chapters
(Also released in a condensed 85-minute feature version)
Buster Crabbe, Jacqueline Wells, E. Alyn Warren, Edward Woods, Philo McCullough, Mathew Betz, Frank Lackteen
Director: Robert Hill
Screenplay: Basil Kickey, George Plympton and Walter Anthony
Producer: Sol Lesser
Based on the character created by Edgar Rice Burroughs
Chapter Titles: (1) The Dive of Death (2) The Storm God Strikes (3) Thundering Death (4) The Pit of Peril (5) Blood Money (6) Voodoo Vengeance (7) Caught by Cannibals (8) The Creeping Terror (9) Eyes of Evil (10) The Death Plunge (11) Harvest of Hate (12) Jungle Justice

THE SWEETHEART OF SIGMA CHI

(Monogram, November 20, 1933) 77 Minutes

Mary Carlisle, *Buster Crabbe,* Charles Starrett, Florence Lake, Eddie Tamblyn, Sally Starr, Mary Blackford, Tom Dugan, Burr McIntosh, Major Goodsell

Director: Edward L. Marin

Screenplay: Luther Reed and Albert E. DeMond

Story: George Waggner

Producer: W. L. Lackey

Suggested by the song by Byron O. Stokes and F. Debleigh Vernor

THE SEARCH FOR BEAUTY

(Paramount, February 2, 1934) 80 Minutes

Buster Crabbe, Ida Lupino, Toby Wing, James Gleason, Robert Armstrong, Gertrude Michael, Roscoe Karns, Verna Hillie, Pop Kenton, Frank McGlynn, Sr.

Director: Erle Kenton

Screenplay: Frank Butler, Claude Binyon and Sam Hellman

Story: David Boehm, Maurine Watkins

Adapted from the play "Love Your Body" by Schuyler E. Grey and Paul R. Milton

YOU'RE TELLING ME

(Paramount, April 4, 1934) 67 Minutes

W. C. Fields, Joan Marsh, *Buster Crabbe,* Adrienne Ames, Louise Carter, Kathleen Howard, Pop Kenton, Del Henderson

Director: Erle Kenton

Screenplay: Walter DeLeon and Paul M. Jones

Story: Julian Street

BADGE OF HONOR

(Mayfair, June 2, 1934) 64 Minutes

Buster Crabbe, Ruth Hall, Ralph Lewis, Betty Blythe, John Trent

Director: Spencer Gordon Bennet

Screenplay: George Morgan

Story: Robert Emmett

Producer: Lester F. Scott, Jr.

WE'RE RICH AGAIN

(RKO-Radio, July 13, 1934) 72 Minutes

Edna May Oliver, Billie Burke, Marian Nixon, Reginald Denny, Joan Marsh, *Buster Crabbe,* Grant Mitchell, Gloria Shea, Edgar Kennedy, Otto Yamaoka, Lenita Lane

Director: William A. Seiter

Screenplay: Ray Harris

Story: Alden Nash

Associate Producer: Glendon Allvine

THE OIL RAIDER

(Mayfair, August 6, 1934) 59 Minutes

Buster Crabbe, Gloria Shea, George Irving, Max Wagner, Emmett Vogan, Harold Minjir, Wally Wales, Tom London

Director: Spencer Gordon Bennet

Screenplay: George Morgan and Homer King Gordon

Story: Rex Taylor

Producer: Lester F. Scott, Jr.

SHE HAD TO CHOOSE

(Majestic, November 1, 1934) 61 Minutes

Buster Crabbe, Isabel Jewell, Sally Blane, Regis Toomey, Maidel Turner, Fuzzy Knight, Arthur Stone, Edward Gargan, Huntley Gordon, Wallis Clark

Director: Ralph Ceder

Screenplay: Houston Branch

Story: Mann Page and Izzola Forrester

Supervisor: Larry Darmour

HOLD 'EM YALE

(Paramount, April, 1935) 65 Minutes

Patricia Ellis, Cesar Romero, *Buster Crabbe,* William Frawley, Andy Devine, George Barbier, Warren Hymer, George E. Stone, Hale Hamilton, Guy Usher, Grant Withers, Gary Owen

Director: Sidney Lanfield

Screenplay: Paul Gerard Smith and Eddie Welch

Story: Damon Runyon

Producer: Charles R. Rogers

HOLLYWOOD HOBBIES

(Paramount, July 5, 1935) 10 Minutes

Richard Arlen, Boris Karloff, Charles Farrell, *Buster Crabbe,* Clark Gable, Jack Holt, James Gleason, Guy Kibbee, Walter Huston, Grantland Rice

Producer: Grantland Rice

Narrator: Ted Husing

WANDERER OF THE WASTELAND

(Paramount, September 9, 1935) 7 Reels

Dean Jagger, Larry *"Buster" Crabbe,* Gail Patrick, Raymond Hatton, Fuzzy Knight, Edward Ellis, Benny Baker, Al St. John, Trixie Frigans, Monte Blue, Charles Walton, Anna Q. Nillson, Tammany Young, Stanley Andrews, Alfred Delcambre, Pat O'Malley, Glenn (Leif) Erikson, Marina Shubert, Kenneth Harlan, Jim Thorpe, Bud Osborne, Robert Burns

Director: Otto Lovering

Story: Zane Grey

Screenplay: Stuart Anthony

Producer: Harold Hurley

NEVADA

(Paramount, November 29, 1935) 7 Reels
Larry *"Buster" Crabbe,* Kathleen Burke, Monte Blue, Raymond Hatton, Glenn (Leif) Erickson, Syd Saylor, William Duncan, Richard Carle, Stanley Andrews, Frank Sheridan, Jack Kennedy, Henry Rocquemore, William L. Thorne, Harry Dunkinson, Barney Furey, William Desmond, Frank Rice, Dutch Hendrian
Director: Charles Barton
Story: Zane Grey - "Nevada"
Screenplay: Barnett Weston, Stuart Anthony

DRIFT FENCE

(Paramount, February 14, 1936) 56 Minutes
(Re-released as "Texas Desperadoes")
Larry *"Buster" Crabbe,* Katherine DeMille, Tom Keene, Benny Baker, Glenn (Leif) Erickson, Stanley Andrews, Effie Ellser, Richard Carle, Jan Duggan, Irving Bacon, Walter Long, Chester Gan, Dick Alexander, Bud Fine, Jack Pennick
Director: Otto Lovering
Story: Zane Grey
Screenplay: Stuart Anthony, Robert Yost
Producer: Harold Hurley

FLASH GORDON

(Universal, March, 1936) 13 Chapters
(also released in a condensed 72-minute feature version as "Rocket Ship")
Buster Crabbe, Jean Rogers, Charles Middleton, Priscilla Lawson, John Lipson, Richard Alexander, Frank Shannon, Duke York, Jr., Earl Askam, Theodore Lorch, James Pierce, Muriel Goodspeed
Director: Frederick Stephani
Screenplay: Frederick Stephani, George Plympton, Basîl Dickey, and Ella O'Neill
Story: Alex Raymond
Chapter Titles: (1) The Planet of Peril (2) The Tunnel of Terror (3) Captured by Shark Men (4) Battling the Sea Beast (5) The Destroying Ray (6) Flaming Torture (7) Shattering Doom (8) Tournament of Death (9) Fighting the Fire Dragon (10) The Unseen Peril (11) In the Claws of the Tigron (12) Trapped in the Turret (13) Rocketing to Earth

Raymond Hatton and Buster Crabbe in **Arizona Raiders** (Paramount, 1936 — later re-released as "Bad Men of Arizona").

169

DESERT GOLD

(Paramount, March 27, 1936) 58 Minutes

Larry *"Buster" Crabbe,* Robert Cummings, Marsha Hunt, Tom Keene, Glenn (Leif) Erikson, Monte Blue, Raymond Hatton, Walter Miller, Frank Mayo, Philip Morris

Director: James Hogan
Story: Zane Grey
Screenplay: Stuart Anthony, Robert Yost
Producer: Harold Hurley

THE ARIZONA RAIDERS

(Paramount, June 28, 1936) 54 Minutes
(Re-released as "Bad Men of Arizona")

Larry *"Buster" Crabbe,* Raymond Hatton, Marsha Hunt, Jane Rhodes, Johnny Downs, Grant Withers, Don Rowan, Arthur Aylesworth, Richard Carle, Herbert Hayward, Petra Silva

Director: James Hogan
Story: "Raiders of Spanish Peaks" - Zane Grey
Screenplay: Robert Yost, John Drafft
Producer: A. M. Botsford

LADY BE CAREFUL

(Paramount, September 4, 1936) 73 Minutes

Lew Ayres, Mary Carlisle, *Buster Crabbe,* Benny Baker, Grant Withers, Jack Chapin, Josephine McKim

Director: Theodore Reed
Screenplay: Dorothy Parker, Alan Campbell, and Harry Ruskin
Story: Kenyon Nicholson and Charles Robinson - "Sailor Beware"

ROSE BOWL

(Paramount, October 30, 1936) 75 Minutes

Eleanore Whitney, Tom Brown, *Buster Crabbe,* William Frawley, Benny Baker, Nydia Westman

Director: Charles Barton
Screenplay: Marguerite Roberts
Story: Francis Wallace - "O'Reilly of Notre Dame"
Producer: A. M. Botsford

ARIZONA MAHONEY

(Paramount, December 4, 1936) 58 Minutes

Larry *"Buster" Crabbe,* June Martel, Robert Cummings, Joe Cook, Marjorie Gateson, John Miljan, Dave Chasen, Irving Bacon, Richard Carlyle, Billie Lee, Fred Kohler, Fuzzy Knight, Si Jenks

Director: James Hogan
Story: "Stairs of Sand" - Zane Grey
Screenplay: Robert Yost, Stuart Anthony

THRILL OF A LIFETIME

(Paramount, January 21, 1937)

Yacht Club Boys, Judy Canova, Ben Blue, Eleanore Whitney, Johnny Downs, Betty Grable, Leif Erikson, *Buster Crabbe,* Franklin Pangborn, Tommy Wonder, Dorothy Lamour

Director: George Archainbaud
Story: Seena Owen and Grant Garrett
Screenplay: Seena Owen, Grant Garrett, and Paul Gerard Smith
Producer: Fanchon

MURDER GOES TO COLLEGE

(Paramount, March 5, 1937) 71 Minutes

Roscoe Karns, Marsha Hunt, Lynne Overman, Astrid Allwyn, Harvey Stephens, *Buster Crabbe,* Earl Fox, Anthony Nace, John Indrisano, Barlowe Borland, Purnell Pratt

Director: Charles Riesner
Story: Kurt Steel
Screenplay: Brian Marlow, Robert Wyler, and Eddie Welch

KING OF GAMBLERS

(Paramount, April 16, 1937) 78 Minutes

Claire Trevor, Lloyd Nolan, Akim Tamiroff, *Buster Crabbe,* Helen Burgess, Porter Hall, Harvey Stephens, Barlowe Borland, Purnell Pratt, Colin Tapley, Paul Fix, Cecil Cunningham, Frank Reicher

Director: Robert Florey
Story: Tiffany Thayer
Screenplay: Doris Anderson

FORLORN RIVER

(Paramount, July 2, 1937) 56 Minutes

Larry *"Buster" Crabbe,* June Martel, John Patterson, Harvey Stephens, Chester Conklin, Lew Kelly, Syd Saylor, William Duncan, Rafael Bennett, Ruth Warren, Lee Powell, Oscar Hendrian, Robert Homans, Purnell Pratt, Larry Lawrence, Tom Long, Merrill McCormack, Vester Pegg

Director: Charles Barton
Story: Zane Grey
Screenplay: Stuart Anthony, Robert Yost

SOPHIE LANG GOES WEST

(Paramount, September 10, 1937) 65 Minutes

Gertrude Michael, Lee Bowman, *Buster Crabbe,* Sandra Storme, Robert Cummings, Barlowe Borland, Jed Prouty, C. Henry Gordon, Rafael Corio, Fred Miller, Herbert Ransom, Nick Lukats, Guy Usher, Archie Twitchell

Director: Charles Riesner
Story: Frederick Irving Anderson
Screenplay: Doris Anderson, Brian Marlow, and Robert Wyler

Buster Crabbe, Jean Rogers, and Beatrice Roberts in **Flash Gordon's Trip to Mars** (Universal, 1938).

FLASH GORDON'S TRIP TO MARS

(Universal, February, 1938) 15 Chapters
(Also released in a condensed 70-minute feature version
entitled "Mars Attacks the World")
Buster Crabbe, Jean Rogers, Charles Middleton, Frank
Shannon, Beatrice Roberts, Donald Kerr, Montague
Shaw, Richard Alexander, Wheeler Oakman, Kane
Richmond, Kenneth Duncan
Director: Ford Beebe and Robert Hill
Story: Alex Raymond
Screenplay: Ray Trampe, Norman S. Hill, Wyndham
Gittens
Chapter Titles: (1) New Worlds to Conquer (2) The
Living Dead (3) Queen of Magic (4) Ancient Enemies
(5) The Boomerang (6) Tree-Men of Mars (7) Prisoner
of Mongo (8) The Black Sapphire of Kalu (9) Symbol
of Death (10) Incense of Forgetfulness (11) Human Bait
(12) Ming the Merciless (13) The Miracle of Magic (14)
A Beast at Bay (15) An Eye for an Eye

DAUGHTER OF SHANGHAI

(Paramount, December 17, 1937) 67 Minutes
Anna May Wong, Philip Ahn, Charles Bickford, *Buster
Crabbe,* Cecil Cunningham, J. Carrol Naish, Anthony
Quinn, Evelyn Brent, Gino Corrado, John Patterson,
Fred Kohler, Frank Sully, Ching Wah Lee, Maurice Liu,
Pierre Watkin, Archie Twitchell, Mrs. Wong Wing,
Ernest Whitman, Guy Bates Post, Virginia Dabney
Director: Robert Florey
Story: Garnet Weston
Screenplay: Gladys Unger and Garnet Weston

TIP-OFF GIRLS

(Paramount, April 1, 1938) 64 Minutes
Lloyd Nolan, Mary Carlisle, Roscoe Karns, *Buster
Crabbe,* J. Carrol Naish, Evelyn Brent, Anthony
Quinn, Benny Baker, Irving Bacon, Harvey Stephens,
Gertrude Short, Archie Twitchell, Barlowe Borland,
Pierre Watkin
Director: Louis King
Story/Screenplay: Maxwell Shane, Robert Yost, and
Stuart Anthony

HUNTED MEN

(Paramount, May 27, 1938) 65 Minutes
Lloyd Nolan, Mary Carlisle, Lynne Overman, J. Carrol Naish, Delmar Watson, *Buster Crabbe,* Anthony Quinn, Johnny Downs, Dorothy Peterson, Lu Miller, Regis Toomey, Fern Emmett, George Davis, Hooper Atchley
Director: Louis King
Story: Albert Duffy and Marian Grant
Screenplay: Horace McCoy and William R. Lipman

RED BARRY

(Universal, October, 1938) 13 Chapters
Buster Crabbe, Frances Robinson, Edna Sedgwick, Syril Delevante, Frank Lackteen, Wade Boteler, Hugh Huntley, Philip Ahn, William Ruhl, William Gould, Wheeler Oakman, Stanley Price, Earle Douglas, Charles Stevens
Director: Ford Beebe and Alan James
Screenplay: Norman Hall and Ray Trampe
Source: King Features comic strip
Chapter Titles: (1) Millions for Defense (2) The Curtain Falls (3) The Decoy (4) High Stakes (5) Desperate Chances (6) The Human Target (7) Midnight Tragedy (8) The Devil's Disguise (9) Between Two Fires (10) The False Trail (11) Heavy Odds (12) The Enemy Within (13) Mission of Mercy

ILLEGAL TRAFFIC

(Paramount, November 4, 1938) 67 Minutes
J. Carrol Naish, Mary Carlisle, Robert Preston, Judith Barrett, Pierre Watkin, *Buster Crabbe,* George McKay, Richard Kenning, Philip Warren
Director: Louis King
Story/Screenplay: Robert Yost, Lewis Foster, and Stuart Anthony

BUCK ROGERS

(Universal, February, 1939) 12 Chapters
(Also released in a condensed 69-minute feature version entitled "Planet Outlaws")
Buster Crabbe, Constance Moore, Jackie Moran, Jack Mulhall, Anthony Warde, C. Montague Shaw, Guy Usher, William Gould, Philson Ahn, Henry Brandon, Wheeler Oakman, Kenne Duncan, Carleton Young, Reed Howes
Directors: Ford Beebe and Saul A. Goodkind
Screenplay: Norman Hall and Ray Trampe
Associate Producer: Barney Sarecky
Source: comic strip by Dick Calkins and Phil Nowlan
Chapter Titles: (1) Tomorrow's World (2) Tragedy on Saturn (3) The Enemy's Stronghold (4) The Sky Patrol (5) The Phantom Plane (6) The Unknown Command (7) Primitive Urge (8) Revolt of the Zuggs (9) Bodies Without Minds (10) Broken Barriers (11) A Prince in Bondage (12) War of the Planets

UNMARRIED

(Paramount, May 26, 1939) 66 Minutes
Buck Jones, Helen Twelvetrees, Donald O'Connor, John Hartley, Robert Armstrong, Sidney Blackmer, *Buster Crabbe,* Edward Pawley, Lucien Littlefield, Jack Roper
Director: Kurt Neumann
Story: Grover Jones and William Slavens McNutt
Screenplay: Lillie Hayward and Brian Marlow

MILLION DOLLAR LEGS

(Paramount, July 14, 1939) 65 Minutes
Betty Grable, John Hartley, Donald O'Connor, Jackie Coogan, *Buster Crabbe,* Peter Hayes, Dorothea Kent, Richard Denning, Philip Warren, Eddie Arnold, Jr., Thurston Hall, Roy Gordon, Matty Kemp, William Tracy, Joyce Mathews, Russ Clark
Director: Nick Grinde
Story: Lewis R. Foster
Screenplay: Lewis R. Foster and Richard English

COLORADO SUNSET

(Republic, July 31, 1939) 61 Minutes
Gene Autry, Smiley Burnette, June Storey, Larry *"Buster" Crabbe,* Barbara Pepper, Robert Barrat, Patsy Montana, Parnell Pratt, William Farnum, Kermit Maynard, Jack Ingram, Elmo Lincoln, Frank Marvin, Ethan Laidlaw, Fred Burns, Jack Kirk, Budd Buster, Ed Cassidy, Slim Whitaker, Murdock McQuarrie, Ralph Peters, The CBS-KMBS Texas Rangers, "Champion"
Director: George Sherman
Story: Luci Ward, Jack Natteford
Screenplay: Betty Burbridge, Stanley Roberts
Associate Producer: William Berke

CALL A MESSENGER

(Universal, September 28, 1939) 65 Minutes
Billy Halop, Huntz Hall, Robert Armstrong, Mary Carlisle, Anne Nagel, Victor Jory, *Buster Crabbe,* El Brendel, Jimmy Butler, George Offerman, Jr.
Director: Arthur Lubin
Story: Sally Sandlin and Michele Kraike
Screenplay: Arthur T. Horman
Associate Producer: Ken Goldsmith

SAILOR'S LADY

(20th Century-Fox, July 5, 1940) 66 Minutes
Nancy Kelly, Jon Hall, Joan Davis, Dana Andrews, Mary Nash, *Buster Crabbe,* Katharine Aldridge, Harry Shannon, Wally Vernon, Bruce Hampton, Charles D. Brown, Selmar Jackson, Ward Bond, Kane Richmond, William B. Davidson, Edmund McDonald, Edgar Dearing
Director: Allan Dwan
Story: Frank Wead
Screenplay: Frederick Hazlitt Brennan

FLASH GORDON CONQUERS THE UNIVERSE

(Universal, 1940) 12 Chapters
Buster Crabbe, Carol Hughes, Charles Middleton, Frank Shannon, Anne Gwynne, Roland Drew, Shirley Deane, Victor Zimmerman, Don Rowan, Michael Mark, Sigurd Nilssen, Lee Powell, Edgar Edwards, Ben Taggart, Harry C. Bradley
Director: Ford Beebe and Ray Taylor
Screenplay: George H. Plympton, Basil Dickey, and Barry Shipman
Source: Alex Raymond's comic strip
Chapter Titles: (1) The Purple Death (2) Freezing Torture (3) Walking Bombs (4) The Destroying Ray (5) The Palace of Horror (6) Flaming Death (7) The Land of the Dead (8) The Fiery Abyss (9) The Pool of Peril (10) The Death Mist (11) Stark Treachery (12) Doom of the Dictator

BILLY THE KID WANTED

(PRC, October 4, 1941) 64 Minutes
Buster Crabbe, Al St. John, Dave O'Brien, Glenn Strange, Choti Sherwood, Charles King, Slim Whitaker, Howard Masters, Joe Newfield, Budd Buster, Frank Ellis, Curley Dresden, Wally West, Ray Henderson, Augie Gomez, Kenne Duncan, Arch Hall
Director: Sherman Scott (Sam Newfield)
Screenplay: Fred Myton
Producer: Sigmund Neufeld

JUNGLE MAN

(PRC, October 10, 1941) 63 Minutes
Buster Crabbe, Charles Middleton, Sheila Darcy, Vince Barnett, Weldon Heyburn
Director: Harry Fraser
Screenplay: Rita Douglas

BILLY THE KID'S ROUND-UP

(PRC, December 12, 1941) 58 Minutes
(Billy the Kid Series)
Buster Crabbe, Al St. John, Carleton Young, Joan Barclay, Glenn Strange, Charles King, Slim Whitaker, John Elliott, Dennis Moore, Kenne Duncan, Curley Dresden, Dick Cramer, Wally West, Tex Palmer, Tex Cooper, Horace B. Carpenter, Jim Mason, Jack Hendricks
Director: Sherman Scott (Sam Newfield)
Screenplay: Fred Myton
Producer: Sigmund Neufeld

BILLY THE KID TRAPPED

(PRC, February 27, 1942) 59 Minutes
(Billy the Kid Series)
Buster Crabbe, Al St. John, Bud McTaggart, Anne Jeffries, Glenn Strange, Walter McGrail, Ted Adams, Jack Ingram, Milt Kibbee, Eddie Phillips, Budd Buster, Jack Kinney, Jimmy Aubrey, Wally West, Art Dillard, Kenne Duncan, Ray Henderson, Carl Mathews, Curley Dresden, Augie Gomez, George Chesebro, Horace B. Carpenter, Herman Hack, James Mason, Hank Bell, Oscar Gahan, Dick Cramer
Director: Sherman Scott (Sam Newfield)
Screenplay: Oliver Drake
Producer: Sigmund Neufeld

BILLY THE KID'S SMOKING GUNS

(PRC, May 1, 1942) 58 Minutes
(Billy the Kid Series)
Buster Crabbe, Al St. John, Dave O'Brien, Joan Barclay, John Merton, Milt Kibbee, Ted Adams, Karl Hackett, Frank Ellis, Slim Whitaker, Budd Buster, Joel Newfield, Bert Dillard
Director: Sherman Scott (Sam Newfield)
Screenplay: George Milton (George Sayre and Milton Raison)
Producer: Sigmund Neufeld

JUNGLE SIREN

(PRC, August 21, 1942) 68 Minutes
Ann Corio, *Buster Crabbe,* Evelyn Wahl, Paul Bryar, Milt Kibbee, Arno Frey, Jess Brooks, Manart Kippen, James Adamson
Director: Sam Newfield
Story: George W. Sayre and Milton Raison
Screenplay: George W. Sayre and Sam Robins

LAW AND ORDER

(PRC, August 21, 1942) 58 Minutes
Buster Crabbe, Al St. John, Tex (Dave) O'Brien, Sarah Padden, Wanda McKay, Charles King, Hal Price, John Merton, Kenne Duncan, Ted Adams, Budd Buster, Kermit Maynard, Art Dillard, Carl Mathews
Director: Sherman Scott (Sam Newfield)
Screenplay: Sam Robins
Producer: Sigmund Neufeld

WILDCAT

(Paramount, August, 1942) 75 Minutes
Richard Arlen, Arline Judge, William Frawley, *Buster Crabbe,* Arthur Hunnicutt, Elisha Cook, Jr., Ralph Sanford, Alec Craig, John Dilson, Will Wright, Billy Benedict
Director: Frank McDonald
Story: North Bigbee
Screenplay: Maxwell Shane and Richard Murphy
Producer: William Rine and William Thomas

SHERIFF OF SAGE VALLEY
(PRC, October 2, 1942) 55 Minutes
(Billy the Kid Series)
Buster Crabbe, Al St. John, Tex (Dave) O'Brien, Maxine Leslie, Charles King, John Merton, Kermit Maynard, Hal Price, Curley Dresden, Jack Kirk, Lynton Brent, Budd Buster, Frank Ellis, Jack Evans, Carl Mathews, Merrill McCormack, Al Taylor, Jack Hendricks, Art Dillard
Director: Sherman Scott (Sam Newfield)
Screenplay: Milton Raison, George W. Sayre
Producer: Sigmund Neufeld

THE MYSTERIOUS RIDER
(PRC, November 20, 1942) 56 Minutes
(Billy the Kid Series) (Reissued in 1947 in a 39-minute version called "Panhandle Trail")
Buster Crabbe, Al St. John, Caroline Burke, John Merton, Kermit Maynard, Jack Ingram, Slim Whitaker, Ted Adams, Guy Wilkerson, Edwin Brien, Frank Ellis, Art Dillard
Director: Sam Newfield
Screenplay: Steve Braxton
Producer: Sigmund Neufeld

THE KID RIDES AGAIN
(PRC, January 27, 1943) 58 Minutes
(Billy the Kid Series)
Buster Crabbe, Al St. John, Iris Meredith, Glenn Strange, Charles King, I. Stanford Jolley, Edward Peil, Ted Adams, Karl Hackett, Kenne Duncan, Curley Dresden, Snub Pollard, John Merton, Slim Whitaker, Art Dillard, Al Haskell
Director: Sherman Scott (Sam Newfield)
Screenplay: Fred Myton
Producer: Sigmund Neufeld

QUEEN OF BROADWAY
(PRC, March 8, 1943) 62 Minutes
Rochelle Hudson, *Buster Crabbe,* Paul Bryar, Emmett Lynn, Donald Mayo, Isabel LaMal, Blanche Rose, Henry Hall, John Dilson, Milt Kibbee, Vince Barnett, Jack Mulhall, Snowflake
Director: Sam Newfield
Story: George Wallace Sayre
Screenplay: Rusty McCullough and George Wallace Sayre
Producer: Bert Sternbach

Buster Crabbe gives Jack Ingram a right-cross in **Mysterious Rider** (PRC, 1942 — later re-released as "Panhandle Trail")

FUGITIVE OF THE PLAINS
(PRC, April 1, 1943) 57 Minutes
(Billy the Kid Series) (Reissued in 1947 in 37-minute version called "Raiders of Red Rock")
Buster Crabbe, Al St. John, Maxine Leslie, Kermit Maynard, Jack Ingram, Karl Hackett, Hal Price, Budd Buster, Artie Ortego, Carl Sepulveda, Art Dillard
Director: Sam Newfield
Screenplay: George Sayre
Producer: Sigmund Neufeld

WESTERN CYCLONE
(PRC, May 14, 1943) 56 Minutes
(Billy the Kid Series)
Buster Crabbe, Al St. John, Marjorie Manners, Karl Hackett, Milt Kibbee, Kermit Maynard, Glenn Strange, Charles King, Hal Price, Frank Ellis, Frank McCarroll, Artie Ortego, Herman Hack, Al Haskell
Director: Sam Newfield
Screenplay: Patricia Harper
Producer: Sigmund Neufeld

CATTLE STAMPEDE
(PRC, August 16, 1943) 58 Minutes
(Billy the Kid Series)
Buster Crabbe, Al St. John, Frances Gladwin, Charles King, Ed Cassidy, Hansel Warner, Ray Bennett, Frank Ellis, Steve Clark, Roy Brent, John Elliott, Budd Buster, Hank Bell, Tex Cooper, Ted Adams, Frank McCarroll, Ray Jones, Rose Plummer, George Morrell, Hal Price
Director: Sam Newfield
Screenplay: Joe O'Donnell
Producer: Sigmund Neufeld

THE RENEGADE
(PRC, August 25, 1943) 58 Minutes
(Billy the Kid Series) (Reissued in 1947 in a 38-minute version called "Code of the Plains")
Buster Crabbe, Al St. John, Lois Ransom, Karl Hackett, Ray Bennett, Frank Hagney, Jack Rockwell, Tom London, George Chesebro, Jimmy Aubrey, Carl Sepulveda, Dan White, Wally West, Silver Harr
Director: Sam Newfield
Story: George Milton
Screenplay: Joe O'Donnell
Producer: Sigmund Neufeld

BLAZING FRONTIER
(PRC, September 4, 1943) 59 Minutes
(Billy the Kid Series)
Buster Crabbe, Al St. John, Marjorie Manners, Milt Kibbee, I. Stanford Jolley, Kermit Maynard, Frank Hagney, George Chesebro, Frank Ellis, Hank Bell, Jimmy Aubrey
Director: Sam Newfield
Screenplay: Patricia Harper
Producer: Sigmund Neufeld

DEVIL RIDERS
(PRC, November 5, 1943)
(Billy Carson Series)
Buster Crabbe, Al St. John, Patty McCarthy, Kermit Maynard, Charles Merton, Frank LaRue, Jack Ingram, George Chesebro, Ed Cassidy, Al Ferguson, Frank Ellis, Bert Dillard, Bud Osborne, Artie Ortego, Herman Hack, Roy Bucko, Buck Bucko
Director: Sam Newfield
Screenplay: Joe O'Donnell
Producer: Sigmund Neufeld

NABONGA
(PRC, January 25, 1944) 72 Minutes
Buster Crabbe, Fifi D'Orsay, Barton MacLane, Julie London, Bryant Washburn, Herbert Rawlinson, Prince Modupe, Jackie Newfield
Director: Sam Newfield
Screenplay: Fred Myton
Producer: Sigmund Neufeld

FRONTIER OUTLAWS
(PRC, March 4, 1944) 56 Minutes
(Billy Carson Series)
Buster Crabbe, Al St. John, Frances Gladwin, Marin Sais, Charles King, Jack Ingram, Kermit Maynard, Edward Cassidy, Emmett Lynn, Budd Buster, Frank Ellis
Director: Sam Newfield
Screenplay: Joe O'Donnell
Producer: Sigmund Neufeld

THUNDERING GUN SLINGERS
(PRC, March 25, 1944) 59 Minutes
(Billy Carson Series)
Buster Crabbe, Al St. John, Frances Gladwin, Karl Hackett, Charles King, Kermit Maynard, Jack Ingram, Budd Buster, George Chesebro
Director: Sam Newfield
Screenplay: Fred Myton
Producer: Sigmund Neufeld

VALLEY OF VENGEANCE
(PRC, May 5, 1944) 56 Minutes
(Billy Carson Series)
Buster Crabbe, Al St. John, Evelyn Finley, Edward Cassidy, Nora Bush, Donald Mayo, David Polonsky, Glenn Strange, Charles King, Jack Ingram, John Merton, Lynton Brent, Bud Osborne, Steve Clark, Budd Buster
Director: Sam Newfield
Screenplay: Joe O'Donnell
Producer: Sigmund Neufeld

A Lobby Card from 1944 picturing Marin Sais, Frances Gladwin, Kermit Maynard, Buster Crabbe, Frank Ellis, Charles King, and Al St. John.

THE CONTENDER
(PRC, May 19, 1944) 66 Minutes
Buster Crabbe, Arline Judge, Julie Gibson, Donald Mayo, Glenn Strange, Milton Kibbee, Roland Drew, Sam Flint, Duke York, Gordon Turner
Director: Sam Newfield
Story: George Sayre, Jay Doten
Screenplay: George Sayre, Jay Doten, and Raymond Schrock

THE DRIFTER
(PRC, June 14, 1944) 62 Minutes
(Billy Carson Series)
Buster Crabbe, Al St. John, Carol Parker, Kermit Maynard, Jack Ingram, Roy Brent, George Chesebro, Ray Bennett, Jimmy Aubrey, Slim Whitaker, Wally West
Director: Sam Newfield
Screenplay: Patricia Harper
Producer: Sigmund Neufeld

FUZZY SETTLES DOWN
(PRC, July 25, 1944) 60 Minutes
(Billy Carson Series)
Buster Crabbe, Al St. John, Patti McCarty, Charles King, John Merton, Frank McCarroll, Hal Price, John Elliott, Edward Cassidy, Robert Hill, Ted Mapes, Tex Palmer
Director: Sam Newfield
Screenplay: Louise Rousseau
Producer: Sigmund Neufeld

RUSTLERS' HIDEOUT
(PRC, September 2, 1944) 60 Minutes
(Billy Carson Series)
Buster Crabbe, Al St. John, Patti McCarty, Charles King, John Merton, Lane Chandler, Terry Frost, Hal Price, Al Ferguson, Frank McCarroll, Edward Cassidy, Bud Osborne
Director: Sam Newfield
Screenplay: Joe O'Donnell
Producer: Sigmund Neufeld

WILD HORSE PHANTOM

(PRC, October 28, 1944) 56 Minutes
(Billy Carson Series)
Buster Crabbe, Al St. John, Elaine Morey, Kermit Maynard, Budd Buster, Hal Price, Robert Meredith, Frank Ellis, Frank McCarroll, Bob Cason, John Elliott
Director: Sam Newfield
Screenplay: George Milton
Producer: Sigmund Neufeld

OATH OF VENGEANCE

(PRC, December 9, 1944) 57 Minutes
(Billy Carson Series)
Buster Crabbe, Al St. John, Mady Lawrence, Jack Ingram, Charles King, Marin Sais, Karl Hackett, Kermit Maynard, Hal Price, Frank Ellis, Budd Buster, Jimmy Aubrey
Director: Sam Newfield
Screenplay: Fred Myton
Producer: Sigmund Neufeld

HIS BROTHER'S GHOST

(PRC, February 3, 1945) 54 Minutes
(Billy Carson Series)
Buster Crabbe, Al St. John, Charles King, Karl Hackett, Archie Hall, Roy Brent, Bud Osborne, Bob Cason, Frank McCarroll, George Morrell
Director: Sam Newfield
Screenplay: George Plympton
Producer: Sigmund Neufeld

SHADOWS OF DEATH

(PRC, April 19, 1945) 60 Minutes
(Billy Carson Series)
Buster Crabbe, Al St. John, Donna Dax, Charles King, Karl Hackett, Edward Peil, Sr., Bob Cason, Frank Ellis, Frank McCarroll
Director: Sam Newfield
Screenplay: Fred Myton
Producer: Sigmund Neufeld

GANGSTER'S DEN

(PRC, June 14, 1945) 55 Minutes
(Billy Carson Series)
Buster Crabbe, Al St. John, Sidney Logan, Charles King, Emmett Lynn, Kermit Maynard, Edward Cassidy, I. Stanford Jolley, George Chesebro, Karl Hackett, Michael Owen, Bob Cason, Wally West
Director: Sam Newfield
Screenplay: George Plympton
Producer: Sigmund Neufeld

STAGECOACH OUTLAWS

(PRC, August 17, 1945) 55 Minutes
(Billy Carson Series)
Buster Crabbe, Al St. John, Frances Gladwin, Kermit Maynard, Ed Cassidy, I. Stanford Jolley, Bob Cason, Bob Kortman, Steve Clark, George Chesebro, Hank Bell
Director: Sam Newfield
Screenplay: Fred Myton
Producer: Sigmund Neufeld

BORDER BADMAN

(PRC, October 10, 1945) 59 Minutes
(Billy Carson Series)
Buster Crabbe, Al St. John, Lorraine Miller, Charles King, Ray Bennett, Archie Hall, Budd Buster, Marilyn Gladstone, Marin Sais, Bud Osborne, Bob Kortman
Director: Sam Newfield
Screenplay: George Milton
Producer: Sigmund Neufeld

FIGHTING BILL CARSON

(PRC, October 31, 1945) 51 Minutes
(Billy Carson Series)
Buster Crabbe, Al St. John, Kay Hughes, I. Stanford Jolley, Kermit Maynard, John L. "Bob" Cason, Budd Buster, Bud Osborne, Charles King
Director: Sam Newfield
Story/Screenplay: Louise Rousseau
Producer: Sigmund Neufeld

PRAIRIE RUSTLERS

(PRC, November 7, 1945) 56 Minutes
(Billy Carson Series)
Buster Crabbe, Al St. John, Evelyn Finley, Karl Hackett, Bud Osborne, Marin Sais, I. Stanford Jolley, Kermit Maynard, Herman Hack, George Morrell, Tex Cooper, Dorothy Vernon
Director: Sam Newfield
Story/Screenplay: Fred Myton
Producer: Sigmund Neufeld

LIGHTNING RAIDERS

(PRC, January 7, 1946) 61 Minutes
(Billy Carson Series)
Buster Crabbe, Al St. John, Mady Lawrence, Ray Brent, Henry Hall, Steve Darrell, Marin Sais, Al Ferguson, Karl Hackett, I. Stanford Jolley
Director: Sam Newfield
Screenplay: Elmer Clifton
Producer: Sigmund Neufeld

Al St. John holds onto Buster Crabbe in **Lightning Raiders** (PRC, 1946).

GENTLEMEN WITH GUNS
(PRC, March 27, 1946) 52 Minutes
(Billy Carson Series)
Buster Crabbe, Al St. John, Patricia Knox, Steve Darnell, George Chesebro, Karl Hackett, Budd Buster, Frank Ellis, George Morrell
Director: Sam Newfield
Screenplay: Fred Myton
Producer: Sigmund Neufeld

TERRORS ON HORSEBACK
(PRC, May 1, 1946) 55 Minutes
(Billy Carson Series)
Buster Crabbe, Al St. John, Patti McCarty, I. Stanford Jolley, Kermit Maynard, Henry Hall, Karl Hackett, Marin Sais, Budd Buster, Steve Karrell, Steve Clark, Bud Osborne, Al Ferguson, George Chesebro, Frank Ellis, Jack Kirk, Lane Bradford
Director: Sam Newfield
Screenplay: George Milton
Producer: Sigmund Neufeld

GHOST OF HIDDEN VALLEY
(PRC, June 5, 1946) 56 Minutes
(Billy Carson Series)
Buster Crabbe, Al St. John, Jean Carlin, John Meredith, Charles King, Karl Hackett, Jimmy Aubrey, John L. "Bob" Cason, Silver Harr, Zon Murray, George Morrell, Bert Dillard, Cecil Trenton
Director: Sam Newfield
Screenplay: Ellen Coyle
Producer: Sigmund Neufeld

PRAIRIE BADMEN
(PRC, July 17, 1946) 55 Minutes
(Billy Carson Series)
Buster Crabbe, Al St. John, Patricia Knox, Charles King, Edward Cassidy, Kermit Maynard, John L. Cason, Steve Clark, Frank Ellis, Budd Buster
Director: Sam Newfield
Screenplay: Fred Myton
Producer: Sigmund Neufeld

OVERLAND RIDERS
(PRC, August 21, 1946) 55 Minutes
(Billy Carson Series)
Buster Crabbe, Al St. John, Patti McCarty, Slim Whitaker, Bud Osborne, Jack O'Shea, Frank Ellis, Al Ferguson, John L. "Bob" Cason, George Chesebro, Lane Bradford, Wally West
Director: Sam Newfield
Screenplay: Ellen Coyle
Producer: Sigmund Neufeld

SWAMP FIRE
(Paramount, September 6, 1946)
Johnny Weissmuller, Virginia Grey, *Buster Crabbe,* Carol Thurston, Pedro DeCordoba, Marcelle Corday, William Edmunds, Edwin Maxwell, Pierre Watkin, Charles Gordon, Frank Fenton
Director: William Pine
Story/Screenplay: Geoffrey Holmes
Producers: William Pine and William Thomas

OUTLAW OF THE PLAINS
(PRC, September 22, 1946) 56 Minutes
(Billy Carson Series)
Buster Crabbe, Al St. John, Patti McCarty, Charles King, Karl Hackett, Jack O'Shea, John L. "Bob" Cason, Bud Osborne, Budd Buster, Roy Brent, Charles "Slim" Whitaker
Director: Sam Newfield
Screenplay: Elmer Clifton
Producer: Sigmund Neufeld

THE SEA HOUND

(Columbia, 1947) 15 Chapters
Buster Crabbe, Jimmy Lloyd, Pamela Blake, Ralph Hodges, Spencer Chan, Robert Barron, Hugh Prosser, Rick Vallin, Jack Ingram, Milton Kibbee, Al Baffert, Stan Blystone, Robert Duncan, Pierce Lyden, Rusty Westcoatt
Directors: Walter B. Eason and Mack Wright
Screenplay: George H. Plympton, Lewis Clay, and Arthur Hoerl
Producer: Sam Katzman
Chapter Titles: (1) Captain Silver Sails Again (2) Spanish Gold (3) The Mystery of the Map (4) Menaced by Ryaks (5) Captain Silver's Strategy (6) The Sea Hound at Bay (7) Rand's Treachery (8) In the Admiral's Lair (9) On the Water Wheel (10) On the Treasure Trail (11) Sea Hound Attacked (12) Dangerous Waters (13) The Panther's Prey (14) The Fatal Doublecross (15) Captain Silver's Last Stand

CAGED FURY

(Paramount, March 5, 1948) 60 Minutes
Richard Denning, Sheila Ryan, *Buster Crabbe,* Mary Beth Hughes, Frank Wilcox, Lane Chandler
Director: William Berke
Story/Screenplay: David Lang
Producers: William Pine and William Thomas

CAPTIVE GIRL

(Columbia, July, 1950) 73 Minutes
Johnny Weissmuller, *Buster Crabbe,* Anita Lhoest, Rick Vallin, John Dehner, Rusty Westcoatt, Nelson Leigh
Director: William Berke
Screenplay: Carroll Young

PIRATES OF THE HIGH SEAS

(Columbia, 1950) 15 Chapters
Buster Crabbe, Lois Hall, Tommy Farrell, Gene Roth, Tris Coffin, Neyle Morrow, Stanley Price, Hugh Prosser, Symona Boniface, William Fawcett, Terry Frost, Lee Roberts, Rusty Westcoatt, Pierce Lyden, Stanford Jolley, Marshall Reed
Directors: Spencer Bennett and Thomas Carr
Screenplay: Joseph F. Poland, David Mathews, George H. Plympton, and Charles R. Condon
Chapter Titles: (1) Mystery Mission (2) Attacked by Pirates (3) Dangerous Depths (4) Blasted to Atoms (5) The Missing Mate (6) Secret of the Ivory Case (7) Captured by Savage (8) The Vanishing Music Box (9) Booby Trap (10) A Savage Snare (11) Sinister Cavern (12) Blast from the Depths (13) Cave In (14) Secret of the Music Box (15) Diamonds from the Sea

KING OF THE CONGO

(Columbia, 1952) 15 Chapters
(also released under the title "The Mighty Thunda")
Buster Crabbe, Gloria Dea, Leonard Penn, Jack Ingram, Rusty Wescoatt, Nick Stuart, Rick Vallin, Neyle Morrow, Bart Davidson, Alex Montoya, Bernie Gozier, William Fawcett, Lee Roberts, Frank Ellis
Directors: Spencer Gordon Bennet and Wallace A. Grissell
Screenplay: George H. Plympton, Royal K. Cole, and Arthur Hoerl
Chapter Titles: (1) Mission of Menace (2) Red Shadows in the Jungle (3) Into the Valley of Mist (4) Thunda Meets his Match (5) Thunda Turns the Tables (6) Thunda's Desperate Chance (7) Thunda Trapped (8) Mission of Evil (9) Menace of the Magnetic Rocks (10) Lair of the Leopard (11) An Ally from the Sky (12) Riding Wild (13) Red Raiders (14) Savage Vengeance (15) Judgment of the Jungle

GUN BROTHERS

(United Artists, September 15, 1956) 79 Minutes
Buster Crabbe, Ann Robinson, Neville Brand, Michael Ansara, Walter Sande, Lita Milan, James Seay, Roy Barcroft, Slim Pickens, Dorothy Ford
Director: Sidney Salkow
Story/Screenplay: Gerald Drayson Adams

THE LAWLESS EIGHTIES

(Ventura/Republic, May 31, 1958) 70 Minutes
Buster Crabbe, John Smith, Marilyn Saris, Ted de Corsia, Anthony Caruso, John Doucette, Frank Ferguson, Sheila Bromley, Walter Reed, Buzz Henry, Will J. White, Bob Swan
Director: Joseph Kane
Story: "Brother Van" - Alson Jesse Smith
Screenplay: Kenneth Gamet
Associate Producer: Rudy Ralston

BADMAN'S COUNTRY

(Peerless/Warners, August 2, 1958) 68 Minutes
George Montgomery, Neville Brand, *Buster Crabbe,* Karin Booth, Gregory Walcott, Malcolm Atterbury, Russell Johnson, Richard Devon, Morris Ankrum, Dan Riss, Lewis Martin, Steve Drexel, Fred Graham, John Harmon, Al Wyatt, Fred Krone, William Bryant, Jack Kinney, Tim Sullivan, LeRoy Johnson, Jack Carol
Director: Fred F. Sears
Screenplay: Orville Hampton
Producer: Robert E. Kent

GUNFIGHTERS OF ABILENE

(United Artists, January, 1960) 67 Minutes
Buster Crabbe, Barton MacLane, Judith Ames, Russell Thorson, Lee Farr, Eugenia Paul, Jan Arvan, Richard Devon, Arthur Space, Kenneth MacDonald, Richard Cutting, Hank Patterson, Reed Howes
Director: Edward L. Cahn
Screenplay: Orville Hampton
Producer: Robert E. Kent

THE BOUNTY KILLER

(Embassy, July 31, 1965) 92 Minutes
(Technicolor) (TechniScope)
Dan Duryea, Rod Cameron, Audrey Dalton, Richard Arlen, *Buster Crabbe,* Fuzzy Knight, Johnny Mack Brown, Bob Steele, Bronco Billy Anderson, Peter Duryea, Eddie Quillan, Norman Willis, Edmund Cobb, I. Stanford Jolley, Frank Lackteen, Dan White, Grady Sutton, Emory Parnell, Duane Ament, Red Morgan, John Reach, Dolores Domasin, Dudley Ross, Ronn Delanor, Tom Kennedy
Director: Spencer G. Bennet
Screenplay: R. Alexander, Leo Gordon
Producer: Alex Gordon

ARIZONA RAIDERS

(Columbia, August 1, 1965) 88 Minutes
(Technicolor) (TechniScope)
Audie Murphy, Michael Dante, Ben Cooper, *Buster Crabbe,* Gloria Talbott, Ray Stricklyn, George Keymas, Fred Krone, Willard Willingham, Red Morgan, Fred Graham
Director: William Witney
Story: Frank Gruber, Richard Schayer
Screenplay: Alex Gottlieb, Mary and Willard Willingham
Producer: Grant Whytock

BUCK ROGERS IN THE 25TH CENTURY

(Glen A. Larson Productions-Bruce Lansbury Productions-Universal-TV/NBC-TV, 1979)
120 Minutes
Gil Gerard, Erin Gray, Tim O'Connor, David Groh, Roddy McDowall, Brianne Leary, Macdonald Carey, Karen Carlson, Michael Mullins, *Buster Crabbe,* Jack Palance, Felix Silla, Mel Blanc, Robert Dowdell, Sheila DeWindt, Don Marshall, William Conrad (narrator)
Director: Michael Caffey
Teleplay: Steve Greenberg, Aubrey Solomon, Cory Applebaum
Producers: John Gaynor, David J. O'Connell
Executive Producer: Glen A. Larson

SWIM TEAM

(Filmtel Ltd./Manson International, 1979)
James Daughton, Stephen Furst, Richard Young, Elise Anne, *Buster Crabbe,* Gunilla Hutton, Guy Fitch
Director/Story/Producer: James Polakof

THE ALIEN DEAD

(Firebird International, 1980) 80 Minutes
Buster Crabbe, Linda Lewis, Raymond Roberts, Mike Bonavia, John Leirier, Rich Vogan
Director: Fred Olen Ray
Screenplay: Fred Olen Ray, Martin Alan Nicholas

THE COMEBACK TRAIL

(Dynamite Entertainment/Rearguard Productions, 1982) 76 Minutes
(Made in 1972; limited release in 1982)
Chuck McCann, *Buster Crabbe,* Ina Balin, Robert Staats, Jara Kahout, Henny Youngman, Irwin Corey, Monit Rock III, Joe Franklin, Lenny Schultz, Hugh Hefner, Mike Geantry
Director/Producer: Harry Hurwitz
Story: Harry Hurwitz, Roy Frumkes, Robert J. Winston

9 ● TIM HOLT

The Aristocratic Cowboy

Sending young Tim Holt over the same trails which had proved profitable to both exhibitors and studio when traveled by his father, Jack Holt, seemed to have possiblities, if **Wagon Train** (1940) was an indication of how he would be used. Tim was a good-looking youth, well built, and had the makings of tremendous appeal with the juvenile traffic. He didn't need whopper stories in the RKO series given him as a result of George O'Brien's reentry into the Navy, and he seemed much more at home in the open spaces than he did when confined to the drawing-room.

RKO had been quite successful with its westerns, first with Tom Keene, then with George O'Brien. And the specials with Harry Carey had been outstandingly good, too. In the silent era, as FBO, the company had made a small fortune with cowboys Tom Mix, Tom Tyler, Bob Steele, Fred Thomson, and lesser stars. Superior programmers were standard fare for the studio, and the films had a quality about them not found in competitive products. Thus, it was good fortune for Holt that he was heaved into the saddle at the youthful age of 22 to play a full-fledged saddle ace in his own series in the declining days of 1939. More good luck was showered on him when the studio signed Ray Whitley as second lead and entrusted Bert Gilroy to produce the series.

After the first four films Lee "Lasses" White replaced Emmett Lynn as comedy relief and proved a popular comic capable of complementing the heroics of Tim and vocalizing of Ray. The production values of Tim's twelve Westerns in his initial series were far above those of most of the competition, being challenged only by the higher-budgeted Gene Autry series at Republic and the William Boyd series of Hopalong Cassidy films at

Paramount. Tim's youth, athletic ability, horsemanship, and refreshing personality caught on with Western fans everywhere. RKO, realizing the appeal of their star, hastened to cast actresses with above-average talent as leading ladies in his pictures.

Tim had been born on February 5, 1919. His real name was Charles John Holt, III, but from early childhood he was known simply as "Tim." His sister Elizabeth Marshall Holt was born in 1920 and she, too, acquired a nickname that all but buried her real one. The movie world knew her as Jennifer, a name she chose for herself after reading Don Byrne's book *Destiny Bay,* in which one of the characters was a girl called Jennifer.

Tim and Jennifer lived a normal, happy childhood for several years, but in 1931 Jack and Margaret Holt decided to separate. Tim elected to stay with his father, while Jennifer and her half-sister Gene went with their mother. Tim entered Beverly Hills High School in 1932, staying only one year before being shipped back east to attend Culver Military Academy in Indiana. He was active in dramatics and played football, polo, squash and tennis, boxed, and, as he put it, was a "gymnast of sorts." He was a member of the Black Horse Troop and the polo team. Upon graduation in 1936 he was awarded the "Gold Spurs," the highest achievement in horsemanship, and graduated *cum laude.*

Tim spent two years at U.C.L.A. while still living with Jack and the two spent much time on Jack's ranch near Fresno. Deciding to give acting a whirl, Tim was appearing in the Westwood Theatre Guild production of the Dutch play, "Papa Is All," in the latter part of 1936 when he decided to apply for a job at Universal,

Tim Holt

hoping to get a job in **The Road Back.** He didn't get the job he sought but he did get a screen test from Walter Wanger which led to a contract and a tiny bit in **History Is Made at Night** (1937). Then came **Stella Dallas** (1937), a film that brought him favorable comment from critics. He was on his way. It should be mentioned, though, that Tim's first screen role was in his father's **The Vanishing Pioneer** (1928). In it he received seventh billing, playing the film's hero as a child, while Jack played the hero as an adult.

In **I Met My Love Again** (1938) Tim plays a clean-cut young college student with eyes for Louise Platt. After giving support to George Brent and Olivia DeHavilland in **Gold Is Where You Find it** (1938), Tim again plays a clean-cut chap who organizes a patriotic group in **Sons of the Legion** (1938) and romances Evelyn Keyes. On a loan to RKO for **The Law West of Tombstone** (1938), Tim turned in a first-rate performance as the youthful bandit in love with Jean Rouverol. He received second billing to Harry Carey. And on loan to John Ford, Tim had a memorable, if short, role, as a young cavalry officer in the classic **Stagecoach** (1939).

Back at RKO, which bought his contract from Wanger, Tim was featured in **Renegade Ranger** (1939), playing the brother of the film's star, George O'Brien. On loan to Universal he did **The Spirit of Culver** (1939). On his own lot he got his first starring role, in **The Rookie Cop** (1939), playing a rookie who trains his dog to identify, track, and attack criminals when commanded. Good roles followed in **The Girl and the Gambler** (1939) and **Fifth Avenue Girl** (1939). He got top billing in **Laddie** (1940), the third picturization of Gene Stratton Porter's tale of saccharine sentimentality and lily-white romance down on the farm. Tim falls in love with the daughter of a newly-arrived Englishman who purchases the adjoining farm.

Swiss Family Robinson (1940) is an appealing picture and the script, despite departures from the Wyss classic, loses none of the heartening flavor of the book. Tim is convincing in the role of one of the sons of Thomas Mitchell and Edna Best.

Tim's next assignment was the Western series already referred to. Following the twelve films made with Ray Whitley, he made six features with Cliff "Ukulele Ike" Edwards as sidekick before entering military service. The pre-war Holt vehicles were solid productions in every way. The plot ingredients were both standard and familiar to all Western audiences, but the mixture was concocted with a skilled hand that displayed the very youthful and personable star at this best, quickly winning Tim a large following. For some time he was fortunate to enjoy the talent of Harry Wilde behind the camera, and the excellent photography of the scenic locations in these early oaters added quality to Tim's films. Too, the films were blessed with expert stuntmen of the caliber of Dave Sharpe and Ben Johnson.

Two of Holt's most widely acclaimed films were completed prior to his entering the service in 1942. In **The Magnificent Ambersons** (1942), directed by Orson Welles, Tim plays a spoiled brat inbred with all the futile, unsocial, arrogant attitudes and behavior characteristic of American working folk who attempted to ape the old continental aristocracies. The film is based on Booth Tarkington's novel of the suburban American magnificence of a family which lost most of its humanity to the pressures of wealth and showy splendor. Tim Holt and Agnes Moorehead get the brunt of the story impact, with Tim demonstrating his dramatic acting mettle in a fine performance; his is a bitterly valid portrayal of the son who scorns work as unbecoming an Amberson. Critics were enthusiastic in their praise of Holt. **Back Street** (1941), made the year before for Universal, had featured Tim as the son who sides with his mother against his father (played by Margaret Sullavan and Charles Boyer) and his acting had also been praised for that endeavor.

The door was open for Tim to do more dramatic roles in big productions, but he chose to remain in the saddle in prairie thrillers. He was, however, coaxed off the range and into a uniform for **Hitler's Children** (1943), one of the great sleepers of movie history. Produced at a cost of $167,000, it grossed over $5 million. One trade paper praised Holt for his masterful performance in a difficult role.

Tim entered the Air Force in late '42 at a time when he was receiving more fan mail than anyone on the RKO lot with the exception of Ginger Rogers. He served with distinction during World War II, flying 59 bombing missions as a B-29 bombardier and earning innumerable citations and medals.

After the war Tim resumed his movie career at RKO, although his first post-war release was John Ford's **My Darling Clementine** (1946) for Fox. He also co-starred in **The Treasure of Sierra Madre** (1948) for director John Huston and Warner Brothers, sharing acting honors with Humphrey Bogart and Walter Huston. It turned out to be one of the best pictures of the year and Tim's performance was hailed by critics and public alike. Offers poured in for roles in major productions, but Holt chose to remain in the corral at RKO, working in minor Westerns and spending as much time as possible in Oklahoma and on the road with his rodeo. Life as a Hollywood glamour star had no appeal for him whatsoever.

With Richard Martin as his sidekick, Tim made 29 slick Westerns in the years 1947-1952 that consistently turned a profit. Even in the Fifties, when drastic

Humphrey Bogart holds a gun on Tim Holt in **Treasure of Sierra Madre** (Warner Bros., 1948).

economies were the order of the day in "B" Westerns, Holt's films were budgeted at close to $90,000 in order to maintain quality. His was one of three series (the others being those of Autry and Rogers) to maintain a high standard of quality to the very end of the "B" era. And the fact that it did is a fine tribute to one of the best actors and most likable fellows ever to sit the saddle as a Western matinee idol.

The Holt films had plenty of action sequences and used location shooting extensively. There was little if any use of the process screens, and very little stock footage was ever used. Production values were high and competent players were chosen for supporting roles. Musical scores, plots, and dialogue content were all several cuts above the competition. In fact the Holt films were about the only films produced by RKO in the early Fifties that were making money. Thus, they were assigned much of the overhead of the company. His pictures consistently grossed $500,000, a sizable profit per picture. Tim was earning an average of $65,000

a year from his films and related efforts. But even though he was the only star consistently making money for them, RKO officials became scared of TV and the collapse of the small town theaters and followed the pattern set by the other studios in discontinuing the horse operas.

Tim ranked in the top ten cowboy stars in popularity in 1941, 1942, and 1943. He again made the big ten in 1948 and remained there until his series ended in 1952, at which time he ranked third in popularity behind Rogers and Autry.

Desert Passage (1952) was Holt's last Western programmer. In 1957 he starred in **The Monster that Challenged the World** for United Artists as a favor to director Arnold Laven. His last film, thirteen years later, was **This Stuff'll Kill Ya!** for Ultima Productions.

From 1948 until his death from cancer on February 15, 1973 Tim lived in Oklahoma except for short periods of time. Personal appearance tours and rodeo work kept

184

him busy for several years. He co-starred with Charles Bronson in a projected TV series for MCA, **Adventure in Java,** but the series failed to materialize although the pilot was aired. In 1952 he married for the third time, to Berdee Stephens, an Oklahoma school teacher. Three children were born to this union, sons Jack and Jay, and daughter Bryanna. Tim also had a son, Lance, by his first wife. During the fifties and sixties Tim worked at various jobs, consistently turning down film offers. He had found more happiness outside Hollywood than he ever had in it and had no desire to return to film making. He finally got into radio and television work in Oklahoma City and was an executive for Radio Station KOPR at his death.

Tim Holt was a man for his time. He epitomized the clean-cut, patriotic, fun-loving youth in his films of the thirties and the handsome, invincible hero on horseback in the forties and fifties. Unlike many other Western performers who needed a gimmick to sustain their popularity, Holt needed only his talent and natural charm. He was a man of the people; he simply did not take to Hollywood's pretentiousness, nor did he take himself seriously as a movie star. He was one of that select group that included Buck Jones, Harry Carey, and Will Rogers—those who seemingly were liked by everyone, even when their backs were turned.

The Holt sagebrushers found favor wherever Westerns were shown, and Tim always turned in a polished job of acting. His screen character was a likeable one but he was quite often tight-lipped and this taciturnity left much of the dialogue as well as the comedy to Richard Martin. Tim's romantic interludes with his leading ladies were business-like and not particularly convincing, as he always seemed anxious to get on with the action at hand. But to those in the audience, it all seemed natural enough. It was easy for the youth to identify with a hero who preferred action to romance. Except for a pair of thin leather gloves, our hero also avoided the fancy clothes worn by other western stars and was quite often seen wearing unfashionable denims, or at least a plain shirt with striped trousers, which added to the realism.

Whenever and wherever Western film connoisseurs gather, throw another log on the fire and talk about the prairie sagas of old, the name of Tim Holt will invariably be recalled as a cowboy who never made a bad shoot-em-up. That's about as nice a way to be remembered as a saddle ace could hope for.

TIM HOLT Filmography

YOUNG HOLLYWOOD
(Pathe, November, 1927) 2 Reels
Erich von Stroheim, Jr., Mike McCoy, Barbara Denny, Mary Jo Desmond, *Tim Holt,* Billy Reid, George Bosworth, Eileen O'Malley
Director: Robert T. Thornby
Producer: Madeline Brandels

THE VANISHING PIONEER
(Famous Players-Lasky/Paramount, August 23, 1928) 6 Reels
Jack Holt, Sally Blane, William Powell, Fred Kohler, Guy Oliver, Roscoe Karns, *Tim Holt,* Marcia Manon
Director: John Waters
Scenario: J. Walter Ruben
Story: Zane Grey

HISTORY IS MADE AT NIGHT
(Wanger/United Artist, April 2, 1937) 11 Reels
Charles Boyer, Jean Arthur, Leo Carrillo, Colin Clive, Ivan Lebedeff, George Meeker, Lucian Prival, *Tim Holt*
Director: Frank Borzage
Screenplay: Gene Towne, Graham Baker

STELLA DALLAS
(Goldwyn/United Artists, August 6, 1937) 12 Reels
Barbara Stanwyck, John Boles, Anne Shirley, Barbara O'Neill, Alan Hale, Marjorie Main, *Tim Holt,* Dickie Jones
Director: King Vidor
Screenplay: Victor Heerman, Sarah U. Mason
Story: Olive Higgins Prouty
Associate Producer: Merritt Hulburd

I MET MY LOVE AGAIN
(Wanger/United Artists, January 28, 1938) 77 Minutes
Joan Bennett, Henry Fonda, Dame May Whitty, Alan Marshal, Louise Platt, Alan Baxter, *Tim Holt,* Dorothy Stickney, Florence Lake, Genee Hall, Alice Cavenna
Directors: Arthur Ripley and Joshua Logan
Screenplay: David Hertz
Story: Ailene Corliss - "Summer Lightning"
Producer: Walter Wanger

GOLD IS WHERE YOU FIND IT

(Warners, February 19, 1938) 90 Minutes

George Brent, Olivia de Havilland, Claude Rains, Margaret Lindsay, John Litel, Marcia Ralston, Barton MacLane, *Tim Holt*, Sidney Toler, Henry O'Neill, Willie Best, Robert McWade, George Hayes, Russell Simpson, Harry Davenport, Clarence Kolb, Moroni Olson, Granville Bates, Robert Homans, Eddie Chandler

Director: Michael Curtiz

Story: Clements Ripley

Screenplay: Warren Duff, Robert Buckner

Producer: Hal B. Wallis

THE RENEGADE RANGER

(RKO, September 16, 1938) 60 Minutes

George O'Brien, Rita Hayworth, *Tim Holt*, Ray Whitley, Lucio Villegas, William Royle, Cecelia Callejo, Neal Hart, Monte Montague, Bob Kortman, Charles Stevens, James Mason, Tom London, Guy Usher, Chris-Pin Martin, Tom Steele, Ken Card, Jack O'Shea, Ray Jones, Bob Burns, Al Haskell, Pete Morrison, Victor Cox

Director: David Howard

Story/Screenplay: Bennett Cohen

Producer: Bert Gilroy

SONS OF THE LEGION

(Paramount, September 23, 1938) 6 Reels

Lynne Overman, Evelyn Keyes, Donald O'Connor, Elizabeth Patterson, William Frawley, *Tim Holt*, Billy Cook, Billy Lee, Edward Pawley, Richard Tucker, Tom Dugan

Director: James Hogan

Story/Screenplay: Lillie Hayward, Lewis Foster, Robert F. McGowan

THE LAW WEST OF TOMBSTONE

(RKO, November 18, 1938) 73 Minutes

Harry Carey, *Tim Holt*, Evelyn Brent, Jean Rouverol, Clarence Kolb, Esther Muir, Bradley Page, Paul Guilfoyle, Robert Moya, Allan Lane, Ward Bond, George Irving, Monte Montague, Bob Kortman, Kermit Maynard (unbilled)

Director: Glenn Tyron

Story: Clarence Upson Young

Screenplay: John Twist, Clarence Upson Young

Producer: Cliff Reid

STAGECOACH

(United Artists, March 3, 1939) 96 Minutes

Claire Trevor, John Wayne, Thomas Mitchell, George Bancroft, Andy Devine, John Carradine, Louise Platt, Donald Meek, Berton Churchill, Tom Tyler, *Tim Holt*, Chris-Pin Martin, Elvira Rios, Bill Cody, Buddy Roosevelt, Yakima Canutt, Paul McVay, Joe Rickson, Harry Tenbrook, Jack Pennick, Kent Odell, William Hopper, Vester Pegg, Ted Lorch, Artie Ortego, Merrill McCormack, Franklyn Farnum, James Mason, Si Jenks, Robert Homans, Chief White Horse, Bryant Washburn, Walter McGrail, Francis Ford, Chief Big Tree, Marga Daighton, Florence Lake, Duke Lee, Cornelius Keefe, Nora Cecil, Lou Mason, Mary Walker, Ed Brady

Director: John Ford

Story: "Stage to Lordsburg" - Ernest Haycox

Screenplay: Dudley Nichols

Producer: Walter Wanger

SPIRIT OF CULVER

(Universal, March 10, 1939) 9 Reels

Jackie Cooper, Freddie Bartholomew, *Tim Holt*, Henry Hull, Andy Devine, Gene Reynolds, Jackie Moran, John Hamilton, Kathryn Kane, Walter Tetley, Marjorie Gateson

Director: Joseph Santley

Screenplay: Nathanael West, Whitney Bolton

Story: George Green, Tom Buckingham, Clarence Marks

Associate Producer: Burt Kelly

THE ROOKIE COP

(RKO-Radio, April 28, 1939) 61 Minutes

Tim Holt, Virginia Weidler, Janet Shaw, Frank M. Thomas, Robert Emmett Keane, Monte Montague, Don Brodie, Ralf Harolde, Muriel Evans, Ace the Wonder Dog, Ralph Stein, Bob Lafferty

Director: David Howard

Screenplay: Morton Grant, Jo Pagano

Story: Guy K. Austin, Earl Johnson

Producer: Bert Gilroy

THE GIRL AND THE GAMBLER

(RKO, June 16, 1939) 63 Minutes

Leo Carrillo, *Tim Holt*, Steffi Duna, Donald MacBride, Chris-Pin Martin, Edward Paquello, Paul Fix, Julian Rivero, Frank Puglia, Esther Muir, Paul Sutton, Charles Stevens, Frank Lackteen, Henry Rocquemore

Director: Lew Landers

Story: "The Blue Ribbon" - Gerald Beaumont

("The Blue Ribbon" was based on Willard Mack's play "The Dove")

Screenplay: Joseph A. Fields, Clarence Upson Young

Producer: Cliff Reid

FIFTH AVENUE GIRL
(RKO-Radio, September 22, 1939) 83 Minutes
Ginger Rogers, James Ellison, Walter Connolly, *Tim Holt*, Veree Teasdale, Franklyn Pangborn, Louis Calhern, Theodore von Eltz, Alexander D'Arcy, Kathryn Adams, Ferike Boros
Director/Producer: Gregory LaCava
Screenplay: Allan Scott

LADDIE
(RKO-Radio, January 18, 1940) 69 Minutes
Tim Holt, Virginia Gilmore, Joan Carroll, Spring Byington, Robert Barrat, Miles Mander, Esther Dale, Sammy McKim, Joan Brodel (later Joan Leslie), Martha O'Driscoll, Rand Brooks, Peter Cushing, Mary Forbes
Director: Jack Hively
Screenplay: Bert Granet and Jerry Cady
Story: Gene Stratton Porter

SWISS FAMILY ROBINSON
(RKO-Radio, February 16, 1940) 93 Minutes
Thomas Mitchell, Edna Best, Freddie Bartholemew, *Tim Holt*, Terry Kilburn, Baby Bobby Quillan
Director: Edward Ludwig
Screenplay: Gene Towne, Graham Baker, Walter Ferris
Story: Johann David Wyss
Producers: Gene Towne and Graham Baker

WAGON TRAIN
(RKO, October 4, 1940) 62 Minutes
Tim Holt, Ray Whitley, Emmett Lynn, Martha O'Driscoll, Bud McTaggart, Cliff Clark, Ellen Lowe, Wade Crosby, Ethan Laidlaw, Monte Montague, Carl Stockdale, Bruce Dane, Glenn Strange
Director: Edward Killy
Story: Bernard McConville
Screenplay: Morton Grant
Producer: Bert Gilroy

Tim Holt ties up villains Cy Kendall and Ernie Adams in **The Fargo Kid** (RKO, 1940).

Virginia Vale and Tim Holt in **Robbers of the Range** (RKO, 1941).

THE FARGO KID

(RKO, December 6, 1940) 63 Minutes
Tim Holt, Ray Whitley, Emmett Lynn, Jane Drummond, Cy Kendall, Ernie Adams, Paul Fix, Paul Scardon, Glenn Strange, Mary MacLaren, Dick Hogan, Carl Stockdale, Harry Harvey, Lee Phelps
Director: Edward Killy
Screenplay: W. C. Tuttle
Producer: Bert Gilroy

I KNOW FOR SURE

(Warner Brothers, circa 1940) 21 Minutes
J. Carroll Naish, Ward Bond, *Tim Holt*, Samuel S. Hinds, Sheppard Studwick, Grant Mitchell

ALONG THE RIO GRANDE

(RKO, February 7, 1941) 61 Minutes
Tim Holt, Ray Whitley, Emmett Lynn, Robert Fiske, Betty Jane Rhodes, Hal Taliaferro, Carl Stockdale, Slim Whitaker, Monte Montague, Ruth Clifford, Harry Humphrey, Ernie Adams
Story: Stuart Antbong
Screenplay: Arthur V. Jones, Morton Grant
Producer: Bert Gilroy

BACK STREET

(Universal, February 27, 1941) 89 Minutes
Charles Boyer, Margaret Sullavan, Richard Carlson, Frank McHugh, *Tim Holt*, Frank Jenks, Esther Dale, Samuel S. Hinds, Peggy Stewart, Nell O'Day, Nella Walker, Cecil Cunningham, Majorie Gateson, Dale Winter, Kitty O'Neil
Director: Robert Stevenson
Story: Fannie Hurst
Screenplay: Bruce Manning and Felix Jackson

ROBBERS OF THE RANGE

(RKO, April 18, 1941) 61 Minutes
Tim Holt, Virginia Vale, Ray Whitley, Emmett Lynn, LeRoy Mason, Howard Hickman, Ernie Adams, Frank LaRue, Ray Bennett, Tom London, Ed Cassidy, Bud Osborne, George Melford, Bud McTaggart, Harry Harvey, Lloyd Ingraham
Director: Edward Killy
Story: Oliver Drake
Screenplay: Morton Grant, Arthur V. Jones
Producer: Bert Gilroy

CYCLONE ON HORSEBACK
(RKO, June 13, 1941) 60 Minutes
Tim Holt, Marjorie Reynolds, Ray Whitley, Lee "Lasses" White, Dennis Moore, Harry Worth, Monte Montague, John Dilson, Lew Kelly, Max Wagner, Terry Frost, Don Kelly, Slim Whitaker
Director: Edward Killy
Story: Tom Gibson
Screenplay: Norton S. Parker
Producer: Bert Gilroy

SIX GUN GOLD
(RKO, August 8, 1941) 57 Minutes
Tim Holt, Ray Whitley, Jan Clayton, Lee "Lasses" White, Lane Chandler, LeRoy Mason, Eddy Waller, Davidson Clark, Harry Harvey, Slim Whitaker, Jim Corey, Fern Emmett
Director: David Howard
Story: Tom Gibson
Screenplay: Norton S. Parker
Producer: Bert Gilroy

THE BANDIT TRAIL
(RKO, October 10, 1941) 60 Minutes
Tim Holt, Ray Whitley, Janet Waldo, Lee "Lasses" White, Morris Ankrum, Roy Barcroft, J. Merrill Holmes, Eddy Waller, Glenn Strange, Frank Ellis, Joseph Eggerton, Guy Usher, Jack Clifford, Bud Osborne, John Merton, Bud Geary, Lew Meehan, Terry Frost, Carl Stockdale, James Farley, Al Ferguson, Armand Wright, Art Dupois, Bert LeBaron
Director: Edward Killy
Screenplay: Norton S. Parker
Producer: Bert Gilroy

DUDE COWBOY
(RKO, December 12, 1941) 59 Minutes
Tim Holt, Marjorie Reynolds, Ray Whitley, Lee "Lasses" White, Louise Currie, Helen Holmes, Eddie Kane, Eddie Dew, Byron Foulger, Tom London, Lloyd Ingraham, Glenn Strange
Director: David Howard
Story/Screenplay: Morton Grant
Producer: Bert Gilroy

RIDING THE WIND
(RKO, February 27, 1942) 60 Minutes
Tim Holt, Ray Whitley, Mary Douglas, Lee "Lasses" White, Eddie Dew, Ernie Adams, Earle Hodgins, Kate Harrington, Charles Phipps, Bud Osborne, Karl Hackett, Hank Worden, Larry Steers, Frank McCarroll, Bob Burns
Director: Edward Killy
Story: Bernard McConville
Screenplay: Morton Grant, Earle Snell
Producer: Bert Gilroy

LAND OF THE OPEN RANGE
(RKO, April 17, 1942) 60 Minutes
Tim Holt, Ray Whitley, Janet Waldo, Lee "Lasses" White, Hobart Cavanaugh, Lee Bonnell, Roy Barcroft, John Elliott, Frank Ellis, Tom London, J. Merrill Holmes
Director: Edward Killy
Story: "Homesteads of Hate" - Lee Bond
Screenplay: Morton Grant
Producer: Bert Gilroy

COME ON, DANGER!
(RKO, June 5, 1942) 58 Minutes
Tim Holt, Frances Neal, Ray Whitley, Lee "Lasses" White, Karl Hackett, Bud McTaggart, Glenn Strange, Evelyn Dickson, Davidson Clark, John Elliott, Slim Whitaker, Kate Harrington, Henry Rocquemore
Director: Edward Killy
Story: Bennett Cohen
Screenplay: Norton S. Parker
Producer: Bert Gilroy

THE MAGNIFICENT AMBERSONS
(Mercury/RKO-Radio, July 10, 1942) 88 Minutes
Joseph Cotten, Delores Costello, Anne Baxter, *Tim Holt,* Agnes Moorehead, Ray Collins, Richard Bennett, Don Dillaway, Dorothy Vaughn, John Elliott, Henry Rocquemore, Billy Elmer, Lew Kelly, John Maguire, James Westernfield, Erskine Sanford
Director/Producer/Screenplay: Orson Welles
Story: Booth Tarkington

THUNDERING HOOFS
(RKO, July 24, 1942) 61 Minutes
Tim Holt, Luana Walters, Ray Whitley, Lee "Lasses" White, Fred Scott, Archie Twitchell, Gordon DeMain, Charles Phipps, Monte Montague, Joe Bernard, Frank Fanning, Frank Ellis, Bob Kortman, Lloyd Ingraham
Director: Lesley Selander
Screenplay: Paul Franklin
Producer: Bert Gilroy

BANDIT RANGER
(RKO, September 25, 1942)
Tim Holt, Cliff Edwards, Joan Barclay, Kenneth Harlan, LeRoy Mason, Glenn Strange, Jack Rockwell, Frank Ellis, Bob Kortman, Bud Geary, Dennis Moore, Russell Wade, Ernie Adams, Lloyd Ingraham, Tom London
Director: Lesley Selander
Screenplay: Bennett Cohen, Morton Grant
Producer: Bert Gilroy

Rarely mentioned as a trio series, the Lee "Lasses" White, Ray Whitley and Tim Holt starrers were above average in budget and story values. Here in **Come On, Danger!** (RKO, 1941).

PIRATES OF THE PRAIRIE
(RKO, November 20, 1942) 57 Minutes
Tim Holt, Cliff Edwards, Nell O'Day, John Elliott, Roy Barcroft, Karl Hackett, Dick Cramer, Edward Cassidy, Eddie Dew, Merrill McCormack, Reed Howes, Charles King, Bud Geary, Lee Shumway, Russell Wade, Ben Corbett, Frank McCarroll, Artie Ortego, George Morrell
Director: Howard Bretherton
Screenplay: Doris Schroeder, J. Benton Cheney
Producer: Bert Gilroy

FIGHTING FRONTIER
(RKO-Radio, January 29, 1943) 57 Minutes
Tim Holt, Cliff Edwards, Ann Summers, Eddie Dew, William Gould, Davidson Clark, Slim Whitaker, Tom London, Monte Montague, Jack Rockwell, Bud Osborne, Russell Wade
Director: Lambert Hillyer
Story: Bernard McConnville
Screenplay: J. Benton Cheney, Norton S. Parker
Producer: Bert Gilroy

HITLER'S CHILDREN
(RKO-Radio, March 19, 1943) 83 Minutes
Tim Holt, Bonita Granville, Kent Smith, Otto Kruger, H. B. Warner, Lloyd Corrigan, Erford Gage, Hans Conried, Nancy Gates, Gavin Muir, Bill Burrud, Jimmy Zaner, Richard Martin, Goetz Van Eyck, John Merton, Max Lucke, Anna Loos, Bessie Wade, Orley Lindgren, Billy Brow, Chris Wren, Egon Brecher, Elas Janssen, William Forrest, Ariel Heath, Rita Corday, Mary Stuart, Roland Varno, Crane Whitley, Edward Van Sloan, Douglas Evans, Carla Boehm, Bruce Cameron, Betty Roadman, Kathleen Wilson, Harry McKim, John Stockton
Director: Edward Dmytryk
Story: Gregor Ziemer - "Education for Death"
Screenplay: Emmet Lavery
Producer: Edward A. Golden

SAGEBRUSH LAW

(RKO-Radio, April 2, 1943)

Tim Holt, Cliff Edwards, Joan Barclay, John Elliott, Ed Cassidy, Karl Hackett, Roy Barcroft, Ernie Adams, John Merton, Bud McTaggart, Edmund Cobb, Otto Hoffman, Cactus Mack, Ben Corbett, Frank McCarroll, Bob McKenzie, Merrill Rodin, Dick Rush, Charles Dorety, Merlyn Nelson, Chester Conklin
Director: Sam Nelson
Screenplay: Bennett Cohen
Producer: Bert Gilroy

THE AVENGING RIDER

(RKO-Radio, May 21, 1943) 55 Minutes

Tim Holt, Cliff Edwards, Ann Summers, Davidson Clark, Norman Willis, Karl Hackett, Earle Hodgins, Ed Cassidy, Kenne Duncan, Bud McTaggart, Bud Osborne, Bob Kortman, Guy Usher, Lloyd Ingraham, David Sharpe
Director: Sam Nelson
Story: Harry O. Hoyt
Screenplay: Morton Grant
Producer: Bert Gilroy

RED RIVER ROBIN HOOD

(RKO-Radio, July 23, 1943)

Tim Holt, Cliff Edwards, Barbara Moffett, Eddie Dew, Otto Koffman, Russell Wade, Tom London, Earle Hodgins, Bud McTaggart, Reed Howes, Kenne Duncan, David Sharpe, Bob McKenzie, Jack Rockwell, Jack Montgomery
Director: Lesley Selander
Story: Whitney J. Stanton
Screenplay: Bennett Cohen
Producer: Bert Gilroy

MY DARLING CLEMENTINE

(20th C.-Fox, December 3, 1946) 97 Minutes

Henry Fonda, Victor Mature, Linda Darnell, Walter Brennan, *Tim Holt,* Cathy Downs, Ward Bond, Alan Mowbray, John Ireland, Roy Roberts, Jane Darwell, Grant Withers, J. Farrell MacDonald, Don Garner, Francis Ford, Ben Hall, Arthur Walsh, Jack Pennick, Louis Mercier, Mickey Simpson, Fred Libby, Harry Woods, Charles Stevens, Russell Simpson, Hank Bell
Director: John Ford
Story: Sam Hellman from book "Wyatt Earp, Frontier Marshal" by Stuart Lake
Screenplay: Samuel G. Engel, Winston Miller
Assistant Director: William Eckhardt
Producer: Samuel G. Engel

THUNDER MOUNTAIN

(RKO, June 15, 1947) 60 Minutes

Tim Holt, Martha Hyer, Richard Martin, Steve Brodie, Richard Powers (Tom Keene), Virginia Owen, Harry Woods, Jason Robards, Sr., Robert Clarke, Harry Harvey
Director: Lew Landers
Story: Zane Grey
Screenplay: Norman Houston
Producer: Herman Schlom

UNDER THE TONTO RIM

(RKO, August 1, 1947) 61 Minutes

Tim Holt, Nan Leslie, Richard Martin, Richard Powers (Tom Keene), Carol Forman, Tonly Barrett, Harry Harvey, Jason Robards, Sr., Lex Barker, Robert Clarke, Jay Norris, Steve Savage, Herman Hack
Director: Lew Landers
Story: Zane Grey
Screenplay: Norman Houston
Producer: Herman Schlom

WILD HORSE MESA

(RKO, November 21, 1947) 60 Minutes

Tim Holt, Nan Leslie, Richard Martin, Richard Powers (Tom Keene), Jason Robards, Sr., Tony Barrett, Harry Woods, William Gould, Robert Bray, Richard Foote, Frank Yaconelli
Director: Wallace Grissell
Story: Zane Grey
Screenplay: Norman Houston
Producer: Herman Schlom

THE TREASURE OF SIERRA MADRE

(Warner Brothers, January 24, 1948) 127 Minutes

Humphrey Bogart, *Tim Holt,* Walter Huston, Barton MacLane, Bruce Bennett, Alfonso Bedoyo, Jacqualine Dalya, Bobby Blake (later Robert Blake), Julian Rivero, John Huston, Harry Vejar, Pat Flaherty, Martin Garralaga, Clifton Young, Ralph Dunn, A. Soto Rangel, Manuel Donde, Jose Torvay, Margarito Luna, and with cameo roles by Ann Sheridan and Jack Holt.
Director/Screenplay: John Huston
Story: B. Traven
Producer: Henry Blanke
Music Score: Max Steiner

WESTERN HERITAGE

(RKO, February 7, 1948) 61 Minutes

Tim Holt, Nan Leslie, Richard Martin, Lois Andrews, Tony Barrett, Walter Reed, Harry Woods, Richard Powers (Tom Keene), Jason Robards, Sr., Robert Bray, Perc Launders, Emmett Lynn
Director: Wallace Grissell
Screenplay: Norman Houston
Producer: Herman Schlom

GUNS OF HATE

(RKO, May 13, 1948) 62 Minutes

Tim Holt, Nan Leslie, Richard Martin, Steve Brodie, Myrna Dell, Tony Barrett, Jim Nolan, Jason Robards, Sr., Robert Bray, Marilyn Mercer

Director: Lesley Selander
Story: Ed Earl Repp
Screenplay: Norman Houston, Ed Earl Repp
Producer: Herman Schlom

THE ARIZONA RANGER

(RKO, May 18, 1948) 63 Minutes

Tim Holt, Jack Holt, Nan Leslie, Richard Martin, Steve Brodie, Paul Hurst, Jim Nolan, Robert Bray, Richard Benedict, William Phipps, Harry Harvey

Director: John Rawlins
Screenplay: Norman Houston
Producer: Herman Schlom

INDIAN AGENT

(RKO, December 11, 1948) 63 Minutes

Tim Holt, Noah Beery, Jr., Richard Martin, Nan Leslie, Lee "Lasses" White, Richard Powers (Tom Keene), Harry Woods, Claudia Drake, Robert Bray, Bud Osborne, Iron Eyes Cody

Director: Lesley Selander
Screenplay: Norman Houston
Producer: Herman Schlom

GUN SMUGGLERS

(RKO, December 28, 1948) 61 Minutes

Tim Holt, Richard Martin, Martha Hyer, Gary Gray, Paul Hurst, Douglas Fowley, Robert Warwick, Don Haggerty, Frank Sully, Robert Bray

Director: Frank McDonald
Screenplay: Norman Houston
Producer: Herman Schlom

BROTHERS IN THE SADDLE

(RKO, February 8, 1949) 60 Minutes

Tim Holt, Richard Martin, Steve Brodie, Virginia Cox, Carol Foreman, Richard Powers (Tom Keene), Stanley Andrews, Robert Bray, Francis McDonald, Emmett Vogan, Monte Montague

Director: Lesley Selander
Screenplay: Norman Houston
Producer: Herman Schlom

RUSTLERS

(RKO, March 1, 1949) 61 Minutes

Tim Holt, Martha Hyer, Richard Martin, Lois Andrews, Steve Brodie, Francis McDonald, Harry Shannon, Addison Richards, Frank Fenton, Robert Bray, Don Haggerty, Monte Montague, Stanley Blystone, Pat Patterson, Mike Jeffers, Tom Lloyd, George Ross, Art Souvern, Bob Robinson

Director: Lesley Selander
Screenplay: Jack Natteford, Luci Ward
Producer: Herman Schlom

STAGECOACH KID

(RKO, June 1, 1949) 60 Minutes

Tim Holt, Richard Martin, Jeff Donnell, Joe Sawyer, Thurston Hall, Carol Hughes, Robert Bray, Robert B. Williams, Kenneth MacDonald, Harry Harvey

Director: Lew Landers
Screenplay: Norman Houston
Producer: Herman Schlom

MASKED RAIDERS

(RKO, August 15, 1949) 60 Minutes

Tim Holt, Richard Martin, Marjorie Lord, Gary Gray, Frank Wilcox, Charles Arnt, Tom Tyler, Harry Woods, Housley Stevenson, Clayton Moore, Bill George

Director: Lesley Selander
Screenplay: Norman Houston
Producer: Herman Schlom

THE MYSTERIOUS DESPERADO

(RKO, September 10, 1949) 61 Minutes

Tim Holt, Richard Martin, Movita, Edward Norris, Frank Wilcox, William Tannen, Robert Livingston, Robert B. Williams, Kenneth MacDonald, Frank Lackteen, Kermit Maynard

Director: Lesley Selander
Screenplay: Norman Houston
Producer: Herman Schlom

RIDERS OF THE RANGE

(RKO, February 11, 1950) 60 Minutes

Tim Holt, Richard Martin, Jacqueline White, Reed Hadley, Robert Barrat, Tom Tyler, Robert Clarke, William Tannen

Director: Lesley Selander
Screenplay: Norman Houston
Producer: Herman Schlom

A sidekick almost handsomer than the hero? Richard Martin sure came close. Here with Tim Holt in **Riders of the Range** (RKO, 1950).

DYNAMITE PASS

(RKO, March 15, 1950) 61 Minutes

Tim Holt, Richard Martin, Lynne Roberts, Regis Toomery, Robert Shayne, Don Harvey, Cleo Moore, John Dehner, Don Haggerty, Ross Elliott, Denver Pyle

Director: Lew Landers

Screenplay: Norman Houston

Producer: Herman Schlom

STORM OVER WYOMING

(RKO, April 22, 1950) 60 Minutes

Tim Holt, Richard Martin, Noreen Nash, Richard Powers (Tom Keene), Betty Underwood, Kenneth MacDonald, Leo MacMahon, Bill Kennedy, Holly Bane, Richard Kean, Don Haggerty

Director: Lesley Selander

Screenplay: Ed Earl Repp

Producer: Herman Schlom

RIDER FROM TUCSON

(RKO, June 7, 1950) 60 Minutes

Tim Holt, Richard Martin, Elaine Riley, Douglas Fowley, Veda Ann Borg, Robert Shayne, William Phipps, Harry Tyler, Marshall Reed, Stuart Randall, Luther Crockett, Dorothy Vaughn

Director: Lesley Selander

Screenplay: Ed Earl Repp

Producer: Herman Schlom

BORDER TREASURE

(RKO, September 16, 1950) 60 Minutes

Tim Holt, Jane Nigh, Richard Martin, John Doucette, House Peters, Jr., Inez Cooper, Julian Rivero, Kenneth MacDonald, Vince Barnett, Robert Payton, David Leonard, Tom Monroe

Director: George Archainbaud

Screenplay: Norman Houston

Producer: Herman Schlom

Edward Cassidy, Kenneth MacDonald and Richard Powers (Tom Keene) look at who Tim Holt has covered in **Storm Over Wyoming** (RKO, 1941).

RIO GRANDE PATROL
(RKO, October 21, 1950) 60 Minutes
Tim Holt, Richard Martin, Jane Nigh, Douglas Fowley,
Cleo Moore, Tom Tyler, Rick Vallin, John Holland,
Larry Johns, Harry Harvey, Forrest Burns
Director: Lesley Selander
Screenplay: Norman Houston
Producer: Herman Schlom

LAW OF THE BADLANDS
(RKO, February 24, 1951) 60 Minutes
Tim Holt, Richard Martin, Joan Dixon, Robert
Livingston, Leonard Penn, Harry Woods, Larry Johns,
Robert Bray, Kenneth MacDonald, John Cliff, Sam
Lufkin, Danny Sands, Art Felix, Booger McCarthy
Director: Lesley Selander
Screenplay: Ed Earl Repp
Producer: Herman Schlom

SADDLE LEGION
(RKO, April 7, 1951) 61 Minutes
Tim Holt, Dorothy Malone, Richard Martin, Robert
Livingston, James Rush, Maurita Hugh, Cliff Clark,
George J. Lewis, Dick Foote, Bob Wilke, Stanley
Andrews, Movita Casteneda
Director: Lesley Selander
Screenplay: Ed Earl Repp
Producer: Herman Schlom

GUNPLAY
(RKO, June 7, 1951) 69 Minutes
Tim Holt, Joan Dixon, Richard Martin, Harper Carter,
Mauritz Hugo, Robert Bice, Marshall Reed, Jack Hill,
Robert Wilke, Leo MacMahon, Cornelius O'Keefe
Director: Lesley Selander
Screenplay: Ed Earl Repp
Producer: Herman Schlom

HIS KIND OF WOMAN
(RKO, July 25, 1951) 120 Minutes
Robert Mitchum, Jane Russell, Vincent Price, *Tim Holt*, Charles McGraw, Raymond Burr, Marjorie Reynolds, Lesley Banning, Jim Backus, Philip Van Zandt, Carleton Young, Dan White, Stacy Harris, John Mylong, Erno Verbes, Richard Berggren, Robert Cornthwaite, Jim Burke, Paul Frees, Joe Granby, Daniel De Laurentis, John Sheehan, Sally Yarnell, Anthony Caruso, Robert Rose, Tod Avery, Paul Fierro, Mickey Simpson, Ed Rand, Jerry James, Barbara Freking, Joy Windsor, Mamie Van Doren, Jerry James, Jerri Jordan, Mary Brewer, Peter Brocco, Mariette Elliott, Saul Goras, Mike Lally, Gerry Ganzer
Director: John Farrow
Story: Frank Fenton and Jack Leonard
Screenplay: Frank Fenton
Producer: Robert Sparks

PISTOL HARVEST
(RKO, August 30, 1951) 60 Minutes
Tim Holt, Richard Martin, Joan Dixon, Guy Edward Hearn, Mauritz Hugo, Robert Clarke, William (Billy) Griffith, Lee Phelps, Bob Wilke, Joan Freeman, Harper Carter, F. Herrick
Director: Lesley Selander
Screenplay: Norman Houston
Producer: Herman Schlom

HOT LEAD
(RKO, October 1, 1951) 60 Minutes
Tim Holt, Richard Martin, Joan Dixon, Ross Elliott, John Dehner, Paul Marion, Lee MacGregor, Stanley Andrews, Paul E. Burns, Bob Wilke, Kenneth MacDonald
Director: Stuart Gilmore
Screenplay: William Lively
Producer: Herman Schlom

OVERLAND TELEGRAPH
(RKO, December 15, 1951) 60 Minutes
Tim Holt, Richard Martin, Gail Davis, George Nader, Mari Blanchard, Hugh Beaumont, Bob Wilke, Fred Graham, Robert Bray, Cliff Clark, Russell Hicks
Director: Lesley Selander
Screenplay: Adele Buffington
Producer: Herman Schlom

TRAIL GUIDE
(RKO, February 15, 1952) 60 Minutes
Tim Holt, Richard Martin, Linda Douglas, Frank Wilcox, Robert Sherwood, John Pickard, Kenneth Mac-Donald, Wendy Waldron, Patricia Wright, Tom London, Mauritz Hugh
Director: Lesley Selander
Screenplay: William Lively
Producer: Herman Schlom

ROAD AGENT
(RKO, March 29, 1952) 60 Minutes
Tim Holt, Richard Martin, Noreen Nash, Mauritz Hugo, Dorothy Patrick, Bob Wilke, Tom Tyler, Guy Edward Hearn, William Tannen, Sam Flint, Forbes Murray, Stanley Blystone, Tom Kennedy
Director: Lesley Selander
Screenplay: Norman Houston
Producer: Herman Schlom

TARGET
(RKO, April 20, 1952) 61 Minutes
Tim Holt, Richard Martin, Linda Douglas, Walter Reed, Harry Harvey, John Hamilton, Lane Bradford, Riley Hill, Mike Ragan
Director: Stuart Gilmore
Screenplay: Norman Houston
Producer: Herman Schlom

DESERT PASSAGE
(RKO, May 30, 1952) 60 Minutes
Tim Holt, Richard Martin, Joan Dixon, Walter Reed, Clayton Moore, Dorothy Patrick, John Dehner, Lane Bradford, Denver Pyle, Francis McDonald
Director: Lesley Selander
Screenplay: Norman Houston
Producer: Herman Schlom

THE MONSTER THAT CHALLENGED THE WORLD
(United Artists, June, 1957)
Tim Holt, Audrey Dalton, Hans Conried, Barbara Darrow, Harlan Ware, Casey Adams, Mimi Gibson, Jody McCrea, Charles Tannen, Milton Parson, Ralph Moody, Gordon Jones, Marjorie Stapp, Dennis McCarthy, Bob Beneveds, Michael Dugan, Mack Williams, Eileen Harley, William Swan, Byron Kane, Hal Taggert, Gil Frye, Can Gachman
Director: Arnold Laven
Story: David Duncan
Screenplay: Pat Fiedler
Producer: Jules V. Levy and Arthur Dalton

THIS STUFF'LL KILL YA!
(Ultima Productions, 1970) 100 Minutes
(EastmanColor)
Jeffrey Allen, *Tim Holt*, Gloria King, Ray Sager, Erich Bradly, Terence McCarthy, Ronna Riddle, Larry Drake, John Garner, Bill Mays, Lee Danser, Pamela Polsgrove, Doffy Candler, Skip Nicholson, Carol Merrell, Pamela Bloomfield, Debbie Gardiner
Director/Producer/Screenplay: Herschell Gordon Lewis
Associate Producer: A. Louise Downe

Johnny Mack Brown

10 ● JOHNNY MACK BROWN

The Affable Cowboy

Johnny Mack Brown is a name familiar to most movie goers over the age of 30, even if they are not students of what is affectionately called the "horse operas." He made quite a name for himself during a 30-year movie career and was one of the more enduring of cowboy stars. Unlike many of his peers, Johnny was a competent actor, equally at home in tuxedo or chaps, and he came into his own as a cowboy star after spending his early movie years as leading man to such beauteous and distinguished ladies as Greta Garbo, Joan Crawford, Mary Pickford, Jean Harlow, and Marion Davies. Johnny was a star at Metro-Goldwyn-Mayer, an honor held by only one other cowboy, Tim McCoy.

For much of his career Johnny was "John," adding the "ny" after having starred in Westerns for many years. But it is as "Johnny" that most fans think of him today. His record as a Western hero is an impressive one: he starred in 121 of 127 Westerns in which he appeared. Adding to this illustrious record are another 40 films in which Johnny appeared as a dramatic actor, many of them for MGM.

Brown hailed from Alabama, where he was born on September 1, 1904. And after 45 years away from the state he still retained traces of the southern drawl that fans came to love. As a football immortal at the University of Alabama, Johnny was elected to the All-American Football Team of 1927. He became an assistant coach at Alabama upon his graduation and was in California for the Rose Bowl game on New Year's day, 1927. Through an actor friend, George Faucett, Johnny secured a screen test at MGM and was given a contract and small parts in several features. He quickly rose to prominent parts as leading man to some of Hollywood's

most gorgeous actresses. One of his most successful silent features was **Our Dancing Daughters** ('28), a jazz-age film that boosted his stock as a leading man considerably and which made a star of Joan Crawford. Brown was subsequently cast in films with Jeanette Loff (**Annapolis**), Norma Shearer (**A Lady of Chance**), Greta Garbo (**A Woman of Affairs** and **The Single Standard**), Mary Pickford (**Coquette**), Leila Hyams (**Hurricane**), Sally O'Neill (**Jazz Heaven**), and Mary Nolan (**Undertow**).

Brown's star was on the rise. He was a fine actor, a perfect physical specimen, good looking, and possessed of sex appeal. MGM co-starred him once more with Joan Crawford, this time in **Montana Moon** ('30), a comedy-western and an all-talking picture. His voice proved satisfactory for sound features, and so MGM proceeded to put him into a big-budget Western titled **Billy the Kid** ('30). It was directed by King Vidor, co-starred Wallace Beery, and was filmed in Metro's widescreen 70-millimeter process on location around Gallup, New Mexico. Johnny, coached by William S. Hart, turned in a memorable performance as the Kid. The story, a fictionalized account of the infamous southwest outlaw, was one of the epics of the early talkies and remains Brown's most noted film.

Next in line for Johnny was a less-auspicious semi-western, **The Great Meadow** ('31), followed by **The Secret Six** ('31), an early spine-tingling gangster film featuring, in addition to Johnny, Clark Gable, Wallace Beery, Jean Harlow, Lewis Stone, Marjorie Rambeau, Ralph Bellamy, and John Miljan. Few Western stars ever kept such company and held their own, but John Mack Brown did.

Johnny Mack Brown as **Billy the Kid** (MGM, 1930) comtemplates a jail break.

Leo Carrillo and Johnny Mack Brown glare at each other over Dorothy Burgess in **Lasca of the Rio Grande** (Universal, 1931).

Leaving MGM in '31, Johnny freelanced for a while, co-starring in **The Last Flight** ('31) at First National, a story of World War I pilots, and **Lasca of the Rio Grande** ('31) at Universal. In the latter film, Johnny is a Texas Ranger, Leo Carrillo is the badman, and Dorothy Burgess is Lasca, a dancehall girl loved by both men. He also made a two-reel football picture for Universal release in '31. Another football film, the full-length **70,000 Witnesses,** was made for Paramount in '32.

Monogram used Johnny in **Flames** ('32) a full decade before they would hire him to carry on in the place of Buck Jones following the latter's death in the Coconut Grove holocaust in Boston in '42. **Malay Nights,** now a much sought-after film by collectors, was made for Mayfair, a Gower Gulch independent studio, in '32. Featured with Brown in this off-beat story was Raymond Hatton, his future sidekick in Monogram Westerns.

Master serial maker Nat Levine hired Johnny to star in the 12-episode serial, **Fighting with Kit Carson,** for Mascot release in '33. Brown was well accepted by Saturday matinee crowds in his first cliffhanger. As usual with Mascot productions, a tremendous cast of competent supporting players pitched in to keep the excitement high and the action pace furious. Noah Beery, Sr. was at his villainous best, while son Noah, Jr. and Betsy King Ross did superb work in their juvenile roles. Lane Chandler, Lafe McKee, Reed Howes, Ernie Adams, and Alan Bridge gave their expected fine performances. Yakima Canutt, Mascot's resident stuntman supreme, was on hand to double and taught Johnny much about making Westerns.

Still freelancing and not as yet typed as a cowboy actor, Johnny worked for First National, Chesterfield, Fox, Tower, Paramount, Showmen, and Columbia in assorted non-Westerns in '33 and '34. As a society dude, he courts Mae West in **Belle of the Nineties;**

199

Louise Stanley and Johnny Mack Brown in a publicity still for **The Oregon Trail** (Universal, 1939).

Saturday's Millions finds him as a football player alongside Robert Young; in **Son of a Sailor** he is a sailor, sharing humorous antics with Joe E. Brown, Thelma Todd, and Frank McHugh; in **Cross Streets** he's an alcoholic who makes his own murder appear to be a suicide to save the reputation of the man whose daughter and wife he loves; **Three on a Honeymoon** is noteworthy in that it featured both Brown and Charles Starrett, another great Western ace yet to find his niche, in a love story with a sea background; Johnny is a football player once again in **St. Louis Woman; Marrying Widows** has him portraying an opportunist who marries for money only to find out his wife has none; and in **Against the Law,** directed by renowned Western director Lambert Hillyer, who would subsequently direct Brown in most of his Monogram Westerns, Johnny is an ambulance driver in love with Sally Blane.

When Universal hired Johnny to star in his second Western serial, **Rustlers of Red Dog,** the fat was in the fire. Johnny was on his way to becoming one of Western filmdom's greatest aces.

Brown possibly could have continued as a dramatic actor but, convinced by his experiences thus far that he was cut out for outdoor films, he signed a contract for a series of eight Westerns to be made by A. W. Hackel for release by Supreme Pictures. They were made in '35 and '36. They were good for an independent series and did well financially—so well, in fact, that Hackel renewed Brown's contract and produced a second series of eight films for release through the newly organized Republic Pictures.

Brown was hardly a slouch as an actor, rider, or fighter; his Westerns were chuck full of brawls, gunfire, and hard riding, and were built around stories which allowed for some display of his acting talents.

Universal again picked Johnny for a starring role in a serial, his third. This time it was one called **Wild West Days** ('37), directed by veteran Cliff Smith, formerly director of Pete Morrison, William S. Hart, and Tom Mix shoot-em-ups in the silent era. In late '37 Brown teamed with John Wayne in Paramount's **Born to the West** and supported Joel McCrea in **Wells Fargo** for the same studio. Cast in the latter as a Confederate officer in love with Frances Dee, Brown is killed trying to capture a gold train, leaving McCrea to get the girl—both on screen and in real life.

Back at Universal he starred in two more serials, **Flaming Frontiers** ('38) and **The Oregon Trail** ('39). He would appear only in features for the remainder of his career. His first programmer western at Universal was **Desperate Trails** ('39). He was supported by funnyman Fuzzy Knight and singing cowpoke Bob Baker, who had just completed his own series of

Westerns. Baker would support Brown in five more features, but after that Brown and Knight would go it alone for another fifteen features before being joined by Tex Ritter for a final seven features.

The Brown Universal features were excellently made films, far above the typical horse opera in production values. Fine musical scores, running inserts, competent editing, believable scripts, good photography, location shooting, and direction by professionals such as Ray Taylor, Ford Beebe, and Joseph H. Lewis combined to make Brown's long-running series one of the finest of the period. Performing feats of agility with convincing realism, and always coming off as a stalwart actor, Brown easily moved into the "Big Ten" of Western stars, remaining there until the demise of the series Western a decade later.

In 1943 Brown signed with Monogram as a replacement for Buck Jones. Raymond Hatton, who had appeared with Jones in the popular "Rough Riders" series, retained his identity as "Sandy Hopkins" and stayed on to ride to greater fame with Johnny, the two making forty-five slam-bang shoot-em-ups together between '43 and '49. The first in the Brown-Hatton series was **The Ghost Rider,** with Johnny portraying Nevada Jack McKenzie, a characterization he would retain until '46 when he and Hatton abandoned their respective roles as McKenzie and Hopkins to play other assorted roles. The team was a popular one in the war and early postwar years. Audiences could always count on lots of action and a generous number of old familiar faces in each film. Lambert Hillyer, who had directed many of the Buck Jones films at Columbia, directed nearly all of the Brown films for Monogram up until '49. Made at a time when movies were still popular and profitable, these little Westerns combined fast and furious action, simple, uncomplicated stories, and the magnetism of Brown and Hatton, coupled with professional competency in both the technical and acting realms, to provide Western buffs with a truly enjoyable cinema experience. Saturday night was something to look forward to when you could throw the kids in the back seat of the family car and take off to the Bijou to see one of Johnny's oaters, coupled with a chapter of some equally exciting cliffhanger and maybe a Three Stooges, Leon Errol, or Edgar Kennedy comedy.

By 1950 Johnny was showing his age and putting on weight, yet his feature films were still making money. Beginning with **West of Wyoming** ('50), Johnny made the remainder of his films without the aid of a comedy sidekick, something few cowboy stars did. Fifteen series westerns were made by Johnny in '50, '51, and '52 and one special, **Short Grass.** Jimmy Ellison, a minor Western star, supported Johnny in the last six of his

Westerns. The last Brown Western for Monogram was **Canyon Ambush,** released on October 12, 1952. Television and mounting production costs, along with a shrinking market, had made "B" Westerns on a series basis a thing of the past. Johnny lasted almost to the end of the "B" era. Autry, Holt, and a few others would hang on for another year or two on a series basis, and occasional "B" films would continue to be made for many years. Johnny himself appeared in three more "Bs" as a guest star.

Brown served as host of a swanky Hollywood restaurant for a while and made several appearances on television over the years. He also traveled with Royal American Shows and made numerous personal appearances. When declining health overtook him he was mainly content to enjoy his retirement and to look back with satisfaction on a lengthy movie career crammed with excitement and achievements. One of the few cowboy stars to be honored with a star implanted on Hollywood Boulevard, Johnny had a secure place in the hearts and minds of thousands of movie fans who remembered the good old days when he and "Rebel," his faithful steed, rode the Hollywood range. That's almost as good as the kiss from the lovely lass at the fadeout, and much longer lasting. Johnny's last years were spent quietly with his wife in their apartment at the posh Park La Brea Towers in Los Angeles.

On November 14, 1974, Johnny Mack Brown, victor in a thousand screen fights, lost his fight for life, a victim of a kidney ailment. He was 70 years old.

JOHNNY MACK BROWN Filmography

SLIDE, KELLY, SLIDE
(MGM, March 12, 1927) 8 Reels
William Haines, Harry Carey, Sally O'Neill, Karl Dane, Junior Coghlan, Paul Kelly, Guinn "Big Boy" Williams, Warner Richmond, Mike Donlin, Tony Lazzeri, *John Mack Brown*
Director: Edward Sedgwick
Screenplay: A. P. Younger

THE BUGLE CALL
(MGM, August 6, 1927) 6 Reels
Jackie Coogan, Claire Windsor, Herbert Rawlinson, Tom O'Brien, Harry Todd, Nelson McDowell, Bodil Rosing, Sarah Padden, *John Mack Brown,* Don Coleman
Director: Edward Sedgwick
Adaptation: Josephine Lovett
Story: C. Gardner Sullivan

MOCKERY
(MGM, August 13, 1927) 7 Reels
Lon Chaney, Ricardo Cortez, Barbara Bedford, Mack Swain, Emily Fitzroy, Charles Puffy, Kai Schmidt, *John Mack Brown*
Director: Benjamin Christensen

AFTER MIDNIGHT
(MGM, August 20, 1927) 7 Reels
Norma Shearer, Gwen Lee, Lawrence Gray, Eddie Sturgis, Phillip Sleeman, *John Mack Brown*
Director: Monta Bell
Scenario: Lorna Moon
Story: Monta Bell

THE FAIR CO-ED
(MGM, October 15, 1927) 7 Reels
Marion Davies, *John Mack Brown,* Jane Winton, Thelma Hill, George Cooper, Noel Francis, Frank Currier, Gene Stone, Lillianne Leighton, Edward Connelly, Jacques Tourneur
Director: Sam Wood
Adaptation: Byron Morgan

THE DIVINE WOMAN
(MGM, January 14, 1928) 8 Reels
Greta Garbo, Lars Hanson, Lowell Sherman, Polly Moran, Dorothy Cumming, *John Mack Brown,* Cesare Gravina, Jean de Briac, Paulette Duval
Director: Victor Seastrom
Scenario: Dorothy Farnum

SOFT LIVING
(Fox, February 5, 1928) 6 Reels
Madge Bellamy, Mary Duncan, Joyce Compton, *John Mack Brown,* Thomas Jefferson, Henry Kolker, Olive Tell, Maine Geary, Tom Dugan, David Wengren, Marjorie Beebe, Leo White
Director: James Tinling
Scenario: Frances Agnew
Story: Grace Mack

SQUARE CROOKS
(Fox, March 4, 1928) 6 Reels
Robert Armstrong, Dorothy Dwan, *John Mack Brown,* Dorothy Appleby, Clarence Burton, Eddie Sturgis, Jackie Combs, Lydia Dickson
Director: Lewis Seiler
Scenario: Becky Gardiner
Producer: Philip Klein

THE PLAY GIRL

(Fox, April 22, 1928) 6 Reels
Madge Bellamy, Walter McGrail, *John Mack Brown,*
Lionel Belmore, Anita Garvin, Thelma Hill, Harry
Tenbrook
Director: Arthur Rosson
Story/Scenario: John Stone

OUR DANCING DAUGHTERS

(Cosmopolitan/MGM, September 1, 1928)
Joan Crawford, Dorothy Sebastian, *John Mack Brown,*
Anita Page, Nils Asther, Kathryn Williams, Eddie
Nugent, Huntley Gordon, Dorothy Cumming, Sam de
Grasse, Mary Gordon, Robert Livingston, Kathlyn
Williams
Director: Harry Beaumont
Story: Josephine Lovett

ANNAPOLIS

(Pathe, November 18, 1928) 8 Reels
John Mack Brown, Jeannette Loff, Hobart Bosworth,
Hugh Allan, William Bakewell, Maurice Ryan,
Charlotte Walker, Fred Applegate
Director: Christy Cabanne
Producer/Screenplay: F. McGrew Willis
Story: Royal S. Pease

A LADY OF CHANCE

(MGM, December 1, 1928) 8 Reels
(part-talking)
Norma Shearer, *John Mack Brown,* Lowell Sherman,
Gwen Lee, Eugenie Besserer
Director: Robert Z. Leonard
Scenario: A. P. Younger

A WOMAN OF AFFAIRS

(MGM, December 12, 1928)
(Sound effects and music score)
Greta Garbo, John Gilbert, Douglas Fairbanks, Jr., *John
Mack Brown,* Lewis Stone, Hobart Bosworth, Dorothy
Sebastian
Director: Clarence Brown
Continuity: Bess Meredyth

COQUETTE

(United Artists, March 30, 1929)
Mary Pickford, Matt Moore, *John Mack Brown,* John
St. Polis, Henry Kolker, Louise Beavers, William Jan-
ney, Robert E. Homans, George Irving
Director: Sam Taylor

THE VALIANT

(Fox, May 12, 1929) 6 Reels
(talking sequences)
Paul Muni, Marguerite Churchill, DeWitt Jennings,
Henry Kolker, Clifford Dempsey, Edith Yorke, George
Pearce, Don Terry, *John Mack Brown*
Director: William K. Howard
Scenario: John Hunter Booth, Tom Barry

THE SINGLE STANDARD

(MGM, July 27, 1929) 8 Reels
(Music score and sound effects)
Greta Garbo, Nils Asther, *John Mack Brown,* Dorothy
Sebastian, Lane Chandler
Director: John S. Robertson
Scenario: Josephine Lovett

HURRICANE

(Columbia, September 30, 1929) 7 Reels
(Sound)
Hobart Bosworth, Leila Hyams, *John Mack Brown,*
Tom O'Brien, Allan Roscoe, Leila McIntyre, Eddy
Chandler, Jack Bourdeaux
Director: Ralph Ince
Continuity: Enid Hibbard
Story: Evelyn Campbell, Norman Springer
Producer: Harry Cohn

JAZZ HEAVEN

(RKO, November 3, 1929) 7 Reels
(Sound)
John Mack Brown, Sally O'Neill, Clyde Cook, Joseph
Cawthorn, Blanche Frederici, Henry Armetta, Albert
Conti, Ole M. Ness, J. Barney Sherry, Adel Watson
Director: Melville Brown
Screenplay: Cyrus Wood, J. Walter Ruben
Story: Pauline Forney, Dudley Murphy

UNDERTOW

(Universal, February 23, 1930) 6 Reels
John Mack Brown, Mary Nolan, Robert Ellis, Audrey
Ferris, Churchill Ross
Director: Harry Pollard
Adaptation: Winifred Reeve, Edward T. Lowe, Jr.

VOICE OF HOLLYWOOD, NO. 7

(Tiffany, March, 1930) 10 Minutes
Jack Duffy, *John Mack Brown,* Lillian Rich, Dorothy
Gulliver, George J. Lewis, Mr. and Mrs. Calvin
Coolidge, Mary Pickford, Mack Sennett, Antonio
Moreno, Will Hays, Duncan Sisters

MONTANA MOON

(MGM, March 20, 1930) 7917 feet
John Mack Brown, Joan Crawford, Cliff Edwards, Dorothy Sebastian, Ricardo Cortez, Benny Rubin, Karl Dane, Lloyd Ingraham
Director/Producer: Malcolm St. Clair
Story/Screenplay: Sylvia Thalberg

BILLY THE KID

(MGM, October 18, 1930) 8808 feet
John Mack Brown, Wallace Beery, Kay Johnson, Karl Dane, Wyndham Standing, Russell Simpson, Blanche Frederici, Roscoe Ates, Warner Richmond, James Marcus, Nelson McDowell, Jack Carlyle, John Beck, Marguerita Padula, Aggie Herring, Soledad Jiminez, Don Coleman, Christopher Martin, Lucille Powers
Director: King Vidor
Story: Walter Noble Burns
Continuity: Wanda Tuchock

THE GREAT MEADOW

(MGM, January 18, 1931) 75 Minutes
John Mack Brown, Eleanor Boardman, Lucille LaVerne, Anita Louise, Gavin Gordon, Guinn Williams, Russell Simpson, Sarah Padden, Helen Jerome Eddy
Director: Charles Brabin
Story: Elizabeth Roberts
Adaptation: Charles Brabin, Edith Ellis

THE SECRET SIX

(Cosmopolitan/MGM, April 18, 1931) 9 Reels
Wallace Beery, Lewis Stone, *John Mack Brown,* Jean Harlow, Marjorie Rambeau, Paul Hurst, Clark Gable, Ralph Bellamy, John Miljan, DeWitt Jennings, Murray Kinnell, Fletcher Norton, Frank McGlynn, Theodore von Eltz, Tom London
Director: George Hill
Story: Frances Marion

THE LAST FLIGHT

(First National, August 29, 1931) 8 Reels
Richard Barthelmess, Helen Chandler, *John Mack Brown,* David Manners, Elliott Nugent, Walter Byron, Yola D'Avril, George Irving, Luis Alberni
Director: William Dieterle
Story: John Monk Saunders - "Single Lady"
Screenplay: John Monk Saunders

LASCA OF THE RIO GRANDE

(Universal, November 2, 1931) 60 Minutes
Leo Carrillo, *John Mack Brown,* Dorothy Burgess, Slim Summerville, Frank Campeau
Director: Edward Laemmle
Story: Tom Reed
Screenplay: Randall Faye

FLAMES

(Monogram, May 30, 1932) 64 Minutes
Noel Francis, *John Mack Brown,* Marjorie Beebe, George Cooper, Richard Tucker, Russell Simpson, Kit Guard, Snowflake
Director: Karl Brown

HOLLYWOOD HALFBACKS

(Universal, July, 1931) 18½ Minutes
Mary Brian, Nick Stuart, *John Mack Brown,* Monty Collins, Raymond Hatton, Joe Bonomo, Arthur Lake, Marjorie White, Betty Compson, Bryant Washburn, Franklin Pangborn, Florence Lake, Albert Conti, Vernon Dent
Director: Charles Lamont
Story: Harry Sauber

THE VANISHING FRONTIER

(Paramount, July 29, 1932) 70 Minutes
John Mack Brown, Evalyn Knapp, Zasu Pitts, Ben Alexander, J. Farrell MacDonald, George Irving, Raymond Hatton, Wallace MacDonald, Joyzelle Joyner, Deacon McDaniels
Director: Phil Rosen
Story/Screenplay: Stuart Anthony

70,000 WITNESSES

(Paramount, September 2, 1932) 8 Reels
John Mack Brown, Phillips Holmes, Dorothy Jordan, Charles Ruggles, J. Farrell MacDonald, Lew Cody, David Landau, Kenneth Thomson, Big Boy Williams, George Rosener, Walter Hiers, Reed Howes, Francis McDonald, Dave O'Brien
Director: Ralph Murphy
Screenplay: Garrett Fort, Robert N. Lee
Story: Cortland Fitzsimmons
Producer: Charles R. Rogers

MALAY NIGHTS

(George W. Weeks Productions/Mayfair, November 1, 1932) 7 Reels
John Mack Brown, Dorothy Burgess, Ralph Ince, Carmelita Geraghty, George Smith, Lionel Belmore, Mary Jane, Raymond Hatton
Director: E. Mason Hooper
Adaptation: John Thomas Neville
Story: Glenn Ellis
Supervision: Cliff Broughton

FIGHTING WITH KIT CARSON

(Mascot, July, 1933) 12 Chapters

John Mack Brown, Noah Beery, Betsy King Ross, Noah Beery, Jr., Tully Marshall, Edmund Breese, Robert Warwick, Edward Hearn, Lafe McKee, Ernie Adams, Al Bridge, Lane Chandler, Reed Howes, Jack Mower, DeWitt Jennings, Maston Williams, Iron Eyes Cody, William Farnum, Frank Ellis, Slim Whitaker

Director: Armand Schaefer, Colbert Clark

Screenplay: Jack Natteford, Barney Sarecky, Colbert Clark, Wyndham Gittens

Producer: Nat Levine

Chapter Titles: (1) The Mystery Riders (2) The White Chief (3) Hidden Gold (4) The Silent Doom (5) Murder Will Out (6) Secret of Iron Mountain (7) Law of the Lawless (8) Red Phantoms (9) The Invisible Enemy (10) Midnight Magic (11) Unmasked (12) The Trail to Glory

SATURDAY'S MILLIONS

(Universal, October 9, 1933) 8 Reels

Leila Hyams, Robert Young, *John Mack Brown,* Grant Mitchell, Andy Devine, Mary Carlisle, Richard Tucker, Joe Sawyer, Lucille Lund, Walter Brennan, Paul Porcasi, Mary Doran, Craig Reynolds, Ernie Nevers, Erny Pinckert, Johnny Baker, Coach Howard Jones, Alan Ladd

Director: Edward Sedgwick

Story: Lucian Cary

Screenplay: Dale Van Every

FEMALE

(First National, November 11, 1933) 60 Minutes

Ruth Chatterton, George Brent, *John Mack Brown,* Laura Hope Crews, Lois Wilson, Gavin Gordon, Edmund Breese, Larry Steers, Milton Kibbee, Charly Grapewin, Jean Muir

Director: Michael Curtiz

Story: Donald Henderson Clark

Screenplay: Gene Markey, Kathryn Scola

SON OF A SAILOR

(First National, December 23, 1933) 8 Reels

Joe E. Brown, Jean Muir, *John Mack Brown,* Frank McHugh, Thelma Todd, Sheila Terry, George Blackwood, Merna Kennedy, Samuel Hinds, Noel Francis, Walter Miller, Henry O'Neill

Director: Lloyd Bacon

Screenplay: Al Cohn, Paul Gerald Smith

CROSS STREETS

(Chesterfield/Invincible, January 22, 1934) 7 Reels

John Mack Brown, Claire Windsor, Anita Louise, Kenneth Thomson, Matty Kemp, Josef Swickard, Niles Welch, Edith Fellows, Mary Gordon, Jerry Madden

Director: Frank R. Strayer

Story: Gordon Morris

Continuity: Anthony Coldeway

HOLLYWOOD ON PARADE NO. B7

(Paramount, February 2, 1934) 1 Reel

John Mack Brown, Willy Pogany, Harry Grene, Bebe Daniels, Mary Pickford, John Boles, William (Buster) Collier, Jr., Robert Woolsey, the Wampas Baby Stars of 1933: Ruth Hall, Patricia Ellis, Lillian Bond, Boots Mallory, Evalyn Knapp, Dorothy Layton, Dorothy Wilson, Mary Carlisle, Marion Shockley, Toshia Mori, Gloria Stuart, Eleanor Holm, Ginger Rogers, Lona Andre

Producer: Louis Lewyn

THREE ON A HONEYMOON

(Fox, March 15, 1934) 65 Minutes

John Mack Brown, Sally Eilers, Charles Starrett, Zasu Pitts, Henrietta Crosman, Irene Hervey, Howard Lally, Russell Simpson, Cornelius Keefe, Winnifred Shaw, Elsie Larson

Director: James Tinling

Story: Ishbel Ross - "Promenade Deck"

Screenplay: Edward Lowe, Raymond Van Sickle, George Wright

Adaptation: Douglas Doty

ST. LOUIS WOMAN

(Showmen's Pictures, April 15, 1934) 8 Reels

John Mack Brown, Jeanette Loff, Earle Fox, Roberta Gale

Director: Al Ray

Story: Elwood Ullman

Screenplay: Jack Natteford

BELLE OF THE NINETIES

(Paramount, September 21, 1934) 8 Reels

Mae West, Roger Pryor, Katherine DeMille, *John Mack Brown,* John Miljan, James Donlan, Tom Herbert, Stuart Holmes, Harry Woods, Ed Gargan, Libby Taylor, Bennie Baker, Warren Hymer, Wade Boteler, George Walsh, Fuzzy Knight, Duke Ellington and his Orchestra

Director: Leo McCarey

Story/Screenplay: Mae West

AGAINST THE LAW

(Columbia, October 25, 1934) 6 Reels

John Mack Brown, Sally Blane, Arthur Hohl, George Meeker, James Bush, Bradley Page, Ward Bond, Al Hill, Hooper Atchley

Director: Lambert Hillyer

Story/Screenplay: Harold Shumate

STAR NIGHT AT COCOANUT GROVE

(MGM, December 1, 1934) 21 Minutes

(Colortone Musical Series)

John Mack Brown, Gary Cooper, Mary Pickford, Bing Crosby, Jack Oakie, Leo Carrillo

MARRYING WIDOWS

(Tower, 1934) 65 Minutes

John Mack Brown, Judith Allen, Minna Gombell, Lucien Littlefield, George Grandee, Sarah Padden, Bert Roach, Charles King, Virginia Sale, Syd Saylor, Gladys Blake, Arthur Hoyt, Nat Carr, Pauline Garon, Otto Hoffman, Emmett Vogan, George O'Hanlon

Director: Sam Newfield

Story: Adele Buffington

RUSTLERS OF RED DOG

(Universal, January, 1935) 12 Chapters

John Mack Brown, Raymond Hatton, Joyce Compton, Walter Miller, Harry Woods, Charles K. French, Fred McKaye, William Desmond, Wally Wales, Chief Thunder Cloud, Slim Whitaker, Art Mix, Jim Corey, Bill Patton, Cliff Lyons, Tex Cooper, Ben Corbett, Hank Bell, Bud Osborne, Edmund Cobb, J. P. McGowan, Monte Montague, Lafe McKee, Artie Ortego, Jim Thorpe, Chief Thunderbird, Ann D'Arcy, Fritzi Burnette, Grace Cunard, Virginia Ainsworth

Director: Louis Friedlander (Lew Landers)

Story: Nathaniel Eddy

Screenplay: George Plympton, Basil Dickey, Ella O'Neill, Nate Gatzert, Vin Moore

Chapter Titles: (1) Hostile Redskins (2) Flaming Arrows (3) Thundering Hoofs (4) Attack at Dawn (5) Buried Alive (6) Flames of Vengeance (7) Into the Depths (8) Paths of Peril (9) The Snake Strikes (10) Riding Wild (11) The Rustlers Clash (12) Law and Order

STARLIT DAYS AT THE LIDO

(MGM, September 23, 1935) 2 Reels

(color) (An MGM Oddity showing the stars enjoying an evening out)

John Mack Brown, Mr. and Mrs. Clark Gable, Richard Barthelmess, Constance Bennett, Robert Montgomery, Francis Lederer, The Radio Rogues, Cliff Edwards, John Boles, Lili Damita, Henry Russe's Band, Reginald Denny (Master of Ceremonies)

Continuity: Alexander Van Dorn

Producer: Louis Lewyn

BRANDED A COWARD

(Supreme/William Steiner, July, 1935)

Johnny Mack Brown, Billie Seward, Syd Saylor, Yakima Canutt, Lee Shumway, Lloyd Ingraham, Roger Williams, Frank McCarroll, Mickey Rentschiler, Rex Downing, Bob Kortman, Ed Peil, Sr., Joe Girard

Director: Sam Newfield

Story: Richard Martinsen

Screenplay: Earle Snell

Producer: A. W. Hackel

BETWEEN MEN

(Supreme/William Steiner, October 29, 1935) 59 Minutes

Johnny Mack Brown, Beth Marion, William Farnum, Earl Dwire, Lloyd Ingraham, Frank Ball, Harry Downing, Horace B. Carpenter, Forrest Taylor, Bud Osborne, Sherry Tansey, Milburn Morante, Artie Ortego

Director/Story: Robert N. Bradbury

Screenplay: Charles Francis Royal

Producer: A. W. Hackel

THE COURAGEOUS AVENGER

(Supreme/William Steiner, December 13, 1935) 58 Minutes

Johnny Mack Brown, Helen Erikson, Warner Richmond, Edward Cassidy, Edward Parker, Frank Ball, Earl Dwire, Forrest Taylor, Robert Burns

Director: Robert N. Bradbury

Story/Screenplay: Charles Francis Royal

Producer: A. W. Hackel

VALLEY OF THE LAWLESS

(Supreme/William Steiner, January 25, 1936) 56 Minutes

Johnny Mack Brown, Joyce Compton, George Hayes, Dennis Meadows (Moore), Bobby Nelson, Frank Hagney, Charles King, Jack Rockwell, Frank Ball, Horace Murphy, Steve Clark, Edward Cassidy, Robert McKenzie, Forrest Taylor, George Morrell, Jack Evans

Director/Screenplay: Robert N. Bradbury

Producer: A. W. Hackel

DESERT PHANTOM

(Supreme/William Steiner, March 10, 1936) 55 Minutes

Johnny Mack Brown, Sheila Manners, Ted Adams, Karl Hackett, Hal Price, Nelson McDowell, Charles King, Forrest Taylor, Frank Ball

Director: S. Roy Luby

Story: E. B. Mann

Screenplay: Earle Snell

Producer: A. W. Hackel

ROGUE OF THE RANGE

(Supreme/William Steiner, April 25, 1936) 58 Minutes

Johnny Mack Brown, Lois January, Alden (Guy) Chase, Phyllis Hume, George Ball, Jack Rockwell, Horace Murphy, Frank Ball, Lloyd Ingraham, Fred Hoose, Forrest Taylor, George Morrell, Blackie Whiteford, Slim Whitaker, Tex Palmer, Horace B. Carpenter, Max Davidson, Art Dillard

Director: S. Roy Luby

Screenplay: Earle Snell

Producer: A. W. Hackel

EVERYMAN'S LAW

(Supreme/William Steiner, June 10, 1936) 62 Minutes
Johnny Mack Brown, Beth Marion, Frank Campeau, Roger Gray, Lloyd Ingraham, John Beck, Horace Murphy, Dick Alexander, Slim Whitaker, Edward Cassidy, Jim Corey, George Morrell, Ralph Bucko, Francis Walker
Director: Albert Ray
Story/Screenplay: Earle Snell
Producer: A. W. Hackel

THE CROOKED TRAIL

(Supreme/William Steiner, July 25, 1936) 60 Minutes
Johnny Mack Brown, Lucile Browne, John Merton, Ted Adams, Charles King, Dick Curtis, John Van Pelt, Edward Cassidy, Horace Murphy, Earl Dwire, Artie Ortego, Hal Price
Director: S. Roy Luby
Screenplay: George Plympton
Producer: A. W. Hackel

UNDERCOVER MAN

(Republic, September 24, 1936) 57 Minutes
Johnny Mack Brown, Suzanne Karen, Ted Adams, Lloyd Ingraham, Horace Murphy, Edward Cassidy, Frank Ball, Margaret Mann, Frank Darien, Dick Morehead, George Morrell, Art Dillard, Jim Corey, Ray Henderson
Director: Albert Ray
Story/Screenplay: Andrew Bennison
Producer: A. W. Hackel

THE GAMBLING TERROR

(Republic, February 15, 1937) 53 Minutes
Johnny Mack Brown, Iris Meredith, Charles King, Horace Murphy, Dick Curtis, Budd Buster, Ted Adams, Earl Dwire, Bobby Nelson, Frank Ellis, Lloyd Ingraham, Emma Tansey, Frank Ball, Sherry Tansey, Steve Clark, George Morrell, Art Dillard, Tex Palmer, Jack Montgomery, Ray Henderson, Clyde McClary, Oscar Gahan, Herman Hack
Director: Sam Newfield
Screenplay: George Plympton, Fred Myton
Producer: A. W. Hackel

Steve Clark goes for his gun as Johnny Mack Brown disarms Warner Richmond in **Trail of Vengeance** (Republic, 1937).

TRAIL OF VENGEANCE

(Republic, March 29, 1937) 58 Minutes

Johnny Mack Brown, Iris Meredith, Warner Richmond, Karl Hackett, Earle Hodgins, Frank LaRue, Frank Ellis, Lew Meehan, Frank Ball, Dick Curtis, Jim Corey, Horace Murphy, Dick Cramer, Steve Clark, Budd Buster, Jack C. Smith, Jack Kirk, Francis Walker, Tex Palmer, Clyde McClary, Wally West, Ray Henderson

Director: Sam Newfield
Screenplay: George Plympton and Fred Myton
Story: E. B. Mann
Producer: A. W. Hackel

LAWLESS LAND

(Republic, April 6, 1937) 55 Minutes

Johnny Mack Brown, Louise Stanley, Horace Murphy, Ted Adams, Julian Rivero, Frank Ball, Ed Cassidy, Anita Camargo, Roger Williams, Frances Kellogg, Chiquita Hernandez Orchestra, Horace B. Carpenter

Director: Albert Ray
Screenplay: Andrew Bennison
Producer: A. W. Hackel

BAR Z BAD MEN

(Republic, April 22, 1937) 51 Minutes

Johnny Mack Brown, Lois January, Tom London, Ernie Adams, Dick Curtis, Jack Rockwell, Milburn Morante, Horace Murphy, Budd Buster, Frank Ball, George Morrell, Tex Palmer, Horace B. Carpenter, Art Dillard, Oscar Gahan

Director: Sam Newfield
Story: James P. Olson
Screenplay: George Plympton
Producer: A. W. Hackel

GUNS IN THE DARK

(Republic, May 13, 1937) 56 Minutes

Johnny Mack Brown, Claire Rochelle, Dick Curtis, Julian Madison, Ted Adams, Sherry Tansey, Slim Whitaker, Lew Meehan, Tex Palmer, Francis Walker, Frank Ellis, Budd Buster, Oscar Gahan, Merrill McCormack, Dick Cramer, Steve Clark, Syd Saylor, Jack C. Smith, Roger Williams, Jim Corey, Chick Hannon

Director: Sam Newfield
Story: E. B. Mann
Screenplay: Charles Francis Royal
Producer: A. W. Hackel

A LAWMAN IS BORN

(Republic, June 21, 1937) 58 Minutes

Johnny Mack Brown, Iris Meredith, Al St. John, Mary MacLaren, Dick Curtis, Earle Hodgins, Charles King, Frank LaRue, Steve Clark, Jack C. Smith, Sherry Tansey, Wally West, Budd Buster, Lew Meehan, Tex Palmer, Warner Richmond, Oscar Gahan

Director: Sam Newfield
Story: Harry Olmstead
Screenplay: George Plympton
Producer: A. W. Hackel

WILD WEST DAYS

(Universal, June, 1937) 13 Chapters

John Mack Brown, Lynn Gilbert, Russell Simpson, Frank Yaconelli, George Shelly, Bob Kortman, Walter Miller, Francis McDonald, Frank McGlynn, Jr., Charles Stevens, Al Bridge, Edward J. LeSaint, Bruce Mitchell, Frank Ellis, Chief Thunderbird, Bud Osborne, Jack Clifford, Hank Bell, Lafe McKee, Joe Girard, William Royle, Mike Morita, Robert McClung, Sidney Bracey, Iron Eyes Cody, Chief Thunder Cloud

Directors: Ford Beebe, Cliff Smith
Story: "Saint Johnson" - W. R. Burnett
Screenplay: Wyndham Gittens, Norman S. Hall, Ray Trampe
Producers: Ben Koenig, Henry MacRae
Chapter Titles: (1) Death Rides the Range (2) The Redskin's Revenge (3) The Brink of Action (4) The Indians Are Coming (5) The Leap for Life (6) Death Stalks the Plains (7) Six Gun Law (8) The Gold Stampede (9) Walls of Fire (10) The Circle of Doom (11) The Thundering Herd (12) Rustlers and Redskins (13) The Rustler's Roundup

BOOTHILL BRIGADE

(Republic, August 2, 1937) 56 Minutes

Johnny Mack Brown, Claire Rochelle, Dick Curtis, Horace Murphy, Ed Cassidy, Frank LaRue, Bobby Nelson, Frank Ball, Steve Clark, Frank Ellis, Lew Meehan, Tex Palmer, Sherry Tansey, Jim Corey

Director: Sam Newfield
Story: Harry Olmstead
Screenplay: George Plympton
Producer: A. W. Hackel

VITAPHONE PICTORIAL REVUE, NEW SERIES NO. 3

(Warner Bros., November 13, 1937) 10 Minutes

Johnny Mack Brown and son Lachlen, Dick Foran, Mickey Rooney, Joe E. Brown

BORN TO THE WEST

(Paramount, December 10, 1937) 59 Minutes
(re-issued as "Hell Town")
John Wayne, Marsha Hunt, *Johnny Mack Brown,* John Patterson, Monte Blue, Syd Saylor, Lucien Littlefield, Nick Lukats, James Craig, Jack Kennedy, Vester Pegg, Earl Dwire, Jim Thorpe, Jennie Boyle, Alan Ladd, Lee Prather, Jack Daley
Director: Charles Barton
Story: "Born to the West" - Zane Grey
Screenplay: Stuart Anthony, Robert Yost

WELLS FARGO

(Paramount, December 31, 1937) 115 Minutes
Joel McCrea, Bob Burns, Frances Dee, Lloyd Nolan, Henry O'Neill, Mary Nash, Ralph Morgan, *Johnny Mack Brown,* Porter Hall, Jack Clark, Clarence Kolb, Robert Cummings, Peggy Stewart, Bernard Siegel, Stanley Fields, Jane Dewey, Frank McGlynn, Barlowe Bourland, Granville Bates, Harry Davenport, Frank Conroy, Brandon Tynan, Frank McGlynn, Sr., David Durand, Scotty Beckett, Jimmy Butler, Dorothy Tennant, Clara Verdera, Edward Earle, Henry Brandon, Harry Stafford, Lucien Littlefield, Helen Dickson, Jerry Tucker, Babs Nelson, Rebecca Wassem, Ronnie Crosby, Erville Anderson, Louis Natheaux, Paul Newlan, Shirley Coats
Director/Producer: Frank Lloyd
Story: Stuart N. Lake
Screenplay: Paul Schoefield, Gerald Geraghty, Frederick Jackson

FLAMING FRONTIERS

(Universal, May, 1938) 54 Minutes 15 Chapters
John Mack Brown, Eleanor Hansen, Ralph Bowman (John Archer), Charles Middleton, Chief Thunder Cloud, Horace Murphy, Charles King, James Blaine, Roy Barcroft, Charles Stevens, William Royle, John Rutherford, Eddy Waller, Edward Cassidy, Michael Slade, Karl Hackett, Iron Eyes Cody, Pat O'Brian, Earle Hodgins, J. P. McGowan, Frank Ellis, Jim Toney, Hank Bell, Horace B. Carpenter, Tom Steele, Slim Whitaker, Frank LaRue, Al Bridge, Blackjack Ward, Ferris Taylor, Jim Farley, Jim Corey, Bob Woodward, Frank Straubinger, Helen Gibson, Sunni Chorre, George Plues, Jack Saunders, Jack Roper, Bill Hazelett
Directors: Ray Taylor, Alan James
Story: "The Tie That Binds" - Peter B. Kyne
Screenplay: Wyndham Gittens, Paul Perez, Basil Dickey, George Pylmpton, Ella O'Neill
Producer: Henry MacRae
Chapter Titles: (1) The River Runs Red (2) Death Rides the Wind (3) Treachery at Eagle Pass (4) A Night of Terror (5) Blood and Gold (6) Trapped by Fire (7) A Human Target (8) The Savage Horde (9) Tool of the Torrent (10) In the Claws of the Cougar (11) The Half Breed's Revenge (12) The Indians Are Coming (13) The Fatal Plunge (14) Dynamite (15) A Duel to Death

THE OREGON TRAIL

(Universal, May, 1939) 15 Chapters
Johnny Mack Brown, Louise Stanley, Fuzzy Knight, Bill Cody, Jr., Edward J. LeSaint, Roy Barcroft, James Blaine, Lane Chandler, Charles King, Jack C. Smith, Forrest Taylor, Charles Stevens, Colin Kelly, Budd Buster, Frank Ellis, Tom London, Iron Eyes Cody, Jim Thorpe, Karl Hackett, Horace Murphy, Tom Steele, Helen Gibson, Jim Toney, Warner Richmond, Kenneth Harlan, George Plues, Tex Young, Chick Hannon, Cactus Mack, Frank LaRue, Lafe McKee, Tom Smith
Director: Ford Beebe, Saul A. Goodkind
Screenplay: Edmund Kelso, George Plympton, Basil Dickey, W. W. Watson
Producer: Henry MacRae
Chapter Titles: (1) The Renegade's Revenge (2) The Flaming Forest (3) The Brink of Disaster (4) Thundering Doom (5) Stampede (6) Indian Vengeance (7) Trail of Treachery (8) Redskin's Revenge (9) The Avalanche of Doom (10) The Plunge of Peril (11) Trapped in the Flames (12) The Baited Trap (13) Crashing Timbers (14) Death in the Night (15) The End of the Trail

DESPERATE TRAILS

(Universal, September 8, 1939) 58 Minutes
Johnny Mack Brown, Bob Baker, Fuzzy Knight, Frances Robinson, Bill Cody, Jr., Russell Simpson, Clarence Wilson, Ed Cassidy, Charles Stevens, Horace Murphy, Ralph Dunn, Tom Smith, Fern Emmett, Anita Camargo, Al Haskell, Frank Ellis, Jack Shannon, Wilbur McCauley, Frank McCarroll, Cliff Lyons, Eddie Parker
Director: Albert Ray
Screenplay: Andrew Bennison
Associate Producer: Albert Ray

OKLAHOMA FRONTIER

(Universal, October 10, 1939) 58 Minutes
Johnny Mack Brown, Bob Baker, Fuzzy Knight, Anne Gwynne, James Blaine, Bob Kortman, Charles King, Harry Tenbrook, Horace Murphy, Lloyd Ingraham, Joe De LaCruz, Anthony Warde, Al Bridge, Robert Cunnings, Sr., Lane Chandler, Hank Worden, Hank Bell, Blackie Whiteford, Roy Harris (Riley Hill), George Magrill, George Chesebro, Tom Smith, The Texas Rangers
Director: Ford Beebe
Screenplay: Ford Beebe
Associate Producer: Albert Ray

CHIP OF THE FLYING U

(Universal, November 29, 1939) 55 Minutes

Johnny Mack Brown, Bob Baker, Fuzzy Knight, Doris Weston, Karl Hackett, Forrest Taylor, Anthony Warde, Henry Hall, Claire Whitney, Ferris Taylor, Cecil Kellogg, Hank Bell, Harry Tenbrook, Chester Conklin, Vic Potel, Hank Worden, Charles K. French, Al Ward, Budd Buster, Frank Ellis, Kermit Maynard, Jack Shannon, Chuck Morrison

Director: Ralph Staub
Story: B. M. Bower
Screenplay: Larry Rhine, Andrew Bennison

RIDERS OF PASCO BASIN

(Universal, April 5, 1940) 56 Minutes

Johnny Mack Brown, Fuzzy Knight, Bob Baker, Frances Robinson, Frank LaRue, Arthur Loft, James Guilfoyle, Lafe McKee, Chuck Morrison, Edward Cassidy, Robert Winkler, William Gould, Ted Adams, Kermit Maynard, David Sharpe, Hank Bell, Edward Peil, John Judd, Gordon Hart, Rudy Sooter and His Californians

Director: Ray Taylor
Story/Screenplay: Ford Beebe

WEST OF CARSON CITY

(Universal, May 13, 1940) 57 Minutes

Johnny Mack Brown, Bob Baker, Fuzzy Knight, Peggy Moran, Harry Woods, Robert Homans, Al Hall, Roy Barcroft, Charles King, Frank Mitchell, Edmund Cobb, Jack Roper, Ted Wells, Jack Shannon, Vic Potel, Kermit Maynard, Ernie Adams, Donald Kerr, Dick Carter, Al Bridge, The Notables Quartet

Director: Ray Taylor
Story; Milt Raison
Screenplay: Milt Raison, Sherman Lowe, Jack Bernhard

BADMAN FROM RED BUTTE

(Universal, May 31, 1940) 58 Minutes

Johnny Mack Brown, Fuzzy Knight, Bob Baker, Anne Gwynne, Lloyd Ingraham, Lafe McKee, Bill Cody, Jr., Buck Moulton, Roy Barcroft, Norman Willis, Earl Hodgins, James Morton, Myra McKinney, Art Mix, Texas Jim Lewis and His Lone Star Cowboys

Director: Ray Taylor
Screenplay: Sam Robins

SON OF ROARING DAN

(Universal, July 26, 1940) 63 Minutes

Johnny Mack Brown, Fuzzy Knight, Nell O'Day, Jeannie Kelly, Robert Homans, Tom Chatterton, John Eldridge, Ethan Laidlaw, Lafe McKee, Dick Alexander, Eddie Polo, Bob Reeves, Chuck Morrison, Frank McCarroll, Lloyd Ingraham, Jack Shannon, Ben Taggert, Ralph Peters, Ralph Dunn, Jack Montgomery, The Texas Rangers

Director: Ford Beebe
Screenplay: Clarence Upson Young
Associate Producer: Joseph Sanford

RAGTIME COWBOY JOE

(Universal, September 20, 1940) 58 Minutes

Johnny Mack Brown, Fuzzy Knight, Nell O'Day, Marilyn (Lynn) Merrick, Dick Curtis, Walter Sodering, Roy Barcroft, Harry Tenbrook, George Plues, Ed Cassidy, Buck Moulton, Harold Goodwin, Wilfred Lucas, Kermit Maynard, Viola Vonn, Jack Clifford, William Gould, Bud Osborne, The Texas Rangers, Bob O'Connor, Eddie Parker, Frank McCarroll, Slim Whitaker

Director: Ray Taylor
Screenplay: Sherman Lowe
Associate Producer: Joseph Sanford

LAW AND ORDER

(Universal, November 28, 1940) 57 Minutes

Johnny Mack Brown, Fuzzy Knight, Nell O'Day, James Craig, Harry Cording, Ethan Laidlaw, Ted Adams, Harry Humphrey, Jimmy Dodd, William Worthington, George Plues, Earle Hodgins, Robert Fiske, Kermit Maynard, Frank McCarroll, Bob Kortman, Frank Ellis, Jim Corey, Lew Meehan, Charles King, The Notables Quartet

Director: Ray Taylor
Story: "Saint Johnson" - W. R. Burnett
Screenplay: Sherman Lowe, Victor McLeod

PONY POST

(Universal, December 1, 1940) 59 Minutes

Johnny Mack Brown, Fuzzy Knight, Nell O'Day, Lane Chandler, Edmund Cobb, Kermit Maynard, Dorothy Short, Tom Chatterton, Stanley Blystone, Jack Rockwell, Ray Teal, Lloyd Ingraham, Charles King, Frank McCarroll, Iron Eyes Cody, Jimmy Wakely and His Rough Riders

Director: Ray Taylor
Story/Screenplay: Sherman Lowe

BOSS OF BULLION CITY

(Universal, January 10, 1941)
Johnny Mack Brown, Fuzzy Knight, Nell O'Day, Maria Montez, Earle Hodgins, Harry Woods, Melvin Lang, Dick Alexander, Karl Hackett, George Humbert, Frank Ellis, Kermit Maynard, Tex Terry, Bob Kortman, Michael Vallon, The Guadalajara Trio, Bill Nestell
Director: Ray Taylor
Story: Arthur St. Claire
Screenplay: Arthur St. Claire, Victor McLeod
Associate Producer: Will Cowan

BURY ME NOT ON THE LONE PRAIRIE

(Universal, March 21, 1941) 57 Minutes
Johnny Mack Brown, Fuzzy Knight, Nell O'Day, Kathryn Adams, Lee Shumway, Frank O'Connor, Ernie Adams, Don House, Pat O'Brien, Bud Osborne, Ed Cassidy, Slim Whitaker, Kermit Maynard, William Desmond, Jack Rockwell, Bob Kortman, Jim Corey, Charles King, Ethan Laidlaw, Harry Cording, Frank Ellis, Jimmy Wakely's Rough Riders
Director: Ray Taylor
Story: Sherman Lowe
Screenplay: Sherman Lowe, Victor McLeod
Associate Producer: Will Cowan

LAW OF THE RANGE

(Universal, June 20, 1941) 59 Minutes
Johnny Mack Brown, Fuzzy Knight, Nell O'Day, Roy Harris (Riley Hill), Pat O'Malley, Elaine Morley, Ethan Laidlaw, Al Bridge, Hal Taliaferro, Jack Rockwell, Charles King, Lucile Walker, Terry Frost, Jim Corey, Bud Osborne, Slim Whitaker, Bob Kortman, The Texas Rangers, Jerome Hart, Jack Casey, Chuck Morrison, Sam Garrett, George Plues, Carl Sepulveda, Harmax Hack
Director: Ray Taylor
Associate Producer: Will Cowan

RAWHIDE RANGER

(Universal, July 18, 1941) 56 Minutes
Johnny Mack Brown, Fuzzy Knight, Nell O'Day, Kathryn Adams, Roy Harris, Harry Cording, Al Bridge, Frank Shannon, Ed Cassidy, Bob Kortman, Chester Gan, James Farley, Jack Rockwell, Frank Ellis, Fred Burns, Tex Palmer, Tex Terry, The Pickard Family, The Texas Rangers
Director: Ray Taylor
Screenplay: Ed Earl Repp
Associate Producer: Will Cowan

MAN FROM MONTANA

(Universal, September 5, 1941) 56 Minutes
Johnny Mack Brown, Fuzzy Knight, Nell O'Day, Butch and Buddy (Billy Lenhart and Kenneth Brown), Jeanne Kelly (Jean Brooks), William Gould, James Blaine, Dick Alexander, Karl Hackett, Edmund Cobb, Frank Ellis, Kermit Maynard, Jack Shannon, Murdock McQuarrie, Charles McMurphy, Blackjack Ward, The King's Men
Director: Ray Taylor
Screenplay: Bennett Cohen
Associate Producer: Will Cowan

THE MASKED RIDER

(Universal, October 24, 1941) 58 Minutes
Johnny Mack Brown, Fuzzy Knight, Nell O'Day, Grant Withers, Virginia Carroll, Guy D'Ennery, Carmela Cansino, Roy Barcroft, Dick Botiller, Fred Cordova, Al Haskell, Rico De Montez, Robert O'Connor, Jose Cansino Dancers, The Quadalajara Trio
Director: Ford Beebe
Story: Sam Robins
Screenplay: Sherman Lowe, Victor McLeod
Associate Producer: Will Cowan

ARIZONA CYCLONE

(Universal, November 14, 1941) 59 Minutes
Johnny Mack Brown, Fuzzy Knight, Nell O'Day, Kathryn Adams, Dick Curtis, Herbert Rawlinson, Buck Moulton, Jack Clifford, Kermit Maynard, Frank Ellis, The Notables, Robert Strange, Glenn Strange, Carl Sepulveda, Chuck Morrison
Director: Joseph H. Lewis
Screenplay: Sherman Lowe
Associate Producer: Will Cowan

FIGHTING BILL FARGO

(Universal, December 9, 1941) 57 Minutes
Johnny Mack Brown, Fuzzy Knight, Nell O'Day, Jeanne Kelly (Jean Brooks), Kenneth Harlan, Ted Adams, James Blaine, Al Bridge, Joseph Eggerton, Bob Kortman, Earle Hodgins, Tex Palmer, Harry Tenbrook, Kermit Maynard, Blackie Whiteford, Merrill McCormack, Bud Osborne, Eddie Dean Trio
Director: Ray Taylor
Story: Paul Franklin
Screenplay: Paul Franklin, Dorcas Cochran, Arthur V. Jones
Associate Producer: Will Cowan

RIDE 'EM COWBOY

(Universal, February 13, 1942) 86 Minutes

Bud Abbott, Lou Costello, Dick Foran, Anne Gwynne, *Johnny Mack Brown*, The Merry Macs, Ella Fitzgerald, Douglass Dumbrille, Samuel S. Hinds, Morris Ankrum, The High Hatters, The Buckaroo Band, The Ranger Chorus, Bob Baker, Richard Lane, Chief Yowlachie, Ted McMichall, Joe McMichall, May Lou Cook, Jody Gilbert, Charles Lane, Russell Hicks, Wade Boteler, James Flavin, Boyd Davis, Eddie Dunn, Isabel Randolph, Tom Hanlon, James Seay, Harold Daniels, Ralph Peters, Linda Brent, Lee Sunrise, Carmela Cansino, Sherman E. Sanders

Director: Arthur Lubin

Story: Edmund L. Hartman

Screenplay: True Boardman, John Grant

Associate Producer: Alex Gottlieb

STAGECOACH BUCKAROO

(Universal, February 13, 1942) 58 Minutes

Johnny Mack Brown, Fuzzy Knight, Nell O'Day, Anne Nagel, Herbert Rawlinson, Glenn Strange, Ernie Adams, Henry Hall, Lloyd Ingraham, Kermit Maynard, Frank Brownlee, Jack C. Smith, Harry Tenbrook, Frank Ellis, Blackie Whiteford, Hank Bell, Ray Jones, Jim Corey, William Nestell, Carl Sepulveda, The Guardsman Quartet

Director: Ray Taylor

Story: "Shotgun Messenger" - Arthur St. Clair

Screenplay: Al Martin

Associate Producer: Will Cowan

THE SILVER BULLET

(Universal, August 5, 1942) 56 Minutes

Johnny Mack Brown, Fuzzy Knight, Jennifer Holt, William Farnum, Rex Lease, LeRoy Mason, Grace Lenard, Claire Whitney, Slim Whitaker, Michael Vallon, Merrill McCormack, Harry Holman, Lloyd Ingraham, Hank Bell, William Desmond, James Farley, Pals of the Golden West (with Nora Lou Martin)

Director: Joseph H. Lewis

Screenplay: Elizabeth Beecher

Story: Oliver Drake

Associate Producer: Will Cowan

BOSS OF HANGTOWN MESA

(Universal, August 21, 1942) 58 Minutes

Johnny Mack Brown, Fuzzy Knight, Helen Deverell, William Farnum, Rex Lease, Hugh Prosser, Michael Vallon, Robert Barron, Henry Hall, Jack C. Smith, Fred Kohler, Jr., Mickey Simpson, Frank Hagney, The Pals of the Golden West

Director: Joseph H. Lewis

Screenplay: Oliver Drake

Producer: Will Cowan

DEEP IN THE HEART OF TEXAS

(Universal, September 25, 1942) 62 Minutes

Johnny Mack Brown, Tex Ritter, Fuzzy Knight, Jennifer Holt, William Farnum, Jimmy Wakely Trio (Jimmy Wakely, Johnny Bond, Scotty Harrell), Harry Woods, Kenneth Harlan, Pat O'Malley, Roy Brent, Edmund Cobb, Earl Hodgins, Budd Buster, Frank Ellis, Tom Smith, Ray Jones, Eddie Polo

Director: Elmer Clifton

Story: Oliver Drake

Screenplay: Grace Norton

Associate Producer: Oliver Drake

LITTLE JOE THE WRANGLER

(Universal, November 13, 1942) 64 Minutes

Johnny Mack Brown, Tex Ritter, Fuzzy Knight, Jennifer Holt, Hal Taliaferro, Glenn Strange, Florine McKinney, James Craven, Ethan Laidlaw, Jimmy Wakely Trio (Jimmy Wakely, Johnny Bond, Scott Harrell)

Director: Lewis Collins

Story: Sherman Lowe

Screenplay: Sherman Lowe, Elizabeth Beecher

Associate Producer: Oliver Drake

THE OLD CHISHOLM TRAIL

(Universal, December 11, 1942) 61 Minutes

Johnny Mack Brown, Tex Ritter, Fuzzy Knight, Jennifer Holt, Mary Correll, Earle Hodgins, Roy Barcroft, Edmund Cobb, Budd Buster, Jimmy Wakely Trio (Jimmy Wakely, Johnny Bond, Scotty Harrell)

Director/Screenplay: Elmer Clifton

Associate Producer: Oliver Drake

TENTING TONIGHT ON THE OLD CAMP GROUND

(Universal, February 5, 1943) 58 Minutes

Johnny Mack Brown, Tex Ritter, Fuzzy Knight, Jennifer Holt, Jimmy Wakely Trio (Jimmy Wakely, Johnny Bond and Scotty Harrell), John Elliott, Earle Hodgins, Rex Lease, Lane Chandler, Hank Worden, Al Bridge, Dennis Moore, Tom London, Bud Osborne, Reed Howes, Lynton Brent, George Plues, Ray Jones, George Eldredge

Director: Lewis Collins

Story: Harry Fraser

Screenplay: Elizabeth Beecher

Associate Producer: Oliver Drake

Tex Ritter, Johnny Mack Brown, Jennifer Holt and Florine McKinney discuss some ore in **Little Joe, the Wrangler** (Universal, 1942).

THE GHOST RIDER

(Monogram, April 2, 1943) 58 Minutes
Johnny Mack Brown, Raymond Hatton, Beverly Boyd, Tom Siedel, Bud Osborne, Milburn Morante, Harry Woods, Edmund Cobb, Charles King, Artie Ortego, George DeNormand, Jack Daley, George Morrell
Director: Wallace Fox
Screenplay: Jess Bowers (Adele Buffington)
Producer: Scott R. Dunlap

CHEYENNE ROUNDUP

(Universal, April 29, 1943) 59 Minutes
Johnny Mack Brown, Fuzzy Knight, Tex Ritter, Jennifer Holt, Jimmy Wakely Trio (Jimmy Wakely, Johnny Bond, Scotty Harrell), Harry Woods, Roy Barcroft, Robert Barron, Budd Buster, Gil Patric, Carl Mathews, Kermit Maynard, William Desmond, Kenne Duncan
Director: Ray Taylor
Story: Elmer Clifton
Screenplay: Elmer Clifton, Bernard McConville

RAIDERS OF SAN JOAQUIN

(Universal, June 4, 1943) 60 Minutes
Johnny Mack Brown, Tex Ritter, Fuzzy Knight, Jennifer Holt, Jimmy Wakely Trio (Jimmy Wakely, Johnny Bond and Scotty Harrell), Henry Hall, Joseph Bernard, George Eldridge, Henry Rocquemore, Carl Sepulveda, John Elliott, Michael Vallon, Jack O'Shea, Jack Ingram, Robert Thompson, Scoop Martin, Roy Brent, Budd Buster, Earle Hodgins, Slim Whitaker
Director: Lewis Collins
Story: Patricia Harper
Screenplay: Elmer Clifton, Morgan Cox
Associate Producer: Oliver Drake

THE STRANGER FROM PECOS

(Monogram, July 16, 1943) 55 Minutes
Johnny Mack Brown, Raymond Hatton, Kirby Grant, Christine McIntyre, Steve Clark, Roy Barcroft, Robert Frazer, Edmund Cobb, Charles King, Bud Osborne, Artie Ortego, Tom London, Kermit Maynard, Milburn Morante, Lynton Brent, Carol Henry, George Morrell
Director: Lambert Hillyer
Screenplay: Jess Bowers (Adele Buffington)
Producer: Scott R. Dunlap

THE LONE STAR TRAIL

(Universal, August 6, 1943) 58 Minutes
Johnny Mack Brown, Tex Ritter, Fuzzy Knight, Jennifer Holt, Earle Hodgins, Jack Ingram, Bob Mitchum, George Eldridge, Michael Vallon, Ethan Laidlaw, Harry Strang, Fred Graham, William Desmond, Henry Rocquemore, Denver Dixon, Eddie Parker, Jimmy Wakely Trio (Jimmy Wakely, Johnny Bond, Scotty Harrell), Billy Engle, Carl Mathews, Bob Reeves, Tom Steele
Director: Ray Taylor
Story: Victor Halperin
Screenplay/Associate Producer: Oliver Drake

SIX GUN GOSPEL

(Monogram, September 3, 1943) 59 Minutes
Johnny Mack Brown, Raymond Hatton, Ina Gest, Eddie Dew, Roy Barcroft, Kenneth MacDonald, Edmund Cobb, Milburn Morante, Artie Ortego, L. W. (Lynton) Brent, Bud Osborne, Kernan Cripps, Jack Daley, Mary MacLaren
Director: Lambert Hillyer
Screenplay: Ed Earl Repp, Jess Bowers (Adele Buffington)
Producer: Scott R. Dunlap

CRAZY HOUSE

(Universal, October 8, 1943) 80 Minutes
Ole Olsen, Chic Johnson, Martha O'Driscoll, Alan Curtis, *Johnny Mack Brown,* Lon Chaney, Jr., Patric Knowles, Percy Kilbride, Cass Daley, Shemp Howard, Edgar Kennedy, Leo Carillo, Allan Jones, Grace McDonald, Robert Paige, Andy Devine, Count Basie and His Band, Thomas Gomez, Marion Hutton, Glenn Miller Singers, Leighton Noble, Andrew Toombes, Ray Walker, Robert Emmett Keane, Franklyn Pangborn, Chester Chute, Billy Gilbert, Richard Lane, Hans Conried, Fred Sanborn, The DeMarcos, Chandra Kaley Dancers, Laison Brothers, The Five Hertzogs, Bobby Brooks, Ward & Van, Terry Sheldon, Harry Powers, Billy Reed, The Delta Rhythm Boys
Director: Edward Cline
Screenplay: Robert Lees and Frederick I. Renaldo

OUTLAWS OF STAMPEDE PASS

(Monogram, October 15, 1943) 58 Minutes
Johnny Mack Brown, Raymond Hatton, Ellen Hall, Harry Woods, Milburn Morante, Edmund Cobb, Sam Flint, Jon Dawson, Charles King, Mauritz Hugo, Art Mix, Cactus Mack, Artie Ortego, Eddie Burns, Bill Wolfe, Hal Price, Dan White, Kansas Moehring, Tex Copper
Director: Wallace Fox
Story: Johnston McCulley
Screenplay: Jess Bowers (Adele Buffington)
Producer: Scott R. Dunlap

THE TEXAS KID

(Monogram, November 26, 1943) 59 Minutes
Johnny Mack Brown, Raymond Hatton, Shirley Patterson, Marshall Reed, Kermit Maynard, Edmund Cobb, Robert Fiske, Stanley Price, Lynton Brent, Bud Osborne, John Judd, Charles King, Cyrus Ring, George J. Lewis
Director: Lambert Hillyer
Story: Lynton Brent
Screenplay: Jess Bowers (Adele Buffington)
Producer: Scott R. Dunlap

RAIDERS OF THE BORDER

(Monogram, January 31, 1944) 58 Minutes
Johnny Mack Brown, Raymond Hatton, Ellen Hall, Craig Woods, Stanley Price, Ray Bennett, Edmund Cobb, Lynton Brent, Dick Alexander, Kermit Maynard, Ernie Adams
Director: John P. McCarthy
Story: Johnston McCulley
Screenplay: Jess Bowers (Adele Buffington)
Producer: Scott R. Dunlap

PARTNERS OF THE TRAIL

(Monogram, March 28, 1944) 57 Minutes
Johnny Mack Brown, Raymond Hatton, Christine McIntyre, Craig Woods, Robert Frazer, Harry L. (Hal) Price, Jack Ingram, Lynton Brent, Ben Corbett, Steve Clark, Marshall Reed, Lloyd Ingraham, Ted Mapes
Director: Lambert Hillyer
Screenplay: Frank Young
Producer: Scott R. Dunlap

LAW MEN

(Monogram, April 25, 1944) 58 Minutes
Johnny Mack Brown, Raymond Hatton, Jan Wiley, Kirby Grant, Robert Frazer, Edmund Cobb, Art Fowler, Hal Price, Marshall Reed, Isabel Withers, Ted Mapes, Steve Clark, Bud Osborne, Ben Corbett, Jack Rockwell, George Morrell, Ray Jones
Director: Lambert Hillyer
Screenplay: Glenn Tyron
Producer: Charles J. Bigelow

RANGE LAW

(Monogram, June 24, 1944) 57 Minutes
Johnny Mack Brown, Raymond Hatton, Sarah Padden, Ellen Hall, Lloyd Ingraham, Marshall Reed, Steve Clark, Jack Ingram, Hugh Prosser, Stanley Price, Art Fowler, Harry (Hal) Price, Ben Corbett, Bud Osborne, Tex Palmer, George Morrell, Lynton Brent, Forrest Taylor, Horace B. Carpenter
Director: Lambert Hillyer
Screenplay: Frank H. Young
Producer: Charles J. Bigelow

WEST OF THE RIO GRANDE
(Monogram, August 5, 1944) 57 Minutes

Johnny Mack Brown, Raymond Hatton, Dennis Moore, Christine McIntyre, Lloyd Ingraham, Kenneth MacDonald, Frank LaRue, Art Fowler, Hugh Prosser, Edmund Cobb, Steve Clark, Jack Rockwell, Hal Price, John Merton, Bob Kortman, Bud Osborne, Pierce Lyden, Lynton Brent
Director: Lambert Hillyer
Story/Screenplay: Betty Burbridge
Producer: Charles J. Bigelow

LAND OF THE OUTLAWS
(Monogram, September 16, 1944) 56 Minutes

Johnny Mack Brown, Raymond Hatton, Stephen Keyes, Nan Holliday, Hugh Prosser, Charles King, John Merton, Steve Clark, Art Fowler, Tom Quinn, Ray Elder, Chick Hannon, Bob Cason, Kansas Moehring, Ben Corbett, George Morrell
Director: Lambert Hillyer
Screenplay: Joe O'Donnell
Producer: Charles J. Bigelow

LAW OF THE VALLEY
(Monogram, November 4, 1944) 52 Minutes

Johnny Mack Brown, Raymond Hatton, Lynne Carver, Edmund Cobb, Charles King, Kirk Barton, Tom Quinn, Marshall Reed, Hal Price, George DeNormand, Steve Clark, George Morrell, Charles McMurphy
Director: Howard Bretherton
Screenplay: Joe O'Donnell
Producer: Charles J. Bigelow

GHOST GUNS
(Monogram, November 17, 1944) 60 Minutes

Johnny Mack Brown, Raymond Hatton, Evelyn Finley, Sarah Padden, Riley Hill, Ernie Adams, Jack Ingram, Tom Quinn, Frank LaRue, John Merton, Bob Cason, Marshall Reed, Steve Clark, George Morrell
Director: Lambert Hillyer
Story: Bennett Cohen
Screenplay: Frank H. Young
Producer: Charles J. Bigelow

A Lobby Card from 1944 showing Johnny Mack Brown, Marshall Reed, Frank LaRue, John Merton and Raymond Hatton.

THE NAVAJO TRAIL

(Monogram, January 5, 1945) 60 Minutes
Johnny Mack Brown, Raymond Hatton, Jennifer Holt, Riley Hill, Edmund Cobb, Charles King, Ray Bennett, Bud Osborne, Tom Quinn, Edward Cassidy, John Carpenter
Director: Howard Bretherton
Story: Frank Young
Screenplay: Jess Bowers (Adele Buffington)
Producer: Charles J. Bigelow

FOREVER YOURS

(Monogram, February 2, 1945) 84 Minutes
(formerly titled "They Shall Have Faith")
Gale Storm, *Johnny Mack Brown,* Sir C. Aubrey Smith, Frank Craven, Conrad Nagel, Mary Boland, Johnny Downs, Catherine McLeod, Selmer Jackson, Matt Willis, Russ Whiteman, Billy Wilderson, Maurice St. Clair, Leo Diamond and His Harmonaires, William Hall
Director: William Nigh

GUN SMOKE

(Monogram, February 16, 1945) 57 Minutes
Johnny Mack Brown, Raymond Hatton, Jennifer Holt, Riley Hill, Frank Ellis, Ray Bennett, Marshall Reed, Steve Clark, Bob Cason, Elmer Napier, Roy Butler, Wen Wright, Demas Sotello, Kansas Moehring, Louis Hart, Chick Hannon
Director: Howard Bretherton
Screenplay: Frank Young
Producer: Charles E. Bigelow

MEN TO REMEMBER

(Columbia, February 25, 1945) 9 Minutes
(Screen Snapshots Series 24, No. 7)
Narrated by Art Baker. Compilation of clips honoring Tom Mix and Will Rogers. *Johnny Mack Brown,* Guinn "Big Boy" Williams, and Charlie Farrell are seen playing polo with Rogers.
Director: Ralph Staub

STRANGER FROM SANTA FE

(Monogram, April 15, 1945) 57 Minutes
Johnny Mack Brown, Raymond Hatton, Beatrice Gray, Jo Ann Curtis, Jack Ingram, Bud Osborne, Jimmie Martin, Steve Clark, Hal Price, John Merton, Tom Quinn, Ray Elder, Eddie Parker, Louis Hart, Jack Rockwell
Director: Lambert Hillyer
Screenplay: Frank Young
Producer: Charles J. Bigelow

FLAME OF THE WEST

(Monogram, June 25, 1945) 70 Minutes
Johnny Mack Brown, Joan Woodbury, Raymond Hatton, Douglass Dumbrille, Lynne Carver, Harry Woods, Riley Hill, Jack Ingram, John Merton, Tom Quinn, Jack Rockwell, Ted Mapes, Bob Duncan, Pierce Lyden, Frank McCarroll, Ray Bennett, Steve Clark, Bud Osborne, Hal Price, Bob Cason, Eddie Parker, Horace B. Carpenter
Director: Lambert Hillyer
Story: Bennett Foster
Screenplay: Adele Buffington
Producer: Scott R. Dunlap

THE LOST TRAIL

(Monogram, October 20, 1945) 53 Minutes
Johnny Mack Brown, Raymond Hatton, Jennifer Holt, Kenneth MacDonald, Riley Hill, Lynton Brent, John Ince, John Bridges, Eddie Parker, Frank McCarroll, Dick Dickinson, Milburn Morante, Frank LaRue, Steve Clark, George Morrell, Carl Mathews, Victor Cox, Cal Shrum and his Rhythm Rangers
Director: Lambert Hillyer
Screenplay: Jess Bowers (Adele Buffington)
Producer: Charles J. Bigelow

FRONTIER FEUD

(Monogram, November 24, 1945) 54 Minutes
Johnny Mack Brown, Raymond Hatton, Christine McIntyre, Dennis Moore, Jack Ingram, Eddie Parker, Frank LaRue, Steve Clark, Jack Rockwell, Mary MacLaren, Edmund Cobb, Lloyd Ingraham, Ted Mapes, Stanley Price, Terry Frost, Dan White, Ray Jones, Charles King, Lynton Brent
Director: Lambert Hillyer
Story: Charles N. Heckelmann
Screenplay: Jess Bowers (Adele Buffington)
Producer: Charles J. Bigelow

BORDER BANDITS

(Monogram, January 12, 1946) 58 Minutes
Johnny Mack Brown, Raymond Hatton, Riley Hill, Rosa Del Rosario, John Merton, Tom Quinn, Frank LaRue, Steve Clark, Charles Stevens, Lucio Villegas, Bud Osborne, Pat R. McGee, I. Stanford Jolley, Ray Jones, Terry Frost, Julia Vilirea
Director: Lambert Hillyer
Screenplay: Frank Young
Producer: Charles J. Bigelow

DRIFTING ALONG
(Monogram, January 26, 1946) 60 Minutes
Johnny Mack Brown, Lynne Carver, Raymond Hatton, Douglas Fowley, Smith Ballew, Milburn Morante, Thornton Edwards, Steve Clark, Marshall Reed, Jack Rockwell, Lynton Brent, Terry Frost, Leonard St. Leo, Ted Mapes, Curt Barrett and the Trailsmen
Director: Derwin Abrahams
Screenplay: Adele Buffington
Producer: Scott R. Dunlap

THE HAUNTED MINE
(Monogram, March 2, 1946) 51 Minutes
Johnny Mack Brown, Raymond Hatton, Linda Johnson, Ray Bennett, Riley Hill, Claire Whitney, John Merton, Marshall Reed, Terry Frost, Lynton Brent, Leonard St. Leo, Frank LaRue, Ray Jones
Director: Derwin Abrahams
Screenplay: Frank Young
Producer: Charles E. Bigelow

UNDER ARIZONA SKIES
(Monogram, April 27, 1946) 59 Minutes
Johnny Mack Brown, Raymond Hatton, Reno Blair (Browne), Riley Hill, Tris Coffin, Reed Howes, Ted Adams, Ray Bennett, Frank LaRue, Steve Clark, Jack Rockwell, Bud Geary, Ted Mapes, Kermit Maynard, Ray Jones, Smith Ballew and the Sons of the Sage
Director: Lambert Hillyer
Screenplay: J. Benton Cheney
Producer: Scott R. Dunlap

THE GENTLEMAN FROM TEXAS
(Monogram, June 8, 1946) 55 Minutes
Johnny Mack Brown, Raymond Hatton, Claudia Drake, Reno Blair (Browne), Christine McIntyre, Curt Barrett and the Trailsmen, Tris Coffin, Marshall Reed, Terry Frost, Jack Rockwell, Steve Clark, Pierce Lyden, Wally West, Artie Ortego, Bill Wolfe, Ted Adams, Lynton Brent, Frank LaRue
Director: Lambert Hillyer
Screenplay: J. Benton Cheney
Producer: Scott R. Dunlap

SCREEN SNAPSHOTS, SERIES 25, NO. 10
Columbia, June 10, 1946) 9½ Minutes
Johnny Mack Brown and son Lachlen
Director: Ralph Staub

TRIGGER FINGERS
(Monogram, September 21, 1946) 56 Minutes
Johnny Mack Brown, Raymond Hatton, Jennifer Holt, Riley Hill, Steve Clark, Eddie Parker, Pierce Lyden, Ted Adams, Cactus Mack, Edward Cassidy, Ray Jones, George Morrell, Frank McCarroll
Director: Lambert Hillyer
Screenplay: Frank H. Young
Producer: Charles J. Bigelow

SHADOWS ON THE RANGE
(Monogram, October 16, 1946) 58 Minutes
Johnny Mack Brown, Raymond Hatton, Jan Bryant, Marshall Reed, John Merton, Jack Perrin, Steve Clark, Terry Frost, Cactus Mack, Pierce Lyden, Ted Adams, Lane Bradford
Director: Lambert Hillyer
Screenplay: Jess Bowers (Adele Buffington)
Producer: Scott R. Dunlap

SILVER RANGE
(Monogram, November 16, 1946) 53 Minutes
Johnny Mack Brown, Raymond Hatton, Jan Bryant, I. Stanford Jolley, Terry Frost, Eddie Parker, Ted Adams, Frank LaRue, Cactus Mack, Lane Bradford, Dee Cooper, Billy Dix, Bill Willmering, George Morrell
Director: Lambert Hillyer
Screenplay: J. Benton Cheney
Producer: Charles J. Bigelow

RAIDERS OF THE SOUTH
(Monogram, January 18, 1947) 55 Minutes
Johnny Mack Brown, Evelyn Brent, Raymond Hatton, Reno Blair, Marshall Reed, John Hamilton, John Merton, Eddie Parker, Frank LaRue, Ted Adams, Pierce Lyden, Cactus Mack, George Morrell, Ray Jones, Artie Ortego, Curt Barrett and the Trailsmen, Billy Dix, Dee Cooper
Director: Lambert Hillyer
Screenplay: J. Benton Cheney
Producer: Scott R. Dunlap

VALLEY OF FEAR
(Monogram, February 15, 1947) 54 Minutes
Johnny Mack Brown, Raymond Hatton, Christine McIntyre, Tris Coffin, Edward Cassidy, Eddie Parker, Edward Peil, Sr., Ted Adams, Pierce Lyden, Steve Darrell, Cactus Mack, Budd Buster, Gary Garrett, Robert O'Bryen, Matt Roubert
Director: Lambert Hillyer
Screenplay: J. Benton Cheney
Producer: Charles J. Bigelow

TRAILING DANGER

(Monogram, March 29, 1947) 58 Minutes

Johnny Mack Brown, Raymond Hatton, Peggy Wynne, Marshall Reed, Patrick Desmond, Steve Darnell, Eddie Parker, Bonnie Jean Parker, Ernie Adams, Bud Osborne, Cactus Mack, Kansas Moehring, Gary Garrett, Dee Cooper, Jack Hendricks, Artie Ortego

Director: Lambert Hillyer
Screenplay: J. Benton Cheney
Producer: Barney Sarecky

LAND OF THE LAWLESS

(Monogram, April 26, 1947) 54 Minutes

Johnny Mack Brown, Raymond Hatton, Christine McIntyre, Tris Coffin, June Harrison, Marshall Reed, I. Stanford Jolley, Steve Clark, Edmund Cobb, Roy Butler, Cactus Mack, Gary Garrett, Carl Sepulveda, Victor Cox

Director: Lambert Hillyer
Screenplay: J. Benton Cheney
Producer: Barney Sarecky

THE LAW COMES TO GUNSIGHT

(Monogram, May 24, 1947) 56 Minutes

Johnny Mack Brown, Raymond Hatton, Reno Blair (Browne), Lanny Rees, Zon Murray, Frank LaRue, Ernie Adams, Kermit Maynard, Ted Adams, Gary Garrett, Lee Roberts, Willard Willingham, Artie Ortego

Director: Lambert Hillyer
Screenplay: J. Benton Cheney
Producer: Barney Sarecky

CODE OF THE SADDLE

(Monogram, June 28, 1947) 53 Minutes

Johnny Mack Brown, Raymond Hatton, Riley Hill, Kay Morley, William Norton Bailey, Zon Murray, Ted Adams, Bud Osborne, Kenne Duncan, Jr., Gary Garrett, Curley Gibson, Jack Hendricks, Boyd Stockman, Bob McElroy, Ray Jones, Chick Hannon

Director: Thomas Carr
Screenplay: Eliot Biggons
Producer: Barney Sarecky

FLASHING GUNS

(Monogram, July 16, 1947) 59 Minutes

Johnny Mack Brown, Raymond Hatton, Jan Bryant, Douglas Evans, James E. Logan, Ted Adams, Edmund Cobb, Norman Jolley, Ken Adams, Gary Garrett, Ray Jones, Jack O'Shea, Steve Clark, Frank LaRue, Jack Rockwell, Riley Hill, Bob Woodward

Director: Lambert Hillyer
Screenplay: Frank H. Young
Producer: Barney Sarecky

SCREEN SNAPSHOTS

(Columbia, September 4, 1947) 9½ Minutes
(Segment called "Hollywood Cowboys")

Buck Jones, Gene Autry, Roy Rogers, Will Rogers, Tom Mix, *John Mack Brown,* Hoot Gibson, William S. Hart, William Boyd, Robert Young, Jackie Coogan

Director: Ralph Staub

PRAIRIE EXPRESS

(Monogram, October 25, 1947) 55 Minutes

Johnny Mack Brown, Raymond Hatton, Virginia Belmont Marshall Reed, William Ruhl, Robert Winkler, Frank LaRue, Ted Adams, Steve Darrell, Ken Adams, Gary Garrett, Hank Worden, Bob McElroy, Carl Mathews, Boyd Stockman, Jack Gibson, Steve Clark, Artie Ortego, I. Stanford Jolley, Jack Hendricks

Director: Lambert Hillyer
Screenplay: Anthony Coldeway, J. Benton Cheney
Producer: Barney Sarecky

GUN TALK

(Monogram, December 20, 1947) 57 Minutes

Johnny Mack Brown, Raymond Hatton, Christine McIntyre, Douglas Evans, Geneva Gray, Wheaton Chambers, Frank LaRue, Ted Adams, Carl Mathews, Zon Murray, Cactus Mack, Carol Henry, Bill Hale, Boyd Stockman, Roy Butler, Bob McElroy

Director: Lambert Hillyer
Screenplay: J. Benton Cheney
Producer: Barney Sarecky

OVERLAND TRAILS

(Monogram, January 31, 1948) 58 Minutes

Johnny Mack Brown, Raymond Hatton, Virginia Belmont, Bill Kennedy, Virginia Carroll, Holly Bane, Ted Adams, Steve Darrell, Sonny Rees, Carl Mathews, Milburn Morante, Bob Woodward, Boyd Stockman, George Peters, Tom London, Pierce Lyden, Roy Butler, Post Park, Marshall Reed, Artie Ortego

Director: Lambert Hillyer
Screenplay: Jess Bowers (Adele Buffington)
Producer: Barney Sarecky

CROSSED TRAILS

(Monogram, April 11, 1948) 53 Minutes

Johnny Mack Brown, Raymond Hatton, Lynne Carver, Douglas Evans, Kathy Frye, Zon Murray, Mary MacLaren, Ted Adams, Steve Clark, Frank LaRue, Milburn Morante, Robert D. (Bob) Woodward, Pierce Lyden, Henry Hall, Hugh Murray, Bud Osborne, Artie Ortego, Boyd Stockman

Director: Lambert Hillyer
Screenplay: Colt Remington (probably Adele Buffington)
Producer: Louis Gray

FRONTIER AGENT

(Monogram, May 16, 1948) 56 Minutes

Johnny Mack Brown, Raymond Hatton, Reno Blair, Kenneth MacDonald, Dennis Moore, Riley Hill, Frank LaRue, Ted Adams, Virginia Carroll, William Ruhl, Kansas Moehring, Bill Hale, Lane Bradford, Bob Woodward, Boyd Stockman

Director: Lambert Hillyer
Screenplay: J. Benton Cheney
Producer: Barney Sarecky

TRIGGERMAN

(Monogram, June 20, 1948) 56 Minutes

Johnny Mack Brown, Raymond Hatton, Virginia Carroll, Bill Kennedy, Marshall Reed, Forrest Matthews, Bob Woodward, Dee Cooper

Director: Howard Bretherton
Screenplay: Ronald Davidson
Producer: Barney Sarecky

BACK TRAIL

(Monogram, July 18, 1948) 57 Minutes

Johnny Mack Brown, Raymond Hatton, Mildred Coles, Marshall Reed, James Horne, Snub Pollard, Ted Adams, Pierce Lyden, George Holmes, Bob Woodward, Carol Henry, William Norton Bailey, George Morrell

Director: Christy Cabanne
Screenplay: J. Benton Cheney
Producer: Barney Sarecky

RANGE JUSTICE

(Monogram, August 7, 1948) 57 Minutes

Johnny Mack Brown, Max Terhune, Felice Ingersoll, Fred Kohler, Jr., Tris Coffin, Riley Hill, Sarah Padden, Eddie Parker, Kenne Duncan, Myron Healey, Bill Hale, Bill Potter, Bob Woodward

Director: Ray Taylor
Screenplay: Ronald Davidson
Producer: Barney Sarecky

THE FIGHTING RANGER

(Monogram, August 15, 1948) 57 Minutes

Johnny Mack Brown, Raymond Hatton, Christine Larson, Marshall Reed, Eddie Parker, Charlie Hughes, I. Stanford Jolley, Milburn Morante, Steve Clark, Bob Woodward, Peter Perkins

Director: Lambert Hillyer
Screenplay: Ronald Davidson
Producer: Barney Sarecky

THE SHERIFF OF MEDICINE BOW

(Monogram, October 3, 1948) 55 Minutes

Johnny Mack Brown, Raymond Hatton, Max Terhune, Evelyn Finley, Bill Kennedy, George J. Lewis, Frank LaRue, Peter Perkins, Carol Henry, Bob Woodward, Ted Adams

Director: Lambert Hillyer
Screenplay: J. Benton Cheney
Producer: Barney Sarecky

GUNNING FOR JUSTICE

(Monogram, November 7, 1948) 55 Minutes

Johnny Mack Brown, Raymond Hatton, Max Terhune, Evelyn Finley, I. Stanford Jolley, House Peters, Jr., Bill Potter, Ted Adams, Bud Osborne, Dan White, Bob Woodward, Carol Henry, Boyd Stockman, Dee Cooper, Artie Ortego

Director: Ray Taylor
Screenplay: J. Benton Cheney
Producer: Barney Sarecky

HIDDEN DANGER

(Monogram, December 12, 1948) 55 Minutes

Johnny Mack Brown, Raymond Hatton, Max Terhune, Christine Larson, Myron Healey, Marshall Reed, Kenne Duncan, Steve Clark, Edmund Cobb, Milburn Morante, Carol Henry, Bill Hale, Bob Woodward, Boyd Stockman, Bill Potter

Director: Ray Taylor
Screenplay: J. Benton Cheney, Eliot Gibbons
Producer: Barney Sarecky

LAW OF THE WEST

(Monogram, February 20, 1949) 54 Minutes

Johnny Mack Brown, Max Terhune, Gerry Patterson, Bill Kennedy, Jack Ingram, Riley Hill, Eddie Parker, Marshall Reed, Kenne Duncan, Jack Harrison, Bud Osborne, Steve Clark, Bob Woodward, Frank Ellis

Director: Ray Taylor
Screenplay: J. Benton Cheney
Producer: Barney Sarecky

TRAIL'S END

(Monogram, April 3, 1949) 57 Minutes

Johnny Mack Brown, Max Terhune, Kay Morley, Douglas Evans, Zon Murray, Myron Healey, Keith Richards, George Chesebro, William Norton Bailey, Carol Henry, Boyd Stockman, Eddie Majors

Director: Lambert Hillyer
Screenplay: J. Benton Cheney
Producer: Barney Sarecky

STAMPEDE

(Allied Artists, May 1, 1949) 76 Minutes

Rod Cameron, *Johnny Mack Brown,* Gale Storm, Don Castle, Don Curtis, John Miljan, Jonathan Hale, John Eldridge, Kenne Duncan, Tim Ryan, Steve Clark, Bob Woodward, Duke York, Artie Ortego, Neal Hart

Director: Lesley Selander
Screenplay: John C. Champion, Blake Edwards
Producers: Scoto R. Dunlap, John C. Champion, Blake Edwards

WEST OF ELDORADO

(Monogram, June 15, 1949) 56 Minutes

Johnny Mack Brown, Max Terhune, Reno Browne, Milburn Morante, Teddy Infurh, Terry Frost, Marshall Reed, Boyd Stockman, Kenne Duncan, Bud Osborne, William Norton Bailey, Artie Ortego, Bill Potter, Bob Woodward

Director: Ray Taylor
Screenplay: Adele Buffington
Producer: Barney Sarecky

WESTERN RENEGADES

(Monogram, October 9, 1949) 56 Minutes

Johnny Mack Brown, Max Terhune, Jane Adams, Hugh Prosser, Constance Worth, Riley Hill, Marshall Reed, Steve Clark, Terry Frost, William Ruhl, Myron Healey, John Merton, Marshall Bradford, Milburn Morante, Chuck Roberson, Lane Bradford, Bill Potter, James Harrison, Dee Cooper

Director: Wallace Fox
Screenplay: Adele Buffington
Producer: Eddie Davis

WEST OF WYOMING

(Monogram, February 19, 1950) 57 Minutes

Johnny Mack Brown, Gail Davis, Milburn Morante, Myron Healey, Dennis Moore, Stanley Andrews, Mary Gordon, Carl Mathews, Paul Cramer, John Merton, Mike Ragan (Holly Bane), Steve Clark, Frank McCarroll, Bud Osborne

Director: Wallace Fox
Screenplay: Adele Buffington
Producer: Eddie Davis

OVER THE BORDER

(Monogram, March 12, 1950) 58 Minutes

Johnny Mack Brown, Wendy Waldron, Myron Healey, Pierre Watkin, Frank Jacquet, Marshall Reed, House Peters, Jr., Milburn Morante, Mike Ragan (Holly Bane), Hank Bell, George DeNormand, Bud Osborne, Herman Hack, Buck Bailey, George Sowards, Carol Henry, Ray Jones, Frank McCarroll, Artie Ortego, Bob Woodward

Director/Producer: Wallace Fox
Screenplay: J. Benton Cheney

SIX GUN MESA

(Monogram, April 30, 1950) 56 Minutes

Johnny Mack Brown, Milburn Morante, Gail Davis, Holly Bane, Steve Clark, Carl Mathews, Bud Osborne, Leonard Penn, George DeNormand, Riley Hill, Marshall Reed, Stanley Blystone, Frank Jacquet, Artie Ortego, Merrill McCormack

Director: Wallace Fox
Screenplay: Adele Buffington
Producer: Eddie Davis

LAW OF THE PANHANDLE

(Monogram, September 17, 1950) 55 Minutes

Johnny Mack Brown, Jane Adams, Riley Hill, Marshall Reed, Myron Healey, Ted Adams, Lee Roberts, Kermit Maynard, Carol Henry, Milburn Morante, Bob Duncan, Boyd Stockman, George DeNormand, Tex Palmer, Ray Jones

Director: Lewis Collins
Screenplay: Joseph Poland
Producer: Jerry Thomas

OUTLAW GOLD

(Monogram, November 26, 1950) 56 Minutes

Johnny Mack Brown, Jane Adams, Myron Healey, Milburn Morante, Marshall Reed, Hugh Prosser, Carol Henry, Bud Osborne, George DeNormand, Frank Jacquet, Carl Mathews, Ray Jones, Steve Clark, Bob Woodward, Merrill McCormack

Director: Wallace Fox
Screenplay: Jack Lewis
Producer: Vincent M. Fennelly

SHORT GRASS

(Allied Artists, December 24, 1950) 82 Minutes

Rod Cameron, Cathy Downs, *Johnny Mack Brown,* Raymond Walburn, Alan Hale, Jr., Morris Ankrum, Jonathan Hale, Harry Woods, Marlo Dwyer, Riley Hill, Jeff York, Stanley Andrews, Jack Ingram, Myron Healey, Tris Coffin, Rory Mallison, Felipe Turich, George J. Lewis, Lee Tung Foo, Kermit Maynard, Lee Roberts, Frank Ellis

Director: Lesley Selander
Story/Screenplay: Tom W. Blackburn
Producer: Scott R. Dunlap

COLORADO AMBUSH

(Monogram, January 14, 1951) 51 Minutes

Johnny Mack Brown, Myron Healey, Lois Hall, Tommy Farrell, Christine McIntyre, Lee Roberts, Marshall Bradford, Lyle Talbot, Joe McGuinn, John Hart, Roy Butler, George DeNormand

Director: Lewis Collins
Screenplay: Myron Healey
Producer: Vincent M. Fennelly

MAN FROM SONORA

(Monogram, March 11, 1951) 54 Minutes
Johnny Mack Brown, Phyllis Coates, Lyle Talbot, House Peters, Jr., Lee Roberts, John Merton, Stanley Price, Dennis Moore, Ray Jones, Pierce Lyden, Sam Flint, George DeNormand
Director: Lewis Collins
Screenplay: Maurice Tombragel
Producer: Vincent M. Fennelly

BLAZING BULLETS

(Frontier Pictures/Monogram, May 6, 1951) 51 Minutes
Johnny Mack Brown, Lois Hall, House Peters, Jr., Stanley Price, Dennis Moore, Edmund Cobb, Milburn Morante, Forrest Taylor, Edward Cassidy, George DeNormand, Carl Mathews
Director: Wallace Fox
Screenplay: George Daniels
Producer: Vincent M. Fennelly

MONTANA DESPERADO

(Frontier Pictures/Monogram, June 24, 1951) 51 Mins.
Johnny Mack Brown, Virginia Herrick, Myron Healey, Marshall Reed, Steve Clark, Edmund Cobb, Lee Roberts, Carl Mathews, Ben Dorbett
Director: Wallace Fox
Screenplay: Dan Ullman
Producer: Vincent M. Fennelly

OKLAHOMA JUSTICE

(Monogram, August 19, 1951)
Johnny Mack Brown, James Ellison, Phyllis Coates, Barbara Allen, Kenne Duncan, Lane Bradford, Marshall Reed, Zon Murray, Stanley Price, I. Stanford Jolley, Bruce Edwards, Richard Avonde, Carl Mathews, Edward Cassidy, Lyle Talbot, George DeNormand
Director: Lewis Collins
Screenplay: Joseph O'Donnell
Producer: Vincent M. Fennelly

WHISTLING HILLS

Frontier Pictures/Monogram, October 7, 1951) 58 Mins.
Johnny Mack Brown, Jimmy Ellison, Noel Neill, Lee Roberts, Pamela Duncan, I. Stanford Jolley, Marshall Reed, Bud Osborne, Pierce Lyden, Frank Ellis, Ray Jones, Merrill McCormack
Director: Derwin Abrahams
Screenplay: Fred Myton
Producer: Vincent M. Fennelly

TEXAS LAWMEN

(Frontier Pictures/Monogram, December 2, 1951) 54 Minutes
Johnny Mack Brown, Jimmy Ellison, I. Stanford Jolley, Lee Roberts, Terry Frost, Marshall Reed, John Hart, Lyle Talbot, Pierce Lyden, Stanley Price
Director: Lewis Collins
Screenplay: Joseph Poland
Producer: Vincent M. Fennelly

TEXAS CITY

(Monogram, January 27, 1952)
Johnny Mack Brown, Jimmy Ellison, Lois Hall, Lyle Talbot, Terry Frost, Marshall Reed, Lorna Thayer, Lane Bradford, Pierce Lyden, John Hart, Bud Osborne, Stanley Price
Director: Lewis Collins
Screenplay: Joseph Poland
Producer: Vincent M. Fennelly

MAN FROM THE BLACK HILLS

(Monogram, March 30, 1952) 51 Minutes
Johnny Mack Brown, Jimmy Ellison, Rand Brooks, Lane Bradford, I. Stanford Jolley, Stanley Andrews, Denver Pyle, Ray Bennett, Robert Bray, Florence Lake, Stanley Price, Joel Allen, Bud Osborne, Merrill McCormack, Roy Bucko, Ralph Bucko
Director: Thomas Carr
Screenplay: Joseph O'Donnell
Producer: Vincent M. Fennelly

DEAD MAN'S TRAIL

(Frontier Pictures/Monogram, July 20, 1952) 59 Minutes
Johnny Mack Brown, Jimmy Ellison, Barbara Allen, Lane Bradford, I. Stanford Jolley, Terry Frost, Gregg Barton, Dale Van Sickel, Richard Avonde, Stanley Price
Director: Lewis Collins
Screenplay: Joseph Poland
Producer: Vincent M. Fennelly

CANYON AMBUSH

(Silvermine/Monogram, October 12, 1952) 53 Minutes
Johnny Mack Brown, Phyllis Coates, Lee Roberts, Dennis Moore, Denver Pyle, Pierce Lyden, Hugh Prosser, Marshall Reed, Stanley Price, Bill Koontz, Frank Ellis, Russ Whiteman, Carol Henry, George DeNormand
Director: Lewis Collins
Screenplay: Joseph Poland
Producer: Vincent M. Fennelly

THE MARSHAL'S DAUGHTER

(United Artists, June 26, 1953) 71 Minutes

Hoot Gibson, Laurie Anders, Harry Lauter, Ken Murray, Robert Bray, Bob Duncan, Forrest Taylor, Tom London, Bruce Norman, Cecil Elliott, Bettie Lou Walters, Francis Ford, Julian Upton, Ted Jordan, Lee Phelps, and guest stars: Preston Foster, *Johnny Mack Brown,* Jimmy Wakely, Buddy Baer

Director: William Berke

Screenplay: Bob Duncan

Producer: Ken Murray

REQUIEM FOR A GUNFIGHTER

(Embassy, June 30, 1965) 91 Minutes

(Technicolor) (TechniScope)

Rod Cameron, Stephen McNally, Mike Mazurki, Olive Sturgess, Tim McCoy, *Johnny Mack Brown,* Bob Steele, Lane Chandler, Raymond Hatton, Chet Douglas, Dick Jones, Chris Hughes, Rand Brooks, Dale Van Sickel, Frank Lackteen, Zon Murray, Ronn Delanor, Edmund Cobb, Margo Williams, Doris Spigel, Dick Alexander, Fred Carson, Red Morgan

Director: Spencer G. Bennet

Story: Evans W. Cornell, Guy J. Tedesco

Screenplay: R. Alexander

Producer: Alex Gordon

THE BOUNTY KILLER

(Embassy, July 31, 1965) 92 Minutes

(Technicolor) (TechniScope)

Dan Duryea, Rod Cameron, Audrey Dalton, Richard Arlen, Buster Crabbe, Fuzzy Knight, *Johnny Mack Brown,* Bob Steele, Bronco Billy Anderson, Peter Duryea, Eddie Quillan, Norman Willis, Edmund Cobb, I. Stanford Jolley, Frank Lackteen, Dan White, Grady Sutton, Emory Parnell, Duane Ament, Red Morgan, John Reach, Dolores Domasin, Dudley Ross, Ronn Delanor, Tom Kennedy

Director: Spencer G. Bennet

Screenplay: R. Alexander, Leo Gordon

Producer: Alex Gordon

APACHE UPRISING

(Paramount, January, 1966) 90 Minutes

(Technicolor) (TechniScope)

Rory Calhoun, Corinne Calvet, John Russell, Lon Chaney, Jr., Gene Evans, Richard Arlen, Robert H. Harris, Arthur Hunnicutt, De Forest Kelly, George Chandler, *Johnny Mack Brown,* Jean Parker, Abel Fernandez, Don Barry, Robert Carricart, Paul Daniel

Director: R. G. Springsteen

Screenplay: Harry Sanford

Producer: A. C. Lyles

11 ● RANDOLPH SCOTT

Perpetuator of Western Realism

Randolph Scott made some fine medium-budget Westerns at Paramount in the Thirties that established him as a Western star of some import; they were realistic, adult-oriented stories not dissimilar to those of William S. Hart and Harry Carey in the silent era. Most of them were based on the popular Zane Grey stories. He became a major Western star in the late Forties and the unofficial "King of the Cowboys" during the Fifties, fighting almost a one-man battle to keep the medium-budget Western alive.

Scott was similar to Hart not only in looks but in mannerisms as well. His Westerns, John Wayne notwithstanding, were the most realistic oaters produced during the Fifties, and he had a tremendous adult following. But his films were sometimes too adult, too realistic and too romantic for the young fans, and he was not looked upon and remembered with the same admiration heaped on Saturday matinee heroes like Buck Jones, Ken Maynard, or Gene Autry. That is not to say that kids did not flock to his films, only that he was not a recipient of the hero-worship accorded the "B" stars. But his talent was not to be denied and he eventually surfaced as the chief perpetuator of the action Western after the fall of the "B," winning universal recognition as one of the saddle opera's all-time great performers on the basis of his consistent box office draw. His popularity kept him among the top twenty-five stars for nearly twenty years and gave him tenth place in 1950, eighth place in 1951, and tenth place in 1952 and 1953 in the Motion Picture Herald's poll of popularity based on *all* Hollywood stars, not just the cowboys.

Randolph Scott was christened George Randolph Scott at his birth on January 23, 1903 in Orange, Virginia. He grew up in Charlotte, North Carolina as the only son (he had five sisters) of a prominent family. He was educated in private schools until he entered Georgia Tech, where he excelled in football until an injury forced him to drop the sport. His last two years of college were spent at the University of North Carolina where he majored in textile engineering, preparing to following in his father's footsteps. But he did not take to the work for which he had prepared himself and, after first taking a tour of Europe for a year following his graduation, told his father he was interested in acting. The elder Scott figured he might as well let the boy get it out of his system and gave him a letter of introduction to Howard Hughes, whom he knew slightly.

In California Scott and a friend who accompanied him spent some time acting like tourists and waiting for a chance to see the elusive Hughes. Eventually Hughes did see them and arranged for both to work as extras in George O'Brien's **Sharp Shooters** (Fox, '28). Through Hughes, Scott met Cecil B. DeMille who tested him for an important role in **Dynamite** (MGM, '29), but the results were not good and, at the urging of DeMille, he enrolled in the Pasadena Community Theatre where he studied and worked for two years. He did, however, appear briefly as an extra in **Dynamite** and in **The Virginian** (Par., '29), a film for which he was hired to coach Gary Cooper in speaking with a southern accent. Other extra parts came his way in John Ford's **The Black Watch** (Fox, '29) and Allan

Randolph Scott

Dwan's **The Far Call** (Fox, '29), but in general his chances to emote were few. Giving up on getting anywhere as an actor, Scott was about to depart for a Hawaiian vacation before returning home when he was offered a stage role in "Under a Virginia Moon." It was followed by a flop, "Oh Judge," and then the romantic lead in "The Broken Wing." The latter play was a hit and Scott was offered screen tests by four studios. He accepted Paramount's offer because he wanted to prove the studio had been wrong it its initial rejection of him. He got a seven-year contract but, before signing, did a quickie called **The Women Men Marry** ('31) for a Poverty Row outfit called Headline Pictures.

After being wasted in small roles in **Sky Bride** (Par., '32) and **The Island of Lost Souls** (Par., '32) he got his chance in **Hot Saturday** (Par., '32), a Nancy Carroll starrer. Better roles followed until he was put into the Zane Grey Western, **Wild Horse Mesa** (Par., '33), a re-make of the Jack Holt silent version. Scott proved adept at saddle heroics and in the next two years made seven more medium-budget Westerns based on the novels of Grey. Actually the films belied their modest budgets, for they appeared to be more expensive productions than what they were, thanks to the panoramic and action footage lifted from the earlier Holt features. The deception was carried to the point of having Randolph (and later, Buster Crabbe when he, too, made a series of Zane Grey Westerns for Paramount) dress exactly as Holt had dressed in order to make use of much of the medium- and long-shot footage of Holt in the sound features. Thus, films budgeted at around $90,000 came off looking like $250,000 productions.

Scott was not yet an exclusively Western star and was adding to his acting laurels with films such as **So Red the Rose** (Par., '33), **Roberta** (RKO, '35), **Follow the Fleet** (RKO, '36), and **And Sudden Death** (Par., '36).

Sally Blane and Randolph Scott look off at **Wild Horse Mesa** (Paramount, 1933).

Binnie Barnes and Randolph Scott look for the **Last of the Mohicans** (United Artists, 1936).

He got back in a Western-type role in **Last of the Mohicans** (United Artists, '36). But it was two years before he again hit the saddle as a cowboy in **The Texans** (Par., '38), again a re-make of a Holt Western (**North of '36**), and again with stock footage from several films cannibalized to make the film appear expensively mounted when it wasn't.

In 1939 Scott had a plum role as a lawman in Fox's **Jesse James;** his transition from dramatic actor to the strong, silent avenger of the range was gradually taking shape. **Frontier Marshall** (Fox, '39), in which he plays famed lawman Wyatt Earp, and **Virginia City** (WB, '40) further strengthened his identification with outdoor dramas. But the die was cast with the release of **When the Daltons Rode** (Univ., '40), the block-buster conservatively-budgeted Western directed by George Marshall. It made money and led to a raft of similar modest-budget but technically superior gems by

Universal that often proved more entertaining than the expensively-mounted oaters of the big studios, in spite of the lack of big money and big names.

Mounted with expansiveness as a super-Western of upper-budget proportions, **Western Union** (Fox, '41) displays some of the most eye-catching exterior panoramas in Technicolor photographed to that time. Scott plays an ex-outlaw who joins the outfit stringing telegraph lines in the 1860s between Omaha and Salt Lake City. He took advantage of every opportunity provided and turned in a characterization that advanced his box office rating. It remains one of his best films.

Belle Starr (Fox, '41) finds Scott as Sam Starr, confederate officer turned outlaw, in another action-full, Technicolor, and money-making tale of the wild frontier. A memorable screen experience was his long drawn-out brawl with John Wayne in **The Spoilers** (Univ., '42). And although he scored in such

226

non-Westerns as **Paris Calling** (Univ., '41), **To the Shores of Tripoli** (Fox, '42), **Corvette K–225** (Univ., '43), **Gung Ho** (Univ., '43), **Captain Kidd** (UA, '45) and **Home Sweet Homicide** (Fox, '46), Scott was spending more and more time in the saddle. After 1945 he would make but two non-Westerns. The transition was now complete. Scott joined the ranks of those reverently or disparagingly labeled "cowboys," joining a genre that claimed such hallowed names as Jones, Mix, Hart, Maynard, Steele, and McCoy. Fast and furious Scott horse operas turned out on relatively modest budgets in the late Forties, released with no special fanfare and made with skill and craftsmanship, proved thoroughly satisfactory to audiences and made good money.

In 1946 Scott teamed with Nat Holt to co-produce his own Westerns. It was a profitable venture, as **Abilene Town** (UA, '46), **Trail Street** (RKO, '47), **Return of the Badmen** (RKO, '48), **Fighting Man of the Plains** (Fox, '49), **Canadian Pacific** (Fox, '49), **The Cariboo Trail** (Fox, '50), and **Rage at Dawn** (RKO, '55) all made lots of money. But it was the Scott-Harry Joe Brown co-production team that walked away with even greater Western honors, beginning in the Forties with **The Gunfighters** ('47), **Coroner Creek** ('48), **The Walking Hills** ('49), and extending through the Fifties with **Ten Wanted Men** ('55), **A Lawless Street** ('55), **Seventh Cavalry** ('56), **The Tall T** ('57), **Buchanan Rides Alone** ('58), **Ride Lonesome** ('59), and **Comanche Station** ('60). All the Scott-Brown films were released through Columbia. Budd Boetticher piloted Randy through seven of them and his competency as a director contributed much to the success of the films, although the part played by good screenplays, able casts, superb photography, pleasant musical scores, intelligent editing, and Scott's own personal magnetism are not to be denied.

With the completion of **Comanche Station** (Col., '60) Scott retired to pursue his various business interests, which reportedly have put him into the $100 million wealth category. But in 1962 he was enticed out of retirement for one last fling, a co-starring effort with old friend Joel McCrea in MGM's **Ride the High Country.** What was supposed to have been merely a run-of-the-mill oater became a Western classic and won acclaim as one of the best pictures of the decade. Scott's performance as the "good lawman turned slightly bad" has been considered his finest portrayal in a long, distinguished career, certainly a fitting farewell movie for one of Hollywood's top money makers who earned the right to stand alongside the other great cowboys of Western filmdom.

Randolph Scott in **A Lawless Street** (Columbia, 1955).

RANDOLPH SCOTT Filmography

SHARP SHOOTERS
(Fox, January 15, 1928) 6 Reels
George O'Brien, Lois Moran, Noah Young, Tom Dugan, William Demarest, Gwen Lee, Josef Swickard, *Randolph Scott* (unbilled)
Director: J. G. Blystone
Scenario: Marion Orth
Story: Randall H. Faye

THE FAR CALL
(Fox, April 28, 1929) 6 Reels, 75 Minutes (Sound)
Charles Morton, Leila Hyams, Arthur Stone, Warren Hymer, Dan Wolheim, Stanley J. Sandford, Ulrich Haupt, Charles Middleton, Pat Hartigan, Charles Gorman, Ivan Linow, Harry Gripp, Sam Baker, Bernard Siegel, Willie Fung, Frank Chew, *Randolph Scott*
Director: Allan Dwan
Scenario: Seton I. Miller
Adaptation: Walter Woods
Story: Edison Marshall

THE BLACK WATCH

(Fox, May 8, 1929) 10 Reels, 93 Minutes
Victor McLaglen, Myrna Loy, David Rollins, Lumsden Hare, Roy D'Arcy, Mitchell Lewis, Cyril Chadwick, Claude King, Francis Ford, Walter Long, David Torrence, Frederick Sullivan, Richard Travers, Pat Somerset, David Percy, Joseph Diskay, *Randolph Scott* (unbilled extra)
Director: John Ford
Screenplay: John Stone
Story: Talbot Mundy - "King of the Khyber Rifles"

THE VIRGINIAN

(Paramount, November 9, 1929) 8717 feet
Gary Cooper, Walter Huston, Richard Arlen, Mary Brian, Chester Conklin, Eugene Pallette, E. H. Calvert, Helen Ware, Vic Potel, Tex Young, Charles Stevens, Jack Pennick, George Chandler, Willie Fung, George Morrell, Ernie Adams, Ethan Laidlaw, Ed Brady, Bob Kortman, James Mason, Fred Burns, Nena Quartero, *Randolph Scott* (unbilled)
Director: Victor Fleming
Story: Owen Wister
Screenplay: Howard Estabrook
Titles: Joseph L. Mankiewicz
Assistant Director: Henry Hathaway
Producer: Louis D. Lighton

DYNAMITE

(MGM, December 13, 1929) 14 Reels (Sound)
Kay Johnson, Charles Bickford, Conrad Nagel, Julia Faye, Muriel McCormack, Joel McCrea, Robert Edeson, William Holden, Henry Stockridge, Leslie Fenton, Barton Hepburn, Ernest Hilliard, June Nash, Nancy Dover, Neely Edwards, Jerry Zier, Rita LeRoy, Tyler Brooke, Clarence Burton, James Farley, Robert T. Haines, Douglas Frazer Scott, Jane Keckley, Blanche Craig, Mary Gordon, Ynez Seabury, Scott Kolk, Fred Walton, *Randolph Scott* (unbilled extra)
Director/Producer: Cecil B. DeMille
Story/Screenplay: Jeanie Macpherson

THE WOMEN MEN MARRY

(Headline Pictures, March 25, 1931) 7 Reels, 67 Minutes
Sally Blane, Natalie Moorhead, Kenneth Harlan, Crauford Kent, Jean De Val, James Aubrey, *Randolph Scott*
Director: Charles Hutchison
Adaptation: John Francis Natteford

SKY BRIDE

(Paramount, April 28, 1932) 78 Minutes, 8 Reels
Virginia Bruce, Frances Dee, Richard Arlen, Jack Oakie, Charles Starrett, Robert Coogan, Louise Closser Hare, Tom Douglas, Harold Goodwin, *Randolph Scott*
Director: Stephen Roberts
Screenplay: Joseph I. Mankiewicz, Agnes Brand Leahy, Grover Jones
Story: Waldermar Young

A SUCCESSFUL CALAMITY

(Warner Brothers, September 17, 1932) 73 Minutes
George Arliss, Mary Astor, Evelyn Knapp, Grant Mitchell, David Torrence, William Janney, Hardie Albright, *Randolph Scott,* Hale Hamilton, Fortunio Bonanova, Nola Luxford, Murray Kinnell, Richard Tucker, Barbara Leonard, Harold Minjur, Harold Waycoff
Director: John G. Adolfi
Adaptation: Austin Parker, Maude Howell, Julian Josephson
Story: Clare Kommer

HERITAGE OF THE DESERT

(Paramount, September 30, 1932) 63 Minutes
Randolph Scott, Sally Blane, Vince Barnett, Guinn Williams, J. Farrell MacDonald, David Landau, Gordon Westcott, Susan Fleming, Charles Stevens, Fred Burns
Director: Henry Hathaway
Story: Zane Grey
Screenplay: Harold Shumate, Frank Partos

HOT SATURDAY

(Paramount, October 27, 1932) 74 Minutes
Nancy Carroll, Cary Grant, *Randolph Scott,* Edward Woods, Lillian Bond, William Collier, Sr., Jane Darwell, Rita LaRoy, Rose Coghlan, II, Oscar Apfel, Grady Sutton, Stanley Smith, Jessie Arnold, Egon Brecher
Director: William Seiter
Screenplay: Seton I. Miller
Adaptation: Josephine Lovett, Joseph Moncure March
Story: Harvey Ferguson

WILD HORSE MESA

(Paramount, November 25, 1932) 65 Minutes
Randolph Scott, Sally Blane, Fred Kohler, James Bush, George Hayes, Charley Grapewin, Buddy Roosevelt, Lucille LaVerne, Jim Thorpe, E. H. Calvert
Director: Henry Hathaway
Story: Zane Grey
Screenplay: Frank Clark, Harold Shumate

THE ISLAND OF LOST SOULS
(Paramount, December 29, 1932) 84 Minutes
Charles Laughton, Bela Lugosi, Richard Arlen, Leila Hyams, Kathleen Burke, Arthur Hohl, Stanley Fields, Robert Kortman, Tetsu Komai, Hans Steinke, Harry Ekezian, Rosemary Grimes, Paul Hurst, George Irving, Joe Bonomo, Constantine Romanoff, Jack Burdette, Robert Milasch, Duke York, Buster Brody, John George, Jack Walters, Bob Kerr, *Randolph Scott,* Evangelus Berbas
Director: Erle C. Kenton
Screenplay: Waldermar Young, Philip Wylie
Story: H. G. Wells - "The Island of Dr. Moreau"

HELLO EVERYBODY!
(Paramount, February 16, 1933) 76 Minutes
Sally Blane, Julia Swayne Gordon, *Randolph Scott,* Jerry Tucker, Marguerite Campbell, William Davidson, George Barbier, Paul Kruger, Charley Grapewin, Fern Emmett, Irving Bacon, Ted Collins, Frank Darien, Edwards Davis, Russell Simpson
Director: William A. Seiter
Screenplay: Dorothy Yost and Lawrence Hazard
Story: Fannie Hurst

THE THUNDERING HERD
(Paramount, March 1, 1933) 59 Minutes
(Reissued as "Buffalo Stampede")
Randolph Scott, Judith Allen, Barton MacLane, Harry Carey, Larry "Buster" Crabbe, Dick Rush, Frank Rice, Buck Connors, Charles Murphy, Noah Beery, Sr., Raymond Hatton, Blanche Frederici, Monte Blue, Al Bridge
Director: Henry Hathaway
Story: Zane Grey
Screenplay: Jack Cunningham, Mary Flannery

MURDERS IN THE ZOO
(Paramount, March 30, 1933) 66 Minutes
Charles Ruggles, Gail Patrick, Lionel Atwill, *Randolph Scott,* John Lodge, Kathleen Burke, Harry Beresford, Edward McWade
Director: Edward Sutherland
Screenplay: Philip Wylie and Seton I. Miller

SUPERNATURAL
(Paramount, May 4, 1933) 64 Minutes
Carole Lombard, Vivienne Osborne, *Randolph Scott,* Alan Dinehart, H. B. Warner, Beryl Mercer, William Farnum, Willard Robertson, George Burr MacAnnan, Lyman Williams
Director: Victor Halperin
Producers: Victor and Edward Halperin
Story/Adaptation: Garnett Weston
Screenplay: Harvey Thew, Brian Marlow

SUNSET PASS
(Paramount, May 26, 1933) 61 Minutes
Randolph Scott, Tom Keene, Kathleen Burke, Harry Carey, Fuzzy Knight, Noah Beery, Vince Barnett, Kent Taylor, Tom London, Pat Farley, Charles Middleton, Bob Kortman, James Mason, Frank Beal, Al Bridge, Leila Bennett, Nelson McDowell, George Barbier, Patricia Farley, Christian J. Frank
Director: Henry Hathaway
Story: Zane Grey
Screenplay: Jack Cunningham, Gerald Geraghty

COCKTAIL HOUR
(Columbia, May 29, 1933) 74 Minutes
Bebe Daniels, *Randolph Scott,* Muriel Kirkland, Jessie Ralph, Sidney Blackmer, Barry Norton, Phillips Smalley, Marjorie Gateson, George Nardelli, Larry Steers, Jay Eaton, Willie Fong, Paul McVey, Oscar Smith
Director: Victor Schertzinger
Screenplay: Gertrude Purcell, Richard Schayer
Story: James K. McGuinnes

MAN OF THE FOREST
(Paramount, August 25, 1933) 62 Minutes
Randolph Scott, Harry Carey, Verna Hillie, Noah Beery, Larry "Buster" Crabbe, Barton MacLane, Guinn Williams, Vince Barnett, Blanche Frederici, Tempe Piggot, Tom Kennedy, Frank McGlynn, Jr., Duke Lee, Lew Kelly, Merrill McCormack
Director: Henry Hathaway
Story: Zane Grey
Screenplay: Jack Cunningham, Harold Shumate

BROKEN DREAMS
(Monogram, January 15, 1934) 70 Minutes
Randolph Scott, Martha Sleeper, Beryl Mercer, Joseph Cawthorne, Buster Phelps, Charlotte Meriam, Sidney Bracy, Adele St. Maur, Phyllis Lee, Martin Burton, Finis Barton, Edward Le Saint, Sam Flint, George Nash
Producer: Ben Verschleiser
Director: Robert Vignola
Story: Olga Printzlau
Screenplay: Maude Fulton

THE LAST ROUNDUP
(Paramount, May 1, 1934) 65 Minutes
Randolph Scott, Barbara Fritchie, Barton MacLane, Fuzzy Knight, Monte Blue, Charles Middleton, Richard Carle, Dick Rush, Ben Corbett, Fred Kohler, James Mason, Bud Osborne, Bob Miles, Buck Connors, Frank Rice, Jim Corey, Sam Allen, Jack M. Holmes
Director: Henry Hathaway
Story: "The Border Legion" - Zane Grey
Screenplay: Jack Cunningham

WAGON WHEELS

(Paramount, September 15, 1934) 56 Minutes

Randolph Scott, Gail Patrick, Billie Lee, Leila Bennett, Jan Duggan, Monte Blue, Raymond Hatton, Olin Howland, J. P. McGowan, James Marcus, Helen Hunt, James Kenton, Alfred Delcambre, John Marston, Sam McDaniels, Howard Wilson, Michael Visaroff, Julian Madison, Eldred Tidbury, E. Alyn Warren, Pauline Moore

Director: Charles Barton
Story: "Fighting Caravans" - Zane Grey
Screenplay: Jack Cunningham, Charles Logan, Carl A. Buss

HOME ON THE RANGE

(Paramount, February 1, 1935) 65 Minutes

Randolph Scott, Ann Sheridan, Dean Jagger, Jackie Coogan, Fuzzy Knight, Ralph Remley, Philip Morris, Frances Sayles, Addison Richards, Clarence Sherwood, Evelyn Brent, Allen Wood, Howard Wilson, Albert Hart, Richard Carle

Director: Arthur Jacobson
Story: Zane Grey
Screenplay: Harold Shumate
Producer: Harold Hurley

ROBERTA

(RKO, February 26, 1935) 12 Reels

Irene Dunne, Fred Astaire, Ginger Rogers, *Randolph Scott,* Helen Westley, Claire Dodd, Victor Varconi, Luis Alberni, Ferdinand Munier, Torben Meyer, Adrian Roseley, Bodil Rosing

Producer: Pandro S. Berman
Director: William A. Seiter
Screenplay: Jane Murfin, Sam Mintz, Allan Scott
Based on the musical play: "Roberta" by Otto Harbach

ROCKY MOUNTAIN MYSTERY

(Paramount, March 1, 1935) 63 Minutes

Randolph Scott, Charles (Chic) Sale, Mrs. Leslie Carter, Kathleen Burke, George Marion, Sr., Ann Sheridan, James C. Eagles, Howard Wilson, Willie Fung, Florence Roberts

Director: Charles Barton
Story: Zane Grey - "Golden Dreams"
Screenplay: Edward E. Paramore, Jr., Ethel Doherty
Producer: Harold Hurley

VILLAGE TALE

(RKO, May 10, 1935) 80 Minutes

Randolph Scott, Kay Johnson, Arthur Hohl, Robert Barrat, Janet Beecher, Edward Ellis, Dorothy Burgess, Andy Clyde, Guinn "Big Boy" Williams, Ray Mayer, T. Roy Barnes, DeWitt Jennings

Director: John Cromwell
Screenplay: Allan Scott
Story: Phil Strong

SHE

(RKO, July 12, 1935) 95 Minutes

Randolph Scott, Helen Gahagan, Helen Mack, Nigel Bruce, Gustav von Seyfferitz, Lumsden Hare, Samuel S. Hinds, Noble Johnson, Jim Thorpe

Producer: Merian C. Cooper
Directors: Irving Pichel, Lansing C. Holden
Adaptation: Ruth Rose
Story: H. Rider Haggard

SO RED THE ROSE

(Paramount, November 22, 1935) 82 Minutes

Margaret Sullavan, *Randolph Scott,* Walter Connolly, Elizabeth Patterson, Janet Beecher, Harry Ellebe, Dickie Moore, Robert Cummings, Charles Starrett, Johnny Downs, Daniel Haynes, Clarence Muse, James Burke, Warner Richmond, Alfred Delcambre

Director: King Vidor
Screenplay: Lawrence Stallings, Maxwell Anderson, Edwin Justus Mayer
Story: Stark Young
Producer: Douglas McLean

PIRATE PARTY ON CATALINA ISLE

(MGM, January 3, 1936) 2 Reels (Technicolor)

Chester Morris, Buddy Rogers and His California Cavaliers, Cary Grant, *Randolph Scott,* Marion Davies, Mickey Rooney, Virginia Bruce, Errol Flynn, Lily Damita, Leon Errol, Robert Armstrong, Sid Silvers, Lee Tracy, Jack Duffy, Vince Barnett, Eddie Peabody, Johnny Downs, Betty Burgess

Producer: Louis Lewyn
Continuity/Dialogue: Alexander Van Dorn

FOLLOW THE FLEET

(RKO, February 20, 1936) 110 Minutes

Fred Astaire, Ginger Rogers, *Randolph Scott,* Harriet Hilliard, Astrid Allwyn, Ray Mayer, Harry Beresford, Addison Randall, Russell Hicks, Brooks Benedict, Lucille Ball, Betty Grable, Joy Hodges, Jennie Gray, Tony Martin, Maxine Jennings, Edward Burns, John Hamilton, Frank Jenks

Director: Mark Sandrich
Story: Hubert Osborne - from play "Shore Leave" as produced by David Belasco
Screenplay: Dwight Taylor, Allan Scott
Producer: Pandro S. Berman

AND SUDDEN DEATH

(Paramount, June 19, 1936) 67 Minutes

Randolph Scott, Frances Drake, Tom Brown, Billie Lee, Fuzzy Knight, Terry Walker, Porter Hall, Charles Quigley, Joseph Sawyer, Oscar Apfel, Maidel Turner, Charles Arnt, Jimmy Conlin, John Hyams, Herbert Evans, Don Rowan, Wilma Francis

Director: Charles Barton
Story: Theodore Reeves, Madeleine Ruthven
Screenplay: Joseph Moncure March

THE LAST OF THE MOHICANS

(United Artists, September 4, 1936) 91 Minutes
Randolph Scott, Binnie Barnes, Henry Wilcoxon, Bruce Cabot, Heather Angel, Philip Reed, Robert Barrat, Hugh Buckler, Willard Robertson, Frank McGlynn, Sr., Will Stanton, William V. Mong, Olaf Hyten Hare, Reginald Barlow, Lionel Belmore
Director: George B. Seitz
Story: James Fenimore Cooper
Screenplay: Philip Dunne
Producer: Edward Small

HIGH, WIDE AND HANDSOME

(Paramount, October 10, 1937) 112 Minutes
Randolph Scott, Irene Dunne, Dorothy Lamour, Elizabeth Patterson, Raymond Walburn, Akim Tamiroff, Charles Bickford, Ben Blue, William Frawley, Alan Hale, Irving Pichel, Stanley Andrews, James Burke, Roger Imhoff, Lucien Littlefield, Purnell Pratt, Edward Gargan
Producer: Arthur Hornblow
Director: Rouben Mamoulian
Story/Screenplay: Oscar Hammerstein, II

REBECCA OF SUNNYBROOK FARM

(20th Century-Fox, March 18, 1938) 80 Minutes
Shirley Temple, Gloria Stuart, *Randolph Scott,* Jack Haley, Phyllis Brooks, Helen Westley, Slim Summerville, Bill Robinson, J. Edward Bromberg, Alan Dinehart, Dixie Dunbar, Raymond Scott Quintet, Paul Hurst, William Demarest, Ruth Gillette, Paul Harvey, Clarence H. Wilson, Sam Hayes, Gary Breckner, Carroll Nye, Franklin Pangborn, William Wagner, Eily Malyon, Mary McCarty
Director: Allan Dwan
Screenplay: Karl Tunbert, Don Ettinger
Story: Kate Douglas Wiggin

COAST GUARD

(Columbia, August 4, 1939) 71 Minutes
Randolph Scott, Frances Dee, Ralph Bellamy, Walter Connolly, Warren Hymer, Robert Middlemass, Stanley Andrews, Edmund MacDonald, Lloyd Whitlock, Ray Mala, John Tyrrell, Lorna Gray (Adrian Booth), Beatrice Curtis, Don Beddoe, Marla Shelton, Claire DuBrey, Lee Phelps, Harry Strang, James Millican, Ann Doran, Adrian Morris, Bob Watson, J. Farrell Mac-Donald, Harry Tyler, Beryl Wallace, Ned Glass, Ray Bailey
Director: Edward Ludwig
Screenplay: Richard Maibaum, Albert Duffy, Harry Segall

THE TEXANS

(Paramount, August 12, 1938) 92 Minutes
Randolph Scott, Joan Bennett, May Robson, Walter Brennan, Robert Cummings, Robert Barrat, Harvey Stephens, Francis Ford, Raymond Hatton, Clarence Wilson, Jack Moore, Chris-Pin Martin, Anna Demetrio, Richard Tucker, Ed Gargan, Otis Harlan, Spencer Charters, Archie Twitchell, William Haade, Irving Bacon, Bill Roberts, Francis MacDonald, William B. Davidson, Jack Perrin, Richard Denning, John Qualen, Ester Howard, Philip Morris, Harry Woods, Wheeler Oakman, Dutch Hendrian, Vera Steadman, Kay Whitehead, Ralph Remley, Frank Cordell, Ernie Adams, Edward LeSaint, Ed Brady, Scoop Martin, Oscar Smith, James Quinn, Everett Brown, Margaret McWade, Virginia Jennings, Jim Burtis, Lon Poff, Laurie Lane
Director: James Hogan
Story: "North of '36" - Emerson Hough
Screenplay: Bertrand Millhauser, Paul Sloane, William Wister Haines
Producer: Lucien Hubbard

JESSE JAMES

(20th C.-Fox, January 27, 1939) 105 Minutes
(Technicolor)
Tyrone Power, Henry Fonda, Nancy Kelly, *Randolph Scott,* Henry Hull, Slim Summerville, J. Edward Bromberg, Brian Donlevy, John Carradine, Donald Meek, John Russell, Jane Darwell, George Chandler, Charles Tannen, Claire Dubrey, Willard Robertson, Harold Goodwin, Ernest Whitman, Eddy Waller, Paul Burns, Spencer Charters, Arthur Aylesworth, Charles Middleton, Charles Halton, Harry Tyler, Virginia Brissac, Edward J. LeSaint, John Elliott, Erville Alderson, George Breakston, Lon Chaney, Jr., Ernest Whitman, James Flavin, Harry Holman, Wylie Grant, Ethan Laidlaw, Don Douglas, George O'Hara
Director: Henry King
Screenplay/Producer: Nunnally Johnson

SUSANNAH OF THE MOUNTIES

(20th C.-Fox, June 23, 1939) 78 Minutes (SepiaTone)
Shirley Temple, *Randolph Scott,* Margaret Lockwood, Martin Good Rider, J. Farrell MacDonald, Maurice Moscovich, Moroni Olson, Victor Jory, Lester Matthews, Leyland Hodges, Herbert Evans, Jack Luden, Charles Irwin, John Sutton, Chief Big Tree
Director: William A. Seiter
Story: Muriel Denison - "Susannah, A Little Girl of the Mounties"
Screenplay: Fidel La Barba, Walter Ferris, Robert Ellis, Helen Logan
Producer: Kenneth MacGowan

FRONTIER MARSHAL

(20th C.-Fox, July 28, 1939) 71 Minutes

Randolph Scott, Nancy Kelly, Cesar Romero, Binnie Barnes, John Carradine, Edward Norris, Eddie Foy, Jr., Ward Bond, Lon Chaney, Jr., Tom Tyler, Joe Sawyer, Del Henderson, Harry Hayden, Harlan Briggs, Dick Alexander, Harry Woods, Dick Cramer, Dick Elliott, Hank Bell

Director: Allan Dwan
Story: "Wyatt Earp, Frontier Marshal" - Stuart Lake
Screenplay: Sam Hellman
Producer: Sol Wurtzel

20,000 MEN A YEAR

(20th C.-Fox, October 27, 1939) 83 Minutes

Randolph Scott, Margaret Lindsay, Preston Foster, George Ernest, Maxie Rosenbloom, Robert Shaw, Mary Healy, Jane Darwell, Kane Richmond, Douglas Wood, Sen Yung, Paul Stanton, Tom Seidel, Edward Gargan, Harry Tyler, Sidney Miller, Edwin Stanley, Holmes Herbert, George Chandler, Selmer Jackson, Carl Stockdale, Harrison Greene, Robert Sherwood, Dave Morris, Matt McHugh, Iva Stewart, The Brewster Twins, Paul Mintz

Director: Alfred E. Green
Screenplay: Lou Breslow and Owen Frances
Story: Frank Wead

VIRGINIA CITY

(Warner Bros., March 23, 1940) 121 Minutes

Errol Flynn, Miriam Hopkins, *Randolph Scott,* Humphrey Bogart, Frank McHugh, Alan Hale, Guinn (Big Boy) Williams, John Litel, Douglass Dumbrille, Moroni Olson, Russell Hicks, Dickie Jones, Frank Wilcox, Russell Simpson, Victor Killian, Charles Middleton

Director: Michael Curtiz
Screenplay: Robert Henry Buckner
Associate Producer: Robert Fellows

MY FAVORITE WIFE

(RKO, May 17, 1940) 121 Minutes

Randolph Scott, Irene Dunne, Cary Grant, Gail Patrick, Ann Shoemaker, Scotty Beckett, Mary Lou Harrington, Donald MacBride, Hugh O'Connell, Granville Bates, Pedro de Cordoba, Brandon Tynan, Leon Belasco, Harold Gerard, Murray Alper, Earl Hodgins, Clive Morgan, Florence Dudley, Cy Ring, Jean Acker, Bert Moorhouse, Joe Cabrillas, Frank Marlow, Thelma Joel, Horace MacMahon, Chester Clute, Cy Kendall, Franco Corsaro, Eli Schmudkler

Director: Garson Kanin
Screenplay: Sam and Bella Spewack
Story: Sam and Bella Spewack and Leo McCarey

WHEN THE DALTONS RODE

(Universal, July 26, 1940) 80 Minutes

Randolph Scott, Kay Francis, Brian Donlevy, George Bancroft, Broderick Crawford, Andy Devine, Stuart Erwin, Frank Albertson, Mary Gordon, Harvey Stevens, Edgar Dearing, Quen Ramsey, Bob McKenzie, Dorothy Granger, Fay McKenzie, Walter Sodering, Mary Ainslee, Erville Alderson, Sally Payne, June Wiklins

Director: George Marshall
Story: "When The Daltons Rode" - Emmett Dalton, Jack Jungmeyer, Sr.
Screenplay: Harold Shumate

PARIS CALLING

(Universal, January 16, 1941) 96 Minutes

Randolph Scott, Elizabeth Bergner, Basil Rathbone, Eduardo Ciannelli, Gale Sondergaard, Lee J. Cobb, Elizabeth Risdon, Charles Arnt, Georges Renavent, William Edmunds, Patrick O'Malley, Georges Hataxa, Paul Leyssac, Paul Bryar, Otto Reichow, Adolph Milar Marion Murray, Grace Lenard, Yvette Bentley, Marcia Ralston, Gene Garrick, Pedro de Cordoba, Ian Wolfe, Rosalind Ivan, Mary Forbes, Howard Hickman, Edward Emerson, Harlan Briggs, Crauford Kent, Philip Van Zandt, Jeff Corey, Roland Varno, Norma Drury, Richard Alexander, Eddie Dew, Eric Alden

Director: Edwin L. Martin
Screenplay: Benjamin Glazer and Charles S. Kaufman
Story: Benjamin Glazer, Charles S. Kaufman, John S. Toldy

WESTERN UNION

(20th Century-Fox, February 21, 1941) 94 Minutes

Robert Young, *Randolph Scott,* Dean Jagger, Virginia Gilmore, John Carradine, Slim Summerville, Chill Wills, Barton MacLane, Russell Hicks, Victor Kilian, Minor Watson, George Chandler, Chief Big Tree, Chief Thunder Cloud, Dick Rich, Harry Strange, Charles Middleton, Addison Richards, Irving Bacon

Director: Fritz Lang
Story: Zane Grey
Screenplay: Robert Carson
Associate Producer: Harry Joe Brown

BELLE STARR

(20th Century-Fox, September 12, 1941) 87 Minutes
Randolph Scott, Gene Tierney, Dana Andrews, John Sheppard, Elizabeth Patterson, Chill Wills, Louise Beavers, Olin Howlin, Paul Burns, Joseph Sawyer, Joseph Downing, Howard Hickman, Charles Trowbridge, James Flavin, Charles Middleton, Clarence Muse, George Melford, Mae Marsh, Herbert Ashley, Norman Willis, Billy Wayne, George Reed, Davidson Clark, Hugh Chapman, Clinton Rosemond
Director: Irvin Cummings
Story: Niven Busch, Cameron Rogers
Screenplay: Lamar Trotti
Associate Producer: Kenneth MacGowan

THE SPOILERS

(Universal, April 10, 1942) 87 Minutes
Marlene Dietrich, *Randolph Scott*, John Wayne, Margaret Lindsay, Harry Carey, Richard Barthelmess, William Farnum, George Cleveland, Samuel S. Hinds, Russell Simpson, Marietta Canty, Jack Norton, Ray Bennett, Forrest Taylor, Art Miles, Charles McMurphy, Charles Halton, Bud Osborne, Robert W. Service
Director: Ray Enright
Story: Rex Beach
Screenplay: Tom Reed
Producer: Frank Lloyd

PITTSBURGH

(Universal, December 11, 1942) 93 Minutes
John Wayne, *Randolph Scott,* Marlene Dietrich, Frank Craven, Louise Allbritton, Shemp Howard, Thomas Gomez, Ludwig Stossel, Samuel S. Hinds, Paul Fix, William Haade, Douglas Fowley, Sammy Stein, Harry Seymour, Charles C. Coleman, Nestor Paiva, Hobart Cavanaugh, Virginia Sale, Wade Boteler, Mira McKinney, Alphonse Mortell, Charles Sherlock, Bess Flowers, Harry Cording, Ray Walker, Charles Arnt, William Gould, John Dilson
Director: Lewis Seiler
Screenplay: Kenneth Gamet, Tom Reed, John Twist
Story: George Owen, Tom Reed

THE DESPERADOES

(Columbia, May 25, 1943) 85 Minutes (Technicolor)
Randolph Scott, Glenn Ford, Claire Trevor, Edgar Buchanan, Guinn (Big Boy) Williams, Evelyn Keyes, Raymond Walburn, Porter Hall, Joan Woodbury, Bernard Nedell, Irving Beacon, Glenn Strange, Ethan Laidlaw, Slim Whitaker, Edward Pawley, Chester Clute, Bill Wolfe, Francis Ford, Tom Smith, Jack Kinney, Silver Harr
Director: Charles Vidor
Story: Max Brand
Screenplay: Robert Carson
Producer: Harry Joe Brown

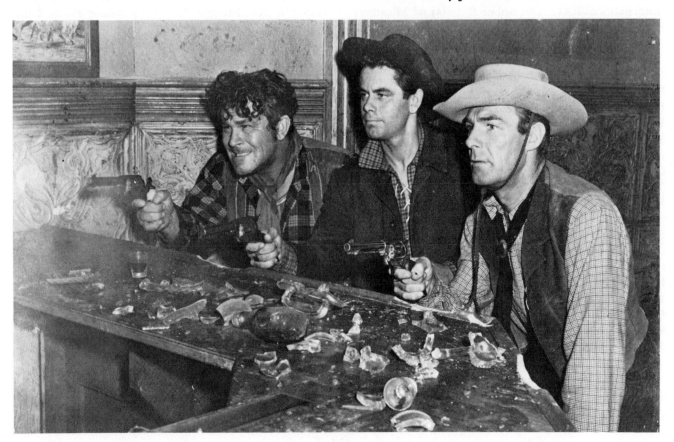

Guinn (Big Boy) Williams, Glenn Ford and Randolph Scott blast away at **The Desperadoes** (Columbia, 1943).

233

CORVETTE K-225

(Universal, September 27, 1943) 99 Minutes

Randolph Scott, Ella Raines, James Brown, Barry Fitzgerald, Andy Devine, Fuzzy Knight, Noah Beery, Jr., Richard Lane, Thomas Gomez, David Bruce, Murray Alper, James Flavin, Walter Sande, Robert Mitchum, Rex Lease, Edmund McDonald, Charles McGraw, Milburn Stone, Jimmie Dodd, Matt Willis, Johnny James, Oliver Blake, Oscar O'Shea, William Forrest, Grandon Rhodes, Ian Wolfe, John Elliott, Peter Lawford, Frank Faylen, Jack Mulhall, George O'Hanlon, John Diggs, Gene O'Donnell, Holmes Herbert, John Frederick, Charles R. Cane, John Mylong, Addison Richards

Director: Richard Rosson

Story/Screenplay: John Rhodes Sturdy

GUNG HO

(Universal, December 20, 1943) 88 Minutes

Randolph Scott, Grace McDonald, Noah Beery, Jr., David Bruce, Sam Levene, J. Carrol Naish, Richard Lane, Milburn Stone, Walter Sande, Louis Jean Heydt, Robert Mitchum, Rod Cameron, Harold London

Director: Ray Enright

Story: W. S. LeFrancois

Screenplay: Lucien Hubbard and Joseph Hoffman

BELLE OF THE YUKON

(International/RKO, December 6, 1944) 84 Minutes

Randolph Scott, Gypsy Rose Lee, Dinah Shore, Bob Burns, Charles Winninger, William Marshall, Guinn "Big Boy" Williams, Robert Armstrong, Florence Bates, Edward Fielding, Wanda McKay, Charles Soldani, Jack Perrin

Director/Producer: William A. Seiter

Story: Houston Branch

Screenplay: James Edward Grant

CHINA SKY

(RKO, April 21, 1945) 78 Minutes

Randolph Scott, Ruth Warrick, Ellen Drew, Anthony Quinn, Carol Thurston, Richard Loo, "Ducky" Looie, Philip Ahn, Benson Fong, H. T. Tsiang, Chin Kuang Chow, James Leong, Jimmy Luno, Gerald Lee, Chung Owen Song, Bob Chinn, Lane Tom, Jr., Harold Fong, Jung Lim, Moy Ming, Audrey Chow, Kermit Maynard, Weaver Levy, Charles Long, Albert Low

Director: Ray Enright

Screenplay: Brenda Weisberg

Story: Pearl S. Buck

CAPTAIN KIDD

(United Artists, August 24, 1945) 89 Minutes

Charles Laughton, *Randolph Scott,* Barbara Britton, John Carradine, Gilbert Roland, Reginald Owen, John Qualen, Henry Daniell, Sheldon Leonard, William Farnum, Abner Biberman, Reginald Sheffield, Edgar Norton, Clifford Brooke, Keith Hitchcock, Frederick Warlock, Ray Teal

Director: Rowland V. Lee

Screenplay: Norman Reilly Raine

Story: Robert N. Lee

ABILENE TOWN

(United Artists, January 11, 1946) 89 Minutes

Randolph Scott, Ann Dvorak, Edgar Buchanan, Rhonda Fleming, Lloyd Bridges, Helen Boyce, Howard Freeman, Richard Hale, Jack Lambert, Hank Patterson, Dick Curtis, Eddy Waller, Buddy Roosevelt

Director: Edwin L. Marin

Story: "Trail Town" - Ernest Haycox

Screenplay: Harold Shumate

Producer: Jules Levey

BADMAN'S TERRITORY

(RKO, April 22, 1946) 98 Minutes

Randolph Scott, Ann Richards, George Hayes, Lawrence Tierney, Tom Tyler, John Halloran, Phil Warren, Steve Brodie, William Moss, James Warren, Isabell Jewell, Morgan Conway, Nestor Paiva, Chief Thunder Cloud, Ray Collins, Virginia Sale, Andrew Tombes, Harry Holman, Richard Hale, Emory Parnell, Ethan Laidlaw, Kermit Maynard, Bud Osborne, Chuck Hamilton, Buddy Roosevelt

Director: Tim Whelan

Screenplay: Jack Natteford, Luci Ward

Producer: Nat Holt

HOME SWEET HOMICIDE

(20th C.-Fox, October, 1946) 85 Minutes

Randolph Scott, Peggy Ann Garner, Lynn Bari, Dean Stockwell, Connie Marshall, James Gleason, Anabel Shaw, Barbara Whiting, John Shepperd (Shepperd Strudwick), Stanley Logan, Olin Howlin, Marietta Canty, Pat Flaherty, Phillip Morris, Lenita Lane, James Seay

Director: Lloyd Bacon

Story: F. Hugh Herbert

Screenplay: Craig Rice

TRAIL STREET

(RKO Radio, February 19, 1947) 84 Minutes

Randolph Scott, Robert Ryan, Anne Jeffreys, George Hayes, Madge Meredith, Steve Brodie, Billy House, Virginia Sale, Harry Woods, Phil Warren, Harry Harvey, Jason Robards, Sr., Forrest Taylor, Kit Guard, Stanley Andrews, Sarah Padden, Frank McGlynn, Jr., Ernie Adams, Roy Butler, Jessie Arnold, Guy Beach, Warren Jackson, Billy Vincent, Frank Austin, Betty Hill, Larry McGrath, Chris Willowbird

Director: Ray Enright
Story: William Corcoran
Screenplay: Norman Houston, Gene Lewis
Producer: Nat Holt

THE GUNFIGHTERS

(Columbia, July 1, 1947) 87 Minutes (CineColor)

Randolph Scott, Barbara Britton, Dorothy Hart, Bruce Cabot, Charley Grapewin, Steven Geray, Forrest Tucker, Charles Kemper, Grant Withers, John Miles, Griff Barnett

Director: George Waggner
Story: "Twin Sombreros" - Zane Grey
Screenplay: Alan LeMay
Producer: Harry Joe Brown

CHRISTMAS EVE

(United Artists, October, 1947) 90 Minutes

Randolph Scott, George Raft, George Brent, Joan Blondell, Virginia Field, Dolores Moran, Ann Harding, Reginald Denny, Carl Harbord, John Litel, Joseph Sawyer, Andrew Tombes, Douglass Dumbrille, Dennis Hoey, Walter Sande, Konstantin Shayne, Claire Whitney, Marie Blake, Molly Lamont, Ernest Hilliard, Al Hill, John Indrisano, Edward Parks, Holly Bane, Soledad Jiminez

Director: Edwin L. Marin
Screenplay: Lawrence Stallings
Story: Lawrence Stallings and Richard M. Landau

ALBUQUERQUE

(Paramount, February 20, 1948) 90 Minutes (CineColor)

Randolph Scott, Barbara Britton, George Hayes, Russell Hayden, Lon Chaney, Jr., Catherine Craig, George Cleveland, Irving Bacon, Bernard Nedell, Karolyn Grimes, Russell Simpson, Jody Gilbert, Dan White, Walter Baldwin, John Halloran

Director: Ray Enright
Story: Luke Short
Screenplay: Gene Lewis, Clarence Upson Young

CORONER CREEK

(Columbia, July 1, 1948) 90 Minutes (CineColor)

Randolph Scott, Marguerite Chapman, George Macready, Sally Eilers, Edgar Buchanan, Barbara Reed, Wallace Ford, Forrest Tucker, William Bishop, Joe Sawyer, Russell Simpson, Douglas Fowley, Lee Bennett, Forrest Taylor, Phil Shumaker, Warren Jackson

Director: Ray Enright
Story: Luke Short
Screenplay: Kenneth Gamet
Producer: Harry Joe Brown

RETURN OF THE BAD MEN

(RKO, July 17, 1948) 96 Minutes

Randolph Scott, Robert Ryan, Anne Jeffreys, George Hayes, Jacqueline White, Richard Powers (Tom Keene), Tom Tyler, Steve Brodie, Robert Bray, Lex Barker, Walter Reed, Michael Harvey, Dan White, Robert Armstrong, Lew Harvey, Gary Gray, Walter Baldwin, Minna Gombell, Warren Jackson, Robert Clarke, Jason Robards, Sr., Ernie Adams, Bud Osborne, Forrest Taylor, Lane Chandler, Charles Stevens, Kenneth MacDonald, Earle Hodgins, Harry Shannon, Larry McGrath, Billy Vincent, Brandon Beach, Ida Moore, John Hamilton

Director: Ray Enright
Screenplay: Charles O'Neal, Jack Natteford, Luci Ward
Producer: Nat Holt

THE WALKING HILLS

(Columbia, March, 1949) 78 Minutes

Randolph Scott, Ella Raines, William Bishop, Edgar Buchanan, Arthur Kennedy, John Ireland, Jerome Courtland, Josh White, Russell Collins, Charles Stevens, Housley Stevenson, Reed Howes

Director: John Sturges
Story/Screenplay: Alan LeMay
Producer: Harry Joe Brown

FIGHTING MAN OF THE PLAINS

(20th C.-Fox, December, 1949) 94 Minutes (Cinecolor)

Randolph Scott, Bill Williams, Victor Jory, Jane Nigh, Dale Robertson, Douglas Kennedy, Joan Taylor, Barry Kroeger, Rhys Williams, Barry Kelly, James Todd, James Millican, Burk Symond, Herbert Rawlinson, J. Farrell MacDonald, Harry Cheshire, James Griffith, Tony Hughes, Kermit Maynard

Director: Edwin L. Marin
Story/Screenplay: Frank Gruber
Producer: Nat Holt

CANADIAN PACIFIC

(20th C.-Fox, 1949) 95 Minutes (CineColor)

Randolph Scott, Jane Wyatt, Nancy Olson, J. Carrol Naish, Victor Jory, Robert Barrat, Don Haggerty, Brandon Rhodes, Mary Kent, John Parrish, John Hamilton, Richard Wessel, Howard Negley, Grandon Rhodes, Walter Sande

Director: Edwin L. Marin

Screenplay: Jack DeWitt and Kenneth Gamet

Story: Jack DeWitt

Producer: Nat Holt

THE DOOLINS OF OKLAHOMA

(Columbia, 1949) 90 Minutes

Randolph Scott, George Macready, Louise Allbritton, John Ireland, Virginia Huston, Charles Kemper, Noah Beery, Jr., Dona Drake, Robert Barrat, Lee Patrick, Griff Barnett, Frank Fenton, Jock Mahoney, James Kirkwood, Robert Osterloh, Virginia Brissac, John Sheehan

Director: Gordon Douglas

Screenplay: Kenneth Gamet

THE NEVADAN

(Columbia, February, 1950) 81 Minutes (CineColor)

Randolph Scott, Dorothy Malone, Forrest Tucker, Frank Faylen, George Macready, Charles Kemper, Jeff Corey, Tom Powers, Jock O'Mahoney, Stanley Andrews, James Kirkwood, Kate Drain Lawson, Olin Howlin, Louis Mason

Director: Gordon Douglas

Screenplay: George W. George, George F. Slavin, Rowland Brown

Producer: Harry Joe Brown

COLT .45

(Warners, May 27, 1950) 70 Minutes (Technicolor)

Randolph Scott, Zachary Scott, Ruth Roman, Lloyd Bridges, Alan Hale, Ian MacDonald, Chief Thunder Cloud, Walter Coy, Luther Crockett, Charles Evans, Buddy Roosevelt, Hal Taliaferro, Art Miles, Barry Reagan, Howard Negley, Aurora Navarro, Paul Newland, Franklin Farnum, Ed Peil, Sr., Jack Watt, Carl Andre, Royden Clark, Clyde Hudkins, Jr., Leroy Johnson, Ben Corbett, Kansas Moehring, Warren Fisk, Forrest R. Colee, Artie Ortego, Richard Brehm, Dick Hudkins, Leo McMahon, Bob Burrows, William Steele

Director: Edward L. Marin

Story/Screenplay: Thomas Blackburn

Producer: Saul Elkins

THE CARIBOO TRAIL

(20th C.-Fox, August 1, 1950) 81 Minutes (CineColor)

Randolph Scott, George Hayes, Bill Williams, Karin Booth, Victor Jory, Douglas Kennedy, Jim Davis, Dale Robertson, Mary Stuart, James Griffith, Lee Tung Foo, Tony Hughes, Mary Kent, Ray Hyke, Kansas Moehring, Dorothy Adams, Jerry Root, Cliff Clark, Fred Libby, Tom Montore, Michael Barret, Kermit Maynard, Smith Ballew

Director: Edwin L. Marin

Story: John Rhodes Sturdy

Screenplay: Frank Gruber

Producer: Nat Holt

SUGARFOOT

(Warners, March 3, 1951) 80 Minutes (Technicolor)

Randolph Scott, Adele Jergens, Raymond Massey, S. Z. Sakall, Robert Warwick, Hugh Sanders, Hope Landin, Hank Worden, Gene Evans, Arthur Hunnicutt, Edward Hearn, John Hamilton, Cliff Clark, Kenneth MacDonald, Dan White, Paul Newland, Philo McCullough

Director: Edwin L. Marin

Story: Clarence Buddington Kelland

Screenplay: Russell Hughes

Producer: Saul Elkins

SANTA FE

(Columbia, April 1, 1951) 89 Minutes (Technicolor)

Randolph Scott, Janis Carter, Jerome Courtland, Peter Thompson, John Archer, Warner Anderson, Roy Roberts, Billy House, Olin Howlin, Allene Roberts, Jock O'Mahoney, Harry Cording, Sven Hugo Borg, Frank Ferguson, Irving Pichel, Harry Tyler, Chief Thunder Cloud, Paul E. Burns, Reed Howes, Charles Meredith, Paul Stanton, Richard Cramer, William Haade, Francis McDonald, Frank O'Connor, Harry Tenbrook, James Mason, Guy Wilkerson, Frank Hagney, William Tannen, James Kirkwood, Stanley Blystone, Edgar Dearing, Al Kunde, Art Loeb, Blackie Whiteford, Bud Fine, Richard Fortune, Lane Chandler, Charles Evans, Chuck Hamilton, George Sherwood, Louis Mason, Roy Butler, Ralph Sanford, William McCormack

Director: Irving Pichel

Story: Louis Stevens from a novel by James Marshall

Screenplay: Kenneth Gamet

Producer: Harry Joe Brown

FORT WORTH

(Warners, July 14, 1951) 80 Minutes (Technicolor)

Randolph Scott, David Brian, Phyllis Thaxter, Helena Carter, Dick Jones, Ray Teal, Lawrence Tolan, Paul Picerni, Emerson Treacy, Bob Steele, Dick Jones, Walter Sande, Chubby Johnson, Kermit Maynard

Director: Edwin L. Marin

Story/Screenplay: John Twist

Producer: Anthony Vellier

STARLIFT

(Warners, 1951) 103 Minutes

Janice Rule, Dick Wesson, Ron Hagerthy, Richard Webb, Hayden Rorke, Howard St. John, Ann Doran, Tommy Farrell, John Maxwell, Don Beddoe, Mary Adams, Bigelowe Sayre, Eleanor Audley, Pat Henry, Gordon Polk, Robert Hammark, Ray Montgomery, Bill Neff, Stan Holbrook, Jill Richards, Joe Turkel, Rush Williams, Brian McKay, Jack Larson, Lyle Clark, Dorothy Kennedy, Jean Dean, Dolores Catle, William Hunt, and guest stars: Doris Day, Gordon MacRae, Virginia Mayo, Gene Nelson, Ruth Roman, James Cagney, Gary Cooper, Virginia Gibson, Phil Harris, Frank Lovejoy, Lucille Norman, Louella Parsons, Jane Wyman, Patrice Wymore, *Randolph Scott*

Director: Roy Del Ruth

Screenplay: John Klorer and Karl Lamb

Story: John Klorer

MAN IN THE SADDLE

(Scott-Brown/Columbia, December 2, 1951) 87 Minutes (Technicolor)

Randolph Scott, Joan Leslie, Ellen Drew, Alexander Knox, Richard Rober, John Russell, Alfonso Bedoya, Guinn "Big Boy" Williams, Clem Bevins, Cameron Mitchell, Richard Crane, Frank Sully, George Lloyd, James Kirkwood, Frank Hagney, Don Beddoe, Tennessee Ernie Ford

Director: Andre de Toth

Story: Ernest Haycox

Screenplay: Kenneth Gamet

Producer: Harry Joe Brown

CARSON CITY

(Warners, June 14, 1952) 87 Minutes (WarnerColor)

Randolph Scott, Lucille Norman, Raymond Massey, Richard Webb, James Millican, Larry Keating, George Cleveland, William Haade, Thurston Hall, Vince Barnett, Don Beddoe, Jack Woody, James Smith, Guy Tongue, Carle Andre, Marlin Nelson, Clyde Hudkins, Sarah Edwards, Iris Adrian, Edmund Cobb, Zon Murray, House Peters, Jr., Pierce Lyden, Kenneth MacDonald

Director: Andre De Toth

Story: Sloan Nibley

Screenplay: Sloan Nibley and Winston Miller

Producer: David Weisbart

Don Beddoe, Richard Webb, Lucille Norman and Randolph Scott hold a discussion in **Carson City** (Warner Bros., 1952).

HANGMAN'S KNOT

(Scott-Brown/Columbia, November 15, 1952) 84 Min. (Technicolor)

Randolph Scott, Donna Reed, Claude Jarman, Jr., Frank Faylen, Glenn Langan, Richard Denning, Lee Marvin, Jeanette Nolan, Clem Bevans, Ray Teal, Guinn "Big Boy" Williams, Monte Blue, John Call, Reed Howes, Edward Earle, Post Park, Frank Hagney, Frank Yaconelli

Director/Screenplay: Roy Huggins
Producer: Harry Joe Brown

THE MAN BEHIND THE GUN

(Warners, January 31, 1952) 82 Minutes (Technicolor)

Randolph Scott, Patrice Wymore, Dick Wesson, Philip Carey, Lina Romay, Roy Roberts, Morris Ankrum, Katherine Warren, Alan Hale, Jr., Douglas Fowley, Tony Caruso, Clancy Cooper, Robert Cabal, James Brown, Reed Howes, Rory Mallinson, John Logan, Vickie Raaf, Lee Morgan, Ray Spiker, Edward Hearn, Terry Frost, Charles Horvath, Art Millian, Rex Lease, Jack Parker, James Bellah, Billy Vincent, Albert Morin, Edward Colemans, Herbert Deans

Director: Felix Feist
Story: Forest Buckner
Screenplay: John Twist
Producer: Robert Sisk

THE STRANGER WORE A GUN

(Columbia, August 15, 1953) 83 Minutes (Technicolor) (3-D)

Randolph Scott, Claire Trevor, Joan Weldon, George Macready, Alfonso Bedoya, Lee Marvin, Ernest Borgnine, Pierre Watkin, Joseph Vitale, Clem Bevins, Roscoe Ates, Paul Maxey, Frank Scannell, Reed Howes, Edward Earle, Guy Wilkerson, Mary Newton, Mary Lou Holloway, Franklin Farnum, Barry Brooks, Tap Canutt, Al Haskell, Frank Hagney, Frank Ellis, Francis McDonald, Phil Tully, Al Hill, Harry Mendoza, Terry Frost, Diana Dawson, Richard Benjamin, Herbert Rawlinson, Britt Wood, Harry Seymour, James Millican, Jack Woody, Rayford Barnes, Rudy Germaine, Edith Evanson, Buy Teague

Director: Andre De Toth
Story: "Yankee Gold" - John Cummingham
Screenplay: Kenneth Gamet
Producers: Harry Joe Brown, Randolph Scott

THUNDER OVER THE PLAINS

(Warners, December 12, 1953) 82 Minutes (WarnerColor)

Randolph Scott, Lex Barker, Phyllis Kirk, Charles McGraw, Henry Hull, Elisha Cook, Jr., Hugh Sanders, Lane Chandler, James Brown, Fess Parker, Richard Benjamin, Mark Dana, Jack Woody, Trevor Bardette, Frank Matts, Steve Darnell, Earle Hodgins, John Carson, Monte Montague, Carl Andre, Charles Horvath, John McKee, Gail Robinson, Boyd Morgan, Gayle Kellogg

Director: Andre de Toth
Screenplay: Russell Hughes
Producer: David Weisbart

RIDING SHOTGUN

(Warners, April 10, 1954) 75 Minutes (WarnerColor)

Randolph Scott, Wayne Morris, Joan Weldon, Joe Sawyer, James Millican, Charles Buchinsky (Bronson), James Bell, Fritz Feld, Richard Garrick, Victor Perrin, John Baer, William Johnstone, Kem Dibbs, Alvin Freeman, Edward Coch, Jr., Eva Lewis, Lonnie Pierce, Mary Lou Holloway, Boyd Morgan, Richard Benjamin, Jay Lawrence, George Ross, Ray Bennett, Jack Kenney, Jack Woody, Allegra Varron, Frosty Royse, Jimmy Mohley, Ruth Whitney, Bud Osborne, Budd Buster, Buddy Roosevelt, Dub Taylor, Joe Brockman, Harry Hines, Clem Fuller, Opan Evard, Morgan Brown, Bob Stephenson

Director: Andre de Toth
Story: Kenneth Perkins
Screenplay: Tom Blackburn
Producer: Ted Sherdeman

THE BOUNTY HUNTER

(Transcona/Warners, September 25, 1954) 79 Minutes (WarnerColor)

Randolph Scott, Dolores Dorn, Marie Windsor, Howard Petrie, Harry Antrim, Robert Keys, Ernest Borgnine, Dub Taylor, Tyler McDuff, Archie Twitchell, Paul Picerni, Phil Chambers, Mary Lou Holloway, Katherine Marlowe, Dorothy Seese, Hope Miller, Guy Teague, Charles Delaney, Gail Robinson, Vincent Perry, Wanda Barbour, Fess Parker, Shirley Whitney

Director: Andre de Toth
Screenplay: Winston Miller
Producer: Sam Bischoff

TEN WANTED MEN

(Scott-Brown, Columbia, February 1, 1955) 80 Minutes (Techicolor)
Randolph Scott, Jocelyn Brando, Richard Boone, Alfonso Bedoya, Donna Martell, Skip Homeier, Clem Bevins, Leo Gordon, Minor Watson, Lester Mathews, Tom Powers, Dennis Weaver, Lee Van Cleef, Louis Jean Heydt, Kathleen Crowley, Boyd "Red" Morgan, Denver Pyle, Francis McDonald, Pat Collins, Paul Maxey, Jack Perrin, Julian Rivero, Carlos Vera, Edna Holland, Reed Howes, Terry Frost, Franklyn Farnum, George Boyce
Director: Bruce Humberstone
Story: Irving Ravetch, Harriet Frank, Jr.
Screenplay: Kenneth Gamet
Producer: Harry Joe Brown

RAGE AT DAWN

(RKO, March 26, 1955) 87 Minutes
(Briefly released under the title "Seven Bad Men")
Randolph Scott, Forrest Tucker, Mala Powers, J. Carrol Naish, Edgar Buchanan, Myron Healey, Howard Petrie, Ray Teal, William Forrest, Denver Pyle, Trevor Bardette, Kenneth Tobey, Chubby Johnson, Richard Garland, Ralph Moody, Guy Prescott, Mike Ragan, Phil Chambers
Director: Tim Whelan
Story: Frank Gruber
Screenplay: Horace McCoy
Producer: Nat Holt

TALL MAN RIDING

(Warners, June 18, 1955) 83 Minutes (WarnerColor)
Randolph Scott, Dorothy Malone, Peggie Castle, William Ching, John Baragrey, Robert Barrat, John Dehner, Paul Richards, Lane Chandler, Mickey Simpson, Joe Bassett, Charles Watts, Russ Conway, Mike Reagan, Carl Andre, John Logan, Guy Hearn, Bill Faucett, Nolan Leary, Phil Rich, Eva Novak, Buddy Roosevelt, Jack Henderson, Bob Peoples, William Bailey, Patrick Henry, Joe Brooks, Vernon Rich, Bob Stephenson, Dub Taylor, Roger Creed
Director: Lesley Selander
Story: Norman A. Fox
Screenplay: Joseph Hoffman
Producer: David Weisbart

A LAWLESS STREET

(Scott-Brown/Columbia, December 15, 1955) 78 Mins. (Technicolor)
Randolph Scott, Angela Lansbury, Warner Anderson, Jean Parker, Wallace Ford, John Emery, James Bell, Ruth Donnelly, Michael Pate, Don Megowan, Jeanette Nolan, Peter Ortiz, Don Carlos, Frank Hagney, Charles Williams, Frank Ferguson, Harry Tyler, Harry Antrim, Jay Lawrence, Reed Howes, Guy Teague, Hal K. Dawson, Pat Collins, Frank Scannell, Stanley Blystone, Barry Brooks, Edwin Chandler, Jack Perrin, Kermit Maynard
Director: Joseph H. Lewis
Story: "Marshal of Medicine Bend" - Brad Ward
Screenplay: Kenneth Gamet
Producers: Harry Joe Brown, Randolph Scott

SEVEN MEN FROM NOW

(Batjac/Warners, August 4, 1956) 78 Minutes (WarnerColor)
Randolph Scott, Gail Russell, Lee Marvin, Walter Reed, John Larch, Donald Barry, Fred Graham, John Barradino John Phillips, Chuck Roberson, Steve Mitchell, Pamela Duncan, Stuart Whitman
Director: Budd Boetticher
Story/Screenplay: Burt Kennedy
Producers: Andrew V. McLaglen and Robert E. Morrison

7TH CAVALRY

(Scott-Brown/Columbia, December, 1956) 75 Minutes (Technicolor)
Randolph Scott, Barbara Hale, Jay C. Flippen, Jeanette Nolan, Frank Faylen, Leo Gordon, Denver Pyle, Harry Carey, Jr., Michael Pate, Donald Curtis, Frank Wilcox, Pat Hogan, Russell Hicks, Peter Ortiz, William Leslie, Jack Parker, Edward F. Stidder, Al Wyatt
Director: Joseph H. Lewis
Story: Glendon F. Swarthout
Screenplay: Peter Packer
Producer: Harry Joe Brown

THE TALL T

(Columbia, April 1, 1957) 78 Minutes (Technicolor)
Randolph Scott, Richard Boone, Maureen O'Sullivan, Arthur Hunnicutt, Skip Homeier, Henry Silva, John Hubbard, Robert Burton, Robert Anderson, Fred E. Sherman, Chris Olsen
Director: Budd Boetticher
Story: Elmore Leonard
Screenplay: Burt Kennedy
Producers: Harry Joe Brown, Randolph Scott

Randolph Scott has just gunned down killer H. M. Wynant in **Decision at Sundown** (Columbia, 1957)

240

SHOOT-OUT AT MEDICINE BEND
(Warners, May 4, 1957) 87 Minutes
Randolph Scott, James Craig, Angie Dickinson, Dani Crayne, James Garner, Gordon Jones, Trevor Bardette, Don Beddoe, Myron Healey, John Alderson, Harry Harvey, Sr., Robert Warwick, Howard Negley, Marshall Bradford, Ann Doran, Daryn Hinton, Dickie Bellis, Edward Hinton, Lane Bradford, Francis Morris, Robert Lynn, Sam Flint, Philip Van Zandt, Guy Wilkerson, Syd Saylor, Harry Rowland, Marjorie Bennett, Jesslyn Fay, Marjorie Stapp, Nancy Kulp, George Meader, Rory Mallinson, Dee Carroll, Gerald Charlebois, Dale Van Sickel, Gil Perkins, Harry Lauter, George Russ, Carol Henry, George Pembrooke, Tom Monroe, John Roy, Buddy Roosevelt, George Bell
Director: Richard L. Bare
Screenplay: John Tucker Battle and D. D. Beauchamp
Producer: Richard Whorf

DECISION AT SUNDOWN
(Columbia, November 10, 1957) 77 Minutes
(Technicolor)
Randolph Scott, John Carroll, Karen Steele, Valerie French, Noah Beery, Jr., John Archer, Andrew Duggan, James Westerfield, John Litel, Ray Teal, Vaughn Taylor, Richard Deacon, H. M. Wynant, Guy Wilkerson
Director: Budd Boetticher
Screenplay: Charles Lang, Jr.
Producers: Harry Joe Brown, Randolph Scott

BUCHANAN RIDES ALONE
(Columbia, August 1, 1958) 78 Minutes (Technicolor)
Randolph Scott, Craig Stevens, Barry Kelley, Tol Avery, Peter Whitney, Manuel Rojab, William Leslie, Don C. Harvey, L. Q. Jones, Robert Anderson, Joe De Santis, Jennifer Holden, Nacho Galindo, Roy Jenson, Frank Scannell, Barbara James, Al Wyatt, Terry Frost, Riley Hill, Leo Ogletree, Jim B. Leon
Director: Budd Boetticher
Story: Charles Lang, Jr. (from Jonas Ward's novel "The Name's Buchanan")
Producers: Harry Joe Brown, Randolph Scott

RIDE LONESOME
(Columbia, February 15, 1959) 75 Minutes
(Eastman Color) (CinemaScope)
Randolph Scott, Karen Steele, Pernell Roberts, James Best, Lee Van Cleef, James Coburn, Duke Johnson, Boyd Stockman, Roy Jenson, Boyd "Red" Morgan, Bennie Dobbins
Director: Budd Boetticher
Screenplay: Burt Kennedy
Producers: Harry Joe Brown, Randolph Scott

WESTBOUND
(Warners, April 25, 1959) 96 Minutes (WarnerColor)
Randolph Scott, Virginia Mayo, Karen Steele, Michael Dante, Andrew Duggan, Michael Pate, Wally Brown, John Day, Walter Barnes, Fred Sherman, Mack Williams, Ed Prentiss, Rory Mallinson, Rudi Dana, Tom Monroe, Jack Perrin, Buddy Roosevelt, Kermit Maynard, May Boss, William A. Green, Jack E. Henderson, Felice Richmond, Creighton Hale, Gertrude Keeler, Walter Reed, Jack C. Williams, Gerald Roberts, John Hudkins, Don Happy, Bobby Herron, Fred Stromscoe
Director: Budd Boetticher
Story: Berne Giler and Albert Shelby LeVino
Screenplay: Berne Giler
Producer: Henry Blanke

COMANCHE STATION
(Columbia, March, 1960) 74 Minutes
(Eastman Color) (CinemaScope)
Randolph Scott, Nancy Gates, Claude Akins, Skip Homeier, Richard Rust, Rand Brooks, Dyke Johnson, Foster Hood, Joe Molina, Vince St. Cyr, Paul Holland
Director: Budd Boetticher
Screenplay: Burt Kennedy
Producers: Harry Joe Brown, Budd Boetticher

RIDE THE HIGH COUNTRY
(Metro-Goldwyn-Mayer, May, 1962) 94 Minutes
(MetroColor) (CinemaScope)
Randolph Scott, Joel McCrea, Mariette Hartley, Ronald Starr, Edgar Buchanan, R. G. Armstrong, John Anderson, L. Q. Jones, Warren Oates, James Drury, John Davis Chandler, Jenie Jackson
Director: Sam Peckinpah
Screenplay: N. B. Stone, Jr.
Producer: Richard E. Lyons

ADDENDUM

TO THE SHORES OF TRIPOLI
(20th Century-Fox, 1942) 82 Minutes
John Payne, Maureen O'Hara, *Randolph Scott,* Nancy Kelly, William Tracy, Maxie Rosenbloom, Harry Morgan, Edmund MacDonald, Russell Hicks, Minor Watson, Michael "Ted" North, Basil Walker, Charles Tannen, Alan Hale, Jr., Margaret Early, Frank Orth, Iris Adrian, Joseph Crehan, John Hamilton, Stanley Andrews, Richard Lane, Gordon Jones, Gaylord "Steve" Pendleton, Anthony Nace, Robert Conway, James C. Morton, Hillary Brooke, Patricia Farr, James Flavin, Knox Manning, Harry Strang, Patrick McVey, Hugh Beaumont
Director: Bruce Humberstone
Screenplay: Lamar Trotti
Story: Steve Fisher
Associate Producer: Milton Sperling
Producer: Darryl F. Zanuck

Charles Starrett

12 ● CHARLES STARRETT

Columbia's Ace of the Open Acres

Charles Starrett, the tall, two-fisted, gun-fanning hero of the hill country that was the West romped through 133 familiarly tailored but meritorious six-shooter dramas for Columbia Pictures, to set both a longevity and quantitative record for a star at a single studio in a continuous series.

Without doubt Starrett was something of an idol, even if he didn't rate with Boyer or Gable on the romantics. He was handsome, definitely personable, a good actor, and a 6'2" 190-pound finely-trained athlete. From his broad, tall stetson to his high-heeled boots, Charles was the typical, albeit mythical, cinematic old-west hero, always standing for the right and the truth and willing to fight for his principles with his fists as well as his guns. There was little of the subtle, psychological stuff in the Starrett movies. The villains were usually rootin'-tootin', tobacco-chewin' varmints shaken loose on society by the broom which swept hell, and Charles, in as dignified a manner as one can do such things, would proceed to pummel and out-shoot the dastards until the range was once more a safe place for the lovely Sunbonnet Sue and her elderly father. No one got talked to death in a Starrett oater, but a lot of baddies got sunlight punched through their innards with hot lead.

Starrett's background was hardly that of a cowboy. He was born on March 28, 1904 in Athol, Massachusetts, the youngest of nine children of Leroy Starrett, founder of the Starrett Precision Tool Company. Charles has never known anything but wealth, yet has never let it affect his personal relationships. Throughout his long career and subsequent retirement years he has had the reputation of being one of the friendliest, most sincerely humble individuals in the movie colony. Starrett was never known to throw a tantrum on the set or speak disparagingly to co-workers or crew. The wranglers and grips got the same courtesy and friendliness from Charles that people of influence got. He simply made no distinctions among people on the basis of money or influence, but acted the gentleman to one and all.

Starrett attended Dartmouth College, where he played varsity football. In 1926 Richard Dix and a Paramount film crew filmed a portion of **The Quarterback** ('26) at Dartmouth, using the varsity squad for several scenes. Thus it is credited as Charles' first film. After graduation he went to New York to pursue an acting career. For three years he toured with a stock company throughout the New England states, finally landing a part in the New York play, "Claire Adams." A Paramount scout saw him and arranged a screen test. He was signed to a contract in 1929.

Fast and Loose ('30) and **The Royal Family of Broadway** ('31), both filmed in the East, were Starrett's first movies. Thereafter he was sent to Paramount's home lot in Hollywood and appeared in **Silence** ('31), **Touchdown** ('31), **Sky Bride** ('32), **Lady and Gent** ('32), **So Red the Rose** ('35), and **Along Came Love** ('36). But his most-remembered films were made on loan-out or as a free-lancer, usually at Poverty Row outfits.

In '32, on loan to MGM, Charles was featured in **The Mask of Fu Manchu,** with Boris Karloff, Lewis Stone, and Myrna Loy sharing the other principal roles. Monogram co-starred him in '33 with Anita Page in the thriller **Jungle Bride,** a satisfactory program picture

Myrna Loy falls in love with Charles Starrett in **The Mask of Fu Manchu** (MGM, 1932).

although suffering from implausible situations and poor direction. Charles' good looks and thespian talents served him well in **Our Betters** (RKO, '33), **Mr. Skitch** (Fox, '33), **Three on a Honeymoon** (Fox, '34), **This Man Is Mine** (RKO, '34), **Call It Luck** (Fox, '34), **Desirable** (WB, '34), and **Gentlemen Are Born** (FN, '34), and it seemed that he might make a career of playing the good-looking, usually clean-cut man about town. Luckily, his work for the independents tended to pull him toward action-oriented films. A good example is **The Viking** ('31), filmed on location in Newfoundland and the Arctic by Varick Friscell, who, along with 20 others, lost his life while attempting to retake some shots. Charles and Louise Huntington center in the love story, but it is the Arctic scenery and wildlife that predominate.

Two railroad pictures helped Charles to become a recognized portrayer of virile men. **Return of Casey Jones** (Mon., '33) is a cheapie and below standard in sound, settings, script, dialogue, and direction, but Starrett and George F. Hayes managed to give good accounts of themselves in the meller. **The Silver Streak** (RKO, '34) is considerably better and contains a thrill for just about every minute of its 85-minute running time. Charles is starred as the engineer at the throttle of the speeding train on a 2,000-mile run from Chicago to Boulder Dam to deliver an iron lung needed to save the life of the railroad president's son.

Chesterfield used Starrett to good advantage in **Murder on the Campus** ('34), directed by Richard Thorpe, and Charles received good reviews as the reporter, sharing plaudits with J. Farrell MacDonald as the policeman he teams up with to rout the murderer. Shirley Grey, the female lead, has little to do, but with her body she really need do nothing to please except smile alluringly and walk across the room.

Starrett stayed around the Gower Gulch studio for further assignments under director Thorpe in **Stolen Sweets** ('34), again with beauteous Shirley Grey. Also for Chesterfield, but under the direction of Charles Lamont, Charles starred in **Sons of Steel** ('35) and **A Shot in the Dark** ('35), keeping company with Polly Ann Young in the former and Marion Shilling in the latter. Both girls made names for themselves as Western heroines. Other "Bs," e.g., **Sweethearts of Sigmi Chi** (Mon., '33), **What Price Crime** (Beacon, '35), and **Make a Million** (Mon., '35), provided Starrett with versatile acting experience and bolstered his name recognition and pulling power in double-harness houses that showed the independent products.

Starrett's out-of-doors heroics really began with **Undercover** ('35), a northwest mountie saga filmed in Canada by Booth Dominions Pictures with action ace Sam Newfield directing. Although a one-shot picture with no intended follow-ups, it did put Charles in a Western-type picture.

In late '35 Columbia was looking for a replacement for the departing Tim McCoy. Of several players tested, Starrett, free-lancing at the time, seemed to have the greatest potential and was signed for a Western series. Columbia president Harry Cohn liked the idea of injecting a little new blood into the Western sweepstakes. His first film in the series was **Gallant Defender** ('35), and for a Western it was rather slow paced. It's got lots of story; in fact, so much that there isn't much time for real shootout showdowns, hard riding, or an occasional exchange of fist sockerooing. Charles makes a personable hero-to-the-rescue, though, while the maiden-in-distress is the wholesome and comely Joan Perry. Gene Autry's impact on Westerns was apparent, for Charles was backed up by a musical group calling themselves The Sons of the Pioneers, which included a skinny fellow named Leonard Slye, better known later to gulch-and-prairie addicts as Roy Rogers.

Starrett's popularity grew rapidly and he soon had a sizable coterie of fans and a firm position in the Western ranks. Good stories, deft direction by Sam Nelson, occasionally spelled by Leon Barsha and others, and plenty of action stuff helped him along. Iris Meredith was quite often the ingenue and Dick Curtis could usually be counted on for the villainy. Music by The Sons of the Pioneers was pleasant and eased in conveniently. By 1940, however, the films had taken on a noticeable sameness, more so than any other series. The same cast of Columbia stock players popped up in each film. But the series remained popular and production standards remain adequate.

In 1940 Paul Franklin put together a screenplay revolving about a masked avenger like Buck Jones' **The**

Phantom Rider (Univ., '36), with no thought at the time of any follow-up films using the character. His story emerged as **The Durango Kid** ('40), typical formula stuff in which Luana Walters, daughter of a homesteader, and others are victims of everything this side of being burned at the stake by a band of baddies. Coming home at the behest of his father, as most sons seem to do in Westerns, Starrett becomes the masked Robin Hood of the nesters. Five years were to elapse before the character was resurrected for Starrett's use again.

Seeking a new angle for the Starrett Westerns, producer Jack Fier launched a new series in '41 in which Charles is a wandering cowboy doctor named Steven Monroe, pausing long enough in each community to straighten out local problems. Stories were based loosely on the book by James L. Rubel. **The Medico of Painted Springs** ('41) was the initial entry, followed by **Thunder Over the Prairies** ('41) and **Prairie Stranger** ('41). The Sons of the Pioneers were gone, as was Iris Meredith—not that they were bad, but it was refreshing to see a Starrett film with a few different faces about. Things looked pretty good for a continuation of the series until legal difficulties arose regarding Rubel's original copyright, and the series was dropped. Starrett reverted to his customary action Westerns, picking up a sidekick in the person of Cliff Edwards and, for a while, Russell Hayden as co-star. Later comic reliefs were Dub Taylor and Arthur Hunnicutt. Various musical groups backed him up, but the Starrett films remained hell-for-leather prairie thrillers with most of the attention focused on Starrett.

In 1945 Colbert Clark took over as executive producer of the Starrett Westerns. Looking around for ideas, he was intrigued by the old **Durango Kid** oater of '40 and decided to try for a little mileage from a re-activation of the character. All agreed that the Starretts needed a change of some sort. Thus, **Return of the Durango Kid** ('45) was scripted by J. Benton Cheney. It was standard fodder for the action trade, spinning its western melodramatics in okay fashion to garner the attention of Saturday matinee audiences. There are some songs tossed in by Tex Harding, who stayed around for a whole season, but all they serve to do is slow down proceedings as Starrett, displaying dazzling virtuosity with a six-gun, goes about his business of bringing a gang of cutthroats to justice. The film was well received in the juvenile market, and a decision was made to continue having Charles portray the character. Thus, a paradox developed. Production quality of the films consistently deteriorated after '45 while the Starrett popularity remained steadfast, a tribute, it must be assumed, to the personal magnetism of the star. Screenplays were probably run off by the

Charles Starrett as The Durango Kid in 1952.

Charles Starrett and Russell Hayden, a mighty Columbia duo in the early '40s.

various writers while galloping down to the office in the morning. Or maybe they didn't even write them down, just remembered them. The Durango stories were the Western stereotype stripped right down to the mare's back.

The theory that the grinding out of the same old plot, with only minor variations, will still result in a successful film, particularly if it happens to be a Western, is nowhere more strongly (and somewhat mistakenly) illustrated than in the Durango Kid series. The same old stagecoach holdup, the same old suave villain masquerading as a benefactor, the same old cattle stampede and a few other standard props were constantly assembled by producer Clark, and while the result probably produced no audible complaints from oater fans, the whole series seemed rather tired. Starrett, however, competently performs his chores in all 63 entries in the long-running Durango series. Smiley Burnette joined Starrett in early 1946 and received second billing in 55 of the Durangos, his buffoonery doing much to enliven the goings-on. As time went along Columbia resorted to the re-use of much footage from previous films—so much so that after 1950 there was almost as much old footage spliced into the films being made as there was new footage. The studio economized in every way imaginable in the years of the final death throes of the series, trying to keep it alive and profitable. In the last year of production the Starrett name was about all the films had in the way of assets, but Charles endured and triumphed over his substandard material. **The Kid from Broken Gun** ('52), the final entry and Starrett's last film, was a formula oater. Involved plotting, with flashbacks within flashbacks, and a vast amount of talk substituting for action, kept it from playing off at the speed demanded by the younger Western fans.

247

Charles Starrett and Smiley Burnette in one of many "Durango Kid" pictures.

Charles Starrett had been at Columbia for 17 years, and for 15 of those years had been voted one of Western filmdom's top money-making stars. He starred in 134 Westerns and 14 non-Westerns, and was featured prominently in 17 other non-Westerns.

When he retired in '52 Charles, still a wealthy man, was able to travel and do many of the things he had wanted to do, though ill health has curtailed his activities in recent years. He had been happily married for over fifty years and is the father of twin sons, now grown and with children of their own. His movie achievements have assured him a place in the minds of Western buffs; his human qualities have assured him a place in their hearts. Charles Starrett was a gentleman, one who took seriously his unique responsibility to the youth who idolized him. The Durango Kid kept the faith.

Charles died on March 23, 1986. He had been having different health problems but was cheerful and active to the end.

CHARLES STARRETT Filmography

THE QUARTERBACK
(Paramount, October 11, 1926) 8 Reels
Richard Dix, Esther Ralston, Harry Beresford, David Butler, Robert W. Craig, Mona Palmer, and the Dartmouth football team of which *Charles Starrett* was a member.
Director: Fred Newmeyer
Adaptation: Ray Harris
Story: William Slavens McNutt, William O. McGeehan

FAST AND LOOSE
(Paramount, January 8, 1930) 7 Reels
Miriam Hopkins, Carole Lombard, Frank Morgan, *Charles Starrett,* Henry Wadsworth, Winifred Harris, Herbert Yost, David Hutcheson, Ilka Chase, Herschell Magail
Director: Fred Newmeyer
Screenplay: Jack Kirkland, Doris Anderson
Story: David Gray and Avery Hopwood - "The Best People"

THE ROYAL FAMILY OF BROADWAY
(Paramount, January 31, 1931) 82 Minutes
Ina Claire, Fredric March, Mary Brian, Henrietta Crosman, *Charles Starrett,* Frank Conroy, Royal C. Stout, Elsie Emond, Murray Alper, Wesley Stark, Hershal Mayall
Directors: George Cukor, Cyril Garner
Screenplay: Herman Mankiewicz, Gertrude Purcell
Story: Edna Ferber and George S. Kaufman - "The Royal Family"

DAMAGED LOVE
(Sono Art/World Wide, March 9, 1931) 79 Minutes
June Collyer, *Charles R. Starrett,* Eloise Taylor, Betty Garde, Charles Trowbridge
Director: Irvin Willat
Story: Thomas W. Broadhurst
Producer: Louis Weiss
Adaptation: Frederic and Fanny Hatton

THE VIKING
(J. D. Williams/Newfoundland Labrador Film Co., April 8, 1931) 75 Minutes (filmed on location in Newfoundland)
Charles Starrett, Louise Huntington, Arthur Vinton, Captain Bob Bartlett, Sir Wilfred Grenfell
Director: George Melford
Adaptation: Garnett Weston
Scenario/Producer: Varick Frissell
Associate Producer: Roy W. Gates

SILENCE
(Paramount, August 29, 1931) 8 Reels
Clive Brook, Marjorie Rambeau, Peggy Shannon, *Charles Starrett,* Willard Robertson, John Wray, Frank Sheridan, Paul Nicholson, John Craig, J. N. Sullivan, Charles Trowbridge, Ben Taggert, Wade Boteler, Robert Homans
Directors: Louis Gosnier, Max Marcin
Story/Scenario: Max Marcin

THE AGE FOR LOVE
(The Caddo Co., Inc./United Artists, October 17, 1931) 81 Minutes
Billie Dove, *Charles Starrett,* Lois Wilson, Edward Everett Horton, Mary Duncan, Adrian Morris, Betty Ross Clarke, Jed Prouty, Joan Standing, Andre Beranger, Cecil Cunningham, Charles Sellon, Alice Moe, Count Pierre de Ramey, Vivian Oakland
Director: Frank Lloyd
Adaptation/Story: Ernest Pascal
Scenario: F. Lloyd, Ernest Pascal
Producer: Howard Hughes

TOUCHDOWN
(Paramount, November 14, 1931) 79 Minutes
Richard Arlen, Peggy Shannon, Jack Oakie, Regis Toomey, *Charles Starrett,* George Barbier, J. Farrell MacDonald, George Irving, Charles D. Brown
Director: Norman McLeod
Story: Francis Wallace - "Stadium"
Screenplay: Grover Jones, William Slavens McNutt

SKY BRIDE
(Paramount, April 28, 1932) 78 Minutes
Virginia Bruce, Frances Dee, Richard Arlen, Jack Oakie, *Charles Starrett,* Robert Coogan, Louise Closser Hare, Tom Douglas, Harold Goodwin, Randolph Scott
Director: Stephen Roberts
Story: Waldemar Young
Screenplay: Joseph L. Mankiewicz, Agnes Brand Leahy, Grover Jones

LADY AND GENT
(Paramount, July 15, 1932) 9 Reels
George Bancroft, Wynne Gibson, *Charles Starrett,* James Gleason, Billy Butts, Morgan Wallace, John Wayne, James Crane, William Halligan, Joyce Compton, Frank McGlynn, Sr., Charles Grapewin, Frederick Wallace, Lew Kelly, Syd Saylor, Russell Powell, Frank Darien, Hal Price, John Beck, A. S. Bryon, Tom Kennedy, Frank Dawson
Director: Stephen Roberts
Screenplay: Grover Jones, William Slavens McNutt

THE MASK OF FU MANCHU
(MGM, November 5, 1932) 67 Minutes
Boris Karloff, Lewis Stone, Myrna Loy, Jean Hersholt, Sir Lionel Barton, David Torrence, *Charles Starrett,* Karen Morley, Ferdinand Gottschalk, C. Montague Shaw, Willie Fung
Director: Charles Brabin (replacing Charles Vidor)
Story: Sax Rohmer (pseudonym of Arthur Sarsfield Ward)
Screenplay: Irene Kuhn, Edgar Allan Woolf, John Willard

JUNGLE BRIDE
(Monogram, February 15, 1933) 68 Minutes
Anita Page, *Charles Starrett,* Kenneth Thompson, Eddie Borden, Gertrude Simpson, Fay Emmett, Clarence Geldert
Directors: Harry O. Hoyt, Albert Kelly
Story: Leah Baird
Producer: Arthur F. Beck

OUR BETTERS

(RKO, March 17, 1933) 9 Reels, 72 Minutes
Constance Bennett, Gilbert Roland, *Charles Starrett,* Anita Louise, Phoebe Foster, Grant Mitchell, Hugh Sinclair, Alan Mowbray, Minor Watson, Violett Kemble-Cooper, Tyrrell Davis, Virginia Howell, Walter Walker, Howard Enthistle
Director: George Cukor
Screenplay: Jane Murfin, Harry Wagstaff Gribble
Producer: David O. Selznick

RETURN OF CASEY JONES

(Chadwick Prod./Monogram, May 22, 1933) 63 Minutes
Charles Starrett, Ruth Hall, Jackie Searle, George Walsh, Margaret Seddon, Robert Elliott, George Hayes, G. D. Wood (Gordon DeMain), George Nash, Anne Howard
Director: J. P. McCarthy
Story: John P. Johns
Adaptation: J. P. McCarthy, Harry O. Jones
Producer: I. E. Chadwick
Supervisor: Trem Carr

SWEETHEART OF SIGMA CHI

(Monogram, November 20, 1933) 77 Minutes
Mary Carlisle, Buster Crabbe, *Charles Starrett,* Florence Lake, Eddie Tamblyn, Sally Starr, Mary Blackford, Tom Dugan, Burr McIntosh, Major Goodsell
Director: Edward L. Marin
Story: George Waggner
Screenplay: Luther Reed and Albert E. DeMond
Producer: W. L. Lackey

MR. SKITCH

(Fox, December 22, 1933) 6,200 feet
Will Rogers, Zasu Pitts, Rochelle Hudson, *Charles Starrett,* Eugene Pallette, Florence Desmond, Harry Green
Director: James Cruze
Story: Anne Cameron - "Green Dice"
Screenplay: Sonya Levine, Ralph Spence

MURDER ON THE CAMPUS

(Chesterfield, January 6, 1934) 7 Reels, 73 Minutes
Shirley Grey, *Charles Starrett,* J. Farrell MacDonald, Ruth Hall, Edward Van Sloan, Maurice Black, Dewey Robinson, Jane Keckley, Harrison Greene
Director: Richard Thorpe
Story: Whitman Chambers - "The Campanile Murders"
Continuity: Andrew Moses
Producer: George R. Batcheller

THREE ON A HONEYMOON

(Fox, March 15, 1934) 70 Minutes
Sally Eilers, Zasu Pitts, *Charles Starrett,* John Mack Brown, Henrietta Crosman, Irene Hervey, Howard Lally, Cornelius Keefe, Winn Shaw, Elsie Larson
Director: James Tinling
Story: Isbel Ross - "Promenade Deck"
Screenplay: Edward T. Lowe, Raymond van Sickle, George Wright
Adaptation: Douglas Doty

STOLEN SWEETS

(Chesterfield, March 27, 1934) 75 Minutes
Sally Blane, *Charles Starrett,* Claude King, Jameson Thomas, Jane Keckley, Phillips Smalley, Tom Ricketts, Johnny Harron, Polly Ann Young, Goodee Montgomery, Maynard Holmes, Aggie Herring
Director: Richard Thorpe
Story/Screenplay: Karl Brown
Producer: George R. Batcheller

THIS MAN IS MINE

(RKO-Pathe, April 5, 1934) 76 Minutes
Irene Dunne, Constance Cummings, Ralph Bellamy, Kay Johnson, *Charles Starrett,* Vivian Tobin, Sidney Blackmer, Louis Mason
Director: John Cromwell
Story: Anne Morrison Chapin - from the play "Love Flies in the Window"
Screenplay: Jane Murfin
Producer: Pandro S. Berman

CALL IT LUCK

(Fox, June 1, 1934) 5,850 feet, 65 Minutes
Pat Peterson, Herbert Mundin, *Charles Starrett,* Gordon Westcott, Georgia Caine, Theodore Von Eltz, Reginald Mason, Ernest Wood, Ray Mayer, Susan Fleming
Director: James Tinling
Story: Dudley Nichols, George Marshall
Screenplay: Dudley Nichols, Lamar Trotti
Adaptation: Joseph Cunningham, Harry McCoy

GREEN EYES

(Chesterfield, June 14, 1934) 63 Minutes
Shirley Grey, *Charles Starrett,* Claude Gillingwater, John Wray, William Bakewell, Dorothy Revier, Ben Hendricks, Jr., Alden Chase, Arthur Clayton, Aggie Herring, Edward Keane, Edward LeSaint, Robert Frazer, John Elliott, Lloyd Whitlock, Elmer Ballard
Director: Richard Thorpe
Story: Harriette Ashbrook - "The Murder of Steven Kester"
Continuity: Andrew Moses
Producer: George R. Batcheller

Charles Starrett and unidentified players in **Stolen Sweets** (Chesterfield, 1934).

ONE IN A MILLION
(Invincible Pictures/Chesterfield, September 15, 1934)
7 Reels, 66 Minutes
Charles Starrett, Dorothy Wilson, Holmes Herbert, Robert Frazer, Gwen Lee, Guinn (Big Boy) Williams, Fred Santley, Frances Sayles, Barbara Rogers
Director: Frank R. Strayer
Screenplay: Karl Brown, Robert Ellis
Producer: Maury M. Cohen

DESIRABLE
(Warner Brothers, September, 1934) 70 Minutes
Jean Muir, George Brent, Verree Teasdale, Arthur Aylesworth, Joan Wheeler, Barbara Leonard, *Charles Starrett,* John Halliday, Jim Miller, Virginia Hammond, Doris Atkinson, Pauline True, Russell Hopton
Director: Archie L. Mayo
Story/Screenplay: Mary McCall, Jr.

GENTLEMEN ARE BORN
(First National/Vitaphone, November 24, 1934)
74 Minutes
Franchot Tone, Jean Muir, Margaret Lindsay, Ann Dvorak, Ross Alexander, Nick (Dick) Foran, *Charles Starrett,* Russell Hicks, Robert Light, Arthur Aylesworth, Henry O'Neill, Addison Richards, Marjorie Gateson, Bradley Page
Director: Alfred E. Green
Story: Robert Lee Johnson
Screenplay: Eugene Solow, Robert Lee Johnson

SILVER STREAK
(RKO Radio, November 30, 1934) 85 Minutes
Charles Starrett, Sally Blane, Hardie Albright, Edgar Kennedy, Irving Pichel, William Farnum, Arthur Lake, Guinn Williams, Doris Dawson, Trevor von Eltz, Murray Kinnel, Harry Allen, James Bradbury
Director: Tommy Atkins
Story: Roger Whately
Screenplay: Roger Whately, H. W. Hanemann, Jack O'Donnell
Associate Producer: Glendon Aklvine

SONS OF STEEL

(Chesterfield, January 11, 1935) 65 Minutes
Charles Starrett, Polly Ann Young, William Bakewell, Walter Walker, Aileen Pringle, Holmes Herbert, Richard Carlyle, Florence Roberts, Adolf Miller, Jack Shutta, Lloyd Ingraham, Edward Le Saint, Tom Rickets, Edgar Norton, Barbara Bedford, Harry Semels, Al Thompson
Director: Charles Lamont
Story/Screenplay: Charles R. Belden
Producer: George R. Batcheller

A SHOT IN THE DARK

(Chesterfield, March 6, 1935) 69 Minutes
Charles Starrett, Robert Warwick, Edward Van Sloan, Marion Shilling, Doris Lloyd, Helen Jerome Eddy, James Bush, Julian Madison, Ralph Brooks, Eddie Tamblyn, Robert McKenzie, George Morrell, Herbert Bunston, Broderick O'Farrell, John Davidson, Jane Keckley
Director: Charles Lamont
Adaptation/Screenplay: Charles S. Belden
Story: Clifford Orr - "The Dartmouth Murders"
Producer: George R. Batcheller

ONE NEW YORK NIGHT

(MGM, April 2, 1935) 71 Minutes
Franchot Tone, Una Merkel, Conrad Nagel, Harvey Stephens, Steffi Duna, *Charles Starrett,* Louise Henry, Tommy Dugan, Harold Huber, Henry Kolker
Producer: Bernard H. Hymon
Director: Jack Conway
Screenplay: Frank Davis
Story: Edwards Childs Carpenter - from play "Order Please" which was based on a play by Walter Hockett

WHAT PRICE CRIME?

(Beacon Pictures, May, 1935)
Charles Starrett, Virginia Cherrill, Noel Madison, Charles Delaney, Jack Mulhall, Nina Guilbert, Henry Rocquemore, Gordon Griffith, John Elliott, Arthur Loft, Earl Tree, Al Baffert, Jack Cowell, Arthur Roland, Edwin Argus, Monte Carter, Lafe McKee
Director: Albert Herman
Story: Al Martin
Producer: Max Alexander
Film Editor: S. Roy Luby

MAKE A MILLION

(Monogram, July 12, 1935) 64 Minutes
Charles Starrett, Pauline Brooks, George E. Stone, James Burke, Guy Usher, Norman Houston, Monte Carter, Jimmy Aubrey, George Cleveland
Director: Lewis D. Collins
Story: Emmett Anthony
Screenplay: Charles Logue
Producer: Trem Carr

SO RED THE ROSE

(Paramount, November 22, 1935) 82 Minutes
Margaret Sullavan, Walter Connolly, Randolph Scott, Elizabeth Patterson, Janet Beecher, Harry Ellerbe, Dickie Moore, Robert Cummings, *Charles Starrett,* Johnny Downs, Daniel Haynes, Clarence Muse, James Burke, Warner Richmond, Alfred Delcambre
Director: King Vidor
Screenplay: Lawrence Stallings, Maxwell Anderson, Edwin Justus Mayer
Story: Stark Young
Producer: Douglas McLean

UNDERCOVER

(Booth Dominions Pictures, 1935)
Charles Starrett, Adrienne Dore, Kenneth Duncan, Wheeler Oakman, Eric Clavering, Phil Brandon, Elliott Lorraine, Austin Moran, Grace Webster, Gilmore Young, Farnham Barter, Muriel Deane
Director: Sam Neufield (Sam Newfield)
Producers: J. R. Booth and Arthur Gottlieb
Production Manager: Jack Chisholm

GALLANT DEFENDER

(Columbia, November 30, 1935) 60 Minutes
Charles Starrett, Joan Perry, Harry Woods, Edward J. LeSaint, Jack Clifford, Al Bridge, George Billings, George Chesebro, Edmund Cobb, Frank Ellis, Jack Rockwell, Tom London, Stanley Blystone, Lew Meehan, Merrill McCormack, Glenn Strange, Al Ferguson, Slim Whitaker, Bud Osborne, Sons of the Pioneers (Roy Rogers, Bob Nolan, Tim Spencer, Hugh and Carl Farr)
Director: David Selman
Story: Peter B. Kyne
Screenplay: Ford Beebe

THE MYSTERIOUS AVENGER

(Columbia, January 17, 1936)
Charles Starrett, Joan Perry, Wheeler Oakman, Edward J. LeSaint, Lafe McKee, Hal Price, Charles Locher (Jon Hall), George Chesebro, Jack Rockwell, Dick Botiller, Edmund Cobb, Sons of the Pioneers (Roy Rogers, Bob Nolan, Hugh Farr, Karl Farr, Tim Spencer)
Director: David Selman
Story: Credited to Peter B. Kyne
Story/Screenplay: Ford Beebe

SECRET PATROL

(Columbia, June 3, 1936) 60 Minutes
Charles Starrett, Finis Barton, J. P. McGowan, Henry Mollinson, LeStrange Millman, Arthur Kerr, Reginald Hincks, Ted Mapes, James McGrath
Director: David Selman
Story: Peter B. Kyne
Screenplay: J. P. McGowan, Robert Watson

CODE OF THE RANGE

(Columbia, October 9, 1936) 55 Minutes

Charles Starrett, Mary Blake, Ed Coxen, Allan Caven, Edward Peil, Sr., Edmund Cobb, Edward J. LeSaint, Ralph McCullough, George Chesebro, Art Mix, Albert J. Smith

Director: C. C. Coleman, Jr.
Story: credited to Peter B. Kyne
Screenplay: Ford Beebe

ALONG CAME LOVE

(Paramount, November 6, 1936) 7 Reels

Irene Hervey, *Charles Starrett,* Doris Kenyon, H. B. Warner, Irene Franklin, Bernadine Hayes, Ferinand Gottschalk, Charles Judels, Frank Reicher, Mathilde Comont

Director: Bert Lytele
Story/Screenplay: Austin Strong, Arthur Caesar
Producer: Richard A. Rowland

THE COWBOY STAR

(Columbia, November 20, 1936) 56 Minutes

Charles Starrett, Iris Meredith, Si Jenks, Marc Lawrence, Edward Peil, Sr., Wally Albright, Ralph McCullough, Dick Terry, Landers Stevens, Winifred Hari, Nick Copeland, Lew Meehan

Director: David Selman
Story: Frank Melford, Cornelius Reece
Screenplay: Frances Guihan

STAMPEDE

(Columbia, November 27, 1936) 58 Minutes

Charles Starrett, Finis Barton, J. P. McGowan, LeStrange Millman, James McGrath, Arthur Kerr, Jack Atkinson, Mike Heppell, Ted Mapes

Director: Ford Beebe
Story: Ford Beebe (credited to Peter B. Kyne)
Screenplay: Robert Watson

Si Jenks watches as Charles Starrett signs autographs for a bunch of lovelies in **The Cowboy Star** (Columbia, 1936).

DODGE CITY TRAIL

(Columbia, December, 1936) 7 Reels

Charles Starrett, Donald Grayson, Marion Weldon, Russell Hicks, Si Jenks, Al Bridge, Art Mix, Ernie Adams, Lew Meehan, Hank Bell, Jack Rockwell, George Chesebro, Blackie Whiteford

Director: C. C. Coleman, Jr.
Screenplay: Harold Shumate
Assistant Director: William E. Mull

WESTBOUND MAIL

(Columbia, January 22, 1937) 54 Minutes

Charles Starrett, Rosalind Keith, Edward Keane, Arthur Stone, Ben Weldon, Al Bridge, George Chesebro, Art Mix

Director: Folmer Blangsted
Story: James P. Hogan
Screenplay: Frances Guihan

TRAPPED

(Columbia, March 5, 1937) 55 Minutes

Charles Starrett, Peggy Stratford, Robert Middlemass, Alan Sears, Ted Oliver, Lew Meehan, Ed Peil, Jack Rockwell, Edward J. LeSaint, Frances Sayles, Art Mix

Director: Leon Barsha
Story: Claude Rister
Screenplay: John Rathmell

TWO GUN LAW

(Columbia, April 7, 1937) 56 Minutes

Charles Starrett, Peggy Stratford, Hank Bell, Edward J. LeSaint, Charles Middleton, Alan Bridge, Lee Prather, Dick Curtis, Vic Potel, George Chesebro, Art Mix, George Morrell, Tex Cooper

Director: Leon Barsha
Story: Norman Sheldon
Screenplay: John Rathmell

TWO-FISTED SHERIFF

(Columbia, June 15, 1937) 60 Minutes

Charles Starrett, Barbara Weeks, Bruce Lane, Ed Peil, Alan Sears, Walter Downing, Ernie Adams, Claire McDowell, Frank Ellis, Robert Walker, George Chesebro, Art Mix, Al Bridge, Dick Botiller, George Morrell, Merrill McCormack, Edmund Cobb, Tex Cooper, Dick Cramer, Dick Alexander, Maston Williams, Ethan Laidlaw, Steve Clark, Wally West, Fred Burns, Charles Brinley

Director: Leon Barsha
Story: William Colt MacDonald
Screenplay: Paul Perez

ONE MAN JUSTICE

(Columbia, July 1, 1937) 59 Minutes

Charles Starrett, Barbara Weeks, Hal Taliaferro (Wally Wales), Jack Clifford, Al Bridge, Walter Downing, Mary Gordon, Jack Lipson, Edmund Cobb, Dick Curtis, Maston Williams, Harry Fleischman, Art Mix, Hank Bell, Steve Clark, Frank Ellis, Ethan Laidlaw, Eddie Laughton, Ted Mapes, Lew Meehan, Merrill McCormack

Director: Leon Barsha
Story: William Colt MacDonald (credited to Peter B. Kyne)
Screenplay: Paul Perez

THE OLD WYOMING TRAIL

(Columbia, November 8, 1937) 56 Minutes

Charles Starrett, Donald Grayson, Barbara Weeks, Dick Curtis, Edward J. LeSaint, Guy Usher, George Chesebro, Edward Peil, Edward Hearn, Art Mix, Slim Whitaker, Alma Chester, Ernie Adams, Dick Botiller, Frank Ellis, Joe Yrigoyen, Charles Brinley, Fred Burns, Si Jenks, Curley Dresden, Ray Whitley, Blackie Whiteford, Tom London, Art Dillard, Ray Jones, Jerome Ward, Ed Javregi, Tex Cooper, Sons of the Pioneers (Bob Nolan, Roy Rogers, Tim Spencer, Hugh and Carl Farr)

Director: Folmer Blangsted
Story: J. Benton Cheney
Screenplay: Ed Earl Repp

OUTLAWS OF THE PRAIRIE

(Columbia, December, 1937) 59 Minutes

Charles Starrett, Donald Grayson, Iris Meredith, Edward J. LeSaint, Hank Bell, Dick Curtis, Norman Willis, Edmund Cobb, Art Mix, Steve Clark, Earle Hodgins, Dick Alexander, Frank Shannon, Fred Burns, Jack Rockwell, Jack Kirk, George Chesebro, Charles LeMoyne, Frank Ellis, Frank McCarroll, Curley Dresden, Vernon Dent, George Morrell, Buel Bryant, Ray Jones, Jim Corey, Blackie Whiteford, Lee Shumway, Bob Burns, Sons of the Pioneers (Bob Nolan, Tim Spencer, Pat Brady, Hugh and Karl Farr)

Director: Sam Nelson
Story: Harry Olstead
Screenplay: Ed Earl Repp

Charles Starrett protects Iris Meredith in **Call of the Rockies** (Columbia, 1938).

CATTLE RAIDERS
(Columbia, February 12, 1938) 61 Minutes
Charles Starrett, Donald Grayson, Iris Meredith, Bob Nolan, Dick Curtis, Allen Brook, Edward J. LeSaint, Edmund Cobb, George Chesebro, Ed Coxen, Steve Clark, Art Mix, Clem Horton, Alan Sears, Ed Peil, Jim Thorpe, Hank Bell, Blackie Whiteford, Sons of the Pioneers, Jack Clifford, Frank Ellis, Curley Dresden, Merrill McCormack, George Morrell, Robert Burns, Wally West, Forrest Taylor, Horace B. Carpenter, James Mason
Director: Sam Nelson
Story: Folmer Blangsted
Screenplay: Joseph Poland, Ed Earl Repp

START CHEERING
(Columbia, March 3, 1938) 78 Minutes
Jimmy Durante, Walter Connolly, Joan Perry, *Charles Starrett,* Professor Quiz, Edward Earle, Gertrude Niesen, Raymond Walburn, Broderick Crawford, Hal LeRoy, Ernest Truex, Virginia Dale, Charley Chase, Jimmy Wallington, Romo Vincent, Gene Morgan, Louise Stanley, Arthur Hoyt, Howard Hickman, Minerva Urecal, Arthur Loft, Nick Lukats, Louis Prima and His Band, Johnny Green and His Orchestra, The 3 Stooges (Curly Howard, Moe Howard, Larry Fine)
Director: Albert S. Rogell
Story: Corey Ford
Screenplay: Eugene Solow, Richard E. Wormser, Phillip Rapp
Associate Producer: Nat Perrin

CALL OF THE ROCKIES
(Columbia, April 30, 1938) 54 Minutes
Charles Starrett, Donald Grayson, Iris Meredith, Bob Nolan, Dick Curtis, Edward J. LeSaint, Edmund Cobb, Art Mix, John Tyrell, George Chesebro, Glenn Strange, Sons of the Pioneers
Director: Alan James
Screenplay: Ed Earl Repp
Producer: Harry Decker

LAW OF THE PLAINS
(Columbia, May 12, 1938) 58 Minutes
Charles Starrett, Iris Meredith, Bob Nolan, Robert Warwick, Dick Curtis, Edward J. LeSaint, Edmund Cobb, Art Mix, Jack Rockwell, George Chesebro, Jack Long, John Tyrell, Sons of the Pioneers
Director: Sam Nelson
Screenplay: Maurice Geraghty

WEST OF CHEYENNE
(Columbia, June 30, 1938) 59 Minutes
Charles Starrett, Iris Meredith, Bob Nolan, Pat Brady, Dick Curtis, Edward LeSaint, Edmund Cobb, Art Mix, John Tyrell, Ernie Adams, Jack Rockwell, Tex Cooper, Sons of the Pioneers
Director: Sam Nelson
Story/Screenplay: Ed Earl Repp

SOUTH OF ARIZONA
(Columbia, July 28, 1938) 56 Minutes
Charles Starrett, Iris Meredith, Bob Nolan, Dick Curtis, Robert Fiske, Edmund Cobb, Art Mix, Dick Botiller, Lafe McKee, Ed Coxen, Hank Bell, Hal Taliaferro, George Morrell, Steve Clark, John Tyrell, Sons of the Pioneers (Bob Nolan, Pat Brady, Hugh and Carl Farr, Lloyd Perryman).
Director: Sam Nelson
Screenplay: Bennett Cohen

THE COLORADO TRAIL
(Columbia, September 8, 1938) 55 Minutes
Charles Starrett, Iris Meredith, Edward J. LeSaint, Al Bridge, Robert Fiske, Dick Curtis, Bob Nolan, Hank Bell, Edward Peil, Sr., Edmund Cobb, Jack Clifford, Dick Botiller, Sons of the Pioneers, Stanley Brown
Director: Sam Nelson
Screenplay: Charles Francis Royal
Producer: Harry Decker

WEST OF THE SANTA FE
(Columbia, October 3, 1938) 57 Minutes
Charles Starrett, Iris Meredith, Dick Curtis, Robert Fiske, LeRoy Mason, Bob Nolan, Hank Bell, Edmund Cobb, Clem Horton, Dick Botiller, Edward Hearn, Edward J. LeSaint, Buck Connors, Bud Osborne, Sons of the Pioneers, Blackie Whiteford, Hal Taliaferro
Director: Sam Nelson
Screenplay: Bennett Cohen

RIO GRANDE
(Columbia, December 8, 1938) 58 Minutes
Charles Starrett, Ann Doran, Bob Nolan, Dick Curtis, Pat Brady, Hank Bell, Art Mix, George Chesebro, Lee Prather, Hal Taliaferro, Edward J. LeSaint, Ed Peil, Sr., Ted Mapes, Harry Strang, Fred Burns, Forrest Taylor, Stanley Brown, George Morrell, Sons of the Pioneers, John Tyrell, Fred Evans
Director: Sam Nelson
Screenplay: Charles Francis Royal

THE THUNDERING WEST
(Columbia, January 12, 1939) 57 Minutes
Charles Starrett, Iris Meredith, Bob Nolan, Hal Taliaferro, Dick Curtis, Hank Bell, Edward J. LeSaint, Blackie Whiteford, Art Mix, Robert Fiske, Edmund Cobb, Ed Peil, Sr., Slim Whitaker, Steve Clark, Fred Burns, Clem Horton, Art Dillard, Art Mix, The Sons of the Pioneers
Director: Sam Nelson
Screenplay: Bennett Cohen
Story: Gibe Lambert Hillyer

TEXAS STAMPEDE
(Columbia, February 9, 1939) 59 Minutes
Charles Starrett, Iris Meredith, Fred Kohler, Jr., Bob Nolan, Lee Prather, Ray Bennett, Blackjack Ward, Hank Bell, Edmund Cobb, Edward Hearn, Ed Coxen, Ernie Adams, Blackie Whiteford, Charles Brinley, Sons of the Pioneers, Dick Botiller, Joe Weaver, Horace B. Carpenter
Director: Sam Nelson
Story: Forrest Sheldon - "The Dawn Trail"
Screenplay: Charles Francis Royal

NORTH OF THE YUKON
(Columbia, March 30, 1939) 59 Minutes
Charles Starrett, Linda Winters (Dorothy Comingore), Bob Nolan and the Sons of the Pioneers, Lane Chandler, Paul Sutton, Robert Fiske, Vernon Steele, Edmund Cobb, Tom London, Dick Botiller, Kenne Duncan, Harry Cording, Hal Taliaferro, Ed Brady
Director: Sam Nelson
Screenplay: Bennett Cohen

SPOILERS OF THE RANGE
(Columbia, April 27, 1939) 57 Minutes
Charles Starrett, Iris Meredith, Dick Curtis, Kenneth MacDonald, Hank Bell, Bob Nolan and the Sons of the Pioneers, Edward J. LeSaint, Forbes Murray, Art Mix, Edmund Cobb, Edward Peil, Sr., Ethan Laidlaw, Charles Brinley, Joe Weaver, Horace B. Carpenter, Carl Sepulveda
Director: C. C. Coleman, Jr.
Story/Screenplay: Paul Franklin

WESTERN CARAVANS
(Columbia, June 15, 1939) 58 Minutes
Charles Starrett, Iris Meredith, Bob Nolan, Russell Simpson, Hal Taliaferro, Dick Curtis, Hank Bell, Sammy McKim, Edmund Cobb, Ethan Laidlaw, Steve Clark, Herman Hack, Charles Brinley, Sons of the Pioneers (Bob Nolan, Pat Brady, Tim Spencer, Hugh and Karl Farr)
Director: Sam Nelson
Screenplay: Bennett Cohen

THE MAN FROM SUNDOWN
(Columbia, July 15, 1939) 58 Minutes
Charles Starrett, Iris Meredith, Richard Fiske, Jack Rockwell, Al Bridge, Dick Botiller, Ernie Adams, Bob Nolan, Robert Fiske, Edward Peil, Sr., Clem Horton, Forrest Dillon, Tex Cooper, Al Haskell, Edward J. LeSaint, Kit Guard, George Chesebro, Oscar Gaham, Frank Ellis, Sons of the Pioneers, Clem Horton, Ernie Adams
Director: Sam Nelson
Story: Paul Franklin

RIDERS OF BLACK RIVER
(Columbia, August 23, 1939) 59 Minutes
Charles Starrett, Iris Meredith, Bob Nolan, Dick Curtis, Stanley Brown, Edmund Cobb, Francis Sayles, Forrest Taylor, George Chesebro, Carl Sepulveda, Ethan Allen, Olin Francis, Master Williams, Sons of the Pioneers, Clem Horton
Director: Norman Deming
Story: Ford Beebe - "The Revenge Rider"
Screenplay: Bennett Cohen

OUTPOST OF THE MOUNTIES
(Columbia, September 14, 1939) 63 Minutes
Charles Starrett, Iris Meredith, Stanley Brown, Kenneth MacDonald, Edmund Cobb, Bob Nolan, Lane Chandler, Dick Curtis, Albert Morin, Hal Taliaferro, Pat O'Hara, Sons of the Pioneers
Director: C. C. Coleman, Jr.
Screenplay: Paul Franklin

THE STRANGER FROM TEXAS
(Columbia, December 8, 1939) 54 Minutes
Charles Starrett, Lorna Gray (Adrian Booth), Richard Fiske, Dick Curtis, Edmund Cobb, Bob Nolan, Al Bridge, Jack Rockwell, Hal Taliaferro, Edward J. LeSaint, Buel Bryant, Art Mix, George Chesebro
Director: Sam Nelson
Story: "The Mysterious Avenger" - Ford Beebe
Screenplay: Paul Franklin

TWO-FISTED RANGERS
(Columbia, January 4, 1940) 62 Minutes
Charles Starrett, Iris Meredith, Bob Nolan and the Sons of the Pioneers, Kenneth MacDonald, Hal Taliaferro, Dick Curtis, Bill Cody, Jr., Ethan Laidlaw, James Craig, Bob Woodward, Francis Walker
Director: Joseph H. Lewis
Screenplay: Fred Myton

BULLETS FOR RUSTLERS
(Columbia, March 5, 1940) 58 Minutes
Charles Starrett, Lorna Gray (Adrian Booth), Bob Nolan, Dick Curtis, Jack Rockwell, Kenneth MacDonald, Edward J. LeSaint, Francis Walker, Eddie Laughton, Lee Prather, Hal Taliaferro, Sons of the Pioneers
Director: Sam Nelson
Screenplay: John Rathmell

BLAZING SIX SHOOTERS
(Columbia, April 4, 1940) 61 Minutes
Charles Starrett, Iris Meredith, Dick Curtis, Bob Nolan, Al Bridge, George Cleveland, Henry Hall, Stanley Brown, John Tyrell, Eddie Laughton, Francis Walker, Edmund Cobb, Bruce Bennett, The Sons of the Pioneers
Director: Joseph H. Lewis
Screenplay: Paul Franklin

TEXAS STAGECOACH
(Columbia, May 23, 1940) 59 Minutes
Charles Starrett, Iris Meredith, Bob Nolan, Dick Curtis, Kenneth MacDonald, Edward J. LeSaint, Harry Cording, Francis Walker, Pat Brady, George Becinita, Don Beddoe, Lillian Lawrence, Fred Burns, Eddie Laughton, The Sons of the Pioneers, Blackie Whiteford, George Chesebro, George Morrell
Director: Joseph H. Lewis
Screenplay: Fred Myton

THE DURANGO KID
(Columbia, August 23, 1940) 60 Minutes
Charles Starrett, Luana Walters, Bob Nolan, Kenneth MacDonald, Francis Walker, Forrest Taylor, Pat Brady, Melvin Lang, Frank LaRue, Jack Rockwell, Sons of the Pioneers, John Tyrell, Steve Clark, Ben Taggart
Director: Lambert Hillyer
Screenplay: Paul Franklin

WEST OF ABILENE
(Columbia, October 21, 1940) 57 Minutes
Charles Starrett, Marjorie Cooley, Bruce Bennett, Bob Nolan, Don Beddoe, William Pawley, Pat Brady, George Cleveland, Forrest Taylor, Bud Osborne, Al Bridge, Frank Ellis, Sons of the Pioneers
Director: Ralph Cedar
Screenplay: Paul Franklin

THUNDERING FRONTIER
(Columbia, December 5, 1940) 57 Minutes
Charles Starrett, Iris Meredith, Bob Nolan, Carl Stockdale, Fred Burns, John Dilson, Alex Callam, Ray Bennett, Blackie Whiteford, John Tyrell, Francis Walker, Pat Brady, Sons of the Pioneers
Director: D. Ross Lederman
Screenplay: Paul Franklin

THE PINTO KID
(Columbia, February 5, 1941) 61 Minutes
Charles Starrett, Louise Currie, Bob Nolan, Paul Sutton, Hank Bell, Francis Walker, Ernie Adams, Jack Rockwell, Pat Brady, Roger Gray, Dick Botiller, Steve Clark, Frank Ellis, Sons of the Pioneers
Director: Lambert Hillyer
Screenplay: Fred Myton
Producer: Jack Fier

OUTLAWS OF THE PANHANDLE
(Columbia, February 27, 1941) 59 Minutes
Charles Starrett, Frances Robinson, Bob Nolan, Richard Fiske, Ray Teal, Lee Prather, Bud Osborne, Pat Brady, Steve Clark, Eddie Laughton, Jack Low, Norman Willis, Blackie Whiteford, Stanley Brown, Sons of the Pioneers
Director: Sam Nelson
Screenplay: Paul Franklin
Producer: Jack Fier

THE MEDICO OF PAINTED SPRINGS
(Columbia, June 26, 1941) 58 Minutes
Charles Starrett, Terry Walker, Richard Fiske, Ray Bennett, Ben Taggert, Bud Osborne, Edmund Cobb, Edith Elliott, Steve Clark, Lloyd Bridges, George Chesebro, Charles Hamilton, Jim Corey, The Simp-Phonie
Director: Lambert Hillyer
Story: James L. Rubel
Screenplay: Winston Miller

THUNDER OVER THE PRAIRIE
(Columbia, July 30, 1941) 60 Minutes
Charles Starrett, Eileen O'Hearn, Cliff Edwards, Carl (Cal) Shrum and His Rhythm Rangers, Stanley Brown, Danny Mummert, David Sharpe, Joe McGuinn, Donald Curtis, Ted Adams, Jack Rockwell, Budd Buster, Horace B. Carpenter
Director: Lambert Hillyer
Story: James L. Rubel
Screenplay: Betty Burbridge
Producer: William Berke

PRAIRIE STRANGER
(Columbia, September 18, 1941) 58 Minutes
Charles Starrett, Cliff "Ukulele Ike" Edwards, Patti McCarty, Forbes Murray, Frank LaRue, Archie Twitchell, Francis Walter, Edmund Cobb, Jim Corey, Russ Powell, George Morrell, Lew Preston and His Ranch Hands
Director: Lambert Hillyer
Story: James Rubel
Screenplay: Winston Miller
Producer: William Berke

THE ROYAL MOUNTED PATROL

(Columbia, November 13, 1941) 59 Minutes

Charles Starrett, Russell Hayden, Wanda McKay, Donald Curtis, Lloyd Bridges, Kermit Maynard, Evan Thomas, Ted Adams, Harrison Greene, Ted Mapes, George Morrell

Director: Lambert Hillyer
Screenplay: Winston Miller
Producer: William Berke

RIDERS OF THE BADLAND

(Columbia, December 18, 1941) 57 Minutes

Charles Starrett, Russell Hayden, Cliff Edwards, Ilene Brewer, Kay Hughes, Roy Barcroft, Rick Anderson, Edith Leach, Ethan Laidlaw, Harry Cording, Hal Price, Ted Mapes, George J. Lewis, John Cason, Edmund Cobb, Francis Walker

Director: Howard Bretherton
Screenplay: Betty Burbridge
Producer: William Berke

WEST OF TOMBSTONE

(Columbia, January 15, 1942) 59 Minutes

Charles Starrett, Russell Hayden, Cliff Edwards, Marcella Martin, Gordon DeMain, Clancy Cooper, Jack Kirk, Budd Buster, Tom London, Francis Walker, Ray Jones, Eddie Laughton, Lloyd Bridges, Ernie Adams, George Morrell

Director: Howard Bretherton
Screenplay: Maurice Geraghty
Producer: William Berke

LAWLESS PLAINSMEN

(Columbia, March 17, 1942) 59 Minutes

Charles Starrett, Russell Hayden, Cliff Edwards, Luana Walters, Ray Bennett, Gwen Kenyon, Frank LaRue, Stanley Brown, Nick Thompson, Eddie Laughton, Carl Mathews

Director: William Berke
Screenplay: Luci Ward
Producer: Jack Fier

DOWN RIO GRANDE WAY

(Columbia, April 23, 1942) 57 Minutes

Charles Starrett, Russell Hayden, Britt Wood, Rose Anne Stevens, Norman Willis, Davidson Clark, Edmund Cobb, Budd Buster, Joseph Eggenton, Paul Newlin, Betty Roadman, William Desmond, Jim Corey, Tom Smith, Steve Clark, Forrest Taylor, Edward Peil, Sr., John Cason, Art Mix, Kermit Maynard, Frank McCarroll

Director: William Berke
Screenplay: Paul Franklin
Producer: Jack Fier

RIDERS OF THE NORTHLAND

(Columbia, June 18, 1942) 58 Minutes

Charles Starrett, Russell Hayden, Cliff Edwards, Shirley Patterson, Lloyd Bridges, Bobby Larson, Kenneth MacDonald, Paul Sutton, Robert O. Davis, Joe McGuinn, Francis Walker, George Filtz, Blackjack Ward, Dick Jensen

Director: William Berke
Screenplay: Paul Franklin
Producer: Jack Fier

BAD MEN OF THE HILLS

(Columbia, August 13, 1942) 58 Minutes

Charles Starrett, Russell Hayden, Cliff Edwards, Luana Walters, Al Bridge, Guy Usher, Joel Friedkin, Norma Jean Wooters, John Shay, Dick Botiller, Art Mix, Jack Ingram, Ben Corbett, Carl Sepulveda, John Cason, Frank Ellis

Director: William Berke
Screenplay: Luci Ward
Producer: Jack Fier

OVERLAND TO DEADWOOD

(Columbia, September 25, 1942) 59 Minutes

Charles Starrett, Russell Hayden, Leslie Brooks, Cliff Edwards, Norman Willis, Francis Walker, Lynton Brent, Matt Willis, June Pickrell, Gordon DeMain, Art Mix, Herman Hack, Bud Osborne, Bud Geary

Director: William Berke
Screenplay: Paul Franklin
Producer: Jack Fier

RIDING THROUGH NEVADA

(Columbia, October 2, 1942)

Charles Starrett, Shirley Patterson, Arthur Hunnicutt, Jimmie Davis and His Rainbow Ramblers, Clancy Cooper, Davidson Clark, Minerva Urecal, Edmund Cobb, Ethan Laidlaw, Kermit Maynard, Art Mix, Stanley Brown

Director: William Berke
Screenplay: Gerald Geraghty
Producer: Jack Fier

PARDON MY GUN

(Columbia, December 1, 1942) 56 Minutes

Charles Starrett, Alma Carroll, Arthur Hunnicutt, Texas Jim Lewis and his Lone Star Cowboys, Noah Beery, Dick Curtis, Lloyd Bridges, Ted Mapes, Dave Harper, Roger Gray, Jack Kirk, Art Mix, George Morrell, Joel Friedkin, Guy Usher, Denver Dixon

Director: William Berke
Story/Screenplay: Wyndham Gittens
Producer: Jack Fier

THE FIGHTING BUCKAROO

(Columbia, February 1, 1943) 58 Minutes

Charles Starrett, Arthur Hunnicutt, Kay Harris, Stanley Brown, Wheeler Oakman, Forrest Taylor, Robert Stevens, Norma Jean Wooters, Roy Butler, Lane Bradford, Ernest Tubb with Johnny Luther's Ranch Boys

Director: William Berke
Screenplay: Luci Ward
Producer: Jack Fier

LAW OF THE NORTHWEST

(Columbia, May 27, 1943) 57 Minutes

Charles Starrett, Shirley Patterson, Arthur Hunnicutt, Stanley Brown, Davidson Clark, Don Curtis, Douglas Levitt, Reginald Barlow, Douglas Drake

Director: William Berke
Screenplay: Luci Ward
Producer: Jack Fier

FRONTIER FURY

(Columbia, June 24, 1943) 55 Minutes

Charles Starrett Arthur Hunnicutt, Roma Aldrich, Clancy Cooper, I. Stanford Jolley, Edmund Cobb, Bruce Bennett, Ted Mapes, Bill Wilkerson, Stanley Brown, Joel Friedkin, Frank LaRue, Lew Meehan, Chief Yowlachie, Johnny Bond, Jimmy Davis and His Singing Buckaroos

Director: William Berke
Screenplay: Betty Burbridge
Producer: Jack Fier

ROBIN HOOD OF THE RANGE

(Columbia, July 29, 1943) 57 Minutes

Charles Starrett, Arthur Hunnicutt, Kay Harris, Jimmy Wakely Trio, Stanley Brown, Kenneth Mac-Donald, Douglas Drake, Bud Osborne, Edward Peil, Sr., Frank LaRue, Frank McCarroll, Ray Jones, Johnny Bond, Merrill McCormack

Director: William Berke
Screenplay: Betty Burbridge
Producer: Jack Fier

HAIL TO THE RANGERS

(Columbia, September 16, 1943) 57 Minutes

Charles Starrett, Arthur Hunnicutt, Leota Atcher, Robert Atcher, Norman Willis, Lloyd Bridges, Ted Adams, Ernie Adams, Tom London, Davidson Clark, Jack Kirk, Edmund Cobb, Budd Buster, Art Mix, Eddie Laughton, Dick Botiller

Director: William Berke
Screenplay: Gerald Geraghty
Producer: Jack Fier

COWBOY IN THE CLOUDS

(Columbia, December 23, 1943)

Charles Starrett, Dub Taylor, Julie Duncan, Jimmy Wakely, Hal Taliaferro, Charles King, Lane Chandler, Davidson Clark, Dick Curtis, Ed Cassidy, Ted Mapes, John Tyrell, Paul Zarema

Director: Benjamin Kline
Screenplay: Elizabeth Beecher
Producer: Jack Fier

COWBOY CANTEEN

(Columbia, February 8, 1944) 72 Minutes

Charles Starrett, Jane Frazee, Vera Vague (Barbara Jo Allen), Tex Ritter, Guinn "Big Boy" Williams, The Mills Brothers, Jimmy Wakely and His Saddle Pals, Chickie and Buck, Roy Acuff and His Smokey Mountain Boys and Girls, the Tailor Maids, Dub Taylor, Max Terhune, Emmett Lynn, Edythe Elliott, Jeff Donnell, Dick Curtis

Director: Lew Landers
Screenplay: Paul Gangelin, Felix Adler
Producer: Jack Fier

SUNDOWN VALLEY

(Columbia, March 23, 1944) 55 Minutes

Charles Starrett, Bud Taylor, Jeanne Bates, Jimmy Wakely, Clancy Cooper, Jesse Arnold, Wheeler Oakman, Jack Ingram, Forrest Taylor, Joel Friedkin, Grace Lenard, Eddie Laughton, The Tennessee Ramblers

Director: Ben Kline
Screenplay: Luci Ward
Producer: Jack Fier

RIDING WEST

(Columbia, May 18, 1944) 58 Minutes
(Filmed in 1943)

Charles Starrett, Arthur Hunnicutt, Shirley Patterson, Clancy Cooper, Steve Clark, Wheeler Oakman, Blackie Whiteford, Bill Wilderson, Johnny Bond, Ernest Tubb

Director: William Berke
Screenplay: Luci Ward
Producer: Jack Fier

COWBOY FROM LONESOME RIVER

(Columbia, September 21, 1944) 55 Minutes

Charles Starrett, Vi Athens, Dub Taylor, Jimmy Wakely, Kenneth MacDonald, Ozie Waters, Arthur Wenzel, Shelby Atkinson, Foy Willing, Al Sloey, Craig Woods, Ian Keith, John Tyrell, Bud Geary, Steve Clark, Jack Rockwell

Director: Ben Kline
Screenplay: Luci Ward
Producer: Jack Fier

CYCLONE PRAIRIE RANGERS

(Columbia, November 9, 1944) 56 Minutes

Charles Starrett, Dub Taylor, Constance Worth, Jimmy Davis, Jimmy Wakely and His Saddle Pals, Foy Willing, Clancy Cooper, Bob Fiske, Ray Bennett, I. Stanford Jolley, Edmund Cobb, Forrest Taylor, Paul Zaremba, Eddie Phillips, John Tyrell, Ted Mapes
Director: Ben Kline
Screenplay: Elizabeth Beecher
Producer: Jack Fier

SADDLE LEATHER LAW

(Columbia, December 21, 1944)

Charles Starrett, Dub Taylor, Vi Athens, Lloyd Bridges, Reed Howes, Robert Kortman, Ted French, Frank LaRue, Edward Cassidy, Steve Clark, Nolan Leary, Budd Buster, Joseph Eggenton, Jimmy Wakely, Salty Holmes, Ted Adams, Frank O'Connor, Franklyn Farnum
Director: Ben Kline
Screenplay: Elizabeth Beecher
Producer: Jack Fier

SAGEBRUSH HEROES

(Columbia, February 1, 1945)

Charles Starrett, Dub Taylor, Constance Worth, Jimmy Wakely and His Saddle Pals, Ozie Waters, Elvin Field, Bobby Larson, Forrest Taylor, Joel Friedkin, Lane Chandler, Paul Zaremba, Eddie Laughton, Johnny Tyrell
Director: Benjamin Kline
Producer: Jack Fier

ROUGH RIDIN' JUSTICE

(Columbia, March 14, 1945) 58 Minutes

Charles Starrett, Dub Taylor, Betty Jane Graham, Jimmy Wakely and His Oklahoma Cowboys, Wheeler Oakman, Jack Ingram, Forrest Taylor, Jack Rockwell, Edmund Cobb, Dan White, Robert Kortman, George Chesebro, Robert Ross, Carl Sepulveda, Butch and Buddy
Director: Derwin Abrahams
Screenplay: Elizabeth Beecher
Producer: Jack Fier

RETURN OF THE DURANGO KID

(Columbia, April 19, 1945) 58 Minutes
(Durango Kid Series)

Charles Starrett, Tex Harding, Jean Stevens, John Calvert, Betty Roadman, Hal Price, Dick Botiller, Britt Wood, Ray Bennett, Paul Conrad, Steve Clark, Carl Sepulveda, Elmo Lincoln, Ted Mapes, Herman Hack, The Jesters
Director: Derwin Abrahams
Screenplay: J. Benton Cheney
Producer: Colbert Clark

BOTH BARRELS BLAZING

(Columbia, May 17, 1945) 57 Minutes
(Durango Kid Series)

Charles Starrett, Tex Harding, Dub Taylor, Pat Parrish, Emmett Lynn, Alan Bridge, Dan White, Edward Howard, The Jesters, Jack Rockwell, Charles King, Robert Barron, Mauritz Hugo
Director: Derwin Abrahams
Screenplay: William Lively
Associate Producer: Colbert Clark

RUSTLERS OF THE BADLANDS

(Columbia, August 16, 1945) 55 Minutes
(Durango Kid Series)

Charles Starrett, Tex Harding, Dub Taylor, Sally Bliss, George Eldredge, Edward Howard, Ray Bennett, Ted Mapes, Karl Hackett, James Nelson, Frank McCarroll, Carl Sepulveda, Steve Clark, Al Trace and His Silly Symphonists
Director: Derwin Abrahams
Story: Richard Hill Wilkinson
Screenplay: J. Benton Cheney
Producer: Colbert Clark

BLAZING THE WESTERN TRAIL

(Columbia, September 18, 1945) 60 Minutes
(Durango Kid Series)

Charles Starrett, Tex Harding, Dub Taylor, Carole Matthews, Alan Bridge, Nolan Leary, Virginia Sale, Steve Clark, Mauritz Hugo, Ethan Laidlaw, Edmund Cobb, Frank LaRue, Forrest Taylor, Francis Walker, Bob Wills and His Texas Playboys
Director: Vernon Keays
Screenplay: J. Benton Cheney
Associate Producer: Colbert Clark

OUTLAWS OF THE ROCKIES

(Columbia, September 18, 1945) 55 Minutes
(Durango Kid Series)

Charles Starrett, Tex Harding, Dub Taylor, Carole Matthews, Philip Van Zandt, I. Stanford Jolley, George Chesebro, Steve Clark, Jack Rockwell, Carolina Cotton, Spade Cooley
Director: Ray Nazarro
Screenplay: J. Benton Cheney
Associate Producer: Colbert Clark

LAWLESS EMPIRE

(Columbia, November 15, 1945) 58 Minutes

Charles Starrett, Tex Harding, Dub Taylor, Mildred Law, Johnny Walsh, John Calvert, Ethan Laidlaw, Forrest Taylor, Jack Rockwell, George Chesebro, Boyd Stockman, Lloyd Ingraham, Jessie Arnold, Tom Chatterton, Ray Jones, Bob Wills and the Texas Playboys
Director: Vernon Keays
Story: Elizabeth Beecher
Screenplay: Bennett Cohen
Associate Producer: Colbert Clark

TEXAS PANHANDLE

(Columbia, December 20, 1945) 57 Minutes
(Durango Kid Series)

Charles Starrett, Tex Harding, Dub Taylor, Nanette Parks, Carolina Cotton, Forrest Taylor, Edward Howard, Ted Mapes, George Chesebro, William Gould, Jack Kirk, Budd Buster, Tex Palmer, Hugh Hooker, Spade Cooley
Director: Ray Nazarro
Screenplay: Ed Earl Repp
Producer: Colbert Clark

FRONTIER GUNLAW

(Columbia, January 31, 1946) 60 Minutes
(Durango Kid Series)

Charles Starrett, Tex Harding, Dub Taylor, Jean Steven, Al Trace and His Silly Symphonists, Weldon Heyburn, Jack Rockwell, Frank LaRue, John Elliott, Bob Kortman, Stanley Price
Director: Derwin Abrahams
Story: Victor McLeon
Screenplay: Bennett Cohen
Producer: Colbert Clark

ROARING RANGERS

(Columbia, February 14, 1946) 55 Minutes
(Durango Kid Series)

Charles Starrett, Smiley Burnette, Adele Roberts, Jack Rockwell, Edward Cassidy, Mickey Kuhn, Edmund Cobb, Ted Mapes, Gerald Mackey, Bob Wilke, Herman Hack, Merle Travis and His Bronco Busters
Director: Ray Nazarro
Screenplay: Barry Shipman
Producer: Colbert Clark

GUNNING FOR VENGEANCE

(Columbia, March 21, 1946) 56 Minutes
(Durango Kid Series)

Charles Starrett, Smiley Burnette, Marjean Neville, Robert Kortman, George Chesebro, Frank LaRue, Lane Chandler, Phyliss Adair, Robert Williams, Jack Kirk, John Tyrell, Curt Barrett and the Trailsmen
Director: Ray Nazarro
Story: Louise Rousseau
Screenplay: Ed Earl Repp
Producer: Colbert Clark

GALLOPING THUNDER

(Columbia, April 25, 1946) 54 Minutes
(Durango Kid Series)

Charles Starrett, Smiley Burnette, Adele Roberts, Richard Bailey, Kermit Maynard, Edmund Cobb, Ray Bennett, Curt Barrett, John Merton, Nolan Leary, Budd Buster, Forrest Taylor, Merle Travis and His Bronco Busters
Director: Ray Nazarro
Screenplay: Ed Earl Repp
Producer: Colbert Clark

TWO-FISTED STRANGER

(Columbia, May 30, 1946) 50 Minutes
(Durango Kid Series)

Charles Starrett, Smiley Burnette, Doris Houck, Charles Murray, Lane Chandler, Ted Mapes, George Chesebro, Jack Rockwell, Herman Hack, I. Stanford Jolley, Edmund Cobb, Davidson Clark, Maudie Prickett, Zeke Clements
Director: Ray Nazarro
Story: Peter Whitehead
Screenplay: Robert Lee Johnson
Producer: Colbert Clark

THE DESERT HORSEMAN

(Columbia, July 11, 1946) 57 Minutes
(Durango Kid Series)

Charles Starrett, Smiley Burnette, Adele Roberts, Richard Bailey, John Merton, George Morgan, Tommy Coats, Jack Kirk, Bud Osborne, Riley Hill, Walt Shrum and His Colorado Hillbillies
Director: Ray Nazarro
Screenplay: Sherman Lowe
Producer: Colbert Clark

HEADING WEST

(Columbia, August 15, 1946) 54 Minutes
(Durango Kid Series)

Charles Starrett, Smiley Burnette, Doris Houck, Norman Willis, Nolan Leary, Bud Geary, Frank McCarroll, John Merton, Tom Chatterton, Hal Taliaferro, Stanley Price, Tommy Coates, Hank Penny and His Plantation Boys
Director: Ray Nazarro
Screenplay: Ed Earl Repp
Producer: Colbert Clark

LANDRUSH

(Columbia, October 18, 1946) 53 Minutes
(Durango Kid Series)

Charles Starrett, Smiley Burnette, Doris Houck, Emmett Lynn, Bud Geary, Stephen Barclay, Robert Kortman, George Chesebro, Bud Osborne, Ozie Waters and His Colorado Rangers
Director: Vernon Keays
Story/Screenplay: Michael Simmons
Producer: Colbert Clark

TERROR TRAIL
(Columbia, November 21, 1945) 55 Minutes
(Durango Kid Series)
Charles Starrett, Smiley Burnette, Barbara Pepper, Lane Chandler, Zon Murray, Elvin Eric Field, Tommy Coates, George Chesebro, Robert Barron, Budd Buster, Bill Clark, Ted Mapes, Ozie Waters and His Colorado Rangers
Director: Ray Nazarro
Story/Screenplay: Ed Earl Repp
Producer: Colbert Clark

THE FIGHTING FRONTIERSMAN
(Columbia, December 10, 1946) 61 Minutes
(Durango Kid Series)
Charles Starrett, Smiley Burnette, Helen Mowery, Emmett Lynn, Robert W. Filmer, George Chesebro, Zon Murray, Jim Diehl, Maudie Prickett, Russell Meeker, Frank Ellis, Ernie Adams, Frank LaRue, Jacques J. O'Mahoney (Jock Mahoney), Hank Newman and the Georgia Crackers
Director: Derwin Abrahams
Screenplay: Ed Earl Repp
Producer: Colbert Clark

SOUTH OF THE CHISHOLM TRAIL
(Columbia, January 30, 1947) 58 Minutes
(Durango Kid Series)
Charles Starrett, Smiley Burnette, Nancy Saunders, Frank Sully, Jim Diehl, Jack Ingram, George Chesebro, Frank LaRue, Jacques J. O'Mahoney (Jock Mahoney), Eddie Parker, Kit Guard, Ray Elder, Hank Newman and His Georgia Crackers
Director: Derwin Abrahams
Story/Screenplay: Michael Simmons
Producer: Colbert Clark

THE LONE HAND TEXAN
(Columbia, March 6, 1947) 54 Minutes
(Durango Kid Series)
Charles Starrett, Smiley Burnette, Mary Newton, Fred Sears, Mustard and Gravy, Maude Prickett, George Chesebro, Robert Stevens, Bob Cason, Jim Diehl, George Russell, Jasper Weldon, Ernest Stokes
Director: Ray Nazarro
Screenplay: Ed Earl Repp
Producer: Colbert Clark

WEST OF DODGE CITY
(Columbia, March 27, 1947) 57 Minutes
(Durango Kid Series)
Charles Starrett, Smiley Burnette, Nancy Saunders, Fred Sears, Glenn Stuart, I. Stanford Jolley, George Chesebro, Bob Wilke, Nolan Leary, Steve Clark, Zon Murray, Marshall Reed, Mustard and Gravy
Director: Ray Nazarro
Screenplay: Bert Horswell
Producer: Colbert Clark

LAW OF THE CANYON
(Columbia, April 24, 1947) 55 Minutes
(Durango Kid Series)
Charles Starrett, Smiley Burnette, Nancy Saunders, Buzz Henry, Fred Sears, George Chesebro, Edmund Cobb, Zon Murray, Jack Kirk, Bob Wilke, Frank Marlo, Texas Jim Lewis and His Lone Star Cowboys
Director: Ray Nazarro
Screenplay: Eileen Gary
Producer: Colbert Clark

PRAIRIE RAIDERS
(Columbia, May 29, 1947) 54 Minutes
(Durango Kid Series)
Charles Starrett, Smiley Burnette, Nancy Saunders, Robert Scott, Hugh Prosser, Lane Bradford, Ray Bennett, Doug Coppin, Steve Clark, Tommy Coates, Frank LaRue, Bob Cason, Ozie Waters and His Colorado Rangers
Director: Derwin Abrahams
Screenplay: Ed Earl Repp
Producer: Colbert Clark

THE STRANGER FROM PONCA CITY
(Columbia, July 3, 1947) 56 Minutes
(Durango Kid Series)
Charles Starrett, Smiley Burnette, Virginia Hunter, Paul Campbell, Jim Diehl, Forrest Taylor, Ted Mapes, Jacques O'Mahoney (Jock Mahoney), Tom McDonough, John Carpenter, Texas Jim Lewis and His Lone Star Cowboys
Director: Derwin Abrahams
Screenplay: Ed Earl Repp
Producer: Colbert Clark

RIDERS OF THE LONE STAR
(Columbia, August 14, 1947) 55 Minutes
(Durango Kid Series)
Charles Starrett, Smiley Burnette, Virginia Hunter, Steve Darrell, Edmund Cobb, Mark Dennis, Lane Bradford, Ted Mapes, George Chesebro, Peter Perkins, Eddie Parker, Curly Williams and His Georgia Peach Pickers
Director: Derwin Abrahams
Screenplay: Barry Shipman
Producer: Colbert Clark

BUCKAROO FROM POWDER RIVER
(Columbia, October 14, 1947) 55 Minutes
(Durango Kid Series)
Charles Starrett, Smiley Burnette, Eve Miller, Forrest Taylor, Paul Campbell, Doug Coppin, Phillip Morris, Casey MacGregor, Ted Adams, Ethan Laidlaw, Frank McCarroll, The Cass County Boys, Kermit Maynard
Director: Ray Nazarro
Screenplay: Norman S. Hall
Producer: Colbert Clark

LAST DAYS OF BOOT HILL
(Columbia, November 11, 1947) 56 Minutes
(Durango Kid Series)
Charles Starrett, Smiley Burnette, Virginia Hunter, Paul Campbell, Mary Newton, Bill Free, J. Courtland Lytton, Bob Wilke, Alan Bridge
Director: Ray Nazzaro
Screenplay: Norman S. Hall
Producer: Colbert Clark

SIX GUN LAW
(Columbia, January 4, 1948) 54 Minutes
(Durango Kid Series)
Charles Starrett, Smiley Burnette, Nancy Saunders, Paul Campbell, Hugh Prosser, George Chesebro, Billy Dix, Bob Wilke, Bob Cason, Ethan Laidlaw, Pierce Lyden, Bud Osborne, Budd Buster, Curly Clements and His Rodeo Rangers
Director: Ray Nazarro
Screenplay: Barry Shipman
Producer: Colbert Clark

PHANTOM VALLEY
(Columbia, February 19, 1948) 53 Minutes
(Durango Kid Series)
Charles Starrett, Smiley Burnette, Virginia Hunter, Sam Flint, Fred Sears, Joel Friedkin, Zon Murray, Robert Filmer, Mikel Conrad, Teddy Infuhr, Jerry Jerome, Ozie Waters and His Colorado Rangers
Director: Ray Nazarro
Screenplay: J. Benton Cheney
Producer: Colbert Clark

WEST OF SONORA
(Columbia, March 25, 1948) 52 Minutes
(Durango Kid Series)
Charles Starrett, Smiley Burnette, Steve Darrell, George Chesebro, Anita Castle, Hal Taliaferro, Bob Wilke, Emmett Lynn, Lynn Farr, Lloyd Ingraham, The Sunshine Boys
Director: Ray Nazarro
Screenplay: Barry Shipman
Producer: Colbert Clark

WHIRLWIND RAIDERS
(Columbia, May 13, 1948) 54 Minutes
(Durango Kid Series)
Charles Starrett, Smiley Burnette, Fred Sears, Nancy Saunders, Don Kay Reynolds, Jack Ingram, Philip Morris, Patrick Hurst, Eddie Parker, Lynn Farr, Arthur Loft, Doye O'Dell and the Radio Rangers
Director: Vernon Keays
Screenplay: Norman S. Hall
Producer: Colbert Clark

BLAZING ACROSS THE PECOS
(Columbia, July 1, 1948) 56 Minutes
(Durango Kid Series)
Charles Starrett, Smiley Burnette, Patricia White, Chief Thunder Cloud, Paul Campbell, Charles Wilson, Thomas Jackson, Pat O'Malley, Jock Mahoney, Frank McCarroll, Pierce Lyden, Paul Conrad, Jack Ingram, Red Arnall and the Western Aces
Director: Ray Nazarro
Screenplay: Norman S. Hall
Producer: Colbert Clark

TRAIL TO LAREDO
(Columbia, August 12, 1948) 54 Minutes
(Durango Kid Series)
Charles Starrett, Smiley Burnette, Jim Bannon, Virginia Maxey, Tommy Ivo, Ethan Laidlaw, Hugh Prosser, Mira McKinney, John Merton, George Chesebro, The Cass County Boys
Director: Ray Nazarro
Screenplay: Barry Shipman
Producer: Colbert Clark

EL DORADO PASS
(Columbia, October 14, 1948) 56 Minutes
(Durango Kid Series)
Charles Starrett, Smiley Burnette, Elena Verdugo, Steve Darrell, Ted Mapes, Rory Mallison, Blackie Whiteford, Shorty Thompson and His Saddle Rockin' Rhythm
Director: Ray Nazarro
Screenplay: Earle Snell
Producer: Colbert Clark

QUICK ON THE TRIGGER
(Columbia, December 2, 1948) 55 Minutes
(Durango Kid Series)
Charles Starrett, Smiley Burnette, Lyle Talbot, Helen Parrish, George Eldredge, Ted Adams, Alan Bridge, Russell Arms, Budd Buster, Tex Cooper, Blackie Whiteford, The Sunshine Boys
Director: Ray Nazarro
Screenplay: Elmer Clifton
Producer: Colbert Clark

CHALLENGE OF THE RANGE
(Columbia, February 3, 1949) 54 Minutes
(Durango Kid Series)
Charles Starrett, Smiley Burnette, Paula Raymond, Billy Halop, Steve Darrell, Henry Hall, Robert Filman, George Chesebro, Frank McCarroll, John (Bob) Cason, John McKay, The Sunshine Boys
Director: Ray Nazarro
Screenplay: Ed Earl Repp
Producer: Colbert Clark

LARAMIE

(Columbia, May 19, 1949) 55 Minutes
(Durango Kid Series)
Charles Starrett, Smiley Burnette, Fred Sears, Tommy Ivo, Marjorie Stapp, Elton Britt, Bob Wilke, George Lloyd, Myrton Healey, Shooting Star, Jay Silverheels, Ethan Laidlaw, Bob Cason
Director: Ray Nazarro
Screenplay: Barry Shipman
Producer: Colbert Clark

THE BLAZING TRAIL

(Columbia, June 5, 1949) 56 Minutes
(Durango Kid Series)
Charles Starrett, Smiley Burnette, Marjorie Stapp, Jock Mahoney, Trevor Bardette, Fred Sears, Steve Darrell, Steve Pendleton, Robert Malcolm, John (Bob) Cason, Hank Penny, Slim Duncan, Frank McCarroll, John Merton, Merrill McCormack
Director: Ray Nazarro
Screenplay: Barry Shipman
Producer: Colbert Clark

SOUTH OF DEATH VALLEY

(Columbia, August 8, 1949) 54 Minutes
(Durango Kid Series)
Charles Starrett, Smiley Burnette, Gail Davis, Clayton Moore, Fred Sears, Lee Roberts, Richard Emory, Jason Robards, Sr., Tommy Duncan and his Western All Stars
Director: Ray Nazarro
Screenplay: Earle Snell
Producer: Colbert Clark

BANDITS OF ELDORADO

(Columbia, October 20, 1949) 56 Minutes
(Durango Kid Series)
Charles Starrett, Smiley Burnette, George J. Lewis, Fred Sears, John Dehner, Clayton Moore, Jock Mahoney, John Doucette, Max Wagner, Henry Kulky, Mustard and Gravy
Director: Ray Nazarro
Screenplay: Barry Shipman
Producer: Colbert Clark

DESERT VIGILANTE

(Columbia, November 8, 1949)
(Durango Kid Series)
Charles Starrett, Smiley Burnette, Peggy Stewart, Tris Coffin, George Chesebro, Jack Ingram, Mary Newton, Paul Campbell, Ted Mapes, I. Stanford Jolley, The Georgia Crackers
Director: Fred F. Sears
Screenplay: Earle Snell
Producer: Colbert Clark

HORSEMEN OF THE SIERRAS

(Columbia, November 22, 1949) 56 Minutes
(Durango Kid Series)
Charles Starrett, Smiley Burnette, T. Texas Tyler, Lois Hall, Tommy Ivo, John Dehner, Jason Robards, Sr., Dan Sheridan, Jock Mahoney, George Chesebro
Director: Fred F. Sears
Screenplay: Barry Shipman
Producer: Colbert Clark

RENEGADES OF THE SAGE

(Columbia, November 24, 1949) 56 Minutes
(Durango Kid Series)
Charles Starrett, Smiley Burnette, Leslie Banning, Trevor Bardette, Douglas Fowley, Jock O'Mahoney, Fred Sears, Jerry Hunt, George Chesebro, Frank McCarroll, Selmer Jackson
Director: Ray Nazarro
Story/Screenplay: Earle Snell
Producer: Colbert Clark

TRAIL OF THE RUSTLERS

(Columbia, February 2, 1950) 55 Minutes
(Durango Kid Series)
Charles Starrett, Smiley Burnette, Gail Davis, Tommy Ivo, Myron Healey, Don Harvey, Mira McKinney, Chuck Roberson, Gene Roth, Blackie Whiteford, Eddie Cletro and His Roundup Boys
Director: Ray Nazarro
Screenplay: Victor Arthur
Producer: Colbert Clark

OUTCASTS OF BLACK MESA

(Columbia, April 13, 1950) 54 Minutes
(Durango Kid Series)
Charles Starrett, Smiley Burnette, Martha Hyer, Richard Bailey, Stanley Andrews, William Haade, Lane Chandler, Chuck Roberson, Ozie Waters
Director: Ray Nazarro
Story: Elmer Clifton
Screenplay: Barry Shipman
Producer: Colbert Clark

TEXAS DYNAMO

(Columbia, June 1, 1950) 54 Minutes
(Durango Kid Series)
Charles Starrett, Smiley Burnette, Lois Hall, Jock O'Mahoney, Slim Duncan, John Dehner, George Chesebro, Marshall Reed, Lane Bradford, Fred Sears, Emil Sitka, Greg Barton
Director: Ray Nazarro
Screenplay: Barry Shipman
Producer: Colbert Clark

Charles Starrett and "The Grand Old Man," Lafe McKee.

STREETS OF GHOST TOWN

(Columbia, August 3, 1950) 54 Minutes
(Durango Kid Series)
Charles Starrett, Smiley Burnette, George Chesebro,
Mary Ellen Kay, Stanley Andrews, Frank Fenton, John
Cason, Don Kay Reynolds, Jack Ingram, Ozie Waters
and His Colorado Rangers
Director: Ray Nazarro
Screenplay: Barry Shipman
Producer: Colbert Clark

ACROSS THE BADLANDS

(Columbia, September 15, 1950) 55 Minutes
(Durango Kid Series)
Charles Starrett, Smiley Burnette, Helen Mowery,
Stanley Andrews, Bob Wilke, Dick Elliott, Hugh
Prosser, Robert W. Cavendish, Charles Evans, Paul
Campbell, Dick Alexander, Harmonica Bill
Director: Fred F. Sears
Screenplay: Barry Shipman
Producer: Colbert Clark

RAIDERS OF TOMAHAWK CREEK

(Columbia, October, 1950) 55 Minutes
(Durango Kid Series)
Charles Starrett, Smiley Burnette, Edgar Dearing, Kay
Buckley, Billy Kimbley, Paul Marion, Paul McGuire,
Bill Hale, Ted Mapes, Lee Morgan
Director: Fred F. Sears
Story: Robert Schaefer
Screenplay: Barry Shipman
Producer: Colbert Clark

LIGHTNING GUNS

(Columbia, December 10, 1950) 55 Minutes
(Durango Kid Series)
Charles Starrett, Smiley Burnette, Gloria Henry,
William Norton Bailey, Edgar Dearing, Raymond
Bond, Jock O'Mahoney, Chuck Roberson, Frank
Griffin, Joel Friedkin, George Chesebro, Merrill
McCormack
Director: Fred Sears
Screenplay: Victor Arthur
Producer: Colbert Clark

FRONTIER OUTPOST
(Columbia, December 29, 1950) 55 Minutes
(Durango Kid Series)
Charles Starrett, Smiley Burnette, Lois Hall, Steve Darrell, Fred Sears, Bob Wilke, Paul Campbell, Jock Mahoney, Bud Osborne, Chuck Roberson, Pierre Watkin, Dick Wessell, Hank Penny, Slim Duncan
Director: Ray Nazarro
Screenplay: Barry Shipman
Producer: Colbert Clark

PRAIRIE ROUNDUP
(Columbia, January 15, 1951) 55 Minutes
Charles Starrett, Smiley Burnette, Mary Castle, Frank Fenton, Lane Chandler, Frank Sully, Paul Campbell, Forrest Taylor, Don Harvey, George Baxter, John Cason, Al Wyatt, Glenn Thompson, Ace Richman, Alan Sears, The Sunshine Boys
Director: Fred F. Sears
Screenplay: Joseph O'Donnell
Producer: Colbert Clark

RIDIN' THE OUTLAW TRAIL
(Columbia, February 23, 1951) 56 Minutes
(Durango Kid Series)
Charles Starrett, Smiley Burnette, Sunny Vickers, Jim Bannon, Edgar Dearing, Peter Thompson, Lee Morgan, Chuck Roberson, Ethan Laidlaw, Pee Wee King and His Golden West Cowboys
Director: Fred F. Sears
Screenplay: Victor Arthur
Producer: Colbert Clark

FORT SAVAGE RAIDERS
(Columbia, March 15, 1951) 54 Minutes
(Durango Kid Series)
Charles Starrett, Smiley Burnette, John Dehner, Trevor Bardette, Peter Thompson, Fred Sears, John Cason, Frank Griffin, Sam Flint, Dusty Walker
Director: Ray Nazarro
Screenplay: Barry Shipman
Producer: Colbert Clark

SNAKE RIVER DESPERADOES
(Columbia, May 30, 1951) 54 Minutes
(Durango Kid Series)
Charles Starrett, Smiley Burnette, Don Reynolds, Tommy Ivo, Monte Blue, Boyd (Red) Morgan, George Chesebro, John Pickard, Charles Hovarth, Sam Flint, Duke York
Director: Fred F. Sears
Screenplay: Barry Shipman
Producer: Colbert Clark

BONANZA TOWN
(Columbia, July 26, 1951) 56 Minutes
(Durango Kid Series)
Charles Starrett, Smiley Burnette, Fred F. Sears, Luther Crockett, Myron Healey, Charles Hovarth, Ted Jordan, Al Wyatt, Marshall Reed, Vernon Dent, Slim Duncan
Director: Fred F. Sears
Screenplay: Barry Shipman, Bart Horswell
Producer: Colbert Clark

CYCLONE FURY
(Columbia, August 19, 1951) 54 Minutes
(Durango Kid Series)
Charles Starrett, Smiley Burnette, Fred F. Sears, Clayton Moore, Bob Wilke, Louis Lettieri, George Chesebro, Frank O'Connor, Merle Travis and His Bronco Busters
Director: Ray Nazarro
Screenplay: Barry Shipman and Ed Earl Repp
Producer: Colbert Clark

THE KID FROM AMARILLO
(Columbia, October 30, 1951) 56 Minutes
(Durango Kid Series)
Charles Starrett, Smiley Burnette, Harry Lauter, Fred Sears, Don Megowan, Scott Lee, Guy Teague, Charles Evans, George J. Lewis, Henry Kulky, George Chesebro, Jerry Scroggins and the Cass County Boys
Director: Ray Nazarro
Screenplay: Barry Shipman
Producer: Colbert Clark

PECOS RIVER
(Columbia, December 15, 1951) 54 Minutes
(Durango Kid Series)
Charles Starrett, Smiley Burnette, Jack (Jock) Mahoney, Delores Sidener, Steve Darrell, Edgar Dearing, Frank Jenks, Paul Campbell, Zon Murray, Maudie Prickett, Eddie Featherstone, Harmonica Bill
Director: Fred F. Sears
Screenplay: Barry Shipman
Producer: Colbert Clark

SMOKY CANYON
(Columbia, January 22, 1952) 55 Minutes
(Durango Kid Series)
Charles Starrett, Smiley Burnette, Jack (Jock) Mahoney, Dani Sue Nolan, Tris Coffin, Larry Hudson, Chris Alcaide, Sandy Sanders, Forrest Taylor, Charles Stevens, LeRoy Johnson
Director: Fred F. Sears
Screenplay: Barry Shipman
Producer: Colbert Clark

THE HAWK OF WILD RIVER
(Columbia, February 28, 1952) 54 Minutes
(Durango Kid Series)
Charles Starrett, Smiley Burnette, Jack (Jock) Mahoney, Clayton Moore, Edwin Parker, Jim Diehl, Lane Chandler, Syd Saylor, John Cason, LeRoy Johnson, Jack Carry, Sam Flint, Donna Hall
Director: Fred F. Sears
Screenplay: Howard J. Green
Producer: Colbert Clark

LARAMIE MOUNTAINS
(Columbia, April 20, 1952) 54 Minutes
(Durango Kid Series)
Charles Starrett, Smiley Burnette, Jack (Jock) Mahoney, Fred Sears, Marshall Reed, Rory Mallison, Zon Murray, John War Eagle, Bob Wilke
Director: Ray Nazarro
Screenplay: Barry Shipman
Producer: Colbert Clark

THE ROUGH, TOUGH WEST
(Columbia, June 15, 1952) 54 Minutes
(Durango Kid Series)
Charles Starrett, Smiley Burnette, Jack (Jock) Mahoney, Carolina Cotten, Marshall Reed, Fred Sears, Bert Arnold, Tommy Ivo, Boyd Morgan, Pee Wee King and His Band, Valeria Fisher
Director: Ray Nazarro
Screenplay: Barry Shipman
Producer: Colbert Clark

JUNCTION CITY
(Columbia, July 12, 1952) 54 Minutes
(Durango Kid Series)
Charles Starrett, Smiley Burnette, Jack (Jock) Mahoney, Kathleen Case, John Dehner, Steve Darrell, George Chesebro, Anita Castle, Mary Newton, Robert Bice, Hal Price, Hal Taliaferro, Chris Alcaide, Bob Woodward, Frank Ellis
Director: Ray Narzarro
Screenplay: Barry Shipman
Producer: Colbert Clark

THE KID FROM BROKEN GUN
(Columbia, August 15, 1952) 56 Minutes
(Durango Kid Series)
Charles Starrett, Smiley Burnette, Jack (Jock) Mahoney, Angela Stevens, Tris Coffin, Myron Healey, Pat O'Malley, Helen Mowery, Chris Alcaide, John Cason, Mauritz Hugo, Edgar Dearing, Eddie Parker
Director: Fred F. Sears
Screenplay: Ed Earl Repp, Barry Shipman
Producer: Colbert Clark

HOLLYWOOD BRONC BUSTERS
(Columbia, 1956) 9 Minutes
(Screen Snapshot Series)
Jack Lemmon, Ralph Staub; Film clips featuring Gene Autry, Rog Rogers, Tom Mix, William Boyd, William S. Hart, Buck Jones, Hoot Gibson, *Charles Starrett*
Director/Producer: Ralph Staub

13 ● WILLIAM BOYD

Hopalong Cassidy to the World

The year 1935 was a momentous one for the program Western. Two events occurred which started new trends that affected range flicks for the next twenty years. First, newcomer Gene Autry zoomed to popularity in a series of musical Westerns made by a newly-formed company called Republic. Secondly, a former big-name silent star, down on his luck, no longer young, and unknown to most Western aficionados, appeared in a series of Westerns quite different in concept and execution from the typical oater, one that set a high standard for the "B" product and popularized the trio-type Western story. Both events were fortuitous for the Western genre, for the Saturday matinee-type hoss opera, while inexorably popular, was suffering from a mild case of staleness. Although the dusty "B" sagas were quite profitable and obviously pleasing, the complaint in some quarters that "once you've seen one, you've seen them all" was not without some foundation.

Since Autry's phenomenal career is discussed in my "Saddle Aces of the Cinema" it will not be pursued here. Rather, we shall devote attention to the second of the two events, the inauguration of the Hopalong Cassidy series starring William Boyd, one of the most debonair and cultured of the movie cowboys.

Harry "Pop" Sherman, a respected and long-time producer, had acquired the movie rights to the Hopalong Cassidy novels of Clarence E. Mulford with the intentions of producing a series of programmers built around the character. The states' rights market was rapidly drying up but Sherman wrangled a distribution agreement out of Paramount, thus assuring his product a larger-than-usual number of bookings. When negotiations fell through with James Gleason, who fitted the

book's description of "Hoppy," the part of Cassidy fell to ex-Cecil B. DeMille protege William Boyd, definitely not the cowboy type and definitely unlike Mulford's salty, uneducated, knavish-but-lovable Cassidy of the books.

Boyd had had an interesting life and career. Born in Cambridge, Ohio in 1898, the son of a laborer, he moved to Oklahoma as a young boy. His parents died while he was still in his teens and he quit school to work at a variety of jobs, most of them menial. On the move and searching for better things, he arrived in Hollywood in 1919. There he found it relatively easy to secure extra work at Famous Players-Lasky studio in DeMille's **Why Change Your Wife?** ('20). Minor parts followed, then more important ones. By 1925 he was receiving good billing in a variety of melodramas. His big break came in 1926 when DeMille starred him in **The Volga Boatman,** a picture that, from the artistic and box-office standpoint, was about as good as anything DeMille had produced to that time. Boyd got rave reviews. Suddenly he was a heart throb and a matinee idol. A succession of estimable and profitable pictures put Boyd into the six-figure salary bracket. He became a man about town living the Hollywood life to its fullest—parties and more parties, fast cars, yachts, fine clothes, a couple of marriages. And then the success bubble burst, through no particular fault of Boyd's.

Another actor named William Boyd, later referred to as William (Stage) Boyd to differentiate the two, was arrested during a wild party and charged with possession of illegal whiskey and gambling equipment. A sex orgy was implied in some newspaper accounts. Bill Boyd's picture was mistakenly run by the papers with

William Boyd and "Topper"

the story instead of the picture of the lesser known Boyd. Bill's career collapsed, aided by the advent of sound and the Depression. He was unable to find work. His fortune went and he turned to drinking heavily, unable to cope with his ill fortune. In two years he made only four movies, one each for small outfits called Liberty and Chesterfield and two for a production company called Winchester, releasing through the newly-organized Republic. The salary he received from these pictures hardly paid his liquor bills.

Pop Sherman had in mind using Boyd either as the chief heavy or as Buck Peters in **Hop-a-Long Cassidy** ('35), but Bill talked himself into the Cassidy role and acquitted himself with aplomb in his first "Hoppy." Actually, it was his third Western; he had starred earlier in his career in **The Last Frontier** (Met., '26) and **The Painted Desert** (Pathe, '31), a couple of better-than-average non-programmers. The latter film is often remembered as the one in which Clark Gable plays the heavy. Neither film required much in the way of horsemanship from Boyd, who could barely sit a saddle.

Seldom has one been snatched from a plunge into the abyss of oblivion as was Bill, but it was not without considerable reservations by Sherman. Bill had to promise that he would lay off the booze and tone down his wild ways for as long as he worked for Sherman, a promise he kept faithfully. Neither man envisioned a series so popular that it would run on and on and on. At best Pop hoped to reap a profit on a six- or eight-film package.

Only in the initial film was there a half-hearted attempt made to conform to Mulford's crusty Cassidy character. Thereafter, Boyd fashioned Cassidy into a literate, moral, gentle and chivalrous cowman quite unlike the character of the books. Mulford's works were used as story bases for the first nineteen films. Thereafter original screenplays were written.

Jimmy Ellison was signed on for the part of Hoppy's young saddle pal, "Johnny Nelson." They complemented each other nicely. Most of Boyd's riding scenes in the initial films were performed in long shot by Cliff Lyons, while the star was busy learning how to ride. In time he was able to handle much of the riding required of his role, though he never became a real horseman. George F. Hayes had minor roles in the first three entries, then was made a permanent member of the Bar 20 outfit, and the Hoppy films became trio-type Westerns with Boyd dominant as range-wise Cassidy, Ellison as the impetuous romantic, and Hayes, as "Windy Halliday," providing a high level brand of comedy. The camaraderie of the three principals proved decidedly popular.

Statistically, 66 Cassidys were made, 41 released by Paramount and 25 by United Artists. Sherman produced the first 54 films, and Boyd produced the last dozen on his own. Ellison dropped out of the series after seven films and was replaced by Russell Hayden who made 27 Hoppys in the role of Lucky Jenkins, before himself being promoted to solo stardom. The third slot in the series was taken in turn by Brad King (5), Jay Kirby (5), Jimmy Rogers (6), George Reeves (1), and Rand Brooks (12). George Hayes was in a total of 22 Hoppys, while Andy Clyde, as the redoubtable sourdough California Carlson, appeared in 36 features.

The Hoppys usually had strong, often ingenious scripting. Sometimes, though, they were just formula stuff, but were made more interesting than usual through intelligent treatment and somewhat different handling. They didn't look like average Westerns. The musical setting helps the cadence and the spirit of the films to a great extent and the photography of Russell Harlan takes fullest adavantage of the scenic vistas of the district at the base of Mt. Whitney, often used as a location for the series. Director Lesley Selander was especially adroit in the management of his scenes, both the intimate affairs and the large ones involving crowds and horses. He neatly interweaved dramatic punch with comedy passages and mass action.

Action was sometimes conspicuous by its absence, until the final reel and the inexorable reckoning with the baddies. Fights were sharp and realistic, the horsemanship thrilling, and the gunplay carried that flair that made self-contained, casual Bill Boyd convincing as well as pleasing.

Boyd played the mature, level-headed cowboy who constantly restrains, in a big brother fashion, the hot-headed cowboy impetuosity of his youthful colleagues—Ellison, Hayden, *et al.* And there was always "Windy" or "California" to pluck them from the trouble caused by their stupidity. Hoppy's equanimity was not lost on even the small fry in the audience. In his characterization as Hoppy, Boyd seemed to be only an ordinary, peaceable, easy-going ranchhand until he had penetrated to the heart of the cattle-rustler's thieving schemes. Then he was suddenly transformed into a galloping, shooting, fighting daredevil, who feared no odds and threw his enemies into a veritable terror.

Hopalong Cassidy and his pals rode again and again to clean up yet another town in the Western sector, and despite the familiarity of the tales, they were told in an interesting and actionful manner that satisfied the Western and action audiences. Harry Sherman's production, mounting, and the scenic backgrounds usually identified with this series made them good attractions in the family houses. Boyd's identity became so completely submerged in his alter ego that many fans knew him only as Hopalong Cassidy, unable to recall his real name. Interestingly, Boyd disliked both Westerns and kids for much of his career but mellowed somewhat toward both as his own personality became immersed in the character he portrayed.

In 1946, after a production hiatus of two years caused by Sherman's discontinuing the series when rising costs threatened its profitability, Boyd bought up the rights to the Cassidy character and made the last twelve Hoppys himself, releasing them through United Artists. Although the first two, **The Devil's Playground** and **Fool's Gold,** compared favorably to the previous Sherman productions in quality, the remaining ten showed the effect of cost-cutting economies. The Hoppys ground to a halt with **Strange Gamble** ('48), 66th in the series.

Before TV became a major force in the entertainment world, Boyd took the biggest gamble of his life, risking every penny he had and could borrow to buy up the TV rights to all the Hoppy features. Then, when TV became big business, he leased the films to NBC, reaping a small fortune. Boyd organized Hopalong Cassidy Enterprises and marketed a multitude of products bearing the Cassidy name. He produced and starred in a series of fifty-two new 30-minute Hoppys especially for television, this time with Rand Brooks and Edgar Buchanan as his cronies. Hopalong Cassidy Enterprises made William Boyd a millionaire.

Boyd made his final screen appearance in a guest cameo dressed as Hoppy for his old boss Cecil B. DeMille in **The Greatest Show on Earth** ('52). Thereafter he lived in retirement with his third wife, Grace Bradley, whom he had married in 1937. His health deteriorated and the last years of his life were spent in seclusion. Boyd wanted his fans to remember him as he had looked on screen when playing Hoppy. He died on September 12, 1972 from Parkinson's disease and congestive heart failure.

Never again will Hoppy set off after the baddies, cutting them off by that well-known gulch, rearing up his detergent-white horse, "Topper," which matched his hair and his image, ivory six-guns at the ready. Hopalong of the fast draw and the impeccable side-saddle manners, the epitome of good triumphing, never a stetson out of place, never a sly pass at a bar girl, always upstanding, always a winner, is gone. Hoppy has ridden into the last sunset, and the genre he was a part of has given way to essays in violence and psychology.

WILLIAM BOYD Filmography

WHY CHANGE YOUR WIFE?
(Artcraft/Famous Players-Lasky Corp., May 2, 1920) 7 Reels
Gloria Swanson, Thomas Meighan, Bebe Daniels, Theodore Kosloff, Sylvia Ashton, Clarence Geldart, Maym Kelso, Lucien Littlefield, Edna Mae Cooper, Jane Wolfe, *William Boyd*
Director/Producer: Cecil B. DeMille
Scenario: Olga Printzlau and Sada Cowan
Story: William C. de Mille

BREWSTER'S MILLIONS
(Famous Players-Lasky/Paramount, January, 1921) 6 Reels
Roscoe "Fatty" Arbuckle, Betty Ross Clark, Fred Huntley, Marian Skinner, James Corrigan, Jean Acker, Charles Ogle, Neely Edwards, *William Boyd*, L. J. McCarthy, Parker McConnell, John MacFarlane
Director: Joseph Henabery
Scenario: Walter Woods

A WISE FOOL
(Famous Players-Lasky/Paramount, June 26, 1921)
James Kirkwood, Alice Hollister, Ann Forrest, Alan Hale, Fred Huntley, *William Boyd,* Truly Shattuck, Harry Duffield, Charles Ogle, John Herdman, Mabel Van Buren
Director: George Melford
Adaptation: Gilbert Parker
Story: Gilbert Parker - "The Money Master"

MOONLIGHT AND HONEYSUCKLE
(Realart Pictures, July, 1921) 5 Reels
Mary Miles Minter, Monte Blue, Willard Louis, Grace Goodall, Guy Oliver, *William Boyd*, Mabel Van Buren
Director: Joseph Henabery
Scenario: Barbara Kent

THE AFFAIRS OF ANATOL
(DeMille-Paramount Special/Dist. by Famous Players-Lasky, September 18, 1921) 9 Reels
Wallace Reid, Gloria Swanson, Elliott Dexter, Bebe Daniels, Monte Blue, Wanda Hawley, Theodore Roberts, Agnes Ayres, Theodore Kosloff, Polly Moran, Raymond Hatton, Julia Faye, Charles Ogle, Winter Hall, Guy Oliver, Ruth Miller, Lucien Littlefield, Zelma Maja, Shannon Day, Elinor Glyn, Lady Parker, *William Boyd,* Maud Wayne, Fred Huntley, Alma Bennett
Producer/Director: Cecil B. DeMille
Scenario: Jeanie MacPherson, Beulah Marie Dix, Lorna Moon, and Elmer Harris
Suggested by Arthur Schnitzler's play "Anatol"

EXIT THE VAMP

(Famous Players-Lasky/Paramount, November 4, 1921) 5 Reels

Ethel Clayton, T. Roy Barnes, Fontaine La Rue, Theodore Roberts, *William Boyd,* Mickey Moore, Mattie Peters

Director: Frank Urson

Story/Adaptation: Clara Beranger

BOBBED HAIR

(Realart Pictures/Paramount, March 12, 1922) 5 Reels

Wanda Hawley, *William Boyd,* Adele Farrington, Leigh Wyant, Jane Starr, Margaret Vilmore, William P. Carleton, Ethel Wales, Junior Coghlan, Robert Kelly

Director: Thomas N. Heffron

Story: Hector Turnbull

Scenario: Harvey Thew

NICE PEOPLE

(Famous Players-Lasky/Paramount, September 4, 1922) 7 Reels

Wallace Reid, Bebe Daniels, Conrad Nagel, Julia Faye, Claire McDowell, Edward Martindel, Eve Southern, Bertram Jones, *William Boyd,* Ethel Wales

Director: William De Mille

Adaptation: Clara Beranger

Story: Rachel Crothers - "Nice People"

MANSLAUGHTER

(Famous Players-Lasky/Paramount, September 24, 1922)

Thomas Meighan, Leatrice Joy, Lois Wilson, John Miltern, George Fawcett, Julia Faye, Edythe Chapman, Jack Mower, Dorothy Cumming, Casson Ferguson, Mickey Moore, James Neill, Sylvia Ashton, Raymond Hatton, Mabel Van Buren, Ethel Wales, Dale Fuller, Edward Martindel, Charles Ogle, Guy Oliver, Shannon Day, Lucien Littlefield, Clarence Burton, *William Boyd,* J. Farrell MacDonald, Theodore von Eltz, Nora Cecil, Madame Sul-Te-Wan, Charles West, Emmett King, Fred Kelsey, Spottiswoode Aitken

Director: Cecil B. DeMille

Adaptation/Scenario: Jeanie Macpherson

Story: Alice Duer Miller - "Manslaughter"

ON THE HIGH SEAS

(Famous Players-Lasky/Paramount, November 5, 1922) 6 Reels

Dorothy Dalton, Jack Holt, Mitchell Lewis, Winter Hall, Michael Dark, Otto Brower, *William Boyd,* James Gordon, Alice Knowland, Vernon Tremaine

Director: Irvin Willat

Adaptation/Scenario: E. Magnus Ingleton

Story: Edward Brewster Sheldon

THE YOUNG RAJAH

(Famous Players-Lasky/Paramount, November 12, 1922) 8 Reels

Rudolph Valentino, Wanda Hawley, Pat Moore, Charles Ogle, Fanny Midgley, Robert Ober, Jack Giddings, Edward Jobson, Josef Swickard, Bertram Grassby, J. Farrell MacDonald, George Periolat, George Field, Maude Wayne, *William Boyd,* Joseph Harrington, Spottiswoode Aitken

Director: Philip Rosen

Adaptation/Scenario: June Mathis

Story: John Ames Mitchell - "Amos Judd"

MICHAEL O'HALLORAN

(Gene Stratton Porter Productions/W. W. Hodkinson Corp., June 10, 1923) 7 Reels

Virginia True Boardman, Ethelyn Irving, Irene Rich, Charles Clary, Claire McDowell, Charles Hill Mailes, Josie Sedgwick, *William Boyd*

Director/Adaptation: James Leo Meechan

Story/Supervisor: Gene Stratton Porter

HOLLYWOOD

(Famous Players-Lasky/Paramount, August 19, 1923) 8 Reels

Hope Drown, Luke Cosgrove, George K. Arthur, Ruby Lafayette, Harris Gordon, Bess Flowers, Eleanor Lawson, King Zany, Roscoe Arbuckle, Gertrude Astor, Mary Astor, Agnes Ayres, Baby Peggy, T. Roy Barnes, Noah Beery, *William Boyd,* Clarence Burton, Robert Cain, Edythe Chapman, Betty Compson, Ricardo Cortez, Viola Dana, Cecil B. DeMille, William De Mille, Jack Holt, Leatrice Joy, Alan Hale, William S. Hart, Ben Turpin, Lois Wilson, Will Rogers, Sennett Girls, Ford Sterling, Anita Stewart, Anna Q. Nilsson, May McAvoy, Robert McKim, Lila Lee, Thomas Meighan, Pola Negri

Director: James Cruze

Adaptation: Tom Geraghty

Story: Frank Condon

THE TEMPLE OF VENUS

(Fox, October 29, 1923) 7 Reels

William Walling, Mary Philbin, Mickey McBan, Alice Day, David Butler, *William Boyd,* Phyllis Haver, Leon Barry, Celeste Lee, Senorita Consuella, Robert Klein, Marilyn Boyd, Frank Keller, Lorraine Eason, Helen Vigil

Director: Henry Otto

Story/Scenario: Henry Otto, Catherine Carr

ENEMIES OF CHILDREN
(Fisher Productions/Mammoth Pictures, December 13, 1923) 6 Reels
Anna Q. Nilsson, George Siegmann, Claire McDowell, Lucy Beaumont, Joseph Dowling, Raymond Hatton, Ward Crane, Charles Wellesley, Virginia Lee Corbin, Kate Price, Boyd Irwin, Eugenie Besserer, *William Boyd*, Mary Anderson
Directors/Adaptation: Lillian Ducey, John M. Voshell
Producer: Victor B. Fisher
Story: George Gibbs - "Youth Triumphant"

CHANGING HUSBANDS
(Famous Players-Lasky/Paramount, June 22, 1924) 7 Reels
Leatrice Joy, Victor Varconi, Raymond Griffith, Julia Faye, Zasu Pitts, Helen Dunbar, *William Boyd*
Directors: Frank Urson, Paul Iribe
Scenario: Sada Cowan, Howard Higgin
Supervisor: Cecil B. De Mille
Story: Elizabeth Alexander - "Roles"

TARNISH
(Goldwyn Pictures/Associated First National, August, 1924) 7 Reels
May McAvoy, Ronald Colman, Marie Prevost, Albert Gran, Mrs. Russ Whytall, Priscilla Bonner, Harry Myers, Kay Deslys, Lydia Yeamans Titus, *William Boyd*, Snitz Edwards
Director: George Fitzmaurice
Scenario: Frances Marion
Story: Gilbert Emery - "Tarnish, a Play in 3 Acts"

FEET OF CLAY
(Famous Players-Lasky Corp., September 28, 1924) 10 Reels
Vera Reynolds, Rod La Rocque, Julia Faye, Ricardo Cortez, Robert Edeson, Theodore Kosloff, Victor Varconi, William Boyd
Director/Producer: Cecil B. DeMille
Scenario: Beulah Marie Kix and Bertram Millhauser
Adapted from novel by Margaretta Tuttle

FORTY WINKS
(Famous Players-Lasky/Paramount, February 2, 1925) 7 Reels
Viola Dana, Raymond Griffith, Theodore Roberts, Cyril Chadwick Anna May Wong, *William Boyd*
Directors: Frank Urson, Paul Iribe
Screenplay: Bertram Millhauser
Story: Cecil B. DeMille and David Belasco - "Lord Chumley"

THE MIDSHIPMAN
(MGM, October 4, 1925) 8 Reels
Ramon Novarro, Harriet Hammond, Wesley Barry, Margaret Seddon, Crauford Kent, Pauline Key, Maurice Ryan, Harold Goodwin, *William Boyd*
Director: Christy Cabanne
Scenario: F. McGrew Willis
Story: Carey Wilson

THE ROAD TO YESTERDAY
(Producers Distributing Corp., November 15, 1925) 10 Reels
Joseph Schildkraut, Jetta Goudal, *William Boyd*, Vera Reynolds, Trixie Friganza, Casson Ferguson, Julia Faye, Clarence Burton, Charles West, Josephine Norman
Director/Producer: Cecil B. DeMille
Scenario: Jeanie Macpherson and Beulah Marie Dix
From the play by Beulah Marie Dix and Evelyn Greenleaf Sutherland

STEEL PREFERRED
(Metropolitan/Producers Dist. Corp., January 3, 1926) 7 Reels
Vera Reynolds, *William Boyd*, Hobart Bosworth, Charlie Murray, Walter Long, William V. Mong, Nigel Barrie, Helene Sullivan, Ben Turpin
Director: James P. Hogan
Adaptation: Elliot J. Clawson
Story: Herschel S. Hall - "Steel Preferred"

THE VOLGA BOATMAN
(Producers Distributing Corp., May 23, 1926) 11 Reels
William Boyd, Elinor Fair, Robert Edeson, Victor Varconi, Julia Faye, Theodore Kosloff, Arthur Rankin
Director/Producer: Cecil B. DeMille
Scenario: Lenore J. Coffee
Story: Konrad Bercovici

EVE'S LEAVES
(De Mille Pictures/Producers Dist. Corp., June 13, 1926) 7 Reels
Leatrice Joy, *William Boyd*, Robert Edeson, Walter Long, Richard Carle, Arthur Hoyt, Sojin, Nambu
Director: Paul Sloane
Adaptation: Elmer Harris
Continuity: Jack Jevne
Story: Harry Chapman Ford - "Eve's Leaves"

THE LAST FRONTIER

(Metropolitan/Producers Dist. Corp., August 16, 1926)
8 Reels

William Boyd, Marguerite De La Motte, Jack Hoxie, Junior Coghlan, Mitchell Lewis, Gladys Brockwell, Frank Lackteen

Director: George B. Seitz
Adaptation: Will M. Ritchey
Story: Courtney Ryley Cooper - "The Last Frontier"

HER MAN O'WAR

(De Mille Pictures/Producers Dist. Corp., August 23, 1926) 6 Reels

Jetta Goudal, *William Boyd,* Jimmie Adams, Grace Darmond, Kay Deslys, Frank Reicher, Michael Vavitch, Robert Edeson, Junior Coghlan

Director: Frank Urson
Scenario: Charles Logue
Supervisor: C. Gardner Sullivan
Story: Fred Jackson - "Black Marriage"

JIM THE CONQUEROR

(Metropolitan/Producers Dist. Corp., January 3, 1927)
6 Reels

William Boyd, Elinor Fair, Walter Long, Tully Marshall, Tom Santschi, Marcelle Corday

Director: George B. Seitz
Screenplay: Will M. Ritchey
Story: Peter B. Kyne - "Jim the Conqueror"

THE YANKEE CLIPPER

(DeMille Pictures/Producers Dist. Corp., March 23, 1927) 8 Reels

William Boyd, Elinor Fair, Junior Coghlan, John Miljan, Walter Long, Louis Payne, Burt McIntosh, George Ovey, William Blaisdell, Clarence Burton, Stanton Heck, Julia Faye, Harry Holden, W. Sousania, James Wang

Director: Rupert Julian
Adaptation: Garrett Fort, Garnett Weston
Story: Denison Clift
Supervisor: C. Gardner Sullivan

TWO ARABIAN NIGHTS

(Caddo Company/United Artists, October 22, 1927)
9 Reels

William Boyd, Mary Astor, Louis Wolheim, Michael Vavitch, Ian Keith, DeWitt Jennings, Michael Visaroff, Boris Karloff

Director: Lewis Milestone
Screenplay: James T. O'Donohue, Wallace Smith
Story: Donald McGibney - "Two Arabian Knights" in *McClure's Magazine*
Supervisor: John W. Considine, Jr.
Producers: Howard Hughes, John W. Considine, Jr.

THE KING OF KINGS

(Pathe Exchange, Inc., April 19, 1927) 18 Reels

H. B. Warner, Dorothy Cumming, Ernest Torrence, Joseph Schildkraut, James Neill, Joseph Striker, Robert Edeson, Sidney D'Albrook, David Imboden, Charles Belcher, Clayton Packard, Robert Ellsworth, Charles Requa, John T. Prince, Jacqueline Logan, Rudolph Schildkraut, Sam DeGrasse, Casson Ferguson, Victor Varconi, Majel Coleman, Montagu Love, *William Boyd,* M. Moore, Theodore Kosloff, George Seigmann, Julia Faye, Josephine Norman, Kenneth Thomson, Alan Brooks, Viola Louie, Muriel McCormac, Clarence Burton, James Mason, May Robson, Dot Farley, Hector Sarno, Leon Holmes

Director/Producer: Cecil B. DeMille
Scenario: Jeanie Macpherson
Story: The Four Gospels of the Holy Bible

DRESS PARADE

(De Mille Pictures/Pathe, October 29, 1927) 7 Reels

William Boyd, Bessie Love, Hugh Allan, Walter Tennyson, Maurice Ryan, Louis Natheaux, Clarence Geldert

Director: Donald Crisp
Screenplay: Douglas Z. Doty
Story: Major Alexander Chilton, Major Robert Glassburn, and Herbert David Walter - "Raw Material"

THE NIGHT FLYER

(Pathe, February 5, 1928) 7 Reels

William Boyd, Jobyna Ralston, Philo McCullough, Ann Schaeffer, De Witt Jennings, John Milerta, Robert Dudley

Director: Walter Lang
Adaptation: Walter Woods
Story: Frank Hamilton Spearman - "Held for Orders: Being Stories of Railroad Life"
Producer: James Cruze

SKYSCRAPER

(De Mille Pictures/Pathe, April 8, 1928) 8 Reels

William Boyd, Alan Hale, Sue Carol, Alberta Vaughn

Adaptation: Elliott Clawson
Story: Dudley Murphy
Supervisor: Walter Woods

THE COP

(De Mille Pictures/Pathe, August 20, 1928) 8 Reels

William Boyd, Alan Hale, Jacqueline Logan, Robert Armstrong, Tom Kennedy, Louis Natheaux, Phil Sleeman

Director: Donald Crisp
Scenario: Tay Garnett
Story: Elliott Clawson
Producer: Ralph Block

POWER

(Pathe, September 23, 1928) 7 Reels
William Boyd, Alan Hale, Jacqueline Logan, Jerry Drew, Joan Bennett, Carole Lombard, Pauline Curley
Director: Howard Higgin
Story/Continuity: Tay Garnett
Producer: Ralph Block

LADY OF THE PAVEMENTS

(Art Cinema Corp./United Artists, January 22, 1929) 90 Minutes (Talking and singing sequences)
Lupe Velez, *William Boyd,* Jetta Goudal, Albert Conti, George Fawcett, Henry Armetta, William Bakewell, Franklin Pangborn
Director: D. W. Griffith
Scenario: Sam Taylor, Gerrit Lloyd
Story: Karl Gustav Vollmoeller - "La Paiva"

THE LEATHERNECK

(Pathe, February 24, 1929) 76 Minutes
Alan Hale, *William Boyd,* Robert Armstrong, Fred Kohler, Diane Ellis, James Aldine, Paul Weigel, Jules Cowles, Wade Lee Shumway, Lloyd Whitlock, Mitchell Lewis
Director: Howard Higgin
Story/Screenplay: Elliott Clawson
Producer: Ralph Block

THE FLYING FOOL

(Pathe, June 23, 1929) 73 Minutes
William Boyd, Marie Prevost, Russell Gleason, Tom O'Brien
Director: Tay Garnett
Story/Adaptation: Elliott Clawson
Supervisor: William Sistrom

THE LOCKED DOOR

(Feature Productions/United Artists, November 16, 1929) 8 Reels (Sound)
Rod La Rocque, Barbara Stanwyck, *William Boyd,* Betty Bronson, Harry Stubbs, Harry Mestayer, Mack Swain, Zasu Pitts, George Bunny, Purnell Pratt, Fred Warren, Charles Sullivan, Edgar Dearing, Mary Ashcraft, Violet Bird, Eleanor Fredericks, Martha Stewart, Virginia McFadden, Lita Chevret, Leona Leigh, Greta von Rue, Dorothy Gowan, Kay English, Edward Dillon
Director: George Fitzmaurice
Scenario: C. Gardner Sullivan
Story: Channing Pollock - "The Sign on the Door"

HIS FIRST COMMAND

(Pathe, December 28, 1929) 65 Minutes
William Boyd, Dorothy Sebastian, Gavin Gordon, Helen Parrish, Alphonse Ethier, Howard Hickman, Paul Hurst, Jules Cowles, Rose Tapley, Mabel Van Buren, Charles Moore
Director: Gregory La Cava
Story/Screenplay: Jack Jungmeyer, James Gleason
Associate Producer: Ralph Block

HIGH VOLTAGE

(Pathe, April 7, 1929) 6 Reels
William Boyd, Owen Moore, Carole Lombard, Diane Ellis, Billy Bevan, Phillips Smalley
Director: Howard Higgin
Screenplay: James Gleason, Kenyon Nicholson
Story: Elliott Clawson
Supervisor: Ralph Block

OFFICER O'BRIEN

(Pathe, January 27, 1930) 72 Minutes
William Boyd, Ernest Torrence, Dorothy Sebastian, Russell Gleason, Clyde Cook, Ralf Harolde, Arthur Housman, Paul Hurst, Tom Maloney, Toyo Fujita
Director: Tay Garnett
Story/Screenplay: Thomas Buckingham
Associate Producer: Ralph Block

THE STORM

(Universal, August 18, 1930) 76 Minutes
Lupe Velez, Paul Cavanaugh, *William Boyd,* Alphonse Ethier, Ernest Adams, Tom London, Nick Thompson, Erin LaBissaniere
Director: William Wyler
Screenplay: Wells Root
Producer: Carl Laemmle

THE PAINTED DESERT

(RKO-Pathe, January 18, 1931) 80 Minutes
William Boyd, Helen Twelvetrees, William Farnum, J. Farrell MacDonald, Clark Gable, William Walling, Wade Boteler, William LeMaire, Dick Cramer, James Mason, Hugh Adams, Jerry Drew, Brady Kline, Charles Sellon, Edward Hearn, Cy Clegg, James Donlan, Al St. John
Director: Howard Higgin
Story/Screenplay: Howard Higgin, Tom Buckingham

BEYOND VICTORY

(RKO-Pathe, April 12, 1931) 70 Minutes
William Boyd, Zasu Pitts, Lew Cody, Marion Shilling, James Gleason, Lissi Arna, Theodore Von Eltz, Mary Carr, Russell Gleason
Director: John Robertson
Story: Horace Jackson, James Gleason
Adaptation: Horace Jackson and James Gleason
Producer: E. D. Derr

BIG GAMBLE

(RKO-Pathe, September 4, 1931) 65 Minutes
William Boyd, Dorothy Sebastian, Warner Oland, William Collier, Jr., James Gleason, Zasu Pitts, June MacCloy, Geneva Mitchell, Ralph Ince, Fred Walton
Director: Fred Niblo
Story: Octavus Roy Cohen
Adaptation: Walter De Leon and F. McGrew Willis

SUICIDE FLEET

(RKO-Pathe, November 20, 1931) 86 Minutes
William Boyd, Robert Armstrong, James Gleason, Ginger Rogers, Harry Bannister, Frank Reicher, Henry Victor
Director: Albert Rogell
Story: H. A. Jones - "The Mystery Ship"
Screenplay: Lew Lipton
Producer: Charles Rogers

CARNIVAL BOAT

(RKO-Pathe, February 12, 1932) 61 Minutes
William Boyd, Ginger Rogers, Fred Kohler, Hobart Bosworth, Marie Prevost, Edgar Kennedy, Harry Sweet, Charles Sellon, Walter Percival, Jack Carlyle, Joe Marba, Eddie Chandler, Bob Perry
Director: Albert Rogell
Story: Marion Jackson and Don Ryan
Screenplay: James Seymour, Ted McCord
Associate Producer: Harry Joe Brown

MEN OF AMERICA

(RKO Radio, December 9, 1932) 57 Minutes
William Boyd, Dorothy Wilson, Ralph Ince, Charles "Chic" Sale, Henry Armetta, Inez Oalange, Theresa Maxwell Conover, Alphonse Ethier
Director: Ralph Ince
Adaptation: Samuel Ornitz and Jack Jungemeter
Story: Humphrey Pearson and Henry McCarthy
Producer: David O. Selznick

LUCKY DEVILS

(RKO-Pathe, February 3, 1933) 70 Minutes
William Boyd, William Gargan, Bruce Cabot, William Bakewell, Creighton Chaney, Bob Rose, Dorothy Wilson, Sylvia Picker, Julie Haydon, Gladden James, Edwin Stanley, Roscoe Ates, Phyllis Fraser, Betty Furness, Alan Roscoe, Charles Gillette
Director: Ralph Ince
Story: Casey Robinson and Bob Rose
Adaptation: Ben Markson and Agnes C. Johnson
Associate Producer: Merian C. Cooper
Producer: David Selznick

EMERGENCY CALL

(RKO-Pathe, May 19, 1933) 70 Minutes
William Boyd, Wynne Gibson, William Gargan, Betty Furness, Reginald Mason, Edwin Maxwell, George E. Stone, Merna Kennedy
Director: Edward Cahn
Screenplay: Houston Branch and Joseph Mankiewicz
Story: John B. Clymer and Mames Ewens

FLAMING GOLD

(RKO-Pathe, September 29, 1933) 54 Minutes
William Boyd, Pat O'Brien, Mae Clarke, Rollo Lloyd, Helen Ware
Director: Ralph Ince
Story: Houston Branch
Screenplay: Malcolm Stuart Boylan, John Goodrich
Associate Producer: Sam Jaffe
Producer: Merian C. Cooper

CHEATERS

(Liberty, January 30, 1934) 68 Minutes
William Boyd, June Collyer, Dorothy Machaill, William Collier, Sr., Alan Mowbray, Guinn Williams, Louise Beavers
Director: Phil Rosen
Story/Screenplay: Adele Buffington
Suggested by "The Peacock Screen" by Fanny Heaslip Lea

PORT OF LOST DREAMS

(Invincible Production/Chesterfield, November 1, 1934) 71 Minutes
William Boyd, Lola Lane, Edward Gargan, George Marion, Harold Huber, Evelyn Carrington, Robert Elliott
Director: Frank Strayer
Story: Robert Ellis
Adaptation: Charles Belden, Norman Markwell
Producer: Maury M. Cohen

HOP-A-LONG CASSIDY

(Paramout, July 30, 1935) 63 Minutes
(First in the Hopalong Cassidy Series—reissued by Screen Guild as "Hopalong Cassidy Enters")
William Boyd, Jimmy Ellison, Paula Stone, Robert Warwick, Charles Middleton, Frank McGlynn, Jr., Kenneth Thompson, George Hayes, James Mason, Frank Campeau, Ted Adams, Willie Fung, Franklyn Farnum, John Merton, Wally West
Director: Howard Bretherton
Story: Clarence E. Mulford
Screenplay: Doris Schroeder
Producer: Harry Sherman

THE EAGLE'S BROOD

(Paramount, October 10, 1935) 59 Minutes
(Hopalong Cassidy Series)
William Boyd, Jimmy Ellison, William Farnum, George Hayes, Addison Richards, Joan Woodbury, Frank Shannon, Dorothy Revier, Paul Fix, Al Lydell, John Merton, Juan Torene, Henry Sylvester
Director: Howard Bretherton
Story: Clarence E. Mulford
Screenplay: Doris Schroeder, Harrison Jacobs
Producer: Harry Sherman

BAR 20 RIDES AGAIN

(Paramount, November 30, 1935) 65 Minutes
(Hopalong Cassidy Series)
William Boyd, Jimmy Ellison, Jean Rouveral, George Hayes, Frank McGlynn, Jr., Howard Lang, Harry Worth, Ethel Wales, Paul Fix, J. P. McGowan, Joe Rickson, Al St. John, John Merton, Frank Layton, Chill Wills and His Avalon Boys
Director: Howard Bretherton
Story: Clarence E. Mulford
Screenplay: Gerald Geraghty, Doris Schroeder
Producer: Harry Sherman

BURNING GOLD

(Winchester/Republic, January 28, 1936) 58 Minutes
William Boyd, Judith Allen, Lloyd Ingraham, Fern Emmett, Frank Mayo
Director: Sam Newfield
Story: Stuart Anthony
Adaptation: Earl Snell

CALL OF THE PRAIRIE

(Paramount, March 6, 1936) 65 Minutes
(Hopalong Cassidy Series)
William Boyd, Jimmy Ellison, Muriel Evans, George Hayes, Al Bridge, Chester Conklin, Hank Mann, Willie Fung, Howard Lang, Al Hill, John Merton, James Mason, Chill Wills and the Avalon Boys
Director: Howard Bretherton
Story: Clarence E. Mulford
Screenplay: Doris Schroeder, Vernon Smith
Producer: Harry Sherman

FEDERAL AGENT

(Winchester/Republic, April 10, 1936) 60 Minutes
William Boyd, Charles A. Browne, Irence Ware, George Cooper, Lenita Lane, Don Alvarado
Director: Sam Newfield
Screenplay: Robert Ellis
Story: Barry Barringer

THREE ON THE TRAIL

(Paramount, April 14, 1936) 67 Minutes
(Hopalong Cassidy Series)
William Boyd, Jimmy Ellison, Onslow Stevens, Muriel Evans, George Hayes, Claude King, William Duncan, Clara Kimball Young, Ernie Adams, Ted Adams, John St. Polis, Al Hill, Jack Rutherford, Lita Cortez, Artie Ortego, Franklyn Farnum, Lew Meehan
Director: Howard Bretherton
Story: Clarence E. Mulford
Screenplay: Doris Schroeder, Vernon Smith
Producer: Harry Sherman

HEART OF THE WEST

(Paramount, July 24, 1936) 60 Minutes
(Hopalong Cassidy Series)
William Boyd, Jimmy Ellison, George Hayes, Lynn Gilbert, Sidney Blackmer, Charles Martin, John Rutherford, Warner Richmond, Walter Miller, Ted Adams, Fred Kohler, Bob McKenzie, John Elliott
Director: Howard Bretherton
Story/Screenplay: Doris Schroeder
Based on characters created by Clarence E. Mulford
Producer: Harry Sherman

HOPALONG CASSIDY RETURNS
(Paramount, October 12, 1936) 71 Minutes
(Hopalong Cassidy Series)

William Boyd, George Hayes, Gail Sheridan, Evelyn Brent, Stephen Morris (Morris Ankrum), William Janney, Irving Bacon, Grant Richards, John Beck, Ernie Adams, Joe Rickson, Claude Smith, Ray Whitley, Fred Burns, Frank Ellis, Robert Burns, Lew Meehan
Director: Nate Watt
Story: Clarence E. Mulford
Screenplay: Harrison Jacobs
Producer: Harry Sherman

TRAIL DUST
(Paramount, December 19, 1936) 77 Minutes
(Hopalong Cassidy Series)

William Boyd, Jimmy Ellison, George Hayes, Gwynne Shipman, Stephen Morris (Morris Ankrum), Britt Wood, Dick Dickinson, Earl Askam, Al Bridge, John Beach, Ted Adams, Tom Halligan, Dan Wolheim, Al St. John, Harold Daniels, Kenneth Harlan, John Elliott, George Chesebro, Emmett Day, Robert Drew
Director: Nate Watt
Story: Clarence E. Mulford
Screenplay: Al Martin
Producer: Harry Sherman

BORDERLAND
(Paramount, February 26, 1937) 82 Minutes
(Hopalong Cassidy Series)

William Boyd, Jimmy Ellison, George Hayes, Stephen Morris (Morris Ankrum), John Beach, George Chesebro, Nora Lane, Charlene Wyatt, Trevor Bardette, Earle Hodgins, Al Bridge, John St. Polis, Edward Cassidy, Slim Whitaker, Cliff Parkinson, Karl Hackett, Robert Walker, Frank Ellis, J. P. McGowan, Jack Evans
Director: Nate Watt
Story: "Bring Me His Ears" - Clarence E. Mulford
Screenplay: Harrison Jacobs
Producer: Harry Sherman

HILLS OF OLD WYOMING
(Paramount, April 16, 1937) 75 Minutes
(Hopalong Cassidy Series)

William Boyd, George Hayes, Stephen Morris (Morris Ankrum), Russell Hayden, Gail Sheridan, Clara Kimball Young, John Beach, Earle Hodgins, George Chesebro, Steve Clemente, Paul Gustine, Leo McMahon, John Powers, James Mason, Chief John Big Tree
Director: Nate Watt
Story: "The Roundup" - Clarence E. Mulford
Screenplay: Maurice Geraghty
Producer: Harry Sherman

NORTH OF THE RIO GRANDE
(Paramount, June 28, 1937) 70 Minutes
(Hopalong Cassidy Series)

William Boyd, George Hayes, Stephen Morris (Morris Ankrum), Russell Hayden, John Beach, Bernadine Hayes, John Rutherford, Walter Long, Lee J. Cobb, Lorraine Randall, Al Ferguson, Lafe McKee
Director: Nate Watt
Story: "Cottonwood Gulch" - Clarence E. Mulford
Screenplay: Joseph O'Donnell
Producer: Harry Sherman

RUSTLER'S VALLEY
(Paramount, July 23, 1937) 60 Minutes
(Hopalong Cassidy Series)

William Boyd, George Hayes, Russell Hayden, Stephen Morris (Morris Ankrum), Muriel Evans, John Beach, Lee J. Cobb, Oscar Apfel, Ted Adams, Bernadine Hayes, John St. Polis, Horace B. Carpenter, John Powers, Al Ferguson
Director: Nate Watt
Story: Clarence E. Mulford
Screenplay: Harry O. Hoyt
Producer: Harry Sherman

HOPALONG RIDES AGAIN
(Paramount, September 30, 1937) 65 Minutes
(Hopalong Cassidy Series)

William Boyd, George Hayes, Russell Hayden, Harry Worth, Nora Lane, William Duncan, Lois Wilde, Billy King, John Rutherford, Ernie Adams, Frank Ellis, Artie Ortego, Ben Corbett, John Beach, Blackjack Ward
Director: Les Selander
Story: Clarence E. Mulford
Screenplay: Norman Houston
Producer: Harry Sherman

TEXAS TRAIL
(Paramount, November 26, 1937) 60 Minutes
(Hopalong Cassidy Series)

William Boyd, George Hayes, Russell Hayden, Judith Allen, Alexander Cross, Robert Kortman, Billy King, Karl Hackett, Jack Rockwell, John Beach, Rafael Bennett, Philo McCullough, Earle Hodgins, Ben Corbett
Director: David Selman
Story: Clarence E. Mulford
Screenplay: Joseph O'Donnell
Producer: Harry Sherman

PARTNERS OF THE PLAINS

(Paramount, January 14, 1938) 68 Minutes
(Hopalong Cassidy Series)

William Boyd, Harvey Clark, Russell Hayden, Gwen Gage, Hilda Plowright, John Warburton, Al Bridge, Al Hill, Earle Hodgins, John Beach, Jim Corey
Director: Lesley Selander
Story: Clarence E. Mulford
Screenplay: Harrison Jacobs
Producer: Harry Sherman

CASSIDY OF BAR 20

(Paramount, February 25, 1938) 56 Minutes
(Hopalong Cassidy Series)

William Boyd, Frank Darien, Russell Hayden, Nora Lane, Robert Fiske, John Elliott, Margaret Marquis, Gertrude Hoffman, Carleton Young, Gordon Hart, Edward Cassidy, Jim Toney
Director: Lesley Selander
Story: Clarence E. Mulford
Screenplay: Norman Houston
Producer: Harry Sherman

HEART OF ARIZONA

(Paramount, April 8, 1938) 68 Minutes
(Hopalong Cassidy Series)

William Boyd, George Hayes, Russell Hayden, Natalie Moorhead, John Elliott, Billy King, Dorothy Short, Lane Chandler, Alden Chase, John Beach, Leo MacMahon, Lee Phelps, Bob McKenzie
Director: Lesley Selander
Story: Clarence E. Mulford
Screenplay: Norman Houston
Producer: Harry Sherman

BAR 20 JUSTICE

(Paramount, June 24, 1938) 70 Minutes
(Hopalong Cassidy Series)

William Boyd, George Hayes, Russell Hayden, Paul Sutton, Gwen Gaze, Pat O'Brien, Joseph De Stefani, William Duncan, Walter Long, John Beach, Bruce Mitchell, Frosty Royce, Jim Toney
Director: Lesley Selander
Story: Clarence E. Mulford
Screenplay: Arnold Belgard, Harrison Jacobs
Producer: Harry Sherman

PRIDE OF THE WEST

(Paramount, July 8, 1938) 56 Minutes
(Hopalong Cassidy Series)

William Boyd, George Hayes, Russell Hayden, Charlotte Field, Earle Hodgins, Billy King, Kenneth Harlan, Glenn Strange, James Craig, Bruce Mitchell, Willie Fung, George Morrell, Earl Askam, Jim Toney, Horace B. Carpenter, Henry Otho
Director: Lesley Selander
Story: Clarence E. Mulford
Screenplay: Nate Watt
Producer: Harry Sherman

IN OLD MEXICO

(Paramount, September 9, 1938) 62 Minutes
(Hopalong Cassidy Series)

William Boyd, George Hayes, Russell Hayden, Betty Amann, Jane Clayton, Al Garcia, Glenn Strange, Trevor Bardette, Anna Demetrio, Tony Roux, Fred Burns, Cliff Parkinson
Director: Edward D. Venturini
Story: Clarence E. Mulford
Screenplay: Harrison Jacobs
Producer: Harry Sherman

THE FRONTIERSMAN

(Paramount, December 16, 1938) 74 Minutes
(Hopalong Cassidy Series)

William Boyd, George Hayes, Russell Hayden, Evelyn Venable, William Duncan, Clara Kimball Young, Charles (Tony) Hughes, Dickie Jones, Roy Barcroft, Emily Fitzroy, John Beach, Blackjack Ward, George Morrell, Jim Corey, Saint Brendan Boys Choir
Director: Lesley Selander
Story: Clarence E. Mulford
Screenplay: Norman Houston, Harrison Jacobs
Producer: Harry Sherman

SUNSET TRAIL

(Paramount, February 24, 1939) 60 Minutes
(Hopalong Cassidy Series)

William Boyd, George Hayes, Russell Hayden, Charlotte Wynters, Jane Clayton, Robert Fiske, Glenn Strange, Kenneth Harlan, Anthony Nace, Kathryn Sheldon, Maurice Cass, Alphonse Ethier, Claudia Smith, Jack Rockwell, Tom London, Jim Toney, Fred Burns, Jerry Jerome, Jim Corey, Frank Ellis, Horace B. Carpenter
Director: Lesley Selander
Story: Clarence E. Mulford
Producer: Harry Sherman

Eddie Dean, Britt Wood, William Boyd, Pedro De Cordoba, Betty Moran and Russell Hayden in **Range War**
(Paramount, 1939)

SILVER ON THE SAGE

(Paramount, March 31, 1939) 68 Minutes
(Hopalong Cassidy Series)
William Boyd, Russell Hayden, George Hayes, Ruth Rogers, Stanley Ridges, Frederick Burton, Hank Bell, Jack Rockwell, Bruce Mitchell, Ed Cassidy, Roy Barcroft, Jim Corey, Sherry Tansey, George Morrell, Frank O'Connor, Buzz Barton, Herman Hack, Dick Dickinson
Director: Lesley Selander
Screenplay: Harrison Jacobs
Producer: Harry Sherman

RENEGADE TRAIL

(Paramount, July 25, 1939) 61 Minutes
(Hopalong Cassidy Series)
William Boyd, George Hayes, Russell Hayden, Charlotte Wynters, Russell Hopton, Sonny Bupp, Jack Rockwell, Roy Barcroft, John Merton, Bob Kortman, Eddie Dean, The King's Men (Ken Darbe, Rad Robinson, John Dobson and Budd Linn)
Director: Lesley Selander
Screenplay: John Rathmell, Harrison Jacobs
Based on characters created by Clarence E. Mulford
Producer: Harry Sherman

RANGE WAR

(Paramount, September 8, 1939) 66 Minutes
(Hopalong Cassidy Series)
William Boyd, Russell Hayden, Willard Robertson, Matt Moore, Pedro De Cordoba, Betty Moran, Britt Wood, Kenneth Harlan, Francis McDonald, Earle Hodgins, Jason Robards, Stanley Price, Eddie Dean, Raphael Bennett, Glenn Strange, George Chesebro, Don Latorre
Director: Lesley Selander
Story: Josef Montaigue
Screenplay: Sam Robins
Producer: Harry Sherman
Based on characters created by Clarence E. Mulford

LAW OF THE PAMPAS

(Paramount, November 3, 1939) 74 Minutes
(Hopalong Cassidy Series)
William Boyd, Sidney Toler, Steffi Duna, Russell Hayden, Sidney Blackmer, Pedro de Cordoba, Jojo La Sadio, Glenn Strange, Eddie Dean, Anna Demetrio, William Duncan, Tony Roux, Martin Garralaga, The King's Men
Director: Nate Watt
Screenplay: Harrison Jacobs
Based on characters created by Clarence E. Mulford
Producer: Harry Sherman

281

SANTA FE MARSHAL
(Paramount, January 26, 1940) 65 Minutes
(Hopalong Cassidy Series)
William Boyd, Russell Hayden, Marjorie Rambeau,
Bernadine Hayes, Earle Hodgins, Britt Wood, Kenneth
Harlan, William Pagan, George Anderson, Jack
Rockwell, Eddie Dean, Fred Graham, Matt Moore,
Duke Green, Billy Jones, Tex Phelps, Cliff Parkinson
Director: Lesley Selander
Screenplay: Harrison Jacobs
Producer: Harry Sherman
Based on characters created by Clarence E. Mulford

THE SHOWDOWN
(Paramount, March 8, 1940) 65 Minutes
(Hopalong Cassidy Series)
William Boyd, Russell Hayden, Britt Wood, Morris
Ankrum, Jane (Jan) Clayton, Wright Kramer, Donald
Kirke, Roy Barcroft, Kermit Maynard, Walter
Shumway, Eddie Dean, The King's Men
Director: Howard Bretherton
Story: Jack Jungmeyer
Based on characters created by Clarence E. Mulford
Screenplay: Howard and Donald Kusel
Producer: Harry Sherman

HIDDEN GOLD
(Paramount, June 7, 1940) 61 Minutes
(Hopalong Cassidy Series)
William Boyd, Russell Hayden, Minor Watson, Ruth
Rogers, Britt Wood, Ethel Wales, Lee Phelps, Roy
Barcroft, George Anderson, Eddie Dean, Raphael
Bennett, Jack Rockwell, Walter Long, Bob Kortman,
Merrill McCormack
Director: Lesley Selander
Screenplay: Jack Merseruau, Gerald Geraghty
Based on characters created by Clarence E. Mulford
Producer: Harry Sherman

STAGECOACH WAR
(Paramount, July 12, 1940) 63 Minutes
(Hopalong Cassidy Series)
William Boyd, Russell Hayden, Julie Carter, J. Farrell
MacDonald, Rad Robinson, Eddy Waller, Frank Lack-
teen, Jack Rockwell, Eddie Dean, Bob Kortman, The
King's Men, Rod Cameron
Director: Lesley Selander
Story: Norman Houston, Henry Olstea
Based on characters created by Clarence E. Mulford
Screenplay: Norman Houston
Producer: Harry Sherman

Russell Hayden, William Boyd and Esther Estrella look at an unidentified player in **Three Men From Texas**
(Paramount, 1940)

THREE MEN FROM TEXAS
(Paramount, November 15, 1940) 70 Minutes
(Hopalong Cassidy Series)
William Boyd, Russell Hayden, Andy Clyde, Esther Estrella, Morris Ankrum, Morgan Wallace, Thornton Edwards, Davidson Clark, Dick Curtis, Glenn Strange, Neyle Marx, Robert Burns, Jim Corey, George Morrell, George Lollier, Frank McCarroll, Lucio Villegas
Director: Lesley Selander
Screenplay: Norton S. Parker
Based on characters created by Clarence E. Mulford
Producer: Harry Sherman

DOOMED CARAVAN
(Paramount, January 10, 1941) 62 Minutes
(Hopalong Cassidy Series)
William Boyd, Russell Hayden, Andy Clyde, Minna Gombell, Morris Ankrum, Georgia Hawkins, Trevor Bardette, Ray Bennett, Ed Cassidy
Director: Lesley Selander
Story/Screenplay: Johnston McCulley, J. Benton Cheney
Based on characters created by Clarence E. Mulford
Producer: Harry Sherman

IN OLD COLORADO
(Paramount, March 14, 1941) 66 Minutes
(Hopalong Cassidy Series)
William Boyd, Russell Hayden, Andy Clyde, Margaret Hayes, Cliff Nazarro, Morris Ankrum, Sarah Padden, Stanley Andrews, Morgan Wallace, Weldon Heyburn, Glenn Strange, Eddy Waller, Philip Van Zandt, James Seay, Henry Wills, Curley Dresden
Director: Howard Bretherton
Screenplay: J. Benton Cheney, Norton S. Parker, Russell Hayden
Based on characters created by Clarence E. Mulford
Producer: Harry Sherman

BORDER VIGILANTES
(Paramount, April 18, 1941) 62 Minutes
(Hopalong Cassidy Series)
William Boyd, Russell Hayden, Andy Clyde, Victor Jory, Morris Ankrum, Frances Gifford, Ethel Wales, Tom Tyler, Hal Taliaferro, Jack Rockwell, Britt Wood, Hank Worden, Hank Bell, Edward Earle, Al Haskell, Curley Dresden, Chuck Morrison, Ted Wells
Director: Derwin Abrahams
Screenplay: J. Benton Cheney
Based on characters created by Clarence E. Mulford
Producer: Harry Sherman

PIRATES ON HORSEBACK
(Paramount, May 31, 1941) 69 Minutes
(Hopalong Cassidy Series)
William Boyd, Russell Hayden, Andy Clyde, Eleanor Stewart, Morris Ankrum, William Haade, Dennis Moore, Henry Hall, Britt Wood, Silvertip Baker
Director: Lesley Selander
Screenplay: Ethel La Blanche, J. Benton Cheney
Based on characters created by Clarence E. Mulford
Producer: Harry Sherman

WIDE OPEN TOWN
(Paramount, August 8, 1941) 78 Minutes
(Hopalong Cassidy Series)
William Boyd, Russell Hayden, Andy Clyde, Evelyn Brent, Victor Jory, Morris Ankrum, Kenneth Harlan, Bernice Kay (Cara Williams), Roy Barcroft, Glenn Strange, Ed Cassidy, Jack Rockwell, Bob Kortman, George Cleveland
Director: Lesley Selander
Screenplay: Harrison Jacobs, J. Benton Cheney
Based on characters created by Clarence E. Mulford
Producer: Harry Sherman

RIDERS OF THE TIMBERLINE
(Paramount, September 17, 1941) 59 Minutes
(Hopalong Cassidy Series)
William Boyd, Brad King, Andy Clyde, J. Farrell Mac-Donald, Eleanor Stewart, Anna Q. Nilsson, Edward Keane, Hal Taliaferro, Victory Jory, Tom Tyler, Mickey Essia, Hank Bell, The Guardsman Quartet
Director: Lesley Selander
Screenplay: J. Benton Cheney
Based on characters created by Clarence E. Mulford
Producer: Harry Sherman

TWILIGHT ON THE TRAIL
(Paramount, September 27, 1941) 58 Minutes
(Hopalong Cassidy Series)
William Boyd, Andy Clyde, Brad King, Wanda McKay, Jack Rockwell, Norman Willis, Robert Kent, Tom London, Bob Kortman, Frank Austin, Clem Fuller, Johnny Powers, Frank Ellis, Bud Osborne, The Jimmy Wakely Trio (Jimmy Wakely, Johnny Bond and Dick Rinehart)
Director: Howard Bretherton
Screenplay: J. Benton Cheney, Ellen Corby and Cecile Kramer
Based on characters created by Clarence E. Mulford
Producer: Harry Sherman

STICK TO YOUR GUNS
(Paramount, September 27, 1941) 63 Minutes
(Hopalong Cassidy Series)
William Boyd, Andy Clyde, Brad King, Jacqueline (Jennifer) Holt, Dick Curtis, Weldon Heyburn, Henry Hall, Joe Whitehead, Bob Card, Jack C. Smith, Homer (Herb) Holcomb, Tom London, Kermit Maynard, Frank Ellis, Jack Rockwell, Mickey Eissa, The Jimmy Wakely Trio (Jimmy Wakely, Johnny Bond and Dick Rinehart)
Director: Lesley Selander
Screenplay: J. Benton Cheney
Based on characters created by Clarence E. Mulford
Producer: Harry Sherman

OUTLAWS OF THE DESERT
(Paramount, November 1, 1941) 66 Minutes
(Hopalong Cassidy Series)
William Boyd, Brad King, Andy Clyde, Forest Stanley, Jean Phillips, Nina Guilbert, Luci Deste, Albert Morin, George Woolsley, George J. Lewis, Duncan Renaldo, Jean Del Val, Mickey Eissa, Jamiel Hasson
Director: Howard Bretherton
Screenplay: J. Benton Cheney, Bernard McConville
Based on characters created by Clarence E. Mulford
Associate Producer: Harry Sherman

SECRETS OF THE WASTELAND
(Paramount, November 15, 1941) 66 Minutes
(Hopalong Cassidy Series)
William Boyd, Andy Clyde, Brad King, Barbara Britton, Douglas Fowley, Keith Richards, Soo Yong, Richard Loo, Lee Tung Foo, Gordon Hart, Hal Price, Jack Rockwell, John Rawlings, Earl Gunn, Roland Got, Ian MacDonald
Director: Derwin Abrahams
Story: Bliss Lomax
Screenplay: Gerald Geraghty
Based on characters created by Clarence E. Mulford
Producer: Harry Sherman

UNDERCOVER MAN
(United Artists, October 23, 1942) 68 Minutes
(Hopalong Cassidy Series)
William Boyd, Andy Clyde, Jay Kirby, Antonio Moreno, Nora Lane, Chris-Pin Martin, Esther Estrella, John Vosper, Eva Puig, Alan Baldwin, Jack Rockwell, Bennett George, Tony Roux, Pierce Lyden, Ted Wells, Martin Garralaga, Joe Dominguez, Earle Hodgins, Frank Ellis
Director: Lesley Selander
Screenplay: J. Benton Cheney
Based on character created by Clarence E. Mulford
Producer: Harry Sherman
(First in this series to be distributed by United Artists, but a Paramount pressbook and advertising posters were prepared and issued on this film.)

HOPPY SERVES A WRIT
(United Artists, March 12, 1943) 67 Minutes
(Hopalong Cassidy Series)
William Boyd, Andy Clyde, Jay Kirby, Victor Jory, George Reeves, Jan Christy, Forbes Murray, Robert Mitchum, Earle Hodgins, Hal Taliaferro, Roy Barcroft, Byron Foulger, Ben Corbett, Art Mix.
Director: George Archainbaud
Screenplay: Gerald Geraghty
Based on characters created by Clarence E. Mulford
Producer: Harry Sherman

BORDER PATROL
(United Artists, April 2, 1943) 60 Minutes
(Hopalong Cassidy Series)
William Boyd, Andy Clyde, Jay Kirby, Claudia Drake, Russell Simpson, Duncan Renaldo, Cliff Parkinson, George Reeves, Robert Mitchum, Pierce Lyden, Merrill McCormack
Director: Lesley Selander
Screenplay: Michael Wilson
Based on characters created by Clarence E. Mulford
Producer: Harry Sherman

THE LEATHER BURNERS
(United Artists, May 28, 1943) 58 Minutes
(Hopalong Cassidy Series)
William Boyd, Andy Clyde, Jay Kirby, Victor Jory, George Reeves, Shelley Spencer, George Givot, Bobby Larson, Hal Taliaferro, Forbes Murray, Bob Mitchum, Bob Kortman, Herman Hack
Director: Joseph E. Henabery
Story: Bliss Lomax
Screenplay: Jo Pagano
Based on characters created by Clarence E. Mulford
Producer: Harry Sherman

COLT COMRADES
(United Artists, June 18, 1943) 67 Minutes
(Hopalong Cassidy Series)
William Boyd, Andy Clyde, Jay Kirby, George Reeves, Gayle Lord, Earle Hodgins, Victor Jory, Douglas Fowley, Herbert Rawlinson, Bob Mitchum
Director: Lesley Selander
Screenplay: Michael Wilson
Based on characters created by Clarence E. Mulford
Producer: Harry Sherman

William Boyd gets ready to climb as Andy Clyde and Jay Kirby protect him in **Border Patrol** (Paramount, 1943)

BAR 20
(United Artists, October 1, 1943) 54 Minutes
(Hopalong Cassidy Series)
William Boyd, Andy Clyde, Dustin Farnum, George Reeves, Victor Jory, Douglas Fowley, Betty Blythe, Bob Mitchum, Francis McDonald, Earle Hodgins, Buck Bucko
Director: Lesley Selander
Screenplay: Morton Grant, Norman Houston, Michael Wilson
Based on characters created by Clarence E. Mulford
Producer: Harry Sherman

FALSE COLORS
(United Artists, November 5, 1943) 65 Minutes
(Hopalong Cassidy Series)
William Boyd, Andy Clyde, Jimmy Rogers, Claudia Drake, Robert Mitchum, Douglass Dumbrille, Roy Barcroft, Glenn Strange, Pierce Lyden, Earle Hodgins, Sam Flint, Tom Siedel, Tom London, George Morrell, Dan White, Elmer Jerome, Ray Jones, Bob Burns, Tom Smith
Director: George Archainbaud
Screenplay: Bennett Cohen
Based on characters created by Clarence E. Mulford
Producer: Harry Sherman

RIDERS OF THE DEADLINE
(United Artists, December 3, 1943) 60 Minutes
(Hopalong Cassidy Series)
William Boyd, Andy Clyde, Jimmy Rogers, Richard Crane, William Halligan, Frances Woodward, Tony Ward (Anthony Warde), Bob Mitchum, Jim Bannon, Hugh Prosser, Herbert Rawlinson, Monte Montana, Earle Hodgins, Bill Beckford, Pierce Lyden, Art Felix, Roy Bucko, Cliff Parkinson
Director: Lesley Selander
Screenplay: Bennett Cohen
Based on characters created by Clarence E. Mulford
Producer: Harry Sherman

LOST CANYON
(United Artists, December 18, 1943) 61 Minutes
(Hopalong Cassidy Series)
William Boyd, Andy Clyde, Jay Kirby, Lola Lane, Douglas Fowley, Herbert Rawlinson, Guy Usher, Karl Hackett, Hugh Prosser, Keith Richards, Herman Hack, Merrill McCormack, George Morrell
Director: Lesley Selander
Story: Clarence E. Mulford
Screenplay: Harry O. Hoyt
Producer: Harry Sherman

TEXAS MASQUERADE
(United Artists, February 18, 1944) 59 Minutes
(Hopalong Cassidy Series)
William Boyd, Andy Clyde, Jimmy Rogers, Mady Correll, Don Costello, Russell Simpson, Nelson Leigh, Francis McDonald, J. Farrell MacDonald, June Pickerell, John Merton, Pierce Lyden, Robert McKenzie, Bill Hunter, Keith Richards, George Morrell
Director: George Archainbaud
Screenplay: Norman Houston
Based on characters created by Clarence E. Mulford
Producer: Harry Sherman

LUMBERJACK
(United Artists, April 28, 1944) 65 Minutes
(Hopalong Cassidy Series)
William Boyd, Andy Clyde, Jimmy Rogers, Douglass Dumbrille, Ellen Hall, Francis McDonald, Herbert Rawlinson, Ethel Wales, John Whitney, Hal Taliaferro, Henry Wills, Charles Morton, Frances Morris, Jack Rockwell, Bob Burns, Hank Worden, Earle Hodgins, Pierce Lyden
Director: Lesley Selander
Screenplay: Norman Houston, Barry Shipman
Based on characters created by Clarence E. Mulford
Producer: Harry Sherman

MYSTERY MAN
(United Artists, May 31, 1944) 58 Minutes
(Hopalong Cassidy Series)
William Boyd, Andy Clyde, Jimmy Rogers, Don Costello, Eleanor Stewart, Francis McDonald, Forrest Taylor, Jack Rockwell, Bill Hunter, John Merton, Pierce Lyden, Bob Burns, Ozie Waters, Art Mix, Hank Bell, Bob Baker, George Morrell
Director: George Archainbaud
Screenplay: J. Benton Cheney
Based on characters created by Clarence E. Mulford
Producer: Harry Sherman

FORTY THIEVES
(United Artists, June 23, 1944) 60 Minutes
(Hopalong Cassidy Series)
William Boyd, Andy Clyde, Jimmy Rogers, Louise Currie, Douglass Dumbrille, Kirk Alyn, Herbert Rawlinson, Robert Frazer, Glenn Strange, Jack Rockwell, Bob Kortman, Hal Taliaferro
Director: Lesley Selander
Screenplay: Michael Wilson, Bernie Kamins
Based on characters created by Clarence E. Mulford
Producer: Harry Sherman

William Boyd, Ethel Wales, Andy Clyde and Frances Morris in a scene from **Lumberjack** (Paramount, 1944)

FOOL'S GOLD
(United Artists, January 31, 1946) 63 Minutes
(Hopalong Cassidy Series)
William Boyd, Andy Clyde, Rand Brooks, Robert Emmett Keane, Jane Randolph, Stephen Barclay, Forbes Murray, Harry Cording, Earle Hodgins, Wee Willie Davis, Ben Corbett, Fred Toones, Bob Bentley, Glen Gallagher
Director: George Archainbaud
Screenplay: Doris Schroeder
Producer: Lewis J. Rachmil

THE DEVIL'S PLAYGROUND
(United Artists, November 15, 1946) 62 Minutes
(Hopalong Cassidy Series)
William Boyd, Andy Clyde, Rand Brooks, Elaine Riley, Robert Elliott, Joseph J. Green, Francis McDonald, Ned Young, Earle Hodgins, George Eldredge, Everett Shields, John George, Glenn Strange
Director: George Archainbaud
Producer: Lewis J. Rachmil

UNEXPECTED GUEST
(United Artists, March 28, 1947) 61 Minutes
(Hopalong Cassidy Series)
William Boyd, Rand Brooks, Andy Clyde, Una O'Connor, Patricia Tate, Ian Wolfe, John Parrish, Earle Hodgins, Bob Williams, Ned Young, Joel Friedkin
Director: George Archainbaud
Screenplay: Ande Lamb
Producer: Lewis J. Rachmil

DANGEROUS VENTURE
(United Artists, May 23, 1947) 59 Minutes
(Hopalong Cassidy Series)
William Boyd, Andy Clyde, Rand Brooks, Fritz Leiber, Douglas Evan, Elaine Riley, Harry Cording, Betty Alexander, Francis McDonald, Neyle Morrow, Patricia Tate, Bob Faust
Director: George Archainbaud
Screenplay: Doris Schroeder
Producer: Lewis J. Rachmil

THE MARAUDERS
(United Artists, July 1, 1947) 63 Minutes
(Hopalong Cassidy Series)
William Boyd, Andy Clyde, Rand Brooks, Ian Wolfe, Dorinda Clifton, Mary Newton, Harry Cording, Earle Hodgins, Richard Bailey, Dick Alexander, Herman Hack
Director: George Archainbaud
Screenplay: Charles Belden
Producer: Lewis J. Rachmil

HOPPY'S HOLIDAY
(United Artists, July 18, 1947) 60 Minutes
(Hopalong Cassidy Series)
William Boyd, Andy Clyde, Rand Brooks, Mary Ware, Andrew Tombes, Leonard Penn, Jeff Corey, Donald Kirke, Holly Bane, Gil Patrick, Frank Henry
Director: George Archainbaud
Story: Ellen Corby, Cecile Kramer
Screenplay: J. Benton Cheney, Bennett Cohen, Ande Lamb
Producer: Lewis J. Rachmil

SCREEN SNAPSHOTS
(Columbia, September 4, 1947) 9½ Minutes
(Segment called "Hollywood Cowboys")
Buck Jones, Gene Autry, Roy Rogers, Will Rogers, Tom Mix, John Mack Brown, Hoot Gibson, William S. Hart, *William Boyd,* Robert Young, Jackie Coogan
Director: Ralph Staub

SILENT CONFLICT
(United Artists, March 19, 1948) 51 Minutes
(Hopalong Cassidy Series)
William Boyd, Andy Clyde, Rand Brooks, Virginia Belmont, Earle Hodgins, James Harrison, Forbes Murray, John Butler, Herbert Rawlinson, Dick Alexander, Don Haggerty
Director: George Archainbaud
Screenplay: Charles Earl Belden
Producer: Lewis Rachmil

THE DEAD DON'T DREAM
(United Artists, April 30, 1948) 68 Minutes
(Hopalong Cassidy Series)
William Boyd, Andy Clyde, Rand Brooks, Mary Ware, Francis McDonald, John Parrish, Leonard Penn, Dick Alexander, Bob Gabriel, Stanley Andrews, Forbes Murray, Don Haggerty
Director: George Archainbaud
Screenplay: Frances Rosenwald
Producer: Lewis J. Rachmil

SINISTER JOURNEY
(United Artists, June 11, 1948) 59 Minutes
(Hopalong Cassidy Series)
William Boyd, Andy Clyde, Rand Brooks, Elaine Riley, John Kellogg, Don Haggerty, Stanley Andrews, Harry Strang, Herbert Rawlinson, John Butler, Will Orleans, Wayne Treadway
Director: George Archainbaud
Screenplay: Doris Schroeder
Producer: Lewis J. Rachmil

William Boyd is ready for action in **The Marauders** (United Artists, 1947).

BORROWED TROUBLE
(United Artists, 1948) 60 Minutes
(Hopalong Cassidy Series)
William Boyd, Andy Clyde, Rand Brooks, Elaine Riley,
John Kellogg
Director: George Archainbaud
Screenplay: Charles Belden
Producer: Lewis J. Rachmil

FALSE PARADISE
(United Artists, September 10, 1948) 60 Minutes
(Hopalong Cassidy Series)
William Boyd, Andy Clyde, Rand Brooks, Elaine Riley,
Joel Friedkin, Cliff Clark, Kenneth MacDonald, Don
Haggerty, Dick Alexander, William Norton Bailey, Zon
Murray, George Eldredge
Director: George Archainbaud
Screenplay: Harrison Jacobs, Doris Schroeder
Producer: Lewis J. Rachmil

STRANGE GAMBLE
(United Artists, October 8, 1948) 62 Minutes
(Last in the Hopalong Cassidy Series)
William Boyd, Andy Clyde, Rand Brooks, Elaine Riley,
Francis McDonald, Paul Fix, William Leicester, Joan
Barton, James Craven, Joel Friedkin, Herbert
Rawlinson, Robert Williams, Albert Morin, Lee Tung
Foo
Director: George Archainbaud
Screenplay: J. Benton Cheney, Bennett Cohen, Ande
Lamb
Producer: Lewis J. Rachmil

THE GREATEST SHOW ON EARTH
(Paramount, January 2, 1952) 153 Minutes.
(Technicolor)
Betty Hutton, Cornel Wilde, Charlton Heston, Dorothy
Lamour, Gloria Grahame, James Stewart, Lyle Bettger,
Henry Wilcoxon, Lawrence Tierney, Emmett Kelly,
John Ringling North, John Kellogg, John Ridgely,
Frank Wilcox, Bob Carson, Lillian Albertson, Julia Faye,
William Boyd, Bing Crosby, Bob Hope, Lane
Chandler, Fred Kohler, Jr., Greta Granstedt, Noel Neill,
John Crawford, Keith Richards, Dolores Hall, Robert
St. Angelo, Davidson Clark, Dorothy Adams, David
Newell, Josephine Whitell, Stanley Andrews, Bess
Flowers, Ottola Nesmith, Ross Bagdasarian, Antoinette
Concello, Cucciola
Director/Producer: Cecil B. DeMille
Screenplay: Fredric M. Frank, Barre Lyndon, and
Theodore St. John
Story: Fredric M. Frank and Frank Cavett

HOLLYWOOD BRONC BUSTERS
(Columbia, 1956) 9 Minutes
(Screen Snapshot Series)
Jack Lemmon, Ralph Staub; Film clips featuring Gene
Autry, Roy Rogers, Tom Mix, *William Boyd,* William
S. Hart, Buck Jones, Hoot Gibson, Charles Starrett
Director/Producer: Ralph Staub

Roy Rogers

14 ● ROY ROGERS

The Yodeling Kid

When Republic released the Roy Rogers starring vehicle **Under Westerrn Stars** in April 1938, a *Variety* review of the film commented favorably upon the several differences that were apparent in that Western compared to the usual run of earlier horse operas. Attributing much of the added appeal to Republic's new Western star, Roy Rogers, as well as to those other essential ingredients—the plot, the action, and the music—the review went on to describe Rogers as "a cowboy who looks like a wrangler, is a looker, an actor and a singer." Pointing out the unusually quick rise to stardom that Rogers (who had made some of his earlier appearances in film under the name of Leonard Slye) had made, going from a minimum number of supporting roles to suddenly having top billing, the reviewer also acknowledged that "he lives up to every expectation and then some." The commentary succinctly but accurately predicted that Rogers was sure to gain almost instant popularity with the Western fans, including the "femme mob," and offered the generous compliment of saying that he "[w]alks away with the film despite the presence of Smiley Burnette and Carol Hughes, and other good supports."

Other reviews were similarly complimentary, definitely an asset for a young star whose career was just being launched.

Rogers was no newcomer to films, however, having been around for three years as backup singer in films. His overnight heave into stardom had been prefaced with many lean, hard, hungry days as he struggled for recognition and a chance to prove himself. Had not Gene Autry been the hard-nosed businessman that he was, the world might not have had a saddle ace called

Roy Rogers. Gene, unhappy with his salary, walked off the lot hoping to bring Republic president Herbert Yates to his knees. Yates, however, had provided himself an ace up the sleeve by signing Rogers as a $75 a week contract player and keeping him under wraps. **Under Western Stars,** intended for Autry, was given to the unknown Rogers in a counter pressure move by Yates. Perhaps everyone won. Roy became a star, Autry untimately got what he wanted, and Yates wound up with two prodigiously valuable properties.

Rogers' early years had been hard ones, as he came from a poor family that was always just a few meals ahead of chronic hunger. His real name was Leonard Slye and he was born in Cincinnati, Ohio on November 5, 1912. His father worked for the U. S. Shoe Company, as did Roy when he dropped out of high school in his junior year. The family moved to Portsmouth when Roy was but a baby and, when he was eight, on a short distance further to a place called Duck Run. It was here that Rogers grew up as a poor farm boy on ten acres from which his dad attempted to scratch a living.

In 1929 Roy traveled to California hoping to find a better life and with a keen desire to become an entertainer. He liked singing, had taught himself to play the guitar, was an expert yodeler, and had considerable experience as a square dance caller. One odd job led to another. Ultimately he helped form a group calling themselves The Rocky Mountaineers; after several name changes they emerged as The Sons of the Pioneers.

Roy's first screen appearance of record was in **Slightly Static** ('35), a Thelma Todd-Patsy Kelly two-reeler for MGM. Several films followed before the group was hired as backup to Charles Starrett at Columbia. When Buck Jones left Universal the studio tested a number of cowboys for a musical Western series, among them Rogers. But he lost out to Bob Baker. Later he was able to land a contract at Republic over about twenty aspirants when that studio, too, tested for singing cowboys. His earlier screen appearances had been as Leonard Slye. For **Wild Horse Rodeo** ('37), a 3-Mesquiteers feature in which he had a small role, his name was changed to Dick Weston, and it was also under this name that he appeared in Autry's **The Old Barn Dance** ('38). But with his stardom came yet another name—Roy Rogers. Eventually he made it his legal one.

Joseph Kane directed all of the Rogers Westerns until mid-1944, and much of the Rogers success is due to Kane's excellent handling of his pictures. Although Roy got to sing five songs in his first film, the musical content was decreased considerably in the rest of the pre-war entries. Autry was still king of the lot and got most of the musical numbers. Roy was put into films featuring historical personalities, and the action in his oatburners is maintained at a fairly good pace, with the usual sprinkling of gunfights, brawls and chasing episodes. There was no pretense of anything more ostentatious than a place on the lower rung of provincial duals. Production was usually handled satisfactorily from the staging as well as the casting angles. Joe Kane knew how to get the most both from his cast and from the budget dollar. Rogers was not a very forceful type, nor in the he-man division does he rate as importantly as others. Few of his films were actually k.o. Westerns, for each one was so similar to the others that it hardly qualified as an unbranded production maverick. But Rogers and bewhiskered George "Gabby" Hayes registerd unusually well as a team for films of the kind

Pauline Moore, Roy Rogers and Bob Steele in a scene from **The Carson City Kid** (Republic, 1940)

292

they made: Rogers as the heroic law defender and Hayes as the sharpshooting comic.

The Carson City Kid ('40) remains this writer's favorite of Rogers' earlier films because of the strong cast and good story. Six sagebrush specialists got cast calls in this one—Rogers, Bob Steele, Noah Beery, Jr., Hal Taliaferro (Wally Wales), Gabby Hayes, and Yakima Canutt—giving the picture unusual name strength with which to bait the marque. In the story Rogers is a reputation gunslinger, chasing Steele, who killed his brother. Steele, under another name, is running a gambling den when they meet, so Rogers hires out as a guard. He eventually forces Steele to show his cards. Along the way, he nurses a friendship with Noah Beery, Jr., George Hayes, and Pauline Moore, the dancehall gal with a 24-carat heart. Equally good action fare was to be found in **Billy the Kid Returns** ('38), **Days of Jesse James** ('39), **Saga of Death Valley** ('39), **Young Bill Hickok** ('40), **The Border Legion** ('40), and **Bad Men of Deadwood** ('41). In fact all of the pre-1943 films of Rogers were solid rangelanders with plenty of old-fashioned Western thrills in old west settings. Sagebrush eaters found little to disapprove of in these rollicking horse frolics set against plenty of scenic background. Most of the elements of vigorous Western drama were embraced and Rogers did some hard riding and neat work generally as the youthful hero. His singing and romantic interludes are pleasant ones, intelligently worked into the stories.

With Autry's entry into military service in '42 and the fact that Herbert Yates was quite taken with the stage play *Oklahoma,* Rogers' films took a decided turn. They became elaborate musicals, usually in a modern setting, and with Roy decked out in the most gosh-awful, garish, effeminate-looking costumery ever foisted on Western audiences, putting Tom Mix and Ken Maynard to shame in the non-realistic western garb contest. Roy not only used his trusty six-guns to good advantage on occasion, but, more often than not, drew his trusty geetar and warbled a couple of dozen ballads at the slightest provocation. Dale Evans was teamed with him in **The Cowboy and the Senorita** ('44) and wound up making 28 Westerns with Rogers, as well as marrying him shortly after the death of his first wife in 1946.

Most of Rogers' post-war films were produced on lavish budgets, filmed in TruColor, and directed by William Witney, who gradually changed Rogers' films from musical extravaganzas to action films with musical interludes, much as they had been before the war. From 1943 through 1954 (although he made no Westerns in '52, '53, or '54) Rogers was ranked by the Motion Picture Herald as the greatest money-making movie cowboy, but no accurate statistics are actually available indicating that his pictures made more money than Autry's, which cost more to produce and which rented for more.

Pals of the Golden West ('51) was Roy's last Republic Western and stacks up as about average for his entries, blending a standard amount of action, four songs and some trite comedy into 67 minutes of footage. In thirteen years he had starred in 81 Westerns for Republic and had played in 12 others as supporting player or guest star. Herbert Yates had decided to discontinue the Rogers series, preferring to sell Roy's old Westerns, along with those of Gene Autry, to television to raise much needed capital to throw away on the money-losing films of his girl friend and later wife, Vera Hruba Ralston.

In 1952 Roy co-starred with Bob Hope and Jane Russell in **Son of Paleface** for Paramount, then turned to television where, between 1952 and 1957, he and wife Dale Evans, along with Pat Brady as comic, made 101 half-hour TV shows. He also did a cameo in Bob Hope's **Alias Jesse James** in '59. Over the years he has managed to stay busy as an entertainer, working in both radio and television, cutting a few records, making hundreds of personal appearances at rodeos and state fairs, etc.

After an absence from the screen of over 20 years (except for the Bob Hope cameo), Roy came back as star of **Mackintosh & T. J.** in 1975 for Penland Productions. It is an amiable family market film, slick and pleasantly corny. It's hard not to appreciate the simple sincerity Rogers brings to the role. Though displaying no great acting ability, Roy is a solid, relaxed screen personality who is always fun to watch, particularly if one's memories go back to the time when Roy and Trigger and Gabby saved the ranch for the pretty maiden time and time again at the Saturday matinee.

Today Rogers is riding the crest of the nostalgia wave and in much demand at film festivals and such. His films in 16mm are eagerly sought after by film collectors, his record "Hoppy, Gene and Me" turned out a hit, and he and Dale still maintain a heavy schedule of personal appearances and television guesting. Both have been inducted into the National Cowboy Hall of Fame. Few stars have been able to maintain their popularity at so high a level for forty years, and the general consensus is that it couldn't happen to a nicer guy. This writer certainly concurs with the majority opinion as he wishes Roy many happy trails yet to ride.

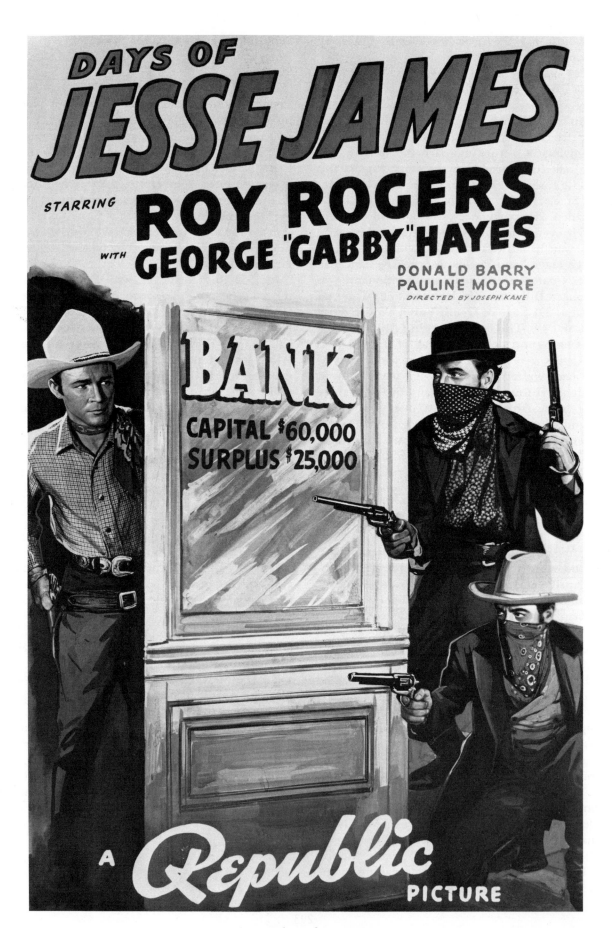

A one sheet from 1939

ROY ROGERS Filmography

SLIGHTLY STATIC
(MGM, September 7, 1935) 2 Reels
(Hal Roach Comedy)
Thelma Todd, Patsy Kelly, Harold Waldridge, Dell Henderson, Kay Hughes, Randall Sisters, Vitaphone Four, Bob Nolan, Leonard Slye (*Roy Rogers*), Verne Spence (Tim Spencer), Hugh Farr, Karl Farr, Ben Taggett, Sidney de Grey, Eddie Craven, Aileen Carlyle, Dorothy Francis, Harry Bowen, Nora Cecil, Carlton E. Griffith, Bobby Burns, Elinor Vandivere, Lorene Carr, Carl Viness, Brooks Burns
Director: William Terhune
Producer: Hal Roach

THE OLD HOMESTEAD
(Liberty, October 5, 1935) 8 Reels
Mary Carlisle, Lawrence Gray, Dorothy Lee, Willard Richardson, Eddie Nugent, Lillian Miles, Fuzzy Knight, Eddie Kane, Harry Conley, Len Slye (*Roy Rogers*), Hugh Farr, Verne Spence (Tim Spencer)
Director: William Nigh
Story/Continuity: W. Scott Darling
Based on: John Russell Corvell's novelized version of the play by Denham Thompson

WAY UP THAR
(Educational, November 8, 1935) 2 Reels
(A Young Romance Comedy)
Joan Davis, Myra Keaton, Louise Keaton, Leonard Slye (*Roy Rogers*), Tim Spencer, Hugh Farr, Karl Farr, Bob Nolan
Director/Producer: Mack Sennett
Story: Oliver Hatch
Adaptation: Hugh Cummings, Joseph Montague, Jr.

TUMBLING TUMBLEWEEDS
(Republic, September 5, 1935) 57 Minutes
Gene Autry, Smiley Burnette, Lucile Browne, Norma Taylor, George Hayes, Edward Hearn, Jack Rockwell, Frankie Marvin, George Chesebro, Eugene Jackson, Charles King, Charles Whitaker, George Burton, Tom London, Cornelius Keefe, Tommy Coats, Cliff Lyons, Bud Pope, Tracy Layne, Bud McClure, Leonard Slye (*Roy Rogers*), George Morrell, Oscar Gahan, "Champion"
Director: Joseph Kane
Story: Alan Ludwig
Screenplay: Ford Beebe
Producer: Nat Levine

GALLANT DEFENDER
(Columbia, November 30, 1935) 60 Minutes
Charles Starrett, Joan Perry, Harry Woods, Edward J. LeSaint, Jack Clifford, Al Bridge, George Billings, George Chesebro, Edmund Cobb, Frank Ellis, Jack Rockwell, Tom London, Stanley Blystone, Lew Meehan, Merrill McCormack, Glenn Strange, Al Ferguson, Slim Whitaker, Bud Osborne, Sons of the Pioneers (Bob Nolan, Leonard Slye [*Roy Rogers*], Tim Spencer, Hugh Farr, Karl Farr)
Director: David Selman
Story: Peter B. Kyne
Screenplay: Ford Beebe

THE MYSTERIOUS AVENGER
(Columbia, January 17, 1936)
Charles Starrett, Joan Perry, Wheeler Oakman, Edward J. LeSaint, Lafe McKee, Hal Price, Charles Locher (Jon Hall), George Chesebro, Jack Rockwell, Dick Botiller, Edmund Cobb, Sons of the Pioneers (Leonard Slye [*Roy Rogers*], Bob Nolan, Hugh Farr, Karl Farr, Tim Spencer)
Director: David Selman
Story: Credited to Peter B. Kyne
Story/Screenplay: Ford Beebe

SONG OF THE SADDLE
(Warners, February 1, 1936) 58 Minutes
Dick Foran, Alma Lloyd, Charles Middleton, Addison Richards, Eddie Shubert, Monte Montague, Vic Potel, Kenneth Harlan, Myrtle Stedman, George Ernest, Pat West, James Farley, Julian Rivero, Bonita Granville, William Desmond, Bud Osborne, Bob Kortman, Sons of the Pioneers (Leonard Slye [*Roy Rogers*], Bob Nolan, Tim Spencer, Hugh and Karl Farr)
Director: Louis King
Screenplay: William Jacobs
Producer: Bryan Foy

RHYTHM OF THE RANGE
(Paramount, July 31, 1936) 85 Minutes
Bing Crosby, Frances Farmer, Bob "Bazooka" Burns, Martha Raye, Samuel S. Hinds, Warren Hymer, Lucille Gleason, George E. Stone, James Burke, Clem Bevans, Leonid Kinsky, Sons of the Pioneers (Leonard Slye [*Roy Rogers*], Bob Nolan, Tim Spencer, Hugh and Karl Farr), Martha Sleeper
Director: Norman Taurog
Story: Mervin Houser
Screenplay: Walter DeLeon, Frances Martin, John Moffitt, Sidney Salkow

THE CALIFORNIA MAIL
(Warners, November 14, 1936) 60 Minutes
Dick Foran, Linda Perry, Edmund Cobb, Tom Brower, James Farley, Gene Alsace (Rocky Camron), Glenn Strange, Bob Woodward, Wilfred Lucas, Fred Burns, Milt Kibbee, Edward Keane, Cliff Saum, Jack Kirk, Lew Meehan, Tex Palmer, Sons of the Pioneers (Leonard Slye [*Roy Rogers*], Bob Nolan, Tim Spencer, Hugh Farr, Karl Farr)
Director: Noel Smith
Story: "The Pony Express Rider" - Harold Buckley, Roy Chanslor
Screenplay: Harold Buckley, Roy Chanslor
Producer: Bryan Foy

THE BIG SHOW
(Republic, November 16, 1936) 59 Minutes
Gene Autry, Smiley Burnette, Kay Hughes, Max Terhune, Sally Payne, William Newill, Charles Judels, Rex King, Harry Worth, Mary Russell, Christine Maple, Jerry Larkin, Jack O'Shea, Wedgewood Norrell, Antrim Short, June Johnson, Grace Durkin, Slim Whitaker, George Chesebro, Edward Hearn, Cliff Lyons, Tracy Layne, Jack Rockwell, Frankie Marvin, Cornelius Keefe, Martin Stevenson, Horace B. Carpenter, Helen Servis, Frances Morris, Richard Beach, Jeanne Lafayette, Art Mix, I. Stanford Jolley, Vic Lacardo, Sally Rand, The SMU 50, Sons of the Pioneers (Leonard Slye [*Roy Rogers*], Bob Nolan, Tim Spencer, Hugh and Karl Farr), The Light Crust Doughboys, The Beverly Hill Billies, The Jones Boys, "Champion"
Director: Mack V. Wright
Story/Screenplay: Dorrell and Stuart McGowan
Producer: Nat Levine

THE OLD CORRAL
(Republic, December 21, 1936) 56 Minutes
Gene Autry, Smiley Burnette, Hope Manning, Cornelius Keefe, Sons of the Pioneers (Leonard Slye [*Roy Rogers*], Bob Nolan, Hugh Farr, Karl Farr, Tim Spencer), Lon Chaney, Jr., John Bradford, Milburn Morante, Abe Lefton, Merrill McCormack, Charles Sullivan, Buddy Roosevelt, Lynton Brent, Oscar and Elmer (Ed Platt and Lou Fulton), Jack Ingram, "Champion"
Director: Joseph Kane
Story: Bernard McConville
Screenplay: Sherman Lowe, Joseph Poland
Producer: Nat Levine

THE OLD WYOMING TRAIL
(Columbia, November 8, 1937) 56 Minutes
Charles Starrett, Donald Grayson, Barbara Weeks, Dick Curtis, Edward J. LeSaint, Guy Usher, George Chesebro, Edward Peil, Edward Hearn, Art Mix, Slim Whitaker, Alma Chester, Ernie Adams, Dick Botiller, Frank Ellis, Joe Yrigoyen, Charles Brinley, Fred Burns, Si Jenks, Curley Dresden, Ray Whitley, Blackie Whiteford, Tom London, Art Dillard, Ray Jones, Jerome Ward, Ed Javregi, Tex Cooper, Sons of the Pioneers (Bob Nolan, Leonard Slye [*Roy Rogers*], Tim Spencer, Hugh and Karl Farr)
Director: Folmer Blangsted
Story: J. Benton Cheney
Screenplay: Ed Earl Repp

WILD HORSE RODEO
(Republic, December 6, 1937) 55 Minutes
(Three Mesquiteers Series)
Bob Livingston, Ray Corrigan, Max Terhune, June Martel, Walter Miller, Edmund Cobb, William Gould, Jack Ingram, Fred "Snowflake" Toones, Henry Isabell, Art Dillard, Ralph Robinson, Dick Weston (*Roy Rogers*), Jack Kirk, Kermit Maynard
Director: George Sherman
Story: Oliver Drake, Gilbert Wright
Screenplay: Betty Burbridge
Producer: Sol C. Siegel

THE OLD BARN DANCE
(Republic, January 29, 1938) 60 Minutes
Gene Autry, Smiley Burnette, Helen Valkis, Sammy McKim, Ivan Miller, Earl Hooper Atchley, Ray Bennett, Carleton Young, Frankie Marvin, Earle Hodgins, Gloria Rich, Dick Weston (*Roy Rogers*), Denver Dixon, The Stafford Sisters, The Maple City Four, Walt Shrum and his Colorado Hillbillies, "Champion"
Director: Joseph Kane
Screenplay: Bernard McConville, Charles Francis Royal
Associate Producer: Sol C. Siegel

UNDER WESTERN STARS
(Republic, April 20, 1938) 65 Minutes
Roy Rogers, Smiley Burnette, Carol Hughes, Guy Usher, Kenneth Harlan, Tom Chatterton, Alden Chase, Brandon Beach, Earl Dwire, Dick Elliott, Jack Rockwell, Frankie Marvin, Slim Whitaker, Jack Ingram, Jean Fowler, Earle Hodgins, Jack Kirk, Fred Burns, Dora Clement, Tex Cooper, Burr Caruth, Curley Dresden, The Maple City Four, Bill Wolfe, "Trigger"
Director: Joseph Kane
Story: Dorrell and Stuart McGowan
Associate Producer: Sol C. Siegel

Jack Rockwell, Smiley Burnette, Roy Rogers, Earl Dwire and players in **Under Western Stars** (Republic, 1938)

BILLY THE KID RETURNS
(Republic, September 4, 1938) 58 Minutes
Roy Rogers, Smiley Burnette, Mary Hart (Lynne Roberts), Fred Kohler, Sr., Morgan Wallace, Wade Boteler, Edwin Stanley, Horace Murphy, Joseph Crehan, Robert Emmett Keane, Al Taylor, George Letz (Montgomery), Chris-Pin Martin, Jim Corey, Lloyd Ingraham, Bob McKenzie, Oscar Gahan, Jack Kirk, Art Dillard, Fred Burns, Betty Roadman, Rudy Sooter, Betty Jane Haney, Patsy Lee Parsons, Ray Nichols, Ralph Dunn, "Trigger"
Director: Joseph Kane
Screenplay: Jack Natteford
Associate Producer: Charles E. Ford

COME ON, RANGERS!
(Republic, November 25, 1938) 57 Minutes
Roy Rogers, Mary Hart, Raymond Hatton, J. Farrell MacDonald, Purnell Pratt, Harry Woods, Bruce McFarlane, Lane Chandler, Lee Powell, Chester Gunnels, Frank McCarroll, Chick Hannon, Jack Kirk, Al Taylor, Horace B. Carpenter, Bob Wilke, Al Ferguson, Ben Corbett, Henry Wills, Allan Cavan, Burr Caruth, "Trigger"
Director: Joseph Kane
Screenplay: Gerald, Geraghty, Jack Natteford
Associate Producer: Charles E. Ford

SHINE ON HARVEST MOON
(Republic, December 30, 1938) 55 Minutes
Roy Rogers, Mary Hart (Lynne Roberts), Lulu Belle and Scotty, Stanley Andrews, William Farnum, Frank Jacquer, Chester Gunnels, Matty Roubert, Pat Henning, Jack Rockwell, Joe Whitehead, David Sharpe, George Letz (Montgomery), "Trigger"
Director: Joseph Kane
Story/Screenplay: Jack Natteford
Associate Producer: Charles E. Ford

ROUGH RIDERS ROUND-UP
(Republic, March 13, 1939) 58 Minutes
Roy Rogers, Mary Hart (Lynne Roberts), Raymond Hatton, Eddie Acuff, William Pawley, Dorothy Sebastian, George Meeker, Jack Rockwell, Guy Usher, George Chesebro, Glenn Strange, Duncan Renaldo, Jack Kirk, Hank Bell, Dorothy Christy, Fred Kelsey, Eddy Waller, John Merton, George Letz (Montgomery), Al Haskell, Frank Ellis, Augie Gomez, Frank McCarroll, Dan White, "Trigger"
Director/Associate Producer: Joseph Kane
Screenplay: Jack Natteford

FRONTIER PONY EXPRESS

(Republic, April 12, 1939) 58 Minutes

Roy Rogers, Mary Hart (Lynne Roberts), Raymond Hatton, Edward Keane, Monte Blue, Donald Dillaway, Noble Johnson, William Royle, Ethel Wales, George Letz (Montgomery), Charles King, Bud Osborne, Fred Burns, Jack Kirk, Bob McKenzie, Ernie Adams, Hank Bell, Jack O'Shea, "Trigger"

Director/Associate Producer: Joseph Kane
Screenplay: Norman S. Hall

SOUTHWARD HO!

(Republic, March 19, 1939) 57 Minutes

Roy Rogers, Mary Hart (Lynne Roberts), George Hayes, Wade Boteler, Arthur Loft, Lane Chandler, Tom London, Ed Brady, Charles Moore, Fred Burns, Frank Ellis, Jack Ingram, Frank McCarroll, Curley Dresden, Jim Corey, Rudy Bowman, George Chesebro, "Trigger"

Director/Associate Producer: Joseph Kane
Story: Jack Natteford, John Rathmell
Screenplay: Gerald Geraghty

IN OLD CALIENTE

(Republic, June 19, 1939) 57 Minutes

Roy Rogers, Mary Hart (Lynne Roberts), George Hayes, Jack LaRue, Katherine DeMille, Frank Puglia, Harry Woods, Paul Marion, Ethel Wales, Merrill McCormack, "Trigger"

Director/Associate Producer: Joseph Kane
Screenplay: Norman Houston, Gerald Geraghty

WALL STREET COWBOY

(Republic, August 6, 1939) 66 Minutes

Roy Rogers, George Hayes, Raymond Hatton, Ann Baldwin, Pierre Watkin, Louisiana Lou, Craig Reynolds, Ivan Miller, Reginald Barlow, Adrian Morris, Jack Roper, Jack Ingram, Fred Burns, Paul Fix, George Chesebro, Ted Mapes, George Letz (Montgomery), "Trigger"

Director/Associate Producer: Joseph Kane
Story: Doris Schroeder
Screenplay: Gerald Geraghty, Norman S. Hall

Roy Rogers and Mary Hart (a.k.a. Lynne Roberts)

THE ARIZONA KID
(Republic, September 29, 1939) 61 Minutes
Roy Rogers, George Hayes, Stuart Hamblen, Sally March, David Kerwin, Earl Dwire, Dorothy Sebastian, Peter Fargo, Fred Burns, Ed Cassidy, Jack Ingram, Ted Mapes, Frank McCarroll, Georgia Simmons, "Trigger"
Director/Associate Producer: Jospeh Kane
Story: Luci Ward
Screenplay: Luci Ward, Gerald Geraghty

JEEPERS CREEPERS
(Republic, October 27, 1939) 69 Minutes
Leon, Frank, June, and Loretta Weaver, Maris Wrixon, Billy Lee, Lucien Littlefield, Thurston Hall, Johnny Arthur, Milton Kibbee, Ralph Sanford, Dan White, *Roy Rogers*
Director: Francis McDonald
Screenplay: Dorrell and Stuart McGowan

SAGA OF DEATH VALLEY
(Republic, November 17, 1939) 58 Minutes
Roy Rogers, George Hayes, Donald Barry, Doris Day, Frank M. Thomas, Jack Ingram, Hal Taliaferro, Lew Kelly, Fern Emmett, Tommy Baker, Buzz Buckley, Horace Murphy, Lane Chandler, Fred Burns, Jimmy Wakely, Johnny Bond, Dick Pinehart, Peter Frago, Ed Brady, Bob Thomas, Matty Roubert, Pasquel Perry, Cactus Mack, Art Dillard, Horace B. Carpenter, Hooper Atchley, Frankie Marvin, Jess Caven, "Trigger"
Director/Associate Producer: Joe Kane
Story: Karen DeWolfe
Screenplay: Stuart Anthony, Karen DeWolfe

DAYS OF JESSE JAMES
(Republic, December 20, 1939) 63 Minutes
Roy Rogers, George Hayes, Pauline Moore, Donald Barry, Harry Woods, Arthur Loft, Wade Boteler, Ethel Wales, Scotty Beckett, Harry Worth, Glenn Strange, Olin Howlin, Monte Blue, Jack Rockwell, Fred Burns, Bud Osborne, Jack Ingram, Carl Sepulveda, Forrest Dillon, Hansel Warner, Lynton Brent, Pasquel Perry, Eddie Acuff, "Trigger"
Director/Associate Producer: Joseph Kane
Story: Jack Natteford
Screenplay: Earle Snell

DARK COMMAND
(Republic, April 5, 1940) 94 Minutes
Claire Trevor, John Wayne, Walter Pidgeon, *Roy Rogers,* George Hayes, Porter Hall, Marjorie Main, Raymond Walburn, Joe Sawyer, Helen MacKellar, J. Farrell MacDonald, Trevor Bardette, Tom London, Dick Alexander, Yakima Canutt, Hal Taliaferro, Edmund Cobb, Edward Hearn, Ernie Adams, Jack Rockwell, Al Bridge, Glenn Strange, Harry Woods, Harry Cording, Frank Hagney, Dick Rich, John Dilson, Clinton Rosemond, Budd Buster, Howard Hickman, John Merton, Al Taylor, Mildred Gover, Jack Low, Ferris Taylor, Edward Earle, Dick Alexander, Joe McGuinn, Harry Strang, Tex Cooper, Jack Montgomery
Director: Raoul Walsh
Story: W. R. Burnett
Screenplay: F. Hugh Herbert, Grover Jones, Lionel Houser
Associate Producer: Sol C. Siegel

YOUNG BUFFALO BILL
(Republic, April 12, 1940) 59 Minutes
Roy Rogers, George Hayes, Pauline Moore, Hugh Sothern, Chief Thunder Cloud, Trevor Bardette, Julian Rivero, Gaylord Pendleton, Wade Boteler, Anna Demetrio, Estrelita Zarco, Hank Bell, William Kellogg, Iron Eyes Cody, Jack O'Shea, George Chesebro, "Trigger"
Director/Associate Producer: Joseph Kane
Story: Norman Houston
Screenplay: Harrison Jacobs, Robert Yost, Gerald Geraghty

THE CARSON CITY KID
(Republic, July 1, 1940) 57 Minutes
Roy Rogers, George Hayes, Bob Steele, Pauline Moore, Noah Beery, Jr., Francis MacDonald, Hal Taliaferro, Arthur Loft, George Rosener, Chester Gan, Hank Bell, Ted Mapes, Jack Ingram, Jack Kirk, Jack Rockwell, Tom Smith, Art Dillard, Hal Price, Yakima Canutt, Kit Guard, Curley Dresden, Oscar Gahan, Chick Hannon, Al Taylor
Director/Associate Producer/Story: Joseph Kane
Screenplay: Robert Yost, Gerald Geraghty

THE RANGER AND THE LADY
(Republic, July 30, 1940) 59 Minutes
Roy Rogers, George Hayes, Jacqueline Wells (Julie Bishop), Harry Woods, Henry Brandon, Noble Johnson, Si Jenks, Ted Mapes, Yakima Canutt, Chuck Baldra, Herman Hack, Chick Hannon, Art Dillard, "Trigger"
Director/Associate Producer: Joseph Kane
Screenplay: Stuart Anthony, Gerald Geraghty

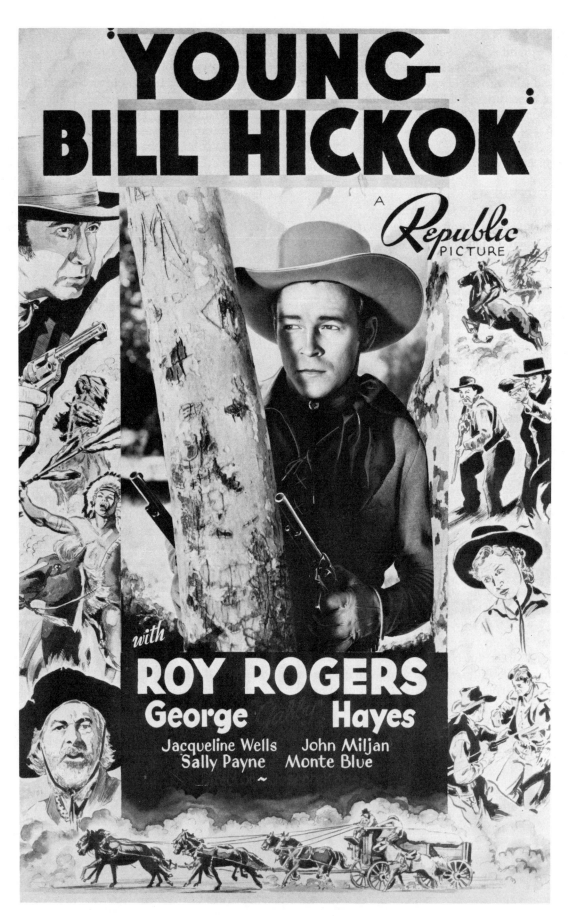

A one sheet from 1940.

COLORADO

(Republic, September 15, 1940) 57 Minutes
Roy Rogers, George Hayes, Pauline Moore, Milburn Stone, Maude Eburne, Hal Taliaferro, Vester Pegg, Fred Burns, Lloyd Ingraham, Jay Novello, Chuck Baldra, Tex Palmer, Joseph Crehan, Edward Cassidy, George Rosener, Robert Fiske, "Trigger"
Director/Associate Producer: Joseph Kane
Screenplay: Louis Stevens, Harrison Jacobs

YOUNG BILL HICKOK

(Republic, October 21, 1940) 59 Minutes
Roy Rogers, George Hayes, Jacqueline Wells, John Miljan, Sally Payne, Archie Twitchell, Monte Blue, Hal Taliaferro, Ethel Wales, Jack Ingram, Monte Montague, Iron Eyes Cody, Fred Burns, Frank Ellis, Slim Whitaker, Jack Kirk, Hank Bell, Henry Willis, Dick Elliott, William Desmond, John Elliott, Jack Rockwell, Bill Wolfe, Tom Smith
Director/Associate Producer: Joseph Kane
Screenplay: Olive Cooper, Norton S. Parker

RODEO DOUGH

(Metro-Goldwyn-Mayer, November 9, 1940)
10 Minutes (Sepiatone)
Sally Payne, Mary Treen and guest appearances by Mickey Rooney, Gene Autry, *Roy Rogers,* Johnny Weissmuller, Joe E. Brown, and Tom Neal
Director: Sammy Lee
Screenplay: Marion Mack
Producer: Louis Lewyn

THE BORDER LEGION

(Republic, December 5, 1940) 58 Minutes
Roy Rogers, George Hayes, Carol Hughes, Joseph Sawyer, Maude Eburne, Jay Novello, Hal Taliaferro, Dick Wessell, Paul Porcasi, Robert Emmett Keane, Ted Mapes, Fred Burns, Post Parks, Art Dillard, Chick Hannon, Charles Baldra
Director/Associate Producer: Joseph Kane
Story: Zane Grey
Screenplay: Olive Cooper, Louis Stevens

George "Gabby" Hayes protects Sally Payne from that "young whippersnapper" Roy Rogers in **Sheriff of Tombstone** (Republic, 1941)

301

ROBIN HOOD OF THE PECOS
(Republic, January 14, 1941) 59 Minutes
Roy Rogers, George Hayes, Marjorie Reynolds, Sally Payne, Cy Kendall, Leigh Whipper, Eddie Acuff, Robert Strange, William Haade, Jay Novello, Roscoe Ates, Jim Corey, Chick Hannon, "Trigger"
Director/Associate Producer: Joseph Kane
Story: Hal Long
Screenplay: Olive Cooper

ARKANSAS JUDGE
(Republic, January 28, 1941) 72 Minutes
Weaver Brothers and Elviry, *Roy Rogers,* Spring Byington, Pauline Moore, Frank M. Thomas, Veda Ann Borg, Eily Malyon, Loretta Weaver, Minerva Urecal, Harrison Greene, George Rosener, Monte Blue, Frank Darien, Russell Hicks, Edwin Stanley
Director: Frank McDonald
Story: "False Witness" - Irving Stone
Screenplay: Dorrell and Stuart McGowan
Associate Producer: Armand Schaefer

IN OLD CHEYENNE
(Republic, March 28, 1941) 58 Minutes
Roy Rogers, George Hayes, Joan Woodbury, Sally Payne, J. Farrell MacDonald, George Rosener, Hal Taliaferro, William Haade, Jack Kirk, Bob Woodward, Jim Corey, Cactus Mack, George Lloyd, Billy Benedict, Jack O'Shea, Edward Peil, Sr., Merrill McCormack, Ted Mapes, Fred Burns, Ben Corbett, Nick Thompson, "Trigger"
Director/Associate Producer: Joseph Kane
Story: John Kraft
Screenplay: Olive Cooper

SHERIFF OF TOMBSTONE
(Republic, May 7, 1941) 56 Minutes
Roy Rogers, George Hayes, Elyse Knox, Harry Woods, Hal Taliaferro, Jay Novello, Roy Barcroft, Jack Rockwell, Addison Richards, Sally Payne, Zeffie Tilbury, Jack Ingram, George Rosenor, Jack Kirk, Frank Ellis, Art Dillard, Herman Hack, Vester Pegg, Al Haskell, Ray Jones, Jess Caven, "Trigger"
Director/Associate Producer: Joseph Kane
Story: James Webb
Screenplay: Olive Cooper

NEVADA CITY
(Republic, June 20, 1941) 58 Minutes
Roy Rogers, George Hayes, Sally Payne, Fred Kohler, Jr., George Cleveland, Billy Lee, Joseph Crehan, Pierre Watkin, Jack Ingram, Art Mix, Syd Saylor, Hank Bell, Yakima Canutt, Rex Lease, Henry Wills, Bob Woodward, Jack Kirk, Fred Burns, "Trigger"
Director/Associate Producer: Joseph Kane
Screenplay: James R. Webb

MEET ROY ROGERS
(Republic, June 24, 1941) 10 Minutes
(Harriet Parsons Series)
Roy Rogers, Gene Autry, Judy Canova, Bill Elliott, George "Gabby" Hayes, Billy Gilbert, Bob Baker, Roscoe Ates, Mary Lee
Director/Producer: Harriet Parsons

BAD MEN OF DEADWOOD
(Republic, September 5, 1941) 61 Minutes
Roy Rogers, George Hayes, Carol Adams, Sally Payne, Henry Brandon, Herbert Rawlinson, Hal Taliaferro, Jay Novello, Horace Murphy, Monte Blue, Ralf Harolde, Jack Kirk, Yakima Canutt, Curley Dresden, Fred Burns, Lynton Brent, Lloyd Ingraham, George Lloyd, Robert Frazer, Archie Twitchell, Karl Hackett, Harry Harvey, Eddie Acuff, Tom London, Jack Rockwell, Ernie Adams, Jack O'Shea, George Morrell, Wally West, Bob Woodward, Pascale Perry, Horace B. Carpenter, Harrison Greene, "Trigger"
Director/Associate Producer: Joseph Kane
Screenplay: James R. Webb

JESSE JAMES AT BAY
(Republic, October 17, 1941) 56 Minutes
Roy Rogers, George Hayes, Gale Storm, Sally Payne, Pierre Watkins, Hal Taliaferro, Roy Barcroft, Jack Kirk, Billy Benedict, Jack O'Shea, Rex Lease, Edward Peil, Sr., Jack Rockwell, Kit Guard, Curley Dresden, Hank Bell, Bill Wolfe, Ivan Miller, Lloyd Ingraham, Karl Hackett, Budd Buster, Fred Burns, Ray Jones, Fern Emmett, Bob Woodward, Chuck Morrison, John Dilson, Chuck Baldra, Blue Washington, Ted Lorch, "Trigger"
Director/Associate Producer: Joseph Kane
Story: Harrison Jacobs
Screenplay: James R. Webb

RED RIVER VALLEY
(Republic, December 12, 1941) 62 Minutes
Roy Rogers, George Hayes, Sally Payne, Trevor Bardette, Bob Nolan, Gale Storm, Robert Homans, Hal Taliaferro, Lynton Brent, Pat Brady, Edward Peil, Sr., Dick Wessell, Jack Rockwell, Ted Mapes, Sons of the Pioneers
Director/Associate Producer: Joseph Kane
Screenplay: Malcolm Stuart Boylin

MAN FROM CHEYENNE
(Republic, January 16, 1942) 60 Minutes
Roy Rogers, George Hayes, Sally Payne, Gale Storm, Lynne Carver, William Haade, Bob Nolan, James Seay, Pat Brady, Jack Ingram, Jack Kirk, Fred Burns, Jack Rockwell, Sons of the Pioneers, Al Taylor, Chick Hannon, Art Dillard, Frank Brownlee, "Trigger"
Director/Associate Producer: Joseph Kane
Screenplay: Winston Miller

SOUTH OF SANTA FE

(Republic, February 17, 1942) 56 Minutes

Roy Rogers, George Hayes, Linda Hayes, Paul Fix, Bobby Beers, Bob Nolan, Pat Brady, Arthur Loft, Charles Miller, Sam Flint, Jack Kirk, Jack Ingram, Hank Bell, Carleton Young, Lynton Brent, Robert Strange, Henry Wills, Jack O'Shea, Merrill McCormack, "Trigger"

Director/Associate Producer: Joseph Kane
Screenplay: James R. Webb

SUNSET ON THE DESERT

(Republic, April 1, 1942) 54 Minutes

Roy Rogers, George Hayes, Lynne Carver, Frank M. Thomas, Bob Nolan, Beryl Wallace, Glenn Strange, Douglas Fowley, Fred Burns, Roy Barcroft, Henry Wills, Forrest Taylor, Bob Woodward, Edward Cassidy, Pat Brady, Cactus Mack, The Sons of the Pioneers, "Trigger"

Director/Associate Producer: Joseph Kane
Screenplay: Gerald Geraghty

ROMANCE OF THE RANGE

(Republic, May 18, 1942) 63 Minutes

Roy Rogers, George Hayes, Sally Payne, Linda Hayes, Bob Nolan and the Sons of the Pioneers, Edward Pawley, Hal Taliaferro, Harry Woods, Glenn Strange, Roy Barcroft, Jack Kirk, Pat Brady, Jack O'Shea, Dick Wessell, Dick Alexander, "Trigger"

Director/Associate Producer: Joseph Kane
Screenplay: J. Benton Cheney

SONS OF THE PIONEERS

(Republic, July 2, 1942) 61 Minutes

Roy Rogers, George Hayes, Maris Wrixon, Sons of the Pioneers, Forrest Taylor, Hal Taliaferro, Minerva Urecal, Bradley Page, Jack O'Shea, Frank Ellis, Tom London, Bob Woodward, Fern Emmett, Chester Conklin, Ken Cooper, Karl Hackett, Fred Burns, "Trigger"

Director/Associate Producer: Joseph Kane
Story: Mauri Grashin, Robert T. Shannon
Screenplay: M. Coates Webster, Mauri Grashin, Robert T. Shannon

SUNSET SERENADE

(Republic, September 14, 1942) 58 Minutes

Roy Rogers, George Hayes, Helen Parrish, Onslow Stevens, Joan Woodbury, Frank M. Thomas, Bob Nolan and the Sons of the Pioneers, Roy Barcroft, Jack Kirk, Dick Wessell, Rex Lease, Jack Ingram, Fred Burns, Budd Buster, Jack Rockwell, "Trigger"

Director/Associate Producer: Joseph Kane
Story: Robert Yost
Screenplay: Earl Felton

HEART OF THE GOLDEN WEST

(Republic, November 16, 1942) 65 Minutes

Roy Rogers, Smiley Burnette, George Hayes, Ruth Terry, Bob Nolan and the Sons of the Pioneers, Walter Catlett, Paul Harvey, Edmund McDonald, Leigh Whipper, Hal Taliaferro, Cactus Mack, Hank Bell, Fred Burns, Carl Mathews, Horace B. Carpenter, Frank McCarroll, Art Dillard, Hall Johnson Choir, "Trigger"

Director/Associate Producer: Joseph Kane
Screenplay: Earl Felton

RIDIN' DOWN THE CANYON

(Republic, December 30, 1942) 55 Minutes

Roy Rogers, George Hayes, Bob Nolan and the Sons of the Pioneers (Pat Brady, Hugh and Karl Farr, Tim Spencer and Lloyd Perryman), Dee "Buzzy" Henry, Linda Hayes, Addison Richards, Lorna Gray (Adrian Booth), Olin Howlin, James Seay, Hal Taliaferro, Forrest Taylor, Roy Barcroft, Art Mix, Art Dillard, "Champion"

Director: Joseph Kane
Story: Robert Williams, Norman Houston
Screenplay: Albert DeMond
Associate Producer: Harry Grey

IDAHO

(Republic, March 10, 1943) 70 Minutes

Roy Rogers, Smiley Burnette, Bob Nolan and the Sons of the Pioneers, Virginia Grey, Harry J. Shannon, Ona Munson, Dick Purcell, The Robert Mitchell Boyschoir, Onslow Stevens, Arthur Hohl, Hal Taliaferro, Rex Lease, Tom London, Jack Ingram, James Bush, "Trigger"

Director/Associate Producer: Joseph Kane
Screenplay: Roy Chanslor, Olive Cooper

KING OF THE COWBOYS

(Republic, April 9, 1943) 67 Minutes

Roy Rogers, Smiley Burnette, Peggy Moran, Bob Nolan and the Sons of the Pioneers, Gerald Mohr, Dorthea Kent, Lloyd Corrigan, James Bush, Russell Hicks, Irving Bacon, Stuart Hamblen, Emmett Vogan, Eddie Dean, Forrest Taylor, Dick Wessell, Jack Kirk, Edward Earle, Yakima Canutt, Charles King, Jack O'Shea, Rex Lease, Bud Geary, Lynton Brent, William Gould, Harry Burns, Earle Hodgins, Dick Rich, Herbert Heyes, Ray Bennett, John Dison, Ed Peil, Sr., Charles Sullivan, Ralph Peters, Jack Ingram, Jack Ray, Kate Lawson, Elmer Jerome, Fred Johnson, Dick Alexander, Harrison Greene, Ed Cassidy, Hugh Sothern, Herbert Rawlinson, "Trigger"

Director: Joseph Kane
Story: Hal Long
Screenplay: Olive Cooper, J. Benton Cheney
Associate Producer: Harry Grey

SONG OF TEXAS

(Republic, June 14, 1943) 69 Minutes

Roy Rogers, Sheila Ryan, Barton MacLane, Harry Shannon, Pat Brady, Arline Judge, Bob Nolan and the Sons of the Pioneers, William Haade, Hal Taliaferro, Yakima Canutt, Tom London, Forrest Taylor, Eve March, Alex Nehera Dancers, "Trigger"

Director: Joseph Kane
Screenplay: Winston Miller
Associate Producer: Harry Grey

SILVER SPURS

(Republic, August 12, 1945) 65 Minutes

Roy Rogers, Smiley Burnette, John Carradine, Phyllis Brooks, Jerome Cowan, Joyce Compton, Bob Nolan and the Sons of the Pioneers, Hal Taliaferro, Jack Kirk, Kermit Maynard, Dick Wessell, Forrest Taylor, Byron Foulger, Charles Wilson, Pat Brady, Jack O'Shea, Slim Whitaker, Arthur Loft, Eddy Waller, Tom London, Bud Osborne, Fred Burns, Henry Wills, "Trigger"

Director: Joseph Kane
Screenplay: John K. Butler, J. Benton Cheney
Associate Producer: Harry Grey

MAN FROM MUSIC MOUNTAIN

(Republic, October 30, 1943) 71 Minutes

Roy Rogers, Bob Nolan and the Sons of the Pioneers, Ruth Terry, Ann Gillis, Paul Kelly, Pat Brady, Paul Harvey, George Cleveland, Renie Riano, Hank Bell, Jay Novello, Hal Taliaferro, I. Stanford Jolley, Jack O'Shea, Tom Smith, Charles Morton, "Trigger"

Director: Joseph Kane
Screenplay: J. Benton Cheney, Bradford Ropes
Associate Producer: Harry Grey

HANDS ACROSS THE BORDER

(Republic, January 5, 1944) 73 Minutes

Roy Rogers, Bob Nolan and the Sons of the Pioneers, Ruth Terry, Guinn (Big Boy) Williams, Onslow Stevens, Mary Treen, Joseph Crehan, Duncan Renaldo, Frederick Burton, LeRoy Mason, Larry Steers, Julian Rivero, Janet Martin, The Wiere Brothers, Roy Barcroft, Kenne Duncan, Jack Kirk, Jack O'Shea, Curley Dresden, "Trigger"

Director: Joseph Kane
Screenplay: Bradford Ropes, J. Benton Cheney
Associate Producer: Harry Grey

THE COWBOY AND THE SENORITA

(Republic, May 12, 1944) 78 Minutes

Roy Rogers, Mary Lee, Dale Evans, John Hubbard, Guinn "Big Boy" Williams, Fuzzy Knight, Dorothy Christy, Lucien Littlefield, Hal Taliaferro, Jack Kirk, Jack O'Shea, Jane Beebe, Ben Rochelle, Bob Nolan and the Sons of the Pioneers, Rex Lease, Lynton Brent, Julian Rivero, Bob Wilke, Wally West, Tito and Corinne Valdes, "Trigger"

Director: Joseph Kane
Story: Bradford Ropes
Screenplay: Gordon Kahn
Associate Producer; Harry Grey

YELLOW ROSE OF TEXAS

(Republic, June 24, 1944) 69 Minutes

Roy Rogers, Dale Evans, George Cleveland, Harry Shannon, Grant Withers, Bob Nolan and the Sons of the Pioneers, William Haade, Weldon Heyburn, Hal Taliaferro, Tom London, Dick Botiller, Janet Martin, Don Kay Reynolds, Bob Wilke, Jack O'Shea, Rex Lease, Emmett Vogan, John Dilson, "Trigger"

Director: Joseph Kane
Screenplay: Jack Townley
Associate Producer: Harry Grey

SONG OF NEVADA

(Republic, August 5, 1944) 75 Minutes

Roy Rogers, Dale Evans, Mary Lee, Bob Nolan and the Sons of the Pioneers, Lloyd Corrigan, Thurston Hall, John Eldridge, Forrest Taylor, George Meeker, Emmett Vogan, LeRoy Mason, William Davidson, Kenne Duncan, Si Jenks, Frank McCarroll, Henry Wills, Jack O'Shea, Helen Talbot, "Trigger"

Director: Joseph Kane
Screenplay: Gordon Kahn, Oliver Cooper
Associate Producer: Harry Grey

SAN FERNANDO VALLEY

(Republic, September 15, 1944) 74 Minutes

Roy Rogers, Dale Evans, Jean Porter, Andrew Tombes, Bob Nolan and the Sons of the Pioneers, Edward Gargan, Dot Farley, LeRoy Mason, Charles Smith, Pierce Lyden, Maxine Doyle, Helen Talbot, Pat Starline, Kay Forrester, Marguerite Blount, Mary Kenyon, Hank Bell, Vernon and Draper, Morell Trio, "Trigger"

Director: John English
Screenplay: Dorrell and Stuart McGowan
Associate Producer: Eddy White

LIGHTS OF OLD SANTA FE

(Republic, November 6, 1944) 76 Minutes

Roy Rogers, George Hayes, Dale Evans, Bob Nolan and the Sons of the Pioneers, Lloyd Corrigan, Richard Powers (Tom Keene), Claire DuBrey, Arthur Loft, Roy Barcroft, Lucien Littlefield, Sam Flint, Pat Brady, Jack Kirk

Director: Frank McDonald
Screenplay: Gordon Kahn, Bob Williams
Associate Producer: Harry Grey

BRAZIL

(Republic, November 20, 1944) 91 Minutes

Tito Guizar, Virginia Bruce, Robert Livingston, Edward Everett Horton, Veloz and Yolanda, Aurora Miranda, Richard Lane, Frank Puglia, Fortunio Bonanvoa, *Roy Rogers*

Director: Joseph Stanley
Story: Richard English
Screenplay: Frank Gill, Jr., Laura Kerr

LAKE PLACID SERENADE

(Republic, December 23, 1944) 85 Minutes

Vera Hruba Ralston, Robert Livingston, Eugene Pallette, Stephanie Bachelor, Vera Vague, Ruth Terry, Walter Catlett, Lloyd Corrigan, Twinkle Watts, *Roy Rogers*

Director: Steve Szekely
Story: Frederick Kohner
Screenplay: Dick Irving Hyland, Doris Gilbert

HOLLYWOOD CANTEEN

(Warner Brothers, December 30, 1944) 121 Minutes

Jack Benny, Eddie Cantor, Jack Carson, Joan Crawford, Joan Leslie, Betty Davis, Faye Emerson, John Garfield, Sidney Greenstreet, Paul Henreid, Peter Lorre, Ida Lupino, Dennis Morgan, Janis Paige, Eleanor Parker, Barbara Stanwyck, Jane Wyman, Jimmy Dorsey and his Orchestra, Sons of the Pioneers, *Roy Rogers*

Director/Screenplay: Delmer Daves

UTAH

(Republic, March 21, 1945) 78 Minutes

Roy Rogers, George Hayes, Dale Evans, Peggy Stewart, Beverly Loyd, Grant Withers, Jill Browning, Vivien Oakland, Hal Taliaferro, Jack Rutherford, Emmett Vogan, Edward Cassidy, Ralph Colby, Bob Nolan and the Sons of the Pioneers, "Trigger"

Director: John English
Story: Gilbert Wright, Betty Burbridge
Screenplay: Jack Townley, John K. Butler
Associate Producer: Donald H. Brown

BELLS OF ROSARITA

(Republic, June 19, 1945) 68 Minutes

Roy Rogers, George Hayes, Dale Evans, Adele Mara, Grant Withers, Janet Martin, Syd Saylor, Addison Richards, Edward Cassidy, Roy Barcroft, Kenne Duncan, Rex Lease, Earle Hodgins, Bob Wilke, Ted Adams, Wally West, Bob Nolan and the Sons of the Pioneers, Robert Mitchell Boyschoir, Poodles Hanaford, Helen Talbot, Hank Bell, Charles Sullivan, Forbes Murray, Eddie Kane, Tom London, Rosemond James, Marin Sais, Barbara Elliott, Sam Ash, Jack Richardson, Marian Kerrigan, "Trigger", and Guest Stars: Bill Elliott, Allan Lane, Don Barry, Robert Livingston, Sunset Carson

Director: Frank McDonald
Screenplay: Jack Townley
Associate Producer: Eddy White

THE MAN FROM OKLAHOMA

(Republic, July 1, 1945) 68 Minutes

Roy Rogers, Dale Evans, George Hayes, Bob Nolan and the Sons of the Pioneers, Roger Pryor, Arthur Loft, Maude Eburne, Sam Flint, Si Jenks, June Bryde, Elaine Lange, Charles Soldani, Edmund Cobb, George Sherwood, Eddie Kane, George Chandler, Wally West, Tex Terry, Bob Wilke, Bobbie Priest, Dorothy Bailer, Rosamond James, Melva Anstead, Beverly Reedy, Geraldine Farnum, "Trigger"

Director: Frank McDonald
Screenplay: John K. Butler
Associate Producer: Louis Gray
Second Unit Director: Yakima Canutt

SUNSET IN EL DORADO

(Republic, September 29, 1945) 65 Minutes

Roy Rogers, George Hayes, Dale Evans, Hardie Albright, Margaret Dumont, Roy Barcroft, Tom London, Stanley Price, Bob Wilke, Ed Cassidy, Dorothy Granger, Bob Nolan and the Sons of the Pioneers, Edmund Cobb, Hank Bell, Jack Kirk, Gino Corrado, Frank Ellis, Tex Cooper, Bert Morehouse, Joe McGuinn, Tex Terry, Bud Osborne, "Trigger"

Director: Frank McDonald
Story: Leon Abrams
Screenplay: John K. Butler
Associate Producer: Louis Gray

DON'T FENCE ME IN

(Republic, October 20, 1945) 71 Minutes

Roy Rogers, Dale Evans, George Hayes, Bob Nolan and the Sons of the Pioneers, Robert Livingston, Moroni Olson, Marc Lawrence, Lucille Gleason, Andrew Tombes, Paul Harvey, Douglas Fowley, Stephen Barclay, Edgar Dearing, Helen Talbot, "Trigger"

Director: John English

Screenplay: Dorrell and Stuart McGowan, John K. Butler

Associate Producer: Donald H. Brown

ALONG THE NAVAJO TRAIL

(Republic, December 15, 1945) 66 Minutes

Roy Rogers, George Hayes, Dale Evans, Estelita Roriguez, Douglas Fowley, Nestor Paiva, Sam Flint, Emmett Vogan, Roy Barcroft, David Cota, Bob Nolan, Pat Brady, Edward Cassidy, Poppy Del Vando, Rosemond James, Tex Terry, Budd Buster, Sons of the Pioneers, "Trigger"

Director: Frank McDonald

Story: William Colt MacDonald

Screenplay: Gerald Geraghty

Associate Producer: Eddy White

SONG OF ARIZONA

(Republic, March 9, 1946) 68 Minutes

Roy Rogers, George Hayes, Dale Evans, Bob Nolan and the Sons of the Pioneers, Lyle Talbot, Tommy Cook, Johnny Calkins, Sarah Edwards, Tommy Ivo, Michael Chapin, Dick Curtis, Edmund Cobb, Tom Quinn, Kid Chissell, Robert Mitchell Boyschoir, "Trigger"

Director: Frank McDonald

Screenplay: M. Coates Webster

Associate Producer: Eddy White

RAINBOW OVER TEXAS

(Republic, May 9, 1946) 65 Minutes

Roy Rogers, George Hayes, Dale Evans, Bob Nolan and the Sons of the Pioneers, Sheldon Leonard, Robert Emmett Keane, Gerald Oliver Smith, Minerva Urecal, George J. Lewis, Kenne Duncan, Pierce Lyden, Dick Elliott, Jo Ann Dean, Bud Osborne, George Chesebro, "Trigger"

Director: Frank McDonald

Story: Max Brand

Screenplay: Gerald Geraghty

Producer: Eddy White

MY PAL TRIGGER

(Republic, July 10, 1946) 79 Minutes

Roy Rogers, George Hayes, Dale Evans, Jack Holt, Bob Nolan and the Sons of the Pioneers, LeRoy Mason, Roy Barcroft, Sam Flint, Kenne Duncan, Ralph Sanford, Francis McDonald, Harlan Briggs, William Haade, Alan Bridge, Paul E. Burns, Frank Reicher, Fred Graham, Ted Mapes, "Trigger"

Director: Frank McDonald

Story: Paul Gangelin

Screenplay: Jack Townley, John K. Butler

Associate Producer: Armand Schaefer

UNDER NEVADA SKIES

(Republic, August 26, 1946) 69 Minutes

Roy Rogers, George Hayes, Dale Evans, Bob Nolan and the Sons of the Pioneers, Douglass Dumbrille, Leyland Hodgson, Tris Coffin, Rudolph Anders, LeRoy Mason, Peter George Lynn, George J. Lewis, Iron Eyes Cody, "Trigger"

Director: Frank McDonald

Screenplay: Paul Gangelin, J. Benton Cheney

Associate Producer: Eddy White

ROLL ON TEXAS MOON

(Republic, September 12, 1946) 68 Minutes

Roy Rogers, George Hayes, Dale Evans, Bob Nolan and the Sons of the Pioneers, Dennis Hoey, Elizabeth Risdon, Francis McDonald, Edward Keane, Kenne Duncan, Tom London, Harry Strang, Edward Cassidy, Lee Shumway, Steve Darrell, Pierce Lyden, "Trigger"

Director: William Witney

Story: Jean Murray

Screenplay: Paul Gangelin, Mauri Grashin

Associate Producer: Eddy White

HOME IN OKLAHOMA

(Republic, November 8, 1946) 72 Minutes

Roy Rogers, George Hayes, Dale Evans, Carol Hughes, Bob Nolan and the Sons of the Pioneers, George Meeker, Lanny Rees, Ruby Dandridge, George Lloyd, Arthur Space, Frank Reicher, George Carleton, "Trigger"

Director: William Witney

Screenplay: Gerald Geraghty

Associate Producer: Eddy White

OUT CALIFORNIA WAY
(Republic, December 5, 1946) 67 Minutes
(TruColor)
Monte Hale, Adrian Booth, Bobby Blake, John Dehner, Nolan Leary, Fred Graham, Tom London, Jimmy Starr, Edward Keane, Bob Wilke, Brooks Benedict, St. Luke's Choristers, Foy Willing and the Riders of the Purple Sage, guest stars: *Roy Rogers,* Allan Lane, Dale Evans, Donald Barry, "Trigger"
Director: Lesley Selander
Story: Barry Shipman
Screenplay: Betty Burbridge
Associate Producer: Louis Gray

HELDORADO
(Republic, December 15, 1946) 70 Minutes
Roy Rogers, George Hayes, Dale Evans, Bob Nolan and the Sons of the Pioneers, LeRoy Mason, Paul Harvey, Rex Lease, Barry Mitchell, John Bagni, John Phillips, James Taggert, Steve Darrell, Doye O'Dell, Charles Williams, Eddie Acuff, Clayton Moore, "Trigger"
Director: William Witney
Screenplay: Gerald Geraghty, Julian Zimet
Associate Producer: Eddy White

APACHE ROSE
(Republic, February 15, 1947) 75 Minutes
(TruColor)
Roy Rogers, Dale Evans, Olin Howlin, Bob Nolan and the Sons of the Pioneers, George Meeker, John Laurenz, Russ Vincent, Minerva Urecal, LeRoy Mason, Donna DeMario, Terry Frost, Conchita Lemus, Tex Terry, "Trigger"
Director: William Witney
Screenplay: Gerald Geraghty
Associate Producer: Eddy White

HIT PARADE OF 1947
(Republic, March 22, 1947) 90 Minutes
Eddie Albert, Constance Moore, Joan Edwards, Gil Lamb, Bill Goodwin, Richard Lane, William Frawley, Woody Herman, Sons of the Pioneer, and guest star: *Roy Rogers*
Director: Francis McDonald
Screenplay: Mary Loos
Story: Parke Levy

BELLS OF SAN ANGELO
(Republic, April 15, 1947)
(TruColor)
Roy Rogers, Dale Evans, Andy Devine, John McGuire, Olaf Hytten, David Sharpe, Fritz Leiber, Hank Patterson, Fred Toones, Eddie Acuff, Dale Van Sickel, Bob Nolan and the Sons of the Pioneers, Silver Harr, Buck Bucko, "Trigger"
Director: William Witney
Story: Paul Gangelin
Screenplay: Sloan Nibley
Associate Producer: Eddy White

SPRINGTIME IN THE SIERRAS
(Republic, July 15, 1947) 75 Minutes
(TruColor)
Roy Rogers, Jane Frazee, Andy Devine, Stephanie Bachelor, Hal Landon, Harry V. Cheshire, Roy Barcroft, Chester Conklin, Hank Patterson, Whitey Christy, Pascale Perry, Bob Woodward, Bob Nolan and the Sons of the Pioneers, "Trigger"
Director: William Witney
Screenplay: Sloan Nibley
Associate Producer: Eddy White

SCREEN SNAPSHOTS
(Columbia, September 4, 1947) 9½ Minutes
(Segment called "Hollywood Cowboys")
Buck Jones, Gene Autry, *Roy Rogers,* Will Rogers, Tom Mix, John Mack Brown, Hoot Gibson, William S. Hart, William Boyd, Robert Young, Jackie Coogan
Director: Ralph Staub

ON THE OLD SPANISH TRAIL
(Republic, October 15, 1947) 75 Minutes
(TruColor)
Roy Rogers, Jane Frazee, Andy Devine, Tito Guizar, Estelita Rodriguez, Bob Nolan and the Sons of the Pioneers, Charles McGraw, Fred Graham, Steve Darrell, Marshall Reed, Wheaton Chambers, "Trigger"
Director: William Witney
Story: Gerald Geraghty
Screenplay: Sloan Nibley
Associate Producer: Eddy White

THE GAY RANCHERO
(Republic, January 10, 1948) 72 Minutes
(TruColor)
Roy Rogers, Tito Guizar, Jane Frazee, Andy Devine, Estelita Rodriguez, George Meeker, LeRoy Mason, Dennis Moore, Keith Richards, Betty Gagnon, Robert Rose, Ken Terrell, Bob Nolan and the Sons of the Pioneers, "Trigger"
Director: William Witney
Screenplay: Sloan Nibley
Associate Producer: Eddy White

UNDER CALIFORNIA STARS
(Republic, May 1, 1948) 70 Minutes
(TruColor)
Roy Rogers, Jane Frazee, Andy Devine, Michael Chapin, Wade Crosby, George Lloyd, House Peters, Jr., Steve Clark, Joseph Carro, Paul Powers, John Wald, Bob Nolan and the Sons of the Pioneers, "Trigger"
Director: William Witney
Screenplay: Sloan Nibley, Paul Gangelin
Associate Producer: Eddy White

EYES OF TEXAS
(Republic, July 15, 1948) 70 Minutes
(TruColor)
Roy Rogers, Lynne Roberts, Andy Devine, Nana Bryant, Roy Barcroft, Danny Morton, Francis Ford, Pascale Perry, Stanley Blystone, Bob Nolan and the Sons of the Pioneers, "Trigger"
Director: William Witney
Screenplay: Sloan Nibley
Associate Producer: Eddy White

MELODY TIME
(Walt Disney Prod./RKO-Radio, July 31, 1945)
75 Minutes (Technicolor)
The Andrews Sisters, Dennis Day, Sons of the Pioneers, Frances Langford, Ethel Smith, Freddy Martin, Fred Waring and his Pennsylvanians, Buddy Clark, Jack Fina, Bobby Driscoll, Luana Patten, Donald Duck, Joe Carioca, *Roy Rogers,* "Trigger"
Supervisor: Ben Sharpsteen

NIGHT TIME IN NEVADA
(Republic, September 5, 1948) 67 Minutes
(TruColor)
Roy Rogers, Andy Devine, Adele Mara, Grant Withers, Marie Harmond (Harmon), Joseph Crehan, George Carleton, Holly Bane, Steve Darrell, Hank Patterson, Jim Nolan, Bob Nolan and the Sons of the Pioneers, Rex Lease, "Trigger"
Director: William Witney
Screenplay: Sloan Nibley
Associate Producer: Eddy White

GRAND CANYON TRAIL
(Republic, November 5, 1948) 67 Minutes
(TruColor)
Roy Rogers, Andy Devine, Jane Frazee, Robert Livingston, Roy Barcroft, Charles Coleman, Emmett Lynn, Ken Terrell, James Finlayson, Tommy Coates, Zon Murray, Foy Willing and the Riders of the Purple Sage, "Trigger"
Director: William Witney
Screenplay: Gerald Geraghty
Associate Producer: Eddy White

THE FAR FRONTIER
(Republic, December 29, 1948) 67 Minutes
(TruColor)
Roy Rogers, Gail Davis, Andy Devine, Francis Ford, Roy Barcroft, Clayton Moore, Robert Strange, Holly Bane, Lane Bradford, John Bagni, Clarence Straight, Edmund Cobb, Tom London, Foy Willing and the Riders of the Purple Sage, "Trigger"
Director: William Witney
Screenplay: Sloan Nibley
Associate Producer: Eddy White

SUSANNA PASS
(Republic, April 29, 1949) 67 Minutes
Roy Rogers, Dale Evans, Estelita Rodriguez, Martin Garralaga, Robert Emmett Keane, Lucien Littlefield, Douglas Fowley, David Sharpe, Robert Bice, Foy Willing and the Riders of the Purple Sage, "Trigger"
Director: William Witney
Screenplay: Sloan Nibley, John K. Butler
Associate Producer: Eddy White

DOWN DAKOTA WAY
(Republic, September 9, 1949) 67 Minutes
(TruColor)
Roy Rogers, Dale Evans, Pat Brady, Monte Montana, Elizabeth Risdon, Byron Barr, James Cardwell, Roy Barcroft, Emmett Vogan, Foy Willing and the Riders of the Purple Sage, "Trigger"
Director: William Witney
Screenplay: John K. Butler, Sloan Nibley
Associate Producer: Eddy White

THE GOLDEN STALLION
(Republic, November 15, 1949) 67 Minutes
Roy Rogers, Dale Evans, Pat Brady, Estelita Rodriguez, Chester Conklin, Douglas Evans, Greg McClure, Frank Fenton, Dale Van Sickel, Clarence Straight, Karl Hackett, Foy Willing and the Riders of the Purple Sage, "Trigger"
Director: William Witney
Screenplay: Sloan Nibley
Associate Producer: Eddy White

BELLS OF CORONADO
(Republic, January 8, 1950) 67 Minutes
(TruColor)
Roy Rogers, Dale Evans, Pat Brady, Grant Withers, Leo Cleary, Clifton Young, Robert Bice, Stuart Randall, John Hamilton, Edmund Cobb, Eddie Lee, Rex Lease, Lane Bradford, Foy Willing and the Riders of the Purple Sage, "Trigger"
Director: William Witney
Screenplay: Sloan Nibley
Associate Producer: Eddy White

TWILIGHT IN THE SIERRAS

(Republic, March 22, 1950) 67 Minutes
(TruColor)

Roy Rogers, Dale Evans, Estelita Rodriguez, Pat Brady, Russ Vincent, George Meeker, Fred Kohler, Jr. Edward Keane, House Peters, Jr., Pierce Lyden, Don Frost, Joseph Carro, William Lester, Bob Burns, Bob Wilke, Foy Willing and the Riders of the Purple Sage, "Trigger"

Director: William Witney
Screenplay: Sloan Nibley
Associate Producer: Eddy White

TRIGGER, JR.

(Republic, June 30, 1950) 68 Minutes
(TruColor)

Roy Rogers, Dale Evans, Pat Brady, Gordon Jones, Grant Withers, Peter Miles, George Cleveland, Frank Fenton, I. Stanford Jolley, Stanley Andrews, The Raylor Lehr Circus, Foy Willing and the Riders of the Purple Sage, "Trigger"

Director: William Witney
Screenplay: Gerald Geraghty
Associate Producer: Eddy White

SUNSET IN THE WEST

(Republic, September 25, 1950) 67 Minutes
(TruColor)

Roy Rogers, Estelita Rodriguez, Penny Edwards, Gordon Jones, Will Wright, Pierre Watkin, Charles LaTorre, William J. Tannen, Gaylord Pendleton, Paul E. Burns, Dorothy Ann White, Foy Willing and the Riders of the Purple Sage, "Trigger"

Director: William Witney
Screenplay: Gerald Geraghty
Associate Producer: Eddy White

NORTH OF THE GREAT DIVIDE

(Republic, November 15, 1950) 67 Minutes

Roy Rogers, Penny Edwards, Gordon Jones, Roy Barcroft, Jack Lambert, Douglas Evans, Keith Richards, Noble Johnson, Iron Eyes Cody, Foy Willing and the Riders of the Purple Sage, "Trigger"

Director: William Witney
Screenplay: Eric Taylor
Associate Producer: Eddy White

Jack Holt, Roy Rogers and Foy Willing examine a busted wagon in **Trail of Robin Hood** (Republic, 1950)

TRAIL OF ROBIN HOOD

(Republic, December 15, 1950) 67 Minutes
(TruColor)

Roy Rogers, Penny Edwards, Gordon Jones, Jack Holt, Emory Parnell, Clifton Young, James Magill, Carol Nugent, George Chesebro, Edward Cassidy, Foy Willing and the Riders of the Purple Sage, "Trigger," and Guest Stars: Tom Tyler, Kermit Maynard, Ray Corrigan, Tom Keene, Monte Hale, Rex Allen, Allan Lane, William Farnum

Director: William Witney
Screenplay: Gerald Geraghty
Associate Producer: Eddy White

SPOILERS OF THE PLAINS

(Republic, February 2, 1951) 68 Minutes

Roy Rogers, Penny Edwards, Gordon Jones, Grant Withers, Fred Kohler, Jr., William Forrest, Don Haggerty, House Peters, Jr., George Meeker, Keith Richards, Foy Willing and the Riders of the Purple Sage, "Trigger"

Director: William Witney
Screenplay: Sloan Nibley
Associate Producer: Eddy White

HEART OF THE ROCKIES

(Republic, March 30, 1951) 67 Minutes

Roy Rogers, Penny Edwards, Gordon Jones, Ralph Morgan, Fred Graham, Mira McKinney, Robert "Buzz" Henry, William Gould, Pete Hern, Rand Brooks, Foy Willing and the Riders of the Purple Sage, "Trigger"

Director: William Witney
Screenplay: Eric Taylor
Associate Producer: Eddy White

IN OLD AMARILLO

(Republic, May 15, 1951) 67 Minutes

Roy Rogers, Estelita Rodriguez, Penny Edwards, Pinky Lee, Roy Barcroft, Pierre Watkin, Ken Howell, Elizabeth Risdon, William Holmes, Kermit Maynard, Alan Bridge, Roy Rogers Riders, "Trigger"

Director: William Witney
Screenplay: Sloan Nibley
Associate Producer: Eddy White

SOUTH OF CALIENTE

(Republic, October 15, 1951) 67 Minutes

Roy Rogers, Dale Evans, Pinky Lee, Douglas Fowley, Pat Brady, Charlita, Ric Roman, Leonard Penn, Willie Best, Frank Richards, Lillian Molieri, George J. Lewis, Marguerite McGill, Roy Rogers Riders, "Trigger"

Director: William Witney
Screenplay: Eric Taylor
Associate Producer: Eddy White

PALS OF THE GOLDEN WEST

(Republic, December 15, 1951) 68 Minutes

Roy Rogers, Dale Evans, Estelita Rodriguez, Pinky Lee, Roy Barcroft, Anthony Caruso, Edwardo Jimenez, Ken Terrell, Emmett Vogan, Maurice Jara, Roy Rogers Riders, "Trigger"

Director: William Witney
Story: Sloan Nibley
Screenplay: Robert DeMond, Eric Taylor
Associate Producer: Eddy White

SON OF PALEFACE

(Paramount, August 1, 1952) 95 Minutes
(Technicolor)

Bob Hope, Jane Russell, *Roy Rogers,* Bill Williams, Lloyd Corrigan, Paul E. Burns, Douglass Dumbrille, Iron Eyes Cody, Harry Von Zell, Wee Willie Davis, Charley Cooley, Hank Mann, Chester Conklin, Jonathan Hale, Oliver Blake, Cecil B. DeMille, Bing Crosby

Director: Frank Tashlin
Screenplay: Frank Tashlin, Robert L. Welch, Joseph Quillan
Producer: Robert L. Welch

HOLLYWOOD BRONC BUSTERS

(Columbia, 1956) 9 Minutes
(Screen Snapshot Series)

Jack Lemmon, Ralph Staub; Film clips featuring Gene Autry, *Roy Rogers,* Tom Mix, William Boyd, William S. Hart, Buck Jones, Hoot Gibson, Charles Starrett

Director/Producer: Ralph Staub

ALIAS JESSE JAMES

(United Artists, April 2, 1959) 92 Minutes
(DeLuxe Color)

Bob Hope, Rhonda Fleming, Wendell Corey, Jim Davis, Gloria Talbot, Will Wright, Mary Young, George E. Stone, Harry Tyler, Emory Parnell, Mike Mazurki, Glenn Strange, Jack Lambert, Sid Melton, James Burke, Joe Vitale, Michael Ross, Nestor Paiva, Dick Alexander, Fred Kohler, Jr., Mickey Finn, and guest stars: *Roy Rogers,* Gary Cooper, Bing Crosby, Ward Bond, James Arness, Hugh O'Brien, Fess Parker, Gail Davis, Jay Silverheels

Director: Norman McLeod
Story: Robert St. Aubrey and Bert Lawrence
Screenplay: D. D. Beauchamp and William Bowers
Producer: Jack Hope

MACINTOSH & T. J.
(Penland Productions, February 5, 1976) 96 Minutes
(Technicolor)
Roy Rogers, Clay O'Brien, Billy Green Bush, Andrew
Robinson, Joan Hackett, James Hampton, Walter
Barnes, Dean Smith, Larry Mahan
Director: Marvin Chomsky
Screenplay: Paul Savage
Producer: Tim Penland
(Film had playdates in mid-central and mid-western
U. S. in the fall of 1975, but officially premiered on
February 5, 1976 in Lubbock, Texas at the Winchester
Theatre.)

Rod Cameron

15 ● ROD CAMERON

A No-Nonsense Saddle Buster

Rod Cameron's complete ease and rugged cinematic ways quickly paid dividends, but it was in Western vehicles that his ability was displayed at its solid best. Certainly his mere screen presence practically fulfilled the Zane Grey ideal—and it was so effortlessly convincing. Cameron, exuding virility, succeeded in making a two-fisted hero plausible and likeable, and he was every inch the symbol of probity, courage, and wholesomeness that his parts usually demanded.

The rugged Canadian star of many a Hollywood second feature could fill a screen as few men can, a fact attributable to his 6'4" frame covered with nearly 200 pounds of muscle. His tall, athletic physique and regular features helped him to find employment in action films; a number of prairie opuses earned him his spurs and identity as a cowboy star in the mid-Forties.

Though often compared with Gary Cooper, James Stewart, and Fred MacMurray in looks, his screen characterizations in the early years were more akin to those of Tom Tyler, another outdoor hero who believed more in action than in words.

The fraternity of Western film fans quickly accepted this powerhouse hero who got on with the job at hand, ably demonstrating his agility and scrapping prowess. Such acceptance by dyed-in-the-wool Western buffs was only extended to those chaps-and-saddle waddies who made sagebrushers on a consistent basis and whose film output, though not necessarily exclusively Western, was predonderantly of the prairie and cactus variety.

But Cameron's versatility enabled him to reach non-Western audiences as well, while still retaining his loyal Western followers. He could put aside the horse for the fast coupe, and the six-shooter for the short, blunt automatic. In black tie and tails, sailor garb, military uniforms, or neckerchief and jeans, it was all the same: Cameron was all man, and his appeal was to those whose movie taste ran to action and adventure sprinkled with ever-so-little romance. The backdrop made little difference, be it desert, ocean, ships, horses, jungle, wild animals, the Las Vegas strip, or New York's lower East Side. Rod's swinging into action was the catalyst that made for a satisfying vicarious movie adventure.

Rod was born Roderick Cox on December 7, 1910 in Calgary, Alberta, where, as they say, one can't steal a chicken without troops of red-coated Northwest Mounted Police on his trail. His father, the late Robert Nathan Cox, was a mechanical engineer. At the time of Rod's birth, the elder Cox and an uncle were dealers in mining equipment in Canada's Peace River district. Two years later the family moved to Toronto, where they remained until Rod was 14. He attended Toronto public schools and, like a lot of kids, worked as a delivery boy and sold newspapers on the street corner.

The elder Cox died in 1925, and shortly thereafter Rod accompanied his mother and his sister, Catherine, two years younger than himself, to New York City, where they resided with one of Rod's uncles. Some time later, they moved to Miami, where Rod attended high school. The hurricane of 1926 caused them to move north to White Plains, New York, and it was here that Rod finished high school.

Because of his height, Rod was a natural for basketball and played center on his school basketball team and tackle with the White Plains semi-pro football squad. He was also an accomplished swimmer and high diver. While at White Plains he appeared in a dozen plays with the Montclair, New Jersey dramatic club but gave little thought to an acting career. Rather, he had since boyhood longed for the glamour of being one of Canada's distinguished redcoats. But an injury suffered during his youthful years made it impossible for him to pass the physical examination.

Disappointed, he proved to himself that, in spite of his failure to pass the mounties' physical, he was still in good condition. The hardest job he could find was that of a sand hog (caisson laborer) in tunnels being constructed under the Hudson River, and he held down this job long enough to satisfy himself that his physical powers were adequate. During the Depression years he worked at many different jobs, whatever he could find to do, and was grateful for the opportunity to work. Ultimately Rod went to California to work for the Metropolitan Water District building a tunnel near Palm Springs. By this time he had become an expert concrete man. For a while he worked for the S. H. Kress & Company in Los Angeles in one of its store's stockroom as training for store managership. Later, he was a purchasing agent for the National Theatre Supply Company.

Becoming interested in the possibilities of movie work, Rod began to pound the pavement in quest of a chance to enter the celluloid world. Doors were not thrown open nor red carpets rolled out before him. Odd jobs kept him eating while he awaited an interview with the legendary and illusive casting director. Through the extravagant praise of a friend who knew the director-writer Edmund Goulding, Rod was able to get a part in the Bette Davis film **The Old Maid.** When the picture was finished he was told how great a job he had done and was invited to the preview. Elated, he showed up for the screening, only to find that his scenes had been left on the cutting-room floor. The giant almost wept, so great was his disillusionment.

Finally Rod got a chance to test at Columbia for **Golden Boy,** but lost out to William Holden. However, Paramount executives saw the test and signed him to a stock contract. His surname was changed to Cameron, family name on his mother's side, and it was intended that he should have a role in Cecil B. DeMille's **Northwest Mounted Police.** His red-coated uniforms were made up, and Rod looked ahead to appearing in scenes with Gary Cooper, Madeleine Carroll and other principals. But circumstances worked against him. He had been put into a Jackie Cooper picture called **Life with Henry** in which, although he had never previously been aboard one, he successfully operated an antiquated 18-ton steamroller. But his occupation as steamroller pilot and adult pal to Jackie Cooper in this "Henry Aldrich" picture took longer than had been anticipated, due to weather conditions postponing Rod's outdoor scenes with the steamroller. The result was that

the Northwest Mounties rode without him—for a while. About halfway through the film an actor died and Rod, about the same size as the man and by this time available, was rushed in to finish the picture, complete with mustache.

For three years Rod played assorted bits and small parts in Paramount films, even appearing in the Hopalong Cassidy Western, **Stagecoach War,** in a very small role. But the parts got bigger and he did some creditable things while at the studio, films such as **The Forest Rangers, Wake Island,** and **The Commandos Strike at Dawn.** He also did an awful lot of tests wherein he would throw lines at the actors or actresses being tested. In this connection his most memorable recollection is of the scenes he did with Ingrid Bergman in the Technicolor tests before the actual shooting on **For Whom the Bell Tolls.** Such tests and the many film assignments as a stock player gave him experience and made a great contribution to his professional education.

When his option came up, with no raise offered, Rod left the studio to free-lance, being picked up by Republic for the starring role as Rex Bennett, American undercover agent, in the now-famous two serials, **G-Men vs. the Black Dragon** and **Secret Service in Darkest Africa,** filmed in 1943. The latter was third most costly of all Republic serials, and both were highly popular with Saturday matinee audiences. As a result, Rod's per picture salary was boosted.

Cameron had fairly good roles in Universal's **Honeymoon Lodge** and United Artists' **The Kansan** before being signed to a long-term contract by Universal after his performance in **Gung Ho,** in which the ex-Calgaryite played the part of Tedrow, the hillbilly. MGM borrowed him for a role in **Mrs. Parkington,** for which he received good notices.

Realizing that Rod would probably make good prairie fodder, Universal cast him as the lead in a series of six Western thrillers produced by Oliver Drake. Fuzzy Knight provided the comic interludes, while Ray Whitley and his Bar-6 Cowboys did the musical segments. Vivian Austin (two films), Jennifer Holt (three), and Marjorie Clements (one) filled the necessary female roles. In the first film, **Boss of Boomtown,** Rod shared the spotlight with a fading Tom Tyler, and they seemed to complement each other adroitly. But the remaining five films (**Trigger Trail, Riders of the Santa Fe, The Old Texas Trail, Beyond the Pecos,** and **Renegades of the Rio Grande**) featured as second banana Eddie Dew, a far less exciting personality than Tyler.

Cameron's acting was restrained and more than satisfactory even in the most desperate inept situations. For the most part direction was good and plots and

Constance Worth gets her hair worked on as Roland Got and Rod Cameron watch in **G-Men vs. the Black Dragon** (Republic, 1943)

counterplots were kept in rapid motion around outstanding casts. Rod generally played with befitting coyness at the start of each film and then unleashed the appropriate whirlwind, gun-blazing, fist-pounding, wrong-righting at the climax. It was a good series from about any viewpoint.

While making the "B" oaters Cameron got the once-in-a-lifetime break that every potential star prays for. Walter Wanger tested him and then offered Rod a very juicy plum in the form of the lead opposite Yvonne De Carlo in **Salome, Where She Danced.** Notable for many gorgeous scenes in Technicolor, the film had strong entertainment value and was replete with romance and the usual Western accoutrements. Obviously the strings were off the bankroll and directors John B. Goodman and Alexander Golitzen had a field day in bringing this one through.

A deluge of fan letters convinced Universal heads that Rod was the fairhaired boy of Hollywood. **Frontier Gal,** a lusty, glorified Western produced for mass audience appeal, served to increase his fan mail by skyrocketing figures. Given the lead as an automatic-toting detective in **The Runaround,** co-starring with Ella Raines, Rod scored another box-office success in what was one of his personal favorite films. Immediately after its completion he did an about-face to return to his former "type" with the starring role opposite Maria Montez in **Pirates of Monterey,** a Technicolor vehicle in which he does a neat job of swashbuckling in a role that calls for riding, swordplay, and other action in addition to a bit of lovemaking. Paul Malvern gave the picture excellent production values, with physical and technical appointments of top quality. The film established Rod as a star of real importance. His fan mail jumped to over 2500 letters a month.

Rod was given nothing to do for eight months, as Universal was going through a reorganization shuffle and no story was made ready for him. Finally he asked

Maria Montez makes eyes at Rod Cameron in **Pirates of Monterey** (Universal, 1947)

for and was given his release. He was besieged with film offers including the lead opposite Yvonne De Carlo in a Technicolor opus titled **River Lady** at, of all studios, Universal, where he made as much money on this one film as he would have made in an entire year under contract to the studio.

Rod next went to Allied Artists where he did the lead in **Panhandle,** a sepia-tone, high-budget Western. As the hero, Cameron is very convincing and easy to take. Though the hero is even more bullet-proof than usual, Rod's easy, quiet yet strongly effective playing makes him and the story believable. There is a shrewd twist of the romantic angle in that one wonders whether Anne Gwynne or Cathy Downs will land the hero.

In quick succession Allied Artists signed the virile star to a two-picture-a-year, five-year contract, and Republic, who had their eye on the rugged star, signed him to the same kind of contract. Twentieth Century-Fox put in their bid for a one-picture-a-year contract. In addition to all these contracts, Columbia and Universal submitted scripts for his agent to read for future pictures, and Rod made plans to produce an independent picture if he could find the time. Rod Cameron, as the old expression goes, "was hot as a sheriff's pistol."

Space does not permit even a comment on all of Cameron's pictures, but several of his better Westerns were **Belle Starr's Daughter, The Plunderers, Brimstone, Yaqui Drums,** and **Stage to Tucson.** There were usually plenty of shootin', fightin', chases, and climatic set-tos between Cameron and the bad guys and the films generally ended with the hero triumphant and the girl in his arms. Cameron proved to be a durable Westerner, never overly flamboyant, who along with Audie Murphy, George Montgomery, Bill Elliott, and Randolph Scott kept the medium-budget Western film alive and profitable during a difficult transitional period.

Douglas Fowley (background) listens to Rod Cameron and Kay Buckley talk in **Stage to Tucson** (Columbia, 1951)

On the personal side, Rod married Doris Stanford, an organist in the Los Angeles church he attended, circa 1937. A daughter, Catherine, was reported born to this union in 1939. The marriage was not a lasting one, and Rod married Angela Alves-Lico on December 7, 1950. He had met the 24-year-old film hopeful when he went to her rescue on June 30th of that year after a minor car accident. But it was a stormy marriage and Angela divorced him on July 6, 1954, giving birth to their son Anthony Roderick on December 29, 1954. The papers made a lot of the fact that Rod "went home to mother"— his wife's mother, that is—after the breakup. It developed that he had more in common with his mother-in-law than with his wife and married Dorothy Alves-Lico in 1960. Evidently the marriage to Dorothy was a happy one, for the two remained married until Rod's death, more than twenty years later.

Rod was one of the first motion picture stars to enter television and starred in a total of three syndicated series, each comprised of one-half hour segments, made by Revue Productions and distributed by MCA-TV. **City Detective** was filmed from 1953 through 1955 and had Rod playing the part of police lieutenant Bart Grant of the New York City Police Department. **State Trooper** found him in Nevada as Rod Blake, chief of the Nevada State Troopers. Produced from 1957 to 1959, this series was the most popular of Rod's three and, according to Rod, a total of 140 segments were filmed. The third and least popular of the trio was **Coronado 9,** filmed in 1959. The background for this series was the San Diego-Coronado Peninsula. Cameron played Dan Adams, a retired naval officer turned private investigator.

For over twenty years Cameron guest starred in various television plays on such programs as Pepsi Cola Playhouse, Studio 57, Fireside Theatre, Loretta Young Show, Star Stage, Crossroads, Laramie, Tales of Wells Fargo, Burke's Law, Perry Mason, Bob Hope Chrysler Theatre, Bonanza, Iron Horse, Name of the Game,

317

Alias Smith and Jones, Adam-12, and Hondo. His estimate of the total number of his television appearances, including his own series, is approximately 400. His last feature film, **Love and the Midnight Auto Supply,** was made in 1978.

Rod eventually retired and he and his wife took up residence in Georgia, so that he could be near his son, a baseball player. In the summer of 1983 he was a guest at the Charlotte Film Festival and seemed to enjoy visiting with his many fans. His death on December 21, 1983 was a shock to his legion of admirers.

For middle-age audiences his craggy face has been a comfort amidst a sea of mostly unrecognizable, unheard of current players and his name in a cast, a fortress in an ever-changing film world.

ROD CAMERON Filmography

THE OLD MAID
(Warner Brothers, September 2, 1939) 95 Minutes
Bette Davis, Miriam Hopkins, George Brent, Donald Crisp, Jane Bryan, Louise Fazenda, James Stephenson, Jerome Cowan, William Lundigan, Cecilia Loftus, Rand Brooks, Janet Shaw, DeWolf Hopper (William Hopper), *Rod Cameron*
Director: Edmund Goulding
Story: Zoe Atkins
Screenplay: Casey Robinson
Producer: Hal B. Wallis
Associate Producer: Henry Blanke
(Cameron is credited with this film, his first, although his scenes were edited out of the release print)

IF I HAD MY WAY
(Universal, April, 1940) 82 Minutes
Bing Crosby, Gloria Jean, Charles Winninger, El Brendel, Allyn Joslyn, Donald Woods, Claire Dodd, Nana Bryant, Moroni Olsen, Kathryn Adams, Blanche Ring, Eddie Leonard, Grace LaRue, Trixie Friganza, Julian Eltinge, Brandon Hurst, Del Henderson, Verna Felton, Emory Parnell, *Rod Cameron*
Director: David Butler
Screenplay: William Conselman and James V. Kern
Producer: David Butler

THOSE WERE THE DAYS
(Paramount, May 31, 1940) 70 Minutes
William Holden, Bonita Granville, Ezra Stone, Judith Barrett, Vaughn Glaser, William Frawley, Lucien Littlefield, Richard Denning, Tom Rutherford, Phillip Terry, Aldrich Bowker, James Seay, Douglas Kennedy, John Laird, John Hartley, Robert Scott, Gaylord Pendleton, Alan Ladd, James Dodd, Wilder Bennett, *Rod Cameron*
Director: Jay Theodore Reed
Story: George Fitch
Screenplay: Don Hartman
Producer: Jay Theodore Reed
Photography: Victor Milner
Film Editor: William Shea

STAGECOACH WAR
(Paramount, July 12, 1940) 63 Minutes
William Boyd, Russell Hayden, Julie Carter, J. Farrell MacDonald, Rad Robinson, Eddy Waller, Frank Lackteen, Jack Rockwell, Eddie Dean, Bob Kortman, The King's Men, *Rod Cameron*
Director: Lesley Selander
Screenplay: Norman Houston
Story: Norman Houston, Henry Olstea
Based on characters created by Clarence E. Mulford
Producer: Harry Sherman

RANGERS OF FORTUNE
(Paramount, September 27, 1940) 80 Minutes
Fred MacMurray, Patricia Morison, Betty Brewer, Albert Dekker, Gilbert Roland, Joseph Schildkraut, Dick Foran, Arthur Allen, Bernard Nedell, Brandon Tynan, Minor Watson, Rosa Turich, *Rod Cameron*
Director: Sam Wood
Story/Screenplay: Frank Butler
Producer: Dale Van Every

THE QUARTERBACK
(Paramount, October 4, 1940) 74 Minutes
Wayne Morris, Virginia Dale, Edgar Kennedy, Lillian Cornell, Alan Mowbray, Jerome Cowan, *Rod Cameron,* William Frawley, Walter Catlett, Frank Burke
Director: H. Bruce Humberstone
Screenplay: Robert Pirosh
Producer: Anthony Veiller

NORTH WEST MOUNTED POLICE
(Paramount, October 22, 1940) 125 Minutes
Gary Cooper, Madeleine Carroll, Paulette Goddard, Preston Foster, Robert Preston, George Bancroft, Lynne Overman, Akim Tamiroff, Walter Hampden, Lon Chaney, Jr., Montague Love, Francis J. McDonald, George E. Stone, Willard Robertson, Regis Toomey, Richard Denning, Douglas Kennedy, Robert Ryan, James Seay, Lane Chandler, Ralph Byrd, Eric Alden, Wallace Reid, Jr., Bud Geary, Evan Thomas, Jack Pennick, *Rod Cameron,* Davidson Clark, Ed Brady, Monte Blue, Mala, Jack Chapin, Chief Thunder Cloud, Harry Burns, Lou Merrill, Clara Blandick, Ynez Seabury, Eva Puig, Julia Faye, Weldon Heyburn, Phillip Terry, George Regas, Jack Luden, Soledad Jiminez, Emory Parnell, William Haade, Nestor Paiva, Donald Curtis, Jane Keckley, Nobel Johnson, Norma Nelson, John Hart, Ethan Laidlaw, Jim Pierce, Kermit Maynard, Franklyn Farnum, James Flavin
Director: Cecil B. DeMille
Story: "Royal Canadian Mounted Police" - R. G. Fetherstonhaugh
Screenplay: Alan LeMay, Jesse Lasky, Jr., C. Gardner Sullivan
Producer: Cecil B. DeMille
Associate Producer: William H. Pine

CHRISTMAS IN JULY
(Paramount, November 25, 1940) 70 Minutes
Dick Powell, Ellen Drew, Raymond Walburn, William Demarest, Ernest Truex, Franklin Pangborn, Harry Hayden, *Rod Cameron,* Michael Morris, Harry Rosenthal, Georgia Caine, Ferike Boros, Julius Tanne, Alan Bridge, Torben Meyer, Lucille Ward, Kay Stewart, Vic Potel, Alexander Carr
Director/Story/Screenplay: Preston Sturges
Producer: Paul Jones

LIFE WITH HENRY
(Paramount, January 27, 1941) 80 Minutes
Jackie Cooper, Lila Ernest, Eddie Bracken, Fred Niblo, Hedda Hopper, Kay Stewart, Moroni Olsen, *Rod Cameron,* Pierre Watkin, Lucien Littlefield, Frank M. Thomas, Etta McDaniel, Hanley Stafford, Edith Johnson, Rand Brooks, Doris Lloyd, Frances Carson, Josephine Whittell, Charlotte Treadway, Thurston Hall, Winifred Harris, Theodore von Eltz, Mary Currier, Wanda McKay
Director/Producer: Jay Theodore Reed
Screenplay: Clifford Goldsmith, Don Hartman
Story: Clarence Goldsmith

THE MONSTER AND THE GIRL
(Paramount, February 21, 1941) 65 Minutes
Ellen Drew, Robert Paige, Paul Lukas, Joseph Calleia, Onslow Stevens, George Zucco, *Rod Cameron,* Philip Terry, Marc Lawrence, Gerald Mohr, Tom Dugan, Willard Robertson, Minor Watson, G. F. Meader, Cliff Edwards
Director: Stuart Heisler
Screenplay: Stuart Anthony
Producer: Jack Moss

I WANTED WINGS
(Paramount, May 30, 1941) 131 Minutes
Ray Milland, William Holden, Brian Donlevy, Wayne Morris, Constance Moore, Veronica Lake, Hedda Hopper, Phil Brown, Harry Davenport, Richard Webb, Herbert Rawlinson, Richard Lane, Addison Richards, Hobart Cavanaugh, Douglas Aylesworth, John Trent, Archie Twitchell, Jack Chapin, Charles Drake, Alan Hale, Jr., Ronny McEvoy, Harlan Warde, *Rod Cameron*
Director: Mitchell Leisen
Screenplay: Richard Maibaun, Lieut. Bierne Lay, Jr., Sid Herzog
Story: Lieut. Bierne Lay, Jr.
Producer: Arthur Hornblow, Jr.

THE PARSON OF PANAMINT
(Paramount, August 22, 1941) 84 Minutes
Charlie Ruggles, Ellen Drew, Phillip Terry, Joseph Schildkraut, Porter Hall, Henry Kolker, Janet Beecher, Paul Hurst, Clem Bevins, Douglas Fowley, Frank Puglia, Minor Watson, Harry Hayden, Russell Hicks, Hal Price, *Rod Cameron*
Director: William McGann, Paul Hurst
Screenplay: Harold Shumate, Adrian Scott
Story: Peter B. Kyne
Producer: Harry Sherman

BUY ME THAT TOWN
(Paramount, October 3, 1941) 70 Minutes
Lloyd Nolan, Constance Moore, Albert Dekker, Sheldon Leonard, Barbara Allen, Ed Brophy, Warren Hymer, Horace MacMahon, Olin Howlin, Richard Carle, *Rod Cameron,* Jack Chapin, Keith Richards, Trevor Bardette, John Harmon, Si Jenks, Jane Keckley, Pierre Watkin, Guy Usher, Broderick O'Farrell, J. W. Johnston, Lillian Yarbo, Russell Hicks
Director: Eugene Forde
Story: Harry A. Gourfain, Murray Boltinoff, Martin Rackin
Screenplay: Gordon Kahn
Producer: Sol C. Siegel
Associate Producer: Eugene Zukor

NOTHING BUT THE TRUTH

(Paramount, October 10, 1941) 90 Minutes

Bob Hope, Paulette Goddard, Edward Arnold, Leif Erickson, Glenn Anders, Helen Vinson, Grant Mitchell, Willie Best, Clarence Kolb, Catherine Doucet, Mary Forbes, Rose Hobart, Leon Belasco, Helen Millard, William Wright, Oscar Smith, Dick Chandler, Catherine Craig, Edward McWade, Keith Richards, James Blane, Jack Egan, *Rod Cameron*

Director: Elliott Nugent
Screenplay: Don Hartman, Ken Englund
Story: James Montgomery, Frederick Isham
Producer: Arthur Hornblow, Jr.

HENRY ALDRICH FOR PRESIDENT

(Paramount, October 24, 1941) 73 Minutes

James Lydon, Charles Smith, June Preisser, Mary Anderson, Martha O'Driscoll, John Litel, *Rod Cameron*, Frank Coghlan, Jr., Lucien Littlefield, Buddy Pepper, Vaughn Glaser, Dick Paxton, Paul Matthews, Frederick Carpenter, Bob Pittard, Bud (Lon) McCallister, Carmen Johnson, Helen Westcott, Rosita Butler, Georgia Lee Settle, Irving Bacon, Lillian Yarbo, Arthur Loft, Sidney Miller, Ruth Robinson, Noel Neill, Christian Rub

Director: Hugh Bennett
Screenplay: Val Burton
Story: Clifford Goldsmith
Producer: Sol C. Siegel

THE NIGHT OF JANUARY 16th

(Paramount, November 28, 1941) 79 Minutes

Robert Preston, Ellen Drew, Nils Asther, Donald Douglas, Margaret Hayes, Clarence Kolb, *Rod Cameron*, Alice White, Roy Gordon, Cecil Kellaway, Harry Hayden, Edwin Stanley, Paul Stanton, Willard Robertson, James Flavin, George Renavent

Director: William Clemens
Story: Based on the play by Ayn Rand
Screenplay: Delmar Daves, Robert Pirosh, Eve Greene
Producer: Sol C. Siegel

MIDNIGHT ANGEL

(Paramount, December, 1941) 76 Minutes

Robert Preston, Martha O'Driscoll, Philip Merivale, Eva Gabor, Louis Jean Heydt, Thurston Hall, Mary Treen, J. Edward Bromberg, Spencer Charters, Cy Kendall, Russell Hicks, Paul Stanton, Clem Bevins, Robert Emmett Keane, Edwin Maxwell, *Rod Cameron*

Director: Ralph Murphy
Story: Franz Spencer, Curt Siodmak
Screenplay: Lester Cole, W. P. Lipscomb
Associate Producer: Burt Kelly
Producer: Sol C. Siegel

NO HANDS ON THE CLOCK

(Paramount, December, 1941) 76 Minutes

Chester Morris, Jean Parker, Rose Hobart, Dick Purcell, Astrid Allwyn, *Rod Cameron,* Loren Baker, Billie Seward, George Watts, James Kirkwood, Robert Middlemass, Frank Faylen, Keye Luke

Director: Frank McDonald
Story: Geoffrey Homes
Screenplay: Maxwell Shane
Producers: William H. Pine, William C. Thomas

THE FLEET'S IN

(Paramount, January, 1942) 93 Minutes

Dorothy Lamour, William Holden, Eddie Bracken, Betty Hutton, Cass Daley, Gil Lamb, Leif Erickson, Jack Norton, Roy Atwell, Harry Barris, Dave Willock, *Rod Cameron*, Jimmy Dundee, Jack Chapin, Bob Everly, Helen O'Connell, Lorraine and Rognan, Betty Jane Rhodes, Jimmy Dorsey and His Band, Barbara Britton, Robert Warwick, Hal K. Dawson, Charlie Williams, Lyle Latell, Stanley Andrews, Chester Clute, Oscar Smith

Director: Victor Schertzinger
Story: Monte Brice, J. Walter Ruben
Screenplay: Walter DeLeon
Associate Producer: Paul Jones

TRUE TO THE ARMY

(Paramount, 1942) 76 Minutes

Judy Canova, Allan Jones, Ann Miller, Jerry Colonna, William Demarest, William Wright, Clarence Kolb, Gordon Jones, *Rod Cameron,* John Miljan, Edward Pawley

Director: Al Rogel
Screenplay: Art Arthur, Bradford Ropes
Adaptation: Edmund Hartmann, Val Burton
Based on a novel by Edward Hope and a play by Howard Lindsay
Producer: Sol C. Siegel

THE REMARKABLE ANDREW

(Paramount, 1942) 80 Minutes

Brian Donlevy, William Holden, Ellen Drew, Montague Love, Gilbert Emery, Brandon Hurst, George Watts, Jimmy Conlon, *Rod Cameron,* Spencer Charters, Richard Webb, Minor Watson, Clyde Fillmore, Thomas A. Ross, Porter Hall, Wallis Clark, Milton Parsons

Director: Stuart Heisler
Screenplay/Story: Dalton Trumbo

WAKE ISLAND

(Paramount, 1942) 87 Minutes

Brian Donlevy, Macdonald Carey, Robert Preston, William Bendix, Albert Dekker, Walter Abel, Mikhail Rasummy, Don Castle, *Rod Cameron*, Bill Goodwin, Barbara Britton, Damian O'Flynn, Frank Albertson, Phillip Terry, Phillip Van Zandt, Jack Chapin, Keith Richards, Willard Robertson, Marvin Jones, Rudy Robies, John Sheehan, Charles Trowbridge, Mary Thomas, Mary Field, Richard Loo, Earl "Tex" Harris, Hillary Brooke, Patti McCarty, William Forrest, Jack Mulhall, Ivan Miller, Hugh Beaumont, Edward Bearle, James (Jim) Brown, Angel Cruz, Anthony Nace, Hollis Bane (Mike Ragan), Frank Faylan, Alan Hale, Jr., Dan Clark

Director: John Farrow
Screenplay: W. R. Burnett, Frank Butler
Associate Producer: Joseph Sistrom
Story: Credited to "Original Story by United States Marine Corps."

PRIORITIES ON PARADE

(Paramount, 1942) 79 Minutes

Ann Miller, Johnnie Johnson, Jerry Colonna, Betty Jane Rhodes, Vera Vague (Barbara Allen), Harry Barris, Eddie Quillan, Dave Willock, Nick Cochrane, *Rod Cameron,* Arthur Loft, The Debonaires

Director: Albert S. Rogell
Screenplay: Art Arthur, Frank Loesser

THE FOREST RANGERS

(Paramount, 1942) 87 Minutes

Fred MacMurray, Paulette Goddard, Susan Hayward, Albert Dekker, Eugene Pallette, Lynne Overman, Regis Toomey, James (Jim) Brown, Clem Bevans, *Rod Cameron*

Director: George Marshall
Screenplay: Harold Shumate
Story: Thelma Strabel

THE COMMANDOS STRIKE AT DAWN

(Columbia, January 7, 1943) 98 Minutes

Paul Muni, Lillian Gish, Anna Lee, Sir Cedric Hardwicke, Robert Coote, Ray Collins, Rosemary DeCamp, Alexander Knox, Elizabeth Fraser, Richard Derr, Erville Anderson, Barbara Everest, *Rod Cameron*, Louis Jean Heydt, George Macready, Arthur Margetson, Ann Carter, Elsa Janssen, Ferdinand Munier, John Arthur Stockton

Director: John Farrow
Screenplay: Irwin Shaw
Story: C. S. Forrester
Producer: Lester Cowan

G-MEN VS. THE BLACK DRAGON

(Republic, January, 1943) 15 Chapters

Rod Cameron, Roland Got, Constance Worth, Nino Pipitone, Noel Cravat, George J. Lewis, Maxine Doyle, Donald Kirke, Ivan Miller, Walter Fenner, C. Montague Shaw, Harry Burns, Forbes Murray, Hooper Atchley, Robert Homans, Allen Jung, Norman Nesbit, John Daheim, Lawrence Grant, Crane Whitley, Eddie Parker, Ken Terrell, Kenneth Harlan, Harry Tauvers, Tom Steele, Peter George Lynn, Stanley Price, Pat O'Malley, Edward Keane, Walter Low, George DeNormand, Charley Phillips, Charles Flynn, William Forrest, Paul Fung, Gil Perkins, Bill Cody, Robert Strange, Ray Parsons, Baron Lichter, Edmund Cobb, Buddy Roosevelt, Eddie Dew, Bud Wolfe, Norman Willis, Walter Thiel, Duke Taylor, Harry Tauvera, Tom Seidel, Arvon Dale, Dale Van Sickel, Virginia Carroll, Mary Bayless, Martin Faust, Bud Geary, John Wallace, Dick French

Director: William Witney
Screenplay: Ronald Davidson, William Lively, Joseph O'Donnell, Joseph Poland
Associate Producer: W. J. O'Sullivan
Chapter Titles: (1) The Yellow Peril (2) Japanese Inquisition (3) Arsenal of Doom (4) Deadly Sorcery (5) Celestial Murder (6) Death and Destruction (7) The Iron Monster (8) Beast of Tokyo (9) Watery Grave (10) The Dragon Strikes (11) Suicide Mission (12) Dead on Arrival (13) Condemned Cargo (14) Flaming Coffin (15) Democracy in Action

SECRET SERVICE IN DARKEST AFRICA

(Republic, June, 1943) 15 Chapters

Rod Cameron, Joan Marsh, Duncan Renaldo, Lionel Royce, Kurt Kreuger, Frederic Brunn, Sigurd Tor, Georges Renavent, Kurt Katch, Ralf Harolde, William Vaughn, William Yetter, Hans Von Morhart, Erwin Goldi, Frederic Worlock, Paul Marion, Ken Terrell, Duke Green, Joe Yrigoyen, Eddie Phillips, Bud Geary, Reed Howes, Carey Loftin, Harry Semels, Tom Steele, Eddie Parker, Leonard Hampton, George Sorel, George J. Lewis, Jack LaRue, George DeNormand, Walter Fenner, Jacques Lory, Jack O'Shea, Buddy Roosevelt, John Davidson, Frank Alten, Nino Bellini, Emily LaRue, Norman Nesbitt, John Royce, Ed Agresti

Director: Spencer Bennet
Screenplay: Royal Cole, Basil Dickey, Jesse Duffy, Ronald Davidson, Joseph O'Donnell, Joseph Poland
Associate Producer: W. J. O'Sullivan
Chapter Titles: (1) North African Intrigue (2) The Charred Witness (3) Double Death (4) The Open Grave (5) Cloaked in Flame (6) Dial of Doom (7) Murder Dungeon (8) Funeral Arrangements Completed (9) Invisible Menace (10) Racing Peril (11) Lightning Terror (12) Ceremonial (13-14) ? (15) New Treachery Unmasked

HONEYMOON LODGE

(Universal, August, 1943) 63 Minutes

David Bruce, Harriet Hilliard, June Vincent, *Rod Cameron,* Franklin Pangborn, Andrew Tombes, Martin Ashe, Ozzie Nelson, Veloz and Yolanda, Tip, Tap, and Toe, Bobby Brooks and quartet, Hattie Noel, Ray Eberle, Joseph Crehan, Selmer Jackson, Margaret Seddon, Robert Dudley, Fay Helm, Mary Eleanor Donahue, Clarence Muse, David Street, Emmett Vogan, Jack Rice, Billy Newell, Herbert Heywood, Charles Jordan, Charles Hall, Alphonse Martell, John Frazer, Francis Sayles, Jack Gardner, Hooper Atchley, Eddie Polo, Willie Thomas
Director: Edward Lilley
Screenplay: Clyde Bruckman
Story: Warren Wilson

THE KANSAN

(United Artists, September 10, 1943) 79 Minutes

Richard Dix, Jane Wyatt, Victor Jory, Albert Dekker, Eugene Pallette, Robert Armstrong, Clem Bevans, *Rod Cameron,* Francis McDonald, Willie Best, Glenn Strange, Douglas Fowley, Jack Norton, Eddy Waller, Ray Bennett, Sam Flint, Merrill McCormack
Director: George Archainbaud
Story: Frank Gruber
Screenplay: Harold Shumate
Producer: Harry Sherman

GUNG HO

(Universal, December 20, 1943) 88 Minutes

Randolph Scott, Grace McDonald, Noah Beery, Jr., David Bruce, Sam Levene, J. Carrol Naish, Richard Lane, Milburn Stone, Walter Sande, Louis Jean Heydt, Robert Mitchum, *Rod Cameron,* Harold London
Director: Ray Enright
Story: W. S. LeFrancois
Screenplay: Lucien Hubbard and Joseph Hoffman

NO TIME FOR LOVE

(Paramount, 1943) 83 Minutes

Claudette Colbert, Fred MacMurray, Ilka Chase, Richard Haydn, Paul McGrath, June Havoc, Marjorie Gateson, Bill Goodwin, Robert Herrick, Morton Lowry, Rhys Williams, Murray Alper, John Kelly, Grant Withers, *Rod Cameron,* Willard Robertson, Arthur Loft, Fred Kohler, Jr., Tom Neal, Sammy Stein, Jack Roper, Frank Moran, Alan Hale, Jr., Ben Taggart, Lillian Randolph, Keith Richards
Director: Mitchell Leisen
Story: Robert Lees, Fred Renaldo
Adaptation: Warren Duff
Screenplay: Claude Binyon
Producer: Mitchell Leisen
Associate Producer: Fred Kohlmar

RIDING HIGH

(Paramount, 1943) 88 Minutes

Dorothy Lamour, Dick Powell, Victor Moore, Cass Daley, Bill Goodwin, *Rod Cameron,* Glen Langan, Milt Britton Band, Louise LaPlanche, Marie McDonald, Andrew Tombes
Director: George Marshall
Screenplay: Walter DeLeon, Arthur Phillips, Art Arthur
Story: James Montgomery

THE GOOD FELLOWS

(Paramount, 1943) 70 Minutes

Helen Walker, Cecil Kellaway, Mabel Paige, James (Jim) Brown, Diana Hale, Kathleen Lockhart, *Rod Cameron,* Irving Bacon
Director: Jo Graham
Story: Based on play "The Good Fellows" by George S. Kaufman and Herman J. Mankiewicz

BOSS OF BOOMTOWN

(Universal, May 22, 1944) 58 Minutes

Rod Cameron, Fuzzy Knight, Tom Tyler, Vivian Austin (Vivian Coe), Ray Whitley, Jack Ingram, Robert Barron, Marie Austin, Max Wagner, Sam Flint, Dick Alexander, Forrest Taylor, Tex Cooper, Hank Bell, Ray Jones, Ray Whitley's Bar-6 Cowboys
Director: Ray Taylor
Screenplay: William Lively
Associate Producer: Oliver Drake

TRIGGER TRAIL

(Universal, June 7, 1944) 59 Minutes

Rod Cameron, Fuzzy Knight, Eddie Dew, Vivian Austin, Ray Whitley and his Bar-6 Cowboys (Ezra Paulette, Lem Giles, and Charley Quirt), Lane Chandler, George Eldridge, Buzzy Henry, Davidson Clark, Michael Vallon, Dick Alexander, Jack Rockwell, Budd Buster, Bud Osborne, Ray Jones, Jack Ingram, Artie Ortego
Director: Lewis Collins
Screenplay: Ed Earl Repp, Patricia Harper
Associate Producer: Oliver Drake

RIDERS OF THE SANTA FE

(Universal, November 10, 1944) 60 Minutes

Rod Cameron, Fuzzy Knight, Eddie Dew, Jennifer Holt, Ray Whitley and his Bar-6 Cowboys, Lane Chandler, Earle Hodgins, George Douglas, Dick Alexander, Budd Buster, Ida Moore, Al Ferguson, Ray Jones, Henry Wills
Director: Wallace Fox
Screenplay: Ande Lamb
Associate Producer: Oliver Drake

MRS. PARKINGTON

(Metro-Goldwyn-Mayer, November, 1944) 124 Minutes
Greer Garson, Walter Pidgeon, Edward Arnold, Agnes Moorehead, Cecil Kellaway, Gladys Cooper, Francis Rafferty, Tom Drake, Dan Duryea, Hugh Marlowe, Selena Royle, Fortunio Bonanova, Lee Patrick, Harry Cording, Celia Travers, Mary Servoss, Tala Birell, Peter Lawford, *Rod Cameron*, Helen Freeman, Gerald Oliver Smith, Ruthe Brady, Byron Foulger, Wallis Clark, Ann Codee, Frank Reicher, Kay Medford, Alma Kruger, Hans Conried, Edward Fielding, Rhea Mitchell, Ivo Henderson, Lee Tung Foo, Marek Windheim, Marcelle Corday, Robert Greig, Gordon Richards, Howard Hickman, Warren Farlan, Doodles Weaver, Rex Evans
Director: Tay Garnett
Screenplay: Robert Thoren, Polly James
Story: Louis Bromfield
Producer: Leon Gordon

THE OLD TEXAS TRAIL

(Universal, December 15, 1944) 60 Minutes
Rod Cameron, Fuzzy Knight, Eddie Dew, Marjorie Clements, Edmund Cobb, Virginia Christine, Ray Whitley and his Bar-6 Cowboys, Joseph J. Greene, George Eldridge, Jack Clifford, Dick Purcell, Harry Strang, Ray Jones, Merle Travis, William Desmond, George Turner (role credited to Terry Frost), Art Fowler, Henry Wills, Terry Frost
Director: Lewis Collins
Screenplay: William Lively
Associate Producer: Oliver Drake

BEYOND THE PECOS

(Universal, April 27, 1945) 58 Minutes
Rod Cameron, Eddie Dew, Fuzzy Knight, Jennifer Holt, Ray Whitley, Eugene Stutenroth (Gene Roth), Robert Homans, Jack Ingram, Frank Jacquet, Henry Wills, Jack Rockwell, Jim Thorpe, Dan White, Al Ferguson, Forrest Taylor, Herman Hack, Artie Ortego, William Desmond, Ray Whitley's Bar-6 Cowboys
Director: Lambert Hillyer
Story: Jay Karth
Screenplay: Bennett Cohen
Associate Producer: Oliver Drake

Fuzzy Knight, Rod Cameron, Robert Homans, Jennifer Holt, unidentified players and Eugene Stutenroth in
Beyond the Pecos (Universal, 1944)

SALOME, WHERE SHE DANCED

(Universal, April 27, 1945) 90 Minutes
(Technicolor)
Yvonne De Carlo, *Rod Cameron,* David Bruce, Walter Slezak, Albert Dekker, Marjorie Rambeau, J. Edward Bromberg, Abner Biberman, John Litel, Ken Katch, Arthur Hohl, Will Wright, Matt McHugh
Director: Charles Lamont
Story: Michael Phillips
Screenplay: Laurence Stallings
Associate Producer: Alexander Golitzen

SWING OUT, SISTER

(Universal, May, 1945) 60 Minutes
Rod Cameron, Billie Burke, Frances Raeburn, Arthur Treacher, Jacqueline de Wit, Samuel S. Hinds, Fuzzy Knight, Milburn Stone, Edgar Dearing, Sam Flint, Constance Purdy, Selina Pettiford, Irene Thomas, Tony Rae, Dee Carroll, Harry Strang, Bill Davidson, Chester Clute, Rex Evans, Eddie Kane, Eddie Hart
Director: Edward Lilley
Screenplay: Henry Blankfort
Story: Eugene Conrad and Edward Dein

RENEGADES OF THE RIO GRANDE

(Universal, June 1, 1945) 57 Minutes
Rod Cameron, Fuzzy Knight, Jennifer Holt, Eddie Dew, Glenn Strange, Ray Whitley, Ethan Laidlaw, Edmund Cobb, Dick Alexander, Iris Clive, John James, Jack Casey, Hal Hart, Dick Botiller, Percy Carson, Ray Whitley's Bar-6 Cowboys
Director: Howard Bretherton
Screenplay: Ande Lamb
Associate Producer: Oliver Drake

FRONTIER GAL

(Universal, December 21, 1945) 84 Minutes
(Technicolor)
Yvonne De Carlo, *Rod Cameron,* Andy Devine, Fuzzy Knight, Sheldon Leonard, Andrew Tombes, Clara Blandick, Beverly Simmons, Frank Lackteen, Claire Carleton, Eddie Dunn, Harold Goodwin, Jack Overman, Jan Wiley, Rex Lease, Jack Ingram, George Eldridge, Joseph Haworth, Lloyd Ingraham, Joseph Bernard, Douglas Carter, Paul Bratti, Edward Howard, Joan Fulton, Jean Trent, Kerry Vaughn, Karen Randle
Director: Charles Lamont
Screenplay: Michael Fessier, Ernest Pagano

THE RUNAROUND

(Universal, June 14, 1946) 86 Minutes
Rod Cameron, Broderick Crawford, Ella Raines, Frank McHugh, Samuel S. Hinds, George Cleveland, Joe Sawyer, Nana Bryant, Dave Willock, Joan Fulton, Charles Coleman, Jack Overman, Dorothy Granger, Jack Rice
Director: Charles Lamont
Screenplay: Arthur T. Horman, Sam Hellman
Story: Arthur T. Horman, Walter Wise
Producer: Joe Gershenson

BELLE STARR'S DAUGHTER

(Alson Productions/20th Century-Fox, November 15, 1947) 85 Minutes
George Montgomery, *Rod Cameron,* Ruth Roman, Wallace Ford, Charles Kemper, William Phipps, Edith King, Chris-Pin Martin, Jack Lambert, Paul Libby, J. Farrell MacDonald, Charles Jewell
Director: Lesley Selander
Screenplay: W. R. Burnett
Producer: Edward L. Alperson

PIRATES OF MONTEREY

(Universal-International, December, 1947) 77 Minutes
(Technicolor)
Maria Montez, *Rod Cameron,* Mikhail Rasumny, Philip Reed, Gilbert Roland, Gale Sondergaard, Tamara Shayne, Robert Warwick, Michael Raffeto, Neyle Morrow, Victor Varconi, Charles Waggenheim, George J. Lewis, Joe Bernard, George Navarro, Victor Romito, Don Driggers, George Magrill
Director: Alfred Werker
Story: Edward T. Lowe, Bradford Ropes
Screenplay: Sam Hellman, Margaret Buell Wilder
Producer: Paul Malvern

PANHANDLE

(Allied Artists, February 1, 1948) 85 Minutes
(Sepiatone)
Rod Cameron, Cathy Downs, Reed Hadley, Anne Gwynne, Blake Edwards, Dick Crockett, Charles Judels, Alex Gerry, Francis McDonald, J. Farrell Mac-Donald, Henry Hall, Stanley Andrews, Jeff York, James Harrison, Charles LaTorre, Frank Dae, Bud Osborne
Director: Lesley Selander
Screenplay/Producers: John C. Champion, Blake Edwards

RIVER LADY

(Universal-International, June, 1948) 78 Minutes
Yvonne De Carlo, *Rod Cameron,* Dan Duryea, Helena Carter, Lloyd Gough, John McIntyre, Florence Bates, Jack Lambert, Esther Somers, Anita Turner, Edmund Cobb, Dewey Robinson, Eddy Waller, Milton Kibbee, Billy Wayne, Jimmy Ames, Edward Earle
Director: George Sherman
Story: Houston Branch, Frank Waters
Screenplay: D. D. Beauchamp, William Bowers
Producer: Leonard Goldstein

STRIKE IT RICH

(Allied Artists, November, 1948) 80 Minutes
Rod Cameron, Bonita Granville, Don Castle, Stuart Erwin, Lloyd Corrigan, Ellen Corby, Emory Parnell, Harry Tyler, Virginia Dale, William Haade, Edward Gargan, Robert Dudley
Director: Lesley Selander
Screenplay: Francis Rosenwald
Producer: Jack Wrather

THE PLUNDERERS

(Republic, December 1, 1948) 87 Minutes
(TruColor)
Rod Cameron, Ilona Massey, Adrian Booth, Forrest Tucker, George Cleveland, Grant Withers, Taylor Holmes, Paul Fix, Francis Ford, James Flavin, Maude Eburne, Russell Hicks, Mary Ruth Wade, Louis R. Faust, Hank Bell, Rex Lease
Director: Joseph Kane
Story: James Edward Grant
Screenplay: Gerald Geraghty, Gerald Adams
Associate Producer: Joseph Kane

STAMPEDE

(Allied Artists, May 1, 1949) 76 Minutes
Rod Cameron, Johnny Mack Brown, Gale Storm, Don Castle, Don Curtis, John Miljan, Jonathan Hale, John Eldredge, Kenne Duncan, Tim Ryan, Steve Clark, Bob Woodward, Duke York, Artie Ortego, Neal Hart
Director: Lesley Selander
Screenplay: John C. Champion, Blake Edwards
Producers: Scott R. Dunlap, John C. Champion, Blake Edwards

BRIMSTONE

(Republic, August 15, 1949) 90 Minutes
Rod Cameron, Adrian Booth, Walter Brennan, Forrest Tucker, Jack Holt, Jim Davis, James Brown, Guinn "Big Boy" Williams, Charlita, Hal Taliaferro
Director: Joseph Kane
Story: Norman S. Hall
Screenplay: Thames Williams
Associate Producer: Joseph Kane

Rod Cameron and Marie Windsor in a dramatic scene in **Dakota Lil** (20th Century-Fox)

DAKOTA LIL

(20th Century-Fox, February 1, 1950) 88 Minutes
(CineColor)

George Montgomery, Marie Windsor, *Rod Cameron,*
John Emery, Wallace Ford, Jack Lambert, Larry Johns,
Marian Martin, James Flavin, J. Farrell MacDonald
Director: Lesley Selander
Story: Frank Gruber
Screenplay: Maurice Geraghty
Producer: Edward L. Alperson

SHORT GRASS

(Allied Artists, December 24, 1950) 82 Minutes

Rod Cameron, Cathy Downs, Johnny Mack Brown,
Raymond Walburn, Alan Hale, Jr., Morris Ankrum,
Jonathan Hale, Harry Woods, Marlo Dwyer, Riley Hill,
Jeff York, Stanley Andrews, Jack Ingram, Myron
Healey, Tris Coffin, Rory Mallison, Felipe Turich,
George J. Lewis, Lee Tung Foo, Kermit Maynard
Director: Lesley Selander
Story/Screenplay: Tom W. Blackburn
Producer: Scott R. Dunlap

STAGE TO TUCSON

(Columbia, January 1, 1951) 82 Minutes
(Technicolor)

Rod Cameron, Wayne Morris, Kay Buckley, Sally
Eilers, Carl Benton Reid, Roy Roberts, Harry Bellaver,
Douglas Fowley, John Pickard, Olin Howlin, Boyd
Stockman, John Sheehan, Reed Howes, James
Kirkwood
Director: Ralph Murphy
Story: Frank Bonham
Screenplay: Bob Williams, Frank Burt, Robert Libott
Producer: Harry Joe Brown

OH SUSANNA

(Republic, March 3, 1951) 90 Minutes
(TruColor)

Rod Cameron, Adrian Booth, Forrest Tucker, Chill
Wills, William Ching, Jim Davis, Wally Cassell, Douglas
Kennedy, James Lydon, William Haade, John Compton,
James Flavin, Charles Stevens, Alan Bridge, Marion
Randolph, Marshall Reed, John Pickard, Ruth Brennan,
Louise Kane
Director: Joseph Kane
Screenplay: Charles Marquis Warren
Associate Producer: Joseph Kane

CAVALRY SCOUT

(Monogram, May 13, 1951) 78 Minutes
(CineColor)

Rod Cameron, Audrey Long, Jim Davis, James
Millican, James Arness, John Doucette, William Phillips,
Stephen Chase, Rory Mallison, Eddy Waller, Paul Bryar
Director: Lesley Selander
Screenplay: Dan Ullman, Thomas Blackburn
Producer: Walter Mirisch

THE SEA HORNET

(Republic, September, 1951) 84 Minutes

Rod Cameron, Adele Mara, Adrian Booth, Chill Wills,
Jim Davis, Richard Jaeckel, James Brown, Grant
Withers, William Ching, William Haade, Hal Taliaferro,
Emil Sitka, Byron Foulger, Monte Blue, Jack Pennick
Director/Producer: Joseph Kane
Story: Gerald Drayson Adams

FORT OSAGE

(Monogram, February 10, 1952) 72 Minutes
(CineColor)

Rod Cameron, Jane Nigh, Morris Ankrum, Douglas
Kennedy, John Ridgely, William Phipps, I. Stanford
Jolley, Dorothy Adams, Francis McDonald, Myron
Healey, Jane Bradford, Iron Eyes Cody, Barbara
Woodell, Russ Conway
Director: Lesley Selander
Story/Screenplay: Dan Ullman
Producer: Walter Mirisch

WAGONS WEST

(Monogram, July 6, 1952) 70 Minutes
(CineColor)

Rod Cameron, Noah Beery, Jr., Peggy Castle, Michael
Chapin, Henry Brandon, Sarah Hayden, Frank
Ferguson, Anne Kimbell, Wheaton Chambers, Riley
Hill, Effie Laird, I. Stanford Jolley, Harry Tyler, Almira
Sessions
Director: Ford Beebe
Screenplay: Dan Ullman
Producer: Vincent M. Fennelly

THE JUNGLE

(Voltaire Productions—A.T.R. Productions/Lippert,
August 1, 1952) 74 Minutes

Rod Cameron, Cesar Romero, Marie Windsor, M. N.
Sulchana, Daniel Abraham, Ramakrishna, Chitradevi
Director: William Berke
Story/Screenplay: Carroll Young
Producer: William Berke

Glenn Strange breaks up a fight between Rod Cameron and Henry Brandon in **Wagons West** (Monogram, 1952)

WOMEN OF THE NORTH COUNTRY
(Republic, September 5, 1952) 92 Minutes
(TruColor)
Ruth Hussey, *Rod Cameron,* John Agar, Gale Storm, J. Carrol Naish, Jim Davis, Jay C. Flippen, Taylor Holmes, Barry Kelley, Grant Withers, Stephen Bekassy, Howard Petrie, Hank Worden, Virginia Brissac
Director/Associate Producer: Joseph Kane
Story: Charles Marquis Warren
Screenplay: Norman Reilly Raine

RIDE THE MAN DOWN
(Republic, January 1, 1953) 90 Minutes
(TruColor)
Brian Donlevy, *Rod Cameron,* Ella Raines, Forrest Tucker, Barbara Britton, Chill Wills, J. Carroll Naish, Jim Davis, Taylor Holmes, James Bell, Paul Fix, Al Caudebec, Roydon Clark, Roy Barcroft, Douglas Kennedy, Chris-Pin Martin, Jack LaRue, Claire Carleton
Director/Associate Producer: Joseph Kane
From the *Saturday Evening Post* **story by** Luke Short
Screenplay: Mary McCall, Jr.

SAN ANTONE
(Republic, January 1, 1953) 90 Minutes
Rod Cameron, Arleen Whelan, Forrest Tucker, Katy Jurado, Rodolfo Acosta, Roy Roberts, Bob Steele, Harry Carey, Jr., James Liburn, Andrew Brennan, Richard Hale, Martin Garralaga, Argentina Brunetti, Douglas Kennedy, Paul Fierro, George Cleveland
Director/Producer: Joseph Kane
Screenplay: Steve Fisher
Story: Curt Carroll - "The Golden Herd"

THE STEEL LADY
(World Films/United Artists, October 9, 1953)
84 Minutes
Rod Cameron, Tab Hunter, John Dehner, John Abbott, Frank Puglia, Antonio Caruso, Christopher Dark, Dick Rich, Charles Victor, Carmen D'Antonio
Director: E. A. Dupont
Screenplay: Richard Schayer
Story: Aubrey Winsberg
Producer: Grant Whytock

327

SOUTHWEST PASSAGE
(Small/United Artists, April 25, 1954) 82 Minutes
(Pathe Color) (3-D)
John Ireland, Joanne Dru, *Rod Cameron*, Guinn Williams, John Dehner, Mark Hanna, Darryl Hickman, Stuart Randall, Morris Ankrum, Kenneth MacDonald, Stanley Andrews
Director: Ray Nazarro
Screenplay: Harry Essex
Producer: Edward Small

HELL'S OUTPOST
(Republic, December 15, 1954) 90 Minutes
Rod Cameron, Joan Leslie, John Russell, Chill Wills, Jim Davis, Kristine Miller, Ben Cooper, Taylor Holmes, Barton MacLane, Ruth Lee, Arthur Q. Bryan, Oliver Blake
Director/Associate Producer: Joseph Kane
Story: "Silver Rock" - Luke Short
Screenplay: Kenneth Gamet

SANTA FE PASSAGE
(Republic, May 12, 1955) 90 Minutes
(TruColor)
John Payne, Faith Domergue, *Rod Cameron*, Slim Pickens, Irene Tedrow, George Keymas, Leo Gordon, Anthony Caruso
Director: William Witney
Screenplay: Lillie Hayward
Story: Clay Fisher in *Esquire* Magazine
Associate Producer: Sidney Picker

DOUBLE JEOPARDY
(Republic, June, 1955) 70 Minutes
Rod Cameron, Gale Robbins, Allison Hayes, Jack Kelly, John Litel, Robert Armstrong, John Gallaudet, Bob Nelson, Minerva Urecal, Tom Powers, Dick Elliott, Fern Hall
Director: R. G. Springsteen
Associate Producer: Rudy Ralston

HEADLINE HUNTERS
(Republic, September, 1955) 70 Minutes
Rod Cameron, Julie Bishop, Ben Cooper, Raymond Greenleaf, Chubby Johnson, John Warburton, Nacho Galindo, Virginia Carroll, Howard Wright, Stuart Randall, Edward Colmans, Joe Besser
Director: William Witney
Screenplay: Frederic Louis Fox, John K. Butler
Associate Producer: William J. O'Sullivan

THE FIGHTING CHANCE
(Republic, October, 1955) 70 Minutes
Rod Cameron, Julie London, Ben Cooper, Taylor Holmes, Howard Wendell, Mel Welles, Bob Steele, Paul Birteh, Carl Milletaire, Rodolfo Hoyos, Jr., John Damler, Sam Scar
Director: William Witney
Screenplay: Houston Branch
Story: Robert Blees
Producer: William J. O'Sullivan

PASSPORT TO REASON
(Mid-Century Productions/Eros Films: Dist. in USA by Astor, June, 1956) 70 Minutes
Rod Cameron, Lois Maxwell, Clifford Evans, Ballard Berkeley, Douglas Wilmer, Andrew Fau, John Collicos, Derek Sydney, Barbara Burke, Marianne Stone
Director: Robert S. Baker
Story: Manning O'Brine

YAQUI DRUMS
(Allied Artists, October 14, 1956) 71 Minutes
Rod Cameron, Mary Castle, J. Carroll Naish, Roy Roberts, Robert Hutt, Denver Pyle, Keith Richards, Ray Walker, Donald Kerr, G. Pat Collins, John Merrick, Paul Fierro, Fred Gabourie, Saul Gorss
Director: Jean Yarbrough
Story: Paul Peil
Screenplay: Jo Pagano, D. D. Beauchamp
Producer: William F. Broidy

SPOILERS OF THE FOREST
(Republic, June 26, 1957) 68 Minutes
Rod Cameron, Vera Ralston, Ray Collins, Hillary Brooke, Edgar Buchanan, Carl Benton Reid, Sheila Bromley, Hank Worden, John Compton, John Alderson, Angela Greene, Paul Stader
Director/Producer: Joseph Kane
Screenplay/Story: Bruce Manning

THE MAN WHO DIED TWICE
(Ventura/Republic, July, 1958) 70 Minutes
Rod Cameron, Vera Ralston, Mike Mazurki, Gerald Milton, Richard Karlan, Louis Jean Heydt, Don Megowan, John Maxwell, Bob Anderson, Paul Picerni, Don Haggerty, Luana Anders, Jesslyn Fax
Director: Joseph Kane
Screenplay: Richard C. Saragian
Producer: Rudy Ralston

THE ELECTRIC MONSTER
(Amalgamated Productions/Columbia, May, 1960)
72 Minutes
Rod Cameron, Mary Murphy, Meredith Edwards, Peter Illing, Carl Jaffe, Kay Ballard, Carl Buering, Roberta Huby, Felix Felton, Larry Cross, Carlo Borelli, Alan Gifford, John McCarthy, Jacqueline Cey, Armande Guinle, Malou Pantera, Pat Clavin
Director: Montgomery Tully
Screenplay: Charles Eric Maine
Producer: Alec C. Snowden

Rod Cameron in **The Gun Hawk** (Allied Artists, 1963)

THE GUN HAWK
(Allied Artists, August 28, 1963) 92 Minutes
(DeLuxe Color)
Rory Calhoun, *Rod Cameron*, Ruta Lee, Rod Lauren, Morgan Woodward, Robert J. (Bob) Wilke, John Litel, Rodolfo Hoyos, Lane Bradford, Glenn Stensel, Joan Connors, Ron Whalen, Lee Bradley, Jody Daniels, Natividad Vacio, Greg Barton, Frank Gardner, Harry Fleer
Director: Edward Ludwig
Screenplay: Jo Heims
Story: Richard Bernstein, Max Steeber
Producer: Richard Bernstein

I SENTIERI DELL'ODIO
(American Title: "Guns of Hate") (1964)
Rod Cameron, Patricia Viterbo, Enzo Girolami (Enzo G. Castellari)
Director/Scenario: Fred Wilson

LE PISTOLE NON DISCUTONO
(American Title: "Guns Don't Argue")
(Jolly Film-Trio Film-Constin Film, 1964)
(May also be known as "Bullets Don't Argue" and "Pistols Don't Say No") (Technicolor)
Rod Cameron, Dick Palmer (Mimmo Palmara), Angel Aranda, Andrew Ray, Vivi Bach, Kay Fischer, Hans Nielsen
Director: Mike Perkins (Mario Caiano)

REQUIEM FOR A GUNFIGHTER
(Embassy, June 30, 1965) 91 Minutes
(Technicolor) (TechniScope)
Rod Cameron, Stephen McNally, Mike Mazurki, Oliver Sturgess, Tim McCoy, Johnny Mack Brown, Bob Steele, Lane Chandler, Raymond Hatton, Chet Douglas, Dick Jones, Chris Hughes, Rand Brooks, Dale Van Sickel, Frank Lackteen, Zon Murray, Ronn Delanor, Edmund Cobb, Margo Williams, Doris Spiegel, Dick Alexander, Fred Carson, Red Morgan
Director: Spencer G. Bennett
Story: Evans W. Cornell, Guy J. Tedesco
Screenplay: R. Alexander
Producer: Alex Gordon

THE BOUNTY KILLER
(Embassy, July 31, 1965) 92 Minutes
(Technicolor) (TechniScope)
Dan Duryea, *Rod Cameron*, Audrey Dalton, Richard Arlen, Buster Crabbe, Fuzzy Knight, Johnny Mack Brown, Bob Steele, Bronco Billy Anderson, Peter Duryea, Eddie Quillan, Norman Willis, Edmund Cobb, I. Stanford Jolley, Frank Lackteen, Dan White, Grady Sutton, Emory Parnell, Duane Ament, Red Morgan, John Reach, Dolores Domasin, Dudley Ross, Ronn Delanor, Tom Kennedy
Director: Spencer G. Bennett
Screenplay: R. Alexander, Leo Gordon
Producer: Alex Gordon

IL PIOMBO E LA CARNE
(American Title: "Bullet in the Flesh")
(Marco Film-Hesperia Film-Cineurop, 1965) 95 Minutes
(EastmanColor)
Rod Cameron, Patricia Viterbo, Thomas Moore (Enzo Girolami), Dan Harrison, Carroll Brown (Bruno Carotenuti)
Director: Fred Wilson (Marino Girolami)
Screenplay: Gino De Santis

WINNETOU UND SEIN FREUND OLD FIREHAND

(American Titles: "Winnetou and His Friend Old Firehand" or "Thunder at the Border")
(USA Distributor: Columbia, 1966) 94 Minutes
Pierre Brice, *Rod Cameron,* Todd Armstrong, Maria Versini, Harald Leipnitz, Nadia Gray, Rik Battaglia, Jorg Marquard, Viktor de Kowa, Walter Wilz
Director: Alfred Vohrer
Story: Karl May

DIE LETZTEN ZWEI VOM RIO BRAVO

(American Titles: "The Two from Rio Grande" or "The Last Two from Rio Bravo")
(Constantin-Jolly-Trio Films, 1967)
(TechniScope)
Rod Cameron, Horst Frank, Vivi Bach, Hans Nielsen, Kai Fischer
Director: Manfred Rieger

EVIL KNIEVEL

(Fanfare Productions, July, 1971) 90 Minutes
George Hamilton, Sue Lyon, Bert Freed, *Rod Cameron,* Dub Taylor, Ron Masak, Hal Baylor, Betty Bronson, Sylvia Hayes, Mary Peters, Judy Baldwin, Kathy Baumann, Kayne Melon, Ben Bentley, Cassie Soloman, Ted Henningsen, Alana Collins, Ellen Tucker, Jan Davis, Inga Nielsen, Robert B. Williams, Lee Le Broux, Roger Edington, Frank Ellis, Paul Sorrenson, John Garwood, Richard Ford Grayling, Mary Grover, Bob Harris, John Haymer, Randee Jensen, Ski Kidwell, Howard Larson, Frank Loverde, Trish Mahoney, John Dale McCutchan, Cliff Medaugh, Eveline Micone, Irwin W. Mosley, Henry Olek, Barbara Parsons, Ralph Schmidt, Pat Setzer, Mike Chak, Joey Viera, Liv Von Linden, John Yates
Director: Marvin Chomsky
Screenplay: Allen Caillou and John Milius
Story: Allan Caillou
Producer: George Hamilton
(Filmed in Los Angeles and Butte, Montana in MetroColor)

THE LAST MOVIE

(Alta Light Productions/Universal, October, 1971)
110 Minutes
Dennis Hopper, Stella Garcia, Julie Adams, Thomas Milian, Don Gordon, Roy Engel, Donna Baccala, Samuel Fuller, Poupee Bocar, Sylvia Miles, Daniel Ades, John Alderman, Michael Anderson, Jr., Rich Aguilar, Tom Baker, Toni Basil, Anna Lynn Brown, *Rod Cameron,* Bernard Caselman, James Contreras, Eddie Donno, Severn Darden, Lou Donelan, Warren Finnerty, Peter Fonda, Fritz Ford, Samya Greene, William (Billy) Gray, Al Hopson, Bud Hassink, George Hill, Kris Kristofferson, John Phillip Law, Ted Markland, Victor Maymudes, Cynthia McAdams, Jim Mitchum, Al Monroe, Jorge Montoro, Owen Orr, Michelle Phillips, Robert Rothwell, Richard Rust, John Stevens, Toni Stern, Dennis Stock, Dean Stockwell, Russ Tamblyn, Alan Warnick, John Buck Wilken
Director: Dennis Hopper
Story: Stewart Stern, Dennis Hopper
Screenplay: Stewart Stern
Producer: Paul Lewis
(Filmed in Technicolor on location in Chinchero, Peru)

PSYCHIC KILLER

(Avco Embassy, November, 1975) 90 Minutes
Paul Burke, Jim Hutton, Julie Adams, Nehemiah Persoff, Neville Brand, Aldo Ray, Della Reese, *Rod Cameron,* Joe Della Sarte, Judith Brown, Mary Wilcox, Whit Bissell, Greydon Clark, Stack Pierce
Director: Raymond Danton
Screenplay: Greydon Clark, Mike Angel, Raymond Danton
Producer: Mardi Rustam

LOVE AND THE MIDNIGHT AUTO SUPPLY

(Producers Capital Presentations/I.P.A., 1978)
Michael Parks, Scott Jacoby, Linda Cristal, Coleen Camp, George McCallister, Monica Gayle, William Adler, and Guest Stars: Rory Calhoun, *Rod Cameron,* John Ireland
Director: James Polakof
Executive Producer: Beverly Johnson

EPILOGUE

The "B" Western died thirty years ago—or did it? Though the horse opry was put to rest by rising production costs, television, dwindling markets, changing mores, and numerous other factors, its demise was only temporary, like that of Dracula or the Frankenstein monster. Today, like the phoenix rising from its ashes in the freshness of youth to live through another fabled cycle of life, the programmer Western, clothed in nostalgic splendor, respectability, and even reverence, has risen from its ashes to thrill again the audiences, now grown wrinkled and gray, who whooped it up on the front-row seats as the heroes of the range vanquished the minions of outlawry in decades long past.

Joining the front-row kids of yesteryear is a younger generation which is seeing the old-time blood-and-guts sagas for the first time, thanks, ironically, to television, which helped to kill the shoot-em-up genre in the first place. And the development and phenomenal popularity of video cassettes has made it possible for film enthusiasts to build their own libraries of vintage prairie flickers as several film producers have rushed in to meet the demand for copies of the old western features that people remember from their youth, or perhaps that they have heard their parents talk about so fondly.

Though the phoenix of antiquity emerged from its ashes as a healthy young bird, ready to soar into new adventures and conquests, the vintage horse opry has risen ghost-like from its grave as simply a resurrected genre, grasping for an extended life in hearts and minds that are once again receptive to the innocence, simplicity, and economy of these films where the hero outfought, out-shot, and out-rode everyone in sight, his horse got second-billing, good scenes, and a few close-ups, and the girl got what little recognition she could muster by simply looking pretty and helpless, without so much as a provocative wriggle of her calico-enshrouded fanny.

Because the movie cowboys exerted such an influence over young boys during seventy-five years of film making, it is providential that most of them were respectable men who reacted positively and sensitively to the unusual demands for model living that their influence over millions of youngsters placed upon their shoulders. Unfortunately, the "B" Western genre, like any other, only in less numbers, had a few stars whose personal life styles were not cinched to allow them to sit tall in the saddle of morality. But, fortunately, these few were far overshadowed by a much larger number of saddle aces of the calibre of Buck Jones, Reb Russell, Roy Rogers, Rex Bell, George O'Brien, Johnny Mack Brown, Fred Thomson, Ray Whitley, and Charles Starrett, to name but a few, who took their favored stations in life as a great and unique opportunity to help youngsters along the rocky, treacherous trail to a meaningful, wholesome adulthood.

They didn't know it then, but as they toiled at creating a cheap fantasy world around crude production methods, long hours and short filming schedules, and ridiculously stringent budgets, the "B" cowboys were creating unique works of art that would outlast in popularity and reverence many of the highly-touted, expensively-made films of the same era. Our stetsons are off to these **Heroes of the Range,** for to think of a movie world in which the programmer western and the beloved cowboy stars never existed is intolerable—a nightmare to end all bad dreams.

NAME INDEX

(Including Companies, Studios, and TV
Series; text only)

Buffalo Bill, Jr. 3
"Bunkie" (a dog) 121, 122
Burbridge, Betty 7
Burgess, Dorothy 199
Burke's Law (TV Series) 317
Burnette, Smiley 247, 248, 291
Buster, Budd 78

-C-

Cameron, Rod 312ff
Canterno, Norma 3
Canutt, Yakima 73, 199, 293
Captain Gallant of the Foreign Legion (TV Series) 166
Carey, Harry 25, 140, 161, 181, 183, 185, 223
Carol, Sue 32
Carr, Trem 7, 44
Carrillo, Leo 199
Carroll, Madeleine 314
Carson-Barnes Circus 105
Cassidy, Edward 194
Cavalier, Nita 12
Chandler, Lane 199
Cheney, J. Benton 245
Chesebro, George 163
Chesterfield Pictures 199, 244, 245, 271
Cisco Kid, The 8
City Detective (TV Series) 317
Clark, Colbert 245, 247
Clark, Steve 55, 207
Clements, Marjorie 314
Clyde, Andy 271, 285, 286
Cohn, Harry 104, 245
Colman, Ronald 8
Colonel Tim McCoy's Real Wild West and Rough Riders of the World 104
Columbia Pictures 27, 104, 140, 164, 199, 201, 227, 243, 245, 247, 248, 314, 316
Conn, Maurice 73
Cooper, Gary 223, 313, 314
Cooper, Jackie 304
Corbett, Ben 114
Corbin, Virginia Lee 109
Cording, Harry 28
Corio, Ann 164
Coronado 9 (TV Series) 317
Cox, Roderick 313
Crabbe, Buster 139, 161ff, 225
Crabbe, Cullen 166
Crawford, Joan 197
Crossroads (TV Series) 317
Curtis, Dick 73, 245
Curwood, James Oliver 72
Custer, Bob 139

-D-

Darro, Frankie 138

Davies, Marion 197
Davis, Bette 314
Davis, Rufe 46, 139, 140
Day, Alice 134
Dean, Eddie 281
De Carlo, Yvonne 315, 316
De Cordoba, Pedro 281
Dee, Frances 161, 201
De Havilland, Olivia 183
De La Motte, Marguerite 122
De Mille, Cecil B. 223, 269, 272, 314
De Shon, Nancy 148
Desmond, William 1, 25
Dew, Eddie 314
Dick Stanley Wild West Show 119
Dix, Richard 103, 243
Dodd, Jimmie 46, 140
Downs, Cathy 316
Drake, Oliver 314
Duncan, William 121
Durango Kid 245, 246, 247, 248
Dwan, Allan 225
Dwire, Earl 297

-E-

Earp, Wyatt 226
Edwards, Cliff "Ukulele Ike" 183, 245
Elliott, Bill 316
Ellis, Frank 176
Ellison, Jimmy 137, 201, 271
Errol, Leon 201
Estrella, Esther 282
Evans, Dale 293

-F-

Fairbanks, Douglas 72
Famous Players-Lasky 2, 269
Farnum, William 25
Faucett, George 197
FBO Studios 41, 43, 138, 140, 181
Fier, Jack 245
Fireside Theatre (TV Series) 317
First National Pictures 73, 199
Fix, Paul 77
Flynn, Lefty 41
Ford, Glenn 137, 233
Ford, John 25, 27, 140, 183, 223
Foster, Helen 4
Fowley, Douglas 317
Fox Pictures 8, 25, 27, 199, 226
Franklin, Paul 245
French, George K. 122
Freuler-Monarch Pictures 140
Friscell, Varick 244
Fritchie, Barbara 35
Frye, Togo 6

Wallace, Beryl 73
Wallace Brothers Circus 140
Walsh, Raoul 8
Walters, Luana 245
Wanger, Walter 183, 315
Warner Bros. Pictures 27
Wayne, John 8, 41, 110, 201, 223, 226
Webb, Harry 45
Webb, Richard 237
Weldon, Marion 55
Welles, Orson 183
West, Mae 199
Westcott, Rusty 166
Weston, Dick 292
Whitaker, Charles 146, 163
White, Lee "Lasses" 181, 190
Whitley, Ray 181, 183, 190, 314, 331
Wilde, Harry 183
Wilkerson, Guy 86
Williams, Guinn (Big Boy) 45, 140, 233
Willing, Foy 309
Willis, Norman 139
Winchester Pictures 271
Windsor, Marie 325
Wilsey, Jay 3
Wilson, Whip 93
Winters, Sally 43, 139
Wood, Britt 281
Woods, Harry 105
Worth, Constance 315
Wray, Fay 132
Wynant, H. M. 240

-Y-

Yates, Herbert 291, 293
Young, Polly Ann 73, 245

337

FILM TITLE INDEX